Accounting in Business Decisions

Theory, Method, and Use

Accounting in Business Decisions

Theory, Method, and Use

HOMER A. BLACK, Ph.D., C.P.A.
Florida State University

JOHN E. CHAMPION, Ph.D., C.P.A.
Florida State University

Prentice-Hall, Inc.

Englewood Cliffs, N. J.   1961

PRINTED IN THE UNITED STATES OF AMERICA

00180

Preface

In recent years there has been mounting criticism of the manner in which much of the subject matter of business administration has been taught. Too much attention, say the critics, has been devoted to description of existing business institutions and practices, and too little to explanation of underlying concepts and analytical method.

Accounting has not been spared from this searching re-examination of course objectives and content. Many have contended that the beginning course in accounting has been designed primarily for the future professional accountant, who will work directly at accumulating and reporting accounting information, and that it has neglected the needs of other students of business administration, who will use that information. The traditional approach in basic accounting textbooks has emphasized the procedures by which financial information is collected, analyzed, summarized, and reported. Lately there has been an increasing number of books dealing chiefly with "managerial" accounting, stressing the use of accounting data by various levels of business management.

Accounting's purposes are to serve as a language for communicating the financial facts about an enterprise to those who have an interest in interpreting and using those facts, and to provide a useful tool for analyzing, controlling, and planning enterprise operations. Perhaps it is impossible in a basic course to serve equally well the needs of all who are concerned with accounting. Nevertheless, we feel that there is a common body of subject matter which is indispensable for everyone. We think that, while the details of accounting procedures are important, both the compiler and the user of accounting information can do their jobs more intelligently if they first gain an understanding of the objectives and basic theory of accounting. Knowing how the results of his work are to be employed, the accountant can be of greater service to the users of those results. Knowing the logical framework of accounting theory and the major problems involved in applying it, the user will be more aware of the potential uses, as well as the limitations, of accounting information.

Our approach, therefore, has been threefold, as denoted by the subtitle "Theory, Method, and Use." We have attempted to present a solid theoretical foundation, focusing our attention upon the basic similarity of the accounting problems faced by different businesses rather than being content to describe their differences. And while we think that accounting method has often received too much attention in the basic course, we recognize the importance of a knowledge of its fundamentals to the nonaccountant as well as to the accountant. We have explained thoroughly a variety of uses of accounting information by business management in appraising, planning, and controlling enterprise operations, but we think that it is improper to present accounting solely as a tool of business management. Some of the same basic material on accounting is also of vital interest to present and prospective stockholders and creditors, and to others who are directly concerned with the financial affairs of businesses, governments, and institutions. The principal difference in the needs of these groups is in the emphasis on certain classes of information.

In our treatment we have recognized the close relationship of accounting to economics, to statistics, and to the functional areas of business. However, courses in those areas are not prerequisites to this text.

Few accounting teachers agree completely upon the particular subject matter which should be included in the basic accounting text and upon its proper sequence. This book is designed to provide a maximum of flexibility to suit the varied preferences of individual instructors. The first 8 chapters of Part I, "Recording and Reporting Financial Events," are an essential unit which deals with the purposes, basic theory, and method of accounting. Beyond them, a number of chapters can be omitted altogether if necessary, or studied in a different sequence, without loss of continuity. For example, even though Chapter 9 discusses the processing of a mass of accounting information in a broad rather than in a highly specialized way, some teachers may wish to omit it. This they can do readily, because no later chapter depends upon it. Part II, "Measuring, Planning, and Controlling Income and Working Capital," deals with appraisal of past enterprise results and with planning for the future, together with some of the special problems involved in measuring and controlling particular current assets. Some instructors may prefer to postpone Chapters 10, 11, and 12, relating to appraisal and to the preparation of the operating budget, until after Chapter 20. Part III, "Measuring, Planning, and Controlling Long-Term Assets and Equities," consists of seven chapters. One or more of the three chapters devoted to comparison of long-range alternatives, though essential in business planning, may be omitted if desired. Chapter 24, 25, or 26, also important to the accountant and the businessman, may also be omitted if necessary.

Appendices at the ends of a number of chapters provide additional material on some of the more technical matters, which not all instructors will wish to assign.

Because of the number of optional chapters, the book may be used for a course of either one or two terms. It is suitable for both college accounting courses and for management development programs. In spite of its flexible arrangement, the book is a unified whole and the discussion flows logically from one chapter to the next.

We have tried to state clearly the basic concepts and principles of accounting and to illustrate their application by means of concrete examples. Chapter 1 begins with an illustrative case, which is intended to arouse the reader's interest in accounting, as it applies to a practical situation of a type with which he is familiar. Illustrative cases are used elsewhere to give extended examples of some of the more complex methods of reporting or analyzing accounting data.

The problem material is designed to teach the student to reason from basic accounting principles by forcing him to apply them in practical situations of increasing difficulty, some of them being unfamiliar to him. The questions and problems are thought-provoking; practically none are of the drill type. The cases are intended to place accounting in its proper perspective as a tool—to afford the student experience in analyzing realistic business situations in order to decide what the principal problems are, to select appropriate accounting methods to aid in solving the problems, and to formulate decisions. Some of the cases are real, some are hypothetical; some are relatively simple, some are more complex. Many accounting teachers prefer to rely largely upon the case method. For them, there is a sufficient number of cases to give the student ample and varied practical experience. For teachers who do not wish to use cases at all, there is a great variety of questions and problems—far more than needed in a single term. We prefer to use a mixture of questions, problems, and cases.

Most of the chapters and problems have been class-tested in preliminary form for more than two years. Our students have generally found them very stimulating, and we feel that they have gained a broader and deeper understanding of accounting than is customary under a procedural approach.

ACKNOWLEDGMENTS

First of all, we should like to acknowledge a profound indebtedness to Professor William A. Paton, of the University of Michigan, and to Professor Harold M. Heckman and the late Professor John F. Burke, of the University of Georgia. Professor Paton's incisive reasoning with respect to accounting theory and his inspired teaching of the philosophy of accounting have been a great stimulus to us. The clear, forceful, practical approach to the teaching of accounting by both Professor Heckman and Professor Burke has given us a worthy model. We also wish to thank sincerely the many other teachers, practitioners, and students of accounting who have influenced our ideas.

Our colleagues and our students have been most patient during the past three years in using the preliminary text material and in making constructive suggestions. We wish to express our appreciation to Professors Finley Belcher, Ross Heck, Gibbes U. Miller, Alice Nichols, Luella Richey, and Edward D. Trembly, all of Florida State University. Particular thanks are due to Professor Nichols for her valuable assistance with the case in Chapter 9, and to Professor Heck for his constructive suggestions on Chapter 24.

Robert Colby and Charles Wynn, accounting students, have been very helpful in collecting material for the cases and problems. Grace Earnest and Jan Lawson worked tirelessly and did an excellent job of typing parts of the manuscript in its preliminary form.

The advice of Professors Jay D. Cook, Jr., of Washington and Lee University, Dean Frank S. Kaulback, Jr., of the University of Virginia, and Professor Leonard E. Morrissey, of Dartmouth College, has been invaluable during the writing of the entire book. Others who assisted ably in one or more stages of its preparation are Professors Paul E. Fertig, of the Ohio State University; Charles T. Horngren, of the University of Chicago; Professor Robert K. Jaedicke, of Harvard University; and Professor George H. Sorter, of the University of Chicago. We are grateful to all of them for their suggestions as to content and method of presentation, and for their help in eliminating inconsistencies.

We are deeply indebted to the American Accounting Association, the American Institute of Certified Public Accountants, the National Association of Accountants, and to many other publishers and companies for their generous permission to quote from their publications and financial reports.

It has been a great pleasure to work with the staff of Prentice-Hall, Inc., because of their friendly cooperation. We especially wish to thank Mr. Wilbur F. Eastman, Jr., Miss Lillian Margot, and Mrs. Frances Dreyer for their encouragement, patience, and aid.

We owe a special debt of gratitude to Barbara Stoutamire for her outstanding work in arranging and typing the material in its final form.

Most importantly, we wish to acknowledge the contribution made by our wives, Clara and Mary, and by our children. Without their support, patience, and understanding, this book could never have been written.

HOMER A. BLACK
JOHN E. CHAMPION

Tallahassee, Florida

Contents

work sheet; Explanations of adjusting entries; Combined adjustment and classification work sheet.

PART TWO · MEASURING, PLANNING, AND CONTROLLING INCOME AND WORKING CAPITAL

come statement, all divisions combined; Using the responsibility reports; Variations in responsibility reports; Summary.

13. Planning and Controlling Cash

Accounting for income versus accounting for cash; Importance of accounting for cash; The cash forecast; Forecasting cash receipts; Forecasting cash disbursements; Basis for cash forecast illustration; Journal entries for budgeted transactions; Budget Work Sheet; Cash Forecast Summary; Using the cash forecast summary. Controlling and Recording Cash: General features of internal check; Internal check in operation; Controlling cash receipts; Controlling cash disbursements; Petty cash; Other cash accounts; Reconciling the bank accounts; Cash in the statement of financial position; Summary. Appendix 13-A, Petty Cash Procedure. Appendix 13-B, Bank Reconciliation Procedure.

14. Measuring and Controlling Receivables

General nature. Measuring Accounts Receivable, Trade: General basis of measurement; Sales discounts; Analysis of quality of accounts receivable; Age distribution of accounts receivable; Estimating uncollectibles from age distribution; Estimating uncollectibles on the basis of credit sales; Writing off uncollectible accounts; Correcting uncollectible account entries; Other deductions from accounts receivable; Special problems in reporting accounts receivable; Detailed records of accounts receivable. Controlling Accounts Receivable, Trade: Internal check of accounts receivable; Measuring past turnover rates; Using the turnover rates; Average collection period; Estimating future turnover rates; Determining credit policy. Measuring Notes Receivable: General basis of measurement; Bills of exchange; Recording receipt of notes; Internal check procedures for notes; Summary. Appendix 14-A, Discounted Notes Receivable: Endorsement without recourse; Endorsement with recourse; Entries at maturity of notes discounted with recourse; Computing the proceeds of discounted notes; Recording endorser's interest revenue or expense; Assigned accounts receivable.

15. Measuring Inventory

Objectives of inventory accounting; Matching costs with revenues; Criteria for evaluating methods of determining inventory cost; Basic illustration for comparing methods; Specific-identification method; Types of assumed cost flows; First-in, first-out (FIFO) method; Last-in, first-out (LIFO) method; Weighted-average method; Comparison of the results of the cost methods; Effect of inventory methods on decisions; Recoverable cost of inventory; The AICPA opinion: lower of cost or market; The AAA view of recoverable inventory cost; Recording reductions of inventory to market; Special problems in measuring inventories; Disclosure of inventories in financial statements; Summary. Appendix 15-A, Application of Lower of Cost or Market; Objections to lower of cost or market.

Objective of inventory planning; Perpetual inventory records as a basis for control; Planning physical quantities; Converting units to money costs; Timing acquisitions; Order point; Standard order quantity; Setting standards for inventory balances; Number of days' supply in inventory; Inventory turnover rate; Inventory control when types of items change; Retail inventory method; The gross margin inventory method; Internal check of inventories; Summary.

Production costs and distribution costs; Uses of unit production costs; Inventory accounts of manufacturers; Periodic and perpetual inventory methods; Cost centers; Direct and indirect production costs; Basic elements of manufactured product cost. Accounting for Historical Costs: Methods of assigning costs to units: job order and process; Illustration of job order cost accounting procedure; Financial statements of a manufacturer; Limitations of the job order cost system; Accounts required in a process cost accounting system; Illustration of process cost accounting procedure. Accounting for Predetermined Costs: Behavior of production costs; Predetermined manufacturing overhead rate; Analyzing the manufacturing overhead variance; Bases for allocating predetermined overhead to products; Standard costs: nature and purposes; Accounting for standard costs; Reporting and using variance information. Direct Costing: Illustration of absorption costing; Illustration of direct costing; Unit costs of distribution and service; Summary.

PART THREE · MEASURING, PLANNING, AND CONTROLLING LONG-TERM ASSETS AND EQUITIES

Capital and revenue expenditures. Depreciation: Objectives; Criteria for judging depreciation methods; Estimating useful life; The straight-line method of depreciation; Production methods of depreciation; Depreciation methods resulting in declining periodic charges; The uniform-rate-on-declining-balance depreciation method; The sum-of-the-years'-digits depreciation method; Evaluation of the declining annual depreciation methods; Comparison of results of depreciation methods; Recording sales of plant and equipment; Recording trades of plant and equipment; Depreciation for individual items or groups; Partial replacements; Revision of depreciation rates; Depletion of natural resources; Amortization of goodwill. Reporting and Interpreting Long-Term Unexpired Costs: General-purpose reporting requirements; Comparison of depreciation with cost; Evidence of deferred maintenance; Turnover of long-lived assets; Internal check; Summary.

Value of $1 at Compound Interest. Appendix 21-B, Present Value of an Annuity of $1 at Compound Interest.

22. Long-Range Planning: Comparing Alternatives   *660*

Types of plans which require no capital investment; Types of plans which require capital investment; Need for a long-range capital additions budget; Rationing capital to specific projects; Ranking projects as to rate of return. Measuring the Rate of Return: Formula for time-adjusted rate of return; Measuring initial net cost of the investment; Estimating differential future receipts; Computing the rate of return; Special problems in estimating the rate of return; Rate of return after income tax. Approximate Methods of Comparing Plans: The payoff period method; Rate of return unadjusted for time differences. Using the Capital Budget: The annual capital additions budget; Administering the capital budget; Appraising the performance of investments; Summary.

23. Estimating the Value of a Business   *685*

Occasions for making an estimate; Limitations of historical cost; Framework for estimating the value of a business; Liquidating value, replacement cost, and discounted earnings; Estimating the value of perpetuities; Estimating the value of a limited-term income stream; Steps in estimating the value of a business; Illustration of estimation process; Recording the purchase of a business; Purchase versus pooling of interests; Summary.

24. Planning and Accounting for Income Taxes   *704*

Different objectives of income taxation and business accounting; Importance of income taxes in business decisions; Effect of taxation on business form; Effect of taxation on business size; Tax saving by means of long-term capital gains; Computing after-tax rate of return on investment; Tax saving in choice of financing methods. Tax Saving by Choice of Accounting Methods: Circumstances in which tax postponement is desirable; Cash versus accrual basis of accounting; Installment sales method; Percentage-of-completion and completed-contract methods; Deductions from accounts receivable; Inventory method; Depreciation method; Other important choices of accounting methods. Other Differences Between Financial and Taxable Income: Nontaxable exchanges; Gains on involuntary conversions; Percentage depletion; Loss carrybacks and carryforwards. Effect of Differences Between Accounting and Income Tax Methods: Influence of taxation on accounting methods; Matching income tax expense with business income; Illustration of methods of accounting for income taxes; Treatment of other income taxes; Summary.

PART FOUR · APPRAISAL OF BUSINESS AND ACCOUNTING

PART 1

RECORDING AND REPORTING
FINANCIAL EVENTS

Chapter 1

Purposes and Nature of Accounting

The need for accounting: an illustrative case

William Daniels had not counted on the sudden turn of events which had left him in complete charge of the retail clothing store owned by his father-in-law, James Lawson. William had graduated several years earlier from a midwestern university. Two years ago he had married Margaret Lawson, and shortly thereafter he had accepted Mr. Lawson's offer of a position as assistant manager of Lawson Clothing Company. Unexpectedly on April 27, however, Mr. Lawson had been paralyzed by a stroke.

Mr. Lawson had never really taken William into his confidence. He had relied on William chiefly to supervise the five sales clerks, to handle incoming shipments of goods, and to assist in making the daily bank deposit. He had kept his business affairs to himself and, as far as William could tell, his financial records were mostly in his head. Still, the business had provided a comfortable living for the Lawson family, and Mr. Lawson seemed to have a good business reputation in the community.

After careful search William had been able to locate the business checkbook, complete with stubs; a file of unpaid bills; and a file of uncollected charge slips for goods sold to customers on account. Mrs. Lawson had given him the combination to the office safe. In the safe William found a bound cash book, with lists of cash receipts and payments in chronological order; a small folder containing several promissory notes signed by customers; and a file of Mr. Lawson's income tax returns for the past few years. Mr. Lawson prided himself on preparing his own returns. William was quite surprised at the small amount of net income subject to tax. Evidently the business had not been doing as well as it had appeared, because he knew that Mr. Lawson was most conscientious in all of his business and tax matters.

April 30 was pay day for the employees. William did not know how much salary each of the employees earned, and although he was aware that deductions from the pay checks had to be made for income tax and social security tax, he was not sure how to determine the amounts. Finally, referring to the check stubs for March salaries, he wrote out the April checks for the same amounts. He hoped that the running bank balance shown on the check stubs was accurate so that the checks would clear. William prepared the checks for the signature of Mrs. Lawson, who was authorized to sign business checks.

Life was hectic for William during the next few days. Each incoming mail brought a stack of unpaid bills. He was not sure whether the business had actually received the items, whether the prices were right, and whether the bills had been paid earlier. Several of the statements were marked "Past Due," and William noted that on others the time period for deducting a discount for prompt payment had expired. He made out checks to pay the bills which seemed most urgent, hoping that the creditors would be honest enough to refund any overpayments, and hoping that the balance in the bank was sufficient to cover the checks. During the next few days William had a call from the landlord, reminding him that the monthly rent payment was due.

William remembered with a start on May 4 that Mr. Lawson was in the habit of sending out monthly statements of account to his charge customers. He was not sure whether the file of uncollected sales slips was complete, or whether it contained items which had already been paid. He could not decide which was worse—to risk offending customers by sending them incorrect statements, or to fail to collect money badly needed by the business. Deciding that the latter was the more objectionable, he and Mrs. Daniels worked several nights preparing and addressing statements.

In the next few weeks new troubles arose. Various items of stock were depleted, and William realized that the store would lose many sales and incur customer ill will during the weeks needed to fill orders. Moreover, he had no idea which items Mr. Lawson had already ordered. Mr. Lawson's medical bills were draining the business bank account severely; his personal assets were barely more than enough to buy groceries. During this time many customers called about their account balances, and although they were usually courteous, William was very embarrassed not to know whether or not their complaints were justified.

Mr. Lawson had left on his desk a form for submitting a quarterly report of employees' payroll taxes withheld. William had wondered about it. Within a few weeks he was disturbed to receive a notice that the quarterly report was overdue. Fortunately, he was able to compile the information needed by a careful reading of the instructions for preparing the form and a laborious analysis of check stubs.

When the bank called on May 28 to report that there were insufficient funds on deposit to cover a $200 check written on the business bank account, it was the last straw for William. The checkbook showed a balance of $282.10, and William had counted on that to tide him over the employees' pay day. In desperation, he called on the bank vice-president, Mr. Dorian, to ask for emergency aid. Mr. Dorian, very sympathetic, said that he had already sensed the situation. He agreed to lend $500 at once on a 60-day note signed by Mrs. Lawson, and indicated that he would advance up to $2,500 more later, if William would furnish him financial statements showing the condition of the business and a financial plan estimating when the loan could be repaid.

William was ashamed to admit that he did not know what details the financial statements should contain. He asked Mr. Dorian to advise him where he might get some help in preparing the statements. The latter named several local firms of Certified Public Accountants and recommended that William engage one of them.

William was afraid, after asking for a rough estimate of what a CPA's fee would be, that the business could not afford to engage one. He knew that the books of the business were inadequate, but felt that this matter was one that ought not to require specialized professional service.

Mr. Dorian warned William that good professional advice was the only kind he could afford. He pointed out that giving professional opinions as to the reliability of business financial statements is just one type of service rendered by CPAs. In addition, he said, CPA firms can give a great deal of constructive advice that will help in managing a business more efficiently. They can design and install an accounting system that will collect the financial information needed by management in operating the business as well as in satisfying the needs of interested third parties like the bank. They can set up controls and safeguards that will help protect business property from dishonesty or mismanagement. They can also help a firm collect information and make analyses that will be of assistance in planning profitable business operations in the future.

Mr. Dorian agreed that it would be rather expensive for William to engage a CPA firm to do his bookkeeping. He advised that William hire a qualified employee who could handle that job. The CPA could help him get started on the right track and assist the business with special problems from time to time, such as the preparation of income tax returns. In his opinion, the money spent for these services would be a good investment, because the fees would be far less than the losses caused by inadequate records and controls.

William considered the matter for a few days, discussed it with some business friends, and finally decided to make an appointment with a CPA firm. He knew that the emergency need of financial statements for the loan had to be met, and he felt that perhaps the firm could suggest how he could improve profits. He was convinced that the business should be earning a much greater return, considering its size and volume of sales.

Purpose of the illustrative case

The plight of William Daniels and the Lawson Clothing Company, though imaginary, is not far-fetched. Businesses often find themselves in similar difficulties, and sometimes in far worse ones. The illustration has been presented to focus attention sharply on some of the needs of businesses, whether large or small, for accounting. It is not intended to imply that accounting is merely a device to help businesses which are in financial trouble. As a matter of fact, accounting serves a continuing need of all types and conditions of businesses as well as of non-business organizations.

Businesses are organized to produce economic wealth. The interrelationships among people within a business, between people and productive facilities, and between a business and outsiders are numerous and complex. Some means is needed of expressing in a systematic, dependable, and understandable way the complex relationships of the business and the results of the multitude of business events. Accounting does this, using as its raw material *financial* events and relationships—those which can be expressed in terms of money.

Definition of accounting

Perhaps the most widely accepted definition of accounting describes it as " . . . the art of recording, classifying, and summarizing in a significant manner and in terms of money, transactions and events which are, in part at least, of a financial character, and interpreting the results thereof."[1] This definition emphasizes the procedures that are used in accounting—recording, classifying, summarizing, and interpreting; the monetary language in which financial information is expressed; and the method of approach in accounting, which centers attention on the individual business transaction. It states *what* accounting does and *how* it does it, but a fuller understanding of the meaning and potential uses of accounting requires an explanation of *why* accounting is carried on and *for whom*.

Accounting is not an end in itself; it is a useful tool. It is a language for

---

[1] American Institute of Certified Public Accountants, Committee on Terminology, *Accounting Terminology Bulletin Number 1, Review and Resumé* (New York: The Institute. 1953), p. 9.

communicating the financial facts about an enterprise or activity to those who have an interest in interpreting and using those facts. It is a means of analyzing and controlling enterprise operations and of planning future action. In order to be useful it must be adapted to the particular needs of each enterprise. These needs arise from the financial information requirements of the various individuals and groups who are affected directly by enterprise operations.

Groups interested in accounting information

(1) The *owners* of a business need to know from time to time what its progress has been toward its objective of earning a profit, as well as what its financial standing is at a given time. This information is useful to them both as a check upon the past performance of the business and as a clue to what is likely to happen in the future. Shares of a business are valuable largely because their owners expect to benefit from future distributions of earnings and from increases in the sales price of the shares.

Potential investors and investors' advisory services examine accounting data for the light they will shed upon the desirability of an investment in the business. Where business ownership is separated from management, as is often true in large corporations whose stock is widely held by the public, owners use accounting reports as a means of checking on the efficiency and faithfulness of their hired managers. An important measure of performance used in this connection is the amount of income of the business, both in absolute terms and relative to the amount invested in the business.

(2) *Management*, whether or not it is the same as owners, relies upon accounting as a device for controlling the operating performance of the business. In a broad sense, accounting provides management controls through the plan of organization and the assignment of powers and responsibilities to the people who carry on the work of the business. In a more specific sense, accounting controls consist of the methods used within a business to safeguard its assets, to check the accuracy and reliability of its accounting information, to promote operating efficiency, and to insure that the policies of management are carried out.[2]

Much of the work of accounting is directed toward helping management in the day-to-day operations of the business: investing and withdrawing of capital by the owners; buying goods, personal services, and productive facilities; borrowing or lending money; selling goods or services; paying debts and collecting debts owed by others; protecting property; and distributing income.

---

[2] American Institute of Certified Public Accountants, Committee on Auditing Procedure, *Internal Control* (New York: The Institute, 1949), p. 6.

Accounting provides a means of evaluating management's performance in carrying on individual activities as well as in conducting the business as a whole. It can include certain guideposts, or standards of performance, to show management whether an activity is proceeding toward accomplishing the business objectives. It can furnish information about undesirable tendencies that need to be corrected. It can also be used as a guide to future action. In this connection accounting forms the basis for financial plans known as *budgets*, and it furnishes information that should be considered in selecting a course of action from such alternatives as whether to make a product or buy it already made; whether to replace a machine, and if so, when; whether to add a new product to the product line; whether to substitute labor-saving machinery for men; whether to change pricing policy; and whether to discontinue a product line or department of the business.

(3) *Creditors* and prospective creditors, such as bankers, bondholders, and suppliers of goods and services, investigate the financial standing of an enterprise before deciding whether to extend credit to it at all, what amount to extend, and under what terms. They pay primary attention to liquidity, the ability of the business to convert its property into money upon short notice without loss; and solvency, the ability to pay debts. They also observe the trend of income over time, which will affect the liquidity and solvency of the business at future dates.

(4) *Governments*, both state and federal, are concerned with the accounting of a business—as taxing bodies, sometimes as customers on cost-plus contracts, and also in many cases as regulatory authorities. Accounting records must make it possible for the government to determine whether the employer has complied with minimum wage laws and the working hours and overtime pay provisions of the Fair Labor Standards Act. Railroads and public utilities must secure the approval of the appropriate regulatory commission for rates charged their customers. They must submit periodic financial reports in the prescribed form to the regulatory bodies. Many companies are required to prepare comprehensive financial reports for the Securities and Exchange Commission before they can offer their capital stock for sale to the public. Companies whose stock is listed on the organized stock exchanges must present financial reports to the exchanges at frequent intervals. Information agencies of the federal government collect financial data of individual businesses and summarize them by types of business to aid businessmen in planning. Examples of such information are the censuses of business conducted by the Bureau of the Census, and the national income statistics compiled by the Department of Commerce.

(5) *Employees* themselves have an important stake in the finances of their company. They are interested in being assured of steady employ-

ment by a financially sound employer, and perhaps also in participating in company profit-sharing and pension plans. Labor unions usually take a more active interest in company financial statements than do individual employees, often using the amount and rate of profits to gauge the employer's ability to pay proposed wage increases and in negotiating for increased benefits.

(6) *Students*, research workers, and other members of the general public analyze enterprise financial statements in connection with various problems they are studying.

This imposing list of groups who have a vital interest in the accounting reports of an enterprise is proof of the public interest in good accounting. Of course, the degree of public interest varies from one business to another, and in the smallest business perhaps only the owner-manager and the Director of Internal Revenue are concerned.

General-purpose and special-purpose accounting reports

The sort of information which one group needs about a particular business is often not the same as that which other groups need. The owner, for example, thinks of income as a measure of the results accomplished by his business during a given time period, while Congress and other taxing authorities think of income as a measure of the ability of a business to pay income taxes. The "income" figures which are reported to these two groups often differ in many important respects, because they are to be used for different purposes.

Another example of a different need is information for management use in planning, such as in estimating future costs and selling prices. These estimates cannot very well form the basis for the general-purpose accounting records.

To serve all of these needs equally well would place an almost impossible burden on the accounting system. The business should take these various requirements into consideration in deciding what classes of information to collect. However, when the requirements of groups differ substantially, the basic system must usually be geared to turn out the information desired by the most important statement users—owners and management—and only incidentally to serve the needs of the other groups. When the general-purpose records and reports of financial status and progress do not furnish the information which some groups need, special-purpose reports can be prepared. They usually require a separate analysis and are often more detailed. Income tax returns, budgets, and comparisons of alternative courses of action are usually such special-purpose reports.

The importance of objectivity in accounting

The reliance which management and groups outside of the business place upon accounting information as a guide to their actions is so great that the facts reported by accounting must be determined impartially and objectively. Indeed, objectivity, the exercise of independent judgment in arriving at conclusions expressed in quantitative terms, is the keystone of accounting.

The accountant's objectivity is evident in his insistence that financial records be based upon actual, verifiable happenings—not plans, hopes, and fears. To be sure, there are occasions when it is not possible to determine positively whether a given event has occurred or what its extent and significance are. In such cases the sound, seasoned, impartial judgment of the accountant is vital.

It is entirely acceptable for the accountant to report different *types* of information for different purposes, but the *quality* of the information must always be reliable. For example, a report to management may contain fifty classifications of expense while the report to stockholders contains only ten. However, the total expense reported to both groups should be the same. The accountant may also arrange statement items in different order in reports prepared for special groups, but the amounts and conclusions should be the same.

Historical accounting data versus estimated future data

If the accounts and reports reflect the accountant's sound, impartial interpretation of the facts, unvarnished by optimism, pessimism, or self-interest, the user of the data has a dependable point of departure from which to make his own judgments reflecting his own interpretations and expectations.

Much accounting information relates to events which have already been completed in the past and which can be measured objectively. Other significant accounting measurements deal with events which are still in progress, such as the continuing use of a building. Accounting measurements dealing with the past use of the building depend to a large extent upon how long the building is expected to be used in the future.

In many business decisions the important figures are future figures—expected prices, volume of sales, and costs. Even though the amounts will be largely a matter of guesswork, the guesses must be made. Often the accountant, because of his knowledge of quantitative analysis, is the logical person to prepare the estimates. Statements of estimated financial data should be clearly identified as such.

Earlier sections have shown how management and others can use accounting information as a guide in their decisions and actions. Although accounting is very important, there is a danger of overemphasizing its usefulness and of failing to recognize some of its important limitations.

Accounting deals with business events and relationships which can be expressed in money amounts, but not all of the important affairs of a business can be described in such terms. Employee morale is a very important factor in business, but the extent to which it does or does not exist cannot be shown by accounting. Other important *qualitative* factors which must be considered in making business decisions, in addition to accounting *quantities*, are relations with customers, the government, and the general public; convenience of the business surroundings; reputation of the business; and many more. Sometimes these qualitative considerations outweigh the importance of quantitative considerations in business decision-making.

The accounting unit, or entity

If the various groups who have a stake in the affairs of a business are to have clear information about its finances, the accountant must be careful to record only those events which relate to the business. The personal and family dealings of the owners have no place in the financial reports of the business. For accounting purposes the business is treated as a complete unit, or *entity*, apart from its owners, creditors, and others. All of its dealings with these groups are recorded from the point of view of the entity. Thus, property formerly belonging to one of the owners as an individual but now put to business use is treated as a receipt of property by the business entity by means of investment. A business should have separate accounting records even though it is unincorporated and has no legal being apart from its owner.

In some cases it is useful to treat parts of a single company as separate accounting entities. If a corporation with three branches in different locations wishes to keep up with the performance of each branch, it can use a separate accounting system to evaluate each as an entity and then combine the results of the branches for a better picture of operations as a whole.

It is usually desirable to keep separate sets of records for each unincorporated business owned by one individual, and law requires separate records for each corporation. When several companies owned by the same person or persons are closely related in operations, it is often worth while to prepare financial statements for the economic *entity* in addition to the separate statements of the individual companies. These statements, called *consolidated financial statements*, are thus prepared for the parent company and its subsidiary companies which are in closely related lines of activity.

The discussion up to this point has dealt almost exclusively with the uses of accounting for the *business* entity. Actually, accounting has much broader application. It is necessary for profit-seeking and nonprofit organizations, whether publicly or privately owned. It is useful for governments, hospitals, schools, and churches. In these nonprofit enterprises the basic accounting entity is the *fund*, which is a group of resources devoted to a particular purpose. An example is a *trust fund* willed by a citizen for the maintenance of a public library. It must be accounted for as a separate unit.

The professional accountant

The terms *accountant* and *Certified Public Accountant* are in almost everyone's vocabulary, but there is a widespread misconception of the nature of the work of each. The typical layman thinks of a CPA as a whiz with figures, a mathematical genius, but in reality the only mathematical processes ordinarily used in accounting are addition, subtraction, multiplication, and division. The idea that the accountant's work consists solely of dealing with figures arises from the fact that business transactions—the raw data of accounting—are expressed in money amounts. However, the figures themselves are not the whole story; it is what they mean that is significant.

A successful accountant must be able to exercise sound judgment within the logical framework of accounting theory, a theory which must have a practical foundation in the usefulness of accounting results. The accountant needs a broad background of knowledge in the fields of general education, statistics, economics, and business administration in addition to specialized knowledge and experience in accounting.

The work of the practicing professional accountant falls into three broad fields: public accounting, internal or private accounting, and governmental accounting. Public accounting, perhaps the best-known, is the practice of the art of accounting by one who offers his services to the public for a fee.

Traditionally, much of the work of the public accountant has consisted of auditing. The function of the public auditor is to serve as an independent, objective examiner of the records and financial statements of his client. In this role he has an obligation to the public as well as to the client. As a result of his examination he expresses an *opinion* as to whether in his judgment the financial statements present *fairly* the results of the client's operations and its financial position. He does not certify that the records and statements are 100 per cent accurate.

Another well-known type of service rendered by the public accountant is tax advice. This service may involve determining the amount of income tax the client owes as a result of past operations, or it may involve tax planning—arranging the affairs of the business so as to minimize legally the income tax bill. Many public accountants also offer clients their expert services in designing and installing accounting systems. In recent years there has been rapid growth in both the quantity and the variety of advisory services offered by public accountants to business management.

The Certified Public Accountant is licensed to offer his services to the public under the laws of the state in which he practices. State requirements vary as to the amount of practical experience needed for certification. To become a CPA in any state, an individual must have passed the uniform examination prepared by the American Institute of Certified Public Accountants. The subjects covered are accounting theory, accounting practice, auditing, and commercial law.

The internal, or private, accountant is an employee of the business firm or nonprofit organization for which he works. Private accounting involves responsibilities ranging all the way from those of the accounting clerk or bookkeeper to the controller. The controller, the top accounting executive, has responsibility for furnishing management with facts useful in controlling operations and in interpreting business results. The duties of the bookkeeper, though essential to the process of recording and communicating financial information, are largely routine. The term *accountant* is usually reserved for individuals with some degree of executive responsibility and a thorough knowledge of accounting theory and practice.

Accountants in federal, state, and local governments work as internal accounting executives or as auditors. They perform duties similar to those of both public and private accountants.

Professional accounting groups and publications

The professional organization to which a majority of Certified Public Accountants belong is the American Institute of Certified Public Accountants (formerly the American Institute of Accountants). CPAs must observe high ethical standards. The American Institute has established "Rules of Professional Conduct" for this purpose. It conducts research on accounting problems and publishes an imposing list of periodicals, bulletins, and books for the benefit of practicing members, businessmen who employ accountants, and students of accounting. One of its publications is the monthly *Journal of Accountancy;* another is a series of authoritative bulletins dealing with special problems in accounting terminology, accounting procedure, and auditing procedure.

The American Accounting Association consists primarily of college accounting teachers. It publishes the quarterly *Accounting Review,* and has issued several significant published statements dealing with accounting concepts and standards.

The National Association of Accountants (formerly the National

Association of Cost Accountants), which publishes the monthly *N.A.A. Bulletin,* is an organization devoted chiefly to the interests of private accountants. Other important professional organizations are the Controllers Institute of America, the Institute of Internal Auditors, the Federal Government Accountants Association, and the Municipal Finance Officers' Association of the United States and Canada.

Accounting is a relatively young and rapidly changing discipline. Periodicals and other current publications form an essential part of its literature. A basic text such as this can only state the fundamentals and general uses of accounting. The reader must refer to current literature for the more technical details and for information on new developments in accounting.

Reasons for studying accounting

Many readers will be interested in following careers as public, private, or government accountants. Most, perhaps, are interested in accounting solely as a useful tool in managing a business or in handling personal investments. Business managers at all levels must have an understanding of accounting—its meaning, its potential uses, and its limitations—if they are to do their work properly. Probably every reader will at one time or another be required to interpret accounting information about the business in which he works or whose stock he owns or is thinking of buying, or the church, school, or governmental unit in whose affairs he is interested.

The extensive description of the nature of accounting and its literature in this chapter has been presented in the belief that the reader can get the most usefulness from accounting if he has some idea of what types of services are available, of what degree of competence and integrity he can expect from an accountant, and of the limits of the applicability of accounting. Later chapters will describe in considerable detail the language for communicating financial facts about business and some suggested methods of using these facts for analyzing past results and planning for the future.

Relation of accounting to law, economics, and statistics

The nature of accounts and reports is strongly influenced by legal requirements. For example, because the law regards a corporation as a separate legal person, accounting must treat the corporation as a separate entity for record-keeping purposes. The accounts of a corporation should, to the extent feasible, show the legal features of stockholders' equity. The accounts of all businesses need to reflect the various classes of liabilities and their important legal provisions, and also the amounts legally owed by customers.

Accounting has a much broader purpose than to show the legal nature of claims, however. As economics deals with wealth, and with man's efforts to create more wealth through business activity, so does accounting. Accounting is designed to show the sources, forms, uses, and changes in the wealth of the particular firm, whereas economics places much of its emphasis on the point of view of society as a whole. The methods of measurement in the two disciplines are also often quite different.

Statistics is broader than accounting in that it refers to the collection, tabulation, analysis, presentation, and interpretation of *any type* of quantitative data,[3] while accounting deals only with business data which can be quantified in terms of money amounts. The classifications which are used for grouping information in accounting are statistical classes which bear the names of economic factors, events, or relationships. Statistics and accounting are similar in their purpose, which is to present information in understandable form, and in their insistence upon objectivity. They differ to a considerable extent in method. However, the information compiled by one discipline is often useful in the other.

Summary

Accounting is justified only to the extent that it is useful. It must furnish needed financial information about the activities of an enterprise to many groups, of whom the most important are usually the managers and the owners. Accounting is flexible, but it must also be dependable. The accountant, whether in public, private, or government practice, must maintain an attitude of impartiality and must exercise sound judgment in arriving at his conclusions.

Although accounting information is useful to individuals who are faced with making decisions about the enterprise, it also has limitations. Its subject matter is economic events and relationships which can be expressed in terms of money, and qualitative factors which cannot be described in this manner often have an important bearing on business decisions.

APPENDIX 1-A

Solution of Accounting Problems and Cases

A most important objective of this text is to help you to become an intelligent user of accounting information. If this objective is to be accom-

---

[3] Kermit O. Hanson, *Managerial Statistics* (Englewood Cliffs, N. J.: Prentice-Hall, Inc., 1955), p. 2.

plished, you must have an opportunity to test your understanding of the ideas presented by applying them to practical situations—accounting questions, problems, and cases. The following suggestions are presented so that you can begin solving problems in the right way.

Approach to problem solving

In tackling a long or complex problem, first be sure that you understand its objective or desired end result. Begin by reading the requirements of the problem, if they are stated, and then read the problem information through carefully, noting mentally or underlining the important facts that relate to the requirements. The requirements may specify the form in which the solution is to be presented; if not, you must visualize the manner in which it will be organized.

Knowing the purpose of the problem and the form of the solution, you should next outline the main steps to take in arriving at the result. In long problems it is often helpful to identify these steps by numbers and then, reading through the problem data a second time, to note beside important information the step of the solution to which it relates.

After planning the outline of your solution, you should proceed to organize its detailed components in logical, neat, and orderly fashion. Although the most useful phases of accounting are analyzing and interpreting results, accuracy in collecting supporting data and in making computations is essential.

The end product of the problem or case is not the mechanical arrangement of the solution, but the conclusions based upon an analysis and interpretation of the data. When you have completed the forms associated with the solution to a problem, examine them to determine their meaning and significance. Only in this way do you put accounting to its intended use.

Purpose and nature of business cases

Business cases are problems which require some positive action by the management of a business. They simulate as nearly as possible in the classroom the process of learning by doing. Their purpose is not to teach facts, rules, and methods, but to teach potential businessmen to think and act when faced with new situations. Cases have three general uses: (1) to focus attention on a principle or issue; (2) to appraise an action already taken; (3) and to provide information as a basis for discussion.

There is almost never a single "correct" answer to a business case. There may be several good ways of solving the business problems, and it may well be that the best way has not yet been discovered. An important part of the case method of teaching is class discussion, in which various individuals in the group contribute toward the analysis of the problem and the decision as to the proper course of action. Each individual learns from the others, and the decision is usually a group decision to which many people have contributed some part. As a rule, the instructor plays a minor role in such class discussions, merely acting as a moderator to keep the discussion on the subject. In the non-directive approach, the instructor refrains from trying to influence the group's thinking or its conclusions. In the directive approach, he may ask pertinent questions that will lead the discussion toward an acceptable conclusion, supply information, or even offer an opinion.

The description of the case situation may contain a great deal of irrelevant information, and this is true to life. In real business one of the important problems is to recognize what the problem is and to select from available information the facts which relate to it. Often in cases some wished-for information is missing, and this, too, is realistic. Many times a businessman must act even though he cannot obtain complete information bearing on a decision, either because there is not enough time or because the needed information is not available.

Approach to case analysis

Usually the instructor asks the individual students to study a case, or to prepare a written analysis of it, before the group discussion.

The student's first step in his individual preparation should be to determine what the problem is and to state it clearly and concisely. This will also be the first part of the later group discussion. The cases in this text are followed by a series of questions relating to the case, but the instructor or students may wish to disregard them. Sometimes the really significant questions are not stated.

The next major step in the solution of the case is to decide what to do about the problem. Divisions of this step may be:

(1) Review the facts in the case which pertain to the business problem;

(2) Review material in the text or in the library which has a bearing on possible solutions;

(3) Outline the alternative solutions, and evaluate them;

(4) Arrive at a decision, state it clearly, and support it with pertinent arguments and evidence.

QUESTIONS AND PROBLEMS

1-1
REQUIRED:

Give a specific example of how the manager of a business can use historical information about the past in planning for the future.

1-2

REQUIRED:

Give an illustration of a type of activity in a retail store, smaller in scope than the whole business, which the manager might fruitfully evaluate by means of accounting.

1-3

REQUIRED:

a. Give a specific illustration of a decision in a retail business which would be based almost entirely upon accounting information.
b. Give an illustration of a decision in a retail business upon which accounting would have little or no bearing.

1-4

REQUIRED:

a. Why is the federal government justified in inspecting the accounting records of a manufacturer who is making weapons under a government contract?
b. What general type of information would the inspector wish?

1-5

REQUIRED:

List several types of special-purpose reports, other than those mentioned in this chapter, which would commonly be drawn from the accounting records.

1-6

REQUIRED:

a. Why do the stockholders of a parent company wish consolidated financial statements?
b. Why are separate statements for the subsidiaries also necessary?

1-7

REQUIRED:

Does an independent auditor undertake to find all of the errors in a company's accounting records as a part of his auditing engagement? Explain.

1-8   Often it is said half-jestingly that an individual keeps two sets of accounting records, one for himself and one for the taxing authorities.

REQUIRED:

a. Would this practice be honest?
b. Would it be useful?
c. Would it be practical?

1-9   A large manufacturing corporation with thousands of stockholders throughout the country is studying its financial reports with the idea of eliminating unnecessary duplication in them. It has been suggested that such duplication might be eliminated by preparing a single set of reports to be used by department heads, top management, and the stockholders.

REQUIRED:

Explain whether this suggested practice would be desirable and practical.

1-10   Engineer to his accountant friend: "Won't high-speed computers, which can perform repetitive calculations almost as fast as lightning, soon make you accountants obsolete?"

REQUIRED:

How should the accountant answer this question?

1-11   The owner of a business, planning to sell it, has requested his Certified Public Accountant to prepare statements for the information of prospective buyers. "Don't use your regular statements," he instructs the CPA, "because I want to get a high price for my business. Make it look as good as possible."

REQUIRED:

a. Would it be proper for the CPA to prepare statements which differ from those he ordinarily prepares for his client at the end of the year?
b. If so, in what general ways might they differ from the regular statements?

1-12   A lawyer who is engaged to represent his client in a suit is under obligation to do his utmost to present information favorable to his client.

REQUIRED:

a. To what extent does the CPA have the same obligation to his client?
b. To what extent does the CPA's obligation to his client differ?

1-13   The financial vice-president of Company X instructs his chief accountant to lean in the direction of understating unfavorable events and overstating favorable ones. "The president is a great pessimist," he says, "and you will be doing him a favor by showing that the company is in a better financial position than it actually is."

REQUIRED:

a. Will the accountant be doing the president a favor if he does as the vice-president suggests? Explain.
b. Will he be doing a disservice to anyone else?
c. Phrase a tactful reply from the accountant to the vice-president.

1-14   "I own every scrap of this business and I don't owe a dime," says the owner of a retail store. "Accounting records would be a waste of time and money for me. I can see what is going on."

REQUIRED:

Explain the possible values of accounting to this proprietor.

1-15

REQUIRED:

Is there any objection to the performance of an audit of Company Y by a Certified Public Accountant who owns one-fourth of the company's capital stock? Explain.

1-16   Mr. Crane owns a 1200-acre farm on which he raises cattle, sheep, vegetables, and grain for home consumption as well as for sale. He raises hunting dogs for pleasure, although he has occasionally sold a few. There are eight tenant houses on the farm, all of which are rented from time to time. Mr. Crane owns a gasoline service station which supplies the needs of the family and the farm vehicles and also sells to the public. He owns shares of stock of the local bank and of several companies listed on the New York Stock Exchange, and he has money on deposit in a checking account and a savings account.

REQUIRED:

a. Outline the general pattern of the accounting records which you think Mr. Crane should have.
b. In what part of the records, if any, should repairs to the farmhouse be accounted for? Alfred Crane's expenses while working toward a degree at the State College of Agriculture?

1-17   John Moore, a Certified Public Accountant, has been engaged by Flick Corporation to perform an annual audit. In addition, the directors of

Flick Corporation have asked him to prepare a five-year earnings forecast to be furnished to prospective investors.

REQUIRED:

a. Under what circumstances, if any, would it be proper for Mr. Moore to prepare such a forecast?

b. How would your answer differ if Mr. Moore were an employee of the Flick Corporation?

1-18

REQUIRED:

a. For each of the following types of business and non-business organizations, name parties other than management and owners who would be interested in accurate accounting information.

b. Give reasons for the usefulness of such information in each case.

(1) Service station
(2) Labor union
(3) City government
(4) State university
(5) Private college
(6) Charitable organization
(7) Public utility
(8) Manufacturing company listed on the New York Stock Exchange
(9) Family-owned corporation
(10) Insurance company
(11) Church

1-19

REQUIRED:

Referring to the Lawson Clothing Company illustration at the beginning of this chapter, list all of the major purposes you can think of for which accounting information about the business would be useful. Approximately how often would each need occur?

CASE 1-1. KENNETH ANDRE

On June 30, 19x2, Kenneth Andre, who was recently awarded a degree in business administration from the state university, received a share of his late father's estate. Included in Kenneth's inheritance was $94,000 in cash and 50 per cent of the outstanding stock of the Superior Furniture Manufacturing Company, a family-owned corporation. Kenneth owned 20 per cent of the outstanding stock previously as a result of a graduation gift, and the remaining 30 per cent is held equally by his mother and sister.

As Kenneth sees it, his alternatives are to sell his shares of the corporation or to continue operating the business. On the advice of the Andre family's attorney, Kenneth has engaged you, an independent Certified Public Accountant, to aid him in making his decision.

In your initial inspection of the company's operations and examination of its records, you discover the following facts:

(1) The company occupies two rented buildings owned by the same individual, one of which is used to house the manufacturing operations and the other serves as a warehouse. The lease agreement, which will expire on September 30,

19x2, contains an option to purchase the land and buildings. The terms of the 20-year lease provide for a monthly rental of $400. If the lessee elects to purchase the property, one-fourth of the total rentals already paid may be applied to the $100,000 purchase price if the option is exercised before the expiration date. The lease is renewable for 20 more years at a monthly rental of $500. Annual property taxes of $900 and average annual maintenance costs of $1,200 are paid by the owner of the property.

(2) Prior to his death, Kenneth's father acted as general manager of the business and personally supervised all advertising and selling.

(3) According to the plant manager, operations have been on a two-shift basis, although these shifts have not been working at full capacity. He also said, "We've got to do something about this old machinery. The maintenance costs and amount of lost time due to breakdowns are terrific."

(4) The warehouse contains a considerable amount of shopworn and obsolete furniture.

(5) Manufacturing materials are purchased on a "hand-to-mouth" basis. The materials used in the manufacture of all the company's products are of a similar type.

(6) Although there are no signs of increasing competition in the local area, sales records indicate a slow but consistent decline in the company's sales.

(7) The company has not maintained records of the unit costs of manufacturing its products. The present records consist of a checkbook, a sales record, an expense record, and an itemized list of prices paid for the major tools and equipment used in the business. Kenneth's father used these records as the basis for determining the company's annual net income for tax purposes.

The only other financial records pertain to the payroll. These records show for each pay period the hours worked, wage rate, gross wages earned, deductions for Social Security taxes and federal income tax, and net pay for each employee.

(8) In your examination of the sales invoice file, you discover that many of the accounts receivable are between six months and two years past due. All sales were subject to a deduction of 2 per cent discount if paid within 10 days, and the full amount was due 30 days from the date of sale.

(9) The company's liabilities consist of several small accounts payable arising from the purchases of materials on credit and installment notes payable to the bank for the purchase of the delivery trucks. All payments have been made when due.

(10) One bookkeeper keeps all accounting records and handles all cash receipts and payments. The bookkeeper prepares the weekly payrolls and also checks all incoming shipments of materials against the invoices.

REQUIRED:

a. What problems face Kenneth Andre?

b. What additional types of information do you need in helping Kenneth reach a decision? How would each type of information be used?

c. How would the information desired by a prospective purchaser of the business differ from your answer in (*b*)?

d. Discuss the major weaknesses in general management, financial management, production, and sales which should be corrected if Kenneth decides to operate the business. Present your suggestions dealing with financial management and accounting in some detail.

e. In what general ways might the $94,000 cash bequest be used in the business?

Chapter 2

Measuring Business Financial Status

Business objectives

The motives of the individuals who shape the policies and make the important decisions of a business are often complex. The most dominant ones are economic. The organizers of a business are induced primarily by the hope of economic rewards to commit their capital, labor, and management ability to the production of goods or services. They expect to receive compensation for their time, energy, and ability and for the use of their property; and they also expect a reward for their assumption of business risks.

The profit motive is the most important one in business, but there are others which often have a great influence on the conduct of business affairs. Some of these are the satisfaction from doing a job well; the desire for the respect of others; the desire to be one's own boss; and, occasionally, the desire for the power to direct and influence others.

The motives of the individuals who control the business are translated into the objectives of the business, which are sometimes stated, sometimes implied. Important business aims are to survive, to grow in absolute terms, and to grow in relation to other firms—to gain a larger share of the market.

The short-run objectives of a business may differ in some degree from its long-range objectives, but the two should be consistent. Enlightened owners and managers realize that the extent to which they accomplish these ends depends upon the actions of their customers, employees, suppliers, and public, who are also motivated by self-interest. To achieve its long-run objectives, the business must attract and retain the patronage of customers on the basis of better quality of goods and services, lower prices, or a similar appeal. A business which recognizes these facts has a better chance of surviving to reach its long-range goals than one which is directed chiefly to earning for its owners the largest possible income in the short run.

Modern businesses are recognizing to an increasing extent their social responsibility, one aspect of which is the importance of their financial health to employees, customers, and the community. In order to survive for the long term, an enterprise must not only attract and keep customers; it must also remain solvent and pay a satisfactory reward to its owners and managers.

Periodic income is an objective measure of the rate at which a business is moving toward its economic goal. The financial position, or status, of a business at any given time is an objective measure of its solvency. These are the two basic classes of information about a business which accounting is designed to provide.

Need for measurement of financial status: an illustrative case

William Daniels, whose difficulties upon unexpectedly finding himself manager of the Lawson Clothing Company were described in Chapter 1, knew that the survival of the business was at stake when he approached Mr. Dorian, the bank vice-president, with a request for a loan. Later, in his initial conference with Mr. Perkins, a partner in the CPA firm of Perkins and Mattox, William learned that among the most important financial information desired by the bank was a statement of the financial status of the business—of the details of the property it owned, the debts it owed, and the equity of its owners. The bank, Mr. Perkins explained, was particularly interested in knowing the likelihood that the business would remain healthy until the proposed loan was repaid.

At first this explanation came as a relief to William, for he did not think it would take long to list all of the property of the clothing company—equipment, furniture, money. But then he remembered that he did not even know for sure what the correct bank balance was. And he had forgotten about the mess in which he had found the records of customers' accounts. Then he thought of the back-breaking job of listing the stock of merchandise, and he began to realize that the task would not be easy.

William told Mr. Perkins that he thought he could get the figures on how much the merchandise and equipment were worth. Most of the stock was marked with its selling price, and he thought that a few telephone calls would suffice to get price quotations on the equipment.

Mr. Perkins informed him that the figures used in the financial statements would have to be based on what the merchandise and equipment actually cost the business, not what they would sell for now. Guesses as to the current value of business property would be too unreliable. Even if good approximations of resale value could be made, it would not be proper to use them in the financial statements. The merchandise might never be sold, and the business did not even expect to sell the equipment, but rather intended to use it.

Although William was somewhat skeptical about the correctness of this opinion, he decided not to pursue the point until he could study the matter further. Besides, he dreaded having Mr. Perkins find out how skimpy the records dealing with actual cost were. The conference concluded with a request by Mr. Perkins that William send him the latest statement of financial status which had been prepared for the company.

William was happy to have additional time to collect the desired information. Again enlisting Mrs. Daniels' aid, he spent many days and nights counting, listing, and searching the paid invoice files for cost information. The task was hopeless for most of the equipment. It had evidently been bought many years ago, because William could not find the appropriate bills or checks. The merchandise problem involved a number of complications. Inventory-taking was constantly interrupted by changes in the quantities as a result of sales and incoming shipments. William could find the invoice costs of some items, but other items had been bought on several different occasions at several different prices. Which items were on hand?

Having done about all he could on the inventory measurement, William racked his brain to think of other types of business property. What about the good reputation Mr. Lawson had built up during all these years? Surely that was worth something. And what about the several years remaining on the store lease? William listed everything he could think of, so as to make the best possible impression on the bank.

Assets and equities

The financial status, or position, of an accounting entity at any given moment is shown by two factors, its *assets* and its *equities*. *Assets* are the economic resources owned by the enterprise which are capable of giving service benefits to its future operations and which can be measured objectively in terms of money. Accounting is concerned with providing information about the *forms* which these assets take (such as cash, accounts receivable, inventories, equipment, and buildings); their *money amounts* ($8,000 in cash); the *sources* from which the business acquires them (owners and creditors); and the *changes* in their forms and amounts ($40 worth of merchandise was sold for $60 cash).

The sources from which a business derives its assets are referred to as *equities*. These sources are of two types, *liabilities* and *owners' equity*. *Liabilities* are the equities of the creditors of the entity. As a rule, they require the payment of a specific amount of money to a particular party at a definite future time, although occasionally the amount of money to be paid is indefinite, they may be settled by some means other than money, the identity of the creditor is not yet known, or the due date is uncertain. Examples of liabilities are notes payable, accounts payable, and bonds payable.

Owners' equity shows the amount of assets which the business has obtained from its owners by way of investment, as well as the amount which has been added or subtracted as a result of business operations. In contrast to *liabilities*, which usually involve specific claims against the business, owners' equity represents an indefinite and residual claim. The owners hope to receive distributions of income if the business is successful and to receive a return of their investment if it is terminated, but they are promised neither. They have a right to receive only whatever income is distributed (in a corporation, only after formal action by the board of directors) or whatever remains at the termination of a business after its liabilities have been paid.

The accounting equation: assets = equities

Assets and equities are merely two different ways of looking at the same set of financial facts about an entity. Assets show the *forms* of the service potentials owned by the entity, while equities show the *sources* of these same service potentials.

EXAMPLE 1: Three individuals organize a business and each invests $5,000 cash in it. What is its financial status immediately after these events?

SOLUTION: The business has an *asset* of $15,000 in the form of cash and, at the same time, *owners' equity* of $15,000, resulting from this investment by the owners.

Because they describe the same facts in different ways, assets and equities must always be equal in money amount. It is often very useful to state this relationship as an equation,

$$\text{Assets} = \text{Equities.}$$

In Example 1, assets of $15,000 cash are exactly equal to the owners' equity of $15,000.

The groups interested in a business need to know how much of the equities are those of business creditors and how much are those of the owners. If the two types of equities are substituted for the total, the expanded equation becomes,

$$\text{Assets} = \text{Liabilities} + \text{Owners' Equity}.$$

EXAMPLE 2:   Immediately after its organization the business in Example 1 buys $5,000 worth of equipment on account. What is its financial status then?

SOLUTION: Assets, $20,000 = Liabilities, $5,000 + Owners' Equity, $15,000. The assets consist of $15,000 cash and $5,000 equipment; the liability is an account payable, and the owners' equity results from the initial investment of the assets.

Sometimes, in accounting analysis, it is helpful in determining an unknown to remember that in an equation any term may be transferred to the opposite side if its sign is changed. Thus, Assets − Liabilities = Owners' Equity; and Assets − Owners' Equity = Liabilities.

EXAMPLE 3:   A business has assets totaling $17,000 and owes debts of $11,000. What is the equity of the owner?

SOLUTION: Assets, $17,000 − Liabilities, $11,000 = Owners' equity, $6,000.

EXAMPLE 4:   A man has built up the assets of a business to $40,000, although his initial investment was only $6,000 and reinvested earnings amounted to $12,000. How much has the business obtained by borrowing?

SOLUTION:

Assets, $40,000 − Owners' Equity, $18,000 = Liabilities, $22,000.

Measurement in terms of money

Useful description of the financial factors and relationships of business requires that, in addition to *form* (described as assets) and *source* (identified as equities), there be some measure of the economic significance, or *amount*, of each. In measuring the amounts of these financial elements, there are three key questions: (1) What elements should be measured? (2) What is the proper yardstick to use? and (3) When should the measurements be made?

The financial elements of a business which are measured by accounting are only those which can be measured objectively in terms of money. The public road in front of a manufacturing plant will be of service benefit to the business because it will give customers, employees, and suppliers access to the plant. It is not an asset, however, because it is not owned by the business. Similarly, the good morale of the employees is not an asset because it cannot be measured dependably.

Why are money amounts used for measuring the productive factors and relationships of a business? A business is formed chiefly to earn a money return for its owners in exchange for its output. Because money has a general command over all goods and services, money amounts are a convenient and suitable yardstick to use in measuring the financial elements of business.

EXAMPLE 5:   A retail business owns 1,200 shirts, 103 suits, a typewriter, and five $20 bills. How much are its assets?

SOLUTION: Different assets can be added together or compared only if they are converted to a common denominator. Stating them in their money equivalents expresses them in terms of such a common denominator.

It is important to recognize that the command of money over particular classes of goods and services (shown by their *prices*) changes from time to time, and that the money prices of these goods and services change in relation to each other. Implied in the use of money for measuring assets and equities is the assumption that money amounts have a constant meaning.

Objective evidence: market transactions

Market transactions—dealings of the business with outsiders—are used as the principal basis for determining both the amount and the timing of accounting measurements. Two parties, the business and the customer, determine by arms'-length bargaining the money amount of the business event. This bargained price is in objective measure suitable for use in accounting.

Market transactions usually determine objectively the money amounts of productive facilities acquired by the business, such as equipment, supplies, materials, merchandise, personal services, and borrowed cash. Often, too, they may be used to measure the amounts of assets which the owners invest in the business.

Acquisition cost

The amount of money which the buyer pays for a productive factor, or the money equivalent of what he agrees to pay later, is the *cost* of the factor as determined by a market transaction. It may be assumed that the factor is worth at least its cost to the purchaser, or he would not have bought it. Initially, then, assets purchased by a business are recorded at their *acquisition cost*, and the related equities are measured by the same yardstick.

Even though assets change form within the business, either by production or use, it is assumed in accounting that they continue to be worth at least their cost to the business unless there is objective evidence to the contrary. Although the appropriate classification for describing the productive factor may change, acquisition cost continues to be used as the basis of measurement.

Often the term *costs* is used to refer to productive factors which are measured in this way. Costs acquired by the business should be classified in such a way as to facilitate tracing their later changes in form within the business, as well as their final disposition.

EXAMPLE 6:   A business buys merchandise for resale, agreeing to pay $500 within 30 days. What effect is there on its assets and equities?

SOLUTION: The business acquires an asset, merchandise, costing $500, and it incurs a corresponding liability, accounts payable, of the same amount.

Cost is more difficult to determine when a business gives something other than money in exchange for an asset. In such cases an attempt is made to estimate what the asset would have cost in money if it had been purchased. The current money equivalent, or fair market value, of the thing used to acquire the new asset is considered to be its cost. That amount measures the sacrifice made by the business in acquiring it.

EXAMPLE 7:   A business exchanges its typewriter for a filing cabinet. What is the cost of the filing cabinet?

SOLUTION: It is reliably determined that the typewriter could have been sold for $80 cash if it had not been traded; therefore, the cost of the filing cabinet is $80.

If the fair market value of the asset given in an exchange cannot be measured reliably, the fair market value of the asset received in exchange is considered to be the next best measure of its cost.

The business transaction

If the operation of a business consisted of a single, brief undertaking, such as a use of resources to buy a block of corporate stock in the hope of a quick speculative gain, the problem of measuring assets and equities would be rather simple. The venture would be in progress for such a short time that there would not be much need for financial statements during its life. It would be satisfactory to measure them at the completion of the venture, when objective information as to their amounts was available.

Most modern businesses are not of this temporary, or venture, type, but are formed with the purpose of operating indefinitely. A retail business does not ordinarily plan to close its doors after it sells the first lot of merchandise. Instead, it will continually replenish and perhaps increase its stock of merchandise. New styles and new lines will supplement the old; new equipment and furnishings will replace the worn-out and obsolete. The business may even open branches in other locations. If operations go according to plan, there will never be a time when all of its assets are in the form of money. That is desirable, but it makes measurement of financial status more difficult.

Even the simplest business is a complex series of overlapping ventures of varying duration. Each venture consists of a cycle of buying an asset, paying for it, selling the product of the business to a customer, collecting for the sale, and buying another asset. The assets during one of these cycles might be shown as follows:

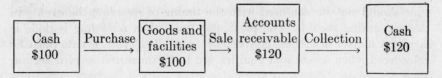

If it were possible to take a still photograph of business operations, the picture would show many individual cycles in progress. Some would have just been completed; others, just begun. In between these extremes would be a host of cycles of various types and sizes in many different stages of completion.

An example of a completed cycle would be a sale just rung up on the cash register. New cycles would be illustrated by merchandise just received from the manufacturer and an insurance policy just purchased. Cycles well under way would be represented by unsold goods on the shelves, accounts receivable not collected, an office desk with one-fourth of its service life gone, and an insurance policy with two-thirds of the protection period expired.

Accounting attempts to measure the effect of business transactions on assets and equities by breaking the complex business activity into identifiable, measurable events. These events, the units of activity for which accounting information is recorded, are called *transactions*.

Some of the principal types of transactions which most businesses think it important to measure are:

(1) Investments in the business by owners;
(2) Withdrawals of investments;
(3) Purchase of productive facilities and services;
(4) Borrowing of money;
(5) Payment of debts owed to others;
(6) Use of facilities and services in production;
(7) Sale of goods and services; and
(8) Collection of debts owed by others.

The effect of each of these types of events on the assets and equities of the business can usually be measured objectively on the basis of market transactions.

Timing of measurements

The preceding section dealt with the very important accounting matter of selecting the events which are to be taken into consideration in measuring financial position at a particular time. The types of transactions which are considered in measuring assets and equities are similar for all businesses. The *selection* of the events which relate to financial status at a given time should not be confused with the timing of *recording* the events in the accounting records. The particular time when recording is done is largely a matter of clerical convenience, but all relevant events must be considered when assets and equities are to be measured as of a certain time.

EXAMPLE 8:   A business keeps a soft drink machine for the convenience of its employees. A few drinks are sold each day, and the coin box is emptied and the supply replenished about once a week. When should the sales be recorded?

SOLUTION: It would be extremely inconvenient to record a sale each time an employee buys a drink. The most convenient time for recording the sales would probably be when the machine is refilled. However, a statement of financial position should include the amount of cash and unsold drinks owned on the date for which the position is determined.

Double-entry accounting

Each business transaction always has a dual effect—it increases an asset or an equity, and it decreases an asset or an equity. Accounting

Summary of Effect of Transactions on the Accounting Equation

Type of Transaction	Assets	= Liabilities	+ Owners' Equity
1. Assets increased and equities increased:			
a. Owners invest an asset	+$10,000		+$10,000
b. An asset is acquired on credit	+ 8,000	+$8,000	
Subtotals	$18,000 =	$8,000	+$10,000
2. Assets decreased and equities decreased:			
a. Owners withdraw an asset	− 100		− 100
Subtotals	$17,900 =	$8,000	+$ 9,900
b. A debt is partially paid	− 5,000	− 5,000	
Subtotals	$12,900 =	$3,000	+$ 9,900
3. Assets increased and assets decreased:			
a. One asset is exchanged for another	− 2,000		
	+ 2,000		
Subtotals	$12,900 =	$3,000	+$ 9,900
4. Equities increased and equities decreased:			
a. One liability is exchanged for another		− 3,000	
		+ 3,000	
Subtotals	$12,900 =	$3,000	+$ 9,900
b. A withdrawal of owners is to be paid later		+ 500	− 500
Subtotals	$12,900 =	$3,500	+$ 9,400
c. A part of a debt is exchanged for owners' equity		− 200	+ 200
Totals	$12,900 =	$3,300	+$ 9,600

These are by no means all of the types of transactions which occur in a given business. They are selected merely to show various combinations of mathematical effect on assets, liabilities, and owners' equity.

Fig. 1.

shows both of the effects of every transaction; that is what is meant by
double-entry accounting. Double-entry accounting preserves the equality
of assets and equities at all times. This is illustrated in Figure 1, a summary of the mathematical effect of various types of transactions on the
accounting equation. The subtotals of assets and equities after each transaction show that their equality has been preserved.

The account

A summary which shows the changes in, and the balance of, each type
of asset and equity about which the business wishes information is called
an *account*. Accounts are the basic classifications for which information is
collected in accounting. The essence of the account is the nature of the
data which it contains, not the physical form in which the data appear.
The principal types of information shown are:

(1) The *account title*, which describes a type of asset or equity;
(2) The amounts of *increases* and *decreases;*
(3) The difference between the two, the *account balance*.

Each business event, or transaction, must be analyzed according to the
particular accounts which it affects, the nature of the change (increase or
decrease), and the amount. The summary of an account distinguishes the
increases from the decreases by recording them in different positions, for
example:

Asset, Cash

	Increases		*Decreases*
(a)	1,000	(b)	300
(d)	900	(c)	500
	1,900		800
Balance, 1,100			

The basic form illustrated above is called a *T-account*, because of its
appearance. It is a useful outline form of account for teaching purposes,
and it is also the skeleton of the account arrangement commonly used in
business practice. The more elaborate form commonly used in practice is
shown in the following illustration.

(ACCOUNT TITLE)

(YEAR) (MO.) (DAY)		(REF.)	(DEBIT AMOUNTS)	(YEAR) (MO.) (DAY)		(REF.)	(CREDIT AMOUNTS)

Increases in assets, such as Cash in the preceding illustration, are recorded on the left-hand side of the account and decreases on the right-hand side. If an asset has any balance at all after a series of transactions have been recorded, the balance appears on the left-hand side of the account as an excess of increases over decreases. The balance of the Cash account in the preceding illustration is $1,100.

A similar account record is used to show the effect of various transactions on each other asset and each equity about which the business wishes information.

Debit and credit

Assets are types of resources owned by the business and equities are their sources. In a sense they are opposites, describing the effect of the same transactions from different points of view. It is customary to show changes in equities in an *opposite* way from changes in assets. To illustrate:

Liability, Notes Payable

	Decreases			*Increases*
(b)	300		(a)	1,000
(c)	500		(d)	900
	800			1,900
		Balance, 1,100		

If a liability or any other equity has a balance, it appears on the right-hand side of the account. In the illustration, the balance of the liability, Notes Payable, is $1,100. This illustration is related to the preceding illustration of the Cash account. Transaction (a) shows how borrowing money in exchange for a promissory note would be recorded: as an increase in the asset, Cash, and as an increase in the liability, Notes Payable. Transaction (b), a payment of money to apply on the debt, involves a decrease in Cash and a decrease in Notes Payable. Transaction (c) is another payment on the debt, and transaction (d) is another loan.

This illustration is oversimplified. In reality, increases in cash would be offset by increases in various other equities in addition to Notes Payable, and by decreases in other assets. Likewise, changes in Notes Payable might be balanced by changes in asset accounts other than Cash and by changes in other equity accounts.

The rule of opposites is very useful in accounting analysis. Assets equal equities, and this equality is preserved in recording each transaction. Furthermore, asset increases and balances appear on the left-hand side of asset accounts, and equity increases and balances appear on the right-hand side of equity accounts. Total changes recorded on the left-hand side of accounts will therefore equal total changes on the right-hand side of accounts, and balances on the left-hand side of accounts (assets) will equal balances on the right-hand side of accounts (equities).

A change shown on the *left-hand* side of any account is called a *debit*, and a change shown on the *right-hand* side of any account is a *credit*. Likewise, balances on the left-hand side of an account (assets) are debit balances and balances on the right-hand side (equities) are credit balances. These rules may be summarized as follows:

Debits (entries on the left) show:	Credits (entries on the right) show:
Increases in assets	Decreases in assets
Decreases in liabilities and owners' equity	Increases in liabilities and owners' equity.

If changes on the left-hand side of accounts always equal changes on the right, and balances on the left-hand side of accounts always equal balances on the right, *debits* (changes on the left-hand side) always equal *credits* (changes on the right-hand side).

The Journal

The account, in which is summarized the effect of all transactions on a particular type of asset or equity, has been described first, but it is usually the second step in recording transactions. For clerical convenience, each transaction is first analyzed to determine its debit and credit effect on particular assets and equities. This analysis is entered in a chronological record, called a *journal*. Then at some convenient later time the effect of transactions on each asset or equity, as shown by the *journal entry*, is recorded in each account. The process of transferring this information from the journal to the accounts is called *posting*.

The essential components of a journal entry are:

(1) The name of the account(s) to be debited;
(2) The name of the account(s) to be credited;
(3) Debit and credit amounts;
(4) Descriptive information about the transaction:
   (a) Date;
   (b) Concise explanation.

In the simplest type of journal record, illustrated in Example 9, the position of the account titles and amounts indicates which are to be debited (those on the left) and which are to be credited (those on the right).

EXAMPLE 9:   A business was organized and the owners invested $10,000 in cash. Show this in journal form.

SOLUTION:

(Date)   (Account Debited)   (Amount Debited)
        (Account Credited)   (Amount Credited)
        (Explanation)

19x1
June 1   A, Cash.........................   10,000
         OE, Owners' Investment......   10,000
        The owners invested cash in the
        business.

There are many more efficient methods of recording business transactions which recur frequently. Some of them are described in Chapter 9. The journal arrangement illustrated above is used in teaching as a brief method of showing the effects of transactions. The abbreviations, "A" for Asset, "L" for Liability, and "OE" for Owners' Equity, are used in this text to help the reader analyze the effects of transactions. They are not used in actual practice. Also, for convenience, later illustrations omit the column headings of journals, shown in parentheses in Example 9, because they are always understood to have the same meaning. The dollar sign, too, is unnecessary; all amounts in a journal entry are expressed in terms of money.

Illustrative journal entries

The following extended illustration shows journal entries for transactions of the types whose effects on assets and equities were summarized in Figure 1. The transactions are those of the Motor Mower Company for the month of June, 19x1. The identifying numbers and letters in parentheses above each journal entry refer to the transaction types of Figure 1.

19x1   (1a)
June   1   A, Cash................................ 10,000
         OE, Owners' Investment.............   10,000
        The business received an investment of cash
        from its owners.

                 (1b)
   2   A, Merchandise.........................   8,000
         L, Accounts Payable.................   8,000
        Purchased 80 lawnmowers for resale on
        credit from the manufacturer at a cost of
        $100 each.

                 (2a)
   4   OE, Owners' Investment.................   100
         A, Cash.............................   100
        The corporation redeemed for cash one stock
        holder's share.

(2b)

June 6 L, Accounts Payable...................... 5,000
             A, Cash............................   5,000
             Made a partial payment to the manufac-
             turer for the lawnmowers.

(3a)

9 A, Notes Receivable...................... 2,000
             A, Cash............................   2,000
             Lent cash to a customer, taking his promis-
             sory note due in 30 days.

(4a)

24 L, Accounts Payable...................... 3,000
             L, Notes Payable......................   3,000
             Gave the lawnmower manufacturer a prom-
             issory note for the balance owed on account.

(4b)

28 OE, Owners' Investment.................. 500
             L, Note Payable to Officer.............   500
             The company reacquired an officer's stock
             in exchange for a promissory note due
             July 14.

(4c)

30 L, Notes Payable........................ 200
             OE, Owners' Investment..............   200
             The manufacturer agreed to accept two
             shares of the company's capital stock in
             partial payment of the promissory note.

Posting to ledger accounts

A collection of the accounts of a business is called a *ledger*. The following illustration shows how the transactions of the Motor Mower Company would appear after they had been posted to simple T-accounts. In actual business practice, each account is usually kept on a separate page, and the various accounts are kept together in a bound volume, a loose-leaf binder, or a file.

A, Cash

19x1	(Debits)			19x1	(Credits)		
June 1		(1a)	10,000	June 4		(2a)	100
				6		(2b)	5,000
				9		(3a)	2,000
	Balance, 2,900						7,100

A, Notes Receivable

19x1					
June 9		(3a)	2,000		

A, Merchandise

19x1			
June 2	(1b)	8,000	

L, Accounts Payable

19x1				19x1			
June 6	(2b)	5,000		June 2		(1b)	8,000
24	(4a)	3,000					
		8,000		Balance, 0			

L, Notes Payable

19x1				19x1			
June 30	(4c)	200		June 24		(4a)	3,000
				Balance, 2,800			

L, Note Payable to Officer

				19x1			
				June 28		(4b)	500

OE, Owners' Investment

19x1				19x1			
June 4	(2a)	100		June 1		(1a)	10,000
28	(4b)	500		30		(4c)	200
		600					10,200
				Balance, 9,600			

The items in parentheses in the ledger accounts are the identifying numbers of the journal entries, included to make cross-reference easier.

Persons studying accounting for the first time often think that the ledger is an unnecessary duplication of the journal—that everything is done twice. It is difficult to show in a textbook illustration why this is not true, because the great number of transactions and the timing of the various steps of accounting are not apparent. The journal shows the entire effect of a single transaction; but if there are numerous transactions, it does not give a clear picture of asset and equity balances. The ledger contains these balances, but it does not show the other accounts affected and the explanatory information contained in the journal analysis of transactions.

List of account balances: the trial balance

Accounting attempts to compress the results of a multitude of transactions in such a way that they can be more easily interpreted. Each journal entry is a complete analysis of the effects of a transaction; each account summarizes the effects of transactions according to type of asset and equity. A list of asset and equity balances resulting from this analysis and summarization is helpful in interpreting the total effects of the business events. Such a list, illustrated below, is called a *trial balance*.

MOTOR MOWER COMPANY
Trial Balance
June 30, 19x1

	(Debits)	(Credits)
A, Cash	$ 2,900	
A, Notes Receivable	2,000	
A, Merchandise	8,000	
L, Notes Payable		$ 2,800
L, Note Payable to Officer		500
OE, Owners' Investment		9,600
Totals	$12,900	$12,900

The total of debit balances must always equal the total of credit balances; otherwise, an error has been made in addition, computing account balances, listing the balances, posting from the journal to the ledger, or journalizing. The fact that the trial balance totals agree is necessary, but not sufficient to prove that the accounts are accurate. The trial balance would still balance if entire transactions were omitted, if the wrong amounts were used, or if the wrong accounts were debited or credited.

Statement of financial position

On the basis of the account balances listed in the preceding trial balance, the following statement of the financial position, or status, of the Motor Mower Company at the end of June was prepared.

MOTOR MOWER COMPANY
Statement of Financial Position
June 30, 19x1

ASSETS		LIABILITIES	
Cash	$2,900	Notes payable	$2,800
Notes receivable	2,000	Note payable, officer	500
Merchandise	8,000	Total liabilities	$ 3,300
		OWNERS' EQUITY	
		Owners' investment	9,600
Total assets	$12,900	Total equities	$12,900

The assets and equities are shown beside each other here to facilitate comparisons, but often the equities are shown below the assets in statements of financial position. Within each half of the statement, the left-hand and right-hand columns are for *details* and *totals*, respectively (not debits and credits).

Summary

Accounting is primarily concerned with the forms, money amounts, sources, and changes of assets which are various types of future service potentials owned by the business. Assets are measured in terms of their money costs as determined in market transactions because such costs are objectively determined.

Assets are always equal to equities because they are merely different ways of looking at the same set of facts. Assets show the forms of service potentials; equities (liabilities and owners' equity) show their sources. In order to distinguish increases from decreases, and asset changes from equity changes, accountants have adopted a custom of showing changes of a given type in the same position: debit (left) and credit (right).

The financial status of a business is measured by analyzing the effect of each business event, or transaction, on assets and equities and summarizing the effects of these transactions in accounts for each type of asset and equity. The account balances are listed in a Trial Balance as a partial check on their accuracy, and then arranged in various types of financial reports. A common report, the Statement of Financial Position, shows the balance of each asset and each equity and their totals as of a certain date.

QUESTIONS AND PROBLEMS

2-1   Mr. Joseph Ballon argues that the only reason why any business is in existence is to earn all of the profit it can.

REQUIRED:

Do you agree with Mr. Ballon's statement? Give reasons for your answer.

2-2   "The total dollar amount of assets on the statement of financial position on any given date indicates what the company is worth at that time."

REQUIRED:

Comment on this statement.

2-3   Mr. Sharlon operated the Sharlon Motel as sole owner, and in addition owned 98% of the capital stock of the Mesomar Hotel. The motel sold the hotel a substantial quantity of furniture which it no longer needed.

REQUIRED:

a. What measurement problems does this transaction create?
b. How would you go about solving them?

2-4   If liability and owners' equity accounts both show sources of assets and both appear on the right-hand side of the statement of financial position, why are they separated into two major sections?

2-5   Liabilities are usually considered to be claims against the assets of a company, and, at the same time, they are sources of assets.

REQUIRED:

Is this statement contradictory? Explain.

2-6   Does the good reputation which a business has built up during the years qualify as an asset? Explain.

2-7   A business has an old machine which is no longer in use stored in its warehouse. The machine is still in good running condition, but far superior machines are now on the market. It could be sold as scrap for about $25, but it would cost at least this much to move it away.

REQUIRED:

Is this machine an asset? Explain.

2-8   *M, N,* and *O* applied for a charter to do business as a corporation in the state in which they resided. Total costs associated with obtaining the charter amounted to $1,500. The charter was granted.

REQUIRED:

a. Did the $1,500 spent result in an asset? Why?
b. If so, to whom did the asset belong?

2-9   The ledger shows the effect of accounting transactions on various types of asset and equity accounts. So does the journal.

REQUIRED:

Explain why both are necessary.

2-10   On September 1, 19x1 the Apex Corporation had its light meter connected and paid a $25 deposit to the electric utility company.

REQUIRED:

a. What accounts would be affected on the books of the Apex Corporation, and in what way?
b. What accounts would be affected on the books of the electric utility company, and in what way?

2-11   In 19x5 the city of Darien has levied a property tax on the Maxwell Manufacturing Co. amounting to $1,200 for the purpose of helping pay off bonds to finance construction of a city hall. A similar tax will have to be levied in each of the years 19x6, 19x7, and 19x8, after which the bonds will be retired.

REQUIRED:

a. From the point of view of the Maxwell Manufacturing Co., is the 19x5 tax an asset? An equity?
b. Is the tax to be levied in the next three years an asset? An equity?

2-12   "Implied in the use of money for measuring assets and equities is the assumption that money amounts have a constant meaning."

REQUIRED:

a. Name two assets for which this assumption would usually be reasonable in preparing a statement of financial position.
b. Name one asset for which this assumption would often be unreasonable.
c. Why is this assumption followed in accounting?
d. What objections do you see to the assumption?

2-13   On September 1, 19x2, total liabilities of an entity were $40,000. On September 2, 19x2, total liabilities amounted to $30,000.

REQUIRED:

a. Illustrate a situation in which the total dollar amount of assets would have changed as a result of the change in liabilities.

b. Illustrate a situation in which the total dollar amount of assets would not have changed as a result of the change in liabilities.

2-14   A company manufactures electric appliances.

REQUIRED:

a. Name one of its liabilities which would be specific as to amount, creditor, and due date.
b. Name a liability which would be specific as to amount and creditor, but indefinite as to due date.
c. Name a liability which would be specific as to creditor, but indefinite as to amount and due date.
d. Name a liability which would be indefinite as to all three.

2-15

REQUIRED:

a. What is the major purpose of a trial balance?
b. If a trial balance is in balance, does this mean that all of the transactions have been recorded correctly? Explain.
c. Explain how the rule of double entry affects the totals of the trial balance.

2-16   Mr. Madison presents the following information from his records to show that assets do not always equal equities:

Assets	$14,000
Liabilities	6,000
Owners' equity	7,900

REQUIRED:

Does this invalidate the rule that assets are always equal to equities? Explain.

2-17

REQUIRED:

a. If on December 31, 19x1, a business owns assets amounting to $68,000 and owes debts of $49,000, what were the major sources of its assets, and how much was derived from each?
b. The owners organized the business by putting in $20,000 of their personal funds on January 1, 19x1. What has happened to the owners' equity during the year? Give possible reasons for any change which may have taken place.

2-18   The Best Hardware Company owns a vacant lot for which it paid $5,000 in a downtown business district. On January 31 the company was offered $10,000 for the property. In another offer, on February 15, the Harris Development Corporation offered a building in a neighboring city in exchange for the vacant lot. The building was recently appraised by the Simon Realty Company at $12,500. The Best Hardware Company accepted the offer of February 15.

REQUIRED:

At what amount should the building be shown on the books of the Best Hardware Company? Explain.

2-19   The owner of a business which had kept no accounting records accumulates the following information, based upon a careful study of the amounts actually paid and owed by the business.

Balance on deposit in the bank	$ 7,100
Amount owed for property taxes	300
Cost of merchandise for sale	8,000
Amount owed to creditor for part of the merchandise	2,000
Lot held for the purpose of erecting a store building	20,000
Mortgage note owed on the lot	15,000

REQUIRED:

a. Determine the amount of the owners' equity of the business.
b. Is this information reliable? Explain.

2-20

REQUIRED:

Use journal form to show the effect of each of the following events on the assets and equities of a millinery shop.

a. On July 18 the owner ordered hats of a total cost of $300 from the manufacturer.
b. On August 7 the hats arrived. Several items had been out of stock, so the total cost of the hats in the shipment was only $240. The manufacturer's credit terms required payment on August 31.
c. The millinery shop was unable to pay for the hats on August 31. Give the entry needed on August 31.
d. On September 25 the millinery shop sent a check for $150 to the manufacturer to apply on the account.

2-21
During the month of May, 19x1, the following transactions took place at the Child's Delight Toy Company.

(1) On May 1, the business was formed. One owner invested $30,000 cash and the other transferred to the toy company his ownership of a building valued at $40,000.
(2) On May 2 the business purchased manufacturing equipment for $20,000 cash.
(3) On May 2 tools were bought for $500 on account.
(4) On May 6 the company obtained a $5,000 cash loan from the bank, giving a promissory note in exchange.
(5) On May 7 materials to be used in the manufacture of toys were purchased on account for $4,000.
(6) The owners decided to offer $1,800 for a lot adjacent to the building, for which the present owner was asking $2,000. The offer was made on May 10.
(7) Some of the materials received in (5) were defective, and on May 11 they were returned to the supplier for credit. According to the supplier's invoice, the returned material cost $50.
(8) On May 17 a payment of $500 was made to the supplier of the materials.
(9) The owners each withdrew $200 cash, a total of $400, for their personal use on May 31.
(10) On May 31 office supplies, which had been ordered on May 21, arrived. Their cost of $150 was to be paid within ten days.

REQUIRED:

a. Prepare journal entries in good form for each of the above transactions.
b. Post the journal entries to T-accounts.
c. Prepare a Statement of Financial Position as of May 31, 19x1.

2-22 Shown below is a Statement of Financial Position of the Quick Drive-in Restaurant as of February 28, 19x1.

Quick Drive-in Restaurant
Statement of Financial Position
February 28, 19x1

ASSETS		EQUITIES	
Cash	$ 250	Owners' Investment	$19,250
Supplies	1,600		
Equipment	3,400		
Land	2,000		
Building	12,000		
Total Assets	$19,250	Total Equities	$19,250

(1) On March 1, 19x1, Ronald Haymaker purchased the business and paid the following prices for its assets to be used in a new business, The Haymaker Drive-in: cash, $250; supplies, $1,500; equipment, $2,000; land, $2,500; and building, $9,000.

(2) Later in the day Mr. Haymaker requested his bank to transfer $1,000 from his personal account to a new account for the new business, The Haymaker Drive-in. The bank complied after getting a signed authorization.

(3) On March 2, 19x1, Mr. Haymaker arranged for the company to borrow $2,000 from his personal friend, Mr. Teagle.

(4) Mr. Teagle delivered the cash on March 3 and accepted the company's ninety-day, non-interest-bearing note.

(5) The business purchased new equipment on account from the Restaurant Supply Company for $1,200 on March 4.

(6) On the same date the company ordered supplies costing $800 from a food wholesaler, the Jeames Wholesale Grocery Company.

(7) On March 5 the business sold for $100 a used electric grill which had been purchased from the Quick Drive-in for $100.

(8) The supplies ordered on March 4 arrived from the wholesaler on March 6. The invoice, $800, included supplies billed at $75 which were not delivered.

(9) On March 7, Mr. Haymaker withdrew $100 cash for personal use.

(10) On March 8 the drive-in purchased for $1,900 cash additional land to be used as a parking lot.

(11) On March 9 six employees were hired. Total payroll would be $840 per month, beginning May 13, when the restaurant would open for business.

(12) On March 10 Mr. Haymaker sent the employees to the Novelty Garment Company to be fitted for uniforms.

(13) The Novelty Garment Company delivered the uniforms to the drive-in two days later and billed the company for $240.

(14) Each of the employees signed a contract to pay for the cost of his uniform, to be deducted in ten equal installments from his future pay checks.

REQUIRED:

a. Prepare journal entries for the above transactions.
b. Post the journal entries to T-accounts.
c. Prepare a Statement of Financial Position as of March 12, 19x1.

2-23 The following statement was prepared from the books of the Regal Realty Company on August 1, 19x1:

Regal Realty Company
Statement of Financial Position
August 1, 19x1

ASSETS			EQUITIES		
Cash............................	$	8,000	Liabilities:		
Rents receivable.............		7,500	Notes payable—bank.......	$	10,000
Land........................		65,000	Mortgages payable.........		90,000
Buildings...................		52,000	Total Liabilities..........		$100,000
			Owners' Equity..............		32,500
Total Assets............		$132,500	Total Equities...........		$132,500

After all transactions during the following week were posted to the accounts, another statement was prepared as follows:

Regal Realty Company
Statement of Financial Position
August 8, 19x1

ASSETS			EQUITIES		
Cash........................	$	3,500	Liabilities:		
Rents receivable.............		4,500	Notes payable—bank.......	$	8,000
Land........................		50,000	Mortgages payable.........		80,000
Buildings...................		60,000	Total Liabilities..........		$ 88,000
			Owners' Equity..............		30,000
Total Assets............		$118,000	Total Equities...........		$118,000

REQUIRED:

a. Prepare journal entries for each of the transactions which might account for the differences between the two statements.
b. Record the August 1 balances in T-accounts and post your journal entries to these accounts to check the accuracy of your solution.

CASE 2-1. KENT LUMBER AND SUPPLY COMPANY

You have just been employed as an accountant by the Kent Lumber and Supply Company, which sells building materials to contractors and homeowners. The business commenced operations on July 1, 19x1, and on June 30, 19x2, you proceed to prepare the annual financial statements.

The bank statement as of June 30, 19x2, shows a balance of $4,500, which agrees with the balance in the company's checkbook. The office safe contains $300 in cash and $200 in undeposited checks, made payable to the Kent Lumber and Supply Company. Included in the undeposited checks is a check for $50, dated July 10, 19x2, which has been credited to a customer's account.

On June 30, 19x2, the total of customers' accounts arising from credit sales amounts to $15,000. Also, the company has received sales orders of $7,500 to be shipped within the next few days. Non-interest-bearing promissory notes, signed by customers and made payable to the business, total $1,500. Advances have been made to employees in the amount of $300. These are supported by written memoranda.

The business purchased office supplies costing $850 for cash during the year. It is estimated that the cost of the supplies used was $600. Merchandise was purchased from suppliers at a total cost of $100,000, of which $32,000 is unpaid at the end of the year. The total lumber inventory as of June 30, 19x2, is $55,000, and the cost of other building supplies available for sale is $8,000. The June 30, 19x2, inventory lists some promotional materials of the type used during the grand-opening celebration. It is estimated that the cost of these unused materials is $200. Suppliers have loaned at no charge demonstration samples, valued at $1,000, for promotional purposes. The company has placed purchase orders for additional lumber and building supplies in the amount of $37,000.

A year ago the company obtained the use of a showroom and warehouses under a ten-year lease agreement at an annual rental of $5,000. Because of its desirable location, the company could easily sublease this property for $8,000 a year. On July 1, 19x1, the company paid two years' advance rent to the landlord. The company is also using power saws and other mill equipment, valued at $12,500, for which it pays rent of $1,200 a year. The rental charge for this equipment has been paid through June 30, 19x2.

During the year office equipment costing $1,500 was purchased for cash. On July 15, 19x1, the company rented two heavy-duty delivery trucks for $400 per month. The company paid a month's rent in advance on that date and has maintained this policy consistently. On June 30, 19x2, the company purchased for $3,000 cash an automobile to be used by the general manager. The list price of this car was $3,600. The company immediately took out a one-year comprehensive coverage insurance policy on the automobile, paying a total premium of $150.

Kent Lumber and Supply Company maintains a bulk-storage tank for the gasoline used by its delivery trucks. The 1,000-gallon tank was first filled on August 1, 19x1. Refills during the remainder of the year totaled 6,000 gallons. The gasoline is purchased at a contract price of 30¢ per gallon. A meter reading on June 30, 19x2, indicated that 6,600 gallons were used during the year.

The CDE Railroad has a railroad siding adjacent to the lumber yard, making it unnecessary for the company to truck the lumber to the main railroad yard. This results in an estimated annual saving of $2,000 in transportation costs.

All employees are paid monthly on the last day of the month. Total monthly salaries are $6,000, all of which have been paid when due.

The telephone company installed a PBX switchboard which cost $1,750. The monthly charge for the use of this equipment, $30, has been paid for every month except June.

The owner of the Kent Lumber and Supply Company originally invested $50,000 cash in the business, and he withdrew $5,000 during the year.

REQUIRED:

a. Prepare a Statement of Financial Position as of June 30, 19x2.
b. List the items which you did not include in the Statement of Financial Position, and give your reasons for excluding them.
c. What has been the increase or decrease in owners' equity since July 1, 19x1? Prepare a schedule to prove your answer.

Chapter **3**

Measuring Business Income

Need for measurement of income: an illustrative case

After several weeks of studying, consulting with Mr. Perkins, of the CPA firm of Perkins and Mattox, and digging into the files and records of the Lawson Clothing Company, William Daniels had been able to prepare what he thought was an accurate statement of the assets and equities of the company as of the last day of May. He had found information bearing on the acquisition cost of assets, which he had used as the basis for measuring the assets owned. From total assets he had subtracted the amount of liabilities owed to determine the amount of owners' equity.

William had decided to do the detailed work of accumulating the financial information himself, and then to engage the CPA firm to render an opinion on its reliability. Mr. Dorian, vice-president of the bank, had asked for a financial plan of the business showing how the proposed loan of $2,500 would be repaid. According to Mr. Perkins, the first step in estimating future results was to get an accurate report of present status and past progress. Then each interested party could estimate the future results by making allowances for known changes in conditions. Income measurement was a very important part of the loan application, he said, because the amount borrowed could be repaid by the business only out of new assets which it earned by means of profitable operations, unless the owners made an additional investment. William would have to convince the bank that the income of the business would bring in enough to finance the drain caused by Mr. Lawson's medical expenses, make necessary payments on the loan, and still leave sufficient assets for carrying on the daily operations of the business.

If measurement of past income was the first step, William asked, for what period of time should it be measured? A month? He did not think that May was a representative month, because sales had slumped during Mr. Lawson's absence. Also, sales in March and April had been much higher than in May because of the demand for Easter merchandise. How about a year, then? William thought that he could find out how much money the business received in the last year as a result of sales, as well as how much it had paid out for expenses. Would that information be sufficient?

The meaning of business income

Although the primary objective of a business is to earn an income, there is disagreement among economists, accountants, and businessmen as to the exact meaning of "business income." The precise definition of income depends to a large extent upon the purpose for which it is being measured. Chapter 1 described some of the needs of owners, management, creditors, and others for income information as an indication of the progress of the enterprise. The following general-purpose definition of income takes into consideration many of these needs, as well as some of the problems of measuring income.

The realized net income of an enterprise measures its effectiveness as an operating unit and is the change in its net assets arising out of (a) the excess or deficiency of revenue compared with related expired cost and (b) other gains or losses to the enterprise from sales, exchanges, or other conversions of assets . . . [1]

Key words in this definition which will be explained in some detail are *realized, net income, net assets, revenue,* and *expired cost.*

A change in an asset or a liability is considered to be *realized* in accounting when it has become sufficiently definite and objective to justify its recognition in the accounts. This recognition may be based upon an exchange transaction, on established trade practices, on the terms of a contract which seems certain to be performed, or on the stability of banking and commercial relationships. [2]

Income may be either positive or negative. If operations are successful, there is a *net income* and a corresponding increase in net assets; if they are unsuccessful, there is a decrease in net assets caused by a *net loss.*

Net assets refers to the amount by which total assets exceed total liabilities; thus, Assets − Liabilities = Net Assets. In the basic accounting equation, Assets − Liabilities = Owners' Equity; therefore, Net Assets = Owners' Equity. If the net assets of a business increase as a result of oper-

---

[1] American Accounting Association, Committee on Accounting Concepts and Standards, *Accounting and Reporting Standards for Corporate Financial Statements, 1957 Revision* (Columbus: The Association, 1957), p. 5.

[2] *Idem.*

ations, the business has earned a *net income;* if they decrease, it has incurred a *net loss.*

Several combinations of directions of change in *total* assets and *total* liabilities will result in *increases* in *net assets,* and several combinations of changes in totals will result in *decreases* in net assets. Some of the various possibilities are illustrated in Figure 2. If these changes in total assets and total liabilities are the result of operations, they are also causes of income, which is a change in *owners' equity* equaling a change in *net assets.* Income, like any equity, is thus a *source* of net assets.

Revenue and expired cost

Income is the net effect on owners' equity resulting from changes in opposite directions, *revenue* and *expired costs.* Revenue measures the net assets which the business receives as a result of its activities; expired cost measures the net assets which it gives up. Revenue increases the net assets and owners' equity of the business; expired costs decrease them. The amount of income is the excess of revenue over expired cost. If revenue is greater, there is a *net income;* if expired cost is greater, there is a *net loss.*

EXAMPLE 1:

> Revenue, \$40,000 − Expense, \$37,000 = Net income, \$3,000
> Revenue, \$40,000 − Expense, \$44,000 = Net loss, \$4,000

When an enterprise sells its products or services to its customers, it receives in exchange new assets in the form of cash or receivables (or, occasionally, reductions in liabilities). The source of this increase in net assets is called *revenue.* Its amount for any period of time is a significant measure of the volume of business activity.

Revenue does not result without effort. The productive assets of a business are used either directly in making the sale or indirectly in making it possible. The business effort put forth, measured by the decrease in net assets, is called *expired cost.*

Operating revenue results from the primary activities of the enterprise, the sale of goods or services. Some businesses, such as retail, wholesale, or manufacturing concerns, receive their principal revenue from selling products. Others, such as telephone companies, hotels, banks, and the professions, obtain revenue chiefly from the sale of services.

Nonoperating revenue results from activities of a business other than the principal ones. Occasionally, for example, a business sells equipment or some other asset which it had held for use rather than for sale. An increase in net assets resulting from such a transaction is a *gain,* a type of nonoperating revenue.

Combinations of Changes in Total Assets and Liabilities Which Will
Result in Changes in Net Assets

	Total Before	Total After	Change	Effect on Net Assets and Income
Net assets increase:				
a. Total assets increase more than total liabilities increase:				
Assets........................	$15,000	$19,000	+$4,000	
− Liabilities.....................	8,000	9,000	+ 1,000	
= Net assets.....................	$ 7,000	$10,000		+$3,000
b. Total assets increase and total liabilities decrease:				
Assets........................	$15,000	$16,000	+$1,000	
− Liabilities.....................	8,000	6,000	− 2,000	
= Net assets.....................	$ 7,000	$10,000		+$3,000
c. Total assets decrease less than liabilities decrease:				
Assets........................	$15,000	$13,000	−$2,000	
− Liabilities.....................	8,000	3,000	− 5,000	
= Net assets.....................	$ 7,000	$10,000		+$3,000
Net assets decrease:				
d. Total assets increase less than total liabilities increase:				
Assets........................	$15,000	$18,000	+$3,000	
− Liabilities.....................	8,000	15,000	+ 7,000	
= Net assets.....................	$ 7,000	$ 3,000		−$4,000
e. Total assets decrease and total liabilities increase:				
Assets........................	$15,000	$14,000	−$1,000	
− Liabilities.....................	8,000	11,000	+ 3,000	
= Net assets.....................	$ 7,000	$ 3,000		−$4,000
f. Total assets decrease more than total liabilities decrease:				
Assets........................	$15,000	$10,000	−$5,000	
− Liabilities.....................	8,000	7,000	− 1,000	
= Net assets.....................	$ 7,000	$ 3,000		−$4,000

Fig. 2.

Expired costs are of two classes, *expenses* and *losses*. *Expenses* are expired costs which are associated with the sale of goods and services and with related business activities. *Costs* which expire without benefit to the business, as when uninsured property is damaged by fire, are *losses*.[3] If the sale of equipment or a similar asset which is held for use results in a decrease in net assets, there is also a loss. Losses are parallel to *nonoperating revenue*, in that they result from business activities other than the primary ones.

Figure 3 shows some examples of types of operating and nonoperating revenues, expenses, and losses.

---

[3] *Ibid.*, p. 6.

Illustrations of Revenue and Expired Costs

A. Trading Enterprise

Revenue from sale of goods....................	$50,000	
Deduct expense associated with selling goods......	40,000	
Net income from operations.........................		$10,000
Add nonoperating revenue:		
Gain on sale of store equipment......................		4,000
Total...		$14,000
Deduct nonoperating expenses and losses:		
Loss on sale of government bonds....................		1,000
Net income...		$13,000

B. Service Enterprise

Revenue from sale of services...................	$80,000	
Deduct expense associated with rendering services	60,000	
Net income from operations.........................		$20,000
Add nonoperating revenue:		
Gain on advantageous settlement of a liability..........		2,000
Total...		$22,000
Deduct nonoperating expenses and losses:		
Loss on adverse judgment on damage suit..............		25,000
Net loss...		($ 3,000)

Fig. 3.

Status accounts and change accounts

Chapter 2 described the accounts which are used to show the *financial status* of a business at any given time as *assets*, which show the forms of resources, and *equities*, which show their sources. Income shows the *changes* in owners' equity which result from the operations of the business. Because income measurement is so important to business, separate accounts are used to accumulate each major type of *revenue* and each type of *expired cost*.

The accounting equation may be expanded to show the effect of these accounts as follows:

$$\text{Assets} = \text{Liabilities} + \overbrace{\text{Owners' Equity}}$$

$$\text{Assets} = \text{Liabilities} + \text{Owners' Investment} + \overbrace{\text{Income}}$$

$$\text{Assets} = \text{Liabilities} + \text{Owners' Investment} + \text{Revenue} - \text{Expense}$$

The accounting period

Income, revenue, and expense, which measure changes in owners' equity, have meaning only if the *period of time* over which the change occurs is known. In order to measure their amounts, it is necessary to decide how long the time period is to be and how to select the events to be considered during that period.

If a business consisted of a single brief undertaking, income could be measured easily. It would be the difference between the net assets available for distribution to the owners at the end of the venture and the amount originally invested. In most cases, however, it is not satisfactory to wait until the termination of a business to compute its income. The income thus measured would be accurate beyond question, but its amount would become known too late to be of much use. The income tax collector requires annual results as a basis for collecting tax. The stockholder and banker need annual and quarterly reports of how the business is doing. The manager needs much more frequent income information to guide him in the day-to-day operation of the enterprise.

EXAMPLE 2:   At the end of a three-year business undertaking, the manager received the following statement:

Net assets available for distribution (= owners' equity) at the end of the venture	$24,000
Net assets invested at the beginning	28,000
Net loss	($ 4,000)

The manager would be justified in objecting to this belated information on the ground that if he had known earlier that such an unprofitable tendency existed, he could have taken action to correct it, or even have discontinued operations.

Income is a *total* change which occurs over a period of time. If too long a period is used, total income does not reveal important changes in income's *rate* and *direction* (net income or net loss).

EXAMPLE 3:   The first information that the owner-manager of a business received about its income was at the end of a year, when he was told that the net income was $24,000. He would have been able to manage the business much more intelligently if he had known monthly income results such as the following:

Month	Income for Month	Annual Rate of Income
January	$10,000 net income	$120,000 net income
February	2,000 net income	24,000 net income
March	(1,000) net loss	(12,000) net loss

The annual rates for each month show what the results for the year would have been if the rate at which income was earned during the month continued for an entire year. If January's results were about normal for a month, receipt of the monthly income reports showing a sharp decline in February would have led the manager to investigate its cause, and perhaps the business would thereafter have earned income more nearly in line with the $120,000 indicated by January's operations.

Just as each year's income is the result of varying rates of earnings for each of 12 months, so is each month's income composed of weekly, daily, and hourly rates. Frequent measurements, up to a practical limit, give better information about the rate at which income is being earned than do infrequent ones, and they give it in time for appropriate action.

Practically all businesses determine income at least once a year. The calendar year, January 1 through December 31, is the most popular basic accounting period, but many companies have recognized the advantages of using their *natural business year.* This period, which varies from one business to another, begins in the slack season, continues through the activities of the busy season, and ends in the slack season a year later. Its use reduces the margin of error in measuring revenue, expired costs, assets, and equities; however, the resulting balances in the Statement of Financial Position may not be representative of the asset and equity balances which prevail during most of the year.

The period for which financial reports are prepared is called the *fiscal period.* An example is the fiscal year beginning June 1, 19x1, and ending May 31, 19x2. Management usually needs detailed reports of income once a month or oftener. Some banks even compute their income every day. In addition, practically all business managements should receive daily reports on the movements of the important components of income, such as major classes of revenue and expense. The more frequent the income reading, the better is management able to determine the direction and rate of business progress. However, the cost of obtaining frequent reports must not exceed the benefit.

Matching revenue and expired cost

Whatever the time period selected for computing the income of a business, it is artificial. Business activity does not come to a sharp conclusion simply because the last day of the accounting period has ended. Instead, there will be quantities of unsold merchandise on hand; shipments in transit to customers; accounts to be collected; bills to be paid; contracts for services, both with customers and with suppliers, in various stages of completion; productive facilities with various fractions of their useful lives expired—in fact, many business activities at many stages of progress.

In the face of this complexity of real business events, arbitrary rules have been made for determining what revenue the business has earned during the accounting period and what costs have expired. Identifying revenue and expired costs consists of three steps:

(1) Selecting a type of event whose occurrence is an appropriate signal for recognizing that the business has realized revenue;

(2) Determining the money amounts of such events which have occurred during the accounting period; and

(3) Measuring the costs which have expired by identifying the benefits received directly with the revenue events.

The third step is called *matching revenue with expired costs,* the principal approach to measuring periodic income. When the two have been matched, they are further identified with the specific accounting period to which they relate.

Timing of revenue realization

What is an appropriate occasion for the business to consider that revenue has been realized? Business progress is measured by the excess of the amount of the net assets which it obtains by producing and selling goods and services over the net assets expended in such production and sale. The actual sale of business output, usually the time when legal title passes, is a very critical event. At this point the business parts with a good or service and receives in exchange a *new asset*, which is usually money or a right to collect money in the near future. The price of the good or service sold is objectively determined in a bargained market transaction.

EXAMPLE 4:   A retail appliance store sells an electric fan for $25 cash. It has revenue of $25, the source of the new asset, cash. If the sale had been on account to a solvent customer, there would still have been revenue of $25, the source of the new asset, accounts receivable.

Businessmen, optimistic by nature, are sometimes inclined to count on favorable events which they hope will happen as though they have already occurred. Occasionally, they tend to be unduly pessimistic. The selection of the sale as an objective event which warrants the recognition of revenue in the accounts helps to neutralize the effect of such optimism and pessimism.

EXAMPLE 5:   A retailer bought a number of men's coats at $25 each, marking them to sell at $40 each. The style proved so popular that the manufacturer raised its price to merchants to $30 a coat. The retailer then marked its selling price up to $50. At the end of its accounting period, the retailer has ten unsold coats on hand. How much revenue has it realized on the unsold coats?

SOLUTION: None. There is no certainty that the coats will be sold at all, or, if so, when; what additional effort will be needed to sell them; or what price they will bring. Only when each coat is sold is there conclusive evidence that there is any revenue and how much there is.

When a business sells a service which, according to contract, is to extend over a definite period of time, it is customary business practice to consider that the revenue is realized at an equal amount per day. Each day's service is, in effect, treated as a separate sale.

EXAMPLE 6:   A bank lends money to a customer for 30 days. The service which the customer receives is the use of the bank's money, for which he agrees to pay *interest*. The bank earns interest revenue of an equal amount each day of the loan's duration.

Convenience in recording revenue realization

As explained earlier, the exact time when a transaction is recorded in the accounts is dictated by clerical convenience. Revenue realized by sale of goods and products should be recorded as soon after the sale as practical, perhaps at the end of each day. When an accounting period ends, it is especially important that the sales of that period all be considered in measuring its revenue.

Revenue earned with the passage of time, such as the bank's interest on a loan, although considered to be *earned* in equal amounts each day, is usually *recorded* when the term of the loan is over. If the accounting period ends before the loan is over, revenue must be recorded for the number of days for which the loan has been outstanding during the period.

Timing of cost expiration

An expense is the part of an asset's cost, or service potential, used up in carrying on the principal activities of the business. Usually expense transactions are considered to be completed when the service benefits of the assets are received by the business.

It is easy to recognize when some types of assets render their services to the business. When goods are transferred to a customer at the time of sale, the service potential of an *asset, merchandise,* is used up as far as the business is concerned and becomes an *expense, cost of goods sold.* At the same time, the business receives revenue in the amount of the sale price. In cases where there is such a direct relationship between revenue and expense, they are regarded in accounting as occurring simultaneously. They are associated directly with each other; that is, they are *matched.*

Many other costs which expire during an accounting period cannot be directly associated with particular sales, even though there is strong evidence that they benefit the business. Examples of these expenses are rent, interest for money borrowed, utilities, and insurance. It is customary to associate expenses of this type with accounting periods in proportion to the part of the service contract which expires during each period.

EXAMPLE 7: A business which uses the calendar year as its accounting period bought a contract for insurance protection for one year beginning October, 19x1, for a total cost of $240. What was its applicable expense for the year 19x1?

SOLUTION: The 19x1 expense was proportionate to the fraction of the service contract which had expired, $3/12$ or $1/4$ of $240, or $60. The remaining $180 of the cost of the insurance policy was an asset at the end of 19x1, a service benefit applicable to future accounting periods.

Other costs expire without any apparent benefit to the revenue-producing operations of the business. Such expirations are *losses*. They may be measured by the amount needed to reduce assets at the end of the year to the proportion of their cost which will presumably benefit future business operations.

EXAMPLE 8:   A machine which was carried on the books at its unexpired cost of $2,200 was damaged in an accident. After the accident its usefulness was severely limited, and it was reliably estimated that a machine with equal service potential for the future could have been acquired for $400. How should these facts be treated in the accounts?

SOLUTION: The amount of the asset's cost which will not benefit the future, $1,800, is a *loss*.

Convenience in recording cost expirations

Criteria for determining which expired costs are associated with the revenue of a given accounting period are (1) direct association with the revenue-producing activities of the period, and (2) lack of potential future service benefit. The time when the actual record of the cost expiration is made in the accounts, like the time of recording revenue, is largely a matter of bookkeeping convenience. In some cases the exact time when the individual cost expirations occur could be determined, but it is not practical to so do.

EXAMPLE 9:   It would be physically possible to match the cost of wrapping supplies with the revenue from the sale of the articles wrapped, but to do so would require an unreasonable amount of time and effort in proportion to the value of the information obtained.

For convenience, the expired cost of supplies used, or small unit costs of merchandise sold, is usually not recorded after each sale transaction. Instead, the *total* expired cost of supplies or merchandise is measured indirectly at the end of the accounting period by the following formula:

Costs Acquired − Costs Unexpired at End of Period
= Costs Expired During Period

EXAMPLE 10:   The X Company had selling supplies costing $200 on hand on December 31, 19x1. During January, 19x2, the company bought additional supplies for $150. It was not practical to record a cost expiration each time supplies were used; therefore, on January 31, an estimate was made which indicated that the supplies still on hand had cost approximately $250. What was the amount of supplies expense for January?

SOLUTION: Cost of supplies on hand at beginning.................. $200
+ Cost of supplies acquired during period................ 150
= Total cost of supplies available for use................ $350
− Cost of supplies not used (estimated cost at end of period). 250
= Expired cost, or expense, of supplies used during the month $100

Illustrative revenue and expense transactions

The illustration of the Motor Mower Company in Chapter 2 is continued for the month of July, 19x1, to show how revenue and expense transactions of the company would be recorded. The company's account balances at the end of June, 19x1, as shown by the trial balance, were as follows:

MOTOR MOWER COMPANY
Trial Balance
June 30, 19x1

	(Debits)	(Credits)
A, Cash	$ 2,900	
A, Notes Receivable	2,000	
A, Merchandise	8,000	
L, Notes Payable		$ 2,800
L, Note Payable to Officer		500
OE, Owners' Equity		9,600
Totals	$12,900	$12,900

The following journal entries record the company's transactions for the month of July.

```
19x1                              (1)
July 1   A, Cash..................................... 150
              OE, Revenue.............................       150
         Sold a lawnmower for cash.
```

Revenue is credited in this entry because it represents an increase in owners' equity. Although the company could very easily determine the cost of the lawnmower which was sold ($80) and immediately record it as an expense, the company prefers for convenience to determine the cost of all goods sold at the end of the period and record it in a single entry. The approach then is the same as that followed for supplies in Example 10.

```
19x1                              (2)
July 1   OE, Rent Expense............................. 310
              A, Cash....................................       310
         Paid building rent for the month.
```

Rent expense is debited to show a decrease in owners' equity. In exchange for the cash payment, the business receives a service benefit in the form of the right to occupy the building for one month. Literally, on July 1 at the time the rent is paid, its cost represents an asset—the cost of a service benefit which applies to the future. The cost of one day's rent ($310/31 days, or $10) is an expense applicable to each day of July. Most likely, however, the business will not need to measure its income and financial status until the end of the month, July 31. On that date the entire service benefit will have been received by the business, and the entire $310 will appropriately be classified as an expense. For convenience, then, the rent for the month is debited to expense at the time of payment, so that no additional entries will be needed at the end of the month.

If the business should wish to prepare financial statements for any shorter interval, such as the period from July 1 to July 10, an additional entry would be needed. The proper amount of expense for that 10-day period would be $100, and the remaining $210 would be an asset on July 10.

19x1		(3)		
July	9	A, Accounts Receivable.............................	450	
		OE, Revenue...............................		450
		Sold three lawnmowers on account for $150 each.		

		(4)		
	9	L, Notes Payable................................	800	
		A, Cash......................................		800
		Made a partial payment on the promissory note owed, and secured an extension of the due date of the remainder.		

		(5)		
	14	L, Note Payable to Officer......	500	
		A, Cash................		500
		Paid the note to the officer due today.		

		(6)		
	17	A, Merchandise..................................	375	
		L, Accounts Payable.........................		375
		Bought three additional lawnmowers on account for $125 each.		

		(7)		
	21	A, Cash..	150	
		A, Accounts Receivable......		150
		Collected for one of the lawnmowers sold on account on July 9.		

		(8)		
	31	OE, Salary Expense.............................	400	
		A, Cash......................................		400
		Paid employees' salaries for the month in cash.		

The rule of convenience is also followed in recording wage and salary payments, as well as other services which are paid for *after* they are rendered. Employees ordinarily work under a contract whereby they are paid at a certain rate per time period—hour, day, week, or month. Usually they are paid at the *end* of a stated interval, such as a month. Literally, each day the business receives an asset, the service of the employee, and incurs an equal liability to pay for it. It is generally assumed in accounting that such services have no benefit to future periods, and that their costs therefore expire the instant they are incurred. A convenient accounting short cut records the entire cost of the service at the end of the contract period or the end of the accounting period, whichever comes first.

EXAMPLE 11: A business employs a night watchman who works every night, earning a salary of $300, which is paid at the end of the month. The following accounting entries *might* be made:

Daily: A, Unused Employee's Services...................   10
        L, Accrued Salaries Payable...................   10
        To record receipt of night watchman's services by the business, and the corresponding liability.

OE, Salary Expense..............................   10
        A, Unused Employee's Services.................   10
        The benefit from watchman's services expired.

End of Month:
L, Accrued Salaries Payable.......................   300
        A, Cash......................................   300
        Paid the liability, which has accumulated at the rate of $10 a day.

BETTER: The foregoing bookkeeping procedure would be unduly cumbersome. Rather, it is customary to reflect the entire series of services at the end of the month in one entry:

OE, Salary Expense..............................   300
        A, Cash......................................   300
        Paid the night watchman's salary, the entire benefit of which applied to the current month.

If an accounting period ends before an employee is paid, the expense and the corresponding liability for the amount he has earned must be recorded in the current period.

EXAMPLE 12: An employee worked for 6 days in December at an agreed rate of $10 a day, but had not been paid on December 31. The necessary entry on December 31 would be:

19x1
Dec. 31   OE, Salary Expense........................   60
         L, Accrued Salaries Payable..............   60
        To record the expense and corresponding liability for exmployee's salary earned but unpaid at the end of the period.

If an employee is paid in advance, the amount paid is debited to an asset, representing a prepayment for a future service benefit.

EXAMPLE 13: On December 31 a company makes a $150 cash advance to a salesman for compensation he expects to earn in January.

19x1
Dec. 31   A, Salary Advances........................   150
         A, Cash................................   150
        To record the asset representing the prepayment of salary expense.

The following transaction illustrates a *compound entry*, one which affects three or more accounts. Total debits in such entries must still equal total credits.

19x1   (9)
July 31   A, Cash.................................... 1,800
          A, Accounts Receivable....................   400
                OE, Revenue..........................   2,200
          Sold 12 mowers for $150 cash each, and two
          of the new type on account for $200 each.

19x1   (10)
July 31   OE, Cost of Goods Sold Expense............. 1,850
                A, Merchandise.......................   1,850
          A count of the unsold mowers on hand on July
          31 showed the following results:

64 at a cost of $100 each.........	$6,400	
1 at a cost of $125..............	125	
Total unexpired cost.............	$6,525	

The expired cost is determined as follows:

Merchandise on hand, June 30....	$8,000
Add cost of July acquisitions.....	375
Total cost of goods available in July........................	$8,375
Deduct ending inventory.........	6,525
Cost of goods sold expense........	$1,850

The T-accounts which result from the July transactions are as follows:

A, Cash

19x1				19x1			
June 30	Balance..............		2,900	July 1		(2)	310
July 1		(1)	150	9		(4)	800
21		(7)	150	14		(5)	500
31		(9)	1,800	31		(8)	400
			5,000				2,010
31	Balance, 2,990						

A, Notes Receivable

19x1			
June 30	Balance..............		2,000

A, Accounts Receivable

19x1				19x1			
July 9		(3)	450	July 21		(7)	150
31		(9)	400				
			850				
31	Balance, 700						

A, Merchandise

19x1				19x1			
June 30	Balance..............		8,000	July 31		(10)	1,850
July 17		(6)	375				
			8,375				
31	Balance, 6,525						

L, Notes Payable

19x1				19x1			
July 9		(4)	800	June 30	Balance..............		2,800
				July 31	Balance, 2,000		

L, Note Payable to Officer

19x1				19x1			
July 14		(5)	500	June 30	Balance..............		500

L, Accounts Payable

				19x1			
				July 17		(6)	375

OE, Owners' Investment

				19x1			
				June 30	Balance..............		9,600

OE, Revenue (July)

				19x1			
				July 1		(1)	150
				9		(3)	450
				31		(9)	2,200
							2,800

OE, Cost of Goods Sold Expense (July)

19x1			
July 31		(10)	1,850

OE, Rent Expense (July)

19x1			
July 1		(2)	310

OE, Salary Expense (July)

19x1			
July 31		(8)	400

The revenue and expense accounts show changes in owners' equity over a period of time, in this case the month of July. To emphasize this fact, the name of the period for which the change is determined has been included parenthetically after each account title. In actual accounting practice it is not necessary to do this, because it is understood that revenue and expense accounts apply to a period, not to a status at a given moment.

All of the asset and liability accounts of the Motor Mower Company at the end of July show the status of each at the *end* of the period. OE, Owners' Investment, shows the status at the *beginning* of the current period. The status of owners' equity at the *end* of the current period may be determined by adding revenue to beginning owners' equity, and then deducting expense.

Income statement

The Trial Balance of the Motor Mower Company at the end of July is as follows:

MOTOR MOWER COMPANY
Trial Balance
July 31, 19x1

	(Debits)	(Credits)
A, Cash	$ 2,990	
A, Notes Receivable	2,000	
A, Accounts Receivable	700	
A, Merchandise	6,525	
L, Notes Payable		$ 2,000
L, Accounts Payable		375
OE, Owners' Investment		9,600
OE, Revenue		2,800
OE, Cost of Goods Sold Expense	1,850	
OE, Rent Expense	310	
OE, Salary Expense	400	
Totals	$14,775	$14,775

The company's financial statements which would be prepared at the end of July are illustrated below.

MOTOR MOWER COMPANY
Income Statement
For the Month Ended July 31, 19x1

Revenue		$2,800
Deduct Expense:		
Cost of Goods Sold Expense	$1,850	
Rent Expense	310	
Salary Expense	400	
Total Expense		2,560
Net Income		$ 240

MOTOR MOWER COMPANY
Statement of Financial Position
July 31, 19x1

ASSETS		LIABILITIES	
Cash	$ 2,990	Notes Payable	$2,000
Notes Receivable	2,000	Accounts Payable	375
Accounts Receivable	700	Total Liabilities	$ 2,375
Merchandise	6,525		
		OWNERS' EQUITY	
		Balance, June 30	$9,600
		Net Income for July	240
		Balance, July 31	9,840
Total Assets	$12,215	Total Equities	$12,215

Since the Income Statement shows changes in owners' equity over a period, it is essential that the title of the statement clearly identify the length of the time period and its ending date. Similarly, the Statement of

Financial Position must show the time period's ending date, at which the financial status existed.

It is customary to use double rulings in accounting to indicate the conclusion of a financial statement or of an account.

Alternative statement titles and forms

Accounting terminology is constantly changing as accountants seek to convey their message more clearly. The reader should recognize that the "Statement of Profit and Loss," still in wide use, is merely another name for the Income Statement. The latter title is preferable because it is broader. Literally, "profit" includes only the excess of selling price over cost and does not include other common components of business income.

The Statement of Financial Position is often called the "Balance Sheet," referring to its content of account balances at the end of the accounting period.

The information contained in the basic illustrations of financial statements in Chapters 2 and 3 has been very limited. More elaborate reports of these types, as well as other specialized types of statements, are needed by management and others. Many representative ones will be described in succeeding chapters.

Summary

Income is the change in the net assets of a business which results from the excess or deficiency of revenue as compared with expired cost as well as from other business gains and losses not associated with the principal activities of the business. *Expired costs* consist of expenses and losses.

Revenue is considered to be realized in the time period when it is assured by means of objective evidence, such as a completed sale. Costs expire in proportion to the service potentials of assets which are used up. In some cases a cost expiration may be clearly associated with the operating activities of the business, in which case it is an *expense*. At other times, a *loss* is indicated by the fact that an asset's potential future benefit is less than its unexpired cost as otherwise measured.

The Income Statement shows the revenue, expense, and resulting net income of a business—all of which are changes in owners' equity—for a specific period of time.

QUESTIONS AND PROBLEMS

3-1 "Periodic income is an objective measure of the rate at which a business is moving toward its economic goal."

REQUIRED:

Why, then, is accounting needed for organizations which are not organized to earn a net income, such as churches and schools?

3-2

REQUIRED:

a. What factors would you consider in selecting the appropriate fiscal year for an automobile manufacturer?

b. For what purposes, if any, would financial reports be needed at more frequent intervals?

3-3 "If you work long enough and hard enough at it, it is possible to determine the exact net income of any business, large or small."

REQUIRED:

Comment on the validity of this statement.

3-4

REQUIRED:

Would information as to how much money the business had received as a result of sales and how much it had paid out for expenses be sufficient for measuring its income? Explain.

3-5 "Net Assets = Owner's Equity;
Change in Net Assets = Net Income."

REQUIRED:

Explain whether or not these formulas are correct.

3-6 A businessman complains that he has suffered a net loss because his cash balance is $7,000 less than it was at the beginning of the year.

REQUIRED:

Explain to the businessman whether his interpretation is correct.

3-7 "Don't hire a fancy accountant to figure your income," Joe Gaines advised his friend. "Do as I do—pay everything by check and let the bank keep your records."

REQUIRED:

a. Can you see any weaknesses in this advice?

b. For what purposes are the records which are kept by the bank useful to its depositors?

3-8 A wealthy individual established a foundation for the purpose of lending money to worthy college students. He did not intend that the fund earn a net income, but merely that it break even. Interest was to be charged on loans solely to cover the operating expenses of the foundation.

REQUIRED:

a. For what purposes, if any, does the foundation need accounting records?

b. Would it be appropriate to measure periodic income for the foundation? Revenue? Expense?

3-9 "The actual sale of business output is a very critical event."

REQUIRED:

a. Is selling more important than manufacturing in accounting? Explain.

b. Is selling more important than organizing the business and acquiring productive facilities? Explain.

3-10

REQUIRED:

a. What would you expect to be the principal expense of a retail store? Of a whole-saler? Of a manufacturer? Of a barber shop? Of a professional football team? Of a casualty insurance company? Of a passenger railroad?

b. What would be the nature of the chief revenue of each of these businesses?

3-11 A weekly newspaper began operations on July 1 and collected for 1,000 one-year subscriptions at $5.20 each during the first three days of the month. Editions were published on July 7, 14, 21, and 28.

REQUIRED:

a. How much revenue, if any, did the newspaper realize in July?

b. Record all of these facts in journal form.

3-12 The Thrifty Shop borrowed $5,000 from the First National Bank on June 1 at a 6% annual interest charge. The first payment on the loan was to be made on the following June 1, when the first year's interest was to be settled.

REQUIRED:

a. At the end of June, how much revenue, if any, had the bank realized?

b. How much expense, if any, did The Thrifty Shop have in June from this arrangement?

c. Record all June transactions for both parties in journal form.

3-13 The word *charge* is a synonym for *debit*. Perhaps every reader has at some time in the past unwittingly given such bookkeeping instructions to a clerk in a retail store as "Charge this to my account," and "Please give me credit for this."

REQUIRED:

a. What account on the books of the store would be debited, what account would be credited, and what would the explanation be for the "charge" entry?

b. What account would be debited, what account would be credited, and for what reason in the second situation?

3-14 Business accounting deals with status and change accounts.

REQUIRED:

List the main types of status accounts that you would expect to find in a retail store, and list the change accounts.

3-15 Necessary preliminary arrangements for the Novelty Shop, prior to its opening for business, included applying for telephone service. The telephone company bills for each month's service at the end of the month. No deposit or installation fee was required.

REQUIRED:

a. Did the installation of the telephone increase the assets of the Novelty Shop?

b. Did it result in an expense at the time of installation?

c. If the monthly service charge is $11, how would this affect the computation of income for the first two weeks?

d. What would be the effect on assets and income if the service charge for the first month were paid in advance at the beginning of the month? Journalize the appropriate entries.

e. What would be the effect on assets and income if an installation charge of $10 were paid at the beginning of the month? Journalize the relevant entries.

3-16 An individual receives his monthly statement from his bank, and enclosed finds two or three "debit" slips.

REQUIRED:

a. What type of account is debited on the bank's books as a result of these slips?
b. If one of these slips is for the bank's $5 service charge for handling the account, what entry should the depositor make?

3-17 The Stallings Manufacturing Company incurred preparatory costs of $50,000 the year before it started manufacturing operations. The company had no revenues during this period.

REQUIRED:

a. Did the company have a loss during this year?
b. What types of costs might have been included in the $50,000?
c. Using the list of costs which you have considered in (b), how would they affect revenues of future periods?

3-18 "Accounting, by recognizing revenue at the time of sale, exaggerates the importance of selling effort and overlooks the importance of production."

REQUIRED:

a. Is this statement true? Explain.
b. Is the approach which accounting uses justified? Explain.

3-19 Mr. Muller bought a share of *R* Mfg. Co. stock, which is actively traded on the stock exchange, for $130 on January 17. Every day he followed the stock quotations with great interest. On January 31 the stock was selling for $142 a share.

REQUIRED:

a. How much was his income during January?
b. During February a market decline set in, and on February 28 the stock was quoted at $114 a share. How much was Mr. Muller's income for February?
c. In March the *R* Mfg. Co. paid a cash dividend of $8 a share. Mr. Muller received the dividend on March 16, and on March 24 he sold the share for $126. What was his income for March?
d. Journalize all of these transactions.

3-20 The Whiz Company was organized on February 1, when its founders invested $12,000 in cash. On February 6 the management paid $7,000 for a lot on which to build its store. Soon thereafter plans for a new shopping center adjacent to the lot were announced. Several would-be purchasers offered prices varying between $15,000 and $18,000 for the lot late in February, but the management elected not to sell. Construction had not been started on February 28.

REQUIRED:

a. How much was the revenue of the Whiz Company for February?
b. What was its asset total on February 28?

3-21 William Wilcox, a farmer, produced 100 bales of cotton during his natural business year, which ended on September 30, 19x1. During the year he sold 30 bales for a total of $4,500. Other farm revenues amounted to $6,000. Total expenses for the period were $7,000. The market price of cotton per bale on September 30, 19x1 was $150.

REQUIRED:

a. What was the total amount of Mr. Wilcox's revenue for the year?
b. What was his income?

c. What problem did Mr. Wilcox have in matching expired costs and realized revenues?

d. Is there any need for deviation from the conventional method of realizing revenues? Explain.

3-22   Richard Drake is a citrus grower in Florida. Although the fruit is picked and sold during only two months of the year, Mr. Drake incurs expenses throughout the year for the care and upkeep of the orchards.

REQUIRED:

What would be some of the problems Mr. Drake would have in determining monthly net income?

3-23   The One-Stop Grocery kept all of its money in a safe in its office. On December 22 the store took in $300 from cash sales. On the morning of December 23 the owner found that a burglar had stolen the money. He called the police and then called the insurance company to take out a burglary insurance policy for an annual premium of $30.

REQUIRED:

a. Record these events in journal form.

b. How would your entries have differed if the grocer had purchased insurance protection some time before the theft?

3-24   A builder formed a construction company in September. After several months' effort, the company completed a residence for a total cost of $19,000 and advertised it for sale. By December 31 the company had received three offers: one of $21,000 cash; one of $22,000 to be paid in monthly installments over 20 years with 5% annual interest; and another of $20,000 cash plus a residential lot worth $2,600. The builder decided to wait for a higher offer, which he seemed certain to get.

REQUIRED:

a. What was the amount of the construction company's revenue for the year?

b. How much were its expenses?

c. What form, if any, did its assets take on December 31?

d. What would revenue, expense, and assets have been if the third offer had been accepted and the sale closed on December 26?

3-25   Mr. Karl has a men's clothing store located adjacent to the State University. He is trying to decide what would be an appropriate accounting year for the business. The peak season of sales is expected to be in the months of September and October, when the students will be selecting their fall wardrobes. A clearance sale of fall goods will be held in January. Spring sales are expected to be rather brisk, followed by another clearance sale in July. The summer school of the University ends on August 15 and the fall term begins on September 20. During this interval most of the shop's personnel will take their vacations.

REQUIRED:

a. What do you think should be the closing date of the store's accounting year?

b. What facts other than those given above should be considered?

3-26   A retail store was organized in November with cash of $4,000, and during the month it bought goods on credit for a total cost of $12,000. By November 30 one-third of the goods had been sold on account for sales prices totaling $7,000. Although one-half of the accounts were collected in November, none of the purchases were paid for. Salaries of $650 and rent of $300 for November were paid in cash.

REQUIRED:

a. How much revenue did the store have in November?
b. What types and amounts of expenses did it incur?
c. What was its income for November?
d. What types and amounts of assets did it have on November 30?
e. Record all of these facts in journal form.

3-27   On the first day of December, the store described in Problem 3-26 closed. All unsold goods were returned to suppliers for full credit. All customers' accounts were collected in full in December, and all debts were paid. Rent, salaries, and other services for December totaling $500 were paid for in cash.

REQUIRED:

a. Record all transactions in journal form.
b. List the revenues and expenses, and determine the income of the store for December.
c. What were its assets at the conclusion of this series of events?

3-28   The Taylor-King Company is a manufacturer of shoes.

REQUIRED:

Use a letter to indicate whether the following events, which affected the Company in 19x1, would result in (a) operating revenue, (b) nonoperating revenue, (c) expense, (d) loss, or (e) none of these.

(1) Cost of organizing the corporation.
(2) Payment of administrative employees' salaries.
(3) Receipt of cash from a bank loan.
(4) Cost of leather purchased to be used in the manufacture of shoes.
(5) Partial expiration of the cost of a building owned and used during the operating period.
(6) Sale of shoes on account.
(7) Sale of shoes for cash.
(8) Cost of materials used in the manufacture of shoes sold.
(9) Cost of damages to an uninsured truck owned by the company.
(10) Cost of damages to a truck with which the company truck collided. The Taylor-King Company was liable for the damages.
(11) Gain from the sale of a machine which had been retired from use three years previously.
(12) Gain from the sale of a machine which was in operation up to the time of sale.
(13) Cost of new machinery.
(14) Proceeds from the collection of accounts receivable.
(15) Withdrawal of cash which had been invested by the owners.
(16) Commissions paid to salesmen.
(17) Damages from a fire in one of the buildings. The building was fully insured.
(18) Investment of additional cash by the owners.
(19) Sale of shoes in exchange for a non-interest-bearing note.
(20) Doubling of the market value of one of its buildings since its acquisition, as the result of an increased demand for commercial property in the area.
(21) Sale of government bonds for less than their cost.
(22) Receipt of an order from a mail-order house for 5,000 pairs of shoes. This was an unusually large order.

3-29   The following events took place at the *ABC* Company, a retailer of hardware, on April 1, 19x1.

(1) The company mailed an order to the *XYZ* Company for merchandise, $10,000, to be delivered immediately.

(2) The company purchased a new office desk for $300.

(3) A contract was signed with Mr. T. R. Sailson, local attorney, for legal services to be rendered when necessary. *ABC* Company agreed to pay Mr. Sailson a retainer fee of $20 per month.

(4) *ABC* Company received an order from the Rolo Corporation for materials, $2,000, to be shipped in two weeks.

(5) Owners of the *ABC* Company invested an additional $20,000 cash in the company.

(6) The company collected $5,000 on accounts receivable.

(7) Paid the Melvin Company $500 for laying tile on the floors of the company office.

(8) Purchased on account six reams of office letterheads, $60.

(9) Purchased a pencil sharpener and a stapler from the Lowlin Company for $10 cash.

(10) Rented a parking lot from Southway Realtors for one year. *ABC* Company agreed to pay $100 per month for the lot each month in advance, and made the April payment.

(11) Assigned parking spaces to the employees of the *ABC* Company and made arrangements to rent parking places to the 15 employees of the neighboring company for $10 per month each. No money was collected at this time.

(12) Borrowed $5,000 for 60 days from the First National Bank. The *ABC* Company signed a promissory note agreeing to pay interest at the rate of 6% per year.

(13) Sold for cash six lawnmowers for $100 each. The company guaranteed the lawnmowers for one year and agreed to service them for 60 days after sale.

(14) Opened a payroll bank account at the Second State Bank. The *ABC* Company informed the bank that the weekly payroll would amount to about $3,800 per week. An initial deposit of $3,800 was made by drawing a check on the company's general bank account.

(15) Called the *City News* and asked for the price of running a want ad for a sales clerk. A price of $5.00 was quoted. The *ABC* Company authorized the *City News* to run the advertisement.

REQUIRED:

Show in journal form how each item affects assets, liabilities, and owners' equity.

3-30

REQUIRED:

a. Provide for the following columns on your answer sheet:

(1) Transaction Number	(2) (3) Assets + −	(4) (5) Liabilities − +	(6) (7) Owners Equity − +	(8) No Change in Totals

b. For each of the following transactions, place check marks in the appropriate columns to indicate the effect of the transaction on the Ragsdale Company's assets, liabilities, and owners' equity (+ increase; − decrease).

(1) The owners invested $100,000 in cash to open the business, The Ragsdale Company.

(2) Purchased a building by paying $20,000 cash and obtaining a bank loan for the balance of the purchase price.

(3) Purchased equipment for cash, $5,000.
(4) Purchased on account merchandise for sale.
(5) Paid salaries to sales clerks.
(6) Made sales on account.
(7) Made sales for cash.
(8) Paid a portion of accounts payable.
(9) Paid utility bill received today.
(10) Made payment on bank loan.
(11) Signed a note for the amount due to a creditor on open account.
(12) Sold a government bond which originally cost $1,000 for $950.
(13) Received telephone bill.
(14) Owners withdrew $2,000.
(15) Collected cash on account from a customer.
(16) Owner invested a desk with a market value of $100.
(17) Received an order to ship merchandise.
(18) Paid for repairs to machinery.
(19) Creditor accepted capital stock in settlement of the amount owed him on account.
(20) Ordered merchandise.

3-31   The Fremont Corporation was organized on March 1, 19x1, when the owners invested $10,000 in cash. Transactions for the month of March are shown below:

March 1	Rented a building, completely furnished, and paid a month's rent in advance, $500.
March 5	Purchased merchandise on account from the Sherman Company for $9,000.
March 1–15	Sold goods on account to various customers during this period, $8,000. Cash sales amounted to $1,500.
	Collections on accounts receivable during this period amounted to $6,000.
March 15	Paid $5,000 to the Sherman Company and signed a 45-day non-interest-bearing promissory note for the balance.
March 18	Paid $50 for stamps, envelopes, and office stationery, which were all used during the month.
March 21	Purchased merchandise on account from the Boggs Company for $4,800.
March 16–31	Sold merchandise on account during this period, $6,000, and sold merchandise for cash, $1,000. Collected $4,000 on account.
March 31	Received a bill for utilities, $75.
	Paid salaries for the month to sales clerks, $650.
	The owners withdrew a total of $750 cash in accordance with a previous agreement.
	A physical inventory was taken on March 31, and the cost of unsold goods on hand was $1,500.

REQUIRED:

a. Prepare journal entries.
b. Post to T-accounts.
c. Prepare a trial balance.
d. Prepare an Income Statement and a Statement of Financial Position.

3-32   Walter Borroughs, owner of a meat market, decided to open another market in a different section of town. He started his new business, which he named

"Borroughs Market No. 2," on Monday, January 2, 19x1. The following are the transactions of Market No. 2 for January.

(1) On January 2, Mr. Borroughs opened a bank account for the new market by depositing $4,000 of his personal funds.

(2) On January 4, the landlord authorized Mr. Borroughs to make certain repairs and alterations to the building, which he would be permitted to deduct from January's rent due at the end of the month. Mr. Borroughs paid $75 cash for these repairs.

(3) On January 5, Mr. Borroughs purchased from the K & Y Company new equipment costing $1,500, paying $250 down and agreeing to pay the balance in 30 days.

(4) A $30 utility deposit was paid to the City Electric Company for connecting the electric and water meters on January 6.

(5) On January 6, Mr. Borroughs placed an order with the Lean Meat Company for 1,200 pounds of meat at a total cost of $660.

(6) Mr. Borroughs hired a butcher and a butcher's helper on January 7 at monthly salaries of $400 and $300, respectively. They were to start work the following day. The butcher requested and received an advance of $35 from Mr. Borroughs. He agreed for Mr. Borroughs to deduct this amount from his first pay check.

(7) On January 7, Lean Meat Company delivered the meat ordered the previous day. The butcher refused 20 pounds of spoiled meat with a cost of $10. Mr. Borroughs called the Lean Meat Company and informed them of the spoilage. They agreed to make an allowance for the cost of the meat, and promised to send a credit memorandum for $10 immediately.

(8) On January 9, Mr. Borroughs transferred poultry costing $20 to the new market from Borroughs Market No. 1.

(9) Additional purchases of meat from the Lean Meat Company during the month were $2,800, and $750 was still unpaid at the end of the month.

(10) It was estimated that the cost of the meat on hand on January 31 was $325.

(11) Employee salaries of $525 were paid for the three weeks ending January 31. Mr. Borroughs deducted the advance to the butcher from his salary.

(12) The market purchased wrapping supplies during the month for $80 cash. It was estimated that three-fourths of the supplies had been used by the end of the month.

(13) Total sales for the month were $5,000. This amount included $600 of sales on credit, of which $350 had been collected by the end of the month.

(14) The unexpired cost of the equipment on January 31 was $1,475.

(15) Rent for the month, $300, became due on the last day of the month, but was not paid.

REQUIRED:

a. Prepare journal entries for each of the transactions of Borroughs Market No. 2.
b. Post the journal entries to T-accounts.
c. Prepare a trial balance.
d. Prepare an Income Statement and a Statement of Financial Position.
e. What items in the financial statements do you think Mr. Borroughs should investigate? Why?

3-33 The following account balances appear in the ledger of the All-Star Sporting Goods Store as of December 31, 19x1:

Salaries	$ 12,000
Cash	2,800
Cost of goods sold	60,000
Store rent	3,600
Utilities	500
Gain on sale of display counters	1,500
Sales	100,000
Sales returns	800
Advertising expense	600
Prepaid insurance	300
Office supplies inventory	150
Loss from water damage	1,200
Licenses and taxes	100
Merchandise inventory	40,000
Accounts payable	5,000
Charitable contributions	50
Taxes payable	900
Depreciation of store equipment	750
Store equipment—unexpired cost	7,500

REQUIRED:

a. Prepare an Income Statement in proper form for the year ending December 31, 19x1.

b. Considering only the accounts given above, how much was the owners' equity without including operating results for the year? How much was the owners' equity including the results of the year's operations?

3-34   The T-accounts below show in summary form the transactions of the Fashion Shoppe for the year 19x1.

REQUIRED:

a. Place the identifying letters A (Asset), L (Liability) and OE (Owners' Equity), whichever is appropriate, to the left of each account title.

b. Determine the balances of the accounts and prepare the three common types of financial statements.

c. Reconstruct in journal form the entries which must have resulted in these account balances, including a brief but plausible explanation.

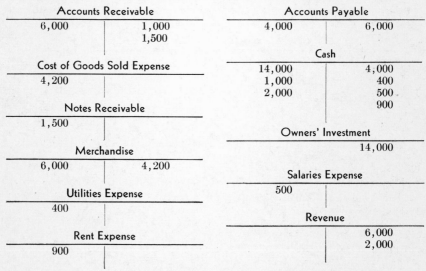

CASE 3-1. PORTER-SLOAN BOAT COMPANY

On June 1, 19x1, John Sloan and Steve Porter received a franchise from the Excellent Boat Company to retail Cruise River boats. Their costs associated with obtaining the franchise, $200, were paid in cash, of which each contributed half. Both of the men had other full-time jobs and had entered into this venture to provide additional income. Steve's father, who was in the farm machinery business, agreed to allow them to display their boats free in a showroom in one of his buildings. John and Steve demonstrated the boats to prospective customers during their off hours. They decided to call their business the Porter-Sloan Boat Company, and on June 5, 19x1, they purchased for cash with personal funds one boat, Model X12453, for $600. Each contributed $300. The boat was listed to sell for $1,095. One week later they purchased on account from the Excellent Boat Company another model, LR65712, which was listed to sell for $1,795, for $1,150. On June 16 they sold the Model LR65712 for cash, $1,700. On June 25 they had an offer of $995 for Model X12453, which they refused.

The two men were quite encouraged when they reviewed their financial situation at the end of the month. Steve stated that they were really doing well because they had $1,700 in cash, more than twice the amount that they had invested.

REQUIRED:

a. Comment on Steve's statement.
b. What was the company's net income for the month?
c. Prepare a statement of financial position on June 30, 19x1.
d. Is the net income for this company a realistic figure? Explain.
e. What are some of the business and accounting problems that the company might face in the future even though the situation now seems to be a very simple arrangement?

Chapter 4

Summarizing Business
Financial Results

Chapter 2 discussed the general bases of
measuring the *financial status* of a business, as shown by its assets and
their sources, liabilities and owners' equity. Chapter 3 described the general methods used in measuring *income*, one of the principal sources of
owners' equity and the primary objective of business. Its determinants,
revenue and expired cost, are considered to be realized when objective,
identifiable events occur. The present chapter deals with other major
components of owners' equity and with special problems of measuring
and summarizing changes in assets and equities.

Components of owner's equity

The owners' equity of a business is derived from two major sources:
direct investment in the business by the owners, and *income retained* in the
business. For the present, these classes of owners' equity will be designated
on the Statement of Financial Position by the titles *Owners' Investment*
and *Retained Income*. A later chapter will deal with modifications of these
account titles which are appropriate for various legal forms of business
organization.

Both Owners' Investment and Retained Income are cumulative in
nature; that is, they show the balance of owners' equity derived from each
source on the date of the Statement of Financial Position. The balance in
Owners' Investment is increased by investments in the business by the
owners, and decreased by disinvestments or withdrawals. The debit and

credit effect of these transactions on the Owners' Investment account (after posting to the ledger) is illustrated as follows:

OE, Owners' Investment

Debits (Decreases)			Credits (Increases)		
19x1			19x1		
Dec. 6	(Withdrawal)	1,000	Jan. 1	(Investment)	10,000
			19x2		
			May 6	(Investment)	4,000
					14,000
				Balance, 13,000	

If these are all of the relevant transactions through December 31, 19x3, Owners' Investment will have a credit balance of $13,000 on that date. If the account has any balance at all, it will be a credit balance, because disinvestments cannot exceed investments.

The balance in Retained Income is increased by the net income of individual accounting periods, decreased by net losses of other accounting periods, and decreased by asset distributions to the owners made possible by the earning of income. These effects may be summarized as follows:

OE, Retained Income

Debits (Decreases)			Credits (Increases)		
19x1			19x2		
Dec. 31	(Net loss)	1,500	Dec. 31	(Net Income)	4,300
19x3			19x3		
Jan. 15	(Income distribution)	2,000	Dec. 31	(Net income)	3,100
		3,500			7,400
				Balance, 3,900	

Retained Income will have a credit balance if the total net income of various accounting periods since the business was organized exceeds the total of net losses and income distributions. If net losses exceed net income, there will be a debit balance in Retained Income, called a *deficit*.

The owners' equity section of the company's Statement of Financial Position at the end of each year would appear as follows:

December 31, 19x1

Owners' Equity:
    Owners' Investment............................ $ 9,000
    Deduct Retained Income (deficit).............. (1,500)
        Total Owners' Equity................................ $ 7,500

December 31, 19x2

Owners' Equity:
    Owners' Investment........................... $13,000
    Add Retained Income.......................... 2,800
        Total Owners' Equity................................ $15,800

December 31, 19x3

Owners' Equity:
    Owners' Investment........................... $13,000
    Add Retained Income.......................... 3,900
        Total Owners' Equity................................ $16,900

In each case, the *net* assets of the company at the end of the year would be equal to total owners' equity.

Income distributions: statement of retained income

The balances in the asset, liability, owners' investment, and retained income accounts cumulate from the time the business is formed. All of them show financial status. Their respective balances in the Statement of Financial Position show the amount of each type of asset owned by the business at the date of the statement, and the sources of these assets by classes of liabilities and owners' equity.

To owners, management, and others, it is important to have detailed information each accounting period about the causes of changes in retained income: income and income distributions. Income, in turn, is the difference between revenues and expired costs. It is customary accounting procedure to keep accounts during the year which show the amount of income distributions, revenues, and expired costs since the beginning of the year. At the end of the year, the last two items are reported to interested parties in the Income Statement, an illustration of which appeared in Chapter 3. After the Income Statement is completed, a Statement of Retained Income, which shows the following classes of items, is prepared:

> Balance of retained income at the beginning of the period
> Add major types of increases
>   Total
> Deduct major types of decreases
> Balance of retained income at the end of the period

The transactions of the Motor Mower Company for the month of July, shown in Chapter 3, are the basis for the Statement of Retained Income which appears below, with one addition. It is assumed that the company paid a cash dividend to its owners on July 31, as reflected by the following journal entry:

```
19x1                              (11)
July 31   OE, Income Distributions........................ 150
              A, Cash..................................       150
              Paid the owners a cash dividend out of income.
```

After this entry has been posted to the ledger accounts, the trial balance will be as follows:

MOTOR MOWER COMPANY
Trial Balance
July 31, 19x1

	(Debits)	(Credits)
A, Cash	$ 2,840	
A, Notes Receivable	2,000	
A, Accounts Receivable	700	
A, Merchandise	6,525	
L, Notes Payable		$ 2,000
L, Accounts Payable		375
OE, Owners' Investment		9,600
OE, Income Distributions	150	
OE, Revenue		2,800
OE, Cost of Goods Sold Expense	1,850	
OE, Rent Expense	310	
OE, Salary Expense	400	
Totals	$14,775	$14,775

The Income Statement and the Statement of Financial Position are as illustrated in Chapter 3, while the Statement of Retained Income is as follows:

MOTOR MOWER COMPANY
Statement of Retained Income
For the Month Ended July 31, 19x1

Retained Income, June 30, 19x1	None
Add Net Income for July (see Income Statement)	$240
Total	$240
Deduct Income Distributions	150
Retained Income, July 31, 19x1	$ 90

It is important that the title of the statement clearly identify the *period* over which the changes in retained income occurred.

Closing the accounts which show changes in owners' equity

After the accounts which show the details of changes in retained income for the accounting period—revenue, expired costs, and income distributions—have been reported to owners, managers, and others by means of the Income Statement and the Statement of Retained Income, they have served their purpose. Revenue and expired cost accounts are then transferred to Income Summary; and Income Summary and Income Distributions are transferred to Retained Income. The balance in Retained Income at the end of the accounting period is the amount which will appear on the Statement of Financial Position. In addition, the accounts which showed changes in owners' equity for the period have zero balances and are ready to be debited or credited to record the changes of the next period. Actually, these accounts are temporary accounts, since they record the changes in owners' equity for only one period, whereas the status accounts remain on the books until they are eliminated.

The process of reducing these "change" account balances to zero and transferring them ultimately to Retained Income is called *closing the books*. Closing entries, like all other entries, are recorded first in the journal and then posted to the ledger. If an account which is to be closed has a credit balance, the closing entry is of the opposite nature: it *debits* the account for the amount of its balance. After this part of the entry has been posted, total debits will equal total credits in the account, and it will have a zero balance; that is, it is *closed*. The account *credited* in this closing entry is the account to which the balance of the closed account is to be transferred, Income Summary or Retained Income, whichever is appropriate.

A revenue account with a balance of $7,500 before closing is used to illustrate the effect of this procedure.

OE, Revenue

(To close)	7,500	(Balance before closing)	7,500
		Balance after closing, 0	

OE, Income Summary

		Revenue balance transferred.....	7,500

If an account to be closed has a debit balance, the closing entry *credits* it and *debits* the account to which it is being transferred, Income Summary or Retained Income.

The following are the closing journal entries of the Motor Mower Company for July 31, 19x1 and the T-accounts after the closing entries have been posted to the ledger.

19x1   (C1)
July 31 OE, Revenue............................... 2,800
              OE, Income Summary...................   2,800
         To close Revenue.

                                        (C2a)
      31 OE, Income Summary....................... 1,850
              OE, Cost of Goods Sold Expense.........   1,850
         To close Cost of Goods Sold Expense.

                                        (C2b)
      31 OE, Income Summary....................... 310
              OE, Rent Expense......................   310
         To close Rent Expense.

                                        (C2c)
      31 OE, Income Summary....................... 400
              OE, Salary Expense....................   400
         To close Salary Expense.

An alternative which saves time in journalizing and posting is to close all expense accounts in one compound entry, as follows:

(C2)

```
July 31   OE, Income Summary........................ 2,560
              OE, Cost of Goods Sold Expense.........          1,850
              OE, Rent Expense......................            310
              OE, Salary Expense....................            400
          To close expense accounts.
```

The ledger accounts affected would then appear as follows:

OE, Income Summary (July)

```
19x1                                    19x1
July 31                (C2)   2,560     July 31              (C1)   2,800
```

OE, Revenue (July)

```
19x1                                    19x1
July 31                (C1)   2,800     July  1              (1)      150
                                              9              (3)      450
                                             31              (9)    2,200
                              ─────                                 ─────
                              2,800                                 2,800
```

OE, Cost of Goods Sold Expense (July)

```
19x1                                    19x1
July 31                (10)   1,850     July 31              (C2)   1,850
```

OE, Rent Expense (July)

```
19x1                                    19x1
July 1                 (2)      310     July 31              (C2)      310
```

OE, Salary Expense (July)

```
19x1                                    19x1
July 31                (8)      400     July 31              (C2)      400
```

At this point Revenue and the three expense accounts have zero balances; they are *closed* and are ready to show the changes in owners' equity for August. The double rulings beneath the totals of each closed account are a conventional method of showing that the account is closed. The Income Summary account has a credit balance of $240, the net income of the month.

The Income Summary balance, which represents net income or net loss, and the Income Distributions balance are then closed to Retained Income.

```
19x1                       (C3)
July 31   OE, Income Summary........................    240
              OE, Retained Income...................           240
          To close Income Summary.

                           (C4)
     31   OE, Retained Income........................    150
              OE, Income Distributions...............           150
          To close Income Distributions.
```

The three accounts affected would then appear as follows:

OE, Retained Income

19x1			19x1		
July 31	(C4)	150	July 31	(C3)	240
			Balance, 90		

OE, Income Summary (July)

19x1			19x1		
July 31	(C2)	2,560	July 31	(C1)	2,800
31	(C3)	240			
		2,800			2,800

OE, Income Distributions (July)

19x1			19x1		
July 31	(11)	150	July 31	(C4)	150

At this point Income Summary and Income Distributions are both closed and are ready to show the changes of August. The credit balance of $90 in Retained Income, the cumulative amount of income retained in the business from its formation to the end of July, 19x1, is the amount shown in the Statement of Financial Position.

The following diagram shows how the basic accounting equation is expanded to provide information on major types of changes in *owners'* equity.

Status Accounts	*Change Accounts*

Assets
=
Liabilities
+
Owners' Equity = $\begin{cases} \text{Owners' Investment} \\ + \\ \text{Retained Income} \end{cases}$

$= \text{Income} - \text{Income Distributions}$
$=$
$\begin{cases} \text{Revenue} \\ - \\ \text{Expired Cost} \end{cases}$

Frequency of the closing process

The illustration of the Motor Mower Company showed the closing of the owners' equity change accounts at the end of a *month*, July. In actual business practice, closing entries are usually made only at the end of the *year*, even though the business prepares monthly financial statements.

EXAMPLE 1:   A business which uses the calendar year as its accounting period closes its books once a year but prepares monthly financial statements for the guidance of management. The credit balance in the Revenue account on January 31 was $14,000, and on February 28 it was $26,200. What did each balance represent?

SOLUTION: The balance at the end of January, $14,000, was the total revenue for the year to date, January 1 through January 31. It was also, of course, the revenue for the month of January. The balance on February 28 was revenue for the year to date, January 1 through February 28. Revenue for February alone could be determined by subtracting the balance at the end of the previous month from the balance at the end of the current month ($26,200 − $14,000 = $12,200).

The balances in the Revenue, Expired Cost, and Income Distributions accounts at any time represent the changes in owners' equity which have occurred since the last closing entries were made. The balance in Retained Income is the cumulative amount of earnings reinvested in the business from its formation through the date of last closing.

The accrual basis of accounting

Often the layman questions the propriety of recognizing revenue in the accounts before cash is received, or of recognizing an expired cost before cash is paid. Under the *accrual basis* of accounting, the method of measuring income described in Chapter 3, revenue is taken into account when the right to receive money or its equivalent accrues to the business as a result of operations. Costs are considered to expire when the business receives a current service benefit, or when the potential benefit to future periods declines. The accrual basis of accounting attempts to translate the flows of cash, described as *receipts* and *payments*, which have occurred in the current or past accounting periods or will occur in future periods, into their equivalent inflow of *revenue* and outflow of *expired cost* in the current period.

The actual *receipt* of money by a business may take place in an earlier period than the *accrual* of revenue, or in the same period, or in a later period.

EXAMPLE 2(a):   In 19x1 a business receives an advance cash deposit of $500 on merchandise which is to be shipped in 19x2. This is a cash receipt of 19x1, but revenue is earned in 19x2, when title to the goods passes to the customer.

EXAMPLE 2(b):   In 19x2 a business sells merchandise on credit for $400 and collects the account before the end of the year. This is both a cash receipt and a revenue of 19x2.

EXAMPLE 2(c):   A business sells merchandise on account for $300 in 19x2 but does not collect the account until 19x3. This is a revenue of 19x2 but a cash receipt of 19x3.

Revenue *accrues* to the business when the business earns the right to receive a new asset which can be measured objectively. In the case of a sale of merchandise, this is the time when title to the goods passes to the customer.

Payment for service benefits received by the business may also take place in the same period as the *cost expiration* or in an earlier or later period.

EXAMPLE 3(a):   On October 1, 19x1, a business paid $1,200 for a one-year insurance policy. Cost expiration applicable to 19x2 is $900, in proportion to the protection received for nine months in 19x2. The cash payment for this amount was made in the previous year.

EXAMPLE 3(b):   In 19x2 a business paid $700 for gasoline, all of which was used in making deliveries during the year. The cash payment and the cost expiration both occurred in 19x2.

EXAMPLE 3(c):   In December, 19x2, a business hired an employee at a pay rate of $20 a day. He worked ten days in December, but was first paid on January 5, 19x3. A cost of $200 expired in 19x2, but the related cash payment was not made until the next year.

Cash receipts include many items that will never become revenue in any accounting period. Cash received from the owners as investment, for example, is *never earned* by the entity. Cash borrowed is a receipt but not a revenue, because the business has an obligation to repay it. Collections of loans previously made to others are not revenue, but the interest is revenue of the periods in which it is earned.

Many cash disbursements, too, are for items that will never become expired costs. Money paid to owners either as a dividend out of income or as a return of capital invested does not represent a cost. A cash repayment of a loan from another is not a cost (although the interest is), just as the receipt of the proceeds of a loan is not revenue. Cash paid out as a loan is likewise not a cost.

Reason for using the accrual basis

The accrual basis of accounting for income is used rather than the cash receipts and payments basis because it is generally considered to give management, owners, and others a better estimate of the performance of a business. Several extreme examples are used to emphasize the shortcomings of cash receipts and payments as a means of measuring income.

EXAMPLE 4:   During 19x1, its first year of operations, a business bought merchandise on account for $10,000, to be paid for in 19x2, and sold all of it for $15,000 cash. What was its income for the year?

SOLUTION:

Cash Receipts and Payments Basis		Accrual Basis	
Receipts....................	$15,000	Revenue....................	$15,000
Deduct payments............	0	Deduct expired cost..........	10,000
Cash gain..................	$15,000	Net income.................	$ 5,000

The net income as determined by the accrual basis is a much better guide of business performance, since it is in proportion to business activity.

EXAMPLE 5:   During 19x3, its first year of operations, a business bought merchandise for $20,000 cash and sold all of it for $30,000 on account. None of the accounts had been collected by the end of the year, but all were owed by reliable people. What was the income for the year?

SOLUTION:

Cash Receipts and Payments Basis		Accrual Basis	
Receipts......................	$ 0	Revenue......................	$30,000
Deduct payments.............	20,000	Deduct expired cost...........	20,000
Cash loss....................	($20,000)	Net income..................	$10,000

Here, again, the accrual basis gives a measure of performance in proportion to the level of business activity.

Although the accrual basis generally furnishes the more useful measure of business income, those concerned with the affairs of a business also need information about its cash receipts, payments, and balance. This information is shown in an asset account, however, and not in an owners' equity account.

Bookkeeping convenience in timing of accrual entries

The income amount reported in the Income Statement at the end of an accounting period should reflect revenue realized during that period rather than cash collections, and expired costs rather than cash payments. Still, bookkeeping effort is often simplified if only market transactions are recorded *during* the period as they take place and additional entries are made at the *end* of the period to reflect accruals properly. These end-of-period adjusting entries to reflect accruals are of four general types:

(1) Debits to record expired costs, offset by credits
    (a) To assets for costs acquired earlier (prepayments);
    (b) To liabilities for amounts to be paid later.
(2) Credits to record earned revenue, offset by debits
    (a) To liabilities for amounts previously collected in advance;
    (b) To assets for amounts to be collected later.

Succeeding paragraphs illustrate the method of accounting for each type of adjustment. In each case, the accounting period is the calendar year, and for simplicity the applicable accounts are assumed to be affected by only one transaction. In reality, a single account may be affected by hundreds of transaction entries and several adjusting entries. Adjustments of a single type which affect a single account should be combined in one entry.

Adjustment for expired cost of asset acquired earlier

```
19x1                        (Entry during the period)
Nov.  1   A, Unexpired Insurance........................ 240
             A, Cash....................................         240
          Purchased for cash a one-year insurance policy
          effective on November 1.
```

No further recognizable event occurs during the accounting period with respect to the insurance policy. The business receives the service, insurance protection, in equal proportions each day; therefore, an equal amount of its cost expires each day. For the accounting year ending December 31, the $40 premium applicable to two months ($\frac{2}{12}$ of $240) should be shown as an expense. The remaining $200 is an unexpired cost applicable to the ten months' protection to be received in 19x2.

19x1   (Adjusting entry at end of period)
Dec. 31   OE, Insurance Expense (19x1).................   40
                 A, Unexpired Insurance.....................   40
          Transferred the expired cost of insurance protec-
          tion to expense.

After this entry has been posted, the accounts affected will appear as follows:

A, Unexpired Insurance

19x1			19x1	
Nov. 1		240	Dec. 31	40
Balance, 200				

OE, Insurance Expense (19x1)

19x1	
Dec. 31	40

In the 19x1 Income Statement, $40 would be included as Insurance Expense; and in the December 31, 19x1, Statement of Financial Position, Unexpired Insurance of $200 would appear as an asset. The $40 balance of the expense would then be closed to Income Summary. The balance of each revenue and expense account to be closed is the balance after the adjusting entry has been made.

The term of the useful life of the insurance policy is set by contract, and is *definite*. On the other hand, the useful life of a physical asset which is acquired for use in the business, such as a piece of equipment, will be long but *indefinite*. Its length depends to some extent upon the effects of physical wear and tear from use, corrosion, and similar factors. More often the useful life ends because the asset becomes obsolete, inadequate for the purpose for which it is being used, or uneconomical to operate as compared with a newer asset.

The expired cost of physical assets such as buildings and equipment is called *depreciation*. *Total depreciation* over such an asset's entire useful life is computed as follows:

(1) Total Depreciation = Acquisition Cost − Salvage Value.

Salvage value is the expected amount for which the asset can be sold when its useful life has ended.

The amount of depreciation assigned to each accounting period is computed thus:

$$(2) \quad \frac{\text{Total Depreciation}}{\text{Number of Time Periods of Life}} = \text{Depreciation per Time Period}$$

EXAMPLE 6: A business acquires for $3,000 a garage which is expected to have a useful life of 10 years and a scrap value of zero at the end of that time. What is the expired cost, or depreciation, for each full year of its life?

SOLUTION: $\dfrac{\text{Cost} - \text{Salvage}}{\text{Number of Periods}} = \dfrac{\$3,000 - 0}{10} = \$300$ per year

If the asset is in use for the entire accounting period, depreciation assigned to the period is $300. If it is in use for only a part of the period, depreciation assigned to the period is determined by multiplying $300 by the appropriate fraction of a year.

The effect of recording depreciation is similar to that of recording expired insurance, transferring an expired cost from an asset to an expense, except for the indefiniteness of the asset's length of life. The following illustration shows the related journal entries and their effect on the ledger accounts.

19x1	(Entry during the period)		
July 1	A, Buildings...............................	3,000	
	A, Cash..............................		3,000
	Purchased a garage which was expected to have a useful life of 10 years and zero salvage value.		

	(Adjusting entry at end of period)		
Dec. 31	OE, Depreciation Expense..................	150	
	A, Buildings.........................		150
	Transferred the expired cost of the garage to expense. Annual depreciation is $300 ($3,000/10), and the garage was in use one-half of a year during this accounting period.		

A, Buildings

19x1			19x1		
July 1		3,000	Dec. 31		150

OE, Depreciation Expense (19x1)

19x1		
Dec. 31		150

In actual accounting practice the credit in the preceding adjusting entry is not made directly to the asset, Buildings account, but to an account which is a deduction from the asset. The use of such an account, entitled *Buildings—Accumulated Depreciation*, is discussed in a later chapter.

Depreciation Expense of $150 would be shown in the 19x1 Income Statement, and Buildings would be shown as an asset with an unexpired cost of $2,850 in the December 31, 19x1, Statement of Financial Position. If the garage is in use for all of the year 19x2, the adjusting entry at the end of that year will affect the same accounts as in 19x1, but will be for $300, a full year's depreciation.

Adjustment for expired cost to be paid for later

On December 1, 19x1, a business engaged a lawyer for a monthly fee of $100, but paid nothing in 19x1.

(Entry during the period—None)

For the accounting period ending December 31, the business has received a service benefit, legal advice, costing $100, for which it owes the lawyer on December 31.

19x1	(Adjusting entry at end of period)		
Dec. 31	OE, Legal Expense	100	
	L, Accounts Payable		100
	To record the expired cost of legal services and the corresponding liability.		

The $100 balance in the Legal Expense account would appear in the 19x1 Income Statement, and the $100 balance in Accounts Payable would appear as a liability in the December 31, 19x1, Statement of Financial Position.

Adjustment for earned revenue previously collected

19x1	(Entry during the period)		
July 1	A, Cash	600	
	L, Subscriptions Collected in Advance		600
	Collected for 100 three-year subscriptions to a monthly magazine at $6 a subscription.		

By the end of 19x1, the business has earned $100 of the amount collected on subscriptions ($6/36$ of $600). It will earn the remaining $500 as it issues the magazine to the subscribers during the next 30 months.

19x1	(Adjusting entry at end of period)		
Dec. 31	L, Subscriptions Collected in Advance	100	
	OE, Revenue		100
	Transferred the earned part of the subscriptions collected from a liability account to revenue.		

The related account balances would then appear as follows:

L, Subscriptions Collected in Advance

19x1			19x1	
Dec. 31		100	July 31	600
			Balance, 500	

OE, Revenue

	19x1	
	Dec. 31	100

The $500 credit balance of Subscriptions Collected in Advance would be shown as a liability in the December 31, 19x1 Statement of Financial Position, and $100 would be shown as revenue in the Income Statement for 19x1.

Adjustment for earned revenue to be collected later

A machine rental business rented a piece of office equipment to a customer on December 1, 19x1. Its customer was to pay the rent of $2 a day when the equipment was returned. On December 31 the customer had not returned the equipment.

(Entry during the period—None)

19x1	(Adjusting entry at end of period)		
Dec. 31	A, Accounts Receivable...................	62	
	OE, Revenue........................		62
	To record the revenue earned but not collected, and the corresponding asset, for 31 days' rent on equipment rented to a customer.		

The year's Income Statement would include the $62 as revenue, and the $62 Accounts Receivable would appear as an asset in the end-of-year Statement of Financial Position.

The going-concern assumption

Chapter 2 argued that the accounting practice of recording an asset at its acquisition cost as determined in a market transaction is justified because the measurement is objectively determined, and because the buyer's purchase of the asset is evidence that he considers its service potential to be at least equal to its cost.

Later accounting within the business assumes that the service potentials of assets continue to be equal to their costs unless there is evidence to the contrary. For assets whose life is determined by contract, such as unexpired insurance, cost is assumed to expire in proportion to the lapse of time. The cost of the future benefit, then, is proportionate to the fraction of the life of the contract which remains.

In other cases, the service lives of assets acquired are expected to be long, but indefinite. Such assets, illustrated by buildings and equipment, are measured initially at their acquisition cost, and thereafter it is generally assumed that their cost expires in proportion to the expiration of their estimated useful lives.

For the purpose of these measurements, it is assumed that the business will continue in operation indefinitely, or at least until its present facilities are used up and its contracts completed. This continuity, or *going-concern*, assumption is in contrast to the assumption that the business will liquidate. Under the going-concern assumption, the market values of these long-lived assets are irrelevant for determining income and financial status. The business does not intend to liquidate, or to *sell* the assets for their market values, but rather to *use* them during their expected useful lives.

EXAMPLE 7:   A merchant buys a cash register on January 1, 19x1, paying $1,000 cash. He expects to use it for 10 years and then junk it. One year later, because of a war shortage, he could sell the register for $1,200. What is the expired cost of the register for 19x1, and its unexpired cost at the end of the year?

SOLUTION: The market value of $1,200 is irrelevant, because the merchant does not intend to sell the register. No matter what its ups and downs in market price during the ten years, the register is expected to be worthless at the end of that time. The expired cost for 19x1 is $100, proportionate to the $\frac{1}{10}$ of the useful life of the asset which has expired; the unexpired cost on December 31, 19x1, is $900. (This allocation of an equal amount of cost to each year of life assumes that each year receives equal service benefits, an assumption which will be examined further in a later chapter.)

There are several reasons why unexpired cost rather than market value is used as the basis for measuring assets.

(1) Market value changes are merely paper gains and losses, not confirmed by actual sale. Before the assets are sold, the direction of price changes may be reversed and their amounts are almost certain to change.

(2) If the accountant wrote the amounts of assets up or down every time their market values changed (assuming that he could get reliable information), he would have time to do little else.

(3) When the assets were finally sold, there would be no way of measuring the amount of gain or loss on them, because the record of their cost would have been obscured by many write-ups and write-downs.

When a concern is on the brink of going out of business, a different approach is in order. The assets are to be sold in the near future, and their market values are of interest, particularly to the creditors. In such situations, special statements of estimated liquidating values (called Statements of Affairs) are often prepared for the guidance of owners, managers, and creditors.

Summary

The owners' equity of a business is derived from Owners' Investment and Retained Income. The latter is the excess of the net income of individual periods over income distributions and periodic net losses. The beginning balance, principal changes during the period, and ending balance of Retained Income are shown in a periodic Statement of Retained Income. After the preparation of the financial statements, the accounts which show changes in owners' equity are closed: Revenue and Expired Cost, to Income; and Income and Income Distributions, to Retained Income.

The accrual basis of accounting is designed to show as revenue the amounts of money which a business has earned the right to receive as a result of operations, and as expense the cost of service benefits which the business has received in the current period. There is often a difference between the accounting period in which an item of revenue is earned and the period in which it is collected, and a similar difference between the period in which a cost expires and the period in which the corresponding cash payment is made. Adjusting entries are sometimes needed at the end of the accounting period so that the revenue and expired cost accounts will include the proper amounts of revenue earned and cost expired during the current period.

Unless there is convincing evidence to the contrary, it may be assumed, in making accounting measurements, that the business will continue in operation indefinitely. On the basis of this assumption, the appropriate yardstick for measuring assets is acquisition cost, or the unexpired fraction thereof, rather than current market value or liquidating value.

QUESTIONS AND PROBLEMS

4-1   If the Statement of Financial Position shows the status of assets and equities at a given time, and the Income Statement shows changes in equities, what does the Statement of Retained Income show?

4-2   "Adjusting entries are always the result of transactions which have occurred but have not been recorded on the accounting books."

REQUIRED:
Do you agree with this statement? Defend your answer.

4-3   Weldon Thorpe, CPA, prepared the financial statements for the McCord Dairy. When the owner of the dairy saw that the company had had a net income of $12,000 for the year, he remarked, "That is impossible. The company is overdrawn $200 at the bank. We don't even have a cash balance, so how could we have that much net income?"

REQUIRED:
Prepare an answer for the owner of the dairy.

4-4   The balance of the Retained Income account for the Blake Company on January 1, 19x1, was $16,000. The balance in this account was $14,000 on December 31, 19x1. Net income for the year was $6,000.

REQUIRED:
Does this situation necessarily indicate an error in the accounting records? Explain.

4-5

REQUIRED:

a. List the main types of *status* and *change* accounts that you would expect to find in a retail hardware store.

b. Which accounts in (*a*) would be closed at the end of the period? Why? To what accounts would they be closed?

4-6   Explain the relation between the following purposes of cash payments of 19x3 and expired costs of 19x3:

a. Repayment of loan from the bank, plus interest.

b. Payment for merchandise bought on account in 19x3.

c. Payment for insurance policy which expires in 19x5.

d. Payment of dividend to stockholders.

e. Cash refund to customer for overpayment of account.

f. Payment for equipment.

g. Payment for 19x3 salaries.

4-7   Explain the relation between the following sources of cash receipts of 19x3 and revenue of 19x3:

a. Issuance of capital stock by the company.

b. Collection of a customer's account for a sale made in 19x1.

c. Sale of merchandise for cash.

d. Cash loan received from the bank.

e. Cash received for sale of equipment used in displaying merchandise.

f. Refund of overpayment inadvertently made to supplier.

4-8   The Vanity Shop signed a 12-month lease for $1,800 on September 1, 19x1, when it moved into its new location. The Shop agreed to pay the amount in advance, but had not paid it by September 30.

REQUIRED:

Explain how this transaction would affect assets, liabilities, and owners' equity on September 30, the date when monthly financial statements were prepared.

4-9   The Newman Department Store hired three additional sales clerks on Monday, July 26, 19x1, to assist in its Anniversary Sale, which lasted two weeks. The sales clerks were paid $360 on August 7. The department store's fiscal year ended on July 31.

REQUIRED:

a. Prepare entries necessary on July 26, July 31, and August 7.

b. What would be the effect on the three principal financial statements if no entries were made until August 7?

4-10   You are in charge of preparing financial statements for the *UVW* Company, and are about to make adjustments at the end of the accounting period.

REQUIRED:

Describe a situation and record the appropriate entries for each of the following types of adjustment:

a. An expense is debited and a liability is credited.

b. An expense is debited and an asset is credited.

c. An asset is debited and revenue is credited.

d. A liability is debited and revenue is credited.

4-11   On November 1 your business borrows $2,000 from the bank, giving a three-month promissory note bearing interest at 6%. Your accounting period ends on December 31.

REQUIRED:

a. Record your necessary entry on November 1.
b. Record your necessary entry, if any, on December 31.
c. How much is *payable* to the bank on December 31? How much is *due*? Explain the difference between these two terms.

4-12   Thomas Shipp and Malcolm Gaines began business on January 1, 19x1, and each invested $15,000 cash in the business. During the first year of operation, the business had a net income of $6,000. On December 24 the business distributed $2,000 cash to each of the two owners. On December 30, 19x1, with the permission of Gaines, Shipp sold his interest in the business to Sydney Elwell for $20,000.

REQUIRED:

a. Show the owners' equity T-accounts of the business for the year.
b. Show how the relevant information would appear in the year-end financial statements.

4-13   The founding of a new business was recorded on January 1, 19x1, using appropriate asset and equity accounts. However, the bookkeeper failed to close the books on December 31, 19x1. He prepared a trial balance on December 31, 19x2.

REQUIRED:

What would the balances in each of the following accounts on that date represent:

a. Cash?
b. Accounts Payable?
c. Merchandise?
d. Expense?
e. Revenue?
f. Retained Income?

4-14   The time when entries for accruals are recorded is largely a matter of clerical convenience.

REQUIRED:

If a business prepares financial statements each month, state when you would record entries for each of the following events, both transactions and adjustments, and show what accounts would be debited and credited.

a. Office supplies are bought about once each month and are used constantly in small amounts every day.
b. Store rent is paid in advance at the beginning of each month.
c. Equipment is rented at a standard rate for each day, and rent is paid early in the following month.
d. Customers are frequently allowed to give the business interest-bearing promissory notes due in 90 days in exchange for merchandise.
e. City business license fees for the current calendar year are paid in January.
f. Property taxes for the entire year are paid in October.
g. The business has five different insurance policies, the premium on each of which is paid a year in advance.
h. Employees are paid once a week on Thursday for work done through the preceding Saturday.

4-15 Company *A* purchased a three-year insurance policy on July 1, 19x1 from Mutual Insurance Co. for $480. The bookkeeper for the company made the following entry in the journal:

19x1
July 1   Insurance Expense............................... 480
               Cash..   480
               Purchased a three-year policy from Mutual Insur-
               ance Co.

On the same date Company *B* purchased an identical policy for the same amount. Its bookkeeper made the following entry:

19x1
July 1   Unexpired Insurance............................ 480
               Cash..   480
               Purchased a three-year policy from Mutual Insur-
               ance Co.

REQUIRED:

a. Which of the bookkeepers made the correct entry? Give reasons for your answer.
b. Assuming that the companies' accounting years ended on December 31, what additional entries would be necessary in each case?

4-16

REQUIRED:

a. From the following list of account balances, state which accounts would be closed at the end of the period on December 31, 19x1, and to which account each would be closed.
b. Assuming that all adjustments have been made, reconstruct the adjusting entries that were probably made.
c. Prepare the three common financial statements.

Account Balances of Turnstill Company

Prepaid insurance..	$ 150
Salaries expense...	350
Rent revenue received in advance.........................	400
Income tax expense.......................................	175
Cash...	770
Equipment..	1,200
Interest revenue...	50
Accrued salaries payable.................................	20
Accrued interest receivable..............................	50
Depreciation expense.....................................	200
Notes receivable...	1,200
Owners' investment.......................................	2,500
Income distributions.....................................	300
Insurance expense..	50
Income tax payable.......................................	175
Sales revenue..	1,800
Rent revenue...	200
Cost of goods sold.......................................	1,200
Retained income, January 1, 19x1.........................	500

4-17 On January 1, 19x1 John Donals paid $3,000 for a three-year fire insurance policy. As of December 31, 19x2 a question has arisen as to the amount of prepaid insurance that should be shown on Donals' Statement of Financial Position.

One proposal is to show prepaid insurance at $600, which is the short-rate cancellation value of the policy on December 31, 19x2.

A second proposal is to show prepaid insurance at $1,000, representing one-third of the original premium cost.

A third proposal is to show prepaid insurance at $1,200, which is the one-year premium cost for a policy for the same amount as the policy in force.

REQUIRED:

You are to discuss each of the proposals as to acceptability, as to the general principle underlying it, and as to its effect on reported income.

(Adapted from AICPA Examination in Theory of Accounts, November 4, 1955.)

CASE 4-1. RANDOM SAMPLE CANDY STORE

REQUIRED:

a. Record the following selected transactions of the Random Sample Candy Store for March, 19x1, in journal form.
b. Summarize the journal entries in T-accounts.
c. Prepare a trial balance at the end of March.
d. Prepare the three basic financial statements for March.
e. The transactions of the Random Sample Candy Store are hypothetical and fragmentary. However, assuming that they were real, do you think the operations of the store for March were successful? Was its financial position at the end of the month strong or weak? Do you notice any matters which require attention or corrective action?

March
 1   George Random began business by depositing $1,500 in the bank.
 1   Mr. Random ordered various candies costing $4,500 from a local wholesaler.
 1   Signed a five-year lease calling for rent of $150 to be paid in advance each month. Gave the landlord a check for the first month's rent.
 1   Bought display equipment costing $3,600 from the manufacturer. Made a cash down payment of $900 and signed a promissory note agreeing to pay the remainder in three equal principal installments on March 31, April 30, and May 30. Accrued interest at the rate of 6% per year on the unpaid principal balance was to be paid at the time each installment was paid. The equipment was expected to be worthless in ten years.
 1   Hired a sales clerk, agreeing to pay her a salary of $175 per month at the end of each month.
 1   Bought wrapping supplies for cash, $40.
 4   The shipment of candy was received from the wholesaler. The total cost of $4,500 was to be paid on March 31 without discount.
 1–31 Total cash sales made to customers throughout the month were $1,800. (Record as one transaction.)
 1–31 Total sales on credit for the month were $600. (Record as one entry.)
 1–31 Total collections on the credit sales during March were $112.
 31   Paid the installment due on the equipment note of March 1, plus interest.
 31   Sent the candy wholesaler a check for $900 and a note promising to pay the remainder, plus 6% annual interest, at the end of six months. Permission to give the note had been received previously.

31   Paid the clerk's salary for the month by check. The clerk had missed
      several days' work; therefore, the check was for only $145.

31   Received a utility bill of $35 for the month, but did not pay it.

31   Mr. Random wrote himself a check on the business bank account for
      personal use, $75, and cashed it at the bank.

1-31 Mr. Random had given candy at various times to prospective customers
      and to his wife. His records showed that the cost of the candy given away
      was $60 and its retail value, $90. Exactly one-fourth of the candy had been
      given to Mrs. Random.

31   Make the entry for equipment use for the month.

31   It had been impractical to keep a record of the cost of each item of mer-
      chandise sold during the month. Mr. Random and his clerk stayed until
      midnight on March 31 counting the unsold merchandise and multiplying
      the quantities of each kind by the wholesale cost. The next day Mr. Ran-
      dom added the figures on a friend's adding machine and arrived at a total
      of $2,700. Wrapping supplies estimated to have cost $15 were also on hand.

CASE 4-2. THE WHITE LAUNDRY COMPANY

The White Laundry Company has not kept adequate accounting records. The
CPA who has been engaged to reconstruct its accounts at the end of November,
19x2, has discovered the following facts:

Unpaid customers' accounts total $950 and unpaid bills to suppliers amount to
$730. The balance in the bank account is $550.

The laundry rents the building it occupies and paid the rent for November,
$200, on November 2.

All laundry equipment and a cash register were bought on December 1, 19x1,
for a lump-sum price of $4,800 cash. The equipment is expected to have a total
useful life of 20 years from the date of purchase.

Soap, wrapping paper, and similar supplies were bought in October, 19x2, for
$300. It is estimated that 1/4 of the original amount is still unused. An order for
$200 worth of additional supplies was placed on November 17, but it has not yet
been filled.

Being short of cash, the laundry borrowed $1,000 from the bank on October 31,
19x2, and signed a note promising to pay the sum borrowed plus 6% interest on
January 31, 19x3. No payment has yet been made.

When the owner opened the business on December 1, 19x1, he invested $3,000
of his own money. He has not withdrawn any money from the business during the
year.

REQUIRED:

a. Prepare a statement of financial position for the White Laundry Company as
   of November 30, 19x2.

b. Prepare a statement of retained income for the year ending on November 30,
   19x2.

c. What additional information would you need to prepare an income statement
   for the year?

CASE 4-3. DR. GEORGE LOWELL

Dr. George Lowell, general practitioner of medicine, lives in a small midwestern
town, where he has maintained an office for 12 years. His office is located next to

the City Pharmacy, which is the only drugstore in the town. In order to attract Dr. Lowell to the community, the City Pharmacy built the doctor's office and furnishes it to him rent-free. Dr. Lowell's father completely equipped his office as a graduation present. Comparable offices in the town rent for $100 a month.

Dr. Lowell is the only doctor in the town. He has one assistant, Miss Rachel Thomas, who serves as nurse and receptionist-bookkeeper. Miss Thomas prides herself on keeping accurate and complete records, which consist of a receipt book, a bank deposit book, a checkbook with detailed stubs, and a daybook in which she keeps a record of all of Dr. Lowell's visits which are to be charged to patients. On a separate page for each patient she keeps a detailed record of all charges and collections. At the beginning of each morning Dr. Lowell reports to Miss Thomas all visits which he has made to patients during the previous evening. He also transfers to her all cash which he collects, so that she can prepare proper receipts and include the cash in the daily deposit in the bank. Miss Thomas prepares and mails monthly statements to patients from the information in the daybook.

Dr. Lowell has requested that Miss Thomas present him with a summary of operations at the end of each week. To arrive at the results for the month, Miss Thomas totals the weekly summaries. Weekly summaries for the month of August, 19x1, appear below.

Week of August 1–6:

Receipts written for cash received:

Office calls	$110.00	
Collections on patients' accounts	240.00	
Refund from Casey Pharmaceutical Company for an over-payment of their July bill	24.50	
Total		$ 374.50

Checks written:

Payment to Golden Medical Company for medical supplies sufficient for three months	$178.16	
Salary of Miss Thomas ($10 per day. Each week, $9 is withheld for income tax and $1.80 for O.A.S. insurance)	49.20	
Salary of the maid, who works in the mornings for Mrs. Lowell and cleans the office in the afternoons. Income tax withheld is $3 and O.A.S. insurance is $0.90	26.10	
Gasoline, oil, etc., paid to Duke Service Station for their July bill	55.00	
Professional dues to a medical society for 19x1	40.00	
Total		$ 248.46
Net income for the week		$ 126.04

Week of August 8–13:

Receipts written for cash received:

Office calls	$ 90.00	
Collections on account	135.00	
Total		$ 225.00

Checks written:

Salary of Miss Thomas	$ 49.20	
Salary of the maid	26.10	
Paid the July utility bill, which includes charges for both residence and office	27.65	
Purchased an electric sterilizer	95.00	
Sent a check to the Valley Camp, which Dr. Lowell's son will attend the next two weeks	60.00	
Total		257.95
Net loss for the week		($ 32.95)

Week of August 15–20:

Receipts written for cash received:

Office calls	$160.00	
Collections on account	350.00	
Check received from a medical journal for an article which Dr. Lowell had contributed in the May issue	100.00	
Income tax refund for previous year	216.00	
Total		$ 826.00

Checks written:

Two-year subscriptions to current periodicals for the office	$ 15.00	
New tires for Dr. Lowell's car	160.00	
City Laundry—Paid July bill	17.35	
To Dr. Lowell for lunch money to entertain a visitor	21.00	
Purchased X-ray film	185.40	
Paid a bill for drugs to Magruder Drug Co., Invoice of August 5	116.12	
Salary of Miss Thomas	49.20	
Salary of the maid	26.10	
Total		$ 590.17
Net income for the week		$ 235.83

Week of August 22–27:

Receipts written for cash received:

Office calls	$150.00	
Collections on account	240.00	
Sale of an old office desk	75.00	
Dividend check from a company in which Dr. Lowell owns stock	48.00	
Total		$ 513.00

Checks written:

Postage	$ 4.40	
Salary of Miss Thomas	49.20	
Salary of maid	26.10	
Paid to City Pharmacy for bandages, gauze, etc	14.58	
Total		$ 94.28
Net income for the week		$ 418.72

Monthly summary:

Receipts written	$1,938.50
Checks written	1,190.86
Net income for the month of August	$ 747.64

Additional data:

Further investigation reveals that Dr. Lowell had 216 office calls in August for which payment was not collected. He charges a standard rate of $5 per office call. Amounts charged to patients for home and hospital visits, according to Dr. Lowell, were $1,665 for the month.

Creditors' statements which arrived in the mail during the week of August 29–September 3 were:

Green Florist Company, flowers for the office for the month of August	$ 20.00
City Laundry, August services	17.40
Duke Service Station, August bill	49.00
Casey Pharmaceutical Company, invoice of August 29 for medical supplies	117.42

Dr. Lowell's deposit book shows that $1,938.50 has been deposited in the bank from August 1 through August 27.

REQUIRED:

a. Do the weekly and monthly financial statements prepared by Miss Thomas for Dr. Lowell give him useful and realistic information? Explain.

b. Do you see where any improvements can be made over the control of Dr. Lowell's assets?

c. Using only the data given here, prepare a more meaningful statement of income for Dr. Lowell. Where expenses are for both home and office, assume that they should be divided equally.

d. What additional information would you need to have to make the income statement more accurate?

e. From the information given, list the assets and the liabilities of Dr. Lowell at the end of August. You need not attempt to show money amounts.

Chapter **5**

Classifying and Measuring
Monetary Assets

The problems involved in classifying assets, equities, and equity changes are not entirely separate from the problems of measuring these financial elements. It is a matter of *classification* to decide whether a particular service potential acquired by the business is an asset (which will benefit future periods), an expired cost (which has benefited the present period), or partly both. The problem of *measuring* the asset or expense is largely solved by proper classification. Usually measurement is largely a matter of apportioning the cost of the service potentials to time periods.

Accounting *measurement* is partly a matter of fact, partly a matter of conventions accepted among accountants, and partly a matter of judgment.[1] For example, the amount of coin and currency owned by the business at any date is *factual* because it can be stated directly in money terms. It is a *convention* to allocate a part of the cost of long-lived assets to each accounting period during which they are used. It is also an accepted custom to measure the amounts earned on contracts for service extending over a definite time period as an equal daily accumulation or accrual. The accountant must exercise judgment in many matters. An example is the estimate that he must make of the expected useful life of a long-lived asset in measuring its periodic depreciation.

If the results of the accounting process are to be meaningful and reliable to management and other users, the accountant must account for factual

---

[1] American Institute of Certified Public Accountants, *Examination of Financial Statements by Independent Public Accountants* (New York: The Institute, 1936), p. 1.

amounts exactly, apply conventions consistently, and exercise judgment impartially.

CLASSIFYING ACCOUNTS

General objectives of classification

Those who decide in what particular accounts financial information is to be classified should consider the purposes to which the information furnished by the accounts is to be devoted. To the extent practical, financial information should be classified initially in such a way that it can readily serve its most important purposes, which are:

(1) To aid in the control of business operations by management at various levels;

(2) To facilitate the accounting for the use of various types of enterprise assets;

(3) To facilitate the appraisal of the financial results of the enterprise by management for its own guidance, and by others as a measure of management's stewardship of the business resources.

External versus internal needs for accounting

General-purpose financial statements, such as the basic Income Statement, Statement of Retained Income, and Statement of Financial Position illustrated in the three preceding chapters, answer some of management's questions about the business, but they are better designed to serve the needs of creditors and investors. The last two groups desire a basis of past performance for estimating what will probably happen to the enterprise in the future as a result of management action, as well as of such external forces as competition and general economic conditions. Business performance is largely out of their control, because the effect upon it of their own decisions as to whether to lend to it or invest in it is usually slight.

It is management's function, on the other hand, to act in such a way as to help the business achieve its objectives. Management actions will have a profound effect on business results. They are based upon answers to the questions:

(1) How well has the business done in comparison with what it should have done?

(2) What is its present financial position?

(3) What can be done to improve its showing in the future?

Generally the information needed by management in answering these questions is more detailed and more complex than that needed by other groups. As a result, management's needs have a greater influence than do those of outsiders on the design of the classification of accounts.

Accounting classification parallels management functions

Accounting is flexible, and the types of information and controls which it provides can be adapted to the needs and objectives of the management of the individual entity. The tailor-made accounting plan of a particular business is called its *accounting system*. It should be designed to aid management in achieving the general objectives of maximizing income and efficiency and minimizing errors, fraud, and waste, as well as in achieving the specific objectives of the business.

Management's functions may be described as a cycle consisting of four phases:

(1) *Determining the objectives* of the business, both for the short-range and the long-range future;
(2) *Planning* how to accomplish the objectives;
(3) *Organizing* the people and things needed to do the work; and
(4) *Controlling* the performance of the work.

Control by management means attempting to keep the business moving toward its objectives at the desired rate. It involves co-ordinating, directing, and supervising work while it is in progress and appraising the quality of its performance after it has been completed.

The manager of a small, simple business may be able to manage informally, carrying out some of his functions directly and observing the performance of others. As organizations grow larger, it becomes increasingly necessary for top management to delegate responsibility to subordinates and to rely upon a formal system for communicating information about how the responsibility is discharged.

Accounting is just such a system of communication. The *objectives* of the business can be translated into accounting terms, such as the desired amount of net income, income distributions, and percentage return on investment. The business *plan* expressed in financial terms is the *budget*, which shows the details of planned activities in terms of revenues, expenses, assets, and equities. Accounting aids in *organizing* the work through the design of the *accounting system*.

In the *control* phase, accounting helps management direct the performance of work by recording, summarizing, and reporting information on what has been done.

The *supervision* feature of accounting consists of *auditing*, which is testing the reliability of the records. This supervision is provided partly by the operation of protective features, or *internal checks*, which are built into the accounting system. In larger businesses additional supervision is provided by an internal audit department, and in most businesses further review comes through the periodic examination of the records by the independent auditor.[2]

Appraisal of business performance is made possible by the *financial statements* discussed in the three preceding chapters, as well as by additional methods of reporting and analysis which are to be presented in later chapters. But appraisal alone does not constitute control, even if it is accompanied by recommendations for corrective action. Management controls the business by taking *action* on the basis of adequate information. Management needs to know where actual results deviate from planned results, who is responsible, what is the cause, and what effects alternative courses of corrective action would have.[3] The accounting system must furnish this information in order to make management control effective.

Appraisal of results is the end of one cycle of management and accounting activity, but it is also a necessary preliminary phase for the next cycle. A business which is already in operation bases its plans for the future to a large extent upon its actual accomplishments of the past, with appropriate modifications for known or expected future changes in internal and external conditions.

Components of the accounting system

An accounting system is an orderly scheme for doing efficiently and accurately the necessary work of providing financial controls and information. The system consists of:

(1) Basic business documents, such as checks and sales tickets, which serve either to originate or to report transactions;

(2) Journals, which analyze the effect of transactions on assets and equities in terms of debits and credits;

(3) Ledgers, which summarize the results of transactions according to each asset or equity affected;

(4) Financial reports; and

(5) The procedures necessary for preparing these records and reports.

---

[2] Chester F. Lay, "The Functional Cycles of Accounting and Management," *N. A. C. A. Bulletin*, June 15, 1949, pp. 1175–1182.

[3] Wyman P. Fiske, "Control of Operations and Investment," in Fiske and Beckett, eds., *Industrial Accountant's Handbook* (Englewood Cliffs, N. J.: Prentice-Hall, Inc., 1954), p. 534.

The work of accounting is done *by* people and *for* other people, and a vital part of the accounting system is the organization of duties and responsibilities among these people. No matter how well the system is designed, it cannot accomplish its objectives unless the people involved perform their duties competently and faithfully.

A very practical limitation on the design of any accounting system is that the cost of operating it must not exceed the value of the information and controls which it provides. Furthermore, the system should be designed to suit the needs of the business—business operations should not be designed to fit the needs of accounting.

Later chapters describe some of the details of the forms and procedures which are used to control operations and to collect and report accounting data. This chapter and the two succeeding ones are concerned primarily with the broad structure of the accounting system and with general problems of classification and measurement which are common to many businesses. All businesses, whether large or small and whether engaged in manufacturing, merchandising goods, or performing a service, need information on the types and amounts of assets, liabilities, and owners' equity and the changes in owners' equity resulting from revenue, expired costs, and income distributions.

The classification of accounts

The backbone which holds the documents, journals, ledgers, reports, and procedures of an accounting system together is the *classification of accounts,* an orderly arrangement listing the accounts which the entity uses for internal management and external reporting purposes.

The type of information which each account collects must be carefully specified, if the data are to be meaningful and dependable. Comparison of the balances of accounts at different times plays a key role in the interpretation of business financial affairs. In order that the information in each account will be collected and interpreted consistently by different people and at different times, the *title* must describe accurately and concisely the nature of the information which the account contains.

To promote consistency in the classification of its financial data, each business should have its own specially prepared *manual of accounts*. The manual provides an orderly list of account titles and their identifying code numbers, a description of the type of information which is to be recorded in each account, and illustrative journal entries for unusual or difficult transactions. Such a manual is especially helpful in large organizations where many people have a part in preparing the source documents for transactions, in recording journal entries and posting them to the ledger, and in preparing and analyzing financial statements.

Bases of classifying accounts

The fundamental classes into which accounts are grouped are *assets* and *equities*. The latter is subdivided into liabilities and owners' equity, which is further broken down into accounts which show owners' investment, retained income, revenue, and expired costs.

Individual assets are classified into accounts according to one or several of the following bases:

(1) Their important physical, legal, or economic features;
(2) The measures of control to which they are subject;
(3) The purposes, or functions, for which they are used;
(4) The individual, or organizational unit, responsible for their custody.

EXAMPLE 1:   Illustrations of classification of assets according to these bases follow.

a. Physical features: Land, buildings, equipment.
b. Legal features: Accounts receivable, notes receivable.
c. Economic features: Merchandise inventory, supplies inventory.
d. Measures of control: Cash, supplies, equipment.
e. Function: Delivery equipment, display equipment, factory building.
f. Lines of responsibility: Supplies or equipment in the custody of each department manager.

Within an industry, the accounts which are needed for general-purpose reporting are very similar from company to company. However, there may be considerable variations in the account classifications within an industry as a result of preferences of different managements for internal operating controls and reports.

The general ledger

The accounts which are needed in the preparation of the customary general-purpose statements compose the *general ledger* of a company. Many of the general ledger accounts contain summary information relating to a large number of assets or equities of a given type. *Accounts Receivable, Trade*, for example, is a general ledger asset account with a debit balance equal to the sum of all amounts owed the business by its customers. In addition, management must have a detailed record of the amount owed by each customer as an aid in collecting these receivables promptly and completely. Such detailed supporting records, or *subsidiary accounts*, for Accounts Receivable, Trade, for Accounts Payable, Trade, and for other general ledger accounts are largely matters of internal procedure.

It is a common practice to arrange the accounts in the classification and in the general ledger in the order in which they appear in the company's general financial statements. The accounts used in the Statement of Financial Position appear first. Within the group of assets, liquid assets are presented first, in the order of the promptness with which they can be converted into cash. Liabilities then appear, in the approximate order of their due dates, followed by owners' equity, classified by type of owner and degree of permanence of the investment. The next group of accounts shows all changes in owners' equity which appear in the Statement of Retained Income. Last are the revenue and expense accounts, which are used in the Income Statement. The accountant can then prepare periodic statements directly from a list of general ledger account balances, or Trial Balance, without rearranging the order of accounts.

For internal purposes, code numbers are used in addition to titles to help locate the accounts in the ledger, to serve on business papers as a shorthand method of identifying the account affected, and to show the relationships between groups of similar accounts. All assets, for example, might be identified by three-digit numbers beginning with *1* (Cash by *101*, and so forth). The particular code numbers used by a company are of little interest to the outsider.

The organization chart and responsibility accounting

Both the financial accounts (assets and equities) and the operating accounts (revenues and expired costs) should be classified according to the individuals who are responsible for taking action to control them. In other words, the account classification and the financial reporting plan should parallel the *organization chart* of the business, which shows the lines of authority within the organization. Action relating to each account in the ledger should be the responsibility of a single individual. One individual may, however, have responsibility for the results shown by more than one account.

EXAMPLE 2:   The *treasurer* of an organization generally has responsibility for the *cash* account: for seeing that the business has adequate cash for its needs, and for insuring that proper safeguards are observed in handling money.

Accounts receivable is usually the responsibility of the *credit manager*. He must see that steps are taken to extend credit only to worthy individuals and to collect accounts owed fully and promptly.

Merchandise inventory may be the responsibility of the *sales manager*. His duty is to see that the quantities and types of goods on hand are in line with the company's requirements for filling future sales orders.

Equipment in the general office would be the responsibility of the *office manager;* in the *sales office*, the responsibility of the *sales manager;* and so on.

Illustrative organization chart

Figure 4 shows the functional divisions which might be appropriate for the Suburban Department Store, a medium-sized business, and for the departments of its Merchandising Division. The chart has been simplified by illustrating only a few merchandising departments and by omitting the departments which compose the Store Superintendent and Personnel, Publicity, and Finance Divisions. Each buyer directs the activities of the sales, inventory control, and clerical personnel within his department.

The lowest level of responsibility which the Suburban Department Store reflects in its formal classification of accounts is the *department*, although the business often makes more detailed analyses of accounting information for special purposes. For example, if each clerk is assigned responsibility for custody of a part of his department's merchandise inventory, an analysis is needed to determine how he discharged that accountability. Likewise, the accountability of each sales clerk for cash is usually established by assigning him a separate cash register, or drawer in a cash register, and by making a special report of the cash transactions which he handles. Such analyses as these usually require more detailed records than it is feasible to keep in the general ledger. In addition, some of the analyses are occasional, rather than continuous, collections of data.

The important point with respect to the classification of accounts is that it should follow the lines of responsibility within the organization, so that reports can be made on how each person has lived up to his responsibility.

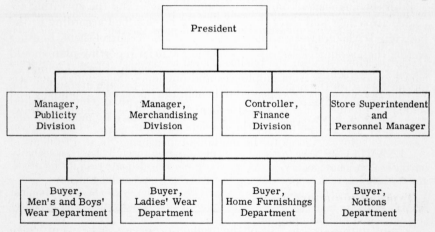

Fig. 4. Suburban Department Store: Organization Chart.

MEASURING MONETARY ASSETS

General and specific assets

In deciding how to measure business assets, it is useful to divide them into two broad groups: *general assets* and *specific assets*.

General assets are those which are available for any use within the business. Cash has a general service potential because it can be used to make any payment the business desires. One step removed from cash are *receivables*, which are claims to certain amounts of money. Cash and claims to cash have general purchasing power and can be used to distribute income to the owners of the business, to pay business debts, or to acquire additional productive factors.

Other types of assets have a rather specific potential for giving service to the business. An example is a store building. It does not represent a claim to a certain amount of money; instead, the business buys it for occupancy rather than for sale and will receive its service benefits through *use*. Prepayments for contractual services, such as insurance, are also specific assets. The *intent* of the business in acquiring such specific assets is important in deciding how to measure them. The fact that a specific asset acquired for use is occasionally sold does not invalidate the general method of measuring it—the going-concern assumption.

Monetary assets and unexpired costs

The objective in measuring general assets is to state each at the amount of general purchasing power which it could bring either immediately or with only a slight delay. Such assets may be referred to as *monetary assets*, because they may be measured in terms of money either directly or with only minor modification.

The specific assets of the business, such as physical resources, unused contractual services from employees and outsiders, and similar facilities which can reasonably be expected to benefit the business in producing and selling its product, may be called *unexpired costs*. This designation draws attention to the availability of these assets for future use, and it also gives important information as to the method of measuring them. Problems of classifying and measuring assets of this type are discussed in Chapter 6.

Types of monetary assets

In most businesses the sale of the product or service is the event which signals that revenue has occurred, and that for practical purposes the aim of the enterprise has been achieved. If the sale is for cash, the business receives a new asset which is readily available for distribution to the owners, for payment of debts, or for purchase of productive services which will again put the cycle of business operations into motion.

If the sale is on credit, the new asset is one step removed from cash. This asset is a legally enforceable claim against the customer for the amount of the sale. It is not as desirable as cash in that some time remains before it will be converted into money, some collection effort is often necessary, and it is occasionally doubtful whether individual amounts will be collected in full. In a majority of businesses these qualifications are relatively minor.

Often a business owns cash balances which are temporarily in excess of its needs. This excess cash may be put to productive use in the form of temporary investments, which are in effect near-cash.

Cash, receivables from customers, and temporary investments differ in legal form and degree of liquidity, but they have two features in common. They are the end results of business operations, and they may be measured in terms of money either directly or with only a slight adjustment.

The proper measure of monetary assets is the amount of money they would currently bring. If there is a substantial waiting period before a claim will be collected in cash, the appropriate measure of the claim is its face amount less interest for the waiting period. If losses are likely to be incurred in collecting claims, these, too, should be deducted in measuring the assets.

Typical monetary assets

The following list of monetary assets is one that applies generally to commercial or industrial concerns. It is not exhaustive, for many other specialized types of assets are frequently owned by such businesses. On the other hand, few individual businesses would have assets of all of the types named.

Assets have debit balances, but the list contains some accounts which have credit balances because they are deductions from assets (or are *contra*-asset accounts). The titles are general; individual businesses often vary their specific account titles to some extent.

	Type of Balance	
	Debit	Credit
Cash...	X	
Temporary Investments.............................	X	
Accounts Receivable, Trade..........................	X	
Accounts Receivable, Trade—Estimated Uncollectibles..		X
Notes Receivable, Trade.............................	X	
Notes Receivable, Trade—Estimated Uncollectibles....		X
Accrued Receivables.................................	X	
Other Receivables...................................	X	

Cash

Cash is the most liquid of all assets. The term *cash* refers only to those items which are available readily and without restriction for payment of obligations arising from the current operations of the business. Cash includes money owned, whether in the form of currency, coin, readily transferable money orders or checks, or demand deposits in bank accounts. Time deposits, or savings accounts, may generally be classified as "*Cash*." Although the bank has the privilege of requiring a waiting period before permitting their withdrawal, it rarely exercises this privilege. Savings accounts are, in effect, readily available to meet general business obligations.

Unused postage is not "Cash," because it is not readily accepted for the payment of debts. Balances on deposit which are available only for the construction of long-lived assets such as buildings or equipment are not "Cash," nor are special bank accounts which are restricted to the payment of long-term debts. Money on deposit in a bank which has failed is not "Cash," because it is not known what proportion of it will be recovered, and when.

There are few problems of measuring the amount of Cash independent of deciding what it includes, because Cash items are stated directly in terms of money amounts. For convenience an entity usually has separate ledger accounts for *Cash on Hand, Petty Cash,* and *Cash in Bank,* and for each bank account, if there is more than one. In financial reports, however, it is satisfactory to lump all of these cash assets together as "Cash on Hand and in Banks." A bank overdraft, it should be noted, is not an asset, but a liability.

Temporary investments

Marketable securities are certificates of ownership or indebtedness owned by the business, which can be sold readily in an established market at a fairly definite price. They may be shares of the capital stock of corporations or promissory notes or bonds owed by corporations or governments. The securities which most often meet the requirement of ready marketability at a reasonably assured price are United States government obligations.

Many businesses with seasonal variations in their volume of activity find that during their slack season more money accumulates than is currently needed for carrying on day-to-day operations. It may be unwise to distribute such temporarily excess funds to the owners or to buy long-lived assets with them, because the business will need them for buying goods and services during the busy season. Idle checking account balances earn no interest. In order to earn a return on the money for the period during which it would otherwise be idle, the company may invest it in highly liquid forms, such as marketable securities, which are classified as *Temporary Investments.* Another need for making a temporary investment occurs when the business is trying to save money to pay a rather large debt which accumulates during the year, such as the quarterly installment of the federal income tax owed by corporations.

Whether investments are classified as temporary or long-term depends upon the intent of the investor. Regardless of the legal life of a security, it is a *temporary investment* if the owner plans to hold it for only a short time, and a *long-term investment* if he plans to hold it indefinitely.

Temporary investments should be measured at their acquisition cost, which includes not only the quoted purchase price of the security but also other costs directly associated with the purchase. If the transaction is handled by a broker, his commission and any postage, insurance, and transfer taxes applicable to the purchase are a part of the cost of the investment.

The accounting entry for the acquisition of a United States government bond having a face amount of $1,000 at a price of 98 (98 per cent of its face amount, or *par*), plus the broker's charge of $9 for commission and postage, would be:

(1)

A, Temporary Investments.............................. 989
    A, Cash.. 989
    Paid $980 plus $9 commission and postage for a U. S. bond
    for short-term investment.

Under normal circumstances, temporary investments continue to be shown in the accounts at cost until they are sold. Interest earned on them is treated as a class of nonoperating revenue. If the bond issuer in the preceding illustration paid interest each three months at a rate of 4% per year, the entry to record the first quarterly interest collection would be:

(2)

A, Cash... 10
    OE, Interest Revenue............................... 10
    Collected quarterly interest on $1,000 U. S. bond.

Since the objective in measuring temporary investments is to show what they would bring in cash, current market price quotations must be considered in reporting their amounts in the Statement of Financial Position. Usually it is sufficient to show the market value parenthetically, thus:

ASSETS

Temporary Investments (market value, $975), at cost.......... $989

If the market value is substantially less than cost, and the condition causing the decline seems to be permanent, Temporary Investments should be reported in the Statement of Financial Position at market value.[4] The accountant should preserve the record of cost in the ledger account so that he can compute the actual gain or loss when the securities are sold.

---

[4] American Institute of Certified Public Accountants, Committee on Accounting Procedure, *Restatement and Revision of Accounting Research Bulletins* (Accounting Research Bulletin No. 43) (New York: The Institute, 1953), p. 23.

Separate general ledger accounts may be used for major types of temporary investments, such as United States bonds, corporate bonds, and corporate stocks, and detailed supporting records should be kept of each block of securities acquired.

Accounts receivable, trade

Claims against customers for sales of goods or services in the ordinary course of business are classified as *Accounts Receivable, Trade*. Usually such sales are made on open account, which means that payment in cash is due according to the seller's customary terms as to time period and rate of discount. In the simplest case, there may be no document supporting the account except a sales ticket. There is no written promise to pay signed by the customer; nevertheless, the seller has a legally enforceable claim against him.

Accounts Receivable, Trade, being monetary assets, should be measured at the amount which they would currently bring in cash.

The following journal entries illustrate the common transactions which affect Accounts Receivable, Trade. They summarize the effect of many similar transactions during a period, which in practice would be recorded individually.

(3)

| A, Accounts Receivable, Trade | 100,000 | |
| OE, Sales Revenue (19x6) | | 100,000 |

To record the effect of total sales on account during the year.

(4)

| A, Cash | 50,000 | |
| OE, Sales Revenue (19x6) | | 50,000 |

To record the effect of total cash sales for the year.

(5)

| A, Cash | 80,000 | |
| A, Accounts Receivable, Trade | | 80,000 |

To record collections on account during the year.

The following T-accounts show the pertinent account balances at the end of 19x6.

A, Accounts Receivable, Trade

| (3) | 100,000 | | (5) | 80,000 |

Balance, 20,000

A, Cash

(4)	50,000
(5)	80,000
	130,000

(Other transactions affecting Cash are omitted.)

OE, Sales Revenue (19x6)

	(3)	100,000
	(4)	50,000
		150,000

A difficult problem in determining the amount of the asset, Accounts Receivable, Trade, is estimating the amount of accounts which will eventually prove to be uncollectible. This problem is discussed later in the chapter.

Notes receivable, trade

A promissory note is an unconditional written promise to pay a stated amount of money to the person owning the note, either on demand or at a determinable future time. *Notes Receivable, Trade* are promissory notes owned by a business as a result of sales to its customers. A note received directly in exchange for goods or services would be recorded in this manner:

(6)

A, Notes Receivable, Trade.....................	600	
OE, Sales Revenue...........................		600
Sold merchandise to A. R. Hope in exchange for a		
3-month, 6% promissory note.		

Occasionally notes are received from customers in settlement of their accounts, particularly if the accounts are past due. Assuming that an entry had been made some time earlier debiting A, Accounts Receivable, Trade, and crediting OE, Sales Revenue, the entry for the receipt of a note would be:

(7)

A, Notes Receivable, Trade.....................	1,200	
A, Accounts Receivable, Trade...............		1,200
Received a 6-month, 6% promissotry note from		
R. A. Ross in settlement of his past-due account.		

A note receivable is often more desirable than an account receivable, for several reasons. It is a written acknowledgment that the amount of the debt is owed, and sometimes accounts receivable are difficult to prove. The holder of a note usually receives interest for the period during which he waits for his money, while the owner of an account does not. The owner of a note receivable can usually obtain cash by selling the note to a bank, transferring ownership by endorsing the note on the back.

A note received from a customer on his past-due account may be less desirable than accounts receivable from other customers because of the indication that the signer of the note is in some financial difficulty. Still, it may be wise to accept the note from him because of its stronger legal position.

Promissory notes received from customers for cash loans and from officers, employees, and stockholders should not be included in Notes Receivable, Trade. Although these notes may be fully collectible, their different origin and quality warrant reporting them as separate items in the financial statements.

Notes Receivable, Trade should be measured at their current cash value. A business can usually sell, or discount at its face amount, a note which bears a reasonable interest rate and which is signed by a financially sound customer. It is justified in recording such a note at face value. A non-interest-bearing note in effect includes in its face interest from the date of issue to date due. Its cash value at the time of receipt is the face amount, minus interest at a reasonable rate for the waiting period. For practical purposes, the amount of such discount is often ignored when the business owns few non-interest-bearing notes and the implied discount on each is relatively small.

The journal entry for the collection of the note in transaction (6) on its maturity date would be:

(8)

A, Cash..	609	
A, Notes Receivable, Trade.................		600
OE, Interest Revenue........................		9

Collected the face amount and 3 months' interest at 6% on the Hope note due today.

Estimated uncollectibles

A business which extends credit expects as a matter of course that some of its customers' accounts and notes will turn out to be worthless. Naturally, it does not know at the time credit is granted which accounts will be uncollectible; otherwise, it would not grant credit. In measuring the amount of collectible accounts or notes receivable at the end of an accounting period, or at any other time when financial statements are being prepared, a business should make an appropriate deduction for the estimated amount of uncollectibles.

The process of estimating uncollectibles involves prediction of what is going to happen to receivables, which are actual claims of the business. As a rule, there is less error in measuring the amount of receivables if a careful, though imperfect, estimate of uncollectibles is made than if no attempt is made to predict the amount of uncollectibles. This prediction is a matter of judgment, and past experience is often a great help in making it.

If there are relatively few individual customers' accounts or notes receivable, the most satisfactory method of estimating the amount of uncollectibles is usually to analyze the quality of each account. This may be done by gathering information bearing on the credit standing of each customer at the date of the measurement.

If there are numerous receivables, it is usually best to use information on past loss experience on accounts receivable as a basis for estimating future uncollectibles. Accurate records of the amounts of receivables which have definitely been determined to be uncollectible are needed. A past loss percentage is then determined by comparing these actual uncollectibles with a factor to which they are presumably related. A common method of estimating compares actual credit losses resulting from the sales of each year with the net sales made on credit for that year.

EXAMPLE 3: The business whose sales transactions were illustrated in entries (3), (4), and (5) wishes to estimate what amount of the $20,000 legally owed it on December 31, 19x6, will ultimately become uncollectible. The balance is composed of several hundred individual customers' accounts. How should the estimate be made?

SOLUTION: A careful analysis should be made of the amount of accounts receivable from the sales of each of the past five years which have turned out to be uncollectible, as well as an analysis of the sales on credit for each year. The percentage of uncollectibles to the credit sales of the appropriate year has been relatively constant from year to year in this case. The summary for the 5-year period shows:

```
Total sales on account, 19x1–19x5.....................  $400,000
Actual uncollectible accounts from these sales...........    4,000
Percentage of loss to credit sales ($4,000/$400,000).......       1%
```

There has been no drastic change in the company's credit policy or in economic conditions recently, so it seems reasonable to assume that about 1% of each year's credit sales will continue to result in uncollectible accounts in the near future.

On this basis, Accounts Receivable, Trade, amounting to $1,000 (1% of 19x6's credit sales of $100,000) may be considered doubtful of collection on December 31, 19x6. The remainder, $19,000 ($20,000 minus $1,000), is the amount of estimated collectible accounts.

It would appear that entry (3) overstates both the asset Accounts Receivable, Trade and 19x6 Sales Revenue by $1,000, the amount of doubtful accounts. A direct entry to correct this overstatement would debit Sales Revenue and credit Accounts Receivable, Trade, for $1,000. However, it is important that a business keep a record of the amounts legally owed it by its customers. After all, that amount is a fact, and the projected amount of uncollectibles is only an estimate. Also, a business does not know which specific accounts will be uncollectible. In addition, a direct reduction of the Sales Revenue balance would result in failure to show in the financial statements information that is important to management. The amount of losses from uncollectible accounts each period is a measure of the performance of the credit manager or other individual who is responsible for approving credit sales. A better entry is:

(9)

OE, Sales Revenue—Losses from Uncollectible Accounts 1,000
   A, Accounts Receivable, Trade—
      Estimated Uncollectibles   1,000
   To record the estimated loss based on 1% of the year's
   sales on account, $100,000.

The account debited, OE, Sales Revenue—Losses from Uncollectible Accounts, is a deduction from (or _contra_ to) the OE, Sales Revenue account. It is shown as a separate account in order to provide valuable information to management and others who read the Income Statement, as follows:

Sales Revenue $150,000
Deduct Losses from Uncollectible Accounts   1,000
Net Sales Revenue $149,000

Similarly, the account credited in entry (9), A, Accounts Receivable, Trade—Estimated Uncollectibles, is a _contra_-asset account. It is a deduction from _total_ Accounts Receivable, not from the individual accounts of any customers. At the moment the identity of the uncollectible accounts is unknown. The presentation in the Statement of Financial Position is as follows:

ASSETS

Accounts Receivable, Trade . . . . $ 20,000
Deduct Estimated Uncollectibles   1,000
Estimated Collectible Accounts . . . . $ 19,000

A new business has no past loss experience upon which to base its estimate of uncollectible accounts. It may either use the experience of other companies in the same industry or analyze each account receivable at the end of the year to judge whether it is collectible. Under either of these methods, the accounts debited and credited would be the same as in entry (9).

Notes Receivable, Trade—Estimated Uncollectibles and other uncollectible receivables are accounted for in the same way as estimated uncollectible accounts, although frequently separate accounts are used for them.

Writing off uncollectible accounts

Follow-up efforts to collect accounts should be carried out regularly throughout the accounting period. When an account is definitely determined to be uncollectible, it should be written off promptly. The decision that a particular account is bad may be based on the customer's discharge from bankruptcy with no assets available to creditors; his death or disappearance; the expiration of the statute of limitations with respect to the debt; the existence of disputed items; or the inability of a collector to secure payment. A typical entry to show that an account is uncollectible follows:

(10)

19x7

Jan. 30   A, Accounts Receivable—Estimated Uncollectibles 120
                 A, Accounts Receivable, Trade.................... 120
                 To write off the uncollectible account of the Amco
                 Corporation.

The preceding entry has no effect upon the income of 19x7, the period in which the account is written off, and no net effect upon assets, as the following comparison shows.

	Before Write-off	After Write-off
Accounts Receivable, debit (assuming no intervening transactions).........................	$20,000	$19,880
Estimated Uncollectibles, credit................	1,000	880
Estimated collectibles.........................	$19,000	$19,000

Income was affected in 19x6 when the total estimated uncollectibles of unknown accounts totaling $1,000, including the $120 sale to the Amco Corporation, were deducted from total sales. The write-off entry avoids an indefinite accumulation of worthless accounts in Accounts Receivable, and it also permits management to compare the actual uncollectibles with the advance estimate in the Estimated Uncollectibles account.

Accrued receivables

Amounts owed to the business on contracts for services extending over a period of time, such as interest for the use of its money and rents and royalties for the use of its property, are called *Accrued Receivables*. Often these amounts are recorded in adjusting entries at the end of the accounting period.

The account for Accrued Interest Receivable should be separate from the account which shows the face amount of the note receivable on which the interest has accumulated.

Other receivables

Businesses often own receivables of more unusual types, such as claims against insurance companies for losses; claims for tax refunds; advances to or accounts receivable from officers, employees, stockholders, and affiliated companies; dividends receivable on investments in corporate stock;

advance payments to suppliers; and many others. A separate account should be kept for each type of receivable of relatively large amount. Each is measured in much the same way as the receivables described in detail in the preceding pages.

Summary

Each individual accounting system should be tailored to provide the financial information and controls needed by the business which it is designated to serve. The classification of accounts should consider both internal and external needs, and it should follow organizational lines. It should facilitate planning for the business as well as appraisal of the manner in which each responsible person within the business has discharged his responsibility.

There are many types of accounts which are common to practically all businesses. This is especially true of assets. For the purpose of solving their problems of measurement, assets may be described as *monetary assets* and *unexpired costs.* The principal objective in measuring monetary assets, which were discussed in detail in this chapter, is to state them at the amount of general purchasing power which they command either immediately or with but a slight delay. Measurement problems of unexpired costs are examined in the next chapter.

QUESTIONS AND PROBLEMS

5-1   Mr. Chambers calls you and requests that you design an accounting system for his business. You agree.

REQUIRED:

List the main points that you would consider and describe the effect that they would have on the design of the system.

5-2   Companies A and B are in the same industry and use an identical classification of accounts, which was suggested by a trade association. Their accounting systems have many important differences.

REQUIRED:

What are some of the principal differences which you would expect to find, and why do they exist?

5-3   Is every bank account cash to the depositor? Explain.

5-4   *a.* How would you distinguish a temporary investment from a permanent investment?

b. What is the major difference between an account receivable and a note receivable?

5-5   "With the appearance of so many types of businesses on the economic scene, a student of accounting will need to take more and more accounting courses to learn how to account for each different type."

REQUIRED:

Do you agree with this statement? Explain.

5-6 Peter Simpson, looking over a Statement of Financial Position of the LMN Company, notices that bonds appear in three different places on the statement: once under a section shown as *Current Assets*, again under a section classified as *Investments*, and a third time under a section labeled *Liabilities*. He cannot understand why bonds would appear on the same statement in three different places.

REQUIRED:

Explain to Peter the reason for classifying bonds in three different sections of the Statement of Financial Position.

5-7 Mr. Donaldson, owner of the Mountain City Variety Store, stated: "I don't include estimated losses of uncollectible accounts receivable on my Income Statement because I don't charge to anyone who won't pay. Besides, even if I did lose some accounts, I don't think that it is proper to estimate the loss because the Income Statement presents facts, not guesses."

REQUIRED:

Comment on Mr. Donaldson's statement.

5-8 The Alpha Company has done a considerable amount of business in a foreign country for the past ten years and has maintained an account in the national bank of that country. During recent months there has been internal strife in the country, and there is danger of civil war breaking out at the time the financial statements are being prepared. The Alpha Company has $210,000 on deposit in the foreign country.

REQUIRED:

a. How would you classify in the Statement of Financial Position the amount on deposit in the foreign country?
b. Would this situation have any effect on the Income Statement being prepared?

5-9 To determine estimated losses on receivables for the accounting year, Mr. Morris, manager of the Wells Company, combines the total dollar amount of accounts receivable and notes receivable owned by the company on the last day of the year and applies a standard rate of loss of 10 per cent each year.

REQUIRED:

a. Do you approve of Mr. Morris's method? Explain.
b. Suggest another method which he might use.

5-10 *J* Company has some seasonally idle money which it wishes to put to work. It elects to purchase United States government securities because of their safety.

REQUIRED:

a. If the company purchases 90-day Treasury bills, how should they be classified in its accounts?
b. How would 30-year bonds purchased be classified?
c. In what respects, if any, do the measurement problems in (*b*) differ from those in (*a*)?

5-11 The Assets section of the Dawn Company's Statement of Financial Position appears as follows:

ASSETS

Accounts Receivable (net of Uncollectibles)................	$24,000
Temporary Investments...................................	8,000
Notes, Accruals, and Other Receivables...................	4,000
Supplies...	600
Prepaid Expenses.......................................	240
Inventory...	30,000
	$66,840
Less Cash Overdraft in Bank............................	470
Total Assets..	$66,370

REQUIRED:

a. What criticisms do you have of the Dawn Company's presentation of Assets?

b. Choosing your own figures for amounts not given, prepare the Asset section in a more desirable form.

5-12   Included in the Statement of Financial Position of the Goldings Corporation on September 30, 19x1, are Accounts Receivable, Trade, $25,000, and Buildings, $50,000.

REQUIRED:

a. Explain to a reader of the statement how the methods of measuring these items differ.

b. What accounts in the Income Statement are related to each of these two accounts?

5-13   On March 1, Retail Co. buys merchandise on account from Wholesale Co. for $800. Wholesale Co.'s credit terms require payment within 30 days.

REQUIRED:

a. What entry should Retail Co. make on March 1? Wholesale Co.?

b. What entry should each make if full payment is made when due?

5-14   Under which, if any, of the account titles used in this chapter would you classify each of the following items selected from published statements?

a. Advances to suppliers on purchase contracts.
b. Cash earmarked to apply on commitments to buy plant and equipment.
c. Prepayments from customers for goods to be delivered later.
d. Deposits to be refunded to customers when they return containers.
e. A bank overdraft.
f. Promissory note from company president for a cash loan.
g. Charge account balances of customers.
h. Loan to subsidiary company, unsupported by a note.
i. Installment note owed by your company for equipment purchased.
j. U. S. Treasury securities—at cost.
k. Customers' installment accounts receivable.

5-15   The Vincent Gift Shop was organized early in 19x1. After checking their credit rating with the city credit bureau, the company opened charge accounts for a select group of customers. On December 31, 19x1, the Accounts Receivable, Trade account in the general ledger showed that a total of $180,000 had been sold on credit up to that date, and that collections on account had been $150,000. The company had no past experience upon which to base an estimate of uncollectible accounts.

REQUIRED:

a. How would you recommend that the company estimate its uncollectible accounts?

b. Using figures of your own selection, prepare the journal entries necessary on December 31, 19x1.

c. If no entry were made for the uncollectible accounts, what effect would this have on the 19x1 Income Statement? On the Statement of Financial Position on December 31, 19x1?

5-16   The following summary shows the K Company's transactions in notes received from customers for merchandise during the year ending December 31, 19x1.

Maker of Note	Face Amount	Interest Rate	Date Received	Term	Due Date
A	$2,000	6%	Jan. 1	6 months	July 1
B	2,500	6%	Aug. 1	6 months	Feb. 1
C	1,500	6%	Oct. 1	2 months	Dec. 1
D	3,000	6%	Dec. 1	3 months	Mar. 1

REQUIRED:

a. Prepare an orderly computation showing the interest earned by K Company for 19x1 and the balances which should be shown in its Statement of Financial Position on December 31, 19x1.

b. Record in journal and T-account form the entries necessary to produce these results.

5-17   You are trying to determine the proper amount of Cash on Hand for inclusion in the Statement of Financial Position on October 31, 19x1. You find the following items in the safe on that date:

(1) Unused postage stamps of a face amount of $20.
(2) A check of a customer for $10 dated October 30.
(3) A check of another customer for $25 dated November 15.
(4) Currency totaling $50.
(5) Coin totaling $12.
(6) Ten bus tokens good for fares which would otherwise cost 10¢ each.
(7) A note signed by the cashier reading, "I owe the cash drawer $15 for a salary advance."
(8) A money order to the company for $8.
(9) A customer's $12 check which his bank had returned marked "Not sufficient funds."

REQUIRED:

a. What amount would you report as Cash on Hand on October 31?

b. How would you classify each of the items which you exclude from Cash on Hand?

5-18   The account balances below are those of the Diran Company at the end of its second year of operations, June 30, 19x3.

Accounts Payable, Trade	$ 17,000
Cost of Goods Sold Expense	135,000
Accounts Receivable, Trade—Estimated Uncollectibles	2,000
Advances from Customers	1,800
Cash	5,000
Dividends Payable	1,000

Salaries Expense	20,000
Accounts Receivable, Trade	16,000
Gain on Sale of Equipment	700
Rent Expense	12,000
Equipment	8,000
Loans to Employees	2,000
Losses from Uncollectible Accounts	2,000
Merchandise Inventory	24,000
Utilities Expense	1,500
Income Distributions	4,000
Interest Expense	400
Advertising Expense	3,000
Interest Revenue	300
Miscellaneous Expense	800
Notes Payable, Bank	10,000
Owners' Investment	35,000
Sales Revenue	161,000
Temporary Investments (cost)	7,100
Retained Income, July 1, 19x2	12,000

On June 30, 19x3, the current market quotation for securities owned was $7,050.

REQUIRED:

a. Reconstruct the June 30, 19x3, Trial Balance.
b. Prepare the three common financial statements.
c. Journalize and post the closing entries.

CASE 5-1. CAPITOL CORPORATION

During 19x4 the Capitol Corporation sold merchandise on account to various customers for $350,000, of which it had collected $275,000 by the end of the year. In addition it made sales of $125,000 for cash. Records for the past three years showed:

	19x1	19x2	19x3
Cash sales	$120,000	$115,000	$125,000
Sales on account	280,000	270,000	320,000
Collections on charge sales by the end of 19x4	278,000	267,600	316,600
Customers' accounts definitely determined to be uncollectible by the end of 19x4	1,350	1,200	1,800

The Corporation has decided to use the average experience of the past three years in reporting its receivables from customers on the financial statements.

REQUIRED:

a. Give in journal form the entries needed to summarize the transactions for 19x4.
b. Post the entries to T-accounts.
c. Illustrate how the appropriate items would appear in the Statement of Financial Position and the Income Statement prepared at the end of 19x4.
d. What weaknesses do you find in the proposed estimate?
e. Recommend another method of estimating uncollectibles which the company might use, and compare its effectiveness with the method which the Capitol Corporation used.

Chapter **6**

Classifying and Measuring
Unexpired Costs

Tangible and intangible resources, prepayments for contractual service from employees and outsiders, and similar specific assets which can reasonably be expected to benefit the business in its future operations may be called *unexpired costs*. The business will derive benefit from some of these unexpired costs, such as merchandise, supplies, equipment, and buildings, through physical use. In other cases the costs provide contractual services which have no physical substance but are necessary or suitable for carrying on the business.

The present chapter deals with problems of classifying and measuring these unexpired costs through three different stages: *acquisition, transformation*, and *expiration*, or final disposition.

CLASSIFYING UNEXPIRED COSTS

Initial classification

When a business first acquires specific assets, or costs, it should classify them in a way that will facilitate later accounting for them in their original form, accounting for any subsequent transformations, and accounting for their final expiration. The principal factors which a business ordinarily considers in deciding what accounts to use for unexpired costs are their physical or economic characteristics, the methods which are needed to safeguard or control them, the organizational unit which has custody of them, and the purpose or use to which they are to be put. Grouping together the costs which are incurred for a similar purpose makes it easier to regroup them appropriately when the purpose has been accomplished.

EXAMPLE 1:   A business has some inventory items which are ready for sale and others which are intended to be used in manufacturing goods for sale. Separate accounts should be kept for *merchandise inventory* and *raw materials inventory*, to show their different nature and to make it possible to identify their expired costs with the function they have served.

EXAMPLE 2:   A business has acquired display equipment to assist in the sale of merchandise, office equipment to be used in general administration, and factory equipment to be used in manufacturing goods for sale. Each of these three types of equipment should be classified in a separate unexpired cost account to show separate responsibilities for their custody, as well as to permit identification of the expired cost with the appropriate function.

A distinction which is important in accounting for unexpired costs is whether they will benefit the business for a short or a long term. *Short-term unexpired costs* are those which are expected to benefit the business for a relatively brief future time. As a rule it will be necessary to replace them continually. *Long-term unexpired costs* last longer and are generally acquired at more irregular intervals.

Short-term unexpired costs. A major class of short-term unexpired costs consists of expendable physical items, or *inventories*. The business holds them for sale directly to its customers, for use in manufacturing its products, or for consumption in carrying on some phase of business activity. The problems of receiving, keeping custody, and issuing all inventories are somewhat alike. Individual accounts are appropriate for inventories of each physical type; for those held for each major purpose; and for those in the custody of each responsible division of the organization.

Another important class of short-term unexpired costs consists of *contractual* services for which the business has paid in advance, or for which it has incurred a liability. Most of these services are for definite periods of time, and it may be assumed that they will be received in equal amounts each day of the contract period. Examples are prepayments for rent, interest, and insurance. The unexpired costs of such contractual services which apply to the near future are called *prepaid expenses*.

Long-term unexpired costs. Physical assets such as land, buildings, and equipment, which are expected to render their services to the business through *use* rather than consumption over an indefinitely long future time, may be called *long-term tangible unexpired costs*. They are also frequently called *fixed assets*. Natural resources, such as timber tracts, oil wells, and mines, are also long-term tangible unexpired costs. Their physical quantity is reduced as they are extracted, like inventories, and they are also usually held for sale.

Another large class of long-term unexpired costs is *intangibles*, such as patents and goodwill. They resemble prepaid expenses in that they have no physical substance and that their potential benefit to the business lies in the rights they confer upon it. On the other hand, they differ from prepaid expenses in the long duration of their expected benefits.

Long-term investments are similar to monetary assets in many ways, except that the intent of the business is to hold them for an indefinitely long period of time. They also involve some additional measurement problems which resemble those associated with unexpired costs.

Common types of unexpired cost accounts. The following is a list of some of the more typical unexpired cost accounts which are found in financial statements, with brief definitions where they are considered necessary.

    (1) INVENTORIES

        (a) Merchandise. Goods which have been purchased by the business and are ready for sale.

        (b) Finished Goods. Goods which have been manufactured by the business and are ready for sale.

        (c) Goods in Process. Goods which are being manufactured for sale but which have not yet been completed.

        (d) Materials. Items, such as raw materials, semi-finished products, or finished parts, which the business has purchased and plans to incorporate physically into its finished product.

        (e) Supplies. Physical items which will be consumed by the business in connection with operations, but which will not physically become a part of the product.

    (2) PREPAID EXPENSES

        (a) Unexpired Insurance.

        (b) Prepaid Rent.

        (c) Prepaid Interest.

        (d) Prepaid Salaries.

    (3) LONG-TERM TANGIBLES

        (a) Land. A site, or location, exclusive of any structures or improvements.

        (b) Buildings. Structures erected on land.

        (c) Land Improvements. Attachments to land other than buildings, such as streets and sidewalks.

        (d) Equipment. A wide variety of physical assets used in carrying on the business, including factory and office machines, automotive equipment, tools, furniture, furnishings, and animals.

    (4) LONG-TERM INTANGIBLES

        (a) Patents. Grants by the United States to an inventor giving him the exclusive right to sell or use his invention for 17 years.

        (b) Copyrights. Exclusive rights to reproduce or sell a literary or artistic work, granted by the United States for 28 years and renewable at the end of that time.

        (c) Trade-marks. Distinguishing symbols used by a company to identify its product. If registered, they have an indefinite legal life.

(d) Franchises. Privileges, often exclusive, granted to a business by a government or a manufacturer. Government franchises permit the owner to use public property; dealer franchises permit the owner to sell the manufacturer's product within a certain territory.

(e) Leaseholds. Long-term contracts for the use of real estate belonging to another.

(f) Leasehold Improvements. Improvements made by the tenant on the landlord's property which, as permanent attachments to the land, belong to the landlord. The tenant has the right to use them during the period of the lease.

(g) Goodwill. The ability of a business to earn more than a normal rate of income on its assets.

(h) Organization Costs. All costs properly incurred in organizing the company, including legal fees, costs of printing corporate stock certificates, incorporation fees paid to governmental agencies, and expenses paid to the promoters of the business.

MEASURING AND RECORDING ACQUISITION COSTS

The proper measure of an unexpired cost at the time it is acquired is the amount paid then, or to be paid later, in cash or its equivalent. *Cash equivalent* is the current value in money of the assets or equities which the business exchanges for the unexpired cost.

Components of acquisition cost of inventories

The amount to be included in the acquisition cost of an inventory item is the sum of the expenditures made directly or indirectly in bringing it to its existing condition and location.[1] In addition to the *net invoice cost* (the amount of the invoice less discounts), inventory properly includes transportation and insurance charges incurred in getting the article to the merchant's place of business. Added components of cost are any excise and sales taxes or import duties which the purchaser has to pay. It is also proper, but often impractical, to include in inventory the cost of purchasing and handling the article and storing it for a reasonable period.

There are many difficulties in applying these rules to an actual problem of inventory measurement. A retailer rarely includes purchasing, handling, and storing cost in the cost of inventory because it is often impossible, or at least impractical, to trace them in a convincing way to the individual

---

[1] American Institute of Certified Public Accountants, Committee on Accounting Procedure, *Restatement and Revision of Accounting Research Bulletins* (Accounting Research Bulletin No. 43) (New York: The Institute, 1953), p. 28.

articles of merchandise to which they apply. In some cases freight, express, postage, or other transportation charges can be traced to specific articles. However, if there are transportation charges of $50 on a mixed incoming shipment consisting of various types of articles of different weight, bulk, and cost, it is an almost impossible (and perhaps useless) task to assign the applicable transportation cost to each item. In such cases the business may add transportation cost to individual items of inventory on the basis of the percentage of the total transportation cost for the accounting period to the net invoice cost of all items purchased during the period.

EXAMPLE 3:

Net invoice cost of all purchases during the accounting period...	$100,000
Total transportation cost on purchases.................	5,000
Per cent of transportation cost to invoice cost...........	5%

How much of this transportation cost applies to Item A, which had a net invoice cost of $20?

SOLUTION:

Net invoice cost of Item A....................................	$20
Add transportation cost at 5% average rate...................	1
Acquisition cost of Item A..................................	$21

Sometimes it is feasible to allocate transportation, handling, and storage costs to individual inventory items on the basis of weight or some other factor which has a direct influence on the amount of transportation cost incurred.

Components of acquisition cost of long-term tangible assets

The acquisition cost of a tangible asset which is expected to yield service benefits over a long term properly includes all costs reasonably incurred in installing it, testing it, and preparing it for use in the business. Usually it is easier to trace transportation costs to individual long-term tangible assets than to inventory.

Expenditures made to rehabilitate assets which are acquired in a run-down condition should be included as a part of their initial cost. However, a careful distinction should be made between the costs of first preparing such assets for business use and the costs incurred later to keep them in operating condition.

EXAMPLE 4:   A used machine was purchased for $600 and was reconditioned prior to use at a cost of $400. What was its acquisition cost?

SOLUTION: The acquisition cost was $1,000, the total amount necessary to prepare the machine for use.

EXAMPLE 5:   If the $400 reconditioning cost were incurred after the machine had been used a year, it is not a part of the acquisition cost of the asset.

It is an expired cost, unless it extends the machine's useful life beyond that originally anticipated, or increases the benefits expected from it in a substantial way, such as providing greater capacity.

Land. Items comprising the cost of land are all of the outlays necessary to obtain legal title to it and to prepare it for use as a location for the business. In addition to the purchase price agreed upon with the seller, land cost includes legal fees, real estate brokers' commissions, cost of title search and title insurance, fees for recording ownership in legal records, and any unpaid back taxes which the purchaser agrees to pay. If a business acquires land containing structures with the expectation of tearing the structures down, the net cost of razing them is an addition to the acquisition cost of land.

EXAMPLE 6:   A company purchased a lot containing an old building for a total cost of $15,000, planning to tear down the old building immediately and replace it with a new one. The cost of demolishing the old building was $3,000, exclusive of scrap, which was sold for $2,000. What was the acquisition cost of the land?

SOLUTION:

Contract price	$15,000
Add cost of demolition	3,000
	$18,000
Deduct proceeds of scrap	2,000
Net acquisition cost of land	$16,000

Natural resources. The acquisition cost of a natural resource includes its purchase cost plus the cost of development incurred up until the asset begins producing. Development costs can easily become excessive; in fact, unproductive explorations, such as dry wells, are a common feature of extractive industries. Such costs should be accumulated as an asset until the production stage is reached. When it becomes clear that the asset will not be productive, its unexpired cost should be shown as a loss.

Components of acquisition cost of intangibles

Patents, copyrights, trade-marks, and franchises. The acquisition cost of patents, copyrights, and trade-marks is either the cash equivalent paid to purchase them or the cost incurred in developing them. The acquisition cost of franchises includes the amounts paid to the grantor of the franchise, together with any legal and similar fees incurred in establishing the right to operate under the franchise.

Leaseholds. The acquisition cost of leaseholds is the amount of rent paid in advance or of costs incurred directly in obtaining the lease. The cost of leasehold improvements includes outlays for purchasing or constructing improvements to the landlord's property which are expected to benefit future periods.

Goodwill should be recorded as an asset only when it is acquired as a part of the assets of a going business, or when there is a purchase and sale of a substantial part of the ownership of a business. Its acquisition cost is the amount of cash, or the cash equivalent of other assets, given in exchange for it.

Organization costs are measured initially at the amount of outlay which can be specifically identified with getting the business organized and legally empowered to carry on its activities.

Discounts

In arriving at the net invoice cost of an asset it is necessary for the purchaser to deduct *trade discounts* and *cash discounts*. *Trade discounts* are a formula for setting the price to a customer. *Cash discounts* are an inducement to the customer to pay promptly.

Many sellers use a series of discounts from a list price as a means of establishing the price to a particular type of customer, such as a retailer or wholesaler. The first discount may be allowed to all dealers, regardless of how many items they buy and when they pay for them. An additional discount is often allowed if large quantities are purchased.

EXAMPLE 7:   The H Stove Works sells stoves which have a suggested retail price of $150 to the final purchaser. The manufacturer allows a discount of 20% of list price to all retail dealers, and an additional discount of $16\frac{2}{3}\%$ to dealers who buy 10 or more stoves. On May 1 the Hardy Furniture Store bought 10 stoves for resale. What was the net invoice cost?

SOLUTION:

Suggested retail price of each stove..........................	$ 150
Deduct dealer discount, 20%...............................	30
Price to any dealer buying one stove.........................	$ 120
Deduct quantity discount to dealers buying 10 or more, $16\frac{2}{3}\%$	20
Price per stove to dealer buying 10 or more...................	$ 100
Multiply by number of stoves bought.......................	✕ 10
Total invoice cost of 10 stoves.............................	$1,000

If no cash discount is offered, that is, if payment terms are "net 30 days,"[2] the Hardy Furniture Store is supposed to pay $1,000 within 30 days from the date of the invoice. The price is still $100 per stove whether the Store pays early, on time, or late. The acquisition should be recorded as follows:

19x1		(1)		
May	1	A, Merchandise Inventory....................	1,000	
		L, Accounts Payable, Trade.............		1,000
		Purchased 10 stoves from H Stove Works,		
		terms n/30.		

---

[2] The term *net* 30 days is a widely used misnomer. Actually, it should be interpreted as *none*, meaning that the purchaser is allowed no discount.

Cash discounts are allowed only if the purchaser pays within the cash discount period. His total payment will be one amount if he qualifies for the discount, and a higher amount if he pays late. The acquisition cost of the inventory item to him in either case is the same: the amount of money that would be needed to pay for it at the time of purchase. Any additional payment for discount lost is a penalty, not a valid addition to an asset.

Common cash discount terms are expressed as "2/10, n/30," or "3/10, E.O.M." The percentage of the deduction and the time period during which it is available, of course, vary from company to company. The payment terms in the first illustration mean that the purchaser will be allowed a reduction of 2 per cent from the price stated on the invoice if he pays within 10 days; otherwise, he must pay the amount of the invoice without cash discount at the end of 30 days. The second illustration means that the purchaser may deduct 3 per cent from the invoice price if he pays by the tenth of the month following the date of the invoice. For a purchase made on May 3 under these terms, the discount would be available until June 10.

Illustration of net price method of recording cash discounts

Assume that the *H* Stove Works initiates a policy of allowing its customers a cash discount under terms of 2/10, n/30. On June 1 the Hardy Furniture Store buys 10 stoves under the same terms as in entry (1), except that a cash discount is available. The amount of money needed to pay for the merchandise at once would be $980 ($1,000 − 2%), and this is the acquisition cost of the asset. The entry would be as follows:

```
19x1                              (2)
June  1   A, Merchandise Inventory...................  980
              L, Accounts Payable, Trade.............        980
          Purchased 10 stoves from H Stove Works,
          terms 2/10, n/30.
```

If the retailer pays within the discount period (any time through June 11), his entry would be

```
19x1                              (3)
June 11   L, Accounts Payable, Trade.................  980
              A, Cash...............................        980
          Paid invoice of June 1 less 2% discount.
```

What entry should he make if he fails to take advantage of the discount and pays on July 1?

The amount of cash discounts available on assets purchased may be large in comparison with net income. For this reason, management and outsiders are interested in the amount of discounts the business loses, whether owing to lack of bank credit or to slowness in processing the paper work needed before payment. The following entry for payment for the purchase in transaction (2) on July 1 without discount gives this information:

19x1		(4)		
July	1	L, Accounts Payable, Trade.................	980	
		OE, Discounts Lost........................	20	
		A, Cash.............................		1,000
		Paid the H Stove Works invoice after the expiration of the discount period.		

Appendix 6-A gives some illustrations which emphasize the importance to businesses of taking cash discounts. Appendix 6-B explains a widely used alternative method of recording cash discounts, the *gross price method*.

Interest paid on asset acquisitions

If there is a time interval between the time an asset is purchased and the time it is paid for, the payment includes implied interest for the waiting period. If the waiting period is short, however, the amount of interest is of little consequence and may be ignored in recording the acquisition cost of the asset.

When an asset is acquired under a payment plan which specifies that interest is being paid, or when the implied amount of interest is substantial, the interest should not be included as a part of the cost of the basic asset. Rather, it should be accounted for as a cost of credit (that is, as *interest*) for the waiting period.

The following entry shows how these costs should be separated.

19x1		(5)		
Jan.	1	A, Equipment............................	960	
		A, Prepaid Interest[3].......................	60	
		L, Notes Payable to Bank..............		1,020
		Bought a machine with a cash price of $960, giving in exchange a note payable due in 12 monthly installments of $85 each. The face of the note included interest to maturity amounting to $60.		

The equipment cost will expire over a useful life which will probably continue for several years. Prepaid Interest will expire during the 12 months for which credit is extended.

---

[3] Some authorities consider such amounts to be a reduction of a liability, such as L, Notes Payable—Discount, rather than an asset. To avoid a complex explanation here, this subject is deferred to a later chapter.

Cost of assets acquired in non-cash exchanges

When the consideration given in exchange for an asset acquired is other than cash, it is customary to use the estimated cash equivalent of the asset parted with to measure the acquisition cost of the new asset. If this *fair market value* of the asset given in exchange cannot be determined readily or reliably, the next best evidence of the cost of the new asset is its own fair market value. If this, too, cannot be determined, it may be necessary to record the new asset on the books at the unexpired cost of the asset which was exchanged for it.

Allocations of cost in joint purchase transactions

When several assets of different types are acquired in a single purchase, a portion of the common cost should be allocated to each asset to facilitate later accounting. The allocation of cost to the individual assets is usually made in the same proportion that the market value of *each* asset bears to the *total* market value of the assets. Or, to state it differently, it is assumed that the ratio of cost to market value of each of the assets is the same.

EXAMPLE 8:   A business acquired land, a building, and merchandise inventory in a lump-sum purchase for $80,000. Separate accounts must be set up for the cost of each asset, because land is not subject to depreciation; the building is subject to depreciation over a long period, but is not expendable; and merchandise inventory is expendable over a relatively short period of time. How should the cost be allocated to each asset?

SOLUTION: The total cost may be allocated to the three assets on the basis of the relative market value of each at the time of purchase. Suppose that an appraiser estimated their market values as follows:

Land	$ 20,000
Building	70,000
Merchandise	10,000
Total market value	$100,000

Considering the total appraised value of $100,000, it would appear that the firm made a good buy; however, the accounts must show only the cost, $80,000. The following table shows how cost would be assigned to each asset in proportion to its appraised value.

	Appraised Value	% of Total Appraised Value	Total Cost	Allocated Cost
Land	$ 20,000	20%	× $80,000	$16,000
Building	70,000	70%	× 80,000	56,000
Merchandise	10,000	10%	× 80,000	8,000
Totals	$100,000	100%		$80,000

MEASURING AND RECORDING COST EXPIRATION

Cost transformation

When an asset in its original form has rendered its service benefit in acquiring still another asset which is expected to benefit the business in future accounting periods, the cost of the original asset is said to have been *transformed*. In the accounting records there is merely a reclassification from one form of unexpired cost to another.

EXAMPLE 9:   A building supply company acquires building materials for sale. They are an unexpired cost, which will ordinarily expire when the materials are sold to a customer. One batch of materials is not sold, but is used in constructing an office building for the business. This part of the cost of the asset, *materials*, is *transformed* to another asset, *buildings*, which is expected to be of benefit to the business in the future.

Reclassification of the costs of assets plays only a minor part in accounting for merchandising companies, but it is very important in construction and manufacturing enterprises. Figure 5 illustrates the flow of costs in a factory. A later chapter is devoted entirely to the complex matter of accounting for manufacturers' inventories.

Cost expiration: product and period costs

A cost *expires* when it contributes a benefit to the revenue of the current accounting period or when it loses its potential to benefit future accounting periods. In some cases a cost can be matched convincingly with the revenue of a given time period because of a direct physical relationship.

EXAMPLE 10:   In 19x1 a retailer bought for resale a table costing $60. In 19x2 he sells it for $100. The cost of the table expires in 19x2 when it can be associated directly with the sales revenue of $100.

Physical traceability of costs may sometimes be misleading, however. It is the *economic relationship* between the cost incurred and the revenue realized that determines whether or not the cost is an expense associated with obtaining the revenue.

EXAMPLE 11:   The manufacturer of the table in Example 10 found it necessary to cut pieces to shape from lumber which contained 50 board feet and which cost $10. The scrap lumber resulting from the process, which was worthless, contained 12 board feet. Although these 12 board feet do not appear *physically* in the product, their cost is *economically* a part of the cost of the table because it is a necessary part of the process of manufacturing it.

Unexpired costs may be classified as *product* costs or *period* costs, according to the methods used for matching them with revenue. Product

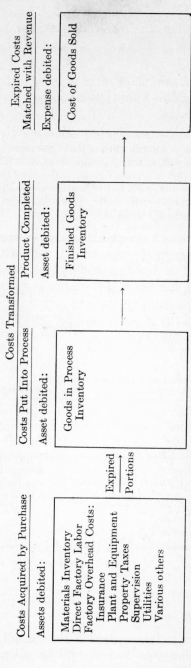

Fig. 5. Flow of Costs in a Manufacturing Enterprise.

costs or inventories, illustrated by the retailer's table, are those that can be associated directly with the physical article that the business is selling. Their benefit is the cash or receivables brought into the business at the time of sale.

The benefits to revenues of many other types of costs cannot be traced to the product in such a direct way, but often they can be identified convincingly with a *time period*.

EXAMPLE 12: A sales clerk is paid a salary of a fixed amount for each time period, such as a week or month. During that time period he may make many successful sales efforts, as well as many unsuccessful ones. His pleasant manner and efficient service in these contacts may be the cause of additional sales in future time periods. Usually, however, such future benefits are so difficult to predict, to identify, or to measure that his entire salary is treated as an expired cost of the *time period* in which he earns the money.

Long-lived assets such as a store building are necessary for carrying on business and thus for earning revenue, but it is pointless to try to estimate how much of the cost of the building should be matched with the revenue from each sale. Instead, the cost of the building is also treated as a *period cost* or, more accurately, a cost common to several periods. Its cost must be distributed fairly to the many accounting periods during which it is used, just as the cost of several assets acquired for a single purchase price must be allocated to the individual assets.

Direct and indirect measurement of expired costs

In some cases it is possible to trace directly the expiration of a given amount of cost and to record the transfer of cost from an asset to an expired cost account while the accounting period is in progress. The amount of the expired cost is then measured *directly*, and the amount of the unexpired cost, or asset, at the end of the period is measured *indirectly* by subtracting the expired cost from the acquisition cost. The method may be summarized in the following T-account:

A, Unexpired Cost

Acquisition cost.................... 500	Expirations traced directly: 35
	100
	15
Balance of unexpired cost measured indirectly, 350	150

There are limitations to this method. If the amount of cost expiration is misstated, the ending asset balance will be misstated by the same amount, but in the opposite direction.

EXAMPLE 13: Assume that the first credit item in the preceding T-account, $35, should have been $55. Expired cost will be *understated* by $20 ($55 −

$35), and unexpired cost at the end of the period will be *overstated* by $20. It should be $330 ($500 − $170) rather than $350.

This method of measuring the unexpired cost will not detect errors in recording the amount of asset acquisitions. It will also fail to record asset decreases which are difficult to trace, such as assets which have been stolen or have become obsolete.

Expired costs may be measured *indirectly* by determining the amount of unexpired cost at the end of the period and subtracting it from the acquisition cost.

EXAMPLE 14:   A business acquired office supplies for a total cost of $100 during an accounting period. At the end of the period the cost of unused supplies on hand was $30. What was the expired cost of supplies used?

SOLUTION:

Acquisition cost, $100 − Unexpired cost, $30 = Expired cost, $70.

If practical, it is desirable to determine the ending balance of the asset both directly and indirectly: to measure the cost expiration, and also to measure the remaining asset balance. Investigation of discrepancies between the results produced by these two general methods gives management valuable information as to weaknesses in procedures for safeguarding assets and for preventing waste, inefficiency, and accounting inaccuracies.

Expiration of inventory costs—perpetual inventory method

The direct method of measuring the cost expiration in the case of inventories is called the *perpetual inventory method.* An entry is made in the asset account, Inventory, each time there is an addition to the asset or a deduction from it. As a result, the ledger account for Inventory should show the unexpired cost of the inventory on hand at any time.

The Hardy Furniture Store illustration for the month of June, 19x1, is continued to show the entries for the perpetual inventory method of accounting. After entry (2) the applicable T-account would be as follows:

A, Merchandise Inventory

19x1			
June 1 (Bought 10 stoves)	(2)	980	

The entry to record the revenue from sales transactions is the same regardless of the method a business uses to account for its inventory costs.

19x1	(6)		
June 5	A, Cash....................................	150	
	OE, Sales Revenue........................		150
	Sold one stove for cash.		

For sales on account, the debit would be to the asset, Accounts Receivable, Trade.

Businesses whose inventories consist of relatively few items, each with a large unit cost, usually find it desirable and practical to keep subsidiary perpetual inventory records for each class of goods. If the Hardy Furniture Store kept such detailed continuous records, the accountant could determine the cost of each stove sold by referring to them and could make the following additional entry at the time of sale:

(7a)

June 5   OE, Cost of Goods Sold Expense................. 98
        A, Merchandise Inventory....................   98
        The inventory was reduced by the expired cost of
        one stove which was sold.

For each sale transaction there would be similar entries for the selling price and the expired cost. The following T-accounts would result if eight stoves were sold during June.

A, Merchandise Inventory

19x1				19x1		
June 1	(Bought 10 stoves)	(2)	980	June, various dates		
				(8 entries of $98)	(7a)	784
	Balance, 196					

OE, Sales Revenue (June)

			19x1		
			June, various dates		
			(8 entries of $150)	(6)	1,200

OE, Cost of Goods Sold Expense (June)

19x1			
June, various dates			
(8 entries of $98)	(7a)	784	

Expiration of inventory costs—periodic inventory method

Most retailers deal in many different articles, each of such relatively small cost that it would be impractical and unduly expensive to keep an up-to-date record of the number and cost of each article on hand. Instead, such businesses rely on a physical count of goods taken periodically, usually once a year, to determine directly the cost of the asset (Merchandise Inventory) on hand at the end of the year and indirectly the expense (Cost of Goods Sold).

Assume that the Hardy Furniture Store did not keep a perpetual inventory record but instead determined the cost of unsold goods on hand at the end of the year by physical count. The method of inventory measurement has no effect on the Sales Revenue account, which would have a balance of $1,200 in either case. Prior to the periodic inventory, the Cost of Goods Sold Expense account would have no balance and Merchandise Inventory would have a debit balance of $980, equal to the cost of goods acquired.

If the periodic inventory taken by physical count on June 30 showed that there were two stoves on hand which had cost $98 each, it would be recorded thus:

```
19x1                              (7b)
June 30   OE, Cost of Goods Sold Expense................. 784
              A, Merchandise Inventory...................       784
          To reduce the asset balance to the cost of inven-
          tory on hand at the end of the year, $196, and
          record the expense for cost of goods sold ($980–
          $196).
```

The ledger accounts would then appear as follows:

A, Merchandise Inventory

19x1				19x1		
June 1	(Bought 10 stoves)	(2)	980	June 30	(7b)	784
	Balance, 196					

OE, Cost of Goods Sold Expense (June)

19x1			
June 30	(7b)	784	

The results show that the expired cost *indirectly* determined at the end of the year by the periodic inventory method is the same as that determined *directly* day by day by the perpetual inventory method. The ending unexpired asset balances are also the same. This is an unrealistically simple example, and in many real cases the results probably would not be identical. The perpetual inventory method records only those events which the accounting staff observes, and some may occur which they do not see. Examples are losses by theft, deterioration, and obsolescence. In addition, there may be clerical errors in recording the cost of individual sales. For these reasons, even if a business maintains a perpetual inventory record, it should confirm it at least once a year by a physical inventory. If the perpetual method is in use, not all of the count needs to be made at one time. It is satisfactory to verify each item on the book record by a physical count of the inventory at some time during the course of the year.

Physical inventory-taking has many purposes other than determining the amount of an expense for the year and the amount of an asset at year-end. It affords a very useful opportunity for the business to determine whether sufficient, insufficient, or excessive quantities of each type of goods are in stock, if certain items are moving too slowly, and if unnecessary damage is occurring because of improper storage conditions. The amount of cost carried forward as an asset at the end of the year should not exceed that which can reasonably be expected to benefit future operations. In this connection, shopworn and obsolete goods on hand at the end of the year should not be measured at their original cost, but at that part of their cost which can be *recovered* through sale.

EXAMPLE 15:   If one of the stoves in the Hardy Furniture Store ending inventory had been damaged and its recoverable cost was only $75, it should be carried in the asset account for Merchandise Inventory at that amount, not at $98. The loss of $23 should be treated as an expired cost of the year in which it occurred.

The perpetual and periodic methods of computing the expired cost of inventories may be summarized as follows:

Known Amounts	Unknown Amount
Perpetual:	
Acquisition Cost − Cost of Goods Sold	= Cost of Ending Inventory
Periodic:	
Acquisition Cost − Cost of Ending Inventory	= Cost of Goods Sold

Expiration of prepaid expenses

Most prepaid expenses are for service contracts of a definite duration. As a rule, their cost expiration is considered to occur in equal amounts each day, but for convenience the *cost expiration* is often recorded at the end of the accounting period. Direct computation of the expired cost as a proportion of the part of the contract which elapsed during the current period, and indirect computation, by determining how much unexpired cost at the end of the period will be of service benefit in the future, should both give the same results.

Some types of prepaid expenses, such as compensation advances to employees, do not always expire directly in proportion to the passage of time. Usually it is rather easy to determine how much the employee has earned, however, and at the same time how much of the prepaid expense has become an expired cost.

Expiration of cost of long-term tangible assets

Most long-term assets have limited service lives. Their costs expire and must be matched against the revenues of the periods in which they render service. The process of allocating this expired cost to periods may be referred to by the general term *cost amortization*, although it is called by different specific names in connection with different types of long-lived assets. The periodic expired cost of buildings and equipment is called *depreciation;* the expired cost of natural resources is called *depletion;* and the expired cost of intangibles such as patents is called *amortization*.

Although the account titles used to describe the cost amortization of long-lived assets are often different, in essence the accounting process is the same: reducing an asset by means of a credit, and reducing owners' equity for the cost expiration by means of a debit.

The total amortization during an asset's life is the difference between its acquisition cost and the expected net proceeds of its disposal at the end of its useful life.

EXAMPLE 16:   A delivery truck with an acquisition cost of $3,000 is expected to be useful for four years and then to be sold for $600. The total expired cost during its life will be $2,400 (Acquisition Cost, $3,000 − Salvage Value, $600).

In some cases the residual value at the end of the asset's life may be ignored, either because its amount is negligible or because the cost of removal is expected to equal the proceeds of disposal.

The allocation of the cost of a long-lived asset to individual accounting periods should accomplish two basic objectives: (1) it should reflect the cost of the benefit which the current period receives from the use of the asset; and (2) it should result in carrying forward as an asset at the end of the current period only that part of the original cost which corresponds to service benefits expected from the asset in future periods.

As a location on the earth's surface, land is expected to be of benefit to its owner indefinitely. For this reason, the total expired cost during its ownership by the business and the expired cost applicable to any accounting period are both zero.

Depreciation

Depreciation may be defined as follows:

Depreciation accounting is a system of accounting which aims to distribute the cost or other basic value of tangible capital assets, less salvage (if any), over the estimated useful life of the unit (which may be a group of assets) in a systematic and rational manner. It is a process of allocation, not of valuation.

Depreciation for the year is the portion of the total charge under such a system that is allocated to the year. Although the allocation may properly take into account occurrences during the year, it is not intended to be a measurement of the effect of all such occurrences.[4]

The length of a depreciable asset's useful life is influenced by the action of physical forces, such as wear, tear, and corrosion. Quite often the useful life ends because the asset becomes obsolete, inadequate for the purpose for which it is being used, or uneconomical to operate as compared with a newer asset. The length of an asset's life involves a *prediction* as to what the future rate of technological improvements will be, an estimate of the future adequacy of the owner's repairs and maintenance, and a forecast of his decision as to when to discard or replace the old asset. Taking into consideration technology and the company's maintenance and replacement policies, the business may be able to estimate the future life of its assets on the basis of its own past experience. The experience of other businesses may serve as a useful guide in estimating useful lives, but the business must consider the particular circumstances under which it uses its own depreciable assets.

By far the most widely used method of assigning depreciation to periods is the *straight-line method*. Under it the estimated life of the asset is expressed in calendar time. The amount of depreciation for a full year of the asset's life is determined by the formula:

$$\text{Annual depreciation } (D) = \frac{\text{Cost } (C) - \text{Net salvage value } (S)}{\text{Estimated life in years } (n)}$$

If the asset is in use during only part of the accounting period, only the appropriate fraction of annual depreciation should be charged to the period's expense.

The straight-line method assumes that each full year receives approximately equal service benefit from the asset. The method derives its name from the fact that a graph of depreciation by years would form a straight line.

Accumulated depreciation account

The acquisition cost of an asset subject to depreciation should be debited to an asset account, such as Buildings or Equipment. The part of the cost which expires during the current accounting period should be transferred from the asset account to an expense account, Depreciation Expense. In an earlier chapter, the credit for the cost expiration entry was, for simplicity, made directly to the asset account. Although that approach helps to emphasize the nature of the credit as a reduction of an asset, it is

---

[4] American Institute of Certified Public Accountants, Committee on Terminology, *Accounting Terminology Bulletin Number 1, Review and Résumé* (New York: The Institute, 1953), p. 25.

not desirable in actual practice. First, the amount of acquisition cost is definitely known and the annual expired cost is an estimate, so it is well to show them in separate accounts. Second, using an asset account to report the amount of cost and an asset-deduction account to record the accumulation of expired cost provides useful information about the amount of physical assets in use. Third, the amount of accumulated depreciation relative to the cost of the assets gives the statement reader valuable clues as to whether the assets are relatively old or new.

The following journal entries show how periodic depreciation should be recorded.

```
19x1                          (8)
July   1   A, Equipment............................ 2,800
               A, Cash.............................          2,800
               Purchased a salesman's automobile for cash.

                              (9)
Dec. 31    OE, Depreciation Expense (19x1)............   300
               A, Equipment—Accumulated Depreciation           300
               To record depreciation of the automobile for
               19x1, computed as follows:

           Cost, $2,800 − Salvage Value, $400
                        = Total Depreciation, $2,400.
           Total depreciation, $2,400
              Estimated life, 4 years
                     = Average depreciation per year, $600.
           Depreciation for 19x1
              = ½ year × Annual Depreciation, $600 = $300.
```

Depreciation Expense of $300 would appear in the 19x1 Income Statement. In the Statement of Financial Position for December 31, 19x1, the asset would appear as follows:

ASSETS

Equipment (cost)................................	$2,800
Deduct Accumulated Depreciation..................	300
Unexpired cost...	$2,500

Depreciation Expense for 19x2, $600, would be recorded in the same manner as in entry (9). The presentation in the Statement of Financial Position at the end of the year would be:

ASSETS

Equipment (cost)................................	$2,800
Deduct Accumulated Depreciation..................	900
Unexpired cost...	$1,900

The credit balance in the Accumulated Depreciation account is cumulative from year to year. As it becomes larger, the unexpired cost of the asset becomes smaller.

Expiration of long-term intangibles

The economically useful life, rather than the legal one, should be used in measuring the expired cost of patents, copyrights, trade-marks, and franchises. Often an invention is useless long before the period of protection granted by the patent expires. The future time period during which copyrights and trade-marks can be expected to benefit the business is often very short or very doubtful.

The acquisition cost of leasehold improvements should be transferred to expense over the remaining term of the lease or the useful life of the improvement, whichever is shorter.

If it appears that the factors acquired in the purchase of a business which are responsible for its above-average return are short-lived, the cost of goodwill should be transferred to expense over an appropriate period of time. Many of the complex questions which are involved in measuring the acquisition and expiration of goodwill are discussed in later chapters.

Organization costs may be expected to benefit the company for as long as it continues in operation. For this reason there are practical grounds for considering "Organization Costs" as a permanent asset, at least until there is evidence that the life of the business is to be terminated. However, because experience shows that the economic life of the typical business is short, it is common accounting practice to transfer a portion of these costs from the asset to an expense over a short period such as five years.

In some cases the expired costs of long-lived assets subject to depletion and cost amortization are credited directly to the asset account. This is often the case when the probable useful life of the asset can be estimated with a high degree of certainty. At other times, asset-deduction accounts, such as Patents—Accumulated Amortization, are used.

LONG-TERM INVESTMENTS

Long-term investments resemble temporary investments because they, too, are usually commitments of funds for the purpose of earning a monetary return on financial instruments. An important difference is that the investor intends to hold them for a long or indefinite period, rather than for a short one. Usually the purpose of the investing company is to earn a return directly in the form of dividends on corporate stocks or interest on corporate or government bonds. However, its purpose in investing may be more indirect, as when it owns some of the stock of another company which is an important customer or an essential source of supply.

Other types of investments which businesses often own are life insurance policies, usually on the lives of key employees, naming the business as beneficiary; holdings of real estate for rental rather than for use; and accumulations of funds to pay off large amounts of debt (*sinking funds*) or to purchase high-cost assets.

Initially, long-term investments should be measured at their acquisition cost. During the long period of ownership there will undoubtedly be fluctuations in the amounts for which they could be sold on the market, reflecting the effect of changes in economic conditions and investor preferences on current rates of interest. These fluctuations in market price should be ignored in the accounting records unless there is an indication that a decline in the market value of an investment is permanent, perhaps because of a weakening of the credit rating of the issuer of the security. For adequate disclosure, the market value should be given parenthetically in the statement of financial position. If the decline appears to be permanent, however, it is likely that there will be a loss when the securities are sold or redeemed in the distant future. The investor should recognize this probable loss by reducing the amount of the asset when the decline occurs.

Long-term investments in bonds should be measured at their *amortized cost*. If the acquisition cost of bonds differs from their maturity value, the *premium* or *discount* should be treated as an adjustment of periodic interest revenue, with a corresponding write-down or write-up, respectively, of the asset, long-term investment.

Because they are rather complex, the accounting entries for bond investments, together with those for bonds payable, are illustrated in a later chapter.

Summary

In contrast to monetary assets, unexpired costs represent commitments of resources to specific types of service potentials. The business is justified in carrying as assets the proportion of these costs which can be expected to benefit the future. The *acquisition cost* of such assets includes all costs incurred which are reasonably necessary to get the asset ready for use or for sale. The *expired cost* of the asset is that part of the acquisition cost which represents its benefits currently received or the loss of its potential to give benefits to the future. In some cases, costs are associated with a *product*, which can then be identified with the revenue of an accounting period by direct association. Other costs are associated only with the *period* in which they expire. Some costs are *transformed;* that is, they have rendered their benefit in their original form, but are reclassified as another asset, such as a manufactured product, which will be matched against revenue as an expired cost in a later period.

The expiration of costs of long-term tangible and intangible assets are variously referred to as *amortization, depreciation,* and *depletion,* but all involve the transfer of cost from an asset to an expired cost account.

APPENDIX 6-A

The Importance of Taking Cash Discounts

A business can ill afford not to take advantage of its cash discounts. In the illustration of the Hardy Furniture Store in Chapter 6 (Illustration of Net Price Method of Recording Cash Discounts), the purchaser could have saved $20 by paying 20 days earlier. A 2% discount for 20 days' prepayment is equivalent to approximately 36% discount for one year (20 days is $\frac{1}{18}$ of 360 days; 18 × 2% is 36%).

If the Hardy Furniture Store's bank credit will permit it to borrow money at 6% annual interest, it could borrow $980 on June 11, take advantage of the purchase discount, and pay the bank back $983.27 on July 1. This is $16.73 less than it would have to pay the H Stove Works if it did not borrow.

The importance of taking discounts is emphasized better by comparing Income Statements for an entire year under two assumptions: (A) that all discounts are taken on the last possible day, and (B) that they are all lost.

	(A) All Discounts Taken		(B) All Discounts Lost	
Sales Revenue....................		$100,000		$100,000
Cost of Goods Sold Expense	$58,800		$58,800	
Other Expenses...........	36,200		36,200	
Discounts Lost...........	0		1,200	
Total Expenses................		95,000		96,200
Net Income....................		$ 5,000		$ 3,800

These amounts are based on the assumption that a 2% cash discount was available on all purchases. Note that the net income is 24% less ($1,200/$5,000) in Case B, when all discounts are lost.

Bank interest charges would have been $196 (6% of $58,800 for 20 days). If the business had borrowed all of the money needed to pay for purchases within the discount period, it would have increased its income $1,004 as compared with Case B, when all discounts are lost.

Aside from its importance to the management and owners of the business, information about the cash discounts lost by a business is important to its creditors. Creditors usually consider a customer's failure to take advantage of available discounts a sign of financial weakness, and may use it as a basis for ceasing to extend credit.

APPENDIX 6-B

The Gross Price Method of Recording Cash Discounts

The net price method of recording cash discounts on purchases results in measuring assets at the amount of money which would be needed to pay for them on the acquisition date. It also focuses the attention of management and other Income Statement users on the loss resulting from the failure to take advantage of cash discounts. However, it is common business practice to record a purchased asset at its *gross invoice cost,* and to treat discounts actually taken by the business as revenue. The following entries show how transactions (2), (3), and (4) of the Hardy Furniture Store, illustrated in Chapter 6, would be recorded under this accounting policy.

```
19x1                          (2a)
June 1    A, Merchandise Inventory.................. 1,000
              L, Accounts Payable, Trade..... ......        1,000
              Purchased 10 stoves from H Stove Works,
              terms 2/10, n/30.

                              (3a)
June 11   L, Accounts Payable, Trade................ 1,000
              A, Cash...............................          980
              OE, Purchase Discount Revenue........           20
              Paid invoice of June 1 less 2% discount.

or                            (4a)
July  1   L, Accounts Payable, Trade................ 1,000
              A, Cash...............................        1,000
              Paid the H Stove Works invoice of June 1
              after the expiration of the discount period.
```

The differences in the effects of the two methods on the financial statements may be summarized as follows:

	Net Price Method	Gross Price Method
Asset, inventory........................	Lower	Higher
Cumulative retained income.................	Lower	Higher
Expired cost of each item in cost of goods sold	Lower	Higher
Loss from discounts not taken..............	Shown	Not shown
Revenue from discounts taken..............	Not shown	Shown

The gross price method is subject to the criticism that it records revenue at the time an asset is paid for rather than when it is sold. Even if the stoves in transaction (3a) had not been sold at the end of the accounting period, $20 of revenue on them would be reported in the Income Statement as Purchase Discount Revenue. Accounting theory recognizes that revenue occurs at the time of *sale,* however, not at the time of *payment* for purchases.

The gross price method is often defended on the ground that it is more practical than the net price method. Consistency demands that if total additions to the asset, inventory, are measured at net cost, each individual item in cost of goods sold and ending inventory should be measured on the same basis. Sometimes this necessitates carrying unit costs of inventory items to several decimal places. For example, a shirt with a gross invoice cost of $2.25, subject to a cash discount of 3%, would have a net invoice cost of $2.1825. Its avoidance of such awkward unit costs is an advantage of the gross price method.

QUESTIONS AND PROBLEMS

6-1   Criticize the following statement: "Assets should be recorded at their market value if it is known; otherwise, they should be recorded at cost."

6-2   The Pinson Company purchased two new machines at a cost of $6,000 each for Department A. The foreman gave these instructions to the machine operators: "Clean those machines carefully every day, and report immediately any and all repairs needed. We don't want any depreciation on them!"

REQUIRED:
Comment on the foreman's instructions.

6-3   *a.* If a company failed to record annual depreciation of $300 for three successive years, what effect would this error have on the Retained Income balance at the end of the third year?

b. If the same company failed to accrue salary expense of $200, payable, but not due, at the end of each of the three years, what effect would this error have on the Retained Income balance at the end of the third year?

6-4   A firm constructed a building for its own use at a total cost of $130,000, all paid in cash. During construction it was necessary to tear out and reconstruct a substantial part of the building because the work was faulty. Under normal conditions, the building should have cost $100,000.

REQUIRED:
a. What was the proper measure of the asset, Building? Explain.
b. Record these facts in journal form.
c. Assuming that the construction period lasted one year, should any depreciation be recorded during this time? Why?

6-5   "*Depreciation for the year* is the portion of the total charge under such a system that is allocated to the year. Although the allocation may properly take into account occurrences during the year, it is not intended to be a measurement of the effect of all such occurrences."

REQUIRED:
a. Give an example of an occurrence during the year that should be taken into account in making the depreciation allocation. Explain how and why it should be considered.
b. Give an example of an occurrence related to a depreciable asset that should not be taken into account in making the depreciation allocation. Explain why it is not applicable.

6-6   Measurement of unexpired costs involves predictions of varying degree.

REQUIRED:

a. Illustrate a type of unexpired cost the measurement of which is fairly certain.
b. Illustrate a type of unexpired cost the measurement of which is subject to a high degree of uncertainty, and explain why it is uncertain.
c. Is the estimate in (b) of any value to management and other users of the financial statements? Explain.

6-7 The Novelty Manufacturing Company buys a patent from an inventor just after it has been issued by the United States Patent Office, paying $1,050 cash. The invention is a fad which seems to have sales possibilities for three years. The accounting period ends six months later.

REQUIRED:

a. Record the acquisition of the patent.
b. Make any other entries needed during the first accounting period.

6-8 Explain why it is desirable to classify the following items in different accounts:

a. Factory building and sales warehouse.
b. Raw materials and shipping supplies.
c. Machinery in Production Dept. 1 and machinery in Production Dept. 2.
d. Prepaid insurance and unused stationery.
e. Merchandise inventory and raw materials.

6-9 Are the amounts of the following accounts which are shown in the Statement of Financial Position facts or estimates? Explain.

a. Accounts Receivable.
b. Cash.
c. Unexpired Insurance.
d. Land.
e. Equipment—Unexpired Cost.
f. Accounts Receivable—Estimated Uncollectibles.

6-10 On July 1, 19x1, a business with seasonally idle cash acquires United States government bonds at their par of $10,000. They mature in five years and pay interest each June 30 and December 31 at the annual rate of 4 per cent.

REQUIRED:

a. Under what account title should these bonds be classified?
b. On what basis should they be measured?
c. Record all of the journal entries that are necessary in 19x1 if the business continues to hold the bonds until the end of the calendar year.
d. Show how all relevant items would appear in the year-end financial statements if the market price of the bonds on December 31 is 98 per cent of par value.

6-11 Your retail store received 20 sweaters from a foreign manufacturer. The invoice contained the following items: List price, $20 each; discount to dealers, 30 per cent; additional discount for purchases of 5 or more, 10 per cent; import duty, $2 per sweater; terms, net 30 days in United States funds. Your firm paid transportation charges of $3 upon receipt of the shipment, as well as $2 for repairing a hole in one of the sweaters.

REQUIRED:

Record these facts in journal entries.

6-12 A builder of residential houses usually has four houses in the process of construction at any given time. The houses require an average of four months each for completion. Usually they are sold within a month after the date of completion.

REQUIRED:

a. What are the principal types of assets which you would expect to find on the books of the builder?

b. Are there any cost transformations in his accounts? Explain and illustrate.

c. What are his principal problems in connection with matching expired cost and revenue, and how would you recommend that he solve them?

6-13 Walter Thompson, treasurer of the recently formed Circle Corporation, received an invoice from his printer itemized as follows:

Printing capital stock certificates.	$100
Printing 10-year bond certificates.	100
Printing letterheads and envelopes.	200
Printing personal calling cards for Mrs. Thompson.	10
	$410

REQUIRED:

a. In what account should the cost of each item be recorded initially?

b. What subsequent accounting treatment would each receive, and what additional information is needed in order to give it?

6-14 Marie's Dress Shoppe bought 5 dozen dresses of a new style at a cost of $40 a dress. Most of the dresses were sold during the season, but at the end of the accounting period there were still 6 on hand which the manager thought could be sold to a bargain basement for $10 each.

REQUIRED:

a. At what amount would you state these unsold dresses in inventory at the end of the year?

b. What additional information is needed in order to give a more complete answer?

6-15 An appliance dealer maintained a perpetual inventory record of television sets. During the year he bought 30 of them at $100 each and sold 20 for cash at $130 each. On December 31, counting his stock, he finds 9 of the T-V sets on hand.

REQUIRED:

Record all of these facts in journal form.

6-16 The Eastman Dime Store received a bill from the City Water Works on December 31 reading: "Services for December, $5. Add 10% penalty if not paid by January 15." On the same date it received an electric bill reading: "December services, $30. Deduct 5% discount if paid by January 15." The Dime Store's accounting period ended on December 31, and neither bill had been paid on that date.

REQUIRED:

a. At what amount should the liability owed for water be shown in the December 31 statements? The liability owed for electricity?

b. Show in journal form the entries needed on December 31.

6-17 On July 1, 19x7, the IM Corporation purchased a bookkeeping machine having a list price of $2,000. In addition, the corporation bought a supply of record forms expected to last about six months for $50, and a service contract for the repair of the machine for one year for $60. The terms of payment were $610 in cash at time of delivery and a promissory note for the balance. On the first of August and of each succeeding month, $100 of the principal of the note was to be paid, together with interest at one per cent of the *original* unpaid balance, $1,500.

REQUIRED:

a. Show in journal form without explanation the entries that are needed on July 1.
b. What information do you need on July 31 to make necessary entries, and how would you obtain it? (Financial statements are prepared monthly.)

6-18   Your company bought a used machine on October 1, 19x1, for $3,000 cash. The seller had acquired it three years earlier for $6,000 and had recorded depreciation of $3,200 on its books up to the time of the sale.

REQUIRED:

a. How much did your company earn by making the purchase?
b. What journal entry is needed to record the purchase of the machine?

6-19   James Gilbert bought 1,000 units of merchandise for resale in his store at a cost of $4 per unit, paying cash. An envious competitor offered him $6 per unit for the entire lot a few days later. Instead, Mr. Gilbert kept the goods and marked them to sell at $12 each. By the end of his accounting period, he had sold 300 for cash at this price. The competitor offered to buy the remainder at $7 each, but again Mr. Gilbert declined.

REQUIRED:

a. Record all of the journal entries necessary to show these facts on the books of Mr. Gilbert.
b. At what amount should he state his ending inventory?

6-20   Upon buying a car for the business use of its executives, the Upton Company is shown the following chart by the dealer:

Cost.	$5,000
Estimated resale value, end of each year:	
First year.	3,500
Second year.	2,600
Third year.	2,000
Fourth year.	1,500
Fifth year.	1,100

The Upton Company plans to use the car for three years and to keep it in excellent condition. The car will probably be driven about the same number of miles each year.

REQUIRED:

a. How much depreciation should be recorded each year?
b. If the company planned to use the car for five years, what would be the proper depreciation each year?

6-21   Webben & Sons, Inc., purchased land, together with a building standing on it, as the site for an additional plant. The corporation obtained bids from several contractors for demolition of the old building and the construction of the new building, but finally rejected all bids and undertook the construction using company labor, facilities, and equipment. Construction was almost completed by the close of the year.

All transactions relating to these properties were charged or credited to an account titled "Real Estate." The various items in that account are summarized below. You decide that separate Land and Buildings accounts should be set up and that all of the items in the Real Estate account should be reclassified.

Indicate the disposition of each numbered item by *printing* beside the item number the *capital letter* which identifies your answer. If you recommend a reclassification involving two or more of the following accounts, list the appropriate capital letters.

Although there may be other appropriate items not listed, you need give them no attention for purposes of this question and should consider only the following four possibilities:

A. Transfer to Land account.
B. Transfer to Buildings account.
C. Transfer to a revenue (or gain) account.
D. Transfer to an expense (or loss) account.

ITEMS CHARGED OR CREDITED TO "REAL ESTATE"

1. Contract price of "package" purchase (land and old building).
2. Legal fees relating to conveyance of title.
3. Invoice cost of materials and supplies used in construction.
4. Direct costs arising from demolition of old building.
5. Discounts earned for early payment of item 3.
6. Total depreciation on equipment used during construction period partially for construction of building and the remainder of the time for regular operations.
7. Total cost of excavation.
8. Proceeds of sale of materials salvaged from razing of old building.
9. Cost of building permits and licenses.
10. Architects' fees.
11. Payment of property taxes on land and old building, owed by the former owner and assumed by the client.
12. Special municipal assessments for sidewalk and street pavings necessitated by the altered use of the site.
13. Premiums for insurance against natural hazards during construction.
14. Premium rebates for certain of the above policies surrendered before completion of construction.
15. Uninsured claims paid for injuries sustained during construction (aggregate amount, $3,000).
16. Installation costs for newly acquired machinery installed in completed wings of the building.
17. Estimated profit on construction of new building to date (computed as follows: Lowest contractor's bid × % of building completion to 12/31 less new-building construction costs to date).

(Adapted from AICPA Examination in Theory of Accounts, November 5, 1954.)

6-22 On July 1, 19x1, Smith Cleaners purchased a delivery truck for cash. The invoice read:

List price of truck	$3,700
Cash discount	800
Net cash	$2,900
State sales tax	87
State automobile license for 19x1	10
Gasoline	5
Total price	$3,002
Settlement:	
Cash on delivery	$3,002

REQUIRED:

a. What entry should Smith Cleaners make to record the purchase?

b. Smith Cleaners finds that it is usually most economical to replace its delivery trucks after three years' use. Typically they can be sold for 20 per cent of their original list price at the end of this time. Make any entries needed on December 31, 19x1.

c. Which of these facts would be shown in the Statement of Financial Position on December 31, 19x1, and how would they be shown?

d. What additional entries would be needed in 19x2?

e. What information would appear in the 19x2 Income Statement? The 19x2 Statement of Financial Position?

6-23 You are examining the financial statements of two companies in the same line of business with a view to buying one or the other. Each shows "Unexpired Cost of Plant and Equipment, $40,000." Upon request, you receive the following additional information:

	Company A	Company B
Plant and Equipment (Cost)	$240,000	$60,000
Accumulated Depreciation	200,000	20,000
	$ 40,000	$40,000

REQUIRED:

a. What does this additional information tell you about each of these companies?

b. What further inquiries would these figures prompt you to make when you visit the plants?

6-24 Your banker is reviewing your financial statements at the end of your first year of business. Coming across an item, "Real Estate, $50,000," he asks you what it represents.

REQUIRED:

a. Why is this title unsatisfactory?

b. What type of classification is needed?

c. What is the nature of the future measurement problem, and how should it be solved?

6-25 The Pure Dairy, whose accounting periods ends on December 31, wishes to acquire a retail outlet. On December 1, 19x1, the dairy pays $500 for an option permitting it to buy a desirable building at any time within 60 days at a total cost of $15,000, of which $5,000 applies to the location. During December the dairy receives a $12,000 loan commitment from the Sure Insurance Company, and the purchase transaction is completed on January 2, 19x2. Here is a summary of the closing statement:

Purchaser's Statement:

Purchase Price		$15,000
Binder		500
Cash at closing required of purchaser		$14,500
To be paid from:		
Proceeds of Sure Ins. Co. loan	$12,000	
Funds of purchaser	2,500	$14,500

Expenses of Purchaser:

Recording Deed......................................	$ 5
Recording First Mortgage.........................	3
Documentary Stamps on Mortgage....................	24
Documentary Stamps on Note Payable................	24
Appraisal Fee......................................	25
Title Insurance....................................	30
Abstract of Title..................................	16
Surveyor...	20
Attorney's Fee.....................................	150
19x2 Property Taxes................................	300
	$597

REQUIRED:

a. How much did the property cost the Pure Dairy? Itemize the components of land cost and building cost.

b. Record all entries needed on December 1, 19x1; during December; on December 31, 19x1; and on January 2, 19x2.

c. If the mortgage note payable to the Sure Insurance Company bears interest at the rate of 5 per cent a year and requires a payment of $1,000 on principal and unpaid interest on January 2, 19x3, make any appropriate entries on December 31, 19x2.

d. The building is expected to have no scrap value at end of its useful life of 25 years. Make the necessary entry on December 31, 19x2.

e. List all items that would appear in the 19x2 Income Statement.

f. Show how each item would appear in the December 31, 19x2 Statement of Financial Position.

6-26   The Pure Dairy bought a used typewriter for its office on July 1, 19x2, paying $100 in cash. It paid a delivery man $3 to deliver it, and then had the typewriter overhauled for $20 prior to using it. At the same time it paid $2 for a new ribbon and $10 for a one-year service contract on the typewriter. The typewriter is expected to last four years and to have no scrap value.

REQUIRED:

a. Record all entries on July 1, 19x2.

b. Make any entries necessary on December 31, 19x2.

c. Show how the relevant facts would appear in the 19x2 financial statements.

d. Show how the relevant facts would appear in the 19x4 financial statements, if everything goes according to expectations.

6-27   The Smart Shop bought two identical lots of merchandise from the Central Supply Co., each costing $200, on terms of 3/10, n/30. The first lot arrived on March 3; the invoice was dated March 2. The second lot, shipped on March 6, arrived on March 8. The Smart Shop sent a check in full payment of the first lot on March 10, but failed to pay the second invoice until March 31.

REQUIRED:

a. Journalize all transactions.

b. If a physical count shows that one-tenth of each lot is unsold on March 31, at what amount should each be included in the inventory?

c. Record the ending inventory under the periodic method.

6-28   Certain transactions of The Williams Company during the month of April, 19x1, appear below:

April 2—Purchased merchandise on account from the Johnson Company, $8,000.
        Terms, 2/10, n/30.

April 5—Purchased from Nanson Machine Co. a machine for use with a list price
of $4,000 and a trade discount of 40 per cent. Terms were 3/15, n/30.

April 10—Purchased for $30,000 cash the tangible assets of a small business. The
market price of the individual assets as determined by an appraiser
were: Land, $5,000; Building, $15,000; Inventory, $15,000; Equipment,
$5,000. Also agreed to pay the owner of the business $2,000 additional
for goodwill, which he claimed was worth $10,000.

April 14—Paid the Johnson Company in full.

April 18—Settled the Nanson Machine Co. bill by paying cash, $2,000, and sign-
ing a 30-day, non-interest-bearing note for the balance. The seller
allowed discount on the partial payment.

April 20—Traded an office desk for a used typewriter. The original cost of the desk
was $300 and the company had recorded depreciation of $100. The
Williams Company had received an offer of $125 for the desk two days
earlier. Fair market value of the typewriter was $135.

REQUIRED:

Journalize the above transactions with a full explanation for each entry.

CASE 6-1. MEADOWS CORPORATION

Meadows Corporation was formed in January of 19x2 to operate an office machine rental service. During January the following transactions occurred:

Cash payments:

    (1) To lawyer for drawing up articles of incorporation, $200.

    (2) To Secretary of State for charter, $50.

    (3) To city for annual business license, $60.

    (4) To State Power Company for January utility bill, $25.

    (5) To Central Printing Company for office supplies and forms sufficient to
last six months, $90.

    (6) To public stenographer for typing publicity material, $50.

    (7) For postage for mailing publicity material, $20.

    (8) For down payment on 20 typewriters purchased for rent to customers,
$1,500. Each typewriter cost $240, and each was expected to have a
useful life of 50 months and a final salvage value of $40. The balance was
to be paid within 60 days.

Bills received but not paid:

    (9) For newspaper advertising, $15.

   (10) For telephone use for the month, $22, including long-distance calls of $8 in
connection with ordering the typewriters in (8).

   (11) For rent of the business building for January, $150.

Promissory notes issued:

   (12) To Janis Equipment Company, note dated January 1, face amount of
$3,000, annual interest rate of 6%, for various machines for rental. The
note required monthly principal payments of $100 on the first of each
month, and the interest was to be computed on the unpaid principal.
The equipment was expected to have a useful life of six years and a
salvage value of $120 at the end of that time.

   (13) To X State Bank for a cash loan of $500 received on January 16, interest
rate of 6%, maturity date of February 15.

Cash received:

(14) From various customers for machine rental applicable to January, $200.

(15) From a customer for machine rental applicable to the period from January 11 to July 11, $120.

(16) From the stockholders by way of investment, $2,000.

(17) From the X State Bank for the cash loan in transaction (13).

Bills issued but not collected:

(18) To customers for rentals applicable to January, $150.

(19) To a customer for rental applicable to the entire months of January, February, and March, $45.

Other data:

(20) The two stockholder-managers had been authorized to receive monthly salaries of $250 each.

REQUIRED:

a. Show journal entries for the January events and for any other items which are necessary to reflect January income and financial status properly.

b. Post the journal entries to T-accounts.

c. Prepare a trial balance.

d. Prepare an Income Statement, a Statement of Retained Income, and a Statement of Financial Position for January.

e. State what general plan you would advise the company to follow in timing the recording of its entries of various types, observing the requirements of clerical convenience.

CASE 6-2. THE BELLFORD OFFICE SUPPLY AND EQUIPMENT COMPANY

The Bellford Office Supply and Equipment Company operates in a large industrial center, selling various types of office supplies and equipment on both a wholesale and a retail basis. The company has been in business for five years, during which time its average annual sales have been $135,000.

It has been the company's policy to ignore all purchase discounts offered by its suppliers. Mr. Bellford, the principal stockholder, considers it advantageous to minimize the amount of the stockholders' investment required by delaying payments for purchases until the last possible date. Discounts available to the company have averaged 2 per cent of the gross invoice price for payment within 10 days of the invoice date, with the gross amount of the invoice typically being due in 30 days. In its accounts the company has treated the gross invoice price as the acquisition cost of merchandise.

A local banker, to whom Mr. Bellford recently applied for a business loan, stated that he considers this policy unwise, since its equivalent annual interest rate is very high. The banker pointed out that two basic methods of accounting for purchase discounts are in wide use: the net price method and the gross price method. He recommended that the company use the former.

Mr. Bellford has asked you to recommend which method should be used in recording the company's purchase discounts. To give concrete illustrations, you have made the following estimates of revenue and expenses for three consecutive future years, which you think will represent the conditions likely to be faced by the company.

| | Projected Future Amounts | | |
	Probable Low	Probable Average	Probable High
Sales.........................	$120,000	$150,000	$180,000
*Beginning inventory.............	32,000	40,000	50,000
*Purchases.....................	80,000	100,000	116,000
*Ending inventory...............	40,000	50,000	58,000
Other expenses.................	49,000	52,000	60,000

* Stated at gross invoice cost.

REQUIRED:

a. Compare the projected annual income that will result from each of the assumed volumes of annual sales, using the two principal methods of recording purchase discounts:

   (1) If the company takes all discounts; and
   (2) If the company loses all discounts.

b. Compare the effects of the two methods on the statements of financial position at the end of each year under all assumptions.

c. Which method would you recommend to Mr. Bellford? Why?

d. What steps might the company take to assure a minimum loss of purchase discounts?

Chapter 7

Classifying and Measuring Equities (Asset Sources)

Chapters 5 and 6 dealt with some of the basic problems involved in classifying and measuring the two principal classes of assets, *monetary assets* and *unexpired costs*. The present chapter considers the chief problems involved in classifying and measuring the two corresponding classes of liabilities, *monetary liabilities* and *deferred credits to income*, as well as the principal types of *owners' equity*.

CLASSIFYING AND MEASURING LIABILITIES

Monetary liabilities and deferred credits to income

Monetary liabilities are the counterparts of monetary assets. They are the legally enforceable claims of outsiders against the enterprise, to be paid in money or money equivalent. Occasionally the amount, due date, or identity of the creditor is unknown.

Deferred credits to income are items resulting from past transactions which are to be used in the measurement of the income of future periods. They generally represent advance collections of revenue which will be earned in a later period, but occasionally they also include past collections which should be deducted from the expenses of future periods in order to match expense with the related revenue.

153

Objectives and bases of classification

The general purposes of classifying liabilities are:

(1) To aid management in planning and controlling the disbursement of enterprise assets for the settlement of debts;

(2) To facilitate accounting for future periodic income; and

(3) To assist management and others in appraising the financial position of the enterprise.

Generally, the most useful bases for classifying liabilities are:

(1) The legal form of the debt instrument (for example, accounts, notes, and bonds payable);

(2) The type of cost which resulted in the liability (for example, interest, taxes, and salaries payable);

(3) The future accounting disposition (for example, deferred revenue); and

(4) The specific identity of the creditor (for example, Account Payable to Abner Company; Note Payable to First State Bank; Federal Income Taxes Payable). This basis of classification is usually used in addition to one of the other three.

Common types of liability accounts

The following is a list of some of the types of liability accounts which are frequently found in financial statements, together with brief definitions where they are considered necessary.

(1) *Monetary liabilities*

    (a) Accounts Payable, Trade. All balances owed to others for goods and supplies purchased on open account and sometimes for services, such as utilities.

    (b) Notes Payable, Trade. The balance of the face amount of promissory notes owed to suppliers of goods, services, and equipment.

    (c) Notes Payable to Banks. Promissory notes to banks, generally arising from cash loans.

    (d) Other notes payable. Separate accounts for notes payable to officers, employees, affiliated companies, and others.

    (e) Dividends Payable. The amount owed by a corporation to its stockholders as a result of an income distribution formally authorized by the board of directors.

    (f) Accrued payables. Liabilities which have accumulated over time but which are to be paid later, such as Accrued Interest

Payable, Accrued Salaries Payable, Accrued Rent Payable, Accrued Property Taxes Payable, and Corporation Income Taxes Payable.

(g) Liabilities as an agent. Employee Income Tax Withheld, Employee Social Security Tax Withheld, Sales Tax Payable, and other items owed in the capacity of a tax-collecting agent for governmental units, together with withholdings for other agencies, such as Union Dues Withheld and Pension Contributions Withheld.

(h) Other payables. Advances to a company by its officers, employees, stockholders, and affiliates not supported by promissory notes or stock certificates.

(i) Estimated liabilities. Liabilities, such as Estimated Warranties Payable, the amount of which is uncertain.

(j) Bonds Payable. Long-term notes issued by a corporation under a formal legal procedure which permits more than one lender to participate in the loan.

(2) *Deferred credits to income*

(a) Deferred revenues. Advances from Customers to apply on future shipments, Rents Collected in Advance, and similar items.

(b) Deferred credits to expense. Bond Premium (according to one point of view). Many accountants consider Unamortized Premium on Bonds Payable to be a deferred credit; others treat it as a part of the long-term liability, Bonds Payable. In either case, it will be treated as a reduction of the interest expense of future periods.

Measuring liabilities

The two chief stages of accounting for liabilities relate to their *incurrence* and their *settlement*.

Liabilities are usually incurred in transactions in which the business receives an asset or incurs an expense or a loss. Initially the proper measure of the liability is the same as that of the asset, expense, or loss: the amount of money or money equivalent that would currently be required to settle the obligation. If there is a substantial waiting period before a liability is to be paid, the appropriate measure of the debt at any time is its maturity amount minus interest for the time remaining until maturity. An additional liability for interest accrues as time passes.

A liability also results from a declaration of a distribution out of income or owners' investment, and occasionally a new liability is created to replace an old one. The basis of measuring such liabilities is also the amount of money or money equivalent currently required to settle them.

Liabilities are customarily settled by *payment* in cash, but creditors may accept assets other than cash, services, other forms of liabilities, or shares of owners' equity in settlement. The consideration given to extinguish a liability, measured in money or money equivalent, may differ from the amount of the debt which is being settled. If the consideration is less than the liability, there is a *gain*, which increases income. If the consideration is greater than the liability, the settlement results in a *loss* and a reduction of net income. Such gains and losses are often associated with the early retirement of bonds payable.

Deferred credits to revenue and expense are allocated to accounting periods in accordance with the principle of matching revenues and related expenses. Their balances are transferred to the revenue or expense accounts of the appropriate periods.

Interest on notes payable

Lenders commonly provide for compensation for the use of their capital by accepting *interest-bearing promissory notes*, which require the payment of the *face* amount of the note at its *maturity*, or due date, together with *interest* at a specified percentage of the face amount of the note for each time period. Interest on notes of short duration is usually paid at maturity. For long-term notes, interest may be due annually, semiannually, or quarterly.

The *interest expense* of the borrower is the difference between the sum he initially receives and the sum he pays back. The same amount is the *interest revenue* of the lender.

Simple interest, or interest based upon the unpaid part of the face amount, may be computed by the formula:

$$I = S(i)(n),$$

where I is the amount of interest;
    S is the initial sum borrowed, or principal;
    i is the interest rate per time period; and
    n is the number of time periods.

EXAMPLE 1: A company borrows \$1,000 from a bank for one year and gives in exchange an interest-bearing promissory note for \$1,000, providing for the payment of interest at the rate of 6 per cent of the face amount per year. What is the interest cost?

SOLUTION: $I = S(i)(n)$

$I = \$1,000(.06)(1)$

$I = \$60.$

Interest computations for fractional periods

Quite often the term of a note bearing simple interest is less than one year, and the appropriate fraction of a year must be substituted for n in the formula for computing interest cost.

EXAMPLE 2:   What is the interest cost of an interest-bearing note of $500 for three months at 6 per cent per year?

SOLUTION: $I = S(i)(n)$

$I = \$500(.06)(\frac{1}{4})$

$I = \$500(.015)$

$I = \$7.50$

Certain combinations of interest rates and time periods lend themselves readily to mental computations of interest. Unless there is a statement to the contrary, interest for a specified number of days is computed as though there were 360 days in the year. Loans for 60 days are quite common, and so is an interest rate of 6 per cent per year. Since 60 days is one-sixth of a year ($\frac{60}{360} = \frac{1}{6}$), the interest cost for 60 days at 6 per cent is one per cent ($\frac{1}{6}$ of 6 per cent) of the principal sum. Interest at one per cent may be computed by multiplying the principal by .01 (or by moving the decimal point two places to the left).

EXAMPLE 3:   What is the interest cost on an interest-bearing note of $662 for 60 days at 6 per cent per year?

SHORT-CUT SOLUTION: Move the decimal point of the principal, $662, two places to the left. The interest cost is $6.62.

Proof: $I = S(i)(n)$

$I = \$662(.06)(\frac{60}{360})$

$I = \$662(.06)(\frac{1}{6})$

$I = \$662(.01)$

$I = \$6.62$

This short-cut method may also be applied to the computation of interest on loans for terms which are convenient multiples of 60 days (30 days is one-half as much, 90 days is one and one-half times as much, and 120 days is twice as much). The interest for 6 days is $\frac{1}{60}$ of the annual amount, and if the annual rate is 6 per cent, interest for 6 days is .001 of the principal. This mental computation can also be applied to periods which are convenient multiples of 6 days. Likewise, mental calculations can be made for interest rates which are convenient multiples of 6 per cent. For example, interest at 3 per cent for 60 days is one-half as much as interest at 6 per cent for 60 days.

Recording interest-bearing notes payable

The following entries are based on the facts of Example 1.

```
19x1                              (1)
Oct.  1  A, Cash................................... 1,000
            L, Notes Payable to Banks.............         1,000
         Borrowed $1,000 on a one-year, 6% note.

                                  (2)
Dec. 31  OE, Interest Expense......................    15
            L, Accrued Interest Payable............         15
         To record the interest expense applicable to
         three months of 19x1 and the corresponding
         liability at the end of the year.
```

In the Income Statement for 19x1, Interest Expense would be shown as $15. In the December 31, 19x1, Statement of Financial Position, the facts would be shown as follows:

LIABILITIES

Notes Payable to Banks................................. $1,000
Accrued Interest Payable...............................   15

Bonds Payable

Bonds are similar to promissory notes in that they represent formal written promises to pay a certain sum of money, the *par* or face amount, at a specified due date, the *maturity*. As a rule, they also involve a promise to pay periodic interest at a stated percentage of the face amount at stated intervals. Corporate bonds usually provide for the semiannual payment of interest. A contract, called an *indenture*, between the borrowing company and the group of creditors, sets forth the terms with which the debtor is to comply. The *trustee*, an intermediary between the borrower and the lender, is appointed to see that the borrower complies with the provisions of the indenture.

Bonds are usually issued for long periods, and during this time the going rate of interest at which money is lent frequently changes. Since the bonds contain a fixed promise to pay a certain dollar amount of "interest" during the entire life of the contract, changes in the current rate of interest are reflected by changes in the market price at which the bonds change hands. If the market interest rate increases, a bond contract promising its holder a fixed number of dollars is worth less. If the market interest rate declines, the value of the bond increases. Thus, an investor may pay more (a *premium*) or less (a *discount*) for a bond than its face amount, which he will collect if he holds the bond until maturity.

The amount of the *premium* paid for a bond is, in effect, an adjustment to reduce the periodic cash payment for "interest" to the true amount of interest reflected in the market price at which the bond changed hands. The borrower treats the premium as a *reduction of interest expense* over the life of the bonds, and the investor accounts for it as a *reduction of interest revenue*. Similarly, bond *discount* is *additional interest expense* to the lender and *additional interest revenue* to the borrower. The entries of the borrower and lender under bond contracts in situations involving both premiums and discounts are illustrated in a later chapter.

CLASSIFYING AND MEASURING OWNERS' EQUITY

General sources of owners' equity

Owners' equity shows the amount of the net assets of the business which have been derived from two principal sources: *owners' investment* in the business and *retained income*. Retained income, in turn, is the cumulative excess of the *income* (positive or negative) of the business over its *income distributions*. Periodic income is the difference between *revenue*, the inflow of net assets into the business in exchange for its products and services, and *expired costs*. *Income distributions* are amounts returned to the owners as a result of successful business operations.

The balance of the owners' investment account and the balance of Retained Income, after closing entries for the period have been made, show the *status*, or cumulative amount, of each at the date of closing.

The Income and Income Distributions accounts show the *changes* that have occurred in owners' equity from the stated causes during the current accounting period. The Income account is used at the end of the period to summarize the revenues and expired costs. Because earning an income is the prime objective of business, management's interest focuses on the details of revenues and expired costs perhaps more than on any other group of accounts. At the end of each accounting period the accounts which show changes in owners' equity, having served their purpose, are closed to the accounts which show the status of owners' equity at the end of the period.

Bases of classification

Legal provisions are the dominant influence on the classification of owners' equity accounts which show owners' investment, retained income, and income distributions. The particular accounts used depend chiefly upon the legal form under which the business is organized—usually, individual proprietorship, partnership, or corporation. For each of these legal forms of business, separate accounts are used to reflect the owners' investment, retained income, and income distributions applicable to groups of owners with different legal rights.

Economic factors are the chief determinants of the particular accounts which are used in classifying revenues and expired costs, and these factors are largely the same whether the business is an individual proprietorship, a partnership, or a corporation.

The basic methods of classifying and measuring owners' equity accounts as they are influenced by the different legal forms of business organization are discussed next.

Owners' equity accounts of sole proprietorships

Up to this point, the titles *owners' investment* and *retained income* have been used to refer to the major sources of owners' equity for any business organization. Economically, these types of owners' equity are the same without regard to the legal form of the business organization. Legally, however, there are important restrictions upon some types of owners' equity which must be reflected in the accounts.

The law does not recognize an *individual proprietorship* as having any status apart from the personal financial affairs of the owner. A creditor of the business may look to the owner's personal assets as well as to those of the business for the satisfaction of his claims, and a personal creditor may depend on the assets of the business as well as on the personal assets of its proprietor. Unless he has special agreements to the contrary with some of his creditors, such as banks, the owner may withdraw business assets for his personal use whether or not the business has any income for the current period or any cumulative retained income. For this reason, it is common practice for the owner's investment and retained income accounts of a sole proprietorship to be merged under the title *Capital*, preceded by the name of the owner. In the interest of managing his business affairs efficiently, however, it is essential that the owner avoid mingling them with his personal financial affairs. And although he is not compelled to do so, he may also wish to maintain separate accounts to show his direct investment and the retained income of the business.

The withdrawals of the individual proprietor, whether they are from retained income or from investment, are usually shown in a *Drawing* account. This account provides useful information about the amount of the owner's withdrawals during the current period.

The following entries illustrate the typical method of recording the owner's investments and withdrawals and the periodic closing entries of a sole proprietorship.

(3)

A, Cash...	10,000	
OE, John Durham, Capital....................		10,000

John Durham invested cash to form a business.

(4)

| OE, John Durham, Drawing (19x1)................ | 300 | |
| A, Cash... .... | | 300 |

The owner withdrew business cash for personal use.

(C1)

| OE, Income (19x1)............................... | 2,100 | |
| OE, John Durham, Capital... . ... | | 2,100 |

The credit balance of the Income account after the
revenue and expense accounts were closed, representing the net income for the period, is closed to the
owner's Capital account.

(C2)

| OE, John Durham, Capital........................ | 300 | |
| OE, John Durham, Drawing (19x1)............. | | 300 |

The debit balance of the Drawing account, showing
the owner's withdrawals during the period, is closed to
the owner's Capital account.

The owners' equity accounts which result from posting these journal
entries are as follows:

OE, John Durham, Capital

(C2)	300		(3)	10,000
			(C1)	2,100
				12,100
		Balance, 11,800		

OE, John Durham, Drawing (19x1)

| (4) | 300 | | (C2) | 300 |

OE, Income (19x1)

		(Balance after closing		
		revenues and ex-		
(C1)	2,100	penses)		2,100

The two accounts which show changes in owners' equity, Drawing and
Income, have now been closed. The $11,800 credit balance in the Capital
account shows the status of John Durham's equity in the business, resulting from direct investment and retained income, at the end of the accounting period.

Owners' equity accounts of partnerships

A *partnership* is an association of two or more persons as co-owners to
carry on a business for the purpose of earning income. Partnerships are

much more complex legally than are proprietorships, but the law does not recognize the partnership as a being or entity apart from its owners.

A legally recognized partnership may result from an express oral or written contract or an implied contract between the co-owners. The rights and obligations of each partner are spelled out in the partnership contract and in the law of the state in which the partnership is organized. It is wise for the partners to specify in their agreement what share of the income each is to receive, along with other important provisions. However, if the partners fail to state how income is to be divided, the law holds that an equal share belongs to each partner. In the absence of a specific provision, a partnership net loss is divided in the same manner as a net income.

Creditors of a partnership, like those of a sole proprietorship, are not limited to the assets of the business in seeking satisfaction of their claims. If the business has insufficient resources for paying its debts, creditors may require that the personal assets of any *general* partner be used for this purpose. If, as a result, a partner is required to pay more than his share of partnership losses as provided in the partnership agreement, he has a claim against his fellow partners for the excess.

In *limited* partnerships, the personal assets of a limited partner may not be seized by partnership creditors. The loss to such a partner is limited by contract to his investment in the business. In all partnerships, however, there must be at least one *general* partner, whose liability for losses is unlimited.

The owners' equity accounts of a partnership are merely multiples of those of a sole proprietorship. If there are two partners, each has a Capital and a Drawing account; and if there are three partners or more, there are three or more sets of Capital and Drawing accounts.

If a partner lends money to the partnership, the equity should be designated as a Loan account, rather than as a part of Capital, to show the temporary nature of the advance. This distinction may be made even more clearly if the partner requires the partnership to give him a promissory note as evidence of the loan.

The following relevant accounts of Marks and Green, before closing, are used as a basis for illustrating the closing entries of a partnership. The partnership agreement provides that Marks shall receive ¼ of the net income of the partnership and Green, ¾.

OE, W. J. Marks, Capital

19x1			
Jan.	1	Balance	14,000
Mar.	7		5,000
			19,000

OE, W. J. Marks, Drawing (19x1)

19x1			
Apr. 9	1,500		
Nov. 26	1,000		
	2,500		

OE, A. L. Green, Capital

		19x1	
		Jan. 1 Balance	18,200

OE, A. L. Green, Drawing (19x1)

19x1			
Dec. 5	2,000		

OE, Income (19x1)

	19x1	
	Dec. 31 (Balance after closing revenues and expenses)	8,000

The closing journal entries are as follows:

(C3)

OE, Income (19x1)...............................	8,000	
OE, W. J. Marks, Capital......................		2,000
OE, A. L. Green, Capital......................		6,000

To close the net income to the partners' capitals in the agreed proportion, ¼ to Marks and ¾ to Green.

(C4)

OE, W. J. Marks, Capital..........................	2,500	
OE, W. J. Marks, Drawing (19x1)...............		2,500

To close Marks' drawing account to his capital.

(C5)

OE, A. L. Green, Capital..	2,000	
OE, A. L. Green, Drawing (19x1)......		2,000

To close Green's drawing account to his capital.

Statement of Partners' Capitals

It is usually desirable to prepare a Statement of Partners' Capitals as one of the general-purpose financial statements of a partnership, in addition to the Income Statement and the Statement of Financial Position. This statement is similar to the Statement of Retained Income, but broader. It begins with the partners' capital balances at the first of the period, shows their additional investments, shares of income, and withdrawals, and concludes with the partners' capital balances at the end of the period. The following statement was prepared from the account balances of Marks and Green. The ending capital balances would then be

MARKS AND GREEN
Statement of Partners' Capitals
For the Year Ended December 31, 19x1

	W. J. Marks	A. L. Green	Totals
Capital balances, January 1.......	$14,000	$18,200	$32,200
Add:			
Additional investments.........	5,000	0	5,000
Share of net income............	2,000	6,000	8,000
Totals......................	$21,000	$24,200	$45,200
Deduct drawings...............	2,500	2,000	4,500
Capital balances, Dec. 31.........	$18,500	$22,200	$40,700

shown in the owners' equity section of the December 31 Statement of Financial Position, cross-referenced to the Statement of Partners' Capitals for further details.

A Statement of Owner's Capital may be prepared for an individual proprietorship if desired, or the details may be shown in the owner's equity section of the Statement of Financial Position.

Owners' equity accounts of corporations

In the eyes of the law, a corporation is a separate legal person which can own property, owe debts, sue, and be sued. The sums invested in the business belong to the corporation, and the debts it contracts are debts of the corporation as a separate person or entity. Creditors can collect their claims only from the assets of the corporation; when these assets are exhausted, the creditors have no recourse against the personal assets of the owners. This means that an owner of a corporation can lose only the sum he invests in the corporation. In a proprietorship or general partnership he can lose all of his investment in the business and all of his personal assets, as well. This *limited liability* feature has induced owners to commit their funds to form the corporations which carry on most of today's business.

The law does not give this privilege of limited liability to corporation owners without exacting from them a corresponding responsibility to creditors. This responsibility is a requirement that the owners' investment in the corporation, on which the creditors rely as a cushion of protection in extending credit, will not be reduced by withdrawals. Distributions to owners can usually be made only to the extent that the corporation has a balance in Retained Income.[1] Of course, net losses may reduce the total

---

[1] This is an oversimplification, because each state has its own legal provisions as to when dividends may be paid. The statement here expresses the general philosophy of these laws.

owners' equity of the corporation below the amount of direct investment, but the limitation of dividends to undistributed earnings provides some assurance that the owners will not voluntarily reduce the margin of protection of the creditors.

Each owner of a corporation receives shares of *capital stock* as evidence of his ownership. If the stockholders of a corporation collectively own 100 shares, an individual who holds one share owns one per cent of the corporation's owners' equity.

The corporation's entry to record the issuance of stock to investors would be:

```
19x1                          (5)
Jan.   5   A, Cash..................................  5,000
               OE, Capital Stock......................         5,000
               Issued shares of capital stock to the owners
               as evidence of their investment.
```

For the present, illustrations will credit the entire amount received upon the issuance of stock to the Capital Stock account. Occasionally this credit is divided between OE, Capital Stock—Par and OE, Capital Stock—Premium, or some other owners' equity account which represents a part of the owners' original investment. Further attention is given to this matter in a later chapter.

If a corporation issues more than one class of stock, separate accounts should be used for each, such as Capital Stock, Preferred, and Capital Stock, Common.

Other typical owners' equity entries for a corporation follow.

```
19x1                          (6)
Dec. 31   OE, Income (19x1)........................  1,800
               OE, Retained Income...................         1,800
               To close the credit balance of the Income
               account, representing the net income of the
               first year of operations, to Retained Income.

19x2                          (7)
Jan. 15   OE, Dividends (19x2)......................   500
               L, Dividends Payable..................          500
               The board of directors declared a dividend
               equal to 10% of the corporation's capital
               stock, to be paid on February 1.

                              (8)
Feb.   1   L, Dividends Payable......................   500
               A, Cash................................          500
               The dividend was paid in cash.

                              (9)
Dec. 31   OE, Retained Income.......................   500
               OE, Dividends (19x2)..................          500
               To close Dividends to Retained Income.
```

(10)

Dec. 31   OE, Retained Income...................... 900
           OE, Income (19x2).....................   900
           To close the debit balance of the Income
           account, representing the net loss of the
           second year, to Retained Income.

Generally a corporation must have a positive, or credit, balance in Retained Income before it can legally declare a dividend. The legality of a proposed dividend is just one factor, however. There can be no dividend unless the board of directors takes formal action to declare one, and the board must be satisfied that the declaration of a dividend is legal, desirable, and practical in view of the corporation's available resources and its other requirements.

Retained Income is often mistakenly thought to be money available for the payment of dividends. Actually, all equities show the *sources* of business assets; the amount of money the business owns is shown in the *Cash* account. Furthermore, the Retained Income balance cannot be identified with any particular asset account or group of assets. Retained income is only one of the sources of net assets in general.

Summary of owners' equity accounts

The following summary compares the accounts which are used to record components of owners' equity for each legal form of business organization.

Type of entry	Equity Effect	Title of Account Used by	
		Proprietorship or Partnership	Corporation
Owners' investment..............	Credit	. . . , Capital	Capital Stock
Owners' disinvestment...........	Debit	. . . , Capital	Capital Stock
Income distributions.............	Debit	. . . , Drawing	Dividends
Income closed..................	{Debit or Credit	. . . , Capital	Retained Income
Income distributions closed.......	Debit	. . . , Capital	Retained Income

Bases of classifying revenues

Businesses need information not only on the total amount of revenue realized during each accounting period, but also on its chief sources. Typical sources of revenue tend to vary according to the industry in which the enterprise is engaged, as well as according to the types of activities which it undertakes. For example, a single business which sells a product, rents property, and lends money has three different basic, or *natural*, classes of revenue.

Revenues are classified for the purpose of enabling management and others to appraise the results of past operations, to plan for the future, and to control operations while they are in progress. As a rule, management is much more interested in a detailed classification of revenues than are other groups, because management must take the necessary steps to earn revenues that will help the business to achieve its objectives.

The classification of revenues should follow the *lines of responsibility* within the organization.

EXAMPLE 4: In the organization chart of the Suburban Department Store shown in Figure 4, page 103, particular responsibility for the control of the total Sales Revenue of the entire business has been delegated by the president to the manager of the merchandising division. The latter, in turn, holds the departmental manager, or buyer, of each of the four merchandising departments responsible for the Sales Revenue of his department. Individual Sales Revenue accounts are needed to show how each department manager discharges his responsibility. Their total shows the performance of the manager of the merchandising division.

Within the area of one manager's responsibility, separate revenue accounts are often needed for each important *activity or class of product*. This information enables the manager to evaluate past results and to decide which segments of his department need additional attention.

EXAMPLE 5:   The buyer of the Ladies' Wear Department of the Suburban Department Store would need information on the sales revenue of major classes of merchandise within his department, such as hats, dresses, shoes, and lingerie. He might also wish separate figures showing the sales revenue resulting from special lots of merchandise.

Revenue accounts can be further subdivided to report the amount attributable to each type of merchandise or to each minor activity. The extent to which detailed classifications of revenue are carried depends largely on the usefulness of the information to management in controlling operations balanced against the cost of obtaining it. Some companies set up ledger accounts to collect information for both major and minor classes of revenue on a continuing basis. Others prefer to keep continuing accounts only for the main types of revenue and to make periodic special analyses to determine the revenue of minor subdivisions, product classes, or activities.

Revenue accounts of different businesses do not differ solely as a result of differences in legal form of organization.

Common types of revenue accounts

The following broad classes of revenue accounts are frequently encountered in various types of businesses. Sub-classes designed to conform to internal organizational lines and to furnish product or activity details differ according to the preferences of the management of each business.

(1) *Sales Revenue.* Owners' equity realized by transferring products to customers.

(2) *Deductions from Sales Revenue.* Debits made to revenue *contra-accounts* to give information helpful to management in evaluating and controlling sales performance:

(a) Sales Returns. Cancellations of the original sales.

(b) Sales Allowances. Price reductions after sales have been made, often to compensate for damages to merchandise.

(c) Sales Discounts. Inducements to customers to pay promptly. If the business records sales at net price, after deducting the available discount, this account is not used. Discounts lost by customers are then credited to a nonoperating revenue account, Revenue from Sales Discounts Forfeited. If it records sales at gross price, Sales Discounts is debited for discounts actually taken by customers. *Trade discounts* on sales, like those on purchases, never appear in the accounts. Only the final price which they help to determine is recorded.

(d) Losses from Uncollectible Accounts. The amount by which Sales Revenue is estimated to be overstated because some of the revenue from sales on credit will never be realized. Many businesses treat such losses as an expense, assigning responsibility for their amount to the department head in charge of granting credit to customers. However, it is not an expired cost like other expenses, but unrealized revenue which was included in the Sales Revenue account.

(3) *Service Revenue.* Owners' equity realized by rendering services to customers. This item is applicable to businesses such as public utilities, whose principal function is to render services rather than to sell products.

(4) *Nonoperating Revenue.* A general classification which includes revenues from incidental sources and gains from disposing of property which is not intended for sale in the ordinary course of operations. Typical examples are:

(a) Interest Revenue.

(b) Rent Revenue.

(c) Royalty Revenue.

(d) Gains on Sale of Miscellaneous Assets. The excess of the sale proceeds of such assets over their unexpired cost.

Bases of classifying expenses

The purposes of classifying expenses parallel those of classifying revenues. The business management needs detailed information on the amount of expenses by types so that it can (1) measure the performance of the individuals who have responsibility for carrying on each phase of business activity, (2) appraise the costs of various segments of enterprise operations, and (3) initiate measures to control these costs.

Businesses show more individuality in their detailed expense accounts than in perhaps any other part of the classification of accounts. Few of these differences result from the legal form of organization. Many differences arise from the features of the industry in which the business is engaged, but most of them are caused by the preferences of the individual company managements for information that will permit them to control business operations effectively.

The customary bases of classifying expenses are according to:

(1) The *object*, or *nature*, of the service benefit used up. Examples are the *salaries* of employees, *supplies* used, and building *rent*.

(2) The *function*, or type of business activity which is carried on with the service benefits used. Examples are *purchasing*, *warehousing*, and *advertising*.

(3) The *organizational unit*, or department within the business, whose manager is responsible for controlling the expense.

As a rule, the expenses of a business are classified along all three of these lines.

Classification of expenses by object

Two advantages of the *object*, or *natural*, basis of classifying expenses are: they make it easy to decide in what account a particular item of expense belongs, and they group together types of expense which are subject to similar measures of control.

EXAMPLE 6: In controlling the cost of *salaries*, business management may seek to hire employees at more advantageous wage rates, or install time clocks to help insure that it is receiving the quantity of labor for which it pays.

EXAMPLE 7: In controlling the price of *supplies* used, management may install a central purchasing department manned by people who are trained in buying effectively. In controlling the quantity of supplies used, management may provide physical safeguards over the custody of supplies and their issuance to the operating departments.

Objects of expense for different companies are fundamentally very similar, but object classifications may be condensed into a few items or expanded into hundreds. The following object classification, recommended to its members by the National Retail Dry Goods Association, is a typical example:

Cost of Goods Sold	Traveling
Payroll	Communication
Rent	Repa·rs
Advertising	Insurance
Taxes	Depreciation
Interest	Professional Services
Supplies	Unclassified
Services Purchased	

Many variations of object classifications are used in business practice. Accounting for payroll costs and the related liability accounts, because of its unusual complications, receives further attention in Appendix 7-A.

Classification of expenses by function

The natural classification of expenses has its advantages, but management soon becomes aware of its limitations when attempting to use it as a guide to action.

EXAMPLE 8:   Upon examining its most recent Income Statement, the president of a company becomes alarmed at the size of the payroll, both in absolute amount and in relation to other expenses and to total revenues. The Payroll Expense object account gives him some clues to the type of remedial action he should take, but it does not tell him where within the organization to take it.

It may first appear to him that individual rates of pay are too high. He is likely to find that there is little that can be done about them because of prevailing wage levels in the community, contracts with the employees' union, and customary relationships among the rates paid to various individuals within the firm.

Usually the most fruitful line of inquiry is to find out whether there are employees who are not needed at all, or whose time can be used more effectively to produce greater income for the business. To answer this question, management must find out what types of work, and how much of it, employees are now performing. The next step will be to decide whether what they are doing needs to be done at all or to look for a better and less costly way of doing it.

The type of analysis described in Example 8 centers attention on *what is being done* with the service benefits used. Expenses classified on this basis are classified according to *function*, or type of activity.

The simplest functional classification of costs includes only *production* and *distribution*. *Production costs*, associated principally with manufacturing, consist of costs incurred in getting the product ready for sale. *Distribution costs* include all costs incurred by a merchandising company after the goods are purchased and are ready for sale and by a manufacturer after goods are produced and are ready for sale.

One widely used classification uses the functions of *selling, administration,* and *financing.* The following functional classification is widely used by retail businesses:

Buying	Sales Force
Stock Control	Handling
Building (store and warehouse)	Delivery
Publicity	Administration[2]

The use of a standard of performance, by which costs actually incurred for a measurable unit of activity are compared with a desirable cost figure, facilitates the appraisal of costs by functions.

EXAMPLE 9: The costs of the delivery function performed by a retailer seemed excessive, both as a percentage of Sales Revenue and as an average cost of delivering one parcel one mile. The manager of the delivery department and the controller initiated a study to determine what could be done to reduce these unit costs.

Classification of expenses by organizational unit

Within a well-organized business, the responsibility for seeing that each function is performed properly is assigned to a single manager. As a result, expenses which are classified according to function are also automatically classified according to *organizational units* within the business. A given organizational unit often has several functions to carry out, but the responsibility for carrying out a single function should not be divided between the managers of different units.

The classification of accounts must be such that the accounts can provide information to each responsible manager and to his superior as to the results of the functions over which he has control. Classification of costs by organizational unit helps to show how this responsibility has been discharged.

Combined basis of classifying expenses

A combined basis of classifying expenses by functions and organizational units is needed to facilitate appraisal of past performance and to localize the responsibility for future action. Additional classification according to object of expense helps the responsible manager to determine what type of action is needed.

---

[2] Rufus Wixon and Walter G. Kell, eds., *Accountants' Handbook,* 4th ed. (New York: The Ronald Press Company, 1956), Ch. 9, p. 7.

EXAMPLE 10: After careful study of the objects of expense, such as salaries, fuel, and repairs, associated with the delivery function referred to in Example 9, the delivery department manager and the controller decided that only insignificant reductions in cost could be expected if the company continued to make its own deliveries. However, a contract was secured with an outside delivery agency at a much lower cost per parcel.

Accounts illustrating the combined basis of classification are:

Buying—Salaries	Stock Control—Salaries
Buying—Supplies	Stock Control—Supplies
Buying—Communication	Stock Control—Insurance

Limitations on classification of expenses

Expense accounts lend themselves to almost endless subclassification, but practical limits must be observed. Individual expense accounts should not be used unless they serve a worthwhile purpose, as contrasted with merely providing interesting information. The classification should not be so elaborate that the balances of individual accounts are insignificantly small.

The contents of individual expense accounts should be defined sharply enough so that an item can be assigned to one or the other without unreasonable difficulty. The items classified within each account should be similar, except that an Unclassified, or Miscellaneous, account always seems to be necessary. Such a Miscellaneous account includes expenses which do not merit separate classification. Its balance should always be relatively small, perhaps not more than one per cent of total expenses. If it becomes substantially larger, further classification of some of its components is needed.

The expense classification should be stable enough so that the results of successive accounting periods are comparable, but it should be elastic enough to permit appropriate changes as the business undertakes new activities, modifies old ones, or requires additional information for effective management.

One of the most important limitations on the extent to which expenses should be classified is the cost of doing the accounting work. Clerical expense increases rapidly as the number of accounts in the classification increases. The cost of obtaining additional details should not be greater than their usefulness warrants.

Other deductions from income

The long lists of revenue, deductions from revenue, and expense accounts in the preceding pages seem deceptively complete. These are types of accounts which many enterprises frequently use. Businesses sometimes encounter more difficult problems in classifying and measuring unusual expenses, losses, and other items. Examples are casualty losses, losses on the disposal of assets held for use rather than for sale, and corrections of errors made in determining the revenues and expenses of past years. For the present, merely let it be said that these special deductions and corrections usually require separate accounts.

Special expense accounts of corporations

The preceding sections of this chapter have emphasized the similarities of the revenue and expense accounts of individual proprietorships, partnerships, and corporations. The expense accounts of corporations which differ from those of unincorporated businesses are few in number, but they are usually significant in amount.

One type of expense which is found in the accounts of a corporation but not in those of other legal forms of business is *Corporate Income Tax*. The Federal government and many states impose an income tax upon the corporation as a separate legal person. Sole proprietorships and partnerships, not being legal persons apart from their owners, are not subject to income tax as business units. However, their owners are subject to the *individual income tax* for their share of the taxable income of proprietorships and partnerships. The latter tax is a personal expense of the individual owners, however, and not an expense of the unincorporated business.

Another type of expense which appears on the books of corporations but not, as a rule, on the books of proprietorships and partnerships is *Management Compensation*, consisting of *Officers' Salaries* and *Directors' Fees*. Even though an individual owns practically all of the stock of a corporation, the salary paid to him as an officer is considered to be compensation of an employee of the corporation, not of an owner. His compensation as an owner takes the form of dividends, a distribution of business income, whereas his salary is an expense, one of the determinants of the amount of business income.

Economically, the managers of businesses which are organized as sole proprietorships and partnerships often have the same relationship to their businesses as do the principal stockholder-managers of corporations. In spite of this, legal and other factors usually dictate that the amounts the proprietors or partners receive as compensation for management services be treated as *income distributions* rather than as expenses. One important factor is that the management salary which an owner pays himself is not determined objectively. Of course, the same limitation applies to the salary which the principal stockholder of a small corporation, acting through the corporation, sets for himself as an employee of the corporation.

It is also rare to find the asset, *Organization Cost,* and the expired part of it, *Amortization of Organization Cost,* in the accounts of proprietorships and partnerships, although they are quite common in the accounts of corporations.

Corporate income taxes, management compensation, and, to a lesser extent, amortization of organization costs are large elements in the measurement of the income of a corporation. Because these items are treated differently in the accounts of different legal forms of business organization, the general-purpose financial statements of a corporation are not comparable to those of an unincorporated business in the same industry. If it is desired to compare the income of such businesses, it may be necessary to use the amount of income of each without consideration of management compensation and corporate income taxes. An alternative is to deduct a reasonable allowance for management salaries from the reported income of the unincorporated business, and then to compare the operating results of the two companies without deducting the corporate income tax.

It is very important to keep these limitations in mind when comparing the financial results of businesses which are organized under different legal forms.

Summary

The owners' equity accounts, which show owners' investments, retained income, and income distributions, differ according to whether the business is incorporated or unincorporated.

The classification of business revenue accounts is not affected by the legal form of organization. As a rule, it is useful to classify the revenues of businesses according to broad source, class of product or activity, and the internal unit of organization which is responsible for the revenue. It is usually desirable to classify expenses along similar lines, showing the object, or nature, of the service benefit used in the performance of each significant function which is assigned to individual managers.

In comparing corporations with unincorporated businesses in the same industry, it is necessary to make allowances for corporate income taxes and management compensation, which are treated as expenses by the former but not by the latter.

APPENDIX 7-A

Accounting for Payroll Costs and Liabilities

Included in the *payroll* object account are salaries, wages, and, occasionally, the costs of employee fringe benefits, such as vacations and contributions to pension funds. *Salaries* refer to amounts of compensation per week or month paid to managerial, professional, and clerical employees. *Wages* refer to the pay earned by employees for labor at a certain rate per hour, day, week, or unit of production. It is usually not important to distinguish salaries from wages in the accounts; it is more important to know what type of work the employee has performed. *Commissions*, which are compensation based upon the quantity or price of items sold by employees, are usually debited to a separate account.

The proper measure of payroll cost is the amount *earned* by the employee during the accounting period, whether or not it has been paid in cash, together with the cost of related fringe benefits.

As a rule, payroll accounting is complicated by the fact that the business must serve as an agent for collecting many types of items, which it withholds from the employees' pay and later pays to the proper organizations. Examples are income taxes, social security taxes, union dues, and hospitalization insurance premiums which are assessed upon the employee but collected by the business. Although the types of such deductions are numerous, in principle they merely involve credits to appropriately labeled liability accounts when they are withheld, and debits to the same accounts when they are paid to the proper organizations. Because the many details of payroll accounting are often confusing, the following illustrative entries are presented.

	(11)		
19x1			
Dec. 31	OE, Salaries Expense.....................	10,000	
	L, Employees' Federal Income Tax Withheld.............................		1,000
	L, Employees' O.A.S. Insurance Withheld		300
	L, Employees' Union Dues Withheld....		100
	A, Cash.............................		8,600

Employees earned salaries of $10,000 for the month of December. Made the required deductions as a collecting agent, and paid the remainder to the employees in cash.

The *Federal Income Tax Withheld* does not constitute an expense of the business, although the total amount of wages earned by the employees does. The amount of employee taxes withheld must be determined separately for each employee, based upon the length of the pay period, the amount of his earnings, the number of personal exemptions to which he is entitled, and the applicable tax rates. Printed tables provide this information readily.

The *Federal Old Age and Survivors' Insurance*, also often called *Social Security Tax*, is assessed in equal amounts upon the employer and the employee. The types of employment and the maximum amount of compensation which are subject to the insurance, as well as the applicable rates, change frequently. The preceding entry was based upon the assumption that the entire gross earnings of the employees for December was subject to O.A.S. insurance, and that the applicable rate was three per cent for both the employee and the business. The entry to record the expense of the business is as follows:

(12)

Dec. 31   OE, Payroll Tax Expense...................   300
        L, Employer's O.A.S. Insurance Payable.   300
        To record the accrual of a business expense
        equal to 3% of employees' insurable wages.

Many businesses are also subject to an *Unemployment Compensation Tax*, part of which is payable to the state and part to the Federal government. Types of covered employment and tax rates are subject to change from time to time. The following entry illustrates the accounts affected:

19x1   (13)

Dec. 31   OE, Payroll Tax Expense...................   300
        L, Federal Unemployment Compensation
           Tax Payable........................   30
        L, State Unemployment Compensation
           Tax Payable........................   270
        To record the accrual of a business expense
        for unemployment compensation tax, pay-
        able to the state at the rate of 2.7% of tax-
        able wages and to the Federal government at
        the rate of 0.3%.

The details of the expense and liability accounts used to record these payroll taxes may be varied to suit the needs of the particular business, but the basic nature of all of them is the same.

The following is a typical entry to record payment of some of these liabilities.

19x2   (14)

Jan. 10   L, Employees' Federal Income Tax Withheld.   1,000
        L, Employees' O.A.S. Insurance Withheld....   300
        L, Employer's O.A.S. Insurance Payable.....   300
           A, Cash...........................   1,600
        Paid the liability for the previous month's
        O.A.S. insurance and employee income tax,
        as required by law.

Businesses must keep carefully detailed records showing for each employee the amount of gross earnings and the various tax, insurance, and other withholdings.

QUESTIONS AND PROBLEMS

7-1 Some of the terms discussed in this chapter are *purchase discounts*, *sales discounts*, *trade discounts*, and *bond discounts*.

REQUIRED:

a. Explain the meaning of each of these types of discounts, carefully differentiating them from one another.

b. Using illustrations of your choice, show how each type of discount would be accounted for:

(1) In the journal;
(2) In the financial statements.

7-2   There are many similarities in the accounts of corporations and partnerships, but a number of significant differences.

REQUIRED:

a. List in parallel columns all of the income statement accounts of a restaurant which would differ according to the legal form of organization.
b. List all of the statement of financial position accounts which would differ.

7-3

REQUIRED:

a. How does a functional classification of expenses resemble a classification along the lines of responsibility?
b. How do the two classifications differ?

7-4

REQUIRED:

Using such reference materials as are available, prepare a list of the principal functional classifications of revenue and expense which would be appropriate for each of the following types of enterprise:

a. A county government.
b. A municipal airport.
c. A telephone company.
d. A machinery manufacturer.
e. A laundry.

7-5   A company with a national sales organization consisting of 120 salesmen, who are grouped in six regional divisions, pays its salesmen a base salary plus a commission at a stated percentage of annual sales above a predetermined quota.

REQUIRED:

Describe in detail how this policy would affect the requirements of the revenue account classification and how you would recommend that these requirements be met.

7-6   Two of the functions which you find listed in the expense classification of a wholesaler are *warehousing* and *shipping*.

REQUIRED:

List the principal object accounts which you would expect to find under each of these headings.

7-7

REQUIRED:

Contrast the meaning of *business net income* as it is determined by the usual accounting practices of:

a. An individual proprietorship.
b. A partnership.

7-8

REQUIRED:

a. What is the difference between an expense and:

   (1) A loss?
   (2) A deduction from revenue?
   (3) An income distribution?

b. Give an example of each.

7-9

REQUIRED:

a. What are the limitations of a functional classification of expenses used without any subclassification?
b. What are the limitations of an expense classification solely along object lines?

7-10   The Flamboyant Company, a large department store chain, has retail outlets in eight cities, each under the supervision of a local manager. It also has a centrally located warehouse which ships merchandise as needed to each of the branches.

REQUIRED:

a. What types of revenue accounts do you think should be included in the company's classification of accounts?
b. What are some of the important features that you would recommend for its expense account classification?

7-11   The Dynamic Sales Company makes its sales primarily as a result of direct contacts by its regional salesmen with retail stores. The company has its sales territories grouped into five regions, each under a manager. The number of salesmen in each region ranges from four to nine. The company sells fewer than a dozen types of products and pays its salesmen a commission on each, the rate of which is a varying per cent of the sales value of the products, depending upon the difficulty of selling and other factors.

REQUIRED:

a. Outline a plan for classifying the revenue of the Dynamic Sales Company. What advantages and limitations are there to your plan?
b. To what extent should the classification of expenses follow your classification of revenues?

7-12   Thurston Corporation has a debit balance of $10 400 in its Retained Income account and a credit balance of $45,000 in its Capital Stock account. The company was founded 12 years ago.

REQUIRED:

a. Explain the meaning of each of these balances.
b. Show how the balances would appear in the corporation's financial statements.

7-13   Johnson Company, Inc., uses the calendar year as its accounting period, closing its books once a year.

REQUIRED:

a. Explain in detail what the following account balances taken from its Trial Balance on March 31, 19x1, mean. Indicate whether each balance is a debit or a credit.

Capital Stock..	$60,000
Retained Income..	20,300
Dividends...	1,500
Dividends Payable......................................	1,500
Sales Revenue..	20,000
Payroll Expense..	4,000
Cost of Goods Sold Expense............................	13,000
All other expenses combined...........................	5,000

b. From these items prepare the Owners' Equity section of the statement of financial position on March 31, 19x1.

7-14 The following accounts appeared in the Trial Balance of a business on December 31, 19x1.

	Debit	Credit
Clark, Capital.................................		$20,200
Clark, Drawing.................................	$6,000	
Dailey, Capital................................		12,000
Dailey, Loan...................................		4,000
Dailey, Drawing................................	5,000	
Income...		10,000

REQUIRED:

a. What was the legal form of organization of the business?
b. Explain the meaning of each account, and indicate in which financial statement it would be shown.
c. Show in journal form the closing entries that would be needed on December 31.
d. Prepare the Owners' Equity section on the December 31 statement of financial position.

7-15 The Grayson Insurance Agency is organized as a partnership. The following operating expense account balances were taken from its trial balance at the end of its accounting period, December 31, 19x1.

REQUIRED:

What constructive suggestions can you make as to the expense classification?

Advertising...	$ 933
Audit and Legal..	160
Automobile...	1,350
Bad Debts..	230
Business Promotions....................................	450
Depreciation, Auto.....................................	800
Depreciation, Furniture and Fixtures...................	320
Insurance..	390
Interest Paid..	240
Lights...	195
Licenses and Memberships..............................	200
Miscellaneous..	2,850
Office Supplies..	250
Postage..	48
Rent...	1,800
Salaries...	5,800
Taxes, Social Security.................................	174
Taxes, Other...	790
Telephone..	120
Telegraph..	12
Water..	36

7-16 Two of the accounts in the general ledger of the Wiley Corporation on December 31, 19x1, appear below:

OE, Owners' Investment

		19x1		
		Jan. 1	Balance	20,000
		May 11		5,000

OE, Retained Income

19x1		19x1		
June 30	6,000	Jan. 1	Balance	17,000
		Dec. 31		8,000

REQUIRED:

a. Explain the origin of the figures in each T-account.
b. Reconstruct the T-accounts as they would appear if the business were a sole proprietorship.
c. What additional information would be needed if the business were a partnership?

7-17 The Morrow Sales Corporation purchased 10 shares of the capital stock of the Taylor Production Company at the date of the latter's organization in order to have a ready source of supply of merchandise. The Taylor Production Company issued 180 shares of stock on this date, each for $100 cash.

REQUIRED:

a. Record the entries of both the Morrow Sales Corporation and the Taylor Production Company at the date the stock was issued.
b. Illustrate how these facts would be shown in the financial statements prepared by each company immediately after the organization.
c. During its first accounting period, the Taylor Production Company earned a net income of $8,000. Give the necessary closing entry on its books, and any entry that is appropriate on the books of the Morrow Sales Corporation.
d. Immediately thereafter the Taylor Production Company declared a dividend of $25 on each share of stock, to be paid in cash two months later. Record the necessary entries on the books of each company.
e. Show how all of the pert nent balances of each company would appear in its statement of financial position immediately after the declaration of the dividend.
f. Show the journal entries needed to record the payment of the dividend in cash.
g. Shortly after the receipt of the dividend, the Morrow Sales Corporation sold its stock in the Taylor Production Company to the Compton Company for $115 per share. Record the appropriate entries on the books of the Morrow Sales Corporation and the Taylor Production Company.

7-18 Three years ago, Walter Kopp and James Lindsey formed a partnership to carry on a business. Recently they have decided to incorporate.

REQUIRED:

a. After the incorporation, what account titles in their ledger will change? How?
b. What additional costs must they expect to incur immediately as a result of the change?
c. Assuming that the operations of the business continue at approximately the same level, how is it possible that the corporation would show a loss, whereas the partnership reported a net income?

d. What principal effects would the change have on the following groups:

(1) The management of the business?
(2) The creditors?
(3) The owners?

7-19   Your company issued bonds on July 1, 19x1, in order to obtain funds to finance the construction of a new building. The face amount of the bonds issued was $50,000; interest was to be paid annually at the rate of 5 per cent of the face of the bonds; and the face amount was to be paid back 10 years from the date the bonds were issued. Because of a sudden change in the going market rate at which money could be borrowed, the issue price of the bonds on July 1, 19x1, was $51,500.

REQUIRED:

a. Record in journal form the entry needed to record the issuance of the bonds on July 1, 19x1.
b. Was the market interest rate more or less than 5 per cent when the bonds were issued?
c. If a statement of financial position were prepared immediately after the issuance of the bonds, how should these facts be shown?

7-20   Realizing that paying off the bonds in Problem 7-19 would be quite a financial burden ten years later, your company started setting aside money each year so that a sufficient amount would be on hand when needed. On June 30, 19x2, it gave a check for $5,000 in exchange for bonds of the Okay Company due in 19x9. The face amount of the bonds was $5,000 and their annual interest rate was 4 per cent payable in cash each March 31.

REQUIRED:

a. Give the journal entry needed to record the purchase of the Okay Company bonds.
b. In a statement of financial position prepared on June 30, 19x2, how should these bonds be classified?
c. Because of changes in the market rate of interest, the Okay Company bonds could have been sold for only $4,750 on December 31, 19x2. How should this fact be reflected in the accounts and statements?
d. What other entries, if any, are needed on December 31, 19x2?

7-21   Barclay and Cottingham, partners, had a written agreement that their income would be divided equally each year. On December 31, 19x1, just prior to the completion of the closing entries, the following accounts appeared on the books of their business.

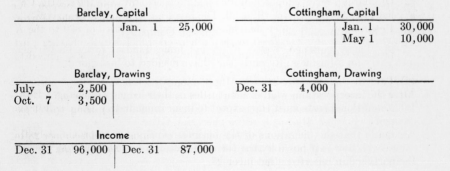

Barclay, Capital				Cottingham, Capital		
	Jan. 1	25,000			Jan. 1	30,000
					May 1	10,000

Barclay, Drawing				Cottingham, Drawing		
July 6	2,500			Dec. 31	4,000	
Oct. 7	3,500					

Income			
Dec. 31	96,000	Dec. 31	87,000

REQUIRED:

a. Give plausible explanations for each of the debits and credits.
b. Complete the closing entries in journal form and post them to the T-accounts.
c. What does each of the balances mean after the closing process is completed?
d. Explain why one of the partners might object to the way the income is divided after the operations of the first year.
e. Suggest alternative methods of dividing the income and give the conditions appropriate for the methods which you suggest.

7-22   The Howard Store, a retailer, made the following purchases during its accounting period ending on December 31, 19x1.

REQUIRED:

Show in journal form how each would be recorded in the records for 19x1.

(1) On November 8 received a shipment from the Davidson Co., list price $1,600, payment terms 2/10, n/30, shipping terms f.o.b. destination (requiring the seller to pay the freight). The invoice was dated November 6. Paid for the shipment on November 15.

(2) On December 17 received a shipment from the Evans Co., list price $4,000, payment terms 2/10, n/30, shipping terms f.o.b. shipping point (requiring the purchaser to pay the freight). Paid transportation charges of $55 on December 17, and paid the amount due on the invoice, which was dated December 14, on December 31.

(3) On January 2, 19x2, received a shipment from the Calvin Company, list price $1,000, payment terms n/20, shipping terms f.o.b. shipping point. The invoice was dated December 28, 19x1, and was paid on January 17, 19x2.

(4) On December 27, 19x1, received a shipment from the Franklin Co., list price $2,000, less trade discounts of 30% and 10%, payment terms 1/10, n/30, shipping terms f.o.b. destination. The invoice was dated December 23. Returned unsatisfactory merchandise having a list price of $200 to the Franklin Co. on December 31. Paid the balance due on the invoice on January 2, 19x2.

7-23

REQUIRED:

Journalize the following isolated 19x2 transactions of the Cosmic Corporation, which was organized several years ago.

(1) Issued additional capital stock to an individual for $4,000 cash.

(2) On March 1 received merchandise bought on account from the K Mfg. Co., list price $600, terms 2/10, n/30. The invoice was dated February 28.

(3) Returned unsatisfactory merchandise having a list price of $60 to the K Mfg. Co. for credit. Agreed to keep other soiled merchandise having a list price of $100 if the price were reduced to $70. The K Mfg. Co. agreed to make the price reduction.

(4) Paid the balance owed the K Mfg. Co. on March 6.

(5) Made a cash advance of $250 to a salesman for travel expenses.

(6) Later the salesman submitted an expense account itemizing travel expenses of $267. He was issued a check for $17.

(7) On December 4 declared a dividend of $5,000 payable on December 28 to stockholders as shown by the corporate records on December 20.

(8) Paid the dividend on December 28.

(9) Sold for $85 an obsolete piece of office equipment which had cost $950 several years ago and on which accumulated depreciation recorded up to the date of sale was $725.

(10) A salesman who was compensated on a commission basis sold merchandise on account for $3,500. Paid his commission of 10% of the sales price.

(11) Sold merchandise on account to a retail customer for $300, plus a retail sales tax of 3 per cent.

(12) Paid employees' weekly payroll in cash. Their gross earnings were $4,000, and deductions for their federal income tax of $530 and Social Security tax of $120 were withheld.

(13) Paid the total sales tax on retail sales for a month, $900, to the State Revenue Department.

(14) Bought a delivery truck for cash as follows: List price, $4,000; cash discount, 5 per cent of list price; sales tax, 3 per cent of net cash price.

(15) Paid an attorney $675 for a bill itemized as follows: Title search on lot purchased, $75; expense of defending company in unsuccessful damage suit brought by customer, $450; fee for securing amendment to the corporate charter to permit the issuance of additional capital stock, $150.

(16) As a result of a blowout, bought a new tire for the delivery truck for $45 cash.

(17) Purchased a heater for the truck costing $110 and anti-freeze costing $8.

(18) Paid $30 for having the company's name and other identifying information painted on the delivery truck.

(19) The estimated federal income tax on the corporation's income for the year was $19,100.

(20) On July 1 paid an insurance premium of $168 for the year beginning on that date. On July 19 received a refund from the insurance company for $18 because of a premium reduction.

CASE 7-1. KELLY AND STARR

James Kelly and Roland Starr formed a partnership on January 2, 19x1, to operate a retail specialty store. Kelly was to receive 30 per cent and Starr 70 per cent of the income of the partnership. Books were to be closed each December 31.

REQUIRED:

a. Record the following transactions for 19x1 in journal form.
b. Post to T accounts.
c. Prepare a trial balance.
d. Prepare an income statement, a statement of partners' capitals, and a statement of financial position.
e. Journalize and post closing entries at the end of the year.
f. Evaluate the first year's operations.

(1) Kelly invested $7,000 cash in the partnership, and Starr invested merchandise which both agreed was worth $10,000.

(2) Merchandise bought on account for resale had a gross invoice cost of $105,000. All purchases were on terms of 2/10, n/30.

(3) Sales for cash totaled $65,000; sales on account were $80,000.

(4) During the year the store failed to take advantage of purchase discounts of $450, but took all others. Unpaid accounts for purchases amounted to $6,000 gross invoice cost on December 31. The discount was still available on all of them.

(5) Collections from charge customers during the year were $60,000. Customers returned for credit merchandise which had been billed to them at $1,800.

(6) The partners estimated that one per cent of their credit sales, after deducting returns, would ultimately result in uncollectible accounts.

(7) Equipment bought on February 1 cost $5,000. The partners signed a note promising to pay this amount, plus interest at 6 per cent per year, on February 1, 19x2. The equipment was expected to have a useful life of 10 years and to have a salvage value of $200 at the end of that time.

(8) Salaries and wages paid in cash during the year amounted to $10,400. Unpaid salaries and wages at the end of December were $250. (Ignore payroll deductions.)

(9) Newspaper advertising paid for in cash amounted to $600. Advertising leaflets were bought for cash, $120, and three-fourths of them were still on hand at the end of the year.

(10) A business license for the year, $75, was bought in January. Property taxes of $350 for 19x1 were still unpaid at the end of the year.

(11) The partners signed a 5-year lease on their building on January 2, 19x1, agreeing to pay monthly rent of $200 in advance at the first of each month. All rent payments were made when due.

(12) The partners received permission from the landlord to install some shelving and other improvements to the building which would be permanently attached to it. The cost of these improvements, $3,600, was paid in cash. It was expected that they would be satisfactory for 10 years from January 2, the date they were installed.

(13) A 3-year fire insurance premium amounting to $1,620 was paid for in advance on January 2, 19x1.

(14) Each partner withdrew $7,500 cash during the year for personal use.

(15) The cost of unsold goods on hand on December 31, determined by physical count, was $21,000. Included in this amount, however, were goods which had been purchased during the year at a net invoice cost of $588 which because of shopwear were expected to bring only $250 after deducting the direct expenses of selling them.

CASE 7-2. THREE SALES DISCOUNT METHODS

The A Company, the B Company, and the C Company each allows its customers a discount of 2 per cent of sales when accounts are paid within 10 days of the date of the invoice.

In its accounts, the A Company debits its customers with 98 per cent of the gross amount billed them. If payment is made within the 10-day period, the customer is credited with the amount paid. If payment for the full amount billed is made after the end of the 10-day period, the customer is credited with 98 per cent of the amount paid, the remaining 2 per cent of the amount received being credited to Revenue from Sales Discounts Not Taken and shown on the income statement as an item of Nonoperating Revenue.

The B Company debits its customers' accounts with the full amount billed them. When proper payment is made within the 10-day period, the customer is credited with the full amount billed, the 2 per cent not remitted being charged to "Discounts on Sales" and shown on the income statement as a deduction from sales.

The bookkeeping procedure of the C Company is the same as that of the B Company, but on the income statement "Discount on Sales" is treated as an element of "Administrative and General Expense."

REQUIRED:

a. Discuss the theory underlying each of the above treatments of sales discounts, and state which method you prefer and why.
b. Using your own figures, prepare journal entries for each method.

(Taken from the AICPA Examination, Theory of Accounts, May, 1948.)

CASE 7-3. JOE HULING AND TOM MELL

Joe Huling had recently received a patent on a gadget with which he had been experimenting for several months. He felt confident that the public was ready for his product, but he did not have sufficient capital to manufacture or sell the article.

Joe recalled reading recently in the newspaper that a friend with whom he had served in the armed forces had inherited a sizable fortune. Fully realizing that he would have to make the sales possibilities of his gadget convincing, Joe decided to approach his friend, Tom Mell, for a loan. He wrote for an appointment and received a reply that Mell would be glad to see him.

After a friendly visit recalling past experiences, Joe got around to the major purpose of his visit. He told Tom about his gadget and his belief that it had excellent sales possibilities. He demonstrated how the gadget worked and handed it over to Tom for inspection.

Tom immediately became excited and remarked that it was most unusual that someone had not thought of the idea before. He agreed with Joe that the public would be attracted. His enthusiasm and interest made it much easier for Joe to ask for a loan of $10,000. Joe offered to pay a premium above the going rate of interest.

Tom indicated a willingness to lend the money. He stated further, however, that he believed that the success of the gadget would depend on an all-out promotional campaign, which would cost much more than the $10,000 requested by Joe. Joe's estimate had included only the cost of getting the product into production on a small scale.

After several hours of discussion, Tom offered to go into business with Joe. He agreed to furnish the necessary capital for the business if Joe would turn over the patent to the business. Tom made it clear that he would have no time to spend in organizing and operating the business and would depend on Joe to spend full time with it. Joe accepted Tom's offer and assured him that he would devote full time to the organization of the business and to its management. They agreed that the sales promotion of the product should be handled by a professional advertising concern.

The young men were quite enthusiastic over the future possibilities of the business. With Joe's patent and technical knowledge and Tom's money, they could only foresee success. Both agreed that the first step was to secure a business license and to begin the organization of the business. They decided to consult a specialist for advice about the form of business organization which they should select.

REQUIRED:

a. Write a report to Tom and Joe pointing out economic and legal factors which should be considered in selecting a form of business organization.
b. What will be their principal accounting problems initially, and how would you suggest that they go about solving them?

Chapter 8

General-Purpose Financial Reports

The need for reports

Unless there is an adequate means of reporting the financial facts of the business, the accounting system cannot adequately accomplish its objectives of aiding management in the control of business operations and furnishing information to persons outside of the business to guide their actions with respect to the business. To be sure, many of the purposes of accounting, such as the safeguards provided by the system of internal control, do not require formal or elaborate financial reports. Even if there were no financial reports at all, accounting would provide a useful repository of information about important business transactions. Succeeding chapters deal with the protective features of the accounting system and give examples of the wide variety of ways in which financial reports can serve the purposes of management. Such reports are often based upon analyses of projected future events, as well as upon the actual financial results of the past.

The accountant must consider the aims of each report in deciding how often it should be prepared, what information it should include, and how the details should be arranged. The present chapter discusses some general standards of financial statement preparation which apply to almost any report. In addition, it emphasizes the considerations which are important in the preparation of general-purpose financial statements which are designed to fulfill the general needs of investors, creditors, and other outsiders as well as those of business management.

Standards of reporting

The users of the general-purpose financial statements need assurance that these reports present reliable information. To provide this assurance, practicing accountants, professional accounting organizations, and groups representing important classes of financial statement users have developed standards of quality for report preparation. These standards must be observed even if the reports are intended to serve only one specific purpose, because a company has no control over the use of its reports after they have been released.

The basic standard for all financial statements is that they must disclose accurately and adequately all important matters which would influence the judgment of an interested and informed user, such as an investor, in arriving at his conclusions.[1] Standards which relate to adequate disclosure are inclusiveness, clarity, timeliness, materiality, and comparability.

Inclusiveness

General-purpose reports should include a summary of all the transactions of the company for the period for which the statements are prepared, accounted for according to the accounting principles previously explained. Reporting needs have an important influence on the particular ledger account classifications used.

General-purpose statements almost always include information about revenue and expense, presented in the Income Statement; assets, liabilities and owners' equity, presented in the Statement of Financial Position; and income, income distributions, and retained income, shown in the Statement of Retained Income. Other widely used statements are the statement of Sources and Uses of Funds, described in a later chapter, and schedules of cost of goods sold, receivables, investments, and plant assets. Not all of these reports are necessary in every case; the accountant must decide which of them will best disclose the information which the user is most likely to need.

Use of any accounting period, whether the natural business year or the calendar year, is an arbitrary way of giving information about where the business stands financially and what its past progress has been. It is arbitrary because few business transactions come sharply to a close at the end of any one period. The period is selected to present a cross-section of a continuing stream of events, so that statement users may form their judg-

---

[1] American Accounting Association, Committee on Concepts and Standards, *Standards of Disclosure for Published Financial Reports*, Supplementary Statement No. 8 (The Association, 1954).

ments about the nature, size, and direction of probable future business events. Considering this purpose, the accountant should by no means close his eyes to significant events which occur in the time between the closing date of the accounting period and the actual date when the statements for the period are completed and issued.

EXAMPLE 1:   An accountant is about to release financial statements for the calendar year 19x1, showing a net income of $50,000, total assets of $1,000,000, and total liabilities of $200,000. Because the work of preparing the statements has been complex, it has taken until January 30, 19x2, to complete them. Suddenly, on January 30, a disaster against which the business carries no insurance destroys all of its physical assets. What is the effect of this event on the financial statements for the year 19x1?

SOLUTION: Under the convention that only transactions completed during the period should be reflected in the accounts, the accountant would not record the loss in 19x1. Would statements prepared on such a basis fill the needs of a prospective merchandise creditor or investor in a distant city who examined the statements in February, 19x2, without first-hand knowledge of the disaster? It seems obvious that the answer is "No." Although the loss should not be shown in the accounting records for 19x1 in the same way as a completed transaction, it should be reported prominently in a descriptive note which forms an essential part of the 19x1 statements.

The disaster should be formally recorded in the accounts in *19x2* by the following type of entry:

```
OE, Loss from Casualty (19x2)......................... xxx
    A, (Various assets destroyed)......................      xxx
```

Footnotes such as that described in Example 1 are integral parts of the financial statements. Examples of other important events occurring after the closing date of the accounting period which ought, nevertheless, to be disclosed in footnotes or elsewhere in the statements are substantial changes in the form of business ownership, mergers, purchase or disposal of major items of property, and adverse decisions of lawsuits which require the company to pay damages.

Often events which occur after the end of a period give definite information about transactions which had been completed at the end of the year, for which the complete facts were unknown at the time. Such information, if available in time, should be used in the accounts and reports of the year just closed. An example would be the determination on January 7, 19x2, that a relatively large account receivable owed the company on December 31, 19x1, was definitely uncollectible.

Footnotes are also used to disclose some matters which have actually taken place in the year whose transactions are being reported but which have not yet reached the status of assets or equities under the accepted principles of accounting. Examples are important purchase contracts and long-term leases which require the payment of a substantial periodic rental in the future.

Clarity of presentation

The terms used in describing financial information and the arrangement of material in the statements must both be clear. Extremes of both brevity and elaborateness should be avoided. Often the exact titles of ledger accounts are inappropriate for use in the financial statements because they are too condensed to be informative.

EXAMPLE 2:   The ledger account "Bonds Payable" would be more adequately disclosed in the statement of financial position as "5% First Mortgage Bonds Payable due July 1, 19x5."

Ledger account titles which are too technical or cumbersome for the statement user should be simplified, but simplicity and conciseness of wording should not be carried to such an extent that exactness of meaning is sacrificed.

It is undesirable to combine so many financial elements under one statement item that important information is buried, and just as undesirable to present so many detailed items that the reader cannot see the forest for the trees.

EXAMPLE 3:   A certain industrial company has 20 types of prepaid expense and 12 different series of bonds payable. It would be more confusing than helpful to itemize these details in a statement of financial position. The items comprising each class should be shown in total as Prepaid Expenses and Bonds Payable, respectively. In addition, the details of the bonds are probably important enough to warrant the use of a supporting schedule, to which the principal statement should refer.

Usually the length of each individual financial statement is limited to one page or two facing pages, but there may be excessive detail even within these limits.

The classification of similar items into groups, the arrangement of items in relation to each other, and the location of subtotals and grand totals may also make the statements clearer. Just as the right-hand column is the most prominent one on the front page of a newspaper, a statement containing a number of figures may use several columns, with the more important amounts appearing toward the right. Varying degrees of indentation of descriptive captions are also used to denote relative importance. Such methods of achieving emphasis in arranging statement items allow the busy reader to look at the more significant amounts first; then, if he wishes, he may examine the details composing the totals.

Timeliness

Financial reports should be made available soon enough to be useful in solving current problems and in appraising the recent performance of business officials and employees. Although important for all financial reports, timeliness is usually more essential for internal reports for management than for external reports. In fact, incomplete details obtained promptly may be more useful to management than complete information received only after great delay. The qualities of completeness and accuracy are of little comfort if the information is furnished too late to prevent avoidable losses.

Many large companies supplement their comprehensive annual financial reports to stockholders with more condensed quarterly reports. In addition, they should release special bulletins to report major financial events affecting the company. Internal reports to management should be much more frequent. Complete financial reports usually need be prepared no oftener than once a month, but practically every management needs daily *flash reports* which summarize concisely such critically important information as the daily volume of sales, the current backlog of customers' orders, and the day's cash receipts, payments, and ending balance.

A company which cannot complete its reports within a reasonable time is not receiving full value for the cost of operating its accounting system. It should either streamline procedures so that the reporting process can be completed more promptly, or reduce to manageable proportions the quantity of information reported.

Materiality

Materiality is a practical guide which helps the accountant decide to what extent to follow recording and reporting methods which would be dictated by strict application of accounting principles. An item in an accounting report is *material* if there is reason to believe that knowledge of it would influence the decisions of an informed user of the report.[2]

Deciding what is material in accounting is a matter of exercising informed judgment, not of applying specific rules. The dividing line between what is material and what is not varies according to the company, the circumstances surrounding the transaction, and the use to which the information is likely to be put. Relative size is more important than absolute size in determining whether an item is material.

EXAMPLE 4:   A chair costing $10 may be an immaterial item of equipment in the financial reports of a company which owns total equipment of $1,000,000 and yet material to a company with total equipment of $1,000. Because its cost will benefit the operations of the business in future years it should, according to

---

[2] *Idem.*

principle, be accounted for as a long-term unexpired cost under the asset, Equipment. However, the clerical cost of checking on the custody of such an asset and of making an annual entry for depreciation might outweigh the usefulness of this proper accounting treatment in the case of the larger company. For convenience, this company would probably debit the cost of such immaterial items directly to an expense account at the time of acquisition.

In deciding whether or not the amount of an item is material, it should be compared not only with other similar items but with the total of items of its class (such as total assets) and with net income. A group of items which are immaterial as single units may be material in the aggregate.

EXAMPLE 5: If the million-dollar company in Example 4 owned several hundred $10 chairs, they would be material when considered together.

Materiality may be qualitative rather than quantitative. A transaction small in amount may be important if it is unexpected or improper, or if it violates a law or contract. It also may be material because, although small, it indicates the probable course of future events or a significant change in business practice.[3]

An illustration which involves both materiality and clarity is the common practice of rounding off amounts in financial statements to the nearest dollar. It is usually easier for the statement reader to grasp the size and relative importance of an amount that has been rounded than of one that is expressed in dollars and cents, as the following table shows:

	(Not rounded)	(Rounded to the nearest dollar)
Cash	$1,726,032.87	$1,726,033
Accounts Receivable, Trade	4,591,191.34	4,591,191
Inventories	7,005,993.96	7,005,994

Although it is not considered acceptable in the primary financial statements, rounding of amounts to the nearest thousand dollars for special analyses would be still clearer, thus:

	(Rounded to the nearest thousand dollars)
Cash	$1,726
Accounts Receivable, Trade	4,591
Inventories	7,006

Sometimes amounts in financial statements give a false appearance of exactness, while actually they are based upon estimates that are only rough approximations. An example is Depreciation, which is measured on

---

[3] *Idem.*

the basis of an indefinite future life which is expressed in whole years and an estimated salvage value in the distant future. Of course, some accounts, such as Cash, can be measured accurately to the penny.

It is customary to maintain the ledger accounts in terms of dollars and cents, and to round amounts only in the financial statements.

Comparability

Raw figures alone usually do not mean much. The informed reader of a financial statement is not especially impressed to learn that the company has earned a net income of $10,000,000. To be meaningful, accounting amounts must be related to appropriate standards of comparison, such as:

(1) The same class of information for the company at other dates;
(2) Related classes of information for the company at the same date;
(3) The same class of information for other companies;
(4) Predetermined goals.

If these comparisons are to be valid, accounting data of the same class must have been collected and measured according to uniform standards of quality, or the reader must be given sufficient information to adjust them to a comparable basis.

EXAMPLE 6: In 19x1 and prior years, a business considered all items of equipment which cost under $10 to be immaterial and debited them to Supplies Expense. If it changed its policy in 19x2 so as to treat all items under $25 as immaterial, its financial statements in 19x2 would not be comparable with those of earlier years. The account balances affected would be the following:

	Comparison of Amounts under New Policy with Those under Old Policy
OE, Supplies Expense	Larger
A, Equipment (cost)	Smaller
A, Equipment—Accumulated Depreciation	Smaller
OE, Depreciation Expense	Smaller

Example 6 is not intended to imply that a company may never make a desirable change in its accounting policies or procedures. The nature of such a departure from consistency should, however, be disclosed clearly in the financial statements, together with sufficient information to enable the reader to use the same basis of accounting in comparing the amounts before and after the change. Changes in accounting methods make comparisons more difficult and should be introduced cautiously.

Comparability of financial-statement items among businesses is also desirable but is subject to many limitations in actual practice. Often many different methods of measuring a particular asset or equity are used by various businesses, some resulting from different operating conditions and others from management preferences. These differences, although sometimes necessary, desirable, and acceptable to professional accounting groups, often place severe limitations on the comparability of financial data of separate companies. When a company uses a method significantly at variance with the prevailing practice in the industry, its general-purpose statements should disclose what method is in use and furnish data for making adjustments to a basis comparable with that of other companies in the industry.

Accounts are kept as if the significance of the monetary unit were constant from one time to another. Costs of assets acquired in different years, for example, are combined as though dollars of the same purchasing power were used to buy them. Changes of individual prices and of general price levels, especially rapid changes, distort the comparability of financial information compiled in such a manner.

Data for extended illustration

The remainder of this chapter explains the purposes, method of preparation, principal uses, and limitations of the three most common types of general-purpose financial statements: the Income Statement, the Statement of Retained Income, and the Statement of Financial Position. It is usually desirable to prepare these statements in the listed order, because the final result of the Income Statement is used in the Statement of Retained Income, and the ending balance of retained income appears in the Statement of Financial Position.

Illustrative statements have been prepared from the trial balance of The Corner Shop, Inc., a retail store, at the end of its second fiscal year, August 31, 19x3. Appropriate end-of-year adjustments for expired costs and accrued revenues have already been made.

One procedure for preparing formal financial statements from an adjusted trial balance is merely to select from the list of balances those which go into each statement. Marking beside each account title in the trial balance letters identifying the statement in which it is to be used (such as *I* for Income Statement, *RI* for Statement of Retained Income, and *FP* for Statement of Financial Position) aids in this process. A more elaborate method, the *Statement Classification Work Sheet*, is illustrated in Appendix 8-A. Under either procedure, account details can be arranged according to the outlines of major statement components, which are presented in the following sections.

THE CORNER SHOP, INC.
Trial Balance after Adjustments
August 31, 19x3

	Debits	Credits
Cash in Bank	$ 2,960	
Petty Cash	100	
Temporary Investments	1,000	
Notes Receivable, Trade	600	
Accounts Receivable, Trade	14,200	
Accounts Receivable, Trade—Estimated Uncollectibles		$ 900
Accrued Interest Receivable	20	
Advances to Employees	200	
Merchandise Inventory	17,600	
Prepaid Expenses	400	
Equipment	6,100	
Equipment—Accumulated Depreciation		500
Cash Surrender Value of Life Insurance	800	
Leasehold Improvements	1,200	
Organization Costs	300	
Notes Payable to Banks		10,000
Accounts Payable, Trade		16,700
Corporate Federal Income Tax Payable		230
Accrued Interest Payable		100
Accrued Social Security Tax Payable		350
Employee Social Security Tax Withheld		50
Employee Federal Income Tax Withheld		200
Capital Stock—Par		15,000
Retained Income, September 1, 19x2		1,030
Dividends	300	
Sales Revenue		116,700
Sales Returns and Allowances	4,100	
Losses from Uncollectible Accounts	900	
Cost of Goods Sold	71,500	
Advertising Expense	4,300	
Communication Expense	1,200	
Depreciation Expense	500	
Discounts Lost Expense	200	
Insurance Expense	600	
Payroll Expense	19,600	
Professional Service Expense	1,400	
Rent Expense	4,668	
Repair Expense	1,412	
Supplies Expense	1,300	
Taxes Expense (Other than Income Tax)	900	
Travel Expense	800	
Miscellaneous Operating Expense	1,600	
Interest Revenue		100
Gains on Sales of Miscellaneous Assets		200
Interest Expense	500	
Loss From Theft	570	
Corporate Federal Income Tax Expense	230	
Totals	$162,060	$162,060

The Income Statement

The purpose of the Income Statement is to show the results of business operations for the period being reported on. It presents information about various classes of revenues, expired costs, and the difference between the two, net income or net loss. In addition to management, present and potential owners and creditors of the business view the final income figure and its detailed determinants as a measure of management's performance in operating the business during the accounting period.

All of the groups interested in the Income Statement are concerned with it as a basis of making decisions as to *future* courses of action, as well as a means of appraising *past* results. Stockholders desire information which will help them estimate the probable future earnings, dividends, and changes in the resale value of their stock. Creditors wish to estimate the degree of financial safety of the business which will exist in the future to assure the payment of their claims. These estimates of the future are *subjective*, based on the judgment of the interested parties. Classification, arrangement, and description of the historical information contained in the statement can assist the analyst in making his interpretations and decisions.

Businessmen and their accountants have somewhat varied preferences as to the exact groupings and captions to be used, but most income statements follow this basic outline:

> Sales revenue
> — Deductions from sales revenue
> = Net sales revenue
>
> — Cost of goods sold expense
> = Gross margin on sales
>
> — Operating expense
> = Income from operations
>
> + Incidental revenue, gains, and corrections
> — Incidental expenses, losses, and corrections
>
> = Net income before income tax
>
> — Corporate income tax
> = Net income

The detailed income statement of The Corner Shop, Inc., shown on page 196, was prepared on the basis of this outline. This form of income statement is called the *multiple-step* form, since various classes of revenue and expense are added or subtracted in succession, and descriptive titles are given to the intervening totals or differences. The significance of some of these groups and captions is discussed in the following section.

Another common arrangement is the *single-step* income statement, in which the total of all expenses and other income deductions is subtracted from the total of all revenues in a single calculation. Advocates of this form contend that the multiple-step statement implies that items deducted first have priority as charges against revenue and that no deductions are attributable to incidental revenues. The single-step form is designed to overcome these objections.

Comments on income statement components

Detailed *deductions from sales revenue* may give valuable hints of weaknesses in the business operations. Excessive *sales returns and allowances* may give a clue to a great hidden cost consisting of lost time of the sales clerks and office force, losses from the return of shopworn merchandise, and customer ill will. A relatively large amount of *losses from uncollectible accounts* may reveal that the credit department has been too lax in extending credit or that the collection department is not doing its job effectively. The balance in this account may even be *too small*. It is sometimes possible that the increased income which would result from a larger volume of sales stimulated by more liberal credit terms would more than outweigh the added loss from uncollectibles.

Cost of goods sold is the major item of expense for most businesses, usually being more than half as great as sales revenue. It is deducted separately in computing gross margin on sales in order to reflect the results of the company's pricing and other sales policies and its purchasing practices.

THE CORNER SHOP, INC.
Income Statement
For the Year Ended August 31, 19x3

Sales revenue		$116,700
Deductions from sales revenue:		
Sales returns and allowances	$ 4,100	
Losses from uncollectible accounts	900	5,000
Net sales revenue		$111,700
Deduct cost of goods sold expense (see Schedule)		71,500
Gross margin on sales		$ 40,200
Deduct operating expenses:		
Advertising	$ 4,300	
Communication	1,200	
Depreciation	500	
Insurance	600	
Payroll	19,600	
Professional service	1,400	
Rent	4,668	
Repairs	1,412	
Supplies	1,300	
Taxes (other than income tax)	900	
Travel	800	
Miscellaneous	1,600	
Total operating expenses		38,280

Income from operations............................ ...	$	1,920
Add incidental revenue and gains:		
Interest revenue............................ $	100	
Gains on sales of miscellaneous assets..........	200	300
Deduct incidental expenses and losses:	$	2,220
Discounts lost............................ $	200	
Interest expense...........................	500	
Loss from theft...........................	570	1,270
Net income before Federal income tax.................... $		950
Corporate Federal income tax expense...................		230
Net income (to Statement of Retained Income) .... $		720

Operating expenses include the costs of carrying on the principal functions of the business. The expenses of The Corner Shop, Inc., are classified only along *object* lines to avoid introducing some rather complex accounting problems at this point.

Income from operations is the difference between revenues from the primary sources and the expenses of the principal activities.

Incidental revenue and gains are *additions* to income from sources other than the principal ones. A common type of incidental revenue is the interest revenue of an industrial company. While revenues represent the total amount received from a source, gains are the excess of amounts received over the costs of miscellaneous assets disposed of. *Incidental expenses and losses* parallel incidental revenues and gains, except that they are *deductions* in computing income.

Corporate Federal income tax is a significant expense of business corporations. It is usually set apart from other expenses in the Income Statement because of its large amóunt, which is frequently more than 50 per cent of net income before deducting the income tax, and because such separate presentation helps the statement reader to estimate the effect of future income taxes more accurately. Business proprietorships and partnerships are not subject to income tax, but their owners must pay personal income taxes on their shares of business earnings.

Extraordinary charges and credits

Neither the preceding outline nor the illustrated Income Statement included *extraordinary charges and credits*. These are "items which in the aggregate are material in relation to the company's net income and are clearly not identifiable with or do not result from the usual or typical business operations of the period." They must be excluded from the measurement of income if including them would result in misleading inferences.[4]

---

[4] American Institute of Certified Public Accountants, Committee on Accounting Procedure, *Restatement and Revision of Accounting Research Bulletins* (Accounting Research Bulletin No. 43) (New York: The Institute, 1953), p. 63.

Three examples of such items are:

(1) Material charges or credits of a nonrecurring nature which are specifically related to operations of prior years, such as adjustments of income taxes of those years;

(2) Material charges or credits resulting from unusual sales of assets not normally held for sale;

(3) Material losses of a nonrecurring nature from hazards which are not usually insured against.[5]

Excluding these charges and credits from the computation of income for the period gives, according to the advocates of this treatment, a measure of the *current operating performance* of the company. Opponents include such items in the determination of an *all-inclusive net income*. They argue that the sum of the net income or net loss reported for each of the years of a company's life should equal the total income for the period, as it does under their method of reporting.

If it were not for the fact that many individuals, newspapers, and financial analysts attach excessive importance to the single figure called the *net income* for the year, these opposing views could be reconciled. The disagreement emphasizes the fact that the income statement is a report, and that in order to get its full meaning the reader must examine its entire contents, not just the concluding income figure.

Limitations of the income statement

The income statement is useful for many purposes, but its user should be fully aware of its limitations. He must remember that, while the current-year income components are measured *objectively*, this measurement is nevertheless based upon the underlying assumptions and conventions of accounting, the principal ones of which are:

(1) That the business is an *entity* apart from its owners;

(2) That the *money unit* is an appropriate common denominator for measuring business results;

(3) That, for purposes of measurement, *continuity* of the business in the indefinite future, rather than liquidation, is the prospect;

(4) That measurements should be based upon *realization*, or objectively verifiable events.

Some of the principal limitations of these assumptions are summarized below.

The dividing line between the affairs of the owners of a business and

---

[5] *Idem.*

those of the business itself is in reality often indistinct, and so are the lines between businesses which are related through common ownership.

Many factors which are important to the success of a business do not lend themselves to measurement in terms of money, and the monetary unit is far from being a stable yardstick.

Income cannot be measured precisely for a business that is going to continue in operation. In an attempt to do so, revenues and costs are allocated to time periods largely on the basis of arbitrary assumptions about relationships and future events which may prove false.[6]

EXAMPLE 7: The periodic amount of depreciation expense and the amount carried forward to future periods as an asset are both based on estimates of useful economic life which are subject to substantial margins of error.

The significance of prospective events to the success of the business often far outweighs that of events which have been completed or are in progress.

In spite of the imperfections of the underlying assumptions of accounting, the Income Statement serves many useful purposes. It gives the user a reliable foundation upon which to base his own judgmental estimates about the future. The user who has studied the principles of accounting is conversant with the general nature and the limitations of the assumptions which have influenced the measurements reported in financial statements.

Schedule of Cost of Goods Sold

Many users of the income statement wish to know the beginning and ending inventory balances and the principal changes in inventory during the period. This information, derived from an analysis of the Merchandise Inventory ledger account, may be presented thus:

THE CORNER SHOP, INC.
Cost of Goods Sold Schedule
Year Ending August 31, 19x3

Additions to merchandise inventory during the year:		
Invoice cost of purchases......................	$74,100	
Transportation in...........................	3,100	
Total cost of purchases............................		$77,200
Deductions:		
Purchase returns and allowances.......................		2,600
Net cost of purchases......................................		$74,600
Add merchandise inventory, beginning of year..............		14,500
Cost of goods available for sale..........................		$89,100
Deduct merchandise inventory, end of year................		17,600
Cost of goods sold (to Income Statement).................		$71,500

[6] *Ibid.*, p. 59.

Often businesses maintain general ledger accounts for the major changes in inventory, such as Purchases, Transportation in, and Purchase Returns and Allowances. Under this procedure, the balance in the Merchandise Inventory account prior to closing entries represents the *beginning* inventory balance. A closing entry is needed to transfer the appropriate amounts from these accounts to Cost of Goods Sold Expense and to set up the cost of the *ending* inventory as an asset in Merchandise Inventory.

If reader interest warrants, schedules similar to the preceding one may be used to report the important changes in receivables, equipment, or any other asset or equity account.

Statement of Retained Income

The outline of the contents of the Statement of Retained Income of a corporation is as follows:

> Retained income balance at beginning of period
> \+ Net income for the period
> or − Net loss for the period
> − Dividends declared during the period
> = Retained income balance at the end of the period

Under the current operating performance view of income, extraordinary charges and credits would also appear in the Statement of Retained Income.

The statement of retained income of The Corner Shop, Inc., is as follows:

THE CORNER SHOP, INC.
Statement of Retained Income
For the Year Ended August 31, 19x3

Retained income balance, September 1, 19x2................	$1,030
Add net income for the year (from Income Statement).......	720
Total...	$1,750
Deduct dividends.......................................	300
Retained income balance, August 31, 19x3.................	$1,450

This statement sometimes also needs to show amounts transferred during the period to or from accounts which reflect *restrictions* (also called *reserves* or *appropriations*) of retained income. Such restrictions of retained income indicate expressed management policy, or sometimes legal requirements, that this segment of owners' equity is to be more or less permanently retained for specific purposes.

EXAMPLE 8: The management of a rapidly growing industrial company which had a Retained Income balance of $320,000 wished to finance a large plant addition by using assets generated as a result of profitable operations. To indicate to its stockholders that a corresponding amount of retained income would not form the basis for dividends, it instructed the accountant to record a formal restriction. The entry was:

```
OE, Retained Income............................  200,000
    OE,  Retained  Income  Restricted  for  Plant
        Expansion................................              200,000
    To transfer a part of Retained Income to an
    account  indicating  management's  reinvestment
    policy.
```

In the year of transfer, this item would appear as a final deduction in the statement of retained income. As long as the restriction continued, the presentation in the statement of financial position would be:

OWNERS' EQUITY

Capital stock................................		$100,000
Retained income:		
Restricted for plant expansion.......	$200,000	
Unrestricted......................	120,000	
Total retained income.....................		320,000
Total owners' equity..............................		$420,000

Statement of Financial Position

The Statement of Financial Position shows the forms of the assets in which the capital of the business is invested at the end of the accounting period and the nature of the equities, or sources, of those assets. Management, investors, and creditors look to this statement for an indication of the strength of the company's resources and the burden of the claims against it. Assets and equities are subclassified chiefly to provide this information. Comparison of successive Statements of Financial Position also shows important trends in the composition of resources by types and sources.

Users of the statement of financial position are interested primarily in forming judgments as to the probable course of future events. The nature of the company's assets and the contractual terms of its liabilities and owners' equities will have a very important influence on its course of business operations, its income, and its financial status in the future.

The outline of headings commonly used in preparing the statements of financial position of corporations is presented below. The illustrated statement of The Corner Shop, Inc., is based on this outline.

ASSETS	LIABILITIES
Current assets	Current liabilities
Investments	Long-term liabilities
Fixed assets	Total liabilities
Intangible assets	
	STOCKHOLDERS' EQUITY
	Capital stock
	Retained income
	Total stockholders' equity
Total assets	Total equities

THE CORNER SHOP, INC.
Statement of Financial Position
August 31, 19x3

ASSETS

Current Assets:

Cash in bank	$ 2,960	
Petty cash	100	
Temporary investments	1,000	
Notes receivable, trade	600	
Accounts receivable, trade $14,200		
Deduct estimated uncollectibles 900		
Estimated collectible accounts	13,300	
Accrued interest receivable	20	
Advances to employees	200	
Merchandise inventory	17,600	
Prepaid expenses	400	
Total current assets		$36,180

Investments:

Cash surrender value of life insurance		800

Fixed Assets:

Equipment (cost)	$ 6,100	
Deduct accumulated depreciation	500	
Unexpired cost		5,600

Intangible Assets:

Leasehold improvements	$ 1,200	
Organization costs	300	
Total intangible assets		1,500
Total assets		$44,080

LIABILITIES

Current Liabilities:

Notes payable to banks (current maturities)	$ 6,000	
Accounts payable, trade	16,700	
Corporate Federal income tax payable	230	
Accrued interest payable	100	
Accrued social security tax payable	350	
Employee social security tax withheld	50	
Employee Federal income tax withheld	200	
Total current liabilities		$23,630

Long-Term Liabilities

Notes payable to banks (noncurrent maturities due 19x3–x7)	4,000	
Total liabilities		$27,630

STOCKHOLDERS' EQUITY

Capital stock, $10 par, authorized, issued, and outstanding, 1,500 shares	$15,000	
Retained income (from Statement of Retained Income)	1,450	
Total stockholders' equity		$16,450
Total equities		$44,080

Current assets and current liabilities

Statement users wish to know whether the business has sufficient assets to pay its liabilities as they come due, with enough remaining to meet payrolls, to purchase supplies, and to pay other day-to-day costs of operation. For this purpose, the Statement of Financial Position groups together the *current assets* (those expected to be available to pay debts and operating costs in the near future) and the *current liabilities* (debts which will have to be paid from current assets in the near future). Deducting current liabilities from current assets (*gross working capital*) leaves *net working capital*. This is the amount of assets available, after paying these debts, to meet the operating needs of the near future.

A comparison with the reader's personal affairs may better explain the meaning of net working capital.

EXAMPLE 9: Suppose that your only means of support is a salary, which you collect once a month. On December 31 you have just received a month's salary of $400 in cash. During December you have made purchases on credit at several stores resulting in total accounts payable of $150. What is your net working capital, and what does it mean?

SOLUTION:

Current assets on December 31............................	$400
− Current liabilities on December 31........................	150
= Net working capital on December 31.....................	$250

You must pay your current liabilities promptly if you are to maintain your credit standing. Your net working capital of $250 is the amount of assets available for meeting your January living costs, such as rent, food, and entertainment. Your operating cycle is one month, the time interval between the periodic replenishments of your assets by receipt of your pay checks.

The length of the *operating cycle* of a business is important in deciding what specific assets and liabilities are current. Businesses are engaged in a continuing round of activities, consisting of purchasing goods for sale or productive factors for use, selling goods or services, collecting for the sales, and paying for the purchases, not necessarily in this sequence. The operating cycle of a given business is the average period of time which elapses from the beginning to the end of this round of activities. For a retail clothing store, it is usually several months; for a tobacco manufacturer, whose product requires a long period of curing, it is several years.

Current assets include cash and other assets which are reasonably expected to be realized in cash or sold or consumed during the normal operating cycle of the business. *Current liabilities* are liabilities which are expected to be paid from current assets during the same interval, or to require the creation of other current liabilities.[7] A business which com-

---

[7] *Ibid.*, pp. 20–21.

pletes several operating cycles in a year uses one year as the dividing line between current and noncurrent assets and liabilities. A business with a longer operating cycle, such as the tobacco manufacturer, might use two years or three years as the dividing line.

Other financial position classifications

Although most businesses use the *current asset* caption in their statements of financial position, their classification of the remaining assets is less uniform.

The *investments* section includes long-term investments, receivables which are not current assets, and items of plant and equipment which are not being used in the business. Sometimes this section is labeled *investments and other assets*.

Fixed assets are assets of relatively long life which the business intends to use in its operations rather than to sell. There is a growing tendency to label this group of assets, *property, plant, and equipment*.

Under the *intangible assets* heading are included long-term intangibles, such as organization costs and goodwill, which were described in Chapter 6. They have all of the principal characteristics of fixed assets except physical substance.

Long-term liabilities are obligations which cannot be classified as current. In the statement of The Corner Shop, Inc., they include the $4,000 principal of notes payable which is to be paid more than a year after the date of the statement. The $6,000 principal of the same notes which is due within the next year is a current liability.

Limitations of the statement of financial position

The Statement of Financial Position does not pretend to show what the business is *worth*. The value of any asset, or of a business as a whole, is subjective. It depends upon a projection of future prospects by the person who is estimating the worth. The expectations of each person making such an evaluation usually differ, and they frequently change from time to time.

The amounts in the Statement of Financial Position are objectively determined measurements about the past based upon the assumptions and conventions of accounting. Most of the individual assets of a business are stated at their *unexpired cost*—that part of their original cost which represents the proportion of the asset's services expected to be received by the business in the future. This statement does, of course, show the cash value of the monetary assets, but they are often a relatively minor part of the total assets. Unless the business intends to cease operations, its most significant determinant of value is its future earning power as a going concern.

The Statement of Financial Position does provide a useful *starting point* for subjective estimates about the future. There is continuity between the past and the future. Many of the contracts, relationships, and productive factors of the business which have shaped past results will continue to influence the business affairs in the future.

Summary

Although the details of the content, form, and arrangement of general-purpose financial statements may vary to suit the circumstances, such statements should meet the reporting standards of adequate disclosure. These standards relate to inclusiveness, clarity, timeliness, materiality, and comparability.

Typical general-purpose statements are the Income Statement, the Statement of Retained Income, and the Statement of Financial Position. Items appearing in these statements should be so grouped as to aid the reader's understanding of the progress and status of the business. The statement user should bear in mind that the Income Statement presents but an imperfect estimate of periodic income. Likewise, the Statement of Financial Position does not portray the current sale value of the business but is based largely on the unexpired costs of assets which are expected to be useful in the future. The primary statements may be supplemented by supporting schedules if additional detail is desired, and a statement classification work sheet may be used to facilitate their preparation.

APPENDIX 8-A

The Statement Classification Work Sheet

Purpose

Source documents of business transactions, journals, and ledgers are all formal, permanent parts of the accounting records. Financial statements, while not a part of the records as such, are also formal documents, usually typewritten or printed for their prospective users. A link between the basic records and the reports is the *work sheet*, an informal aid in summarizing and classifying information for presentation in the formal reports.

The work sheet is a means to an end, not an end in itself. It should be prepared only if it will facilitate the summarization and reporting process. Its design is flexible. It should be so arranged as to group information for ready transfer to the financial statements.

Method of preparation

The steps in preparing a classification work sheet suitable for The Corner Shop, Inc., *preliminary* to the preparation of its three formal financial statements, are:

(1) Secure a sheet of columnar analysis paper with a description column and at least eight money columns.

(2) Write a heading identifying the company, the nature of the work sheet, and the accounting period.

(3) Label the description column "Ledger Account Title."

(4) Label the first *pair* of money columns "Trial Balance after Adjustments," and additional pairs of columns with the title of each formal financial statement in which the account balances are to be used. In the present case, pairs of columns are needed for:

    (a) Income Statement;

    (b) Statement of Retained Income;

    (c) Statement of Financial Position.

(5) Label the first column of each pair "Debit" and the second, "Credit."

(6) Record each ledger account title and enter its balance as a debit or credit, as appropriate, in the Trial Balance after Adjustments columns.

(7) Add the columns. The debit total should equal the credit total. A separate Trial Balance is not necessary.

(8) Starting at the top, extend each account balance to the appropriate column for the financial statement in which that account is to be used. (Example: Cash, a debit in Trial Balance after Adjustments, is also a debit in the Statement of Financial Position columns.)

(9) (a) Compute subtotals of the Income Statement columns. If the credit total is the larger, revenue exceeds expense and there is a *net income;* if the debit total is the larger, there is a *net loss.*

    (b) Enter the net income in the debit Income Statement column and in the credit Statement of Retained Income column. The effect is to *balance* the pair of Income Statement columns and *transfer* the net income to the Statement of Retained Income columns. (If there is a net loss, enter

MERLIN, INC.
Statement Classification Work Sheet
For the Year Ended December 31, 19x2

Ledger Account Title	Trial Balance After Adjustments		Income Statement		Statement of Retained Income		Statement of Financial Position	
	Debits	Credits	Debits	Credits	Debits	Credits	Debits	Credits
Cash	2,000						2,000	
Accounts Receivable, Trade	12,000						12,000	
—Estimated Uncollectibles		500						500
Merchandise Inventory	20,000						20,000	
Accounts Payable, Trade		11,000						11,000
Capital Stock		15,000						15,000
Retained Income (January 1)		5,300				5,300		
Dividends	1,500				1,500			
Sales Revenue		60,000		60,000				
Losses from Uncollectibles	400		400					
Cost of Goods Sold Expense	40,000		40,000					
Rent Expense	1,800		1,800					
Salary Expense	6,000		6,000					
Other Expenses	8,100		8,100					
Totals	91,800	91,800	56,300	60,000				
Net Income, to Retained Income			3,700			3,700		
Totals			60,000	60,000	1,500	9,000		
Ending Retained Income, to Financial Position					7,500			7,500
Totals					9,000	9,000	34,000	34,000

its amount as a credit in the Income Statement columns and a debit in Retained Income.)

(c) Total the Income Statement columns.

(10) (a) Compute subtotals of the Statement of Retained Income columns. If the credit total is larger, there is a *positive balance* of retained income at the end of the period; if the debit total is larger, there is a *deficit*.

(b) Enter the positive balance as a debit in Retained Income to balance the pair of columns, and transfer it as a credit to the Statement of Financial Position columns. (If there is a deficit, enter its amount as a credit in the Retained Income and a debit in the Statement of Financial Position columns.)

(c) Total the Retained Income columns.

(11) Add the debit and credit Statement of Financial Position columns. Their totals should be equal. If they are not, an error has been made somewhere on the work sheet.

The condensed illustration shows how this procedure would be applied in the preparation of a statement classification work sheet for Merlin, Inc.

Use

After the statement classification work sheet has been completed and any errors have been corrected, it is ready to be used in the preparation of the formal financial statements. Each statement is prepared from the items classified in the appropriate pair of columns in the work sheet. Thus, all items in the Income Statement columns of the work sheet, and only those items, are used in the preparation of the formal Income Statement. Placing a check mark beside each item in the work sheet as it is used in the financial statements helps to prevent omissions and duplications. The formal statements are classified and arranged according to the illustrations in Chapter 8, but their components should be the same as those on the work sheet. For example, Accounts Receivable, Trade—Estimated Uncollectibles is a credit of $500 in the Statement of Financial Position columns of the work sheet but a *deduction from the related asset* in the formal statement.

Additional columns may be added to classify the items to be used in each supporting schedule. For example, if there are many *selling expenses*, they may be grouped together in a separate debit column preceding the Income Statement columns. The total of this column is transferred to the Income Statement debit column as *total selling expenses*.

Similar modifications of the columns used may be made to conform to the particular statements which are being prepared for a partnership or proprietorship.

QUESTIONS AND PROBLEMS

8-1 What is the major difference between the heading of an income statement and that of a statement of financial position?

8-2 What difficulties would be caused by rounding off amounts in transaction entries and ledger accounts to the nearest dollar?

8-3 The accounting period is an arbitrary device for showing a cross-section of a continuing series of business events.

REQUIRED:

a. List the types of transactions of a retail furniture store which would typically be completed entirely within one accounting year.
b. List the types of transactions of the furniture store which would usually extend beyond the end of a fiscal year.

8-4 The general ledger trial balance of a wholesale company consisted of about 100 accounts. The accounting department prepared monthly statements for the use of management, usually issuing them around the 20th of the following month. The accounting department frequently had to spend several days in locating errors so that the trial balance would balance, or in finding the causes of discrepancies in the records.

REQUIRED:

a. What criticism can you make of this situation?
b. What constructive suggestions can you offer?

8-5 A company has engaged a consultant on accounting systems to make recommendations for revising its chart of general ledger accounts.

REQUIRED:

a. In what respect should the consultant consider the standard of materiality in devising the new list of accounts?
b. What bearing does the standard of consistency have on this case? How would you recommend that it be observed, assuming that the company plans to change from an object to a combined functional-and-object classification of expenses?

8-6 Referring to recent published financial statements in your library, find examples of the following, and summarize the practices briefly:

(1) Clarity of terminology.
(2) Excessive simplicity of terminology.
(3) Excessive complexity of terminology.
(4) Excessive condensation of material.
(5) Excessive detail.
(6) Good arrangement.
(7) Poor arrangement.
(8) Violations of consistency between periods.

8-7 "It is impossible to measure income exactly for any business which plans to continue in operation."

REQUIRED:

a. Do you agree with this statement? Why?
b. List items on an income statement which can be measured with a high degree of accuracy.
c. List items on an income statement which are subject to a relatively large margin of error.

8-8 "The statement of financial position does not show what the business is worth at the date of the statement."

REQUIRED:

a. List items on a statement of financial position which do reflect current market values.
b. List items on the statement which do not reflect current values.
c. Should all assets be reported at their current worth? Explain.

8-9 The Largo Corporation is preparing financial statements for the year 19x5.

REQUIRED:

Describe how the following facts should be shown in these statements, and why.

a. The corporation changed its method of computing the cost of its inventory on January 1, 19x5, to the last-in, first-out method. In previous years it had measured inventory by the first-in, first-out method.
b. During 19x5 the corporation was required to pay additional Federal income tax for 19x2 because the Internal Revenue Service disallowed certain deductions that had been claimed in computing the income subject to tax.
c. During 19x5 the accountant discovered that the accrued salaries payable determined at the end of 19x4 had been substantially understated.
d. During 19x5 the corporation changed its method of measuring depreciation on equipment to the diminishing-balance method, so that larger amounts of depreciation would be charged to expense during the early years of an asset's life. The method formerly in use was the straight-line method, which treated an equal amount as depreciation each year.

8-10 "Grouping object of expense accounts into functional classifications in the income statement gives the reader the impression that some expenses are more important than others."

REQUIRED:

Comment.

8-11

REQUIRED:

State how you would classify the following items in the statement of financial position of Beauchamp and Meecham, retail grocers, for December 31, 19x1:

(1) Goodwill
(2) Payroll bank account.
(3) Liability for additional Federal income taxes for previous years.
(4) Pensions payable to employees who retire in the future. No employees have yet retired.
(5) Loan from Beauchamp. The company did not give him a promissory note, nor does the loan bear interest.
(6) Note payable to Z Insurance Company maturing in one lump sum on July 5, 19x4.
(7) Bank account accumulated under the terms of the note in (6) to pay the principal when it becomes due.
(8) Note payable to Seventh National Bank in equal installments on May 1, 19x2, May 1, 19x3, and May 1, 19x4.

8-12 In the standard short-form audit report usually issued by Certified Public Accountants, the opinion paragraph reads:

"In our opinion, the accompanying statement of financial position and statements of income and retained income present fairly the financial position of the X Company at December 31, 19x1, and the results of its operations for

the year then ended, in conformity with generally accepted accounting principles applied on a basis consistent with that of the preceding year."

REQUIRED:

a. What is meant by the terms:

  (1) Present fairly?
  (2) Generally accepted accounting principles?
  (3) Basis consistent with?

b. If there are inconsistencies between the financial statements of two years, what
action do you think the CPA should take?

8-13 Under the Current Liabilities section of the statement of financial
position of the Morton Company, there appears an account, Notes Payable,
$7,000. Closer investigation reveals that the note is a 60-day, 6 per cent note,
payable to the First National Bank. It has been renewed by the bank eleven
times. The manager of the Morton Company explains that the bank is willing to
renew the note indefinitely as long as interest is paid when due. He also states that
the company intends to continue to renew the note in the future, because there
will be a constant need for working capital, and the company is in no position to
liquidate the note at the present time.

REQUIRED:

a. How would you classify the note on the statement of financial position? Why?

b. Explain how improper classification of this item might affect the interpretation
of the statement of financial position.

8-14 Late in 19x1 a retail store decided to sell its store property and lease
another location. The store building had cost $60,000 ten years prior to the sale
and the land had cost $25,000. The accounting records had been kept on the basis
of an estimated useful life of 40 years for the building and no salvage value. The
property was sold for $82,000 cash, of which $30,000 applied to the land. Immediately after selling the property, the company signed a 20-year lease on another
location. The terms of the lease required payment of $4,000 annual rental at the
beginning of each year. The first payment was made when due on December 1,
19x1.

REQUIRED:

a. Show in journal form the entries needed to record the sale of the real estate and
the lease of the new property.

b. Show how this information would be disclosed in the financial statements of
the retailer for 19x1.

8-15 The cashier-bookkeeper of the Waine Company carefully completed
accurate financial statements for the company as of the end of its year, December
31, 19x1, leaving them on the president's desk on January 10. Total assets as
shown by the balance sheet were $300,000 and net income was $21,000. The bookkeeper-cashier did not report to work on January 11, and an investigation soon
disclosed that he had departed with $15,000 of the company's cash. He was not
bonded. Efforts to trace him were fruitless.

REQUIRED:

a. What consideration, if any, should be given to this situation in the reports of
19x1?

b. What accounting record, if any, should be made in 19x1? 19x2?

c. What would be your answer to (a) if the amount involved were $1,500? $15?

8-16 The following are the statements of financial position of three corporations. Although the purposes of each of the statements are similar, the corporations
use different formats for presenting their financial data.

THE BORDEN COMPANY

Consolidated Balance Sheet

December 31

ASSETS	1959	1958
CURRENT ASSETS:		
Cash	$ 36,294,489	$ 40,899,899
United States Government Securities	16,712,208	16,396,874
Receivables	61,668,206	58,486,257
(Less Reserves—1959, $2,825,019; 1958, $2,420,451)		
Inventories (Note 2) :		
Finished Goods	40,051,958	38,403,345
Materials and Supplies	29,464,176	28,608,363
Total Inventories	$ 69,516,134	$ 67,011,708
Total Current Assets	$184,191,037	$182.794,738
INVESTMENTS AND OTHER ASSETS:		
Unconsolidated Foreign Subsidiaries . (Note 1)	$ 1,723,147	$ 1,723,147
Securities on Deposit	1,693,160	1,517,862
(Pursuant to Workmen's Compensation Laws, etc.)		
Mortgages, Receivables, etc.	7,202,289	5,955,059
Total	$ 10,618,596	$ 9,196,068
Less Reserves	334,202	324,477
Net Investments and Other Assets	$ 10,284,394	$ 8,871,591
PROPERTY AND EQUIPMENT	$305,407,468	$292,358,752
Less Reserves for Depreciation	142,375,018	139,211,991
Net Property and Equipment	$163,032,450	$153,146,761
DEFERRED CHARGES	$ 3,361,678	$ 2,639,991
INTANGIBLES	$ 2,753,457	$ 1,370,715
TOTAL	$363,623,016	$348,823,796

See page 21 for notes to financial statements.

and Consolidated Subsidiaries

LIABILITIES	December 31	
	1959	1958
CURRENT LIABILITIES:		
Accounts Payable	$ 40,356,426	$ 39,847,806
Accrued Accounts:		
Taxes (after deducting Treasury Bills equal to U.S. Federal Income Taxes—1959, $13,100,000; 1958, $15,900,000) . . .	3,888,413	3,545,946
Other	15,527,309	15,145,897
Total Current Liabilities	$ 59,772,148	$ 58,539,649
LONG-TERM DEBT (Note 3):		
The Borden Company—2⅞% Debentures due 1981	$ 47,000,000	$ 49,000,000
Subsidiary—3½% Note due 1973	1,200,000	1,250,000
Total Long-Term Debt	$ 48,200,000	$ 50,250,000
RESERVES:		
Insurance, etc.	$ 6,893,260	$ 7,329,930
Deferred Federal Taxes on Income (Note 7)	3,187,143	799,543
Total Reserves	$ 10,080,403	$ 8,129,473
CAPITAL STOCK AND SURPLUS (Note 4):		
Capital Stock—par value $15 per share		
Authorized 8,000,000 shares		
1959 1958		
Issued 5,133,074 shares 5,083,757 shares		
Less Treasury Stock 233,074 " 223,757 "		
Outstanding 4,900,000 shares 4,860,000 shares . .	$ 73,500,000	$ 72,900,000
Capital Surplus	38,426,829	37,213,184
Earned Surplus (Earnings retained for use in the business)	133,643,636	121,791,490
Total Capital Stock and Surplus	$245,570,465	$231,904,674
TOTAL	$363,623,016	$348,823,796

Balance Sheet

FLORIDA POWER

ASSETS	1956	1955
UTILITY PLANT (see Note 1)	$359,505,047	$320,092,807
INVESTMENT AND FUND ACCOUNTS:		
Other physical property	$ 739,276	$ 488,071
Investment in subsidiary	477,220	477,220
Other investments and special funds	164,930	152,020
Total investment and fund accounts	$ 1,381,426	$ 1,117,311
CURRENT ASSETS:		
Cash in banks	$ 6,872,066	$ 3,494,302
Special deposits . . . . . . :	1,177,329	1,176,655
Working funds	165,260	184,088
United States Government short-term obligations	19,980,738	13,500,000
Accounts receivable—Customers and miscellaneous	7,827,006	6,726,973
Materials and supplies	6,128,135	5,643,480
Prepayments	853,557	893,226
Other current assets	438,178	245,636
Total current assets	$ 43,442,269	$ 31,864,360
DEFERRED DEBITS	$ 310,254	$ 82,612
CAPITAL STOCK EXPENSE	$ 958,002	$ 957,875
TOTAL	$405,596,998	$354,114,965

The accompanying Notes to Financial Statements should be considered in conjunction with the above statement.

DECEMBER 31, 1956 and 1955

& LIGHT COMPANY

LIABILITIES	1956	1955
CAPITAL STOCK AND SURPLUS:		
Preferred stock (details shown in Note 2)	$ 36,250,000	$ 36,250,000
Premium on preferred stock	118,450	118,450
Common stock, no par—Authorized, 20,000,000 shares; issued and outstanding, 6,000,000 shares	90,000,000	90,000,000
Earned surplus—Restricted (future Federal income taxes)—see Note 3	4,215,559	2,355,559
Earned surplus—Not restricted	19,847,177	11,632,691
Total capital stock and surplus	$150,431,186	$140,356,700
LONG-TERM DEBT (details for 1956 shown in Note 4)	$148,601,000	$119,163,000
Total capitalization	$299,032,186	$259,519,700
CURRENT LIABILITIES:		
Accounts payable	$ 3,586,046	$ 2,896,281
Taxes accrued	18,691,692	17,313,195
Interest accrued (including amounts for which cash is in special deposits: 1956, $1,058,799; 1955, $1,068,478)	1,800,052	1,594,783
Other current liabilities	1,449,507	1,935,182
Sub-total	$ 25,527,297	$ 23,739,441
Customers' deposits	11,462,886	10,174,817
Total current liabilities	$ 36,990,183	$ 33,914,258
DEFERRED CREDITS		
Unamortized premium on debt	$ 1,390,716	$ 1,423,292
Customers' advances for construction	247,391	158,203
Total deferred credits	$ 1,638,107	$ 1,581,495
RESERVES:		
Property retirement	$ 54,158,073	$ 46,635,760
Amortization of utility plant acquisition adjustments	5,071,947	4,582,078
Amortization of limited-term investments	68,689	60,343
Storm damage (see Note 5)	6,658,267	5,938,267
Uncollectible accounts	191,219	184,089
Inventory adjustment	161,240	185,273
Injuries and damages	711,861	739,085
Total reserves	$ 67,021,296	$ 58,324,895
CONTRIBUTIONS IN AID OF CONSTRUCTION	$ 915,226	$ 774,617
TOTAL	$405,596,998	$354,114,965

The accompanying Notes to Financial Statements should be considered in conjunction with the above statement.

Source: Florida Power and Light Company Annual Report, 1956.

Consolidated statement of financial position:

		Nov. 1, 1958	Nov. 2, 1957
Current assets	Cash..	$ 24,949,530	$ 15,583,268
	Accounts and notes receivable (less allowance for doubtful accounts $1,468,875 in 1958, $1,817,542 in 1957)............	80,899,034	82,846,691
	Inventories—certain products valued at cost on basis of "last-in, first-out", balance of products and supplies either at the lower of cost or market or at market less allowance for selling expense.		
	Products—note 2...................................	107,085,293	126,623,977
	Supplies...	11,296,187	15,070,277
		$224,230,044	**$240,124,213**
Current liabilities	Notes payable...	$ —	$ 27,249,134
	Accounts payable, including payrolls, interest, etc............	32,753,530	30,634,522
	Reserve for Federal income taxes.........................	7,916,119	3,206,383
	General and social security taxes........................	4,484,989	4,898,984
	Long term debt and subordinated long term debt payable within one year—notes 5 and 6.............................	3,633,246	6,718,409
		$ 48,787,884	**$ 72,707,432**
Working capital	Current assets less current liabilities......................	**$175,442,160**	**$167,416,781**
	Ratio of current assets to current liabilities..............	4.60	3.30
Investments	Foreign subsidiary companies—note 4......................	306,415	18,371,266
	International Packers Limited—note 4.....................	16,187,276	—
	Funds deposited with trustees of first mortgage bonds......	569,609	622,897
	All other investments (at cost or less)—note 8..............	4,241,771	4,385,460
		$ 21,305,071	**$ 23,379,623**
Plant and equipment	Land.................................... } At less than cost {	$ 22,426,322	$ 24,586,783
	Buildings, machinery and fixed equipment..	243,417,021	249,741,097
	Accumulated depreciation................................	(120,182,898)	(119,055,597)
	Refrigerator cars, delivery equipment, tools, etc.—at cost less accumulated depreciation.............................	18,242,073	20,120,185
		$163,902,518	**$175,392,468**
Deferred charges	....	**3,058,269**	**3,721,225**
	Total assets — less current liabilities	**$363,708,018**	**$369,910,097**

(See Notes to Financial Statements)

long term debt and common stock equity

ARMOUR AND COMPANY AND CONSOLIDATED SUBSIDIARY COMPANIES

at November 1, 1958 and November 2, 1957

		Nov. 1, 1958	Nov. 2, 1957
Long term debt (note 5)	First Mortgage Twenty-Five Year 2¾% Sinking Fund Bonds, Series F, due July 1, 1971..................	$ 42,500,000	$ 45,000,000
	First Mortgage 3% Sinking Fund Bonds, Series G, due July 1, 1971.......................................	10,206,000	10,446,000
	3½% Sinking Fund Debentures, due September 1, 1968...	26,000,000	28,000,000
	Purchase Money Notes, payments due in installments to 1968...	1,006,977	1,145,223
		$ 79,712,977	$ 84,591,223
Subordinated long term debt (note 6)	3½% Cumulative Income Debentures (Subordinated), due November 1, 1972...............................	16,954,000	18,339,000
	5% Cumulative Income Subordinated Debentures, due November 1, 1984...............................	58,463,520	59,181,800
		$155,130,497	$162,112,023
Common stock (note 7)	Par value $5 per share—authorized 15,000,000 shares, issued 4,677,409 shares at November 1, 1958..............	$ 23,387,045	$ 23,387,052
Capital and paid-in surplus (note 7)	Parent company and consolidated subsidiary companies...	39,370,463	39,370,463
	Foreign subsidiary companies (undistributed earnings)....	—	149,296
Earnings employed in the business (note 1)	....	145,820,013	144,891,263
		$208,577,521	$207,798,074
	Total long term debt and common stock equity......	$363,708,018	$369,910,097

Source: Armour and Company Annual Report, 1958.

REQUIRED:

a. In your opinion, which statement presents the financial information most clearly?

b. What are the principal advantages and features of each form of presentation?

c. Explain the probable reasons for the presentation of the assets and equities of the Florida Power and Light Company in reverse order.

d. What are the principal advantages, if any, of deducting the current liabilities from the current assets on the asset side, as illustrated in the statement of Armour and Company?

e. In the interest of clarity, what additional modifications to the common form of presentation would you suggest?

f. What types of financial position information do you think management will need in addition to that presented in these statements?

8-17   Early in 19x2, before the financial statements of the Cooke Department Store for 19x1 were issued, the events described below occurred.

(1) Estimated uncollectible accounts from 19x1 sales were $1,200 (out of credit sales of $100,000), based on prior years' experience. By the time the 19x1 statements were completed and ready for release, specific accounts amounting to $1,500 had already proved uncollectible, and it was thought that $300 more would be bad.

(2) A typewriter, one of several owned by the store, was being depreciated on the basis of an estimated life of 10 years. Its original cost was $200, and it was expected to have a useful life of three years from the end of 19x1. Early in 19x2 an employee dropped it, damaging it so badly that it had to be junked.

(3) Some fashion items carried in inventory, having an original cost of $1,200, were shown in the December 31, 19x1, statement of financial position at $400, which was thought to be their recoverable cost. They were actually sold in the first week of January for $250.

(4) A building which had cost $10,000 and on which $4,000 of depreciation had been accumulated was sold for $8,000.

(5) Merchandise costing $10,000 was damaged by fire during the first week of January. Merchandise costing $6,000 was a total loss, but was insured to the extent of $5,000. It was estimated that the remaining merchandise could be sold for $1,500.

REQUIRED:

a. What effect, if any, would the above transactions have on the 19x1 financial statements?

b. For each of the transactions, what entry, if any, would be necessary in 19x2?

8-18

MATSON MANUFACTURING COMPANY
Statement of Assets and Liabilities

ASSETS

Cash on hand and in bank	$ 10,000
Receivables, net	28,000
Inventories	73,000
Securities	11,000
Prepaid expenses and accrued items	700
Real estate	112,000
Intangibles	54,000
	$288,700

LIABILITIES

Accounts payable	$ 17,000
Notes payable	25,000
Miscellaneous payables	4,000
Bonds payable	50,000
Estimated income taxes payable	6,500
Stockholders' investment	186,200
	$288,700

REQUIRED:

a. Criticize the illustrated statement of the Matson Manufacturing Company, listing all errors you find in form, classification, and presentation.

b. Prepare in good form an acceptable statement of financial position. Assume appropriate figures for unknown items.

8-19

REQUIRED:

Using the following information, prepare an income statement, classified according to the functions of Selling, Delivery, and General Administration, for the Grinn Plumbing Supply Company for the year ending December 31, 19x1.

Store rent	$ 3,600
Uncollectible accounts	500
Interest expense	150
Sales	200,000
Salesmen's salaries	15,000
Federal income taxes	15,000
Purchases	140,000
Advertising expense	1,000
Loss on sale of office equipment	300
Sales returns and allowances	400
Office salaries	10,500
Merchandise inventory, January 1	60,000
Merchandise inventory, December 31	92,000
Purchase discounts	720
Depreciation—office equipment	250
Interest income	200
Purchase returns and allowances	1,280
Insurance expense	350
Payroll taxes	1,950
Sales discounts	600
Freight in	4,000
Depreciation—delivery trucks	1,200
Gasoline and other delivery expense	1,500
Loss due to fire damage	600
Miscellaneous office expenses	1,700
Gain on sale of delivery truck	100
Miscellaneous selling expense	2,200
Manager's salary	7,500
Office rent	1,200

8-20 The following is the income statement for the Aycock Department Store for 19x1:

THE AYCOCK DEPARTMENT STORE
Statement of Income
For the Year Ended December 31, 19x1

Sales...			$185,000
Less: Losses from uncollectibles.................	$	925	
Sales discounts...........................		2,000	
Returned sales and allowances......		3,500	6,425
Net sales..			$178,575
Less operating expenses:			
Cost of goods sold..........................	$107,400		
Salaries and wages.........................	22,500		
Advertising.................................	1,200		
Depreciation...............................	12,000		
Utilities.....................................	750		
Property taxes..............................	1,100		
Repairs and maintenance....................	1,825		
Miscellaneous..............................	475	147,250	
Net operating income...........................			$ 31,325
Less other expenses:			
Interest expense.............................	$	400	
Loss on sale of equipment...................		900	1,300
			$ 30,025
Add other revenue:			
Rent revenue..			5,000
Net income before income taxes.........................			$ 35,025
Income taxes....................................			12,713
Net income after income taxes.........................			$ 22,312

REQUIRED:

a. Criticize the way in which this income statement is classified.

b. Has there been a proper matching of expired costs with realized revenues in arriving at the figure for *net operating income?*

c. Is it desirable to classify an income statement in one form for one group of users and in another form for other groups? Explain.

d. Explain why *income tax* is presented separately from other expenses at the end of the statement.

8-21   The transactions below relate to Highland Manufacturing Company. Assume that all of the transactions occurred in 19x1, and that the company follows the *all-inclusive concept* when preparing its income statement at the end of its accounting year.

(1) The company paid $25,000 for goodwill when it purchased a small competing company during the year. It immediately wrote the cost of the goodwill down to $1.

(2) The company received a check for $7,000 from the United States Treasury as an adjustment of ncome taxes overpaid in prior years.

(3) A decision was handed down by the courts in a suit in which the Highland Manufacturing Company, the defendant, was charged with using the trade slogan of another company. The courts held in favor of the plaintiff, and the company was ordered by the court to pay $15,000 plus court costs of $2,000.

(4) On December 21 a $40,000 dividend was declared to stockholders of record on December 30. The dividend was to be paid on January 7.

(5) The company sold scrap iron and broken tools for $800.

(6) During the year a flash flood caused damage to the main office building making it necessary to spend $600 for repairs.

(7) At a meeting in November the board of directors decided to install, effective January 1, a perpetual method for controlling its inventory. Previously the periodic method had been used.

(8) During the year the company sold a fully depreciated machine for $400. It also sold a building lot for $8,000. The company had purchased this lot four years earlier for $10,000.

(9) Organization costs which had been carried on the books of the company at $6,500 since the year of organization were written off.

(10) Interest of $2,000 was received on $50,000 of United States Government bonds owned by the company. At their November meeting, the directors decided to sell the bonds shortly after the beginning of the new year.

REQUIRED:

a. For each of the numbered transactions, you are to determine which financial statement is affected, if any, and how.

b. To what extent would each of the standards of disclosure apply to each of the foregoing events?

8-22   The following trial balance is that of the People's Department Store. It was taken from the general ledger on December 31, 19x2, after all transaction and adjusting entries for the year had been recorded.

	Debits	Credits
Accounts receivable, trade.....................	$ 8,900	
Accounts payable, trade......................		$ 13,150
*Accrued liabilities............................		1,680
Accumulated depreciation.....................		37,870
Advertising.................................	8,500	
Cash.......................................	6,300	
*Cash surrender value of life insurance..........	2,120	
Capital stock, par $5.........................		50,000
*4% Debentures due 19x4–19x8...............		25,000
*4% Debentures due in 19x3..................		6,000
*Damages paid to injured customer............	5,000	
*Dividends declared..........................	21,250	
Dividends payable...........................		7,250
Depreciation................................	6,840	
Cost of goods sold...........................	117,400	
*Corporate Federal income tax.................	5,840	
Equipment..................................	82,320	
Estimated uncollectible accounts..............		360
*Federal taxes accrued.......................		5,840
*Gain on sale of marketable securities..........		120
Insurance...................................	5,300	
Interest expense.............................	1,350	
Interest revenue.............................		400
*Leasehold improvements.....................	9,650	
Losses from uncollectible accounts.............	360	
*Marketable securities held for plant expansion (Market, $9,950)........................	9,800	

	Debits	Credits
Merchandise inventory (last-in, first-out cost method)..............................	31,000	
Miscellaneous operating expense..............	3,850	
Notes payable to banks (due in 90 days).......		10,000
*Prepaid insurance premiums..................	1,100	
Rent expense.................................	8,400	
Repairs and maintenance.....................	1,790	
*Retained income............................		17,520
*Revenue from subleased space................		600
Salaries and wages..........................	20,000	
Sales returns and allowances.................	3,400	
*Sales discounts.............................	1,020	
Sales revenue................................		206,500
*Stock of associated company..................	12,450	
Taxes (other than income tax)..............	6,700	
*Utilities....................................	1,650	
	$382,290	$382,290

REQUIRED:

a. Prepare the following statements, carefully classified and in good form:

   (1) Income statement.
   (2) Statement of retained income.
   (3) Statement of financial position.

The use of a statement classification work sheet is optional.

b. Explain what each item in the trial balance marked by an asterisk means, and why you classified it as you did.

c. What suggestions can you make for improving the account terminology?

d. Why is a trial balance not a satisfactory financial report?

e. List the accounts that would have had different titles or balances if the People's Department Store had been organized as a partnership, and state what the appropriate partnership account titles would have been.

8-23 The following trial balance was prepared by an employee of the Hatchford Appliance Store on December 31, 19x1:

HATCHFORD APPLIANCE STORE
Trial Balance
December 31, 19x1

Capital stock		$100,000
Wages and salaries	$ 25,000	
Rent expense	4,000	
Cash in bank	28,000	
Insurance expired	600	
Office equipment	8,000	
Office supplies on hand	300	
Sales revenue		300,000
Notes payable		5,000
Accrued interest receivable	250	
Petty cash	200	
Office supplies used	900	
Prepaid insurance	100	
Gain on sale of equipment		1,500
Advances to employees	750	
Land	4,000	
Sales returns and allowances	1,100	
Federal income taxes payable		12,000
Store equipment	10,000	
Merchandise inventory	75,000	
Advertising expense	2,500	
Depreciation—office equipment	400	
Discounts lost	800	
Dividends	12,000	
Cost of goods sold	220,000	
Interest revenue		500
Organization cost	2,000	
Depreciation—store equipment	500	
Maintenance	3,000	
Accrued salaries payable		450
Losses from uncollectible accounts	750	
Employee Federal income tax withheld		2,500
Employee social security tax withheld		750
Accrued social security tax payable		750
Federal income tax expense	12,000	
Temporary investments	15,000	
Accounts receivable, trade	55,000	
Accounts payable, trade		33,000
Retained income		27,050
Accrued interest payable		50
Accounts receivable, trade—estimated uncollectibles		1,100
Advances on sales contracts		4,500
Loss from fire	2,000	
Notes receivable—trade	5,000	
Totals	$489,150	$489,150

REQUIRED:

a Prepare classified general-purpose financial statements, making such changes in terminology as you think appropriate. The use of a classification work sheet is optional.

b. Which statement items might properly be condensed in a published annual statement?

BULLOCK'S, INC.

STATEMENT OF FINANCIAL POSITION

ASSETS

	FEBRUARY 1, 1958	FEBRUARY 2, 1957
CURRENT ASSETS		
Cash	$ 5,138,815	$ 4,237,898
U.S. Government securities — at cost plus accrued interest . .	5,959,935	7,151,987
Accounts receivable from customers, less allowances for doubtful accounts, returns, etc.	21,812,877	22,182,757
Merchandise inventories — Note A	17,254,813	17,567,881
Supplies	695,097	778,303
Prepaid taxes, insurance, and sundry	968,346	881,661
TOTAL CURRENT ASSETS	$51,829,883	$52,800,487
OTHER ASSETS		
Stocks and other securities	$ 482,932	$ 483,732
Notes, sundry accounts, and deposits	528,407	500,396
Estimated future income tax benefits available upon distribution of stock under Incentive Compensation Plans — Note B . .	625,651	450,876
TOTAL OTHER ASSETS	$ 1,636,990	$ 1,435,004
PROPERTY AND EQUIPMENT — on the basis of cost		
Land and leaseholds	$ 6,384,461	$ 6,367,932
Buildings and improvements	29,701,080	27,133,760
Furniture, fixtures, and equipment	16,228,633	15,421,924
	$52,314,174	$48,923,616
Less allowances for depreciation and amortization	23,065,327	21,558,369
TOTAL PROPERTY AND EQUIPMENT	$29,248,847	$27,365,247
	$82,715,720	$81,600,738

See Notes to Financial Statements

FEBRUARY 1, 1958 AND FEBRUARY 2, 1957

LIABILITIES AND STOCKHOLDERS' INVESTMENT

	FEBRUARY 1, 1958	FEBRUARY 2, 1957
CURRENT LIABILITIES		
Accounts payable and accrued expenses	$ 7,188,415	$ 7,733,212
Salaries and wages, and taxes, etc. withheld from employes . .	3,185,151	3,371,653
Taxes, other than taxes on income	1,293,059	1,239,300
Federal taxes on income — estimated — Note C	5,205,000	6,070,000
Current portion of long-term debt	600,000	510,000
TOTAL CURRENT LIABILITIES	$17,471,625	$18,924,165
LONG-TERM DEBT (less current portion) — Note D . . .	$ 6,800,000	$ 7,430,000
RESERVES — for self-insurance	$ 211,392	$ 195,153
STOCKHOLDERS' INVESTMENT		
Capital stock:		
Cumulative Preferred, 4% Series, par value $100 a share, redeemable at $106 a share; outstanding 63,833 shares at February 1, 1958, and 64,279 shares at February 2, 1957; authorized 40,000 shares in addition to those outstanding — Note E	$ 6,383,300	$ 6,427,900
Common, par value $10 a share; authorized 1,500,000 shares; outstanding 1,223,951 shares at February 1, 1958, and 1,188,873 shares at February 2, 1957 — Notes B and F . .	14,128,368	13,777,588
Capital in excess of par value of capital stock — Note F . . .	1,087,418	—
Earnings retained for use in the business — Note D	36,633,617	34,845,932
TOTAL STOCKHOLDERS' INVESTMENT	$58,232,703	$55,051,420
COMMITMENTS — Note G		
	$82,715,720	$81,600,738

See Notes to Financial Statements

STATEMENT OF INCOME
AND EARNINGS RETAINED FOR USE IN THE BUSINESS

BULLOCK'S, INC.

	FISCAL YEAR ENDED	
	FEBRUARY 1, 1958 (52 WEEKS)	FEBRUARY 2, 1957 (53 WEEKS)
Net sales (including sales of leased sections)	$135,874,873	$138,310,506
Cost of goods sold, selling, administrative and general expenses .	$120,137,520	$121,799,669
Contributions to Profit Sharing Retirement Benefit Payments Plans	1,059,979	1,162,968
Depreciation and amortization	2,123,277	1,991,045
Interest on long-term debt	225,806	251,421
Miscellaneous income, less other deductions	(118,879)	(118,821)
	$123,427,703	$125,086,282
INCOME BEFORE FEDERAL INCOME TAXES	$ 12,447,170	$ 13,224,224
Federal taxes on income — estimated — Note B	6,578,094	7,029,997
NET INCOME	$ 5,869,076	$ 6,194,227
Earnings retained for use in the business at beginning of year . .	34,845,932	31,259,803
	$ 40,715,008	$ 37,454,030
Less dividends declared:		
Stock dividend — Note F	1,438,198	—
Cash dividends on Preferred Stock — $4 a share	255,868	259,360
Cash dividends on Common Stock — $2 a share	2,387,325	2,348,738
EARNINGS RETAINED FOR USE IN THE BUSINESS AT END OF YEAR	$ 36,633,617	$ 34,845,932

See Notes to Financial Statements

Source: Bullock's, Inc. Annual Report, 1958.

NOTES TO FINANCIAL STATEMENTS

NOTE A—INVENTORIES

Merchandise inventories are valued at cost as determined under the last-in, first-out (Lifo) method. Inventories so valued are $2,346,865 less at February 1, 1958, and $2,267,758 less at February 2, 1957, than would be the case if the conventional retail method were followed.

NOTE B—RETIREMENT AND INCENTIVE COMPENSATION PLANS

Profit Sharing Retirement Benefit Payments Plans are in effect to provide retirement income for qualifying employes. It is estimated at February 1, 1958, that approximately $400,000 will be necessary to fund the remaining cost of benefits for service prior to adoption of the Plans.

Under Incentive Compensation Plans a part of the annual compensation of certain executives is retained by the Company for payment generally after retirement or death of the executive. The Company holds 24,694 shares of its Common Stock for eventual distribution in settlement of the liability to participants in these Plans.

The increase in the amount for estimated future tax benefits under Incentive Compensation Plans has been classified in the statement of income as a credit against costs and expenses.

NOTE C—INCOME TAXES

Federal income tax returns of the Company for the years subsequent to January 28, 1956, are subject to review by the Internal Revenue Service.

NOTE D—LONG-TERM DEBT AND DIVIDEND LIMITATION

Long-term debt at February 1, 1958, was represented by an unsecured note. The loan agreement applicable thereto permits the payment of cash dividends on Common Stock up to 100% of net income (as defined in the agreement) earned since January 31, 1949, plus $2,500,000. Under this limitation $18,862,217 of earnings retained for use in the business was unrestricted at February 1, 1958, for cash dividends on Common Stock. The note bears 3% interest; principal payments are due annually on August 15th in amounts ranging from $600,000 in 1958, to $750,000 in 1963, and $3,300,000 (final payment) in 1964.

Under the terms of a credit agreement (no borrowings thereunder outstanding at February 1,

1958), a group of banks has agreed to lend to the Company up to $10,000,000 outstanding at any one time until January 31, 1959, and to lend to the Company on January 31, 1959, an amount up to the unterminated amount of its $10,000,000 commitment, payable in five equal annual installments commencing January 31, 1960. Such agreement contains the same restrictions as to payments of dividends as does the loan agreement referred to in the preceding paragraph.

NOTE E—SINKING FUND FOR PREFERRED STOCK

The Company is required to set aside $160,000 by May 1st of each year for the redemption of Preferred Stock. At February 1, 1958, the May, 1958, requirement and $25,700 of the 1959 requirement had been met.

On February 5, 1957, a 3% stock dividend was declared on Common Stock. Accordingly, Common Stock account was increased $350,780 (par value of 35,078 shares distributed) and the excess ($31 a share; $1,087,418 in the aggregate) of the approximate quoted market price over the par value of the shares distributed was credited to capital in excess of par value of capital stock; the total of these amounts ($1,438,198) was transferred from earnings retained for use in the business.

NOTE G—COMMITMENTS

The Company occupies premises held under twenty-six lease agreements which provide for cash rentals plus taxes, insurance, and maintenance. Seven of these leases provide for rental based upon sales. The aggregate minimum annual cash rentals are as follows:

One lease expiring within three years	$ 10,000
Thirteen leases expiring from twelve to twenty-five years	1,153,653
Twelve leases expiring from twenty-six to forty-eight years . . .	329,942
	$1,493,595

The Company has authorized expenditures of approximately $14,000,000 (a substantial portion of which was committed for at February 1, 1958) in connection with additions and improvements.

REQUIRED:

a. Referring to the illustrated financial statements of Bullock's, Inc., answer the following questions:

   (1) How can you explain why the company uses such an unusual fiscal period? What effect does this have on comparability of information? What advantages does it have?
   (2) Why is *Miscellaneous income, less other deductions* a negative amount?
   (3) How does the treatment of U. S. Government securities differ from the customary treatment?
   (4) Why do you suppose allowances are made for returns under *Accounts receivable?*
   (5) What is the purpose of footnote A?
   (6) What would be a better title for *Supplies?*
   (7) What caption or captions would you substitute for *Other Assets?*
   (8) What was the total principal amount of *Long-Term Debt?*
   (9) What do you suppose is the nature of *Reserves—for self-insurance?*
   (10) Why is there a caption for *Commitments* but no amount? What does it mean?
   (11) Comment on other features of the statements that in your opinion are noteworthy.
   (12) How much was the company worth on February 1, 1958? On February 2, 1957?

b. State what principal accounting assumptions underlie each item in the financial statements, and comment upon the resulting limitations of the usefulness of the statements.

   8-25   The Southern Swimming Pool Company is owned and operated by three partners: Walter Berger, Fred Clark, and Herbert Dane. The company, which constructs small swimming pools for families, was organized on January 1, 19x1, when the partners made the following capital contributions:

Berger	$20,000
Clark	20,000
Dane	10,000
Total	$50,000

It was agreed that annual salaries as follows would be allowed the partners: Berger, $7,500; Clark, $6,000; and Dane, $5,000. After allowing salaries, the remaining income is to be distributed in the ratio of the partners' capital contributions at the beginning of the year.

The trial balance as of December 31, 19x1 appears below:

SOUTHERN SWIMMING POOL COMPANY
Trial Balance
December 31, 19x1

Cash	$ 5,000	
Accounts receivable	40,000	
Inventory—December 31, 19x1	35,000	
Prepaid insurance	1,000	
Trucks	6,500	
Construction sheds	5,000	
Tools	3,500	
Accounts payable		$ 12,000
Accrued wages payable		500
Note payable to Dane		5,000
Sales revenue		150,000
Cost of sales	104,500	
Depreciation expense	2,000	
Insurance expense	500	
Office expense	3,000	
Rent expense	1,500	
Berger—Drawing	6,000	
Clark—Drawing	4,000	
Dane—Drawing	5,000	
Berger—Capital		20,000
Clark—Capital		25,000
Dane—Capital		10,000
Totals	$222,500	$222,500

The partnership being short of cash, on October 1 Dane made a temporary advance of $5,000. The partnership gave him in exchange a promissory note due in one year, bearing interest at the rate of 6 per cent a year. It was understood that the note would, if necessary, be renewed at maturity. No entry relating to the note other than to record its receipt has been made in the accounts.

REQUIRED:

a. Prepare formal financial statements for the partnership.
b. Journalize the necessary closing entries.
c. Assume that the business was organized as a corporation on January 1, 19x1, that all salaries were paid in cash, and that an income distribution of 50 per cent of the net income (if any) was declared on December 31, 19x1, to be paid on January 10, 19x2. Prepare a trial balance to reflect these assumptions.
d. Prepare formal financial statements for the corporation described in (c).
e. Discuss in detail the limitations of comparability between the financial statements in (a) and those in (d).
f. Journalize closing entries for the corporation.

CASE 8-1. ATLAS PUBLISHING COMPANY, INC.

The Atlas Publishing Company, Inc., publishes a monthly magazine called *Roar*. Its principal sources of revenue are magazine subscriptions, sales to newsstands, and sales of advertising space in the magazine. *Roar's* circulation is approximately 2,000,000 copies per year. The company sells its own advertising space and handles its own distribution.

Management is interested in the net income from each issue of the magazine; therefore, financial statements are prepared monthly. There is particular interest in the amounts of the principal classes of revenues and expenses which can be associated directly with each monthly issue. Other revenue and expense items which accrue during the month, but which are not directly related to the particular issue, are reported separately.

The company's statement of financial position as of February 28, 19x1, is illustrated.

ATLAS PUBLISHING COMPANY, INC.
Statement of Financial Position
February 28, 19x1

ASSETS		EQUITIES	
Cash	$ 15,000	*Liabilities:*	
Subscriptions receivable	40,000	Accounts payable	$ 85,000
Accounts receivable—		Notes payable	60,000
advertisers	98,000	Estimated income taxes	
Accounts receivable—		payable	15,000
newsstands	25,000	Royalties payable	30,000
Accounts receivable—officers	1,000	Accrued salaries payable	3,500
Notes receivable	10,000	Deferred subscription	
Inventory	60,000	revenue	120,000
Machinery and equipment	150,000	Deferred advertising revenue	50,000
Office equipment	20,000	Total liabilities	$363,500
Delivery trucks	65,000		
Prepaid insurance	3,500		
Prepaid advertising	3,000	*Stockholders' equity:*	
Temporary investments	15,000	Capital stock	$100,000
Deferred promotion expenses	11,000	Retained income	53,000
			$153,000
	$516,500		$516,500

The following selected transactions occurred in March, 19x1:

(1) Received one-year subscriptions beginning with the March issue, and billed the subscribers a total of $52,000. Collected $24,000 of this amount during the month.

(2) Sold $45,000 of advertising space in issues for the nine months beginning with April. Advertising space in the March issue was sold for $70,000 cash during the month.

(3) Collected subscriptions receivable of $32,000 and accounts of $70,000 due from advertisers.

(4) Collected accounts receivable from newsdealers in the amount of $12,500.

(5) Loans of $2,000 were made to officers of the company.

(6) Paid $13,500 to writers for accepted articles which will appear in later issues of *Roar*.

(7) Signed a contract with Mr. Roy Goms, a cartoonist, to purchase two cartoons monthly at $100 each for the next 24 months. Presented Mr. Goms with a check for the two cartoons appearing in the March issue.

(8) Purchased paper, ink, and other printing supplies for $16,500 cash.

(9) Depreciation for the month was as follows:

Machinery and equipment.. $1,200
Office equipment... 200
Delivery trucks... 1,000

(10) A 3-year fire insurance policy was taken out on February 1, 19x1, for a total premium of $3,600.

(11) The $3,000 balance in the prepaid advertising account represents the cost of advertising the March issue in newspapers and other publications.

(12) The deferred promotion expenses represents the cost of circulars mailed on February 1 to promote the sale of the magazine. It was decided at that time to allocate the cost to the next 12 issues.

(13) Paid $25,000 of accounts payable and $10,000 of notes payable.

(14) Estimated income taxes for the month are $12,000.

(15) Total salaries and wages earned by employees during the month amounted to $34,000, of which $30,000 was paid in cash.

(16) Of the deferred subscription revenue balance on February 28, $18,000 applies to the March issue, as does $10,000 of the deferred advertising revenue balance on that date.

(17) The cost of inventories on hand on March 31 was $30,200.

REQUIRED:

a. Make all of the necessary entries for March in the permanent accounting records of the Atlas Publishing Company, Inc.

b. Present classified financial statements as of March 31, 19x1.

c. Write a report to the management suggesting how the information in the reports might be used in directing business operations, and explaining which specific accounts are subject to a relatively wide margin of error in measurement, and why.

Chapter **9**

Processing a Mass of Accounting Data

Chapter 2 described how accounting measures the financial progress and status of an entity by breaking its complex activities into identifiable, measurable financial *transactions*. Accounting is a process of *condensing* and *summarizing* a multitude of enterprise transactions in such a way that their significance can be more readily understood by those who are concerned with the affairs of the enterprise.

This chapter deals with some of the general methods of condensing and summarizing financial details. These methods may be referred to as *distribution* methods, or procedures for grouping the numerous details of business transactions according to the accounts which they affect. Distribution begins with the raw data of transactions in the source documents, and ends when the facts are summarized under appropriate account titles in the financial reports. The examples presented in this chapter should by no means be considered as ideals, but merely as illustrations of the general features of distribution methods. These methods, like other details of the accounting system, should be tailored to the requirements of the particular company. One needs to be a specialist in system design in order to keep up with the many refinements which are constantly taking place in distribution methods.

Basic stages of the distribution process

The following are the principal customary steps in the process of collecting and summarizing financial data:

(1) Preparation of *source documents*, the first records of transactions, which serve to initiate transactions or to report them after they have occurred;

(2) Preparation of *journal entries*, which analyze each transaction in terms of its debit and credit effect on the assets and equities of the enterprise;

(3) Posting the debit and credit parts of the journal entries to a *ledger*, which contains a separate *account* of the debits and credits to each type of asset and equity;

(4) Preparation of a *trial balance*, which lists the balances of all of the accounts at the end of the accounting period, and perhaps of a *work sheet*, which aids in the preparation of formal financial statements by grouping together the account balances which are to be used in each statement;

(5) Preparation of formal *financial statements*, such as the income statement, the statement of retained income, the statement of financial position, and various special types of reports for internal and external use.

During an accounting period even a moderate-sized business may have *thousands* of individual sales, purchases, receipts, payments, and other transactions. By means of the distribution process, these may be condensed into *hundreds* of journal entries, which are then further condensed into *tens* of ledger account balances and financial statement items. In this final stage of condensation and orderly arrangement, the summarized information about business transactions is meaningful to the reader of the financial statements.

Need for time-saving methods

Earlier and later chapters in this book make extensive use of the *general journal entry* as a device for analyzing and explaining the effect of various types of business events on the assets and equities. The following is an example of the form used:

```
19x1
Mar. 1   A, Accounts Receivable...........................  19
              OE, Sales Revenue...........................        19
         Sold merchandise on account to Alfred Adams.
```

This form is very useful teaching device for showing the effects of various *types* of events on the financial elements. However, in actual business practice, when the *number* of transactions of a given type is very great, the form is cumbersome. Even the smallest business makes thousands of individual sales on account during an accounting period and also completes thousands of several other common types of transactions. If each transaction were recorded in the manner illustrated above, journalizing would consume a great deal of time. Then, if each of the thousands of debits and credits were transferred separately to the ledger accounts, a vast amount of time would also be required for posting. There would also be many opportunities for errors in posting individual amounts.

It is obvious that more efficient methods of journalizing and posting are needed for practically any business. The remainder of this chapter describes some of the general features of these methods, as well as of means of preparing source documents and financial statements more efficiently. Some of these time-saving methods are *manual*, while others involve the use of *machines*.

Time saving in preparing source documents

The first record of a business transaction is usually contained in a *source document*, such as a sales invoice, purchase invoice, check, or receipt. When much descriptive information is needed about each event, the source document often consists of a standardized form, on which the particular information about each transaction is written at the time the transaction occurs. Frequently several copies of the source document are prepared to furnish information about the transaction to the individuals inside and outside of the business who are principally concerned.

EXAMPLE 1:   At the time of a sale on account, the customer's name, address, the date, the quantity and description of the articles sold, the unit prices, and the total amount of the sale are usually written on a printed sales invoice form. The original may go to the customer, a copy to the accounts receivable bookkeeper, and a copy to the bookkeeper who records sales revenue.

The following are some examples of time-saving methods which may be used in the preparation of source documents:

(1) Use of *billing machines* which can compute the *extension* (price multiplied by quantity) for each item sold, and the *footing* (total of the extensions).

(2) Use of sales invoices *preprinted with quantities and prices* for goods which are frequently sold in standard amounts. If, for example, customers frequently order a gross of item K at a time, a supply of invoices containing the description, quantity, and extension can be printed in advance. At the time of sale only the customer's name and address and the date need be recorded.

(3) Use of *mechanical registers*, such as the cash register. The only record at the time of each cash sale transaction is made when the cashier depresses the keys which indicate the amount of the sale. The machine lists the amount of each individual sale on a tape, which is locked within the machine, and at the same time accumulates a total of all cash sales. Usually the single figure representing the total cash sales for the day, perhaps from thousands of transactions, is recorded as *one journal entry*.

(4) Use of the *same form in two or more stages* of a complex transaction, or use of equipment which permits the preparation of the source document, journal entry, ledger record, and perhaps other records in a single writing. For example, the employee's pay check, a payroll journal, and an entry on the continuous earnings record of the employee can be prepared in one writing.

Special journals

When a particular type of transaction recurs frequently, its details can usually be distributed to the appropriate accounts more efficiently by means of a *special journal*, in which only that type of transaction is recorded. For example, many businesses find that their large number of sales on account warrants the use of a special *Sales Journal*, such as the following:

SALES JOURNAL   Page 7

Date	Invoice Number	Customer's Name	Posted	Debit Accounts Receivable, Credit Sales Revenue
19x1				
Mar. 1	115	Adams, Alfred.........	✓	19
1	116	Warren, James.........	✓	12
1	117	Carver, W. J..........	✓	112
1	118	McIntosh, O. R........	✓	5
2	119	Mathis Company......	✓	94
2	120	Barker, Carolyn.......	✓	10
2	121	Davis, John W.........	✓	47
3	122	Adams, Alfred.........	✓	33
31	206	Madison Mfg. Co......	✓	215
31	207	Ehrlich, J. K..........	✓	7
31	208	Magnuson, Alice.......	✓	80
31		Monthly total.......	✓	8,450

(3) (70)

A separate account of the amount owed by each customer must be maintained in the *Accounts Receivable subsidiary ledger*, a separate group of accounts whose total balances must agree with the balance in Accounts Receivable, Trade, the *general ledger controlling account.* The check marks in the "Posted" column denote that the amounts have been recorded in the individual customers' accounts. This should be done frequently—perhaps daily—so that the customer's account balances will be current.

The numerals (3) and (70) below the total sales on account for the month indicate that this amount has been posted at the end of the month as a *debit* to general ledger account number 3, Accounts Receivable, and also as a *credit* to general ledger account number 70, Sales Revenue. The general ledger accounts would then appear as follows:

A, Accounts Receivable (Account #3)			OE, Sales Revenue (Account #70)		
19x1			19x1		
Feb. 28	Balance	10,200	Mar. 31	S7	8,450
Mar. 31	S7	8,450			

The notation "S7" in the posting reference column of the ledger accounts is an abbreviation for "Sales Journal, page 7."

Advantages of specialized journals

Among the advantages of specialized journals are the following:

(1) They save time in recording journal entries. In the illustrated sales journal, the act of writing an amount in the money column is sufficient to indicate that Accounts Receivable is to be debited and Sales Revenue is to be credited. The names of these accounts to be debited and credited need not be written for each entry since they are already printed at the top of the column. Also, it is not necessary to write the amount of each transaction twice, because it is understood that the amount to be debited and the amount to be credited are the same.

(2) They save time in posting to the ledger. Assume, in the illustration, that there were 200 sales on account during the month. Posting only the column total as a debit to Accounts Receivable, Trade, and as a credit to Sales Revenue requires 199 fewer debit postings and 199 fewer credit postings than would be required if each debit and credit were posted individually. No saving is made in this illustration in posting to the subsidiary accounts receivable ledger.

(3) Duties of keeping special journals may be divided among several employees, each of whom is a specialist in recording one type of transaction.

(4) Relatively unskilled employees may be used to keep each special journal.

A business may use a special journal for any type of transaction which occurs frequently. The particular journals which are used in a given business depend chiefly upon the nature of its transactions and their frequency, and upon the number of classifications and the nature of details that are needed in the accounts and reports. Types of special journals which are frequently found in practice are:

Cash Receipts Journals
Cash Payments Journals

Sales Journals
Purchases Journals
Sales Returns and Allowances Journals
Purchase Returns and Allowances Journals
Notes Receivable Registers
Notes Payable Registers

No matter how many specialized journals a business uses, there are almost always unusual transactions which cannot be recorded in any of them. For this reason, every business should have a *General Journal* in addition to the special journals. It is ordinarily used to record adjusting and closing entries, corrections, and unusual or complex transactions which affect many accounts or require an extended explanation.

Special columns in journals

A *special column* in a journal is one which is used to collect all of the debits, or all of the credits, to a particular account. The total of each column is then posted periodically—usually once a month—as a single debit or credit to the appropriate account.

The single money column in the Sales Journal is a special column whose amounts always represent debits to Accounts Receivable and credits to Sales. Several special columns are often used in a given special journal, and special columns are often appropriate in a general journal. They should be used whenever the transactions recorded in a particular journal involve frequent debits or credits to a given account.

A *Cash Receipts Journal* is a specialized journal which usually has more than one special column. By definition, each cash receipts transaction involves a *debit to Cash;* therefore, a special column for *Cash, Debit* is needed. Other special columns are needed for accounts which are often debited or credited in cash receipts transactions. It is usually desirable, in addition, to provide a *Miscellaneous Debit* and a *Miscellaneous Credit* column to record debits and credits to accounts which are infrequently affected in cash receipts transactions.

The illustration on page 238 shows how transactions would be journalized in a Cash Receipts Journal. When there are special columns for both the account debited and the account credited in a transaction, the bookkeeper does not have to write the name of either account in journalizing the transaction. Furthermore, no individual posting to the general ledger is needed for transaction amounts in these special columns. Examples of such transactions are the *cash sales* on the first line and the *collection on account* from Marshall Burke on the second line. A credit to the individual customer's account in the Accounts Receivable subsidiary ledger must be posted for the latter type of transaction.

CASH RECEIPTS JOURNAL

Page 5

Date	Explanation	Cash Debit	Accounts Receivable Posted	Accounts Receivable Credit	Sales Credit	Misc. Title	Misc. LF	Misc. Debit	Misc. Credit
19x1 Mar. 1	Cash sales	680			680				
1	Burke, Marshall	55	✓	55					
1	Edison, Miriam	20	✓	20					
2	Mathis Company	200	✓	200					
2	Tollman, Augustus	27	✓	27					
2	Issuance of capital stock	5,000				Capital Stock	60		5,000
2	Collection of note and interest	1,020				Notes Receivable	4		1,000
						Interest Revenue	75		20
2	Cash sales	900			900				
3	Magnuson, Alice	8	✓	8					
3	Property tax refund	50				Property Taxes	93		50
3	Borrowed on note	2,970				Notes Payable	41		3,000
						Interest Expense	95	30	
3	Cash sales	550			550				
31	Evander, Mary	70	✓	70					
31	Capitol Sales Co	300	✓	300					
31	Cash sales	1,300			1,300				
	Monthly totals	45,200		7,100	27,430			830	11,500
		(1)		(3)	(70)			(X)	(X)

Summary:

Debits:
Cash................ 45,200
Miscellaneous....... 830
    Total debits.... 46,030

Credits:
Accounts Receivable. 7,100
Sales............... 27,430
Miscellaneous....... 11,500
    Total credits... 46,030

(X)—Miscellaneous Accounts columns are not posted in total. Each account is posted individually.

When accounts for which there are no special columns are debited or credited, the name of the account affected and the amount are recorded in the "Miscellaneous Accounts" section. Each such amount must be posted individually to the general ledger, and the number of the appropriate ledger account should be written in the "LF" (ledger folio) column to show that this has been done.

At the end of the month, all columns should be totaled and a summary should be prepared to prove the equality of debit and credit column totals. No totals should be posted until this proof has been completed; otherwise, errors might be carried forward into the ledger, where they would be difficult to locate. The totals of the special columns—Cash Debit, Accounts Receivable Credit, and Sales Credit—are then posted to the respective general ledger accounts and the account numbers are written below the column totals. "(X)" under each of the Miscellaneous column totals indicates that the totals are not to be posted; their component amounts must be posted individually.

After this additional posting, the Accounts Receivable and Sales Revenue accounts would appear as follows:

A, Accounts Receivable

					(Account #3)
19x1				19x1	
Feb. 28	Balance		10,200	Mar. 31	CR5 7,100
Mar. 31		S7	8,450		

OE, Sales Revenue

		(Account #70)
19x1		
Mar. 31	S7	8,450
31	CR5	27,430

The number and variety of special columns used in journals differ widely from one business to another.

Short cuts in journalizing

Time is often saved by journalizing only the *total of a batch* of source documents. If sales on account numbered dozens or hundreds each day, for example, the business might record only the daily total in the sales journal. Posting to the individual customers' accounts in the Accounts Receivable subsidiary ledger would then be made directly from copies of the sales invoices.

Time can also be saved in journalizing by recording in the cash receipts journal only the daily totals of collections on account, and posting individual credits to customers' accounts directly from duplicate copies of receipts or other source documents. Journalizing and posting should be done separately by different individuals, if possible.

The use of special journals and special columns results in time saving in both journalizing and posting, whether the work is done by hand or by bookkeeping machine.

Ledgerless bookkeeping

One method of saving time in posting is *ledgerless bookkeeping*, which means not posting to the ledger at all. Instead, copies of basic source documents related to each account are filed together, and the information in the open items in the file can be used at any time to determine the account balance.

EXAMPLE 2:   A certain company which has thousands of individual customers does not post to individual ledger accounts for them, but instead maintains a file of the unpaid invoices owed by each. Its procedure consists of the following steps:

(a) Making one entry in the sales journal each day to debit Accounts Receivable and credit Sales Revenue for the total of the day's sales on account, usually recorded on several hundred invoices.

(b) Filing two copies of each unpaid invoice in a separate section for each customer. If a customer has an unpaid balance at the beginning of the month, there would already be a ticket for that amount in his file.

(c) Making one entry in the cash receipts journal each day to debit Cash and credit Accounts Receivable for the total of cash remittances.

(d) Matching copies of the cash remittance ticket for each customer with the appropriate invoice or invoices in his file, marking the invoices "Paid," and transferring them to a paid invoice file. When the amount of a remittance is not exactly equal to the amount of the invoice, the remittance ticket is filed in the customer's unpaid invoice file.

(e) Once a month the balance owed by each customer is determined by adding the debit items (beginning balance and unpaid invoices of the current month) and subtracting the credit items (partial cash payments on account). A statement is mailed to the customer showing his balance at the end of the month, supported by copies of the unpaid invoices. A copy of the statement is filed in the open invoice file to show the account balance at the end of the period.

(f) A total of the unpaid customer's balances is obtained and compared with the balance in the Accounts Receivable controlling account in the general ledger.

The preceding illustration is intended merely to describe the general features of ledgerless bookkeeping. Often more detailed steps in the processes of filing and proving balances are required, and many other variations of the basic plan are in use. One alternative is to carry a cumulative balance of each customer's account forward from ticket to ticket as each new item is added to the file.

Although ledgerless bookkeeping saves time, it is not without disadvantages. If source documents are lost, the accounts will be out of balance and the error will be difficult to discover. Also, it is practically impossible to tell at a later date, when the documents have been transferred to another file (such as the "Paid" file in Example 2), what changes occurred in an account during a given period. For these reasons, ledgerless bookkeeping is rarely used for the general ledger. Its use is ordinarily restricted to classes of accounts which have many individual subsidiary units, such as accounts receivable and accounts payable.

MACHINE ACCOUNTING

Three general types of machines are available for collecting and summarizing accounting information: *electromechanical equipment*, *punched-card equipment*, and *electronic equipment.* There are many makes and models of these machines, ranging from the relatively small, simple, and inexpensive to the large, complex, and costly. Technological changes in these types of machines have been particularly rapid in recent years. The following discussion describes only in a general way the accounting functions which may be performed by each type of machine.

Electromechanical equipment

Two basic operations are involved in distributing information about business transactions to the appropriate accounts: (1) *Listing*, or writing the descriptive information, such as the date, a reference to the source document, and the amount, and (2) *adding* or *subtracting* the amounts.[1]

The simplest type of accounting equipment has only *one register;* that is, it is capable of accumulating only one total at a time. Such a machine is suitable for relatively simple bookkeeping operations.

EXAMPLE 3: A bookkeeping machine with a single *vertical* register may be used for recording transactions in the sales journal illustrated earlier in this chapter. The process would consist of recording a date, brief descriptive information or reference, and an amount for each sale. At the end of a "run," or continuous series of entries journalized at one time, the machine provides a total which can be recorded in the journal, avoiding the necessity of adding the transaction amounts in a separate operation.

Accounting equipment which has *two or more registers* can be used to accumulate the totals of several columns at a time. Several registers which accumulate *vertical* totals would be appropriate for recording entries in a multi-columnar journal.

---

[1] Cecil Gillespie, *Accounting Systems: Procedures and Methods* (Englewood Cliffs, N. J.: Prentice-Hall, Inc., 1951), p. 258.

A machine which has a *horizontal register* (a crossfooter) may be used to compute the difference between debits and credits on a single line. Such a machine is especially useful in posting items to an account and at the same time computing the new balance of the account.

EXAMPLE 4:   A machine with a crossfooter can be used to post debits for sales on account to each customer's account in the Accounts Receivable subsidiary ledger. The previous balance is recorded in the machine, then the debit for the current transaction is recorded, and the machine then computes the ending balance. A similar approach can be used for posting credits.

A machine with a crossfooter is especially useful to banks, which need current balances of their depositors' accounts.

Machines with several registers can be used to post transactions and compute account balances, at the same time accumulating the total debits and total credits to several different accounts.

Many types of electromechanical accounting equipment are *semiautomatic*, being designed to print a total when the operator presses the proper key. Still others print totals or move from one stage of operation to the next *automatically* on the basis of a set, or sets, of instructions built into the machine or its attachments.

Electromechanical machines increase the accuracy and legibility of accounting records, as well as the speed with which the work is done. They facilitate *proofs* of the accuracy of journalizing and posting. They also provide an excellent opportunity to perform several stages of accounting work, such as the preparation of an original source document, journal, and ledger, with one writing.

Punched-card equipment

Distributing the details of accounting transactions to the appropriate accounts and reports consists of the following three basic stages: (1) recording transaction information on a source document; (2) classifying the information on the source documents according to the accounts affected; (3) summarizing the resulting account balances. Punched-card equipment is designed to complete these stages accurately, automatically, and at high speed. It is also useful for recording, classifying, and summarizing statistical data other than accounting data.

(1) *Recording information.* Transaction information is *recorded* on a *punched card* of standardized size and shape, like that illustrated in Figure 6. Instead of being written or printed on the card, however, alphabetical and numerical information is shown on the card by means of *punched holes.* Each card has from 80 to 90 columns in which information can be punched. A column, or group of columns, is used to record each class of

information. For example, the first 12 columns might be used to record the customer's name and the next 6, to record the amount of the sale. A number is recorded by a single punch in a column, and a letter, by a combination of two punches.

The punched card may be the original source document of a transaction. For example, many organizations use punched cards for *payments by check*. In other cases, the information on various sizes and shapes of source documents, such as *purchase invoices*, is transferred to punched cards. Several punched cards may be needed to record the information on a single source document. For example, a separate card may be required for *each account* to be debited for the purchase, and another card may be required for the total credit to Accounts Payable.

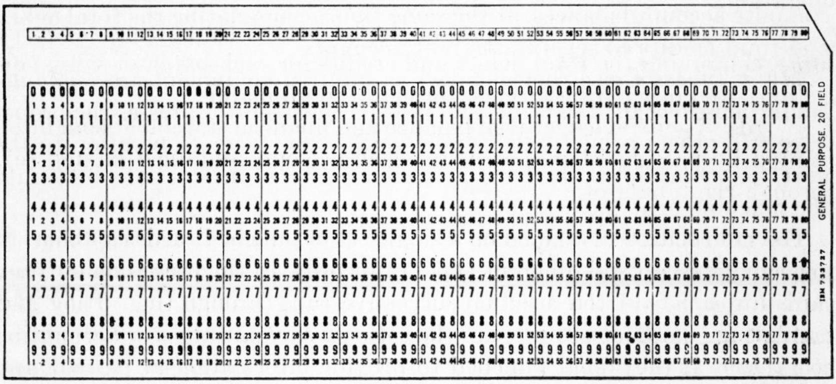

Courtesy of International Business Machines Corporation.

Fig. 6. Punched Card.

The machine which is used to punch the cards is operated by a keyboard similar to that of a typewriter. Cards can also be punched automatically as copies of other cards, or as by-products of other machine operations.

(2) *Classifying information*. The information contained on the punched cards is classified according to the accounts affected by means of a *sorter*. The cards are passed through the sorting machine, which senses the holes punched in the cards and causes them to drop into the appropriate pocket. As a rule, the cards must be passed through the sorter several times to accomplish one complete classification, because most machines can only sort for one vertical column of information at a time.

(3) *Summarizing information*. The information contained on the punched cards, classified in groups according to the account affected, can be summarized by passing the cards through a *tabulator*. By means of an electrically wired control panel, the tabulator can be given a variety of instructions, such as to list items, to select items of a given type, to add,

and to subtract. The usual accounting records and reports might be prepared by the tabulator as follows:

(a) A *journal*, such as a sales journal, might be printed by passing all of the punched cards for the sales of a period through the tabulator, which would list each item and obtain a total. A variation would be to sort the cards according to each of several different sales revenue classifications, and obtain a list of each. As an alternative, sometimes the machine is instructed to accumulate details but to print only totals.

(b) An *accounts receivable subsidiary ledger* might be printed by passing the punched cards for sales and those for cash collections on account, sorted by customer, through the tabulator. The tabulator could print a ledger account form and a customer's statement form in the same operation.

(c) *General ledger accounts* might be posted by passing *summary cards*, containing the total debits and credits for each batch of sales, collections, and other transactions, through the tabulator.

(d) A general ledger trial balance and financial statements might be printed by passing *balance cards* for each account, obtained in step (c), through the tabulator.

The information contained on a single set of punched cards can be used to accumulate several different types of records. In the preceding outline, cards for each sale were used on successive runs through the sorting and tabulating equipment to prepare the *sales journal* and the *accounts receivable ledger*. If they were punched to provide information as to *salesman* and *geographical area*, successive runs could also summarize information according to these classifications.

Electronic equipment

Electronic computers are designed to receive a mass of *input* data, store it for future use, perform arithmetic operations upon it, make logical decisions regarding it, and supply the information, or *output*, which results from these operations, all at a very high rate of speed. The following quotation gives an idea of the operating speed of a computer in comparison with that of electromechanical equipment:

It has been estimated that the speed of an ordinary adding machine could be increased by about 20 per cent by converting its operations from electromechanical to electronic methods, retaining, of course, the human operator; by also replacing the human operator by an electronic operator the speed could be increased 10,000-fold.[2]

[2] Eldred A. Johnson, *Accounting Systems in Modern Business* (New York: McGraw-Hill Book Company, Inc., 1959), p. 284.

Because of the rapid rate of technological change in the field of computers, machines of greatly increased capacity and rates of speed are continually being developed.

Computers can perform the same basic functions as electromechanical and punched-card equipment, but they have several additional features of great importance:

(1) They have internal memory units in which data, sometimes consisting of millions of digits, may be stored for future use in processing information.

(2) Besides performing the addition and subtraction operations which can be performed by electromechanical and punched-card equipment, electronic computers can multiply and divide.

(3) Computers can make logical decisions: determining whether two items being compared are equal in amount or have the same algebraic sign, the computers can thereafter perform one set of procedures if one condition exists and another set of procedures if a different condition is found.[3]

Computers are designed to receive at an early point, information which is to be used in many stages of data processing, to store it, and thereafter to reuse it in later stages without the necessity of having it recopied. The information may be fed into the computers by means of *punched cards*, *punched tape* (in which the location of a hole has a certain meaning), or *magnetic tape* (in which the existence of magnetized spots at particular locations on metallic tape has a particular meaning),[4] depending upon the make or model of the computer.

All of the machines in a given processing system are designed to respond to the same code. Once the computers begin processing data, they are controlled by automatic, electronic directions.[5] Machines early in the processing cycle may feed information to those later in the cycle, which perform operations according to their instructions.

Selection of accounting machines

As might be expected, the cost of accounting machines increases approximately in proportion to the increase in the complexity of the information which they can process and the efficiency with which they can process it. Punched-card equipment is generally more expensive than electromechanical equipment, and electronic computers are more expensive still.

---

[3] *Ibid.*, p. 283.
[4] *Ibid.*, pp. 242, 244.
[5] *Ibid.*, p. 284.

Many types of accounting equipment can be obtained by lease as well as by purchase, sometimes under a lease-purchase plan.

The selection of accounting machines, like that of all other parts of the accounting system, must be made by balancing two opposing factors: (1) the effectiveness of the machine in doing the particular job and (2) the cost of getting the job done. Although the most advanced designs of electronic computers can usually accomplish a given task more quickly than can other types of equipment, they are not appropriate except for handling a large volume of data. As a rule, they are practical only for large organizations. The organization which has a computer may find it undesirable to use it for any but a few types of transactions of high frequency. At the other end of the scale, some businesses may not need any accounting equipment at all, although usually they can appropriately use some of the time-saving methods of keeping manual records.

Other factors which should be considered in selecting particular accounting methods, in addition to the quantity of source data and the cost of processing the information, are the nature of the information needed, the safeguards and proofs which are needed, and the quality of the personnel who are available to do the work.

Machines and the future of accounting

Occasionally the opinion is voiced that high-speed electronic computers will soon make accountants obsolete. Certainly, such machines now perform many clerical operations that were once performed by people. Rather than displacing accountants, however, it would seem that such machines, where it is feasible to introduce them, free the accountants from much of the drudgery of *highly repetitive clerical work*. As a result, accountants have more time for the important functions of *analyzing* and *interpreting* the results of enterprise operations. There is an increasing tendency for the modern business to require accountants of broad background with the ability and experience necessary to make reasoned judgments.

High-speed data-processing equipment makes it possible for the businessman to collect and use types of information which would not have been available to him at all under slower methods.

As pointed out in the preceding section, there are many small and medium-sized businesses which will not find the use of electronic equipment for accounting feasible in the foreseeable future.

Summary

Accounting is a process of condensing and summarizing numerous enterprise transactions and presenting the results in such a way that they can be understood and used by those who are concerned with enterprise affairs. The steps in the condensation and summarization process, referred to as the *accounting cycle*, are: preparation of source documents, recording journal entries, posting to ledger accounts, and preparation of a trial balance and financial statements.

The transactions of each business usually are of a relatively few types, some of which recur with high frequency. Manual as well as machine methods are available for saving time and increasing accuracy in each step of accounting. Some of the manual methods consist of preparing several records at a single writing; using special journals for transactions of a given type; using special columns for accounts which are frequently debited or credited; summarizing information according to batches and journalizing the batch total; and omitting journals or ledgers altogether. Types of machines available range from the electromechanical bookkeeping machine with a single register, to multiple-register machines, punched-card equipment, and, ultimately, to electronic equipment.

The methods and machines appropriate in a given case depend upon the nature of the information required, the volume of raw data to be processed, the controls needed by management, the ability of the accounting personnel, and the cost of obtaining the information by the particular method or machine.

APPENDIX 9-A

Transaction or Adjustment Work Sheet

Appendix 8-A, "The Statement Classification Work Sheet," illustrated an orderly method for classifying adjusted account balances according to the formal financial statements in which they are to be used. As a rule, there is a pair of debit and credit columns for each statement which is to be prepared. Each adjusted account balance is extended from the trial balance to *one* of these classification columns.

Another type of work sheet which is frequently useful is the *transaction work sheet*, or *adjustment work sheet*. It summarizes on one page the effect on account balances of a number of entries. In some cases it is desirable to have a quick summary of the effect of a number of transactions without the necessity of recording journal entries, posting them to the ledger, and taking a trial balance. Another common use of this type of work sheet is to summarize the effect of end-of-period adjustments on the unadjusted trial balance amounts preliminary to the preparation of formal financial statements.

When adjustments are made on a work sheet, they must be recorded later in the permanent accounting records, the journal and the ledger. Statements can be prepared more quickly when a work sheet is used, without waiting for the formal entries to be completed. The work sheet adjusting entries are tentative at first. Any errors in them can be corrected before the statements are prepared and before the final adjusting entries are made in the accounts.

Variations in timing of adjustments

The Trial Balance after Adjustments of Merlin, Inc., shown in the Statement Classification Work Sheet illustrated in Appendix 8-A, might have been taken directly from the ledger accounts at the end of the period if it was the practice of the company to record adjusting entries before taking a trial balance. Some companies follow this practice, especially for types of accrual and expired cost adjustments which are needed regularly.

Other accountants prefer to record a Trial Balance before Adjustments on the work sheet. They determine what adjustments are needed by examining the account titles in the trial balance. For example, balances in *prepaid expense* or *prepaid revenue* accounts probably require adjustment. If the company owns any notes receivable or notes payable, adjustments are most likely needed for *accrued interest revenue* or *accrued interest expense*.

Method of preparing an adjustment work sheet

The steps in preparing an adjustment work sheet are as follows:

(1) Use a columnar analysis sheet with a description column and at least six money columns.

(2) Write a heading identifying the company, the nature of the work sheet, and the accounting period.

(3) Label the description column "Ledger Account Title."

(4) Label pairs of money columns "Trial Balance before Adjustments," "Adjustments," and "Trial Balance after Adjustments." Identify the first column of each pair as "Debit" and the second column as "Credit."

(5) Record a trial balance from the ledger in the first pair of columns.

(6) In the pair of Adjustment columns, record the debits and credits of each adjusting entry which is needed.

(a) Identify the debit and credit members of each adjusting entry by the same letter, such as *a*, *b*, and so forth.

(b) At the bottom of the work sheet, or on a separate sheet, write beside the letter for each adjusting entry a brief explanation of the entry.

(c) Total the debit and credit Adjustment columns. The totals should be equal.

(7) Starting at the top, compute the adjusted balance of each account and extend it to the appropriate column of the Trial Balance after Adjustments. The totals of the Trial Balance after Adjustments columns should be equal.

J. A. BURTON
Adjustment Work Sheet
For the Year Ended December 31, 19x3

Ledger Account Title	Trial Balance Before Adjustments		Adjustments		Trial Balance After Adjustments	
	Debits	Credits	Debits	Credits	Debits	Credits
Cash........................	2,600				2,600	
Accounts Receivable, Trade.....	15,000				15,000	
—Estimated Uncollectibles......		200		a 500		700
Notes Receivable, Trade........	3,000				3,000	
Merchandise Inventory.........	20,000				20,000	
Unexpired Insurance...........	900			f 750	150	
Equipment...................	6,000				6,000	
—Accumulated Depreciation....		1,800		c 600		2,400
Accounts Payable, Trade........		12,000				12,000
J. A. Burton, Capital...........		32,500				32,500
J. A. Burton, Drawing..........	8,800				8,800	
Sales Revenue................		90,000				90,000
Cost of Goods Sold Expense.....	60,000				60,000	
Rent Expense.................	3,300		d 300		3,600	
Salary Expense...............	15,000		e 200		15,200	
Other Expense................	2,000				2,000	
Interest Revenue..............		100		b 40		140
Totals.....................	136,600	136,600				
Loss from Uncollectibles........			a 500		500	
Accrued Interest Receivable.....			b 40		40	
Depreciation Expense..........			c 600		600	
Accrued Rent Payable..........				d 300		300
Accrued Salaries Payable.......				e 200		200
Insurance Expense.............			f 750		750	
Totals.....................			2,390	2,390	138,240	138,240

Explanations of adjusting entries

The explanations of the adjusting entries are an integral part of the work sheet. The following adjustments pertain to the illustrated work sheet of J. A. Burton, a single proprietorship.

a   To record an expected loss of one per cent of sales on account for the year,
    $50,000. (The previous balance in Accounts Receivable—Estimated Uncol-
    lectibles applies to doubtful accounts from prior years which are still on the
    books.)
b   To record accrued interest receivable on Notes Receivable, computed as
    follows:

    Note dated October 2, 90 days' interest on $2,000 at 6%......... $30
    Note dated November 1, 60 days' interest on $1,000 at 6%....... 10
       Total.. $40

c   To record annual depreciation at 10 per cent of the cost of equipment.
d   To record unpaid rent for December, $300.
e   To record accrued but unpaid salaries of employees for the last few days of
    December, $200.
f   To record expired insurance premiums of $750.

If the adjusting entries affect accounts which are not listed in the Trial
Balance columns, their titles are added in the first blank lines below the
Trial Balance totals. The items on a line constitute a record of the account
balance and adjustments to it. In computing the adjusted balance, debit
adjustments are *added* to previous debit balances, and credit adjustments
are *added* to previous credit balances. Adjustments of a nature opposite to
the previous balance are *subtracted* from it.

Combined adjustment and classification work sheet

A common form of work sheet is used to serve two purposes: to summarize the effect of adjustments, and to classify the adjusted balances
according to the financial statements in which they are to be used. The
following example shows how such a work sheet for J. A. Burton would
appear. The statements to be prepared are the income statement, statement of capital, and statement of financial position. A pair of columns is
provided for each on the work sheet. The use of a pair of Trial Balance
after Adjustments columns is optional. If the adjustments are few in number, it is probably unnecessary.

The following steps are needed to complete the work sheet, after the
adjusting entries have been recorded as explained in the first six steps in
the section "Method of preparing an adjustment work sheet":

(7) Starting at the top, compute the adjusted balance of each account
and extend it to the appropriate column for the financial statement in
which that account is to be used.

(8) (a) Compute subtotals of the Income Statement columns. If the
credit total is the larger, there is a *net income;* if the debit total is the
larger, there is a *net loss.*

J. A. BURTON
Adjustment and Classification Work Sheet
For the Year Ended December 31, 19x3

Ledger Account Title	Trial Balance Before Adjustments Debits	Credits	Adjustments Debits	Credits	Income Statement Debits	Credits	Statement of Capital Debits	Credits	Statement of Financial Position Debits	Credits
Cash	2,600								2,600	
Accounts Receivable, Trade	15,000								15,000	
—Estimated Uncollectibles		200		a 500						700
Notes Receivable, Trade	3,000								3,000	
Merchandise Inventory	20,000								20,000	
Unexpired Insurance	900			f 750					150	
Equipment	6,000								6,000	
—Accumulated Depreciation		1,800		c 600						2,400
Accounts Payable, Trade		12,000								12,000
J. A. Burton, Capital		32,500						32,500		
J. A. Burton, Drawing	8,800						8,800			
Sales Revenue		90,000				90,000				
Cost of Goods Sold Expense	60,000				60,000					
Rent Expense	3,300		d 300		3,600					
Salary Expense	15,000		e 200		15,200					
Other Expense	2,000				2,000					
Interest Revenue		100		b 40		140				
Totals	136,600	136,600								
Loss from Uncollectibles			a 500		500					
Accrued Interest Receivable			b 40						40	
Depreciation Expense			c 600		600					
Accrued Rent Payable				d 300						300
Accrued Salaries Payable				e 200						200
Insurance Expense			f 750		750					
Totals			2,390	2,390	82,650	90,140				
Net Income—to Capital					7,490			7,490		
Totals					90,140	90,140	8,800	39,990		
Ending Capital—to Statement of Financial Position							31,190			31,190
Totals							39,990	39,990	46,790	46,790

(b) Enter the net income in the debit Income Statement column and in the credit Statement of Capital column. (If there is a net loss, enter its amount as a credit in Income and a debit in Statement of Capital.)

(c) Total the Income Statement columns.

(9) (a) Compute subtotals of the Statement of Capital columns. If the credit total is larger, as is usually the case, there is a *positive balance* in the Capital account at the end of the period. If the debit total is larger, there is a *capital deficiency*.

(b) Enter the positive balance as a debit in the Statement of Capital columns and as a credit in the Statement of Financial Position columns.

(c) Total the Statement of Capital columns.

(10) Add and balance the debit and credit Statement of Financial Position columns.

After the work sheet has been completed, the financial statements should be prepared by selecting and arranging the items classified for use in each. Then the adjustments should be recorded in permanent form in the journal and ledger, as should the closing entries.

QUESTIONS AND PROBLEMS

9-1 This chapter has emphasized how special journals and accounting machines can be used to condense and summarize financial data.

REQUIRED:

Explain how these methods can also improve the system of safeguarding the assets of the business.

9-2

REQUIRED:

a. Explain the difference between a *special journal* and a *general journal*.
b. Explain what is meant by a *controlling account*.
c. List as many accounts as you can which might be controlling accounts in a moderately large company, and describe the general nature of the subsidiary ledger of each.

9-3 The controller of a large company is convinced that electronic equipment would be the most efficient means of condensing and summarizing the company's financial data.

REQUIRED:

Why might it be desirable for the company to lease the equipment rather than to purchase it?

9-4 "A small company which depends on manual methods of recording and classifying financial data cannot expect to have financial statements as complete and as current as those of a large company which uses the latest electronic equipment."

REQUIRED:

Comment on this statement.

9-5 The *XYZ* Company does not keep a general ledger record or subsidiary accounts for accounts payable during the accounting period. Instead, when each invoice is paid during the period, the company debits the appropriate asset or expense account and credits Cash. At the end of each accounting period, adjustments are made to record on the books the amounts of all unpaid bills.

REQUIRED:

a. What advantages do you see in this method? What disadvantages?
b. Is the company using the accrual basis of accounting in its financial statements? Explain.

9-6 "Punched-card and electronic equipment not only make it possible to do the accounting work more rapidly; they also permit a business to gather useful information which it might not be feasible to collect by manual methods."

REQUIRED:

Give an example of one type of such useful information.

9-7 A company which has 500 charge customers has maintained its Accounts Receivable ledger in pen and ink. It is now considering using an electric bookkeeping machine.

REQUIRED:

a. Will the machine improve the accuracy of posting? Explain.
b. What advantages is the machine likely to provide?

9-8 A retail automobile dealer sold new and used cars and also did motor and body repair work. The dealer sold about 30 cars a month and took in exchange installment notes receivable with terms ranging from 3 to 36 months. As a rule there would be about 20 repair orders a day, of which about one-fourth were for cash. The dealer's bookkeeper opened a ledger page for each automobile purchaser, and another for each repair customer. He copied in the customer's ledger account information from each invoice and sent each repair customer an itemized monthly statement.

REQUIRED:

a. What controlling and subsidiary accounts would seem to be appropriate in this situation?
b. What special journals would you recommend, and what principal columns would you suggest for each journal?
c. What time-saving procedures can you suggest, other than purchase of a bookkeeping machine?

9-9 By preparing several accounting records at one writing, the bookkeeper can save time and minimize errors in the records.

REQUIRED:

a. Explain how this can be done in connection with the accounts receivable of a small company which does not own an accounting machine.
b. Explain how this can be done in connection with the accounts receivable of a medium-sized company which owns an electromechanical machine.
c. Explain how this can be done in connection with the accounts receivable of a large company which owns punched-card equipment.

9-10 The Merion Appliance Company, a retailer, sells a large number of small appliances for cash. Its suppliers consist of a number of manufacturers and distributors. The management of the company likes to know the amount of gross margin on three classes of appliances, which it designates as classes A, B, and C, respectively. The company keeps its accounting records by hand.

REQUIRED:

a. What journals would you recommend for the company?

b. Explain specifically how the requirement of gross margin information would affect your design of the company's journals.

9-11   The Williams Manufacturing Company sells three classes of products in five sales territories, each under the direction of a sales manager. It employs 30 traveling salesmen, each of whom receives a sales commission. It would like to make an analysis of the proportion of its sales to large and to small customers, considering a small customer as one who buys less than $50 worth of merchandise at a time. All sales are made on account, and the typical invoice contains more than one class of product.

REQUIRED:

a. Describe how the company could use punched cards in collecting information about its accounts receivable and sales revenue.

b. What classifications of sales revenue seem to be appropriate for this company, and how would you suggest that they be made?

9-12   A retail business has used a single-column sales journal, kept manually, to record sales on account. The number of sales has increased to such an extent that this procedure has become cumbersome, yet the company does not feel that it can afford a machine.

REQUIRED:

Describe two ways in which this company can save time in collecting sales and accounts receivable information.

9-13   A medium-sized hospital employs a chief accountant and four office clerks, one of whom devotes full time to maintaining patients' accounts receivable by hand and to typing periodic statements of account for the patient or his insurance company. This work is especially time-consuming because charges to patients are of 16 different types, some of which are made several times during a single illness. The accounts receivable subsidiary ledger is rarely in agreement with the controlling account, and the bookkeeper often spends hours looking for errors.

REQUIRED:

a. Outline some of the advantages that this hospital could expect from the use of an electric bookkeeping machine.

b. What are some of the problems that would be encountered in installing such a machine?

c. What types of cost would be reduced and what types would be increased if the machine were installed?

9-14   A wholesaler maintains the following books of original entry:

Cash Receipts Journal
Cash Payments Journal
Purchases Journal
Sales Journal
Sales Returns and Allowances Journal
General Journal

REQUIRED:

List the types of entries that you would expect to find in its General Journal.

9-15 The Marginal Company maintains a pen-and-ink Sales Journal with the following money columns: Accounts Receivable Debit, Sales Department A Credit, and Sales Department B Credit. The company makes about 100 sales on account each month.

REQUIRED:

a. Record the following sales transactions as though they were all of the sales on account of the Marginal Company during the month of November, 19x8:

(1) Invoice #1105	Nov. 1, 19x8
Sold to: J. E. Dawson	
Items: Dept. A............ $100	
Dept. B............ 20	
Total............ $120	
(2) Invoice #1106	Nov. 1, 19x8
Sold to: N. K. Barnes Company	
Items: Dept. A............ $500	
(3) Invoice #1107	Nov. 1, 19x8
Sold to: Magic Motors	
Items: Dept. A............ $ 50	
Dept. B............ 300	
Total............ $350	
(4) Invoice #1108	Nov. 2, 19x8
Sold to: Monroe Company	
Items: Dept. B............ $800	
(5) Invoice #1109	Nov. 2, 19x8
Sold to: Adams Mfg. Co.	
Items: Dept. A............ $400	
Dept. B............ 350	
Total............ $750	

b. Describe the posting procedure that is necessary for individual items.

c. Total the journal, and describe the necessary end-of-month posting procedure.

d. The state in which the Marginal Company is located levied a 3 per cent sales tax effective January 1, 19x9. What changes in the sales journal would you then recommend?

e. What manual methods would you suggest if the sales invoices numbered 500 a month?

9-16 The Akins Co. maintains the following books of original entry (among others which are not relevant to this problem):

Purchases Journal with a single money column labeled "Merchandise Debit, Accounts Payable Credit."

Cash Payments Journal with money columns for Cash Credit, Accounts Payable Debit, Accrued Wages Payable Debit, and Miscellaneous Accounts Debit and Credit.

General Journal with one debit and one credit column.

After closing entries for the fiscal year ended April 30, 19x1, were made, the credit balance in the Accounts Payable controlling account was $7,500. The subsidiary ledger contained a separate ledger page showing the date, posting reference, debit amounts, credit amounts, and balance of each creditor's account. The balances on April 30, 19x1, were as follows:

	Debit	Credit
Barker Co...		$1,000
Darron Sales Corp.................................		400
Fryer, M. J.......................................	$200	
N-T Products.....................................		2,500
Odell, James.....................................		3,000
Warren, M. E....................................		800
Totals...	$200	$7,700

No cash discounts were available on any of these balances.

REQUIRED:

a. Enter the April 30 balances of the controlling and subsidiary ledger accounts of the Akins Co. in ledger account forms.
b. Journalize the transactions listed below in the appropriate journals.
c. Post to the appropriate general ledger and subsidiary ledger accounts.
d. Prepare a trial balance of the resulting general ledger accounts and a schedule of Accounts Payable subsidiary ledger balances.
e. If transactions of the types illustrated were five times as frequent during a month, what modifications of these journals would you recommend?

Transactions:

May 1—Paid the Barker Co. balance of $1,000 in cash.
     1—Gave James Odell a 30-day, 6% promissory note for the balance owed him.
     2—Returned to N-T Products unsatisfactory merchandise billed at $500. Paid freight of $20 on the return shipment. The Akins Co. mailed N-T Products a debit memorandum for $520 for the two items described.
     3—Purchased merchandise having a list price of $2,000, terms 2/10, n/30, from the Barker Co.
     4—Received merchandise from M. J. Fryer listed at $400, minus a quantity discount of 10%.
     7—Received a credit memorandum of $520 from N-T Products for the items returned on May 2.
     8—Purchased delivery equipment on account from the Mansfield Equipment Co., $800, terms net 30 days.
     9—M. E. Warren owed the Akins Co. $500 for merchandise which had been sold to him and properly recorded in April. Both agreed to apply Mr. Warren's account against the balance owed by the Akins Co., and the latter mailed Mr. Warren a check for the difference.
    11—Paid the Barker Co. invoice of May 3 in full.
    12—Purchased merchandise of a list price of $700 from Darron Sales Corp., terms 2/10, n/30.
    18—Purchased merchandise of a list price of $600 from M. E. Warren, terms net 30 days, f.o.b. destination. Paid transportation charges of $15 by check.
    20—Returned unsatisfactory merchandise having a list price of $100, received on May 12, to Darron Sales Corp.
    31—Paid the note due Odell.
    31—The monthly payroll consisted of gross salaries of $1,500. Deductions were $200 for employees' Federal income tax and $45 for Old Age and Survivors' Insurance. The company follows the practice of recording the accrual of the payroll in the General Journal. It draws one check for the net amount to be paid the employees, fills pay envelopes, and records the payment in the Cash Payments Journal.

9-17   The trial balance of the Tri-State Machine Company, after its transactions for the fiscal year ended June 30, 19x3, have been posted but before adjustments have been recorded, is as follows:

TRI-STATE MACHINE COMPANY
Trial Balance
For the Year Ended June 30, 19x3

	Debits	Credits
Cash..	$ 15,000	
Accounts Receivable..	110,000	
Accounts Receivable—Estimated Uncollectibles...		$ 1,500
Notes Receivable..	5,000	
Merchandise Inventory......................................	150,000	
Prepaid Expenses..	10,000	
Land..	40,000	
Plant and Equipment...	200,000	
Plant and Equipment—Accumulated Depreciation		60,000
Goodwill..	25,000	
Accounts Payable..		80,000
Notes Payable...		75,000
Capital Stock, $100 par.....................................		150,000
Sales...		400,000
Sales Returns and Allowances................................	8,000	
Cost of Goods Sold..	260,000	
Other Operating Expenses....................................	30,000	
Salary Expense..	40,000	
Interest Revenue..		200
Interest Expense..	2,500	
Gain on Sale of Land..		3,000
Retained Income, July 1, 19x2...............................		125,800
Totals...	$895,500	$895,500

Other available information is as follows:

(1) The balance provided for estimated uncollectibles now on the books is considered sufficient for accounts of prior years which are still uncollected. In addition, $\frac{1}{2}$ of 1 per cent of the sales of the current year are expected to result in uncollectible accounts.

(2) Interest accrued but uncollected on the notes receivable amounts to $100.

(3) The proper amount of prepaid expenses at the end of the year is $8,000. Any difference is applicable to Other Operating Expenses.

(4) The annual depreciation rate applicable to Plant and Equipment is 5 per cent. All items were in use during the entire year.

(5) Accrued but unpaid interest on notes payable amounts to $1,000. The principal of the notes is due in equal annual installments of $15,000, beginning December 31, 19x3.

(6) On June 25, 19x3, the board of directors declared a dividend of $5,000 to be paid on July 15, 19x3 to persons who owned the company's stock on June 30, 19x3.

(7) Corporate income tax may be assumed to be 50 per cent of the net income before deducting income tax.

REQUIRED:

a. Prepare a work sheet to summarize the adjustments and other entries which have not been included in the Trial Balance amounts. Use classification columns for Income Statement, Statement of Retained Income, and Statement of Financial Position.

b. Prepare classified statements by using the work sheet.

9-18   One week before his personal income tax return for 19x3 is due to be filed, James Tazeman suddenly discovers that his part-time bookkeeper has not made any journal entries or posted to the general ledger since December 31, 19x2. Sales on account and cash collections have been recorded properly in the accounts receivable ledger. Mr. Tazeman calls upon you to summarize quickly the information in basic documents so that he can file his tax return on time. You decide that there would not be time to journalize all transactions and post them within a week, and therefore elect to prepare a transaction work sheet, classifying the December 31, 19x3, balances according to whether they are to be used in the Income Statement, Statement of Capital, or Statement of Financial Position.

The ledger accounts, which contain no entries after December 31, 19x2, show the following balances:

Cash	$ 1,100
Accounts Receivable	9,000
Accounts Receivable—Estimated Uncollectibles	200
Merchandise Inventory	14,000
Equipment	5,000
Equipment—Accumulated Depreciation	2,000
Accounts Payable	6,000
6% Notes Payable	3,000
James Tazeman, Capital	17,900

You prepare adding-machine lists of various source documents for 19x3, and obtain the following totals:

(1) Invoices of sales on account, $80,000.
(2) Deposit tickets:

Collections from customers on account	$78,000
Cash sales	20,000
Additional investment by Mr. Tazeman	3,000

(3) Purchase invoices:

Merchandise bought on account	$70,000
Equipment bought on account	1,000

(4) Check stubs:

Payments for merchandise bought on account	$66,000
Payments for equipment	1,000
Payments on notes payable, including interest to November 1 of $150	2,150
Cash withdrawals of Mr. Tazeman	2,400
Mr. Tazeman's personal income tax of 19x2	5,000
Employees' salaries	8,000
Rent	2,400
Other expenses	6,000

(5) Additional information:

Merchandise inventory, Dec. 31, 19x3	$16,000
Accounts definitely uncollectible	400
Accounts probably uncollectible	300
Depreciation, 10% of cost per full year, and half this rate for items bought or sold during the year	?
Prepaid expenses (included in payments for other expenses)	1,200

REQUIRED:

a. Prepare a work sheet to determine the amounts of Mr. Tazeman's assets, equities, and equity changes for 19x3.

b. Prepare formal classified statements for Mr. Tazeman for the year ended December 31, 19x3.

CASE 9-1. FRANKLIN COMPANY

This case is designed to provide an extended review of journalizing, posting, and statement preparation, and practice in the use of the special columns and special journals which were discussed in this chapter. The necessary transaction information, journals, ledger accounts, and other forms appear in the workbook which accompanies this text.

PART 2

MEASURING, PLANNING, AND CONTROLLING INCOME AND WORKING CAPITAL

Chapter **10**

Appraising Past Operating Results

Use of accounting in making decisions

No matter how well the accounting system is designed or how adequately the statements summarize the financial affairs of the business, accounting still fails to achieve its purpose unless its information is put to use. The use may be in helping management decide upon and carry out actions needed for operation of the business, or in guiding investors and creditors in deciding whether to invest in or lend to the business.

Chapter 5 explained how the design of the accounting system should be tailored to assist management in the functions of determining the objectives of the business, planning how to accomplish them, organizing the people and facilities to do the work, and controlling the performance of the work. Accounting is especially useful in the *control* phase of this cycle as an aid in co-ordinating, directing, and supervising work during its performance and later in *appraising* the results. Logically, planning is the first phase, but plans for a business which is already in existence can be made much more effectively if an appraisal of past results is used as a guide in formulating them. For this reason, the present chapter is devoted to accounting's role in appraisal, as a prelude to the several succeeding chapters, which are concerned principally with the use of accounting in planning.

Regardless of the thoroughness with which the accountant has reported and analyzed the financial information of the business, the user of the statements must make his own interpretations of the data and form his own conclusions. This chapter explains some of the more significant types of comparisons which will assist the statement user in interpreting the financial results.

Need for appraising operating results—an illustrative case

Sound Center, Inc., retails high-fidelity sets. The capital stock of the company, which has been in operation for a number of years, is owned by the Winkle family, heirs of the deceased former owner-manager. Mr. Farley, who has been the manager of the company for the past two years, does not own any of the company's stock. His compensation consists of an annual salary of $8,000 and a commission of one per cent of the sales of the business. The sales clerks also receive a base salary, as well as a commission of three per cent of sales.

The Winkles have become increasingly dissatisfied with the amount of their annual dividends from the company, and have privately discussed the possibility of hiring a new manager to replace Mr. Farley. They are particularly upset because a competitor in the community has been prospering, while the results of Sound Center, Inc., have been poor. As a majority of the board of directors, they have asked Mr. Farley to prepare a careful analysis of the company's operating results and financial status for discussion at the meeting of the board on January 10, 19x4. Mr. Farley requested the company's accountant to prepare statements comparing the financial results of the business for the past two years to aid in this discussion. These statements appear on pages 267–268.

Mr. Farley has sensed the growing impatience of the board of directors, but he feels that he has done as well as could be expected in managing the business, considering its neglected state at the time of Mr. George Winkle's death. He hopes to convince the board that his policies are just beginning to bear fruit in increased revenues and profits, and that even better results can be expected in the future. Mr. Farley knows that the two questions uppermost in the minds of the directors on January 10 will be:

(1) *How well has the business done in comparison with what could be expected of it?*

(2) *What can be done to improve future performance?*

In the days remaining until the board meeting, Mr. Farley is busily preparing analyses that will help him answer these questions.

BASES AND METHODS OF COMPARISON

The need for comparisons

Account titles and balances alone are usually not sufficient to give a clear understanding of the operating results and financial status of a business. The statement reader must have some frame of reference, some standard of comparison, by which to measure both the over-all results and the individual financial elements of the enterprise. An amount has significance only if it is compared with some other related amount. The following types of comparison are useful in analyzing financial information:

(1) Comparison with another balance of the same company for the same accounting period. *Example 1:* Comparing net income with sales revenue.

(2) Comparison with the corresponding balance or relationship of the same company for an earlier accounting period. *Example 2:* Comparing net income for 19x3 with net income for 19x2.

(3) Comparison with the corresponding balance or relationship of another company for the same accounting period. *Example 3:* Comparing the sales revenue for Company *A* with that of Company *B*.

(4) Comparison of the actual amount of a given financial category with the planned amount. *Example 4:* Comparing actual sales with budgeted sales for 19x3.

(5) Comparison of the actual results with some standard which represents a norm or desirable level of achievement. *Example 5:* Comparing the actual labor cost of a manufacturing operation with an engineering standard.

Comparisons of the financial data of a business may be in the form of individual relationships, tables of figures and relationships, or charts and graphs.

Computing individual relationships

The relationship between two amounts, such as *a* and *b*, which are being compared may be expressed as a *ratio* or as a *percentage*. The ratio of *a* to *b* expresses how many units of *a* there are for each *one* unit of *b*. The percentage of *a* to *b* (%) shows how many units of *a* there are for each *one hundred* units of *b*.

The formulas for these computations are:

$$\text{Ratio of } a \text{ to } b = \frac{a}{b}$$

$$\text{Percentage of } a \text{ to } b = 100 \left(\frac{a}{b}\right)$$

Any ratio may be converted to a percentage by multiplying it by 100; any percentage may be converted to a ratio by dividing it by 100.

EXAMPLE 6: Cost of goods sold expense of Sound Center, Inc., for 19x3 amounted to \$100,500 and sales were \$150,000. What was the ratio of cost of goods sold to sales? The percentage?

SOLUTION: $\text{Ratio} = \dfrac{\text{Cost of goods sold}}{\text{Sales}} = \dfrac{\$100,500}{\$150,000} = .67$

$\text{Percentage} = 100 \left(\dfrac{\text{Cost of goods sold}}{\text{Sales}} \right) = 100 \left(\dfrac{\$100,500}{\$150,000} \right) = 100(.67) = 67\%$

Cost of goods sold for the year was \$0.67 for each dollar of sales, or \$67 for each \$100 of sales.

The use of averages

In comparing the amount of one item with other items of the same class, it is often desirable to select a typical, or *average*, item which is representative of the other items in the group. Three common methods of measuring the average item which is to be used as a standard of comparison are the *arithmetic mean*, the *median*, and the *mode*.

The *arithmetic mean* of a group of measurements may be computed by dividing the sum of the measurements by the number of items.

The *median* is the middle value of a series of numbers which have been arrayed in the order of their size.

The *mode* is the value which appears most frequently in a series of numbers.

EXAMPLE 7: The owner of a restaurant wished to determine the amount of its typical lunch check. He arranged the checks for one day in the order of their size, from smallest to largest, and listed the amounts as follows:

\$0.40	\$0.65	\$0.75
.50	.70	.80
.50	.70	.80
.55	.70	.85
.60	.75	.90
.60	.75	1.00
.65	.75	1.10

What was the average amount of a lunch check?

SOLUTION: (a) The arithmetic mean would be computed by dividing the sum of the amounts, \$15.00, by the number of items, 21. The result is approximately \$0.7143, or \$0.71 if rounded to the nearest cent.

(b) The median is the eleventh item in the series, \$0.70.

(c) The mode is \$0.75, which occurs four times.

Determining which method is appropriate for measuring the average number of a group depends upon the use which is to be made of the resulting information and the qualities of the numbers which comprise the class. In drawing conclusions about a class of information on the basis of an average, the analyst must be certain that the average is actually representative of that class. For example, the day selected in the preceding example may not be a typical day for the restaurant.

Averages based upon accounting information usually have to be computed in a special analysis. Debits and credits in journal entries and ledger accounts are often totals of classes of information. The sales of the restaurant in Example 7 would probably be recorded in the journal in one item which represented the total sales for the day.

Comparative financial statements

One of the basic methods of comparison is to present the data of a business for successive accounting periods in tabular form. The accompanying *comparative financial statements* of Sound Center, Inc., illustrate this method.

The following quotation emphasizes the important role played by comparative statements in analyzing and interpreting the finances of business:

The presentation of comparative financial statements in annual and other reports enhances the usefulness of such reports and brings out more clearly the nature and trends of current changes affecting the enterprise. Such presentation emphasizes the fact that statements for a series of periods are far more significant than those for a single period and that the accounts for one period are but an installment of what is essentially a continuous history.[1]

SOUND CENTER, INC.
Income Statement

	For the Years Ended	
	December 31, 19x3	December 31, 19x2
Net sales revenue.	$150,000	$120,000
Deduct cost of goods sold expense.	100,500	80,400
Gross margin on sales.	$ 49,500	$ 39,600
Deduct operating expense:		
Advertising.	$ 3,900	$ 2,000
Commissions on sales.	6,000	4,800
Depreciation.	1,000	1,000
Insurance.	2,000	2,000
Rent.	6,000	6,000
Salary, manager.	8,000	8,000
Salaries, other.	13,860	12,360
Supplies.	1,740	1,500
Taxes (other than income tax).	1,900	1,840
Miscellaneous.	2,100	1,980
Total operating expense.	$ 46,500	$ 41,480
Income (loss) before Federal income tax.	$ 3,000	($ 1,880)
Corporate Federal income tax expense.	900	0
Net income (loss) (to Statement of Retained Income).	$ 2,100	($ 1,880)

---

[1] AICPA, Committee on Accounting Procedure, *ARB No. 43, op. cit.*, p. 15.

SOUND CENTER, INC.
Statement of Retained Income

	For the Years Ended	
	December 31, 19x3	December 31, 19x2
Retained income at beginning of year..................	$ 28,300	$30,930
Add net income, or deduct net loss for the year (from Income Statement)...............................	2,100	(1,880)
	$ 30,400	$29,050
Deduct dividends....................................	1,500	750
Retained income at end of year (to Statement of Financial Position)................................	$ 28,900	$28,300

SOUND CENTER, INC.
Statement of Financial Position

	December 31	
ASSETS	19x3	19x2
Current Assets:		
Cash...	$ 5,000	$ 6,000
Accounts receivable, trade.........................	36,500	34,600
Deduct estimated uncollectibles.................(	3,000)	(2,800)
Merchandise inventory............................	51,000	49,000
Prepaid expenses................................	4,000	4,200
Total current assets...........................	$ 93,500	$91,000
Fixed Assets:		
Equipment (cost)................................	$ 14,000	$11,500
Deduct accumulated depreciation................(	5,500)	(4,500)
Total fixed assets.............................	$ 8,500	$ 7,000
Total assets................................	$102,000	$98,000
LIABILITIES		
Current Liabilities:		
Notes payable to banks...........................	$ 5,000	$ 4,500
Accounts payable, trade...........................	25,600	24,500
Corporate Federal income tax payable..............	900	800
Accrued liabilities................................	2,100	2,200
Total current liabilities........................	$ 33,600	$32,000
Long-Term Liabilities:		
Long-term notes payable..........................	9,500	7,700
Total liabilities..............................	$ 43,100	$39,700
STOCKHOLDERS' EQUITY		
Capital stock, $50 par, 600 shares...................	$ 30,000	$30,000
Retained income (from Statement of Retained Income)	28,900	28,300
Total stockholders' equity......................	$ 58,900	$58,300
Total equities..............................	$102,000	$98,000

Graphic comparisons

It is often difficult for the statement analyst to get an accurate idea of the relationships of financial elements just from tables of amounts, percentages, and ratios. Visual aids such as the *line graph* (Figure 7a), the *bar chart* (Figure 7b), and the *pictogram* (Figure 8) convey quickly informa-

TREND OF TRAFFIC REVENUES

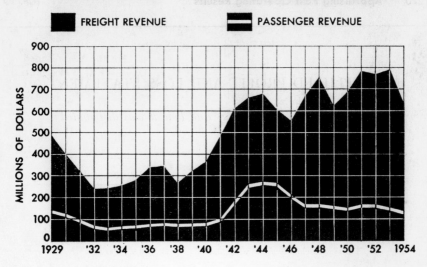

■ FREIGHT REVENUE   ▬ PASSENGER REVENUE

Total revenues were 18 percent below the previous year,
representing a decrease of $159,300,000 freight revenue
and a decrease of $15,600,000 in passenger revenue.

Source: Pennsylvania Railroad Annual Report, 1954.

Fig. 7a.

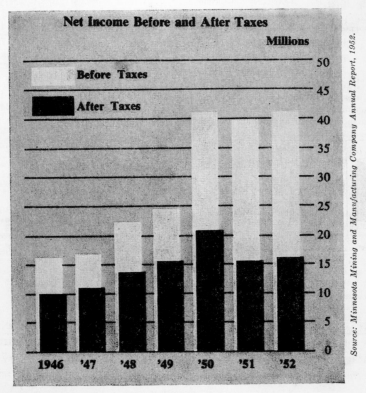

Fig. 7b.
269

SIMPLIFIED PROFIT AND LOSS STATEMENT

The Sylvania Sales Dollar and how it was distributed

SYLVANIA TOOK IN

From sale of products and services $293,267,408   100%

IT COST SYLVANIA

For raw materials of many kinds	100,847,899	
For manufacturing, selling and other expenses .	45,395,695	
For new machinery as old wears out	6,877,000	
For taxes (exclusive of social security taxes) .	16,955,651	
For interest on debentures and loans . . .	2,478,469	
For wages, salaries and non-wage labor costs .	111,176,513	
These items total	$283,731,227	97%
Leaving as Net Income	$ 9,536,181	3%

SYLVANIA DISTRIBUTED

To stockholders as dividends 6,104,927*   2%

THERE REMAINED

To be reinvested in the business . . . . . $ 3,431,254   1%

*In addition a 10% stock dividend was issued on the common stock.

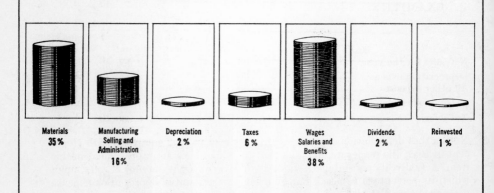

| Materials 35% | Manufacturing Selling and Administration 16% | Depreciation 2% | Taxes 6% | Wages Salaries and Benefits 38% | Dividends 2% | Reinvested 1% |

Source: Sylvania Electric Products, Inc. Annual Report, 1953.

Fig. 8.

tion about business relationships which would require the use of long and complex tables or descriptions.

Analysis of composition

Ratios and percentages may be used to compare the size of the components of an accounting category with the total of that category. One common comparison of this type is to determine the percentage of each principal expense and of net income to net sales. The same procedure would be used as in Example 6, which showed the calculation of the percentage of cost of goods sold to net sales. The total percentages of each of the components of the net sales dollar would add up to 100 per cent. The individual percentages are often recorded in a separate column beside the corresponding amounts in the financial statements (see Figure 8 for an example) to facilitate interpretation by the reader.

Percentages of this type help the analyst judge the size of each of the components relative to their total and to each other. A comparison with the percentages for similar items for the preceding year shows changes in the composition of the total from one year to the next.

When there is a cause-and-effect relationship between the individual components and their total, analysis of composition is often meaningful and useful. An outstanding example of such an analysis is determining the relationship of variable expenses to sales, which will be discussed in detail in Chapter 11. However, percentages of composition are quite often misinterpreted, and for that reason they should be used with caution. The following example shows how percentages of composition might lead to an erroneous interpretation.

EXAMPLE 8:

	19x2		19x1	
	Amount	Per cent of Net Sales	Amount	Per cent of Net Sales
Net sales for the year..............	$100,000	100%	$50,000	100%
Depreciation expense...............	$ 5,000	5	$ 5,000	10
All other expenses.................	80,000	80	44,000	88
Total expenses..................	$ 85,000	85	$49,000	98
Net income......................	$ 15,000	15%	$ 1,000	2%

Noting that depreciation expense was five per cent in 19x2 compared with 10 per cent in 19x1, the reader might think that there had been an improvement in this item. Actually, its percentage is smaller solely because the amount of sales, upon which its percentage is based, has doubled. The amount of depreciation expense has not changed at all.

Analysis of change

Comparisons of the financial results of one period with those of the same company for an earlier period are often made by computing the amounts of change and entering them in a column of the financial statements beside the amounts which are being compared.

EXAMPLE 9:   Sales of Sound Center, Inc., as shown by its comparative Income Statement, were $120,000 in 19x2 and $150,000 in 19x3, indicating an increase of $30,000.

Such comparisons are often of limited value, because they do not show the size of the change *relative* to the size of the amounts involved. It is more meaningful to compute a percentage of change, or a ratio of one amount to the other. It is important to use the proper base year in making these comparisons—the earlier year in both types of comparison. The appropriate formulas are:

$$\text{Percentage of change} = 100\left(\frac{\text{Amount of change}}{\text{Base-year amount}}\right)$$

$$\text{Ratio of later year to earlier} = \frac{\text{Amount for later year}}{\text{Base-year amount}}$$

EXAMPLE 10:   The *percentage* of increase in sales of Sound Center, Inc., from 19x2 to 19x3 is determined as follows:

$$100\left(\frac{\text{Amount of change}}{\text{Base-year amount}}\right) = 100\left(\frac{+\$30,000}{\$120,000}\right) = 100(+.25) = +25\%.$$

The *ratio* of Sound Center's 19x3 sales to those of 19x2 is computed thus:

$$\frac{\text{Amount for later year}}{\text{Base-year amount}} = \frac{\$150,000}{\$120,000} = 1.25$$

Sometimes percentages of change cannot be computed, as when the item amounted to zero in the base year. In other cases, percentages are difficult to interpret because of their size.

EXAMPLE 11:   The net income of Company *C* increased from $10 in 19x1 to $4,000 in 19x2. The percentage of increase is 39,900%. In such a case it would be easier to interpret a ratio showing that the *increase* was 399 times as much as the income of the base year, or that the *amount* of the income for the second year was 400 times as great as that of the first year.

Percentages of change and ratios for a series of successive years are much more useful than for a single year in making comparisons over time. These methods of comparison are intended to give the reader an idea of the direction in which the company's financial results are moving and the rate of change. Estimates of future results on the basis of such past comparisons must be made very cautiously, however, because the factors which have resulted in the past relationships may not continue to operate in the same way. In order to interpret the figures about a business, the individual must be familiar with the operating conditions which lie behind them and with the plans of management and the changed conditions which are likely to exist in the future.

It is often just as difficult to interpret percentages, unaccompanied by absolute amounts, as it is to understand the significance of amounts without relating them to a standard of comparison. It is of little significance to determine that net income in 19x2 is 10 per cent larger than in 19x1 if the net income is totally inadequate in both years in comparison with the amount of assets invested in the business. As someone has aptly remarked, "It is *money*, not percentages, that you deposit in the bank."

When an analyst compares the operating results or financial position of a business with its own financial data for an earlier period, he assumes that the data have been compiled in a comparable manner by means of accounting, and that the real factors at work on the two dates are reasonably similar. In interpreting the meaning of changes, the analyst must make proper allowances for factors which have, in fact, changed.

EXAMPLE 12:   Sales of $150,000 of Sound Center, Inc., for 19x3 would be better than sales of $120,000 for 19x2 only if all other factors affecting the business remained unchanged. If there has been a relatively greater increase elsewhere in the economy as a result of rapidly increasing prices or some other cause, the amount of increase may even be unsatisfactory. Likewise, if expenses have increased out of proportion to revenues, the change is unsatisfactory.

Comparisons with other businesses

Individuals who are analyzing the results or prospects of a company often do so by comparing selected items derived from its financial statements with those of similar companies. For this purpose, an effort is made to select a typical, or average, company whose results are representative of those of the companies in the industry.

There are many published sources of information which show averages of financial ratios and percentages for particular industries. One of the best-known sources is Dun & Bradstreet, Inc., which publishes frequent information relating to 14 selected ratios for a number of lines of manufacturing, wholesaling, and retailing business. The representative measures used in these ratios are the *medians*, or middle numbers for each industry; the *upper quartiles*, or dividing line between the highest one-fourth and the next-highest one-fourth of businesses in the industry; and the *lower quartiles*, the dividing line between the lowest one-fourth and the next lowest.[2] In many industries, the trade association compiles similar information on averages for the industry.

Industry averages are often very useful in evaluating the status or performance of a given company, but the user must be fully aware of their limitations. The company being analyzed may not be similar to the group

---

[2] Published in Roy A. Foulke, *The Genesis of the Fourteen Important Ratios* (Dun & Bradstreet, Inc., 1955) and other Dun & Bradstreet publications.

represented by the average in size, geographical location, functions, or other important characteristics. A further limitation of comparability is imposed by differences in accounting methods between companies, a matter which was discussed in Chapter 8.

Comparisons with predetermined goals and with ideals

One basis of comparison that is very useful to management in appraising actual financial results is the goal, or planned achievement of the business for the period. Later chapters explain how departures of actual results from the plan can be used by management in deciding upon future action.

The often limited validity of comparisons of current financial results with those of the same company at other times, with those of other companies at the same time, and with planned results has led management and other interested groups to try to develop standards of comparison which express *what the company should have done under the circumstances*. Such standards may be based upon the assumption of *ideal* conditions or upon the *normal* conditions which the company faces. Standards of this type are highly developed in many manufacturing companies, especially as to the material and labor components of manufactured products. They receive detailed attention in Chapter 17, "Accounting for Manufacturing Inventories."

Limitations of comparisons

The variety of comparisons which could be made for any company is almost endless, but there are practical limitations upon the number which should be made in any given case. The following are some of the principal requisites and limitations of comparisons.

(1) Each comparison should be meaningful. The amounts compared should represent events, economic factors, or conditions which are related to each other. The figures alone do not tell the whole story, and the person who analyzes and interprets them must be familiar with the actual physical operating conditions of the company if his interpretations are to be valid.

(2) Each comparison should be useful and its proper use should be understood by the user. The time spent making comparisons is wasted unless they are actually put to use in interpreting the affairs of the business. If they are potentially useful but are not being used, management and others should be educated to their value.

(3) The data being compared should be comparable, both as to method of collection and as to the conditions in effect.

(4) The figures selected for comparison should be representative.

(5) The cost of making the analyses should not exceed the benefit to be gained from them. If they are of limited significance, they might well be omitted. The number of comparisons is not the important thing; a few comparisons analyzed thoroughly are of much greater value than a large number merely glanced at superficially.

(6) The comparisons should be used as a basis for decisions and actions. Mathematical analysis of financial data does not solve business problems. The analysis may indicate that some trouble exists or even help to pinpoint its cause, but the remedy can come only through appropriate management action.

MEASURES FOR APPRAISING OPERATING RESULTS

Rate of income on stockholders' equity

Because of the dominance of the income objective in business, one of the most widely used measures of business operating performance is the *rate* (or percentage) *of income as compared with stockholders' equity*. This is one of a number of useful comparisons which determine a *rate of change*. The general formula is:

$$\text{Rate of change} = \frac{\text{Amount of Change during Period}}{\text{Typical Balance at a Given Time during Period}}$$

The specific formula appropriate for the present comparison is:

$$\frac{\text{Rate of Income on}}{\text{Stockholders' Equity}} = \frac{\text{Net Income for the Period}}{\text{Typical Balance of Stockholders' Equity}}$$

EXAMPLE 13: What was the rate of income on stockholders' equity of Sound Center, Inc., for 19x3?

SOLUTION: $\dfrac{\text{Income}}{\text{Average Stockholders' Equity}} = \dfrac{\$2,100}{\$58,600} = .036 \text{ or } 3.6\%$

The average used was the arithmetic mean of the beginning and ending totals of stockholders' equity $\left(\dfrac{\$58,300 + \$58,900}{2}\right)$.

The arithmetic mean is usually a more representative measure of the balance of stockholders' equity throughout the period than is either the beginning or ending balance alone. Its use assumes that the changes which have occurred during the period have been of uniform amounts, evenly spaced. If they have not been, the arithmetic mean of the beginning and ending balances of each month may be a more typical balance.

The rate of return on stockholders' equity is a measure of the profitability with which management has used the capital of the stockholders. It may be compared with the rate of return of the same company for earlier periods, with that of similar companies, and with the planned rate, with due attention given to the limits of comparability. The point of view is that of the corporation, not of the stockholders as individuals. Rarely, and only by coincidence, will the total amounts which stockholders have paid for their shares equal the total stockholders' equity on the books of the corporation.

Unusual items, such as extraordinary charges and credits, which are sometimes used in the measurement of net income, cannot be expected to recur with the same degree of certainty as can operating revenues and expenses. The interpreter of the statement should, therefore assign them a different weight. This is facilitated by computing a *rate of income before extraordinary items* in addition to the final rate of income.

Earnings per share

A widely used, and often misused, measure of the operat ng performance of corporations is the amount of *earnings per share* of capital stock. The formula is,

$$\text{Earnings per Share} = \frac{\text{Net Income}}{\text{Average Number of Shares Outstanding}}$$

Again, the arithmetic mean of the number of shares outstanding during the year is likely to be more representative than the number outstanding at either the beginning or the end of the year.

EXAMPLE 14:   The computation of earnings per share for Sound Center, Inc., for 19x3 is made as follows:

$$\frac{\text{Net Income}}{\text{Average Number of Shares Outstanding}} = \frac{\$2,100}{600} = \$3.50$$

This measure is sometimes used to compare the results of companies whose shares of stock are not comparable. Unless there is a basis for expressing the stock of the two companies in a common denominator, it is impossible to determine, from the information given, which company's results were better. One such common denominator is the percentage of the earnings per share of each company to the current market value of one of its shares.

EXAMPLE 15:   Earnings of Company *A* were $10 per share in 19x1, while those of Company *B*, a similar company, were $1 per share. Were the results of *A* 10 times as good as those of *B*?

SOLUTION: Current market quotations were $100 a share for the stock of Company A and $5 a share for Company B. The rates of earnings to the current market value of the stock of each were as follows:

	Company A	Company B
Earnings per share............................	$ 10	$1
Divided by current market price..............	$100	$5
Equals current rate of return................	10%	20%

It now appears that the results of Company B were twice as good as those of Company A, in relation to market prices. However, since market price depends to a large extent upon expected earnings, stockholders apparently think Company A's prospects are better.

Effect of leverage on return to stockholders

A business can increase the rate of return on stockholders' equity above that earned on the total assets of the business by the effective use of *leverage*, or *trading on the equity*. If a business which earns income at the rate of 6 per cent on all assets can obtain some of these assets by borrowing at an interest rate lower than 6 per cent, the rate of return on stockholders' equity will be higher than 6 per cent.

The extent to which a company has made effective use of borrowed capital can be measured by comparing (1) the percentage of net income before deducting interest and income tax expenses to total equities with (2) the percentage of net income to stockholders' equity.

EXAMPLE 16:   Companies C and D were the same size and they operated under identical conditions except as to the sources of their assets, which were as follows:

	Company C	Company D
Total liabilities..	$ 0	$ 40,000
Total stockholders' equity.............................	100,000	60,000
Total equities..	$100,000	$100,000

Their operating results for 19x1 were as follows:

7.0%   9.33%

	Company C	Company D
Net income before deducting interest and income tax expense...	$ 10,000	$ 10,000
Interest expense at 5%................................	0	2,000
Net income before income tax.........................	$ 10,000	$ 8,000
Income tax at 30%....................................	3,000	2,400
Net income...	$ 7,000	$ 5,600

The rate of return on stockholders' equity of Company C is 7 per cent ($7,000/ $100,000) and that of D is 9.33 per cent ($5,600/$60,000). This difference is due solely to the favorable operation of leverage.

A word of caution is in order. Leverage can operate unfavorably and even disastrously. If the rate of return on all assets is less than that paid to lenders as interest (in Example 16, 5 per cent), the effect of borrowing will be to *reduce* the percentage of net income to stockholders' investment.

EXAMPLE 17:   If Company D's rate of return on all assets in Example 16 were 3 per cent ($3,000) instead of 10 per cent, its net income before income tax would have been $1,000 and its net income, $700, only a 1.17 per cent return on the stockholders' equity of $60,000. By comparison, the stockholders of a company financed entirely by owners' equity would have earned 3 per cent.

Interest on borrowed funds is an expense which must be paid whether or not there is any net income. If it is not paid, the company will be subjected to financial embarrassment or failure. For this reason, businesses subject to wide fluctuations in their periodic income should borrow sparingly and should maintain a cushion of stockholders' equity sufficient to absorb probable losses.

Another type of contract in which leverage operates to a significant extent is the acquisition of the use, though not the ownership, of real estate by means of a long-term lease at a fixed rental.

Effect of income taxes on return to stockholders

Example 16 demonstrated how corporate income tax reduces the rate of return on stockholders' equity below the rate of return earned on all equities. Its effect on Company D was rather complex, because interest expense is deductible in computing the amount of income tax expense. For this reason, Company D's income tax expense was lower than that of Company C ($2,400, as compared with $3,000).

Many times, because of the dissimilar objectives of measuring business income and taxable income, there are significant differences between the amount of income in the income statement and the amount of taxable income upon which the income tax expense was computed. There are also frequent differences in the tax rates which apply to various segments of taxable income. For these reasons, comparisons of the net income of a company from time to time, and between companies at the same time, are often meaningless. In such cases it is useful to compute the *percentage of income before deducting income tax* to stockholders' equity or to total equities.

Rate of income on total assets

Comparisons of various measures of the income of a business with its stockholders' equity have one important limitation in common: they do not show the efficiency with which management has employed the assets of the business, without regard to their source. A measure designed to give this information is the *percentage of net income before deducting interest and income tax to total assets* (or, what amounts to the same thing, the percentage as compared to total equities). The formula is,

Percentage of Income before Interest and Tax to Total Assets

$$= \frac{\text{Net Income before Interest and Tax}}{\text{Average Total Assets}} = \frac{I}{A}$$

EXAMPLE 18:   The computation for Sound Center, Inc., is made as follows:

$$\frac{I}{A} = \frac{\$3,000}{\$100,000} = 3\%$$

The average total assets figure used is the arithmetic mean of the beginning total asset balance of $98,000 and the ending balance of $102,000. Interest expense has not been added back to net income because none is shown in the income statement, although it is quite possible that some interest is included in Miscellaneous Expense.

The use of this percentage facilitates comparison of the operating results of companies which are in the same line of business but which are financed differently. This measure alone does not show the full picture of the performance of the management of the business, however. It should be supplemented by the percentage of income on stockholders' equity to show the effectiveness of the business in financing and in managing income tax matters.

Mathematically, there are many possible ways of increasing the rate of return of a business.

EXAMPLE 19:   Some of the possible combinations of changes in amounts which would increase the rate of return (before interest and taxes) of Sound Center, Inc., from 3 per cent to 6 per cent are:

(a) Increase the *amount* of income while using the same average total assets:

$$\frac{I}{A} = \frac{\$6,000}{\$100,000} = 6\% \text{ return}$$

It is unlikely, however, that the amount of income could be changed without some effect on assets.

(b) *Reduce* the amount of assets employed while continuing to earn the same dollar income:

$$\frac{I}{A} = \frac{\$3,000}{\$50,000} = 6\% \text{ return}$$

There would be an additional problem of finding a worthwhile investment for the assets released from the business.

(c) Increase the amount of income relative to the amount of assets employed while both are changing:

$$\frac{I}{A} = \frac{\$9,000}{\$150,000} = 6\% \text{ return}$$

Components of rate of income as a basis for action

While the rate of return on assets is useful for showing whether the performance of the business as a whole is up to expectations, it does not pinpoint the trouble spots or indicate the type of corrective managerial action that is needed. It is necessary to investigate further to determine which specific revenues, expenses, assets, or equities need attention.

Top management can evaluate the performance of its individual department or division managers by computing the rate of return on assets of each such internal unit. This is done by dividing the income of each unit by the assets which it used in earning the income.

In planning specific management action to increase the rate of return, it is useful, as a starting point, to break the rate-of-return formula into its two principal components, the *net margin percentage* and the *number of asset turnovers*.

The formula for computing the *net margin percentage* is:

$$\frac{\text{Income}}{\text{Revenue}} = \frac{I}{R}$$

The net margin percentage is a measure of the profitability of each turnover of the average amount of assets used by the business at any given time.

The formula for computing the *number of asset turnovers* is:

$$\frac{\text{Revenue}}{\text{Average Total Assets}} = \frac{R}{A}$$

Turnover shows how hard the assets of the business, on the average, are worked. Turnover is a measure of change which is used in many types of financial analysis. The general formula is,

$$\text{Turnover} = \frac{\text{Amount of Change}}{\text{Average Balance}}$$

The product of these two formulas is the rate of return on average assets:

$$\frac{I}{R} \times \frac{R}{A} = \frac{I}{A}$$

Revenue in the denominator of the first fraction cancels revenue in the numerator of the second.

EXAMPLE 20:   (a) The net margin percentage of Sound Center, Inc., for 19x3 was:

$$\frac{I}{R} = \frac{\$3,000}{\$150,000} = 2\%$$

(b) The number of asset turnovers was:

$$\frac{R}{A} = \frac{\$150,000}{\$100,000} = 1.5 \text{ asset turnovers}$$

(c) The product of these two results was:

$$\frac{I}{R} \times \frac{R}{A} = 2\% \times 1.5 = 3\%, \text{ the rate of return on assets}$$

A business may earn a satisfactory rate of return even though its net margin percentage is low, if it has a high rate of turnover. Food retailers usually operate under such conditions. On the other hand, adequate income may result from a combination of high margin and low turnover, illustrated by the typical operations of a jewelry store.

EXAMPLE 21:

	Grocery Store	Jewelry Store
Financial Statement Data:		
Sales revenue	$500,000	$100,000
Net income before interest and income tax	5,000	5,000
Average total assets	50,000	50,000
Comparisons:		
Rate of return on total assets	10%	10%
Net margin percentage	1%	5%
Number of asset turnovers	10	2

An increase in the rate of return on assets may result from an increase in the net margin percentage, an increase in the number of turnovers, or a favorable combination of changes in both.

EXAMPLE 22:   Here are some of the mathematical possibilities which confront Mr. Farley in attempting to increase the rate of net income of Sound Center, Inc., from 3 per cent to 6 per cent:

New Net Margin %		New Number of Turnovers	Desired Rate of Return
1.0%	×	6.0	6%
1.5%	×	4.0	6%
2.0%	×	3.0	6%
3.0%	×	2.0	6%
4.0%	×	1.5	6%
6.0%	×	1.0	6%

Further refinements of these two components of the rate of return are needed to provide useful guides to management in deciding upon future courses of action. Income is not the result of the operation of a single homogeneous set of factors, but the *difference* between two types of flows which have opposite effects: *revenue*, which tends to increase income, and *expense*, which tends to reduce it. The behavior of the amounts of various classes of revenue and expense stems from many complex causes, and separate types of action upon each class are often needed to improve operating results. Likewise, the amounts of each type of asset used in carrying on business operations respond to many complex influences. Succeeding chapters show how management should proceed to plan for an increased rate of return in view of these many complications.

Summary

Appraisal of the past results of a business is designed to answer two principal questions: (1) How well has the business done in comparison with what could be expected of it? and (2) What can be done to improve future performance? Comparisons of several types help to provide answers to these questions: comparisons with other items in the financial statements of the company at the same time, comparisons with the corresponding results of the company at earlier periods, comparisons with the corresponding results of other similar companies, comparisons of actual results with planned results, and comparison of actual results with a desired standard of performance.

Comparisons alone do not tell the whole story, and they are but a prelude to management action. Comparisons should be meaningful, useful, and reliable, and the cost of making and using them should not exceed the resulting benefit.

One useful measure of past performance is the rate of income on stockholders' equity, which measures the operating results of the business from the point of view of the stockholder. Perhaps even more useful is the rate of income on all assets, and its components, the net margin percentage and the number of asset turnovers. These measures indicate management's efficiency in the administration of assets, regardless of source, and they provide valuable clues as to where and how managerial action can be taken to improve results in the future.

QUESTIONS AND PROBLEMS

10-1   The percentage of net income to stockholders' equity for your company for 19x1 was the highest of all companies in its industry.
REQUIRED:
Was its operating performance satisfactory? Explain.

10-2   Company Y's net income was 10 per cent of sales of 19x5, while Company Z's was 4 per cent.
REQUIRED:
Under what circumstances would you consider Y's showing better? Z's?

10-3   Company K's statement of financial position at the end of 19x5 shows capital stock of $10,000,000 and retained income of $40,000,000. You are discussing its financial affairs with another stockholder, who is impressed by the amazing profitability of the company.

REQUIRED:

a. What does the information given tell you about the past financial history and policy of the company?

b. What does it tell you about the recent and prospective profitability of the company?

10-4

REQUIRED:

a. List four types of credits and debits which you might expect to find classified as "nonrecurring" items in an income statement.

b. How would each of these items affect your appraisal of the company's operating results for the past year?

c. How would they affect your estimate of the company's future prospects?

10-5   On a given day, the stock of the Superior Oil Company of California was changing hands on the New York Stock Exchange at $1,720 a share, while that of Sinclair was selling at $59.75.

REQUIRED:

a. How can you explain the fact that the Superior Oil stock was worth so much more?

b. The previous day, Superior stock had sold at $1,730.25 and the Sinclair, at $60.75. Which had undergone the greatest price change?

c. If an individual had bought one share of Superior stock on the first day and sold it on the second, what would be the effect on the corporation's books? (Disregard brokerage fees and transfer taxes.)

10-6   Percentages are often used in the analysis and interpretation of financial statements.

REQUIRED:

a. Illustrate two specific ways in which percentages may be used in analyzing the results of operations.

b. What are the principal advantages of the use of percentages?

c. What are their chief limitations?

10-7

REQUIRED:

a. When comparing the financial results of a business over a period of years, which is more useful, a study of the changes in absolute dollar amounts or of the changes expressed in percentages? Explain.

b. Illustrate a situation in which the method you preferred in (a) leads to confusion in statement interpretation. How would you correct this defect?

10-8   Paul Brent owns 100 shares of the stock of A Company. Upon receiving its published income statement for 19x2, Paul calculated that his proportionate share of the net income of the company, based upon the earnings-per-share figure, represented a 12 per cent return on his investment. He was perplexed, however, to find upon reading in the financial comments of the annual report that the company's return on total stockholders' equity was 8 per cent.

REQUIRED:

Explain to Paul how it is possible for both percentages to be correct.

10-9   On December 31, 19x3, the statement of financial position of Company R showed total assets of $200,000, total liabilities of $100,000, and owners' equity of $100,000. On the same date, the statement of Company S disclosed total assets of $200,000 and no liabilities. The average interest rate paid by Company R was 5 per cent. The net income before interest and income taxes was $14,000 for Company R and $16,000 for Company S.

REQUIRED:

a. On the basis of the information given, in which company did the management seem to be more efficient? Explain.
b. Which company earned the greater return for its owners?
c. To what extent has leverage been used effectively?
d. Under what conditions would the use of leverage by Company R be inappropriate?
e. How does income tax affect the results of leverage?
f. Assume that the net income before interest and taxes for Company R for 19x4 was $2,000, and that all other balances were the same as in 19x3. Analyze and comment upon the results.

10-10   William Foster sold 500 shares of S Company capital stock, for which he had paid a total of $5,000, to George Hanson for $6,000.

REQUIRED:

a. What factors should George Hanson consider before he decides to buy the stock?
b. Why did he probably decide to pay $6,000 for it?
c. Why was Foster probably willing to sell it for $6,000?
d. When stock changes hands at a price different from that received by the corporation, is there any direct effect on the corporation's accounts?
e. Is a sale such as that in (d) of any importance to the corporation?

10-11   It is often difficult to evaluate the profitability of single proprietorships, partnerships, and family corporations because the dividing line between reward for management services and return on capital is not distinct.

REQUIRED:

a. Why is this statement true?
b. How would you suggest that the problem be solved?
c. Why is this problem of less significance in large publicly owned corporations?

10-12   The manager of the Milham Company, upon reviewing the company's 19x2 income statement and a supporting analysis prepared by the accountant, noticed that Losses from Uncollectible Accounts amounted to 1.2 per cent of net sales in 19x2, whereas they were only 0.7 per cent of net sales in 19x1.

REQUIRED:

a. Was the performance of the company in granting credit and making collections worse in 19x2 than in 19x1? Explain.
b. What additional information do you need in order to give a more conclusive answer to (a)?

10-13   Which single measure of operating performance discussed in this chapter do you think would be of greatest interest to each of the following:

(1) The president of the company?
(2) The manager of a branch of the company?
(3) A stockholder?
(4) A large supplier of raw materials on credit?
(5) An employee in the shipping department?
(6) A large customer?

10-14   One of the first questions that any financial statement analyst seeks to answer is, "Is the business earning a satisfactory income?"

REQUIRED:

a. Why, then, should a reader of the financial statements know whether the business prepares its statements according to the all-inclusive concept or the current operating performance concept?
b. Which of the two methods do you think would give the statement analyst more accurate information about the net income of the business? Explain.

10-15   This chapter discusses several different measures of the rate of income of a business.

REQUIRED:

a. For what purpose is the rate of income on stockholders' equity useful?
b. Under what circumstances would it be satisfactory to compute the rate of income on stockholders' equity?
c. What are the principal limitations of the rate of income on stockholders' equity?
d. For what purpose is the percentage of income, before deducting interest and income taxes, to stockholders' equity useful?
e. Does the method of comparison in (d) imply that income taxes and interest expense are not important? If not, how can you justify its use?
f. For what purpose is the percentage of income, before deducting interest and income taxes, to total assets useful?
g. Which method should be used in appraising the operating performance of a business, that in (a), (d), or (f)? Explain.

CASE 10-1. BEST-BUYS, INCORPORATED

The comparative financial statements of Best Buys, Incorporated, for the three years ended December 31, 19x1, 19x2, and 19x3 are given.

REQUIRED:

The board of directors desires an analysis, from the point of view of both management and stockholders, of the operating performance of the company for 19x3. You are to prepare a detailed report to the directors, consisting of the following parts for *each* of the lettered requirements listed below:

(1) Comparative ratios or percentages, as appropriate. Ratios should be rounded to the nearest thousandth (.016) and percentages to the *nearest* tenth of a per cent (1.6%).
(2) A brief explanation of the meaning of the comparisons in (1), from the point of view of both management and stockholders.
(3) A brief explanation of the principal limitations of the comparisons in (1).

a. Percentage of income to stockholders' equity for 19x3, and a comparison with the results of preceding years.
b. Percentage of income, before interest and income taxes, to total assets for 19x3, and a comparison with earlier years.
c. The effectiveness of the use of financial leverage.
d. Number of asset turnovers for 19x3 and prior years.
e. Percentage of net margin to sales for 19x3 and prior years.
f. Composition of net sales (percentage of each item in the income statement to net sales) for 19x3, and the change in composition in the three-year period.

BEST-BUYS, INCORPORATED
Income Statement
For the Year Ended December 31:

	19x3		19x2		19x1	
Gross revenue from sales		$1,200,000		$1,400,000		$1,000,000
Sales returns and allowances	$ 7,000		$ 6,000		$ 5,000	
Sales discounts	18,000		24,000		15,000	
Losses from uncollectible accounts	2,000	27,000	2,000	32,000	1,000	21,000
Net revenue from sales		$1,173,000		$1,368,000		$ 979,000
Cost of goods sold		800,000		900,000		600,000
Gross margin on sales		$ 373,000		468,000		$ 379,000
Operating expenses:						
Wages and salaries	$120,000		$110,000		$100,000	
Depreciation—buildings	50,000		50,000		50,000	
Depreciation—equipment	30,000		22,000		25,000	
Advertising expense	13,000		15,000		10,000	
Rent expense	12,000		12,000		12,000	
Insurance expense	3,000		3,000		3,000	
Supplies expense	37,000		33,000		24,000	
Payroll taxes expense	8,000		7,000		6,000	
Maintenance expense	6,000		6,000		5,000	
Transportation expense	5,000		3,500		4,000	
Total operating expenses		284,000		261,500		239,000
Income from operations		$ 89,000		$ 206,500		$ 140,000
Other revenue and gains:						
Interest revenue	$ 4,000		$ 15,000		$ 6,000	
Gain on sale of miscellaneous assets	21,500	25,500		15,000	11,000	17,000
		$ 114,500		$ 221,500		$ 157,000
Other expenses and losses:						
Interest on bonds payable	$ 20,000		$ 20,000		$ 20,000	
Interest on notes payable	1,500		2,500		2,000	
Loss on sale of miscellaneous assets		21,500	23,000	45,500		22,000
Net income before Federal income tax		$ 93,000		$ 176,000		$ 135,000
Corporate Federal income tax expense		42,860		86,020		64,700
Net income (to Statement of Retained Income)		$ 50,140		89,980		$ 70,300

BEST-BUYS, INCORPORATED
Statement of Retained Income

	For the Year Ended December 31		
	19x3	19x2	19x1
Retained income at beginning of year.............	$480,280	$445,300	$425,000
Net income for the year (from Income Statement).	50,140	89,980	70,300
Total.........	$530,420	$535,280	$495,300
Deduct dividends.............................	35,000	55,000	50,000
Retained income at end of year (to Statement of Financial Position).........................	$495,420	$480,280	$445,300

BEST-BUYS, INCORPORATED
Statement of Financial Position

	December 31		
ASSETS	19x3	19x2	19x1
Current assets:			
Cash.................................	$ 60,000	$ 50,000	$ 75,000
Accounts receivable....................	300,000	260,000	220,000
Less estimated uncollectibles............(	4,000) (	3,000) (	2,000)
Notes receivable.......................	20,000	20,000	25,000
Inventories...........................	350,000	410,000	430,000
Temporary investments.................	60,000	280,000	100,000
Accrued interest receivable.............	1,000	3,000	2,000
Unexpired insurance...................	1,000	1,000	
Supplies inventories....................	8,000	5,000	10,000
Total current assets..................	$ 796,000	$1,026,000	$ 860,000
Fixed assets:			
Land.................................	$ 100,000	$ 50,000	$ 50,000
Buildings.............................	1,000,000	1,000,000	1,000,000
Less accumulated depreciation.......... (	300,000) (	250,000) (	200,000)
Equipment........	634,000	485,000	300,000)
Less accumulated depreciation......... (	90,000) (	65,000) (	50,000)
Total fixed assets....................	$1,344,000	$1,220,000	$1,100,000
Other assets:			
Organization costs....................	$ 100,000	$ 100,000	$ 100,000
Total assets...........................	$2,240,000	$2,346,000	$2,060,000
EQUITIES			
Liabilities:			
Current liabilities:			
Accounts payable, trade..............	$ 422,720	$ 475,700	$ 257,000
Notes payable, trade.................	18,000	35,000	22,000
Notes payable, banks.................	5,000	8,000	10,000
Accrued interest payable.............	1,000	1,000	1,000
Accrued salaries payable.............	2,000	6,000	8,000
Accrued payroll taxes payable........	3,000	4,000	2,000
Estimated Federal income taxes payable	42,860	86,020	64,700
Total current liabilities.............	$ 494,580	$ 615,720	$ 364,700
Long-term liabilities:			
4% bonds payable, due 19x9.....	$ 500,000	$ 500,000	$ 500,000
Total liabilities...................	$ 994,580	$1,115,720	$ 864,700
Stockholders' equity:			
Capital stock, $100 par; authorized, issued, and outstanding, 7,500 shares.........	$ 750,000	$ 750,000	$ 750,000
Retained income (from Statement of Retained Income)..................	495,420	480,280	445,300
Total stockholders' equity..........	$1,245,420	$1,230,280	$1,195,300
Total equities.......................	$2,240,000	$2,346,000	$2,060,000

CASE 10-2. SOUND CENTER, INC. (A)

Refer to the comparative financial statements of Sound Center, Inc., which are illustrated in Chapter 10, and the accompanying descriptive information.

REQUIRED:

a. What are some of the detailed questions which Mr. Farley could anticipate that the board of directors would ask at the meeting on January 10?

b. Prepare the analyses which you think Mr. Farley should have prepared in advance of the meeting.

c What conclusions can you form on the basis of these analyses?

CASE 10-3. THE NOVELTY STORE

Shortly after the close of their second year of operations, the three directors and stockholders of The Novelty Store met to discuss the results of the year's operations, to take action in connection with a dividend to stockholders, and to make plans for the year which was just beginning. Each had just received a copy of financial statements which the accountant had prepared, showing in adjacent columns the income, retained income, and financial position of the Store for the years ended June 30, 19x5, and 19x4. These statements are illustrated as Exhibits A, B, and C, respectively.

Calvin Borman, who served as President and General Manager of the Store, owned 30 per cent of the company's stock, for which he had paid $6,000 at the time of organization. William Dalton, the Vice-President, had acquired 40 per cent of the stock for $8,000. His only participation in the business was in the role of a member of the board of directors. John Farnham, whose stock ownership was identical with that of Borman, acted as Secretary-Treasurer and Assistant General Manager of the corporation.

Mr. Borman called the meeting to order and asked if there were any comments on the financial statements.

Mr. Dalton, quickly making calculations on the back of one of the statements, exclaimed, "The business has really done well, in my opinion. Last year earnings per share were $43.15 and this year they are $68.45. That is an increase of approximately 60 per cent over last year. You can talk all you like, but that is *the figure* that counts in my book."

Mr. Farnham frowned slightly and said, "I disagree with you, Bill. Earnings per share have increased, but our return on our total equity has only increased a little more than 10 per cent. Actually, that's not very good."

"Both of you gentlemen are talking about our improvement. It looks to me as though we are worse off this year than at the same time last year. Our cash in the bank was over $5,000 then, and now we only have $1,700," remarked Mr. Borman. He continued, "It just doesn't make sense to me that our sales went up $60,000 last year, and our cash went down! And if you calculate net income as a percentage of sales, it is 5.3 per cent this year compared with 4.3 per cent for last year—60,000 more dollars of sales, yet only a one per cent increase in profits."

"I'm convinced of one thing already," said Mr. Farnham. "You can't analyze the results of a company by trying to summarize everything through the use of one or two ratios. We had better examine these three statements separately and review their individual components so that we can see what we have done, and what plans we wish to make for next year."

"I guess you're right, John," replied Mr. Dalton. "I was all set to make a motion that we declare a big dividend on the basis of my calculated earnings per share, but Calvin has made me realize that we don't have any cash for paying a dividend, even though we have had a nice income this year. I'm puzzled myself about this cash business. Not only did our net income and sales increase, but you remember that we sold $5,000 worth of government bonds last year. Perhaps we made a mistake in distributing such a large portion of our net income in dividends this year."

THE NOVELTY STORE
Income Statement

EXHIBIT A

	For the Year Ended	
	June 30, 19x5	June 30, 19x4
Credits:		
Sales.........................	$260,000	$200,000
Interest received..................	0	200
Gain on sale of U. S. bonds...........	0	260
Total credits....................	$260,000	$200,460
Deduct debits:		
Advertising.......................	$ 9,000	$ 6,500
Cost of goods sold..................	155,000	121,000
Depreciation......................	2,000	1,500
Discounts lost.....................	190	270
Insurance.........................	1,100	900
Interest paid......................	1,300	900
Loss from uncollectible accounts.......	4,150	1,700
Loss from theft....................	0	800
Payroll...........................	41,600	34,200
Miscellaneous.....................	2,600	3,000
Rent.............................	10,400	8,000
Sales returns and allowances..........	11,000	7,500
Taxes, income.....................	5,870	2,760
Taxes, all other....................	2,100	2,800
Total debits.....................	$246,310	$191,830
Net income.......................	$ 13,690	$ 8,630

THE NOVELTY STORE
Statement of Retained Income

EXHIBIT B

	For the Year Ended	
	June 30, 19x5	June 30, 19x4
Credits:		
Beginning balance..................	$ 8,630	$ 0
Net income.......................	13,690	8,630
Total credits....................	$ 22,320	$ 8,630
Deduct debits:		
Dividends.........................	8,210	0
Ending balance....................	$ 14,110	$ 8,630

The three men sat quietly for a few minutes and finally Mr. Borman spoke. "You know, boys, we have all of the company's financial statements right before us; yet it is amazing how our interpretations have differed. I think we've all been working conscientiously, but we have not used our financial information effectively. We need to have an expert help us analyze our performance for the last two years, and I'm certain that it would help us to understand future financial reports as well as help in planning future action. What do you think?"

There was unanimous agreement that Mr. Borman's suggestion would be followed through.

THE NOVELTY STORE

Statement of Financial Position

EXHIBIT C

	June 30	
	19x5	19x4
Debits		
Accounts receivable......................	$28,800	$22,900
Advances to employees....................	900	350
Cash.....................................	1,700	5,150
Equipment................................	20,000	15,000
Merchandise inventory....................	24,100	25,200
Organization costs.......................	500	500
Unexpired insurance......................	400	200
United States bonds due in 19x9..........	0	5,000
Total debits.........................	$76,400	$74,300
Credits		
Accounts payable.........................	$15,250	$23,470
Accrued interest payable.................	120	140
Accrued payroll taxes....................	1,400	1,100
Accumulated depreciation.................	3,500	1,500
Capital stock, $100 par..................	20,000	20,000
Corporate Federal income tax payable.....	5,870	2,760
Estimated uncollectible accounts.........	4,150	1,700
Notes payable to bank, due in six months..	12,000	15,000
Retained income..........................	14,110	8,630
Total credits........................	$76,400	$74,300

REQUIRED:

a. Present statements in classified form, suitable for management's use in analysis.
b. Write a report to the board of directors analyzing the performance of the company, supporting your analysis by the specific comparisons which you think are appropriate.

CASE 10-4. ANALYSIS OF RATE OF RETURN

Part I. The du Pont Chart System[3]

The E. I. du Pont de Nemours Company has used its *executive committee charts*, a chart system designed to streamline internal financial reporting, for more than 30 years. Each of the approximately 350 charts used is presented at least four times a year to the executive committee, which consists of the company president and eight vice-presidents. The charts supplement the customary financial statements.

---

[3] Adapted from C. A. Kline, Jr. and Howard L. Hessler, "The du Pont Chart System for Appraising Operating Performance," from *N.A.C.A. Bulletin*, 1952 Conference Proceedings, Copyright 1952 by the National Association of Cost Accountants. Adapted by permission of the National Association of Accountants.

A separate series of charts is maintained for each of the company's 10 operating departments. More than one series of charts is maintained for departments whose operations are diverse.

The du Pont management thinks that the effectiveness of each department's effort may be judged best in terms of *return on investment*. Therefore, each chart series emphasizes the percentage return on investment and its components, *gross profit on sales* and *turnover*.

The formula for deriving the percentage return on investment is outlined in Exhibit A.

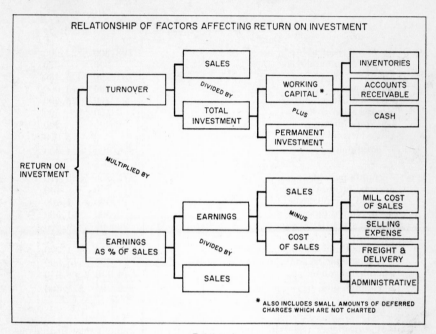

Exhibit A.

Cost of sales includes expenses, freight and delivery, and administrative expenses, in addition to production costs. *Earnings as a per cent of sales*, representing the "gross profit" as thus determined, and *percentage return on investment* are both based on earnings before Federal income taxes, although net earnings after taxes is often determined in a supplementary calculation.

The manager of an operating department can improve his results by working existing investment harder (increasing turnover) or by reducing costs (increasing earnings as a per cent of sales), assuming that both factors are within his control and that there are no changes in pricing policy or capital investment.

The charts are designed to show current and anticipated performance against a background of past results. All plottings are presented on an annual basis. The results of the preceding 10 years are plotted on the left side of the chart, and the current year's actual results and estimates are plotted on the right side.

Each series of charts includes the following basic charts:

(1) Master chart;
(2) Chart of sales (and transfers) and earnings;

(3) Chart of expenses as a per cent of sales;
(4) Investment chart; and
(5) Current asset charts.

A hypothetical master chart for the ABC Department is illustrated in Exhibit B.

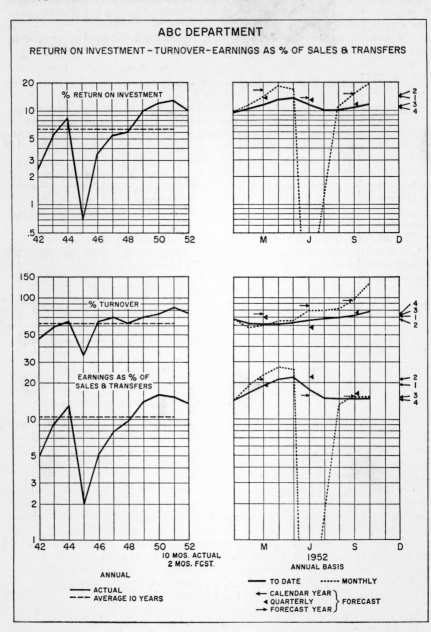

Exhibit B.

The du Pont Company makes four complete forecasts of the following items each year: sales, cost of sales, earnings, and investment. All forecasts are made for the ensuing 12-month period at the following times:

Forecast No.	Made in	Period Covered
1	January	January 1 to December 31
2	April	April 1 to March 31 of the following year
3	July	July 1 to June 30 of the following year
4	October	October 1 to September 30 of the following year

The master chart illustrated is based on actual performance for the period from January through October of 1952. In the upper right-hand field, the end of the solid line on the October ordinate reflects the annual per cent return on investment based on actual performance to October 31. The dotted line shows annual per cent return on investment *on an annual basis* (derived by multiplying each month's actual performance by 12). Arrows indicate the forecasts for the calendar year, the forecast year, and each quarter.

An analysis of changes in the two principal factors which determine percentage return on investment, changes in turnover and changes in earnings as a per cent of sales, requires further analysis of individual changes in working capital, permanent investment, sales, and cost of sales. A complete series of the company's charts would show the causes of the steady increases in percentage return on investment since 1948.

The du Pont chart system reports the results of *operating* management. If the business is to prosper, management must produce a profit on capital assigned to it, regardless of its source. The over-all liability and owners' equity position of the business is the responsibility of *financial* management.

Part II. Application to Jordan Manufacturing Company

Comparative income statements and statements of financial position of the Jordan Manufacturing Company appear below:

JORDAN MANUFACTURING COMPANY
Income Statement

	For the Year Ended December 31		
	19x3	19x2	19x1
Net sales............................	$500,000	$475,000	$300,000
Cost of sales:			
Mill cost of sales.................	325,000	285,000	180,000
Selling expense...................	60,000	38,000	30,000
Freight and delivery..............	25,000	23,750	15,000
Administrative expense...........	50,000	50,000	50,000
Total cost of sales..............	$460,000	$396,750	$275,000
Earnings before taxes..............	$ 40,000	$ 78,250	$ 25,000

JORDAN MANUFACTURING COMPANY
Statement of Financial Position

| | December 31 | | |
ASSETS	19x3	19x2	19x1
Current assets:			
Cash..........................	$ 9,000	$ 8,000	$ 6,000
Accounts receivable..............	14,000	10,000	12,000
Inventories......................	25,000	20,000	15,000
Prepaid expenses.................	2,000	2,000	1,000
Total current assets...........	$ 50,000	$ 40,000	$ 34,000
Fixed assets:			
Land.........................	$ 3,000	$ 3,000	$ 3,000
Buildings........................	25,000	25,000	25,000
Machinery and equipment.........	32,000	32,000	23,000
Total fixed assets...............	$ 60,000	$ 60,000	$ 51,000
Total assets......................	$110,000	$100,000	$ 85,000
EQUITIES			
Liabilities:			
Accounts payable..............	$ 15,000	$ 10,000	$ 15,000
Stockholders' equity:			
Capital stock....................	$ 50,000	$ 50,000	$ 50,000
Retained income.................	45,000	40,000	20,000
Total stockholders' equity.......	$ 95,000	$ 90,000	$ 70,000
Total equities....................	$110,000	$100,000	$ 85,000

The effects of depreciation and Federal income taxes are not considered in this case.

The management of the Jordan Company established the following ending inventory standards based on anticipated procurement, transportation, storage, production, and sales conditions:

19x1..	$18,000
19x2..	24,000
19x3..	24,000

REQUIRED:

a. Compute the percentage return on investment of the Jordan Company for each of the three years in accordance with the principles established in Part I. Plot the results on a master chart similar to the one illustrated.

b. Analyze as completely as possible the causes of changes in percentage return on investment. Include in this analysis a comparison of the percentages of the various expenses to net sales.

c. Compare the strong and weak points of the du Pont chart system with the internal reporting methods described in this text.

Chapter 11

Planning Future Business Operations

Appraisal of the past operating results of a business is a very important preliminary step in planning future action, because it helps to determine which phases of the business need improvement. The present chapter shows how an analysis of past results may be used to help predict the effect of alternative courses of business action on the future rate of return. For this purpose, the two principal components of the rate of return, the *net margin percentage* and the *number of asset turnovers*, are further analyzed to show the expected behavior of revenue, expense, and assets in response to various courses of action.

Relevance of past and future amounts

It cannot be emphasized too strongly that the amounts which are relevant to business planning are the *expected future* revenues, expenses, assets, and equities. Predicting future amounts is subject to a considerable degree of uncertainty. Two general methods of approach are used in estimating the future financial elements: *statistical analysis of past results* and *judgmental estimates about the future*. The planner must not forget that accounting amounts represent *what has happened in the past*, and he must modify them where necessary to reflect changes in contracts or operating conditions which are already in effect, or which are expected to be in effect in the future.

Some future elements can be estimated reliably on the basis of continuing contracts for the purchase or sale of goods and services, and others can be estimated on the basis of the unexpired costs of the assets which the business already owns. These can be supplemented by judgment estimates of amounts which are subject to more uncertainty. Although subjective estimates made carefully by a judicious use of *both* past statistics and judgment are essential in planning and controlling business operations, they are less reliable than objective data about the past.

Prediction by association

Knowledge of the *cause-and-effect relationships* among the determinants of the future rate of return of a business is of great assistance in estimating their future amounts. If, for example, it can be established that changes in the amount of an expense are closely related to changes in the amount of sales revenue, the future amount of the expense can be predicted reliably if the future amount of the revenue can be predicted. This is done by multiplying the estimated amount of revenue by a ratio expressing the *degree of relationship* of the expense to revenue.

EXAMPLE 1:   Sound Center, Inc. (refer to illustrated financial statements and descriptive material in Chapter 10) pays its salesmen a commission of 3 per cent of sales and its manager one per cent. If Mr. Farley, the manager, estimates that sales for next year, 19x4, will be $175,000, how much will commission expense be?

SOLUTION: Commission Expense = .04(Sales) = .04($175,000) = $7,000.

This relationship, with continuing contracts, will hold true for any volume of sales.

In Example 1, the amount of commissions expense *depends* upon the amount of sales revenue; therefore, commissions expense is the *dependent variable* in this relationship and sales revenue is the *independent* variable. The *degree* of relationship between the two, or *correlation*, is perfect. At any volume of sales, the company would be one hundred per cent accurate in predicting that commission expense would be .04 of sales revenue.

Expenses perfectly variable with revenue

Expenses which change in almost exact proportion to changes in revenue are called *variable* expenses. Few expenses in actual business vary perfectly with sales revenue. In the illustrated case, the relationship will exist only as long as the contract remains unchanged. Figure 9 shows this relationship graphically. In such a graph, it is customary to show the amounts of the independent variable along the horizontal, or X, axis, and those of the dependent variable along the vertical, or Y, axis. The diagonal line shows the relationship of commission expense to sales. Its location was determined by plotting points for the amount of sales commission for each amount of sales, at $50,000 intervals, and then drawing a line to

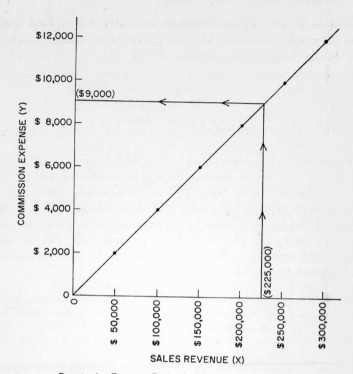

Fig. 9. An Expense Perfectly Variable with Revenue.

connect these points. The graph can also be used to *predict* the amount of commission expense at any volume of sales.

EXAMPLE 2: If the sales of Sound Center, Inc., for next year are expected to be $225,000, determine from the graph how much commission expense will be.

SOLUTION: From the point on the *X*-axis representing sales of $225,000, follow a vertical line to the line of relationship. Then follow a horizontal line to the *Y*-axis, and the reading at that point, $9,000, is the estimated amount of commission expense if sales are expected to be $225,000.

The graph is used to illustrate the general relationship of variable expenses to sales and is, of course, not needed to predict the amount of commission expense in this instance. It is a simple matter to compute its amount by multiplying any expected volume of sales by .04. The specific formula is:

$$Y = .04X$$

Expenses perfectly nonvariable with revenue

At the opposite extreme in their degree of relationship to revenue are *perfectly nonvariable expenses*, those which do not change at all in response to changes in revenue. These expenses are often called *fixed expenses*, because their total amounts are not expected to change as revenue changes during the planning period.

EXAMPLE 3: Sound Center, Inc., has signed a 10-year lease providing for the payment of $6,000 annual rental. The lease expires December 31, 19x9. If sales are expected to increase from $150,000 in 19x3 to $175,000 in 19x4, what will be the change in rent expense?

SOLUTION: None. Rent expense will be $6,000 next year and each of the succeeding five years if the present contract remains in effect.

The absence of a constant relationship between a perfectly nonvariable expense, such as rent in the illustration, and sales revenue is shown graphically in Figure 10. In Example 3, although rent expense does not vary at

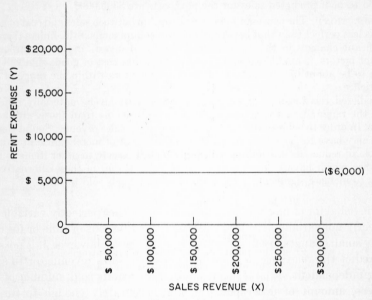

Fig. 10. An Expense Perfectly Nonvariable with Revenue.

all with changes in sales, it accrues in equal daily amounts, and therefore varies in direct proportion to the passage of *time*.

Degrees of variability

There are few examples of business expenses which can be expected to vary perfectly with sales revenue even for short periods of time, and none which can be expected to vary perfectly in the long run. The 4 per cent commission rate in Example 1 will not remain unchanged indefinitely. On the other hand, there are no expenses which can be expected to remain perfectly fixed in total for very long periods of time. The lease contract in Example 3 will terminate in 6 more years, when a new annual rental is likely to come into effect. Moreover, the business can change the total amount of rent expense even before then by leasing additional property.

The behavior of some types of expense is perfectly predictable (either completely variable or completely nonvariable) if changes in the amount of sales revenue are relatively small, but unpredictable in varying degree when the changes in revenue are relatively large.

EXAMPLE 4:   The sales of Sound Center, Inc., have ranged between $90,000 and $180,000 for the past few years. During this time, cost of goods sold expense has ranged between 66 per cent and 68 per cent of sales. During 19x2 and 19x3, sales were entirely of one class of hi-fi set which Sound Center, Inc., bought for $335 each and sold for $500 each. What can cost of goods sold expense be expected to be if predicted sales for the next year are $300,000?

SOLUTION: The cause-and-effect relationship between sales and cost of goods sold is less perfect than that between sales and commissions. Still, unless there are significant changes in the conditions of supply, demand, and other important market factors, it might reasonably be assumed that cost of goods sold will continue to be about 67 per cent for future sales amounts within the range of past experience.

Predicted relationships of expenses to revenue at levels materially different from the range of past experience are much less reliable than those within this range. In order to achieve the substantial increase in sales revenue, Sound Center, Inc., may have to (1) reduce its unit acquisition cost of merchandise in order to be able to reduce its unit selling price, or (2) shift largely to other items of merchandise which have a lower unit gross margin. Either of these alternatives is likely to increase significantly the ratio of cost of goods sold to sales.

The behavior of most classes of expense is neither perfectly variable nor perfectly nonvariable, even for relatively short periods of time or for relatively small changes in sales revenue. In many cases, however, it is possible to predict the relationship of such expenses to sales revenue, or to some other independent variable, such as number of units sold, number of employees, amount of floor space, or time, accurately enough to furnish management a useful guide in deciding which alternative business plan to follow. This is especially true of plans for short periods such as the next month, quarter, or year.

It is ordinarily useful to recognize four types of expense behavior in estimating their amounts for the near future:

(1) Fixed in amount by contract, management policy, or operating conditions and not subject to change during the planning period. (Example: A 10-year lease at a fixed annual rental.)

(2) Fixed in amount by contract, management policy, or operating conditions but subject to change during the planning period. (Examples: The planned amount of advertising of Sound Center, Inc., or its planned

amount of charitable contributions, both of which are usually set by management policy but which are subject to change.)

(3) Variable directly or indirectly with sales revenue or with some other financial element. (Example: A business borrows on short-term notes to finance seasonal changes in its inventories. The inventory balance should vary with expected future sales, and the amount of interest expense should vary with the amount of inventory.)

(4) Mixed, consisting of both a fixed component and a variable component. (Example: Other Salaries of Sound Center, Inc. This item consists partly of compensation for general office work, which may be expected to remain relatively constant without regard to the volume of sales; partly of the salaries of veteran sales clerks, whom Mr. Farley would feel obliged to retain even if sales declined drastically; and partly of compensation to additional sales clerks who are hired during periods of peak activity.)

Determining behavior of expenses

The future behavior of some types of expense can be estimated accurately by reasoning or by the use of relationships which are set by law (property tax rates) or by contract (commissions). The future amount of expenses whose composition and behavior are more complex can often be predicted reliably by means of graphs or formulas which have been derived from an analysis of past accounting and statistical data.

Data for illustration. Mr. Farley, manager of Sound Center, Inc., in preparing plans for 19x4, is trying to determine whether there is a predictable relationship between Other Salaries and Sales Revenue. He has taken the following information from the ledger accounts for 19x3:

| | Actual Results for 19x3 | |
Month	Sales (X)	Other Salaries (Y)
January	$ 13,000	$ 1,170
February	11,000	1,090
March	12,000	1,130
April	10,000	1,040
May	10,000	1,030
June	9,000	970
July	8,000	930
August	7,000	880
September	10,000	1,040
October	15,000	1,270
November	20,000	1,530
December	25,000	1,780
Totals	$150,000	$13,860

Predicting behavior by scattergraph. A *statistical scattergraph* may be used to determine visually whether there seems to be any consistent relationship between two variables. This is done in Figure 11 for the 19x3 monthly Sales and Other Salaries of Sound Center, Inc. Each dot shows the Sales Revenue and the corresponding expense for a month. It can readily be seen that a line connecting the dots would be almost straight, indicating that there was a close relationship last year between changes in the amount of Other Salaries and changes in the amount of Sales. Assuming that the same pattern of relationship can be expected to continue in 19x4, a straight line fitted to the dots in the scattergraph can be used to predict the amount of Other Salaries, if estimated Sales Revenue for the year or for any month is given. The method is the same as that illustrated in Example 2, except that in the present case the estimate is unlikely to be perfect.

Predicting behavior by formula. If it seems reasonably accurate to show the relationship between two variables by a straight line, the mathematical formula for the straight line may be used to predict the amount of the dependent variable, Y (Other Salaries, in this illustration) on the basis of the estimated amount of the independent variable, X (Sales Revenue, in this case). The formula for a straight line is:

$$Y = a + bX,$$

where a is a constant representing the fixed component of the dependent variable for any value of X and b is the ratio of the variable component of the dependent variable to any value of X.

The location of the line of relationship may be determined by the *method of least squares*, which, though beyond the scope of this book, is treated in elementary statistics texts. The approximate formula for the straight line may be derived from the statistical scattergraph by the following steps (see Figure 11):

(1) Fit a straight line visually to the dots of the scattergraph. Approximately half of the dots should be above and half below the line.

(2) Extend the line to the Y-axis. The amount at the point of intersection is a, the constant component of Y for any value of X. (In this illustration, the constant component of Y seems to be approximately $530 per month.)

(3) Compute the average amount (arithmetic mean) of X and Y per month from the given data. (The average monthly amounts are: S, Sales, $12,500; and Y, Other Salaries, $1,155.)

(4) Subtract a, the fixed monthly component of Y, from the average monthly amount of Y to determine b, the variable component, for the average month. $1,155 (average monthly amount of Other Salaries) − $530 (the monthly fixed component) = $625, the variable component for the average month.

(5) Compute the relationship of b, the average monthly variable com-

ponent of Y, to the average monthly amount of X. \$625 (average monthly variable component of Other Salaries) ÷ \$12,500 (average monthly Sales) = .05, the ratio of the variable component of Other Salaries to Sales Revenue.

(6) Substitute the values of a and b, which were computed from past experience, in the formula for the straight line ($Y = a + bX$):

$$Y = \$530 + .05X$$

The formula may now be used to predict the future amount of Y for any

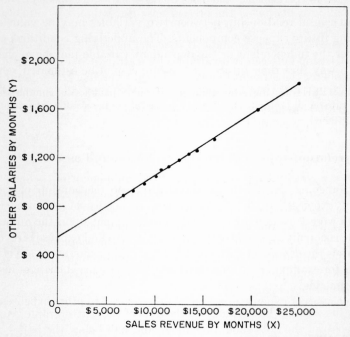

Fig. 11. Scattergraph Showing Relationship of Other Salaries to Sales Revenue.

assumed amount of X. (If Mr. Farley estimates that sales of Sound Center, Inc. (X) will be \$15,000 for January, 19x4, Other Salaries may be estimated as follows: Other Salaries (Y) = \$530 + .05(\$15,000) = \$530 + \$750 = \$1,280, the estimated amount of Other Salaries for January, 19x4.)

Limitations of assumed relationships

Even though an analysis of past results shows a high degree of relationship between the amounts of two variables, such as an expense and sales revenue, the relationship may not be one of cause and effect. The close association of the two amounts may result from coincidence. This is especially true when the relationship is determined on the basis of a limited number of observations of past data. Sometimes judgment is sufficient to determine whether such a relationship is causal or merely coincidental.

EXAMPLE 5:   The illustrated relationship of Other Salaries to Sales in the case of Sound Center, Inc., should be viewed principally as a demonstration of method. Actually, Mr. Farley's judgment estimate of future salary expenses is likely to be more accurate than the more refined technique. Either analysis would have been facilitated if the monthly amounts of Other Salaries had been subdivided into major groups by type of behavior, such as Office Salaries, Sales Clerks' Salaries (Permanent), and Sales Clerks' Salaries (Temporary).

A past causal relationship between two variables may be valueless in predicting future expense components. The underlying conditions affecting either the independent or the dependent variable may have changed in such a way that their future relationship cannot be estimated reliably.

EXAMPLE 6:   A business which has formerly paid a sales commission at a uniform rate on all products changes to a policy of paying a different rate on each class of product.

Interrelationships of revenues, expenses, and assets

The foregoing discussion has illustrated the relationship of various types of expense to sales revenue, and especially of expenses whose amounts were considered to depend to some extent upon the amount of sales. Occasionally, the relationship between sales and expense is reversed, and sales is the *dependent* variable. Changes in the amounts of advertising expense, for example, can often be shown to have caused changes in sales, with a time lag.

Some classes of expense are more closely related to other expenses than to sales.

EXAMPLE 7:   ,Employer's payroll tax expense tends to vary closely with changes in total salary expense. Because the latter includes some components which are variable and others which are nonvariable with sales revenue, it is difficult to predict the relationship of payroll tax expense to sales. It is easier to estimate its amount in relation to estimated salaries.

Other classes of expense are closely related to the amounts of assets or liabilities.

EXAMPLE 8:   The amount of depreciation expense depends upon the cost of depreciable assets, their estimated life, and the passage of time. The amount of interest expense depends upon the face amount of liabilities, their rate of interest, and the passage of time.

In order to estimate the amount of assets needed to carry on the planned level of business activity, one must predict the behavior of individual assets in response to changes in the amounts of revenue, expense, and other factors. This estimate enables management to make plans for financing and obtaining the needed assets, and also to estimate the antici- pated percentage of income to assets.

The amounts of some assets are closely related, either directly or in- directly, to the amount of revenue.

EXAMPLE 9:   New accounts receivable result from sales on account, and therefore the amount of the accounts receivable balance at any time is related to the amount of credit sales made in earlier periods. If the amount of credit sales varies closely with the total amount of sales, the amount of accounts receivable is also closely related, with a time lag, to the amount of sales.

The amounts of still other assets are closely related to the amounts of expenses.

EXAMPLE 10:   A business generally plans to have on hand enough inven- tory to provide for its withdrawals from stock (sales or issues) in the near future and to leave a desired minimum balance. Since inventory is measured at cost, the amount of the asset Merchandise Inventory should bear a close relationship to the expected Cost of Goods Sold Expense of the near future.

Components of account balances: quantity and price

In analyzing the results of past operations and predicting those of the future, it is often useful to remember that each homogeneous class of costs and revenues is the product of multiplying the *quantity* of items bought or sold by the unit *price*.

EXAMPLE 11:   The units composing the Sales Revenue account of Sound Center, Inc., for 19x3 were homogeneous, each consisting of a high-fidelity set which was sold for $500. The composition of the account was:

Quantity, 300 sets × Unit Price, $500 = Total Revenue, $150,000.

EXAMPLE 12:   The units composing the Cost of Goods Sold account were also homogeneous, consisting of identical sets which had cost $335 each. The com- position of the account was:

Quantity, 300 sets × Unit Cost, $335 = Total Cost of Goods Sold, $100,500.

Knowledge of the components of such a homogeneous account enables the analyst to project the effect upon future account balances of various expected or planned changes in quantity alone, in price alone, or in both. Some of the various possibilities for increasing income by increasing the gross margin (the excess of Sales Revenue over Cost of Goods Sold) which might have occurred to Mr. Farley, of Sound Center, Inc., are shown in Figure 12. They are merely representative of types of effect, and not of likely results of the indicated actions. For comparison, all changes in the illustration are designed to produce an increase of $33,000 in the gross

Type of Action	Quantity Sold	Sales Price	Resulting Amounts			
			Sales (Q × P)	Cost Price	Total Cost (Q × P)	Gross Margin
Sales revenue alone increased by:						
a. Increasing unit sales price $110.........	300	$610	$183,000	$335	$100,500	$82,500
b. Increasing quantity sold by 200......	500	500	250,000	335	167,500	82,500
c. Increasing unit sales price $85 and increasing quantity sold by 30.........	330	585	193,050	335	110,550	82,500
d. Decreasing unit sales price $82.50 and increasing quantity sold by 700.......	1,000	417.50	417,500	335	335,000	82,500
Cost of goods sold alone decreased by:						
e. Decreasing unit cost price $110........	300	500	150,000	225	67,500	82,500
Both sales and cost price changed:						
f. Increasing margin per unit:						
Unit sales price increased $50 and unit cost price decreased $35...........	330	550	181,500	300	99,000	82,500
g. Decreasing margin per unit:						
Unit sales price decreased $25 and unit cost price decreased $10........	550	475	261,250	325	178,750	82,500

Note: Present unit sales price is $500.
Present unit cost of goods sold is $335.
Present quantity sold is 300 units.

Fig. 12. Combinations of Changes to Increase Gross Margin $33,000.

margin of Sound Center, Inc.—from $49,500 in 19x3 to a planned amount of $82,500 in 19x4.

In an actual business situation, the extent to which additional quantities can be sold or individual sales prices can be changed successfully depends on the demand for the product and the probable reaction of competitors. Sometimes a business can increase its sales by price cuts or by stronger sales efforts. At other times, any increase in sales other than as a result of a natural growth of demand is likely to be at the expense of competitors, who will probably retaliate.

Like revenue, many expense amounts are the product of a *quantity* and a *price* per unit. Cost of goods sold is an example: the expense is the product of the number of units sold and the cost of each unit. Other examples are electricity expense (number of kilowatt hours used multiplied by the unit cost per KWH), employees' compensation (wages per time period multiplied by the number of time periods worked), and supplies (the number of items used multiplied by the unit cost). Efforts to reduce such expenses can be directed toward reducing the quantity of each service used, the cost price per unit, or a combination of both.

Components of account balances: mix

Analysis of past and prospective changes in the balances of homogeneous accounts is complex enough, but analysis of the composition and behavior of most of the actual accounts of businesses is further complicated by the factor of *mix*, the relative proportions of the different elements of an account. Most account balances do not consist of a single type of item whose units are identical as to price and quantity, but of many dissimilar items with different prices and quantities. The Sales Revenue account of even a small retail business, for example, might consist of the aggregate of the sales revenues of thousands of different types of merchandise. The sales revenue of each type of merchandise is, in turn, the product of its price and its quantity. Furthermore, the prices of even a single class of merchandise often change during the period, and the composition of total sales revenue is then heterogeneous even for each such class of merchandise.

The following example shows how a change in the *mix*, or composition, of sales can result in a change in gross margin even though the unit cost prices and sales prices of each class of goods sold remain unchanged.

EXAMPLE 13:   A manufacturing company sold two classes of products, Product A and Product B. Product A, which cost $6 a unit to manufacture, sold for $10 a unit. Product B, with a unit cost of $8, sold for $10. In 19x1, the total sales revenue was divided equally between the two classes of products. In 19x2, although total sales revenue was the same as in 19x1, sales of Product A comprised 80 per cent of the total and sales of Product B, 20 per cent. The result was to increase the percentage of gross margin on the same total volume of sales from 30 per cent to 36 per cent and its amount from $30,000 to $36,000, as the following tabulation shows.

	19x1 Mix		19x2 Mix	
	50% A,	50% B	80% A,	20% B
Sales revenue:				
Product A..............	$50,000		$80,000	
Product B..............	50,000		20,000	
Total................		$100,000		$100,000
Deduct cost of goods sold:				
Product A (60% of sales).	$30,000		$48,000	
Product B (80% of sales).	40,000	70,000	16,000	64,000
Gross margin.............		$ 30,000		$ 36,000

Most businesses would find it impractical to use a separate account for each component of revenue and expense which differs from others in quantity or price. Otherwise, a conglomerate mixture such as that which composes an account like Office Supplies would require dozens of minor sub-accounts. It is more practical to group together items whose amounts are governed by similar factors, and to use individual accounts only for those items which are material when considered alone. Then it is possible to estimate the future income and rate of return of the business by considering relatively few factors.

EXAMPLE 14: The tobacco counter of a retail store usually handles hundreds of different brands and types of articles, but they usually fall into two or three important classes of behavior as to the percentage of gross margin to sales. For internal analysis, the use of accounts for these two or three types of behavior should be sufficient.

When an account balance is composed of a mixture of dissimilar items, the analyst must watch for significant changes in mix which have occurred or are about to occur. He must consider them carefully in his appraisal of past results and his plans for the future.

Statement of Marginal Income

The Statement of Marginal Income is a simple expression of the relationships between income statement components. It is useful despite its many shortcomings. Its basic components are:

Sales revenue

— Expenses which vary with sales revenue

= Marginal income (or contribution to nonvariable expense and income)

— Expenses which do not vary with sales revenue:
  a. Expenses fixed by past action, not subject to change in the period
  b. Expenses fixed by past action, subject to change in the period

= Net income before income tax

— Income tax expense (which varies approximately with net income
    before income tax)

= Net income

It is usually satisfactory to omit the final deduction, income tax expense, in estimating the effect of alternative future plans on the income of the business. If a given management action will increase the net income before tax, it will generally increase the net income after tax in somewhat the same proportion. There are many important exceptions to this statement, which, because of their complexity, are discussed along with other income tax matters in Chapter 24.

The accompanying illustration shows a Statement of Marginal Income for the Sound Center, Inc., for 19x3.

SOUND CENTER, INC.
Statement of Marginal Income
For the Year Ended December 31, 19x3

	Amount		Per Cent of Net Sales
Net sales revenue................................		$150,000	100.0%
Deduct variable expenses:			
Cost of goods sold...........................	$100,500		67.0%
Commissions on sales......................	6,000		4.0
Salaries, other (partial)...................	7,500		5.0
Supplies (partial)..........................	1,200		0.8
Taxes, other than income tax (partial).....	300		0.2
Miscellaneous (partial)....................	600		0.4
Total variable expenses................		116,100	77.4
Contribution to nonvariable expense and income.....................................		$ 33,900	22.6%
Deduct nonvariable expenses:			
Fixed for the period:			
Depreciation...........................	$ 1,000		
Insurance.............................	2,000		
Rent..................................	6,000		
Salary, manager.......................	8,000		
Salaries, other (partial)................	6,360		
Supplies (partial)......................	540		
Taxes, other than income tax (partial)..	1,600		
Miscellaneous (partial).................	1,500		
Total expenses fixed for the period....	$ 27,000		
Fixed by management policy:			
Advertising............................	3,900		
Total nonvariable expenses...........		30,900	
Net income before income tax...............		$ 3,000	

The failure to compute the percentages of total nonvariable expenses and net income before income tax to net sales revenue in the Statement of Marginal Income was intentional. Such percentages would be valueless in predicting the respective amounts for any net sales volume other than $150,000. The percentage of nonvariable expenses to net sales, if computed, would be different for each volume of sales. The important thing to remember in estimating the future amount of *nonvariable expenses* is that they tend to *remain unchanged in total*, while *variable expenses* tend to *change in total in exact proportion to changes in net sales*.

Comments on components of the statement of marginal income

The amounts in the Statement of Marginal Income of Sound Center, Inc., were derived from the comparative financial statements illustrated in Chapter 10, and from the analysis earlier in this chapter. All amounts are hypothetical, and unrealistically simple behavior has been assumed to simplify explanations of appropriate analytical methods.

The derivation of the following account balances has been discussed earlier in this chapter:

> Net sales revenue
> Cost of goods sold expense
> Commissions on sales
> Salaries, other
> Rent
> Salary, manager

Succeeding paragraphs consider problems involved in analyzing the behavior of the other income statement items.

Advertising is usually a cause, rather than an effect, of changes in sales revenue. Sound Center, Inc., increased its advertising expense from $2,000 in 19x2 to $3,900 in 19x3, perhaps as a result of a definite management policy. Management will have to determine the planned amount for 19x4 in the same way by balancing two factors: the amount of advertising effort needed to maintain or increase sales revenue, and the amount of marginal income that is available to cover advertising expenses.

Supplies, taxes other than income tax, and miscellaneous expense were all divided into nonvariable elements and elements which varied in response to changes in sales. The analysis was as follows:

	Supplies	Taxes, Other	Miscellaneous
Total expense in 19x3...............	$ 1,740	$ 1,900	$ 2,100
− Total expense in 19x2...............	1,500	1,840	1,980
= Amount of change in expense.......	+$ 240	+$ 60	+$ 120
÷ Amount of change in net sales......	+ 30,000	+ 30,000	+ 30,000
= Per cent of change in expense to change in net sales...............	0.8%	0.2%	0.4%
Total expense in 19x3...............	$ 1,740	$ 1,900	$ 2,100

	Supplies	Taxes, Other	Miscellaneous
— Total variable component:			
0.8% of 19x3 sales of $150,000....	1,200		
0.2% of 19x3 sales		300	
0.4% of 19x3 sales			600
= Fixed component of expense........	$ 540	$ 1,600	$ 1,500

The method used in estimating the fixed components of each of these three expenses and the relationship of their variable components to sales revenue is of limited validity. In effect, it determines the location of a straight line, $Y = a + bX$, or Supplies = $540 + .008 (estimated sales), from the position of only two points (supplies expense in relation to sales in 19x2 and supplies expense in relation to sales in 19x3). The relationship between expenses and sales could be determined more reliably by using the 19x1 amounts also, but there are still limitations in using only three points. Furthermore, the underlying factors which cause changes in the amounts of such heterogeneous accounts as these are unlikely to continue to operate in a predictable fashion. Mr. Farley could probably get a better idea of the future amount of each by estimating the behavior of its principal components. Other taxes, for example, consist partly of licenses, which are usually fixed in amount; partly of property taxes, which vary with insurable assets; and partly of payroll taxes, which vary with salaries and wages.

Depreciation, although classified as a fixed expense in the statement, is subject to change if the amounts and classes of depreciable assets owned by the business change during the planning period. *Insurance*, too, will change in response to changes in the amounts of insurable property or to changes in applicable insurance rates. Classifying these two items as fixed implies that few changes in the amounts of depreciable property or insurable risks are anticipated during the planning period. Even if they do change, the change would be related to assets more closely than to sales. A revised figure for each such expense should be used for planning purposes to the extent that significant changes can be expected.

Predicting the effect of alternative actions on income

The arrangement used in the marginal income statement, together with the amounts of nonvariable expenses and the percentages of variable expenses to sales, may be used in predicting the effect of alternative courses of future business action. The *estimated future amounts and relationships* are needed for this purpose. In subsequent illustrations it is assumed that the conditions and relationships of Sound Center, Inc., which existed in 19x3 will continue in 19x4, except for stated specific changes, which are introduced one at a time. The existing relationships may be expressed by the formula:

(1) $$S - V - F = I,$$

where S is net sales revenue;
  V is variable expenses;
  F is fixed expenses; and
  I is net income before income tax.

This form of the equation is used in the conventional income statement. Other useful forms of the equation are:

(2) $$S - V = F + I$$

This is similar to the computation made in the statement of marginal income. $(S - V)$, yields the amount of *marginal income*, or the contribution to fixed expense and income.

(3) $$S = V + F + I \text{ (assumed to be zero)}$$

This is the form for determining the "break-even" sales volume—the point at which sales revenue will just equal the total of variable and fixed expenses.

The following sections illustrate the use of the formula in estimating the effect of several general types of business action which might be considered as a means of increasing business income.

(1) *Sales volume increased.* It is unlikely that a significant increase of this type would take place without some stimulus, such as price reductions or increased sales effort. If it did occur as a result of external causes alone, however, it would be almost certain to cause some early changes in the requirements of the business for facilities, which would be reflected in fixed costs. Its effect is illustrated in the following example.

EXAMPLE 15: What would be the effect on the 19x4 income of Sound Center, Inc., if sales volume increased 20 per cent while the ratio of variable expenses to sales and the amount of fixed expenses remained unchanged?

SOLUTION: $S - V - F = I$

$$S = 1.20(\$150,000)$$
$$V = .774S \text{ (from Statement of Marginal Income)}$$
$$F = \$30,900 \text{ (from Statement of Marginal Income)}$$

Substituting in the formula:

$\$180,000 - .774(\$180,000) - \$30,900 = I$
  $\$180,000 - \$139,320 - \$30,900 = \$9,780$, the expected income for 19x4.

ALTERNATE SOLUTION: Unless sales price is changed in relation to cost, the ratio of marginal income $(S - V)$ to sales will remain the same. For the Sound Center, this ratio is $.226S$. An alternate solution is:

$$.226S \text{ (Marginal Income)} - F = I$$
$$.226(\$180,000) - \$30,900 = I$$
$$\$40,680 - \$30,900 = \$9,780.$$

Conclusion: This action would increase net income before income tax from $3,000 to $9,780.

(2) *Marginal income percentage increased.* An action to increase the percentage of marginal income (sales − variable expenses) to sales might take one of the following forms:

(a) Unit sales price increased without a corresponding effect on variable costs per unit;

(b) Unit variable costs decreased without a corresponding effect on sales price per unit;

(c) A favorable combination of (a) and (b), including changes in mix.

The effect of any of these possibilities on net income can be estimated easily by use of the *marginal income percentage*, developed in the alternative solution to Example 15.

EXAMPLE 16:   What would be the effect on the 19x4 income of Sound Center, Inc., if the ratio of variable expenses to sales is reduced to 75 per cent by means of a price increase, a reduction of variable costs per unit, or a favorable combination of the two? Assume that sales volume in dollars remains the same.

SOLUTION: Marginal Income $- F = I$

$$.25S - \$30,900 = I$$
$$.25(\$150,000) - \$30,900 = I$$
$$\$37,500 - \$30,900 = I$$
$$\$6,600 = I$$

Conclusion: This action would increase net income before income tax from $3,000 to $6,600.

(3) *Fixed costs decreased.* An effect of this type might be expected to result from more efficient use of money and long-lived facilities, or from changes in long-term contracts for services.

EXAMPLE 17:   What would be the effect on the 19x4 income of Sound Center, Inc., if the company is able to secure the services of a new manager just as efficient as Mr. Farley for a salary of $6,000 a year?

SOLUTION: It is unnecessary to use the formula in this case, because there is no effect on sales revenue, variable expenses, or marginal income. The only effect, is to reduce fixed expenses by $2,000, and consequently to increase net income before tax by $2,000.

Estimating action needed to produce desired income

If it is desired to find out the extent of an action which is needed to produce a desired amount of net income before tax, the basic approach is the same as in the preceding section.

EXAMPLE 18:   If the desired net income before taxes of Sound Center, Inc., for 19x4 is $10,000 and all other factors are expected to behave as they did in 19x3, what sales volume would be needed?

SOLUTION:

$$S - V = F + I$$
$$.226S = \$30,900 + \$10,000$$
$$S = \frac{\$40,900}{.226}$$
$$S = \$181,000$$

(The computation results in an amount of $180,973.45. This is an illustration of false accuracy, because sales of the company increase in multiples of $500.)

Estimating volume of sales needed to break even

In appraising the existing situation of the business and in evaluating alternative ways of improving it, business management often finds it useful to know the *break-even point*. This point is the volume of sales at which revenues are expected to be exactly equal to total expenses, with no net income. To express it differently:

$$S - V - F = 0$$

or

$$S - V = F$$

The break-even point can be expressed in terms of dollars of sales or units of sales, if just one type of unit is involved. The objective of a business is to earn an income, not to break even. Nevertheless, knowledge of the break-even point may be useful to management in the following situations:

(1) Estimating how large an increase in sales volume, or increase in marginal income percentage, or decrease in fixed expenses, is needed to convert operations at a loss to profitable operations. If the business is now earning a net income, management may wish to know how great an unfavorable change is needed to cause operations to become unprofitable.

EXAMPLE 19:   In appraising the risk of the business, the management of Sound Center, Inc., wishes to know how much sales could decline before operations resulted in a net loss. It is assumed that all other factors remain unchanged.

SOLUTION:

$$S - V = F$$

$$S - .774S = \$30,900$$

$$.226S = \$30,900$$

$$S = \frac{\$30,900}{.226}$$

$$S = \$136,726 \text{ (rounded)}$$

Proof of computation: Resulting income statement:

Sales...	$136,726
Deduct variable expenses, 77.4% of sales..................	105,826
Marginal income...	$ 30,900
Deduct nonvariable expenses...........................	30,900
Net income..	$ 0

Conclusion: A decline in the sales of Sound Center, Inc., from $150,000 to $136,726 would result in zero income. This would be a decline of approximately 8.8% of sales.

(2) Estimating the degree of risk associated with a proposed change in (a) nonvariable expenses or (b) percentage of marginal income to sales.

EXAMPLE 20:   The present break-even sales volume of Sound Center, Inc., is $136,726, computed in Example 19. Mr. Farley is thinking of recommending a $3,000 increase in the amount spent for advertising in an effort to increase sales volume. If this change is made, what volume of sales will be needed in order to break even?

SOLUTION:

$$.226S = \$30,900 + \$3,000$$

$$.226S = \$33,900$$

$$S = \frac{\$33,900}{.226}$$

$$S = \$150,000$$

This result could have been determined without using a formula. Under the present circumstances, there is a contribution margin of $3,000 to fixed expenses and income. The proposed expenditure would equal this exactly.

Conclusion: Adding the proposed $3,000 to nonvariable expenses would mean that the sales would have be to a minimum of $150,000 before expenses were covered, rather than the $136,726 needed now.

EXAMPLE 21:   What would the break-even point of Sound Center, Inc., be if the marginal income percentage were reduced from 22.6 per cent of sales to 20 per cent?

SOLUTION:

$$.20S = \$30,900$$

$$S = \frac{\$30,900}{.20}$$

$$S = \$154,500$$

Conclusion: The break-even point would be increased from sales revenue of $136,726 to sales revenue of $154,500.

Break-even chart

A graph showing the relationship of sales revenue, expenses, and income for various volumes of sales is frequently referred to as a *break-even chart*. Figure 13 is a break-even chart illustrating this relationship of Sound Center, Inc., for 19x3.

The point at which the sales revenue and total expense lines cross in the graph is the break-even point—the volume at which there is zero income.

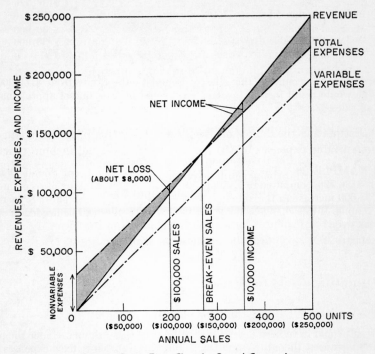

Fig. 13. Break-Even Chart for Sound Center, Inc.

The vertical line labeled "Break-Even Sales" shows that this point is reached for Sound Center, Inc., when unit sales are 274 and dollar sales, at $500 per set, are approximately $137,000 (the break-even point as computed by formula is $136,726). If more than 274 sets are sold, there will be a net income, represented by the vertical distance between the revenue and the total expenses lines.

The break-even chart can also be used to estimate the amount of income or loss which will result from a given volume of sales, or the amount of sales revenue required to produce a given amount of net income or net loss. The vertical line labeled "$10,000 Income" shows that there is expected to be a net income before income tax of $10,000 when sales are about 360 units, or $180,000. (In Example 18 it was computed that sales of 362 units, or $181,000, would be needed to yield a net income of $10,000.)

The vertical line labeled "$100,000 Sales" shows that a net loss of about $8,000 can be expected if sales fall to 200 units. (Computation by the formula shows that at this sales volume variable expenses would be .774 of sales, or $77,400; fixed expenses would be $30,900; and total expenses, $108,300. This would result in a net loss of $8,300 when compared with total revenue of $100,000.)

The break-even chart can be used to give a quick approximation of the income effects of various possible levels of sales. Computation by formula would be somewhat longer. Usually the estimates made in projecting the future amounts of fixed expenses and the relationship of variable expenses to sales revenue are rough enough so that the approximation provided by the graph is sufficiently accurate to be used alone.

Limitations of formula and graphic predictions of income

Use of the formula based upon the fixed-variable analysis of expenses and the relationship of variable expenses to sales, and use of the break-even chart are both subject to the same limitations. To the extent that there are significant unexpected changes in the quantity, price, or mix of any revenues or expenses, or significant changes in the interrelationships of expenses and revenues, the predictions are inaccurate.

Estimating assets to be used

Chapter 10 pointed out that, for planning purposes, the rate of return on the assets of a business should be analyzed into its two principal components: the net margin percentage, and the number of asset turnovers. Chapter 11 has been devoted almost entirely to methods of estimating a particular measure of net income, the *net income before income tax*. The chief problems which are involved in appraising and predicting the other principal determinant of the rate of return—the number of asset turnovers —are discussed in later chapters as they apply to particular assets such as cash, accounts receivable, and inventories.

Summary

In business planning, the appropriate amounts are *future amounts*. Accounting data about the past often provide a useful starting point in estimating future revenues, expenses, assets, and equities. Often there is a close relationship between two variables, such as an expense and revenue, two expenses, or revenue and an asset. The degree of this relationship can be determined from accounting records by observing the behavior of the two variables in the past. In terms of their short-run behavior in response to changes in the amount of revenue, expenses may be classified as *variable* (those which are expected to change in proportion to changes in revenue) and *nonvariable* or *fixed* (those which are not expected to change as a result of revenue changes during the period for which plans are being made).

If the relationships which existed between two variables in the past can be expected to continue, future expense and income can be estimated if the estimated amount of revenue is known. The general formula is

$$S - V - F = I,$$

or some convenient rearrangement of it. The expected components of income can be computed by the formula, or they can be estimated visually from a *break-even chart*.

It is important to keep the limitations of the variable-nonvariable analysis, and predictions based thereon, fully in mind. The data do relate to the past, and future conditions are almost certain to change in some respects, perhaps materially enough to invalidate the conclusions based on the analysis of past results.

QUESTIONS AND PROBLEMS

11-1 "The objective of business is to maximize the rate of return on the assets used in the business."

REQUIRED:

Criticize this statement.

11-2 The rate of return on assets employed in the business is used as a measure of the effectiveness of management.

REQUIRED:

a. What are its strong points?

b. What are its limitations?

11-3 *B* Company had total assets of $120,000 at the beginning of the year and $160,000 at the end.

REQUIRED:

What amount of income before federal income tax would be required to yield a return of 8 per cent on assets?

11-4 Chapter 11 distinguishes between accounts whose balances are homogeneous and those whose balances are heterogeneous.

REQUIRED:

a. Explain why this distinction is important in business planning.

b. Illustrate two accounts whose contents are homogeneous and two which are heterogeneous.

c. Is it practical to keep historical accounting records in such a way that they will be ideally suited to planning for the future? Explain.

11-5 Determining the existence and degree of past relationships between two variables often assists in estimating the amount of future income.

REQUIRED:

Give an example of each of the following:

a. An expense which varies closely with sales revenue.
b. An expense which varies closely with another expense.
c. An expense which varies closely with an asset balance.
d. An expense which varies closely with a liability.
e. An asset which varies closely with revenue.
f. An expense which varies with the passage of time.
g. A revenue which varies in some measure with an expense.

11-6 "All expense account balances either vary in proportion to changes in sales revenue, or remain fixed in amount for short periods."

REQUIRED:

Comment on the validity of this statement.

11-7 "In the very short run, all expenses are fixed; in the long run, all are variable."

REQUIRED:

a. Explain whether or not this statement is correct.
b. If it is correct, of what use is it in business planning?

11-8

REQUIRED:

Name three major types of action which a company can follow in order to increase its net income.

11-9 A company doubled its net income in one year, yet its rate of return to owners decreased at the same time.

REQUIRED:

Using figures of your own choice, illustrate whether or not this is possible.

11-10 "In planning ways of increasing the rate of return of the business, the income statement is more important than the statement of financial position."

REQUIRED:

Do you agree with this statement? Why?

11-11

REQUIRED:

Illustrate how the following could occur:

a. A company's sales volume increased, but its net income decreased.
b. A company's sales volume increased and its variable costs also increased.
c. A company's sales volume increased and its variable costs decreased.

11-12 The management of a business is attempting to plan its operations for the near future.

REQUIRED:

a. Why is it useful for it to classify its expenses as variable and nonvariable?
b. What are some of the main difficulties involved in making this classification?

11-13 How would you expect the amount of loss from uncollectible accounts to behave as sales volume increased? Explain.

11-14 "The formula for estimating income is exact, whereas the graphic method of estimation is only approximate."

REQUIRED:

Comment on the validity of this statement.

11-15 If it is impossible to predict business income accurately, why should management even attempt to do so? Why should stockholders?

11-16 A company sells two products, X and Y. Product X yields a gross margin which is 60 per cent of sales revenue, and Product Y's gross margin rate is 55 per cent. Other variable expenses which are associated with the two products amount to 15 per cent of X and 25 per cent of Y.

REQUIRED:

a. If no other important considerations are involved, which product would the company prefer to sell?
b. Explain what other important considerations may be involved and how they would affect your choice of products.

11-17 Two sandwich shops were located side by side in a college town. Although both occupied buildings of the same size and charged the same prices for their sandwiches, Shop A had three times as many employees. It prided itself on its rapid service. To a passerby it would appear that Shop B was always as busy as A, yet A consistently earned greater net income.

REQUIRED:

How can this be explained?

11-18 In 19x1 a business showed the following components in its financial statements:

Average liabilities	$ 80,000
Average retained income	15,000
Average capital stock	85,000
Revenue	200,000
Fixed expense	40,000
Variable expense	120,000

The effect of income taxes was not included in these data. The items listed are expected to behave in the same way in 19x2 as they did in 19x1, except for the changes itemized below. These proposed changes are alternatives to one another, not consecutive in effect.

REQUIRED:

a. State the formula for estimating the company's net income for 19x2.
b. What would the net income be if sales for 19x2 were expected to be $250,000?
c. What is the break-even point under present conditions?
d. If the maximum amount of sales which can be accommodated with present facilities is $300,000, what is the company's maximum potential rate of income

before tax? (Assume that this revenue can be attained without an increase in average assets.)

e. If an alternate source of supply will result in reducing the cost of goods sold at the present volume of sales by $10,000, what would be the effect on (1) income at the present volume, (2) break-even point, (3) income at the maximum potential volume?

f. If an expense of $10,000 that is now fixed can be transferred to the variable category by a new contract, what would be the effect on (1) income at the present volume, (2) break-even point, (3) rate of return at the maximum potential volume? (Assume that the change would reduce the average investment in assets by $2,000.)

11-19   The chief accountant of the Hopton Department Store prepared an analysis of the percentage to net sales of each item in the income statements of the company for the current and preceding years. In reviewing the statements, one of the members of the board of directors noticed that cost of goods sold was 66 per cent of sales in 19x2, while it had been 63 per cent of sales in 19x1. He was concerned over the large increase and asked the president to explain the reasons for it.

REQUIRED:

a. What are some of the types of causes which the president might offer in explaining the change?
b. For each of your causes in (a), state what its general effects might be on each of the following: (1) revenues, (2) expenses, (3) marginal income, (4) rate of income before tax to assets.
c. For each of the causes in (a), as analyzed in (b), would you conclude that its effects on the income of the business are good or bad? Explain.

11-20   The Zeroid Company, which sells a single product, has kept the following records of its operating results for the past three years:

	19x3	19x2	19x1
Sales......................	$2,000,000	$1,800,000	$2,400,000
Cost of goods sold............	1,200,000	1,080,000	1,440,000
Officers' salaries.............	50,000	50,000	50,000
Salesmen's commissions.......	100,000	90,000	120,000
Heat.......................	15,000	18,600	12,000
Depreciation of equipment....	24,000	22,000	22,000
Other fixed expenses..........	250,000	250,000	250,000
Other variable expenses.......	280,000	252,000	336,000

REQUIRED:

a. Prepare an estimated income statement if sales for 19x4 are expected to be 10 per cent more than in 19x3.
b. Prepare an estimated income statement for 19x4 if sales are expected to be $1,600,000 and cost of goods sold is expected to become 55 per cent of sales.
c. Prepare an estimated income statement for 19x4 if the company sold its building, thereby reducing fixed expenses $110,000 a year, and signed a lease at an annual rental of $90,000 a year.
d. Would you recommend that the company take the action in (c), on the basis of the information given? What other information is needed?

11-21   The following is an analysis of the variable expenses of the Colson Company for 19x1 and 19x2. The percentages are based upon the net sales of each year.

Expense	19x1 Amount	19x1 Per Cent of Sales	19x2 Amount	19x2 Per Cent of Sales
Cost of goods sold	$120,000	60.0%	$195,000	65.0%
Sales salaries	5,000	2.5%	10,000	3.3%
Sales commissions	6,000	3.0%	9,000	3.0%
Advertising	500	.25%	2,000	.67%
Supplies	2,000	1.0%	3,000	1.0%
Taxes (other than income)	4,000	2.0%	6,000	2.0%
Discounts lost	—	—	500	.17%
Loss on uncollectible accounts	2,000	1.0%	6,000	2.0%
Miscellaneous expenses	200	.1%	500	.17%
Total variable expenses	$139,700	69.85%	$232,000	77.31%

REQUIRED:

a. Are all of these expenses likely to be perfectly variable during the next year? Explain any exceptions carefully.
b. If nonvariable expenses during 19x1 and 19x2 amounted to $50,000, and if depreciation in 19x3 is expected to increase $3,000 because of the acquisition of some new equipment, determine, by constructing a graph, what the company's new break-even point is.
c. Compute both the old and the new break-even points by formula.
d. How can management use the information relating to the break-even point?
e. What are the principal limitations of the break-even calculation?

11-22 The statements of financial position of two similar companies in the same industry, as of December 31, 19x1, are as follows:

ASSETS	Company A	Company B
Cash	$ 50,000	$175,000
Accounts receivable	75,000	250,000
Inventories	150,000	250,000
Land	100,000	
Plant and equipment	$1,000,000	
Less accumulated depreciation	300,000	
	700,000	
Prepaid expenses	5,000	5,000
	$1,080,000	$680,000

LIABILITIES AND OWNERS' EQUITY		
Accounts payable	$ 60,000	$ 90,000
Notes payable	20,000	100,000
30-year, six per cent first mortgage bonds payable	750,000	
Owners' investment	100,000	100,000
Retained income	150,000	390,000
	$1,080,000	$680,000

The annual sales for each company are approximately the same. The net income of each, before deducting interest and income taxes, was 10 per cent of sales in 19x1.

REQUIRED:

a. Explain in detail in what way you would expect the fixed expenses of the two to differ.
b. In what way would their net margin percentages probably differ?

c. Assuming that the net income of each before income tax and interest was $80,000:

(1) Compute the rate of return before interest and tax on total assets;
(2) Compute the number of asset turnovers;
(3) Assuming an average income tax rate of 50 per cent of net income before income tax, compute the rate of return of each company to its owners.

d. What differences in the policies of the two companies can you detect from the illustrated statements?

CASE 11-1. SOUND CENTER, INC. (B)

The basic data for this case are contained in the financial statements of Sound Center, Inc., which were illustrated in Chapters 10 and 11, and the supporting discussion.

Part A, Sales Commission Policy

REQUIRED:

a. Why do you suppose Sound Center, Inc., paid a commission on sales to its salesmen?
b. What disadvantages are there to this practice?
c. Why was a commission paid to Mr. Farley?
d. What revisions in the commission plan of the Center would you suggest?
e. How would your revisions affect the components of the formula for predicting the Center's income for 19x4?

Part B, Change of Store Location

Sound Center, Inc., has an opportunity to move to a more desirable location requiring a five-year lease at an annual rental of $4,000 or 3 per cent of sales, whichever is greater. The move would cost about $1,000 and redecorating expenses, to be borne by the tenant, would cost $3,000. The new quarters should not require further redecoration for five years. The present quarters would not require redecoration during that period.

REQUIRED:

a. Analyze the effect of the move on income if sales increased 20 per cent in the new location, with no increase in asset investment.
b. What would be the effect of the move, as compared with remaining in the present location, on income if sales declined 20 per cent in the new location as a result of a general business recession?
c. Would you advise the move, considering the results of your analysis in (a) and (b) and the fact that the new location contained 20 per cent less floor space?

Part C, Miscellaneous Alternative Plans

Assume, for the purpose of comparison, that the following three alternatives, and no others, face the management of Sound Center, Inc., at the beginning of 19x4.

Plan I. One proposal is to reduce the base salary of Mr. Farley $1,000 per year and that of sales clerks another $1,000, while increasing Mr. Farley's commission to 2 per cent of sales and increasing that of the clerks to 5 per cent. The increased sales effort is expected to result in a 20 per cent increase in number of sets sold, with no change in the amount of assets invested.

Plan II. A second plan is to redecorate and install some expensive sound equipment which would make demonstrations more effective. The redecoration is expected to cost $4,000 and the equipment $5,000. It would not be necessary to decorate again during the remaining 6 years of the lease. The equipment would have a trade-in value of $500 at the end of its useful life, expected to be 5 years. With these changes, the selling price per set could be increased $20 and the volume could be maintained. The average investment in assets would be increased by $10,000.

Plan III. A third alternative would involve purchasing sets from a different manufacturer for $15 per set less than the present cost and selling them for $475 a set. Records costing $2,000 would be given away each year to stimulate sales. This plan is expected to increase sales by 100 sets a year, with no change in the average amount of assets invested.

REQUIRED:

a. Evaluate each of the three plans on the basis of answers to the following questions, supported by any other factors which you think are relevant:

  (1) How would it affect the rate of return if the expected results materialized?
  (2) How would it affect the break-even sales volume, and of what significance would this effect be?
  (3) How would it affect the maximum rate of return that the business could earn if capacity sales in the present location are assumed to be 500 sets?
  (4) What would be the rate of return under the plan if the present physical volume of sales continued?
  (5) What unusual accounting problems or business risks would it involve?

b. Which of these plans would you recommend, if they were the only alternatives available? Why?
c. List some of the other alternative courses of action which seem to be available, and state in general how they would affect the estimated revenues, expenses, assets, and rate of return of Sound Center, Inc., for 19x4.

CASE 11-2. JACK RONSOM

Jack Ronsom has lived for several years in a small town in a southern state, where he is supervisor of a state park. One of his lifelong ambitions has been to have his own business, and for years he has been watching for what he would consider the right opportunity. Mr. Ronsom's present home town, with a population of approximately 3,000, is 75 miles from a large city. It is located near several other state- and privately-owned parks and a number of large lakes and resorts which are fast becoming national tourist attractions. During the spring and summer months, thousands of people are attracted to the area, some staying for several weeks. During the past two or three years, the attendance in the area has increased, especially in the slack season.

Mr. Ronsom believes that a first-class sporting goods store is sorely needed in this area. Many of the tourists neglect to bring adequate clothes and sports equipment for their visit. Several merchants in the town carry a few items of sports wear, and some of the hardware stores have a limited selection of sports equipment and fishing supplies. However, there is not a sporting goods store with adequate selection within a fifty-mile radius. Mr. Ronsom thinks that the type of store which he has in mind should sell sporting equipment, summer playclothes and informal clothing, and picnic supplies.

For several months he has gathered information which he thinks is relevant for planning his proposed business venture. Lacking accurate statistics, he has made rough estimates of attendance in the area throughout the year. During the spring and summer months, the principal attractions for tourists are swimming, boating, fishing, and picnicking. During the fall months, fishing, hunting, and mountain climbing are preferred. Throughout the year thousands of people stop by just to enjoy the scenery and the delightful climate of the area. Mr. Ronsom estimates that average attendance for the spring and summer months of 19x1 was 200,000 people per month, and average attendance during the fall and winter months was 50,000 per month. During the past five years, the average annual growth in attendance has ranged from 10 per cent to 15 per cent.

Mr. Ronsom wishes to locate his business in the center of the area. He has carefully planned the amount of capital which he thinks he will need to organize his store. He plans to finance the business principally by using $25,000 of personal savings. By shopping around, he has found a desirable plot of land which the owner is willing to sell for $5,000. He has discussed his building needs with a local contractor, whose rough cost estimate for the type of building suggested by Mr. Ronsom was $15,000. Mr. Ronsom plans to finance two-thirds of the cost of the building by a five-year loan from a mortgage loan association. He estimates that the cost of furniture and equipment will be $2,000. He anticipates that most of the remainder of his initial investment will be needed to finance the purchase of merchandise.

Mr. Ronsom and his wife plan to devote full time to the business, and he thinks hat one full-time sales clerk will be sufficient. During the peak season of the busy summer months, he will be able to hire high school students from the local area. He plans to use his own automobile for routine business operations, including buying trips.

Mr. Ronsom expects the principal expense of the business to be the cost of merchandise, which he estimates will be 50 per cent of selling price. The cost of utilities in the area is relatively small, and Mr. Ronsom predicts that advertising, supplies, summer salaries for clerks, and other miscellaneous expenses will not exceed 15 per cent of sales. His major worry is the drop in attendance which takes place during the winter months.

Mr. Ronsom has prepared an estimate of his expenses for the first year, grouped into two categories—those which will be more or less fixed throughout the year, and those which will vary with sales. He realizes that his figures are not absolutely accurate, but he thinks that they will be a satisfactory guide to enable him to decide whether the venture will be profitable. His estimates are as follows:

Fixed expenses:

Depreciation of building (The building is expected to have a 30-year life with no salvage value)...	$ 500
Depreciation of equipment (Estimated life, 10 years, no salvage value).....	200
Interest on the loan...	600
Insurance...	300
Full-time clerk's salary........	3,600
Taxes (other than income tax)...	400
Utilities (based on a $25-per-month average).............................	300

Mr. Ronsom will be giving up a job which pays him an annual salary of $6,000 in order to operate the business. He thinks that he should earn at least a 10 per cent return on the capital which he is investing.

REQUIRED:

a. Using the estimates which Mr. Ronsom has made, what is his break-even point?
b. Prepare a break-even chart for Mr. Ronsom.
c. What are the chief uses of such a prediction? The shortcomings?
d. How much would the sales of the sporting goods store have to be in order to fulfill Mr. Ronsom's expectations?
e. Do you consider Mr. Ronsom's estimates reasonable? Would you classify the income determinants differently? Has he omitted any major expenses?
f. Point out any other major factors which Mr. Ronsom should have considered.
g. Assuming that he decides to organize the business, what accounting period would you recommend for Mr. Ronsom? Why?
h. What general types of accounting records would you recommend for the business?
i. What types of financial statements should be prepared, and how often?

Chapter 12

The Operating Budget

Purpose and components of the budget

A *budget* is a financial plan of an organization or a part of an organization. *Budgetary control* is highly useful to management in striving to achieve the objectives of the business. It consists of the following principal steps:

(1) Preparation of a plan which is in accordance with the goals of the business;
(2) Comparison of actual results with the planned results;
(3) Explanation of deviations from the plan;
(4) Appropriate action.

Just as a business should determine what its long-range objectives are, so should it have a *long-range budget* showing how they are to be carried out. The distant future cannot be planned as accurately as can the near future, of course, and the long-range budget is merely a broad outline of goals and major financial elements. The budget for the next year can be more specific, and the plans for the next month can be prepared in considerable detail. Planned revenues and the expenses which are expected to be associated with their realization compose the *operating budget*, while the assets to be used by the business and the sources from which they are to be derived form the *financial budget*.

The budgetary controls of businesses can range from the very simple and informal to the very elaborate. The budget, like other components of the accounting system, should be tailored to the needs of the particular business.

326

The budget and responsibility accounting

A budget should be more than a plan on paper; it should also be a vital instrument for control by management. If the plan is to be fulfilled, the *responsibility* for doing so must be assigned to the *people* who are to carry it out, the managers of the organization. Each person who is assigned responsibility for directing the actions of others toward accomplishing the business plan must understand how his responsibility fits into the over-all objectives of the business. Each such manager needs to know what is expected of him in the operation of the business. He must have the necessary *authority* to direct the work of the employees under him so as to meet this responsibility.

So that appropriate action can be taken when needed to keep operations on the right track, each level of responsibility must receive *timely financial reports* of its actual performance in comparison with its expected performance. Reports to a given manager should be in sufficient detail to point out the principal strong and weak points of the activities for which he is responsible. Reports to the next higher level of management should be in less detail, summarizing the performance of each manager who is responsible to the same superior.

If actual results are to be compared with planned results, accounts for actual revenues, expenses, assets, and equities in the ledger must be classified along the same lines as the budget. Both budgeted and actual financial elements must be classified according to the individuals who are responsible for taking action to control them.

Setting the over-all income goal

The management of a business should decide what its long-range objectives are in terms of growth, share of the market, and income. It is appropriate to express the income goal as a percentage of the total assets used to earn it. Sometimes management needs to plan gradual increases in the annual rate of income in order to attain the company's ultimate income objective.

EXAMPLE 1: If a business which earned a before-tax income of eight per cent on assets in 19x1 wishes to earn 20 per cent in the future, its goals might be 11 per cent in 19x2, 14 per cent in 19x3, 17 per cent in 19x4, and 20 per cent in 19x5 and later years.

Changes in general economic conditions, particularly in the cost of capital, and in the operating conditions affecting the enterprise may dictate annual goals above or below the desired long-term average rate of income.

Chapters 10 and 11 showed how the manager of a business might use the rate of return on the assets of the business in appraising its past results and planning for its future. The rate was converted into a planning device by breaking it into two parts, the *net margin percentage* and the *number of asset turnovers*, and by separating expenses into their *variable* and *nonvariable* components. This made it easier to estimate the effects of alternative courses of action on revenues, expenses, and the amount and rate of income.

The business financial plan can also be useful to management in *controlling* operations. In a small business with a single level of management, reports comparing actual results with the budgetary plan can be relatively simple. The manager can control satisfactorily by relying principally on *observation* of what is going on. Nevertheless, he can make good use of budgetary performance reports to insure that his observations are reliable.

Setting income goals for subdivisions

In larger businesses it is impossible for one man to supervise directly the work of all employees. The top manager must delegate to intermediate managers the responsibility for supervising groups of employees who perform related work. Each intermediate manager must answer to the next higher level of management for the effectiveness of his department's results. The larger the business, the greater is the required number of management levels.

The business should set goals for each subdivision and then prepare a formal financial plan for their accomplishment. The goal of each revenue-producing division of the business may be expressed as a rate of return on the total assets used by the division.

Direct and common financial elements

When the divisions or branches are at different locations, it is often possible to tell without question which revenues, expenses, and assets apply to each. Such items are *directly* applicable, or traceable without question, to the division. Other items cannot be traced directly.

EXAMPLE 2:   The expenses of the top administrative office of a manufacturing company with three plants in different locations apply to all of the plants in common. These different administrative expenses associated with each plant cannot be traced in a direct and convincing way. Likewise, the assets used in the general offices are common to all of the plants of the company.

If the common expenses, revenues, and assets are to be associated with the several subdivisions, the apportionment must be made on some arbitrary basis. The basis should be designed to show how much of the *common* financial elements is each subdivision's responsibility. To avoid such arbitrary and often meaningless allocations, businesses often plan and report the actual results of their subdivisions on the basis of only the *direct* revenues, expenses, and assets—those which are *directly traceable* to each subdivision.

The following condensed illustrations show how the direct revenues, direct expenses, and contributions to common expenses of subdivisions might be organized in either financial plans or actual financial statements.

PLANT A
ISIS MANUFACTURING COMPANY
Summary of Planned Performance
For the Year 19x1

Expected direct sales revenue..	$200,000
Deduct expected direct expenses......................................	160,000
Contribution to common expenses and income of the entire company...	$ 40,000
Average total assets used directly by Plant A.........................	$160,000
Contribution to common expenses and income as a per cent of direct assets...	25%

Summaries of the same type would be prepared for Plants B and C.

ISIS MANUFACTURING COMPANY
Summary of Planned Performance
For the Year 19x1

Expected contributions to common expenses and income:	
Plant A...	$ 40,000
Plant B...	70,000
Plant C...	10,000
Total contributions to common expenses and income....	$120,000
Deduct expected expenses common to all branches:	
Expenses of home office.................................	35,000
Net income of company as a whole, before income tax.......	$ 85,000
Average total assets used by the entire company....................	$500,000
Net income before tax as a per cent of total assets..................	17%

The objective of each branch is to maximize the amount and rate of its *contribution* to common expenses and income. The contribution goals of the various divisions would total more than the income goal of the business as a whole, because the division figures do not reflect a share of common costs and income taxes.

Many business subdivisions, such as production, accounting, and personnel departments, do not produce revenue directly. Their goals must be set in terms of the total costs for which each is responsible. Improvement in their performance is often measured in terms of the reduction of expense per unit of work done.

The plans of businesses and the appraisal of results must consider standards of *quality* of performance as well as the *quantitative* measures of revenue, expense, and rate of return.

Controllable and noncontrollable financial elements

It is an established principle of management that an individual who is to be held responsible for a result must be given the authority necessary to accomplish it. Accounting reports to each level of management follow this principle by dividing revenues, expenses, and assets into two groups: those which are *controllable* by that specific level of management, and those which are *noncontrollable* at that level. An item is *controllable* by a department or division manager if he has the responsibility and authority to take action which will change its amount to a significant extent. From his standpoint it is *noncontrollable* if he cannot change its amount significantly, even if someone higher in the organization can. Rarely are the amounts of financial elements *completely* controllable by anyone.

Whether or not a given financial element is controllable by a given manager depends partly on the division of authority and responsibility in the particular firm, partly on the length of the time period in question, and partly on the nature of the item.

EXAMPLE 3:   The buyer of a merchandising department in a department store can control payroll expense to some extent if he has authority to hire or discharge part-time sales clerks as sales volume changes. He can control advertising expense if he has authority to decide the number, frequency, size, and types of advertisements of the goods for sale by his department. He cannot control payroll expense if he is not consulted about the number of employees assigned to his department, or advertising expense if he has nothing to do with determining the number and types of advertisements. Both expenses are then controllable by the level of management which decides what quantity and types of each service to buy.

The buyer can control the amount of the investment in inventory, within the limits set by his superior, by the manner in which he directs the functions of buying and selling within the department.

All financial elements are controllable to some extent by some level of the management of the business, if a long enough time period is considered. For very short periods, however, the amounts of a number of financial elements are not subject to change by anyone within the business.

EXAMPLE 4:   The departmental buyer in Example 3 cannot control the amount of periodic depreciation expense, or the amount invested in the asset equipment, if he does not have the responsibility for making decisions regarding equipment acquisitions and disposals. If such decisions are made by the president, the asset equipment and depreciation expense are controllable by the president in the long run. However, for short periods even he may be powerless to control their amounts.

Distinction between controllable and variable expenses. The classification of expenses as controllable or noncontrollable should not be confused with the variable-nonvariable grouping, although the two bases of classification are very similar. The latter distinguishes variable expenses, *which change in proportion to changes in sales volume, from nonvariable expenses,* whose behavior is not related to changes in sales volume. An expense may be variable from the point of view of the business as a whole but noncontrollable by a department manager because he cannot change its amount. On the other hand, equipment depreciation, a nonvariable expense, can be controlled over time by the action of the manager who has authority to buy equipment.

Distinction between direct and controllable expenses. There are important differences between the *direct* revenues, expenses, and assets of a business subdivision and the *controllable* elements.

EXAMPLE 5:   The asset, equipment, and its periodic depreciation are both *directly traceable* to a given department if the equipment is used solely in that department. However, the items are *noncontrollable* at that level unless the department head makes decisions related to equipment.

Distinction between common expenses and nonvariable expenses. Common expenses are those which cannot be identified convincingly with the operations of any particular unit of the businesses, whereas *nonvariable* expenses are those which do not change in proportion to changes in revenue. A common expense may be variable or nonvariable, and a nonvariable expense may be direct or common.

EXAMPLE 6:   A company has a national sales office but ships goods sold directly from each of three branch manufacturing plants. If it pays its national sales manager a commission based upon sales, the expense *varies* with total sales revenue but is *common* to all three plants.

Allocations of common financial elements

By definition, *common* revenues, expenses, and assets cannot be traced directly to the units of the organization, but sometimes assigning their amounts to the units serves useful management purposes. Such *allocations* attempt to associate the behavior of the common financial element with some factor which seems to cause changes in its amount. The common element is then allocated to each organization unit in proportion to the unit's use of the causal factor.

EXAMPLE 7:   A department store occupies a single building, for which it pays an annual rent of $12,000. Each of the four department heads has shown tendencies to spread the merchandise of his department over a wide area, with resulting inefficient space utilization. The president thinks that it will soon be necessary to acquire a larger building at a higher rent unless the wasteful tendency is corrected. He feels that the present volume of merchandise handled could, through efficient planning, be accommodated in less space. In order to make the department managers conscious of the cost of occupying building space, he instructs the accountant to develop a fair basis for charging rent to each department. How should the allocation be made?

SOLUTION: An obvious basis for allocating rent expense would be in proportion to the floor space occupied by each department. If Department A occupies $\frac{1}{4}$ of the total floor space, it would seem reasonable to charge $\frac{1}{4}$ of the rent expense, or $3,000, to Department A. For more complex figures, an alternate approach can be used.

a. $\dfrac{\text{Total number of square feet of floor space}}{\text{Total rent expense}}$ = Rent per square foot

b. Number of square feet in department $\times$ Rent per square foot
$$= \text{Rent expense of department}$$

The fairness as well as the usefulness of such arbitrary bases of classification is often limited.

EXAMPLE 8:   The manager of Department A objected to the charging of rent to departments on the basis of square feet of floor space. He contended that his department, being in a relatively inaccessible location near the rear of the store, should pay a lower rate of rent than departments in better locations.

The manager of Department C thought that the charge should be based on cubic feet of space, rather than square feet. The ceilings were somewhat lower in his department than elsewhere in the store, with the result that his available space for wall displays and shelf storage was less.

Allocations are useful if they help management in accomplishing its objectives more than would the alternatives of not allocating, or of reporting the common elements in some other fashion. Sometimes a compromise approach is followed: reporting to department managers their individual direct revenues, expenses, and assets, followed by the total common expenses and assets of the business. The purpose is to impress upon them the fact that the organization as a whole must earn enough revenues to cover common expenses as well as direct departmental expenses, and it must earn an adequate return on all assets, not just those directly used in specific operating departments.

Preparing the operating budget

In modern budgeting practice, it is customary to ask each individual who is responsible for managing a segment of business operations to prepare his own tentative budget for the items under his control. The theory is that the individuals who are to execute the business plans will exert greater effort to accomplish goals which they have participated in setting. There are, of course, limits to this approach. The budget supervisor should examine the details of departmental estimates for evidence of over-optimism, over-pessimism, or wasteful planning. He should review the parts of the plan to see that they are coordinated with each other where necessary and are reasonable in view of the availability of labor, merchandise, facilities, and funds. He should determine whether the planned margin of revenue over controllable expenses, the percentage of this margin to assets used by the department, and the budgeted rate of return for the business as a whole are consistent with the objectives. If he thinks they are not, he should recommend action to bring the departmental and over-all plans into line with the enterprise goals or, if necessary, to revise the goals. It is important that the department head understand the reasons for any changes in his budget and that he continue to feel that the plan is his own, not one imposed upon him from above.

The present chapter discusses only a part of the budgetary process, the preparation of the *operating budget* of revenue and expense for the next year.

The forecast budget and the flexible budget

One form of the operating budget, the *forecast budget*, is useful for *planning* future business activities. Another form, the *flexible budget*, is useful as a standard for *appraising* actual results.

In making plans for the future, management considers many important alternative courses of action which will have varied effects upon revenues, expenses, assets, and equities. The tentative decisions regarding some of the more important alternatives are often reflected in the preliminary budgets. For various reasons, components of these preliminary budgets may be unsatisfactory to management: (1) the prospective income may be inadequate, (2) they may not be properly coordinated with other important phases of the budget, (3) the necessary funds for financing the plans may not be available, or (4) important external factors, such as the general level of economic activity, conditions in the specific industry, or actions of competitors may change significantly. The budget often goes through several partial and complete revisions in its preliminary stages before it becomes the accepted plan of action of the business for the coming period. When this stage is reached, it is expressed in final form as the *forecast budget*, showing in detail the operating results which management expects to accomplish during the budget period.

Once a forecast budget has been completed, it serves as a guide to various levels of management in initiating action to carry out the plans. However, it is not satisfactory to prepare a budget at the beginning of the period and then leave it as a rigid plan of action. Important unforeseen changes in internal or external conditions may necessitate budget revisions during the budget period.

As time segments of the budget period elapse, it is essential that management receive information on its actual results in comparison with the plan. If the basic budget period is a year, for example, management may wish monthly reports of performance.

A comparison of actual operating performance with the forecast budget would show management *what the business did* in comparison with *what it planned to do*.

EXAMPLE 9:   *F* Company's forecast budget for 19x2 included sales revenue of $2,400,000, spaced evenly through the 12 months. Actual sales for January were $180,000, or $20,000 less than the budgeted amount.

A comparison of actual performance with planned performance is useful for sales revenue, but is inapplicable for expenses which vary in proportion to sales.

EXAMPLE 10:   In its forecast budget for 19x2, *F* Company had shown forecast cost of goods sold for January of $120,000, or 60 per cent of sales, but actual cost of goods sold amounted to $111,000. Was the performance on this expense item $9,000 better than expected?

SOLUTION: No, because cost of goods sold should bear a constant relationship to sales, 60 per cent in this illustration. If sales were less than the forecast, cost of goods sold should also have been less than the forecast, maintaining the 60 per cent relationship. Considering that sales for the month were actually $180,000, cost of goods sold should have been $108,000 (60 per cent of $180,000). The cost of goods sold was actually $3,000 too much, considering the level of sales volume actually attained.

A form of the budget which compares *what the business actually did* with *what it should have done under the circumstances* is called the *flexible budget.* While the forecast budget contains the plans for a single level of revenue and expense, the flexible budget permits comparisons of actual expenses with standards of what the expenses should have been at any level of operations actually achieved.

The flexible budget consists principally of a formula for estimating the behavior of each expense for any level of sales revenue, based upon analyses of the type discussed in Chapter 11. The formula for each individual expense may consist of a nonvariable amount alone, a ratio expressing the relationship of the expense to sales, or a combination of both. These standards can usually be applied more objectively if they are determined in advance of the period, rather than when the actual results are known. The latter approach tends to encourage excessive excuse-making.

The sales forecast

The logical starting point in preparing the operating budget is the *sales forecast*. Revenue is a critical element in projecting income, because it is the independent variable which influences the behavior of many important expense components. Variations in sales revenue from one period to another are often influenced markedly by external factors such as booms, recessions, and wars. Many businesses, especially those whose sales seem to be causally related to national income, base their estimates largely on the estimated total national income, or on total expected sales of the industry. The probable effect upon sales of changes within the business must also be carefully considered.

Often the record of actual past sales is a useful starting point in budgeting the sales for the future. Appropriate upward or downward adjustments should be made to allow for expected changes in internal and external conditions. Separate estimates should be made for sales of individual product classes to permit the planner to budget sales more accurately, to show what supplies and facilities are needed, and to coordinate the purchase and sales plans for the various types of products.

Basis for extended illustration

The remainder of this chapter is devoted principally to showing how to prepare the operating budget, how to report actual performance to various levels of responsibility, and how to appraise operating performance against the standard of the flexible budget. The data relate to Suburban Department Store, whose organization chart was illustrated in Chapter 5. The levels of responsibility for this store are:

Top Level	*Middle Level*	*Lower Level*
	Division Managers:	
	Publicity	
	Finance	
President	Store Superintendent and	
	Personnel	
	Merchandising	Department Buyers:
		Men's and Boys' Wear
		Ladies' Wear
		Home Furnishings
		Notions

In the illustrations, only one detailed departmental budget is shown: that of the Men's and Boys' Wear Department. The departmental budgets and reports of the other three departments of the Merchandising Division would be similar. Division budgetary and actual information is shown in detail only for the Merchandising Division in the following illustrations.

Departmental budget

Responsibility for control. The buyers of the merchandising departments of the Suburban Department Store have considerable latitude in selecting the types of goods they will feature, determining their sources of supply, setting the mark-up percentages used to arrive at selling prices, deciding when to make additional mark-ups or mark-downs in selling prices, varying the number of sales clerks, and selecting the number and frequency of promotional devices. The following condensed list shows which revenues and expenses the manager of the Merchandising Division considers to be controllable by each buyer under these circumstances:

Controllable:
  Sales revenue
  Expenses:
    Cost of goods sold
    Payroll
    Supplies
    Publicity
Non-controllable:
  Depreciation of equipment (a direct expense)
  All other expenses

Departmental sales forecast. The buyer of the Men's and Boys' Wear Department of the Suburban Department Store noted that annual sales in the past had increased about 5 per cent as a result of city population growth, which was expected to continue in 19x2. Considering this and an increase of almost 3 per cent in clothing prices which had taken place in 19x1, he estimated that revenues for the department would be 8 per cent higher in 19x2 than they were in 19x1. After a careful analysis of the distribution of past sales by months, he and the accountant together prepared the following sales budget for 19x2 by multiplying each past month's sales by 1.08.

SUBURBAN DEPARTMENT STORE
Men's and Boys' Wear Department
Sales Budget by Months
Year Ending December 31, 19x2

	Budgeted Sales		
	Men's Wear	Boys' Wear	Dept. Total
January	$ 10,200	$ 7,300	$ 17,500
February	7,800	4,700	12,500
March	10,800	7,200	18,000
April	15,000	10,000	25,000
May	17,700	7,300	25,000
June	12,000	8,000	20,000
July	9,000	6,000	15,000
August	3,900	8,600	12,500
September	9,600	10,400	20,000
October	15,000	7,500	22,500
November	17,400	7,600	25,000
December	21,600	15,400	37,000
Total for year	$150,000	$100,000	$250,000

Departmental expense budget. Although past records can be used for estimating the variable and nonvariable components of the departmental expenses, it is easy to exaggerate their importance. They show what the business *has done*, but they are quite often unsuitable measures of what it *can do*. Budgeted revenues and expenses should give effect to improvements which can be made. Budgeted variable expenses should consider possible savings, which will change the percentage relationship of variable expenses to sales.

The following expense standards were set on the basis of past experience and planned improvements.

SUBURBAN DEPARTMENT STORE
Men's and Boys' Wear Department
Controllable Expense Standards
For the Year Ending December 31, 19x2

		% of Sales
Cost of goods sold:		
Men's Wear (60% of $150,000 sales)	$ 90,000	
Boys' Wear (70% of $100,000 sales)	70,000	
Total for forecasted sales	$160,000	
Total forecasted sales	250,000	
Departmental cost percentage, based on planned mix		64%
Supplies		1%
Publicity		4%
Payroll (variable portion)		8%
Total		77%
Payroll fixed portion, applicable to buyer, assistant buyer, and other permanent employees)	$18,000	

(*Note:* Payroll, when considered as a single expense, is controllable because it amount can be changed to some extent by the departmental buyer. When it is split however, one component is controllable and the other is not.)

The department head in this instance has no control over the amount of depreciation of equipment, but the amount is directly traceable to the department. To provide useful information, and also to help insure that it is included in the budget for the entire store, it is listed in the departmental budget as a separate item. Such nonvariable expenses generally do not change greatly during the budget year, but the budget should incorporate expected changes in them resulting from asset additions, retirements, or substitutions.

Summary of departmental operating budget. The following is a summary of the departmental operating budget.

SUBURBAN DEPARTMENT STORE
Men's and Boys' Wear Department
Operating Budget
For the Year Ending December 31, 19x2

(All figures are estimates.)	Men's Wear	Boys' Wear	Total	
Sales revenue	$150,000	$100,000	$250,000	100%
Deduct cost of goods sold	90,000 (60%)	70,000 (70%)	160,000	64%
Gross margin	$ 60,000	$ 30,000	$ 90,000	36%
Deduct controllable expenses:				
Supplies			$ 2,500	1%
Publicity			10,000	4%
Payroll (variable)			20,000	8%
Totals			$ 32,500	13%
Departmental margin for noncontrollable expenses			$ 57,500	23%
Deduct direct, noncontrollable expenses:				
Depreciation of equipment			$ 2,400	
Payroll (nonvariable)			18,000	
Total			$ 20,400	
Departmental contribution to common expense and income			$ 37,100	

Operating budget for the entire business

The basic procedure used in preparing the departmental operating budget for the Men's and Boys' Wear Department would apply to the other departments of the Merchandising Division. These four departmental budgets, plus the budget for the division office, would comprise the budget for the division. Some condensation would usually be appropriate in the divisional budget, which would then be combined with the budgets of the other three divisions to form the operating budget of Suburban Department Store as a whole.

The following is an illustration of a highly condensed operating budget which might be submitted to the president and the board of directors.

SUBURBAN DEPARTMENT STORE
Budgeted Income Statement
For the Year Ending December 31, 19x2

Expected sales revenue		$1,000,000
Deduct expected cost of goods sold		600,000
Estimated gross margin		$ 400,000
Deduct estimated expenses controllable by division managers:		
Merchandising	$150,000	
Publicity	41,000	
Finance	38,000	
Store Superintendent and Personnel	32,000	261,000
Margin for noncontrollable expenses and income		$ 139,000
Deduct expenses noncontrollable by divisions:		
Administration	$ 40,000	
Occupancy	22,000	62,000
Estimated net income before income tax		$ 77,000
Deduct estimated Federal income tax		34,000
Estimated net income		$ 43,000

Summary of effect of planned transactions on the accounts

Difficult as it is to estimate the detailed components of net income for a business on the basis of past records and knowledge of changes in contracts and conditions, it is more difficult to estimate the resulting effects on the balances of assets and equities. Nevertheless, these estimates must be made for several reasons:

(1) Management needs to know the amount of assets that will be needed to carry out the budgetary plans, so that it can make necessary arrangements for obtaining them.

(2) Limitations of available funds may make it impossible to carry out tentative operating plans, requiring a revision in the operating budget.

(3) The balances of many asset and equity accounts which will result from planned revenues and expenses will, in turn, affect the amounts of

other components of the income statement. An example is interest on borrowed money.

(4) It is easy to overlook some important components of the operating budget or the financial budget unless a systematic procedure is followed to guard against such omissions.

One or both of the following methods may be used to test the effect of the tentative operating budget on the financial accounts and to insure completeness of the plans:

(1) A *transaction work sheet*, which traces the effect of the proposed budget on the accounts. The work sheet consists of the following columns:

Account Title	Balance, End of Current Year		Proposed Transactions Next Year		Resulting Balances End of Next Year	
	Debit	Credit	Debit	Credit	Debit	Credit

The work sheet can be extended to provide additional pairs of columns for *classifying* information needed in the preparation of the budgeted income statement, statement of retained income, and statement of financial position. A detailed illustration of such a budgetary work sheet is presented in Chapter 13, where the method of estimating the balances of some of the principal asset and equity accounts is discussed.

(2) *Budgeted financial statements.* These may be prepared instead of, or in addition to, the transaction work sheet.

REPORTING BUDGETARY OPERATIONS

Need for report of budgetary operations

Frequent comparisons of actual results with budgeted results are essential to successful control of operations by management. The budget is practically worthless as an instrument of control if an entire year passes before operating figures can be compared with it.

Contents of responsibility reports

Timely periodic reports should be submitted to each level of management, showing how that level actually performed in discharging its responsibilities. The general contents of such reports should show:

(1) What the responsible manager's unit did;
(2) What it was expected to do (on the basis of the forecast budget);

(3) What it should have done under the circumstances (on the basis of the flexible budget).

Reports for each department manager should give the details of his department's budgeted and actual performance as an aid in locating specific weak spots in operations. The reports to the next higher level of management, such as the division head, should present more condensed information about the performance of each department, because the division head is not concerned with the details of departmental operations. Instead, he looks to the head of the department to attend to the details within his area of responsibility in such a way as to achieve the objectives of the department. Reports on the performance of divisions are similarly condensed when submitted to the next higher level. If the need arises, these summary reports to higher levels of management can be supplemented by copies of the more detailed reports which are presented to lower levels.

To show how budgetary performance information might be reported to various levels of management, the following statements for Suburban Department Store for March, 19x2, are presented on succeeding pages:

(1) Operating Statement, Men's and Boys' Wear Department;
(2) Operating Statement, Merchandising Division;
(3) Income Statement, All Divisions Combined.

The title "Operating Statement" is used in the first two illustrations to emphasize that the final figure in each is not income, but a margin after deducting only those expenses which are directly applicable to the department or division.

Operating Statement, Men's and Boys' Wear Department. The illustrated statement for the month of March contains the following principal amounts for the month of March only, as well as for the year to date:

(a) Actual revenues and expenses;
(b) The total differences between actual revenues and expenses and the corresponding amounts in the forecast budget;
(c) The part of the total difference caused by the difference of the actual sales volume from the forecasted sales volume;
(d) The part of the total difference which is presumably the result of failure to keep expenses under control at the sales volume actually attained.

Derivation of the figures in the departmental operating statement. A department head who had used such statements for several months would soon understand how the differences from the forecast budget were computed. The supporting schedule, "Computation of Variances from Budget,"

SUBURBAN DEPARTMENT STORE
Men's and Boys' Wear Department
Operating Statement
March, 19x2, and the Three Months to Date

A. E. Curry, Buyer

Description	March Actual Results	March — Credit (Debit) Differences from Forecast: Total	Due to Volume	Due to Efficiency	January through March Actual Results	Jan–Mar — Credit (Debit) Differences from Forecast: Total	Due to Volume	Due to Efficiency
Sales revenue (net):								
Men's Wear	$9,000	($1,800)	($1,800)	0	$26,000	($2,800)	($2,800)	0
Boys' Wear	8,000	800	800	0	20,500	1,300	1,300	0
Total	$17,000	($1,000)	($1,000)	0	$46,500	($1,500)	($1,500)	0
Deduct cost of goods sold:								
Men's Wear	$5,580	$900	$1,080	($180)	$17,000	$280	$1,680	($1,400)
Boys' Wear	5,600	560	(560)	0	14,000	560	(910)	350
Total	$11,180	$340	$520	($180)	$31,000	($280)	770	($1,050)
Gross margin	$5,820	($660)	($480)	($180)	$15,500	($1,780)	($730)	($1,050)
Deduct expenses controllable at department level:								
Supplies	$174	$6	$10	($4)	$410	$70	$15	$55
Publicity	670	50	40	10	1,800	120	60	60
Payroll (variable portion)	1,540	(100)	80	(180)	4,000	(160)	120	(280)
Total controllable expenses	$2,384	($44)	$130	($174)	$6,210	$30	195	($165)
Margin for noncontrollable expenses	$3,436	($704)	($350)	($354)	$9,290	($1,750)	535	($1,215)
Deduct direct, noncontrollable expenses:								
Payroll (fixed portion)	$1,600	($100)	0	($100)	$4,600	($100)	0	($100)
Depreciation of equipment	200	0	0	0	600	0	0	0
Total direct, noncontrollable expenses	$1,800	($100)	0	($100)	$5,200	($100)	0	($100)
Departmental margin	$1,636	($804)	($350)	($454)	$4,090	($1,850)	($535)	($1,315)

shows how these differences were determined for the Men's and Boys' Wear Department.

The total credit or debit difference from the forecast budget is computed by comparing the actual results in Column 2 with the forecasted amounts in Column 1. For example, sales revenue, Men's Wear, was expected to be a credit of $10,800; actually, it was a credit of $9,000, a *debit* difference (an under-achievement) of $1,800. Similarly, cost of goods sold expense, Men's Wear, was expected to be a debit of $6,480 but was actually $5,580, a *credit* difference of $900 (similar to a saving).

All sales revenue differences may be explained as being caused by differences of the actual dollar sales volume from the forecast. Their amounts are entered in Column 5.

Each expense which tends to vary in direct proportion to sales revenue could be expected to be lower than its forecasted amount if sales are lower, and to be higher if sales exceed the forecasted amount. Column 4 shows the expected percentage relationship of each expense item to sales. Column 6 shows the flexible budget allowance for these items, determined by multiplying the actual sales volume by the expected percentage of each variable expense to sales. For example, cost of goods sold, Men's Wear, could be expected to be 60 per cent of the sales of that department at any volume; therefore, since sales of the department were $9,000, cost of goods sold should have been $5,400. Similarly, cost of goods sold for Boys' Wear should have been 70 per cent of that department's actual sales of $8,000. Supplies, likewise, should have been 1 per cent of *total* sales of $17,000.

Since nonvariable expenses are not expected to change in proportion to changes in sales, the flexible budget allowance for them would be the same as the forecast budget amount. For example, depreciation of equipment was expected to be $2,400 in the forecast budget for the year. Since it is a nonvariable expense, the forecast and the flexible budget amounts for it for a single month are both $200.

The credit or debit difference due to efficiency, shown in Column 7, is the difference between the actual result in Column 2 and the flexible budget allowance, in Column 6, for the corresponding expense item at the sales volume actually reached. For example, actual cost of goods sold expense in the Men's Wear Department was $5,580, $180 in excess of the $5,400 allowed by the flexible budget for the actual volume of that department. Publicity, at an actual amount of $670, was $10 less than the flexible budget allowance of $680.

The sum of the difference due to volume in Column 5 and the difference due to efficiency in Column 7 must equal the total difference of the actual results from the forecast budget as shown in Column 3. For example, the variable portion of payroll expense was $100 *more* than the forecast budget (a debit difference). This item would have been expected to be $80 *less* (a credit difference) than the forecast budget because sales volume was

SUBURBAN DEPARTMENT STORE
Men's and Boys' Wear Department
Computation of Variances from Budget
March, 19x2

	(1) Forecast Budget	(2) Actual Results	(3) Total Credit (Debit) Difference from Forecast	(4) Allowed Percentages of Sales	(5) Credit (Debit) Difference Due to Volume	(6) Flexible Budget Allowance at Actual Volume	(7) Credit (Debit) Difference Due to Efficiency (Col. 6 Minus Col. 2)
Sales revenue (credit):							
Men's Wear	$10,800	$ 9,000	($1,800)		($1,800)	$ 9,000	
Boys' Wear	7,200	8,000	800		800	8,000	0
Total	$18,000	$17,000	($1,000)		($1,000)	$17,000	
Deduct cost of goods sold (debit):							
Men's Wear	$ 6,480	$ 5,580	$ 900	60%	$1,080	$ 5,400	($180)
Boys' Wear	5,040	5,600	(560)	70%	($ 560)	5,600	0
Total	$11,520	$11,180	$ 340		$ 520	$11,000	($180)
Gross margin (credit):							
Men's Wear	$ 4,320	$ 3,420	($ 900)	40%	($ 720)	$ 3,600	($180)
Boys' Wear	2,160	2,400	240	30%	240	2,400	0
Total	$ 6,480	$ 5,820	($ 660)		($ 480)	$ 6,000	($180)
Deduct controllable expenses (debit):							
Supplies	$ 180	$ 174	$ 6	1%	$ 10	$ 170	$ 4
Publicity	720	670	50	4%	40	680	10
Payroll (variable portion)	1,440	1,540	(100)	8%	80	1,360	($180)
Total	$ 2,340	$ 2,384	($ 44)		$ 130	$ 2,210	($174)
Margin for noncontrollable expenses	$ 4,140	$ 3,436	($ 704)		($ 350)	$ 3,790	($354)
Deduct direct noncontrollable expense:							
Payroll (fixed portion)	$ 1,500	$ 1,600	($ 100)		0	$ 1,500	($100)
Depreciation	200	200	0		0	200	0
Total	$ 1,700	$ 1,800	($ 100)		0	$ 1,700	($100)
Departmental margin	$ 2,440	$ 1,636	($ 804)		($ 350)	$ 2,090	($454)

(handwritten annotations: "(4) × (17,000)" pointing to Column (6); "(2) − (6)" pointing to Column (7))

down; therefore, the debit difference due to operating inefficiency at the level of sales actually reached was $180. A debit efficiency difference of $180 minus a credit volume difference of $80 equals a net debit difference of $100.

Similar operating statements would be submitted to the buyers of the Ladies' Wear, Home Furnishings, and Notions Departments.

Operating statement, Merchandising Division

The manager of the Merchandising Division of the Suburban Department Store receives a monthly operating statement of the type illustrated, showing in summary form the results of the departments under his control. In addition, he receives a more detailed report of the expenses within the division office for which he is directly responsible.

The top line of the Merchandising Division statement is the same as the fifth- from-the-last line of amounts in the Men's and Boys' Wear Department statement. The division head has authority to control to some extent the amounts of equipment depreciation and fixed salaries of the departments of his division because he makes decisions regarding equipment acquisitions and disposals and hiring, firing, and pay changes of permanent employees. These two items of expense are also reported to each department head, even though they are not directly controllable by him, because top management wishes the department heads to be aware of the amounts of such direct expenses. These amounts, combined with those for similar expenses of other departments, are reported as being controllable at the division level.

The performance of the departments is reported to the division manager in summary form rather than in detail, for two reasons. First, he gets a better over-all view of the performance of the division when details are omitted. Second, if the full details of a department's operating results are reported to the division head, the department head may tend to dodge responsibility for taking the corrective action which the figures indicate is necessary. He may assume that his superior will study the figures and tell him what to do about them. With departmental details omitted from the division statements, the division head can expect more initiative from the department head in providing a detailed explanation of his operating results.

Reports to department and division managers in divisions other than the Merchandising Division are devoted primarily to expenses, although the Controller is responsible for the amount of interest revenue and other division heads occasionally deal with incidental revenues. Otherwise, the general format of these responsibility reports is similar to that of the Merchandising Division reports.

SUBURBAN DEPARTMENT STORE
Merchandising Division
Operating Statement
March, 19x2, and the Three Months to Date

O. H. Bergen, Manager

Description	March Actual Results	March Credit (Debit) Difference from Forecast — Total	March Credit (Debit) Difference from Forecast — Due to Volume	March Credit (Debit) Difference from Forecast — Due to Efficiency	January through March Actual Results	January through March Credit (Debit) Difference from Forecast — Total	January through March Credit (Debit) Difference from Forecast — Due to Volume	January through March Credit (Debit) Difference from Forecast — Due to Efficiency
Departmental margins for noncontrollable expenses:								
Men's and Boys' Wear	$ 3,436	($ 704)	($ 350)	($ 354)	$ 9,290	($1,750)	($ 535)	($1,215)
Ladies' Wear	4,000	(500)	(600)	100	15,000	(400)	(250)	(150)
Home Furnishings	5,000	400	50	350	18,000	1,500	(200)	1,700
Notions	4,100	200	(120)	320	13,500	800	700	100
Total	$16,536	($ 604)	($1,020)	$ 416	$55,790	$ 150	($ 285)	$ 435
Deduct expenses controllable at division level:								
Payroll	$ 4,000	($ 400)	$ 0	($ 400)	$11,000	($ 900)	$ 0	($ 900)
Depreciation of equipment	1,500	100	0	100	4,500	200	0	200
Supplies	150	20	(12)	32	400	(10)	(25)	15
Total	$ 5,650	($ 280)	($ 12)	($ 268)	$15,900	($ 710)	($ 25)	($ 685)
Divisional margin for noncontrollable expense and income	$10,886	($ 884)	($1,032)	$ 148	$39,890	($ 560)	($ 310)	($ 250)

Income statement, all divisions combined

The president of the Suburban Department Store receives the illustrated summary of the performance of all of the divisions, together with an itemization of the expenses and revenues of the president's office, which are directly under his control. Note that the amounts on the top line of the combined income statement are the same as those on the last line of the divisional operating statement of the Merchandising Division.

The principal purpose of the illustrated divisional statement and the company-wide statement is to show how the final results of a subdivision flow in summary form into the more condensed report to the next higher level of management. The reader should not attempt to determine how the individual differences in the last two statements were computed.

Using the responsibility reports

The illustrated reports to various levels of management apply the principle of *exception*—that is, they call each manager's attention to specific parts of his area's operations which are out of line with the company's plans. By reporting the dollar amounts of variations from the budget, they emphasize those points where the potential to increase income is apparently greatest.

Upon receiving the report of his area of responsibility, the manager should investigate to determine the causes of differences from the budget and the nature of appropriate corrective action needed. The causes may have been *external to the business*, such as a general change in cost or selling prices, and the manager may have been powerless to do anything about them. Sometimes *errors are made in budgeting*, with the result that a debit or credit difference from the budget is not attributable to inefficiency or good performance at all. Sometimes the causes of differences may be internal as far as the business is concerned, but *external to the particular department* whose results are being reported. Quite often, though, the *department head has some control* over the quantity, price, or mix of the revenue or expense item in question.

Often it is desirable to include space in the reports for the responsible individual to explain briefly the probable cause of substantial differences from the budget. In other cases, a verbal report by him to his superior is sufficient. Reports alone, however, cannot control expenses and revenues. What is needed is *action*. The action needed to be taken may be merely to revise the budget for future periods on the basis of the better information that is now available. Quite often it involves definite steps to increase revenues, decrease costs, or make a favorable combination of changes in both revenues and costs.

SUBURBAN DEPARTMENT STORE
Income Statement, All Divisions Combined
March, 19x2, and the Three Months to Date

J. C. Vining, President

Description	March				January through March			
		Credit (Debit) Difference from Forecast				Credit (Debit) Difference from Forecast		
	Actual Results	Total	Due to Volume	Due to Efficiency	Actual Results	Total	Due to Volume	Due to Efficiency
Merchandising Division's margin	$10,886	($884)	($1,032)	$148	$39,890	($560)	($ 310)	($250)
Deduct expenses controllable by other divisions:								
Publicity	$ 3,000	$100	$ 0	$100	$ 8,500	$300	$ 0	$300
Finance	2,500	(50)	0	(50)	7,000	500	0	500
Store Superintendent and Personnel	2,200	200	0	200	6,500	(600)	0	(600)
Total	$ 7,700	$250	$ 0	$250	$22,000	$200	0	$200
Combined divisional margin	$ 3,186	($634)	($1,032)	$398	$17,890	($360)	($ 310)	($ 50)
Deduct expenses controllable at president's level:								
Administrative	$ 3,300	($150)	$ 0	($150)	$ 9,500	($120)	$ 0	($120)
Occupancy	1,786	100	0	100	5,790	210	0	210
Total	$ 5,086	($ 50)	$ 0	($ 50)	$15,290	$ 90	$ 0	$ 90
Net income (loss) before income tax	($ 1,900)	($684)	($1,032)	$348	$ 2,600	($270)	($ 310)	$ 40
Deduct estimated Federal income tax	760	274	413	(139)	1,040	108	124	(16)
Net income (loss)	($ 1,140)	($410)	($ 619)	$209	$ 1,560	($162)	($ 186)	$ 24

EXAMPLE 11: Upon receiving the March operating statement of the Men's and Boys' Wear Department, illustrated on page 341, Mr. Curry, the buyer, would probably look first at the amount by which his department failed to achieve its forecasted margin for the month. This deficiency was $804, and the cumulative deficiency for the year to date was even greater, $1,850. Of these deficiencies, $704 for March alone and $1,750 for the three months to date were due to items largely under Mr. Curry's control.

Looking further, Mr. Curry would note that practically all of the deficiency for March, $660, and more than the cumulative deficiency, $1,780, were caused by lower gross margins than anticipated. Sales of boys' wear for the month were $800 greater than expected, and cost of goods sold for this class of goods was exactly as expected, 70 per cent of selling price. Sales of men's wear, however, lagged $1,800 behind the budgeted amount, with the result that sales for the department as a whole were $1,000 lower than the forecast budget figure for March. A change in the sales mix, shifting sales from the relatively high-margin (40 per cent of sales) men's wear to the relatively low-margin (30 per cent of sales) boys' wear, would itself explain some of the decrease in gross margin. Even if the entire $1,800 loss in sales of men's wear had been gained by boys' wear, the departmental gross margin would have been $180 less than forecast $(1,800 \times (40\% - 30\%))$ as a result of the change in mix. The actual difference may be attributed to the following causes:

Net decline in sales of men's wear:
Expected gross margin, 40%, × sales decline of $1,000 . . . . $400
Change in sales mix:
Shift of $800 of sales to boys' wear, with decline of 10% in gross margin   80
Reduced margin for men's wear:
Expected margin for actual sales, $3,600 (40% of $9,000), minus actual
margin, $3,420   180
Total decline in departmental gross margin $660

Mr. Curry should attempt to determine the causes for the shift of sales between classes of goods, for the net decline, and for the reduced margin on men's wear. He should then plan appropriate corrective action. In addition, there is apparently some room for improvement in the other expenses which are controllable at the department level.

Variations in responsibility reports

Although the financial reports prepared by businesses for external users such as stockholders and creditors follow a fairly uniform pattern, internal reports for management differ widely. The reader should not assume that the form of the responsibility reports of the Suburban Department Store is standard or even widely used. The illustrations are intended merely to show how reports to various levels of management are tied together. The nature and behavior of expenses and the division of responsibility for them vary from one business to another, and different managers have different preferences as to the types of information to be reported to them and the manner in which it is reported. Internal reports to management should be tailored to fit the peculiarities of the business and the wishes of the persons to whom the reports are addressed.

Some managers may desire columns, both for the month and for the year to date, which show the percentage deviation of each item from the budget. These percentages help the reader interpret the relative size of each departure from budgeted amounts. It may also be desirable to compare actual results for the current period and the current year to date with those for the corresponding periods last year. This can usually be done effectively by placing the current year's and the previous year's reports side by side, or by overlapping them.

In addition to the more formal monthly reports, various levels of management usually need frequent, but brief, reports of critical factors. The treasurer needs to know daily cash balances; the foreman in charge of an important manufacturing operation needs to know the daily amount of loss from scrap or defective work. Because the operating foreman tends to think more in physical than in monetary terms, reports to him are often more effective if they are expressed in such physical terms as the number of pounds of scrap or the number of defective units rather than in dollars of cost.

Restraint must be exercised in adding information to the existing reports and in initiating new reports. A few well-chosen figures that can actually be interpreted and used are much better than an unintelligible mass of figures.

Summary

The budget—the financial plan for an organization or a division—should be carefully developed to follow the lines of authority and responsibility within the organization. The long-range budget, prepared in general terms, should be consistent with the long-range objectives of the business. The operating budget, composed of the planned revenues and expenses for a short planning period, and the financial budget, composed of the needed business assets and their expected sources, should be carefully tied in with the long-range budget.

In assigning responsibility to particular managers, it is often well to classify financial elements as those that are directly traceable to a given manager's unit and those that are common to several units. In addition, it is useful in budgeting and reporting to report separately the expenses which are controllable to a significant extent by the manager in question and those which are noncontrollable at his level.

Reports of budgetary performance are vital in helping the organization carry out its plans. They may compare actual results (what the unit did) with the forecast budget (what it planned to do) and with the flexible budget (what it should have done under the circumstances). The responsible manager should investigate the causes of these differences, plan appropriate corrective action, and then initiate the action.

QUESTIONS AND PROBLEMS

12-1   The accountant of a company presented an income statement showing the contribution of each division to common expenses and income. The president remarked that the contributions of the divisions totaled more than the net income of the business, and asked for an explanation.

REQUIRED:

What explanation should the accountant have given?

12-2   The manager of a small manufacturing company made the following remark: "Budgets are a waste of time, because nobody can predict accurately what is going to happen in the future. And besides, budgets tie management's hands if changes need to be made because of unexpected operating conditions."

REQUIRED:

Draft a reply to this manager.

12-3   The proprietor of a small sandwich shop complains that his sales of sandwiches have been increasing steadily every month, but that he is finding it more and more difficult to pay his bills.

REQUIRED:

a. What course of action would you recommend to this proprietor?
b. What would you expect to be the general causes of his difficulty?

12-4   The X Retail Store has the six following operating departments, each headed by a manager: Sales Department A, Sales Department B, Sales Department C, Finance, Maintenance, and Personnel. The department heads are responsible directly to the president, who is interested in evaluating the effectiveness of each department manager in contributing to the store's income.

REQUIRED:

a. How would you suggest that the performance of the three selling department managers be evaluated?
b. How would you suggest that the performance of the three other department managers be evaluated?
c. Prepare an outline form of statement which might be used to report the monthly results of the Finance Department.

12-5   The manager of a department of a retail store learned that cost of goods sold expense was 1 per cent larger than the budgeted figure for a certain month, while supplies expense was 5 per cent larger.

REQUIRED:

a. On which of the two should he focus primary attention? Why?
b. What possible explanations could he find for the two variations from the budgeted amounts?

12-6   Many different types of budgets are discussed in this chapter.

REQUIRED:

Explain how the following (1) are different from each other and (2) are related to each other:

a. Long-range budget and operating budget.
b. Operating budget and financial budget.
c. Operating budget and forecast budget.
d. Forecast budget and flexible budget.

12-7

REQUIRED:

a. Give an example of an expense of a retail store which is direct and noncontrollable at the department level.

b. Give an example of an expense of a retail chain which is direct and noncontrollable at the branch manager's level.

c. Would it serve any useful purpose to report these direct, noncontrollable expenses to the respective managers in (a) and (b)? Explain.

12-8 The accounting department of a large manufacturing company prepared monthly operating reports for each department foreman. Copies of these reports, together with a summary of them, were submitted to the division manager. The president received a summary of operations for the company as a whole, supported by copies of all the division managers' and foremen's reports.

REQUIRED:

What is the reason for such a plan?

12-9 The Nalis Company is in the process of preparing its operating budget for the coming year. Many of the projected amounts depend largely upon the expected amount of sales.

REQUIRED:

How should the company go about estimating its sales for the budget period?

12-10 Department A has stayed within its budget on every single item, while Department B has exceeded its budgeted figures for more than half of the items.

REQUIRED:

Should the manager of Department A be commended because his department has operated more effectively than Department B? Explain.

12-11 The Tarey Company is preparing its budget for the coming fiscal year.

REQUIRED:

How should it forecast the amounts for each of the following:

(1) Advertising expense?
(2) Transportation out expense?
(3) Depreciation expense?
(4) Interest expense?
(5) Losses from uncollectibles?
(6) Cost of goods sold expense?

12-12 The management of Freeman Variety Store is faced with a decision as to whether to continue operating its lunch counter. Separate records have been kept for this department, showing its revenue, direct expenses, and share of such common expenses as heat, light, rent, insurance, property taxes, and administrative expense. Considering all of these items, the department has operated at a rather large net loss for the past four years.

REQUIRED:

a. Outline a form of statement which you think management should use in making its decision.

b. What nonfinancial factors should be considered in making the decision?

c. List the steps which management should follow in making the decision.

12-13 "It is much easier to prepare a sales forecast for a given period than to estimate the various expenses for that period."

REQUIRED:

Is this a true statement? Explain.

12-14 "An operating budget must necessarily be based upon estimates of the future. If the estimates are inaccurate, the budget is useless as a device for management control."

REQUIRED:

Discuss the validity of this statement.

12-15 A nationwide company with manufacturing plants and sales offices in many cities has decided to prepare financial reports for the manager in charge of each office, showing allocated common expenses as well as directly traceable items.

REQUIRED:

On what basis would you recommend that each of the following be allocated:

(1) President's salary?
(2) Total fire and theft insurance premiums?
(3) Cost of nationwide advertising?
(4) Income tax?
(5) Cost of installing the entire accounting system?
(6) Interest expense?
(7) Cost of training understudies for key executives?
(8) Cost of a company park in Kentucky available for the use of any employee?
(9) Rent of the central office in Pittsburgh?

12-16

REQUIRED:

Prepare a sales forecast by months for the Mammoth Products Company for the first quarter of 19x5 from the following information.

The company sells two products, S and N. The former is seasonal, the latter is not. In 19x4, sales of N were 24,000 units at $40 a unit. Sales of S were 20,000 units. The company's total sales were $1,200,000. Unit sales of S by months are shown below.

January	2,000	May	1,000	September	800
February	2,400	June	600	October	1,600
March	3,000	July	1,200	November	1,600
April	2,000	August	1,400	December	2,400

The seasonal pattern is expected to continue. The physical volume of S is expected to increase 20 per cent during 19x5, but sales prices are expected to be less by $2 a unit. Both unit prices and physical volume of N are expected to be 10 per cent greater in 19x5.

12-17 Gammon Sales Company prepared the following budget for 19x4:

	Total	Product 1	Product 2	Product 3
Sales	$100,000	$50,000	$30,000	$20,000
Cost of goods sold	67,000	30,000	21,000	16,000
Gross margin	$ 33,000	$20,000	$ 9,000	$ 4,000
Variable operating expenses	15,000	7,500	4,500	3,000
Contribution to nonvariable expenses	$ 18,000	$12,500	$ 4,500	$ 1,000
Nonvariable expenses	12,000			
Net income before income tax	$ 6,000			

Actual sales for the year were $110,000, but there was a net loss of $500. Sales of Product 1 were $20,000; of Product 2, $20,000; and of Product 3, $70,000. Variable and nonvariable expenses behaved exactly as they were expected to.

REQUIRED:

Prepare an analysis of the reason or reasons for the disappointing results.

12-18 The Perdu Company prepares monthly reports to help department managers control their costs. Just before the end of 19x1, the following budget for Dept. A was prepared for January, 19x2:

Sales..		$6,500
Cost of goods sold.....................................		3,900
Gross margin..		$2,600
Direct operating expense:		
Variable......................................	$1,300	
Nonvariable...................................	1,200	2,500
Contribution to indirect expense......................		$ 100

The actual results for January were:

Sales..	$8,500
Cost of goods sold.....................................	5,300
Gross margin..	$3,200
Direct operating expense..............................	3,000
Contribution to indirect expense......................	$ 200

REQUIRED:

a. Prepare a report to the manager of Dept. A analyzing the effectiveness of his operations for the month.

b. Comment on any significant phases of the operating results.

12-18 The Taylor Wholesale Grocery Company operates three branches in neighboring cities. At the end of the fiscal year, the chief accountant prepared financial statements for each branch, and the summary presented to the president of the company is shown below.

TAYLOR WHOLESALE GROCERY COMPANY
Income Statement
For the Year Ended December 31, 19x5

	Branch A	Branch B	Branch C
Sales revenue...............................	$150,000	$100,000	$200,000
Deduct direct expenses:			
Cost of goods sold..........................	$ 90,000	$ 62,000	$110,000
Payroll....................................	17,000	13,000	19,000
Supplies..................................	200	150	225
Utilities......................................	550	450	600
Transportation out and delivery..............	2,500	1,900	3,100
Depreciation of plant and equipment..........	10,000	9,600	11,250
	$120,250	$ 87,100	$144,175
Branch contribution to common expenses and income.	$ 29,750	$ 12,900	$ 55,825
Deduct expenses common to all branches:			
Advertising expense.........................	$ 6,000	$ 4,000	$ 8,000
General and administrative salaries (allocated equally)...................................	15,000	15,000	15,000
Other administrative expenses...............	1,000	1,000	1,000
Total common expenses........................	$ 22,000	$ 20,000	$ 24,000
Net income (loss) before income tax............	$ 7,750	($ 7,100)	$ 31,825

REQUIRED:

a. What are the advantages of the type of statement illustrated from the point of view of (1) the branch managers and (2) the president?
b. What are the disadvantages of the illustrated statement form?
c. Explain how expenses common to all branches have been allocated. Do you agree with this basis of allocation? If not, what would you have done?
d. Select examples of the following types of expenses, from the point of view of the branch managers:

   (1) Direct and controllable.
   (2) Direct and noncontrollable.
   (3) Common and noncontrollable.
   (4) Variable and noncontrollable.
   (5) Variable and direct.
   (6) Nonvariable and controllable.

e. Since Branch B shows a net loss for the period, should this branch be eliminated? Submit an analysis to support your answer.

   12-19   Refer to the operating statement of the Men's and Boys' Wear Department of the Suburban Department Store for the month of March, 19x2.

REQUIRED:

Assume that you are the buyer of the department, and that the manager of the Merchandising Division has asked you to prepare a written report explaining the reason for each difference of revenue and expense items from the budget. Write such a report, using plausible assumptions as to the underlying causes for the differences from the forecast budget.

CASE 12-1. THE COTTER MANUFACTURING CO.

The Cotter Manufacturing Co. maintains a central administrative office in New York City and has manufacturing plants and warehouses in Atlanta and Chicago. Advertising and other forms of sales effort, accounting, and general administration are carried on at the home office. After orders are received in New York, they are routed to either Atlanta or Chicago for filling. Shipments are made directly from the branches to the customers. Invoices are prepared at the branches but are collected by the home office. All cash payments are made by the home office.

The Cotter Manufacturing Co. has followed the practice of allocating all common expenses to the two branches on the basis of the sales of each. Assets common to the branches are also allocated. The following statements were prepared for 19x1.

COTTER MANUFACTURING COMPANY
Income Statement (Partial)
Year Ended March 31, 19x1

		Atlanta Branch	Chicago Branch
		(000 omitted in all amounts)	
Sales		$6,000	$9,000
Cost of goods sold		3,600	5,850
Gross margin		$2,400	$3,150
Operating expense:			
Accounting	$120		$180
Advertising	360		540
Billing	55		120
Collection	100		150
Finance	180		270
General Administration	360		540
Selling	500		750
Shipping	120		180
Storing	200		450
Total operating expense		1,995	3,180
Net income (loss) before income tax		$ 405	($ 30)

Cost of goods sold of each branch includes all costs incurred up to the time the goods are completed, including factory overhead.

COTTER MANUFACTURING COMPANY
Statement of Financial Position (Partial)
March 31, 19x1

	Atlanta Branch	Chicago Branch
ASSETS	(000 omitted in all amounts)	
Cash	$ 120	$ 180
Accounts receivable, trade (less estimated uncollectibles)	250	200
Inventories	360	540
Buildings and equipment—factory	400	500
Buildings and equipment—selling and administrative	140	210
Total assets	$1,270	$1,630

REQUIRED:

a. Which items in the statements are directly assignable to the branches, and which items are common?

b. Are the reports a good example of responsibility reporting? If not, how would you improve them?

c. Using columnar analysis paper, prepare an income statement emphasizing the contribution of each branch to common expenses. Use the following columns: "Total" (two columns), "Atlanta Branch" (two columns) and "Chicago Branch" (two columns).

d. On the basis of the original statements and your revised statement, compare the profitability and efficiency of the two branches.

e. If it were considered appropriate to allocate common items, what basis of allocation would you recommend for each item? Why?

f. What reports and analyses would you suggest for evaluating the performance of the New York office?

CASE 12-2. STATE ELECTRICAL SUPPLY CO.

A wholesaler of electrical parts and supplies prepared the following condensed financial statements for 19x3.

STATE ELECTRICAL SUPPLY CO.
Combined Statement of Income and Retained Income
Year Ended December 31, 19x3

Sales revenue		$1,200,000
Deduct cost of goods sold		876,000
Gross margin		$ 324,000
Deduct operating expense:		
Nonvariable	$194,000	
Variable with physical volume	120,000	314,000
Net income before income tax		$ 10,000
Federal income tax		3,000
Net income		$ 7,000
Add retained income, December 31, 19x2		18,000
		$ 25,000
Deduct dividends		6,000
Retained income, December 31, 19x3		$ 19,000

STATE ELECTRICAL SUPPLY CO.
Statement of Financial Position
December 31, 19x3

ASSETS

Current Assets:

Cash	$ 39,000	
Accounts receivable, trade (less uncollectible accounts)	96,000	
Merchandise inventory	290,000	
Total current assets		$425,000

Fixed Assets:

Land	$ 25,000	
Buildings and equipment (less accumulated depreciation)	150,000	
Total fixed assets		175,000
Total assets		$600,000

LIABILITIES

Current Liabilities:

Notes payable to banks	$110,000	
Accounts payable, trade	125,000	
Accrued liabilities	16,000	
Total current liabilities		$251,000

Long-term Liabilities:

Mortgage note payable		90,000
Total liabilities		$341,000

STOCKHOLDERS' EQUITY

Capital stock	$240,000	
Retained income	19,000	
Total stockholders' equity		259,000
Total equities		$600,000

Mr. Dobbs, the president of the company, notes that total sales of electrical parts and supplies in the company's trade area have been increasing at the rate of about 10 per cent a year, and he expects this rate to continue. However, the State Electrical Supply Co. has not kept its share of the market.

The most successful competitor usually earns a before-tax net income of 15 per cent of total assets. Mr. Dobbs would like the State Electrical Supply Co. to achieve the same level of performance within two years. He thinks that if the selling price of each unit is changed so that the gross margin will be 25 per cent of sales, the physical volume sold can be increased 50 per cent. This would involve no changes in the unit cost of goods sold or sales mix. Mr. Dobbs is considering the two following methods of handling this expected increase in volume:

Plan 1. Cash and accounts receivable balances at the end of 19x4 would have the same relationship to 19x4 sales as their ending balances for 19x3 have to 19x3 sales. Merchandise inventory at the end of 19x4 would be the same percentage of 19x4 cost of goods sold as the 19x3 ending inventory is of 19x3 cost of goods sold. The existing building and equipment are adequate to handle a 30 per cent increase in the physical volume of goods on hand at any time. The additional 20 per cent increase in volume would require leasing additional facilities at an annual rental of $15,000 on a 5-year lease. There would be no change in the behavior of variable operating expenses. Funds to finance the increase in assets can be obtained without difficulty.

Plan 2. The increase in sales resulting from the new pricing policy can be handled within the present plant capacity by more efficient ordering, better coordination of sales and deliveries, more effective credit and collection policies, and other similar measures. A management consulting firm would charge $30,000 to point out ways of accomplishing these improvements. Each asset's balance at the end of 19x4 would be the same as at the end of 19x3.

REQUIRED:

a. Determine the percentage return (before income tax) on assets, the number of asset turnovers, and the percentage of the net margin to sales of the State Electrical Supply Co. for 19x3. Carry computations to two decimal places.
b. If Plan 1 is used in 19x4, what progress would the company make toward its goals?
c. What progress would it make under Plan 2?
d. What would be the proper accounting treatment of the management consulting fee?
e. Which plan, or combination of plans, would you recommend? Why? What is the effect of your recommendation on the company's two-year progress toward its goal?

CASE 12-3. BONANZA STORES CORPORATION

Bonanza Stores Corporation operates 10 supermarkets in a large metropolitan area. Most of the stores have been purchased from independent grocers who were in financial difficulty. As a result of the company's expert management and excellent reputation in the area, the corporation has prospered in recent years and now has over 5,000 stockholders.

In addition to selling groceries, meat, and produce, the company's stores sell a line of high mark-up, nonfood items. The company realized an increase in sales volume several years ago when trading stamps were first offered with all purchases.

On January 1, 19x1, Bonanza Stores Corporation purchased another store, its eleventh. The store had formerly been owned by A. L. Jones and James T. Goodman, who had operated it on a supermarket basis. Although the business had a substantial sales volume, its income was far below the average of similar grocery stores. The former owners decided that they could no longer compete with the chain stores, which they thought had the advantages of mass purchasing. They agreed to sell the assets of their business to Bonanza Stores Corporation for $220,000.

As accountant for the Bonanza Stores Corporation, you and the newly appointed manager of Store No. 11 proceed to analyze the operating results of the store under the old management. Your purposes are to decide upon the necessary changes in financial and operating policies and to prepare a sales forecast and an operating budget for the year 19x1.

The following income statement was prepared by Mr. Jones and Mr. Goodman for the year ended December 31, 19x0. For comparison purposes, you have computed a standard of performance, expressed in terms of the percentages of the various types of expenses to sales. This standard is based on the average past performance of the company's other 10 stores.

STORE NO. 11
BONANZA STORES CORPORATION
Income Statement
For the Year Ended December 31, 19x0

		Actual Results of Store #11	Standard Company Percentages
Net Sales........................		$1,341,700	100.00%
Deduct cost of goods sold...........		1,151,900	81.50
Gross margin on sales (Schedule 1)...		$189,800	18.50
Deduct operating expenses:			
Advertising expenses.............		$ 10,400	1.00
Bank service charge expense.......		300	0.02
Depreciation expense:			
Building......................	$ 6,200		
Fixtures and equipment........	5,400		
Vehicles.....................	5,200	16,800	1.37
Insurance expense................		2,500	0.13
Laundry expense..................		2,100	0.15
Licenses and fees expense.........		150	0.01
Payroll tax expense..............		4,485	0.29
Repairs and maintenance expense..		1,900	0.13
Salary expense:			
Managers......................	$10,400		
Employees....................	84,000	94,400	6.00
Supplies expense:			
Office........................	$ 400		
Store........................	10,600	11,000	0.90
Trading stamp expense...........		26,835	2.00
Utilities expense.................		8,200	0.60
Total operating expenses........		179,070	12.60
Net income from operations.........		$ 10,730	5.90
Deduct incidental expense:			
Interest expense.................		5,200	0.40
Net income before income tax.......		$ 5,530	5.50%

STORE NO. 11
BONANZA STORES CORPORATION
Gross Margin on Sales
For the Year Ended December 31, 19x0   Schedule 1

| | Departments | | | |
	Grocery	Meat	Produce	Total
Net sales	$756,800	$460,600	$124,300	$1,341,700
Cost of goods sold	658,000	397,500	96,400	1,151,900
Gross margin on sales	$ 98,800	$ 63,100	$ 27,900	$ 189,800

With the addition of an extensive line of nonfood items, the operations of Store No. 11 will be accounted for on a four-department basis. Sales mix is of crucial importance to a supermarket of this type, since the gross margins for the various sales categories differ widely. Following are comparisons of the sales mix and gross margins achieved by Store No. 11 during 19x0 and the standard goals of the Bonanza Stores Corporation.

Sales Mix

Department	19x0 Actual Per Cent of Total Sales	Standard Per Cent of Total Sales
Grocery	56.4%	60%
Meat	34.3	25
Produce	9.3	10
Nonfood items	—	5
	100.0%	100%

Gross Margins to Net Sales

Department	19x0 Actual	Company Standard
Grocery	13.1%	15%
Meat	13.7	20
Produce	22.4	25
Nonfood items	—	40%

The management of Bonanza Stores Corporation sets sales goals of $1,400,000 for 19x1 and $1,500,000 for 19x2 for Store No. 11. Departmental forecasts are to be based on the company's standard sales mix.

Operating expenses are classified as variable and nonvariable according to the predominant nature of the expense. It is company policy to spend one per cent of the forecasted sales amount for advertising. Insurance expense includes premiums on fire, workmen's compensation, and public liability policies. Salary expense includes salaries and year-end bonuses paid to the store manager and department managers based on a percentage of actual sales in excess of established annual quotas.

Actual results for Store No. 11 for 19x1 were as follows:

Net sales:
Grocery ... $820,000
Meat ... 335,000
Produce ... 165,000
Nonfood items ... 80,000

Cost of sales:

Grocery	697,000
Meat	268,000
Produce	123,750
Nonfood items	36,000
Advertising expense	13,300
Bank service charges	360

Depreciation expense:

Buildings	6,200
Fixtures and equipment	8,600
Vehicles	5,200
Insurance expense	1,750
Laundry expense	2,400
Licenses and fees expense	150
Payroll tax expense	4,370
Repairs and maintenance expense	5,600

Salary expense:

Officers	12,000
Employees	80,000

Supplies expense:

Office	800
Store	9,000
Trading stamp expense	27,200
Utilities expense	8,400
Interest expense	3,200

REQUIRED:

a. Compare the operating results of Store No. 11 for 19x0, under the former management, with the Bonanza Stores Corporation's standards. What areas apparently need greatest management attention?

b. Prepare an operating budget for Store No. 11 for 19x1.

c. Prepare a report comparing the actual results of 19x1 with the operating budget, identifying differences due to volume and those associated with efficiency.

d. Comment upon the causes of the major deviations of actual results from planned results.

e. What segments of operations should receive special attention in 19x2, and what general type of action would you recommend?

Chapter **13**

Planning and Controlling Cash

Accounting for income versus accounting for cash

Earlier chapters have pointed out how *income*, the basic objective of business activity, is measured. It is the difference between *revenue*, the inflow of assets in exchange for the products or services of the business entity, and *expense*, the outflow or expiration of business assets associated with making such sales. The inflow and outflow of cash, matters of central interest in this chapter, are called *receipts* and *disbursements*, respectively.

It should again be emphasized that there is no direct relationship between the amount of periodic income, or net change in owners' equity which results from operations, and the net change in cash. A business may find its cash decreasing even though operations are very profitable, and a cash increase may accompany a net loss. This is true because under the *accrual basis* of accounting, revenue is taken into account when the right to receive money or its equivalent accrues to the business as a result of operations, and expense is considered to occur when the business receives a service benefit.

Importance of accounting for cash

The reader should not assume from the distinctions just made that accounting for cash is unimportant. Although income and cash change, or *cash flow*, are not the same, control of both is vital. Management must be able to plan cash receipts so that money will be available in the quantities and at the times needed for making payments. There must be reliable estimates of the amounts of cash that will be available from time to time for making discretionary payments, such as purchasing new plant facilities, making short-term investments, and paying dividends.

Accounting records of actual cash receipts, payments, and balances contain essential information about the liquid resources owned by the company and their changes over time. Equally important, the accounting system can provide reasonable safeguards to insure that business cash is used for proper business purposes and is not wasted, misused, or stolen. Although there should be similar accounting measures to protect other assets, accounting control of cash is of critical importance. Money is universally attractive; it can be transported easily, concealed, and put to improper use.

The cash forecast

One of the most important parts of any company's budget is the *cash forecast*. Its purpose is to show the probable amount of cash receipts and payments during future time periods and the expected cash balance at the end of each period. There should usually be a cash forecast for the next year and for each quarter of the year. Monthly forecasts are desirable for at least the next quarter, and if a business finds itself in a tight cash position, it may wish to prepare weekly cash forecasts for the next month.

Although the expected sales for the period covered by the budget is a key figure in planning, good historical records of cash are also essential. Such records provide information about past relationships that is helpful in estimating the effect of the volume of activity on future cash receipts and payments.

Forecasting cash receipts

Operations are a very important source of business cash receipts. The operating cash receipts come primarily from sales, with a time lag needed for collecting sales made on credit. Factors affecting the extent of this lag are the company's credit terms, its collection efforts, the habits of its customers, and economic conditions. An analysis of past records will show what proportion of a month's sales have typically been collected in the month of sale and in each following month. With proper allowances for important changes in the conditions affecting collections, these percentages can be used to estimate the cash receipts from customers in each future period.

Other sources of cash receipts are *incidental revenues*, such as interest, and *refunds* of payments made in earlier periods. Cash receipts records of past periods may be helpful in disclosing the probable nature and extent of such future receipts.

Nonoperating sources of receipts include the proceeds of sales of assets other than merchandise, such as investment securities and fixed assets; funds received on loan; and additional sums invested in the business by its owners. The amounts and timing of such receipts are usually irregular, and the amount which can be expected in the budget period should be estimated on the basis of definite plans.

Forecasting cash disbursements

Expected cash disbursements depend mainly upon the planned sales volume, the credit terms applicable to purchases of goods, services, and facilities, and the policy of the business relating to prompt payment. The net result of these factors can usually be determined by studying past records to determine when payments for particular types of purchases were ordinarily made. The largest single type of payment of a merchandising company is usually that for goods bought for resale. The amount of merchandise purchased, in turn, depends upon the expected sales of the budget period, the desired level of the ending inventory, and the amount of merchandise on hand at the beginning of the period.

There are usually many other important purposes of cash payments, but, in estimating their future timing by periods, it is usually satisfactory to classify them as either *required* or *discretionary*. *Required payments* are of two general types:

(1) Those which for all practical purposes are fixed by law, or by contracts which the business has previously made.

EXAMPLE 1: Payments for rent, interest, and principal payments on loans with definite due dates are required by contract to be made at specific times. Payments for taxes are governed by law.

The timing and amounts of payments of this type may be determined by referring to the related contract or law.

(2) Those for variable items, whose amount is largely set by the level of sales.

EXAMPLE 2: Payments for utilities and salaries must be made periodically according to contract, but their amounts vary to some extent according to the quantity of the service used.

The timing and amounts of payments of this type may be estimated from the terms of the contracts and the expected volume of sales.

Other cash disbursements are largely *discretionary*. That is, management has some leeway in deciding how much the payment is to be, when it is to be made, or even whether it is to be made at all.

EXAMPLE 3: Management has discretion as to the timing of early payment of liabilities. It has considerable discretion in both the timing and the amount of dividends, purchases of securities for investment, and purchases of fixed assets.

In formulating definite plans for discretionary cash payments and receipts, management should first compute the difference between the cash which will become available from operations and the cash which will be needed for required payments. The following illustration shows how this may be done.

	Case A	Case B
Estimated Cash Available:		
Beginning cash balance......................	$10,000	$10,000
Receipts from operations......................	75,000	75,000
Total cash available........................	$85,000	$85,000
Estimated Cash Required:		
Required payments............................	$82,000	$62,000
Desired ending balance........................	15,000	15,000
Total cash required..........................	$97,000	$77,000
Cash available for discretionary payments.........		$ 8,000
Additional cash required........................	$12,000	

In Case A, $12,000 additional cash must be obtained from borrowing, additional investment of owners, or sale of assets other than merchandise. In Case B, $8,000 cash will apparently be available for such discretionary uses as payment of dividends, purchase of securities or fixed assets, or early repayment of loans.

The ending cash balance should be sufficient to make payments which will be necessary before the cash is replenished. Its amount should be based upon the expected cash receipts and payments of the following period. Often banks help determine this amount by requiring their depositors to keep a specified minimum cash balance in the bank at all times as a condition for making a loan.

Basis for cash forecast illustration

The following statement of financial position of the Tranton Company as of December 31, 19x1, and additional data relating to its plans for January, 19x2, form the basis for preparing the cash forecast of the company for the month of January, 19x2.

TRANTON COMPANY
Statement of Financial Position
December 31, 19x1

ASSETS

Current Assets:		
Cash...		$ 60,700
Accounts receivable, trade	$112,500	
Deduct estimated uncollectibles................	6,000	106,500
Merchandise inventory.....................................		150,000
Prepaid expense...		15,800
Total current assets..		$333,000

Fixed Assets:

Store fixtures and equipment.............................	$ 80,000	
Deduct accumulated depreciation.........................	35,000	45,000
Total assets..		$378,000

LIABILITIES

Current Liabilities:

Accounts payable, trade................................	$ 70,000	
6% Notes payable to banks.............................	90,000	
Accrued interest payable..............................	3,150	
Federal income tax payable............................	12,500	
Taxes payable, other..................................	3,700	
Dividends payable.....................................	2,000	
Total current liabilities..............................		$181,350

Long-term Liabilities:

6% Notes payable maturing 19x3–x7............................		50,000
Total liabilities.......................................		$231,350

STOCKHOLDERS' EQUITY

Capital stock, $100 par.................................	$100,000	
Retained income.......................................	46,650	
Total stockholders' equity.............................		146,650
Total equities..		$378,000

Journal entries for budgeted transactions

The following paragraphs explain how the amounts for each *budgeted transaction* for the month of January would be determined and show their effect on the accounts of the Tranton Company in journal form. In the next section, these projected transactions are summarized in such a way as to facilitate the preparation of a cash forecast for January, a budgeted income statement for January, and a budgeted statement of financial position as of January 31, 19x2.

(1) *Sales forecast.* The company's records show that sales in the past have consistently been about 40 per cent for cash and 60 per cent on account. Budgeted sales for the first four months of 19x2 are:

	Total	40% Cash	60% Credit
January........................	$ 70,000	$28,000	$42,000
February......................	50,000	20,000	30,000
March.........................	80,000	32,000	48,000
April..........................	110,000	44,000	66,000

The company sends monthly statements to its customers on the last day of the month. An analysis of cash receipts and sales by months indicates that 70 per cent of the charge sales of a given month are usually collected in the following month; 29 per cent are collected in the second following month; and one per cent are never collected. The balance of Accounts Receivable, Trade, on December 31, 19x1, consists of the following items:

100% of December charge sales of $90,000................	$ 90,000
30% of November charge sales of $60,000................	18,000
1% of January–October charge sales of $450,000........	4,500
Balance, December 31, 19x1..........................	$112,500

Cash receipts from sales in January, 19x2, should include $28,000 for cash sales and $80,400 for collections on account, computed as follows:

70% of December charge sales of $90,000	$ 63,000
29% of November charge sales of $60,000	17,400
Total January collections on account	$ 80,400

Collections for later months are computed in the same manner. The following entries show the effect of this information.

(a)

A, Accounts Receivable, Trade	42,000	
OE, Sales Revenue		42,000
Estimated sales on account for January.		

(b)

A, Cash	28,000	
OE, Sales Revenue		28,000
Estimated cash sales for January.		

(c)

A, Cash	80,400	
A, Accounts Receivable, Trade		80,400
Estimated collections of January 1 accounts receivable in January.		

(d)

OE, Loss from Uncollectible Accounts	420	
A, Accounts Receivable—Estimated Uncollectibles		420
Estimated uncollectible accounts are 1% of sales on account.		

(2) *Merchandise inventory forecast.* The Tranton Company buys all of its merchandise on terms of 2/10, n/30. Payment for supplies and other items bought from outsiders is due in the month following purchase without discount. The store takes all discounts on the last day of the discount period and pays other bills just before the expiration of the credit period. It makes purchases evenly throughout each month. At the end of any month, it plans to have an inventory of goods on hand sufficient to fill the expected sales of the following three months. The average cost of goods sold for the store as a whole is 60 per cent of sales.

The required purchases for January are computed as follows:

	Selling price	Cost, 60%
Merchandise required:		
Desired ending inventory, January 31, equal to expected sales of:		
February	$ 50,000	
March	80,000	
April	110,000	
Total	$240,000	$144,000
Add expected January sales	70,000	42,000
Total merchandise required in January		$186,000
Deduct merchandise available in beginning inventory		150,000
Required purchases in January		$ 36,000

Cash payments required as a result of January merchandise purchases will be $24,000 in January and $12,000 in February. Since purchases are made evenly throughout the month, on January 31 the discount period will not have expired for the purchases made during the last ten days (one-third) of the month.

The following entries summarize the effect of these estimates.

(e)

```
A, Merchandise Inventory...................... ..  36,000
    L, Accounts Payable, Trade....................          36,000
    Estimated purchases on account in January.
```

(f)

```
L, Accounts Payable, Trade....................... 24,000
    A, Cash......................................          24,000
    Estimated payments for January purchses:
```

(g)

```
OE, Cost of Goods Sold Expense................... 42,000
    A, Merchandise Inventory......................          42,000
    Estimated cost of goods sold.
```

(3) *Forecasted payments of beginning liability balances.* Accounts Payable, Trade, consisted of one-third of the December merchandise purchases plus other items normally bought on credit, both of which were to be paid for in January.

The Notes Payable to Banks were for a term of 90 days. The bank had agreed that they might be renewed for 90 days in January upon the payment of three months' interest. None of the principal of the $50,000 long-term notes was due in 19x2, and the interest was payable once a year in March. No payment on principal would be required in January.

The Federal income taxes for a given year are assumed to be payable ½ by the following March 15 and ½ by June 15. No payment would be required in January.

Taxes Payable, Other, consisted of taxes withheld from the pay of employees and payroll taxes on the employer. Both of these must usually be paid to the appropriate government in the month following collection.

A dividend had been declared by the board of directors in December, 19x1, payable to the stockholders in January.

The following entries summarize the effect of these expected payments.

(h)

```
L, Accounts Payable, Trade....................... 70,000
    A, Cash......................................          70,000
    Expected payment of beginning accounts payable.
```

(i)

```
L, Accrued Interest Payable...................... 1,350
    A, Cash......................................          1,350
    Expected payment of 3 months' interest.
```

(j)

```
L, Taxes Payable, Other.......................... 3,700
    A, Cash......................................          3,700
    Expected payment of December taxes.
```

(k)

| L, Dividends Payable............................... | 2,000 | |
| A, Cash.. | | 2,000 |

Expected payment of December dividend.

(4) *Forecasted payments of current expenses.* The following entries record the expected payment in January of current expenses.

(l)

OE, Payroll Expense.............................	15,200	
A, Cash.		12,800
L, Taxes Payable, Other........................		2,400

Gross wages expected to be earned by employees in January, minus payroll tax withholdings.

(m)

| OE, Rent Expense................................ | 800 | |
| A, Cash......... .... | | 800 |

Expected rent payment in January.

(5) *Forecasted expense accruals.* The following entries record the effect of expenses which are expected to accrue in January but which will be payable in February.

(n)

OE, Advertising Expense..........................	850	
OE, Purchased Service Expense....................	1,300	
OE, Supplies Expense............................	1,050	
OE, Miscellaneous Expense.	1,000	
L, Accounts Payable, Trade....................		4,200

Estimated expense accruals payable in February.

(o)

| OE, Tax Expense, Other.......................... | 600 | |
| L, Taxes Payable, Other....... .... | | 600 |

Estimated employer payroll tax accruals payable in February.

Interest on the notes payable accrues in equal daily amounts in January, as shown by the following entry, but is payable at irregular intervals set by the terms of the notes.

(p)

| OE, Interest Expense............................. | 700 | |
| L, Accrued Interest Payable.................... | | 700 |

Estimated interest accruals in January as follows:

6% of Notes Payable to Banks, $90,000, for one month.........................	$450
6% of Long-Term Notes Payable, $50,000, for one month.......	250
Total...........................	$700

The additional accrual of income tax expense in January, recorded below, is assumed to be 40 per cent of the net income before income tax, and to be payable in the following year, 19x3.

(q)

OE, Federal Income Tax Expense.................	1,672	
L, Accrued Income Tax Payable...............		1,672

Estimated income tax accrual in January.

(6) *Forecasted purchase of assets.* Insurance premiums are usually paid in advance for at least a year. It is assumed in the following entry that all policies expire at the end of January, and will be renewed at a higher rate.

(r)

A, Prepaid Expense.............................	12,600	
A, Cash..		12,600

Expected payment of annual insurance premiums.

There were no purchases of long-lived assets expected in January. Projected purchases of long-lived assets would be recorded by debiting the asset and crediting cash or a liability.

(7) *Forecasted asset cost expirations.* In the following entry it is assumed that $900 of insurance premiums expire in January and that none of the other prepaid expense items expire during the month.

(s)

OE, Insurance Expense.........................	900	
A, Prepaid Expense...........................		900

Estimated insurance expiration in January.

Depreciation expense requires special comment. The cash payment for an asset which is subject to depreciation occurs when the asset is bought or when installment payments, which have no direct relationship to periodic depreciation expense, are made. Depreciation expense is that portion of the asset's cost which is allocated to each period of its useful life, and it does not require a cash payment. Depreciation for January is assumed to be $1,000.

(t)

OE, Depreciation Expense.......................	1,000	
A, Store Fixtures and Equipment—Accumulated Depreciation...............................		1,000

Estimated January depreciation.

Budget Work Sheet

The illustrated Budget Work Sheet begins with the asset and equity balances of the Tranton Company on January 1, summarizes the effects of the planned transactions for January which were illustrated in the preceding journal entries, and classifies the resulting January 31 balances according to the formal financial statements in which they would be used. A projected income statement, statement of retained income, and statement of financial position could be prepared in proper form from the information contained in the last six columns of the work sheet.

TRANTON COMPANY
Budget Work Sheet
For the Month Ending January 31, 19x2

	Actual Balances January 1, 19x2		Projected January Transactions		Income Statement Items		Retained Income Statement Items		Statement of Financial Position Items	
	Debit	Credit	Debit	Credit	Debit	Credit	Debit	Credit	Debit	Credit
A, Cash..........	60,700		b 28,000 c 80,400	f 24,000 h 70,000 i 1,350 j 3,700 k 2,000 l 12,800 m 800 r 12,600					41,850	
A, Accounts Receivable, Trade........	112,500		a 42,000	c 80,400					74,100	
A, —Estimated Uncollectibles........		6,000		d 420						6,420
A, Merchandise Inventory........	150,000		e 36,000	g 42,000					144,000	
A, Prepaid Expense........	15,800		r 12,600	s 900					27,500	
A, Store Fixtures and Equipment........	80,000								80,000	
A, —Accumulated Depreciation........		35,000		t 1,000						36,000
L, Accounts Payable, Trade........		70,000	f 24,000 h 70,000	e 36,000 n 4,200						16,200
L, 6% Notes Payable to Banks........		90,000								90,000
L, Accrued Interest Payable........		3,150	i 1,350	p 700						2,500
L, Accrued Income Tax Payable........		12,500		q 1,672						14,172
L, Taxes Payable, Other........		3,700	j 3,700	o 600						
L, Dividends, Payable........		2,000	k 2,000	l 2,400						3,000

Account	Trial Balance Dr	Trial Balance Cr	Entries Dr	Entries Cr	Income Statement Dr	Income Statement Cr	Retained Income Dr	Retained Income Cr	Financial Position Dr	Financial Position Cr
L, 6% Long-Term Notes Payable		50,000								50,000
OE, Capital Stock		100,000								100,000
OE, Retained Income		46,650						46,650		
Totals	419,000	419,000								
OE, Sales Revenue				a 42,000 / b 28,000		70,000				
OE, Loss from Uncollectible Accounts			d 420		420					
OE, Cost of Goods Sold Expense			g 42,000		42,000					
OE, Payroll Expense			l 15,200		15,200					
OE, Rent Expense			m 800		800					
OE, Advertising Expense			n 850		850					
OE, Purchased Service Expense			n 1,300		1,300					
OE, Supplies Expense			n 1,050		1,050					
OE, Miscellaneous Expense			n 1,000		1,000					
OE, Tax Expense, Other			o 600		600					
OE, Interest Expense			p 700		700					
OE, Federal Income Tax Expense			q 1,672		1,672					
OE, Insurance Expense			s 900		900					
OE, Depreciation Expense			t 1,000		1,000					
Totals			367,542	367,542	67,492	70,000				
Estimated Net Income—to Retained Income					2,508			2,508		
Totals					70,000	70,000		49,158		
Estimated ending Retained Income—to Statement of Financial Position							49,158	0		49,158
Totals							49,158	49,158	367,450	367,450

The budget work sheet may be prepared by entering the debits and credits of projected transactions directly on the work sheet, omitting the preparation of separate journal entries. If this is done, a legend should accompany the work sheet, giving for each letter a brief explanation of the transaction.

The illustrated budget work sheet should be regarded as tentative. If the projected net income which it shows is unsatisfactory, if the projected balances of various assets are too small or too large, or if projected relationships between assets and equities are undesirable, management should revise its plans in an attempt to attain more desirable results. A final budget work sheet which incorporates these revised plans would then be useful.

Cash Forecast Summary

A Cash Forecast Summary of the following type may be prepared for the use of management, on the basis of the budget entries which affect Cash.

TRANTON COMPANY
Cash Forecast Summary
For the Month Ending January 31, 19x2

Estimated cash available:

From operations:

Cash sales...	$28,000	
Collections for charge sales of prior months.................	80,400	
Total estimated receipts from operations...........................		$108,400
Add beginning cash balance...		60,700
Estimated total cash available....................................		$169,100

Estimated cash required:

Required payments:

Liabilities of preceding month:		
Accounts payable, trade.................................	$70,000	
Taxes payable, other...................................	3,700	
Dividends payable......................................	2,000	
Liabilities of current month:		
Merchandise purchases.............................	24,000	
Payroll...	12,800	
Rent..	800	
Irregular payments:		
Accrued interest payable.............................	1,350	
Insurance premiums paid.............................	12,600	
Total required payments..		$127,250
Add desired ending cash balance...................................		25,000
Estimated total cash required....................................		$152,250

Difference:

Cash available for discretionary payments (if cash available is greater than cash required)... $ 16,850

or

Additional cash required (if cash required is greater than cash available).. 0

Using the cash forecast summary

The cash forecast summary, like the budget work sheet, may be regarded as tentative. Management can use it as a basis for deciding what discretionary payments to make during the coming budget period or where to obtain needed additional funds.

The cash forecast summary of the Tranton Company indicates that there is expected to be $16,850 of cash available in January for making discretionary payments. Before deciding what use to make of this excess, however, management needs to know how long it is likely to be available. Monthly cash forecasts for later months should be prepared in the same manner as the January forecast. The individual monthly increases and decreases expected for available cash should be added to the beginning cash balance to give a cumulative balance, as shown in the following table:

TRANTON COMPANY
Estimated Cash Balance by Months
For the Year Ending December 31, 19x2

Month	Estimated Receipts from Operations	Estimated Payments Required	Monthly Cash Increase (+) or Decrease (−)	Cumulative Cash Balance
January 1 balance..........				+$60,700
January..................	$108,400	$127,250	−$18,850	+ 41,850
February.................	90,000	98,000	− 8,000	+ 33,850
March...................	80,000	100,000	− 20,000	+ 13,850
April....................	70,000	85,000	− 15,000	− 1,150
May.....................	90,000	100,000	− 10,000	− 11,150
June....................	70,000	55,000	+ 15,000	+ 3,850
July....................	80,000	60,000	+ 20,000	+ 23,850
August..................	60,000	50,000	+ 10,000	+ 33,850
September...............	55,000	47,000	+ 8,000	+ 41,850
October.................	65,000	56,000	+ 9,000	+ 50,850
November...............	75,000	70,000	+ 5,000	+ 55,850
December...............	100,000	90,000	+ 10,000	+ 65,850
Total for year............	$943,400	$938,250	+$ 5,150	

The table shows that, if no discretionary payments are made and no cash is received from additional sources, the Tranton Company will probably need to borrow $11,150 ($25,000 desired balance minus $13,850 expected balance) at the end of March in order to maintain its cash balance at the desired level. It will need to borrow even more in April and May. If the $16,850 which the cash forecast shows will probably be available at the end of January for discretionary payments ($41,850 expected balance minus $25,000 desired balance) is spent, that much additional cash must become available in March, April, and May.

The graph in Figure 14 shows more readily the amount of cash that will probably be available for discretionary payments and the amount of

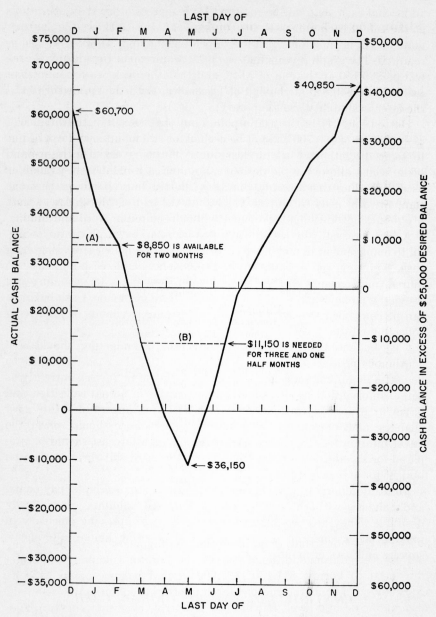

Fig. 14. Tranton Company: Estimated Cash Balance by Months For the Year Ending December 31, 19x2.

additional cash that will be required from sources other than operations at the end of each month of the coming year. It also shows the approximate length of time for which the respective amounts will be available or required. The graph reveals that the peak requirement for additional cash will be $36,150 at the end of May, and that the peak seasonal excess of cash will be $40,850 at the end of December. Both the requirement and the later availability are temporary.

Dotted line (A) in the graph points out that $8,850 of the January 1 cash balance of $60,700 will not be needed for two months, and can be put to some discretionary use at least until February 28. The right-hand scale, which allows for the desired minimum cash balance of $25,000, is used in finding this amount. Similarly, dotted line (B) shows that the company will need to borrow $11,150 at the end of March for at least $3\frac{1}{2}$ months. Additional borrowings will be required in April and May.

A cash forecast, whether in statement, tabular, or graphic form, is useful to management in making decisions and setting policies for controlling cash. Knowing well in advance the probable available cash and cash required, management can make more intelligent plans for spending and providing money than if reliable estimates were not made. Cash balances can be controlled to some extent by postponing payments or improving collection efforts.

Cash budgeting, as well as all other phases of budgeting, should be a continuous process of planning for the future. If the cash forecast is to be useful in guiding management action, it should be revised currently as actual information becomes available. Analysis of actual collection and payment experience facilitates more accurate estimates of future cash changes, and, of course, the projected cash balance should reflect the latest information. As each month passes, a cash forecast should be prepared for an additional future month so that there will always be a cash budget for a year in advance.

Monthly reports to management comparing actual receipts, payments, and balances with the corresponding budgeted amounts are generally desirable. They are useful in estimating needs, improving efficiency in making collections and payments, and in choosing among alternative sources and uses of money.

CONTROLLING AND RECORDING CASH

General features of internal check

Cash is so important to a business that the accounting records must give accurate, up-to-date information about it. In addition, adequate safeguards must be built into both the physical handling of and the recording procedures for cash receipts, payments, and balances. The features of organization and the methods and facilities that are used to prevent errors, dishonesty, and waste in dealing with cash and other business assets, or to detect them promptly if they do occur, compose the system of *internal check*.

The value of a good system of internal check in *deterring* errors, fraud, and waste is undoubtedly greater than its value in *detecting* them. One of its basic objectives is to remove the opportunity to commit irregularities or to use assets in a manner contrary to the objectives of the business. How well it can accomplish this is a practical matter. Rarely is a system designed so perfectly that it will foil all fraudulent schemes. Sometimes the cost of the cure is greater than the probable cost of the disease, and management may elect to take a calculated risk by not incurring the extra cost of a foolproof system.

Many accounting procedures are designed so that errors will be detected automatically as a part of routine proofs of clerical work. The detection and prevention of wasteful use of assets is a much more difficult, although a no less important, matter. Constant vigilance by management is needed to help insure that cash and other assets are employed efficiently and profitably. The various means of comparing the actual performance of the business with the planned performance, described in other chapters, are very effective in promoting the profitable use of assets.

Internal check procedures are tailored to the particular business entity more than perhaps any other feature of the accounting system. They depend upon the size and type of the business, the physical location of its parts, the number, ability, and character of its employees, and the wishes of management. However, the following rules, which have been developed from the experience of many businesses, apply to most businesses and to most types of assets.

(1) Duties should be so assigned that no one individual has complete control over a transaction, over a business asset, or over the records accounting for them.

EXAMPLE 4: No one employee should be solely responsible for making sales, collecting for them, and recording them in the journals and ledgers. In such a case it would be too easy for him to misappropriate cash or merchandise and falsify the records to conceal the shortage. Errors and waste, likewise, would often go undetected.

EXAMPLE 5: No one employee should be responsible for collecting cash, paying it out, and having custody of the cash balance. Such joint duties would enable him to take cash receipts and cover the shortage by reporting fictitious cash payments. Independent verification of his work would make it easier to discover errors and inefficiency.

(2) Duties should be organized so that one employee, acting independently, verifies the work of another while carrying the necessary work forward. This does not mean that the second employee duplicates the work of the first, but rather that checks and balances which promote honesty and accuracy are built into their work procedures.

EXAMPLE 6:   The following organization of duties is designed to prevent or detect errors, fraud, and waste in handling the mail cash receipts of a medium-sized or large organization:

The *mail clerk* opens the mail and lists cash remittances in triplicate, giving the names and amounts. His total of receipts is the amount for which employees subsequently handling the money or records are accountable.

The *accounts receivable bookkeeper* receives a copy of the remittance list from the mail clerk and posts credits in the individual customers' ledger accounts. The total of credits posted must equal total remittances.

The *cash receipts bookkeeper* receives a copy of the remittance list and makes cash journal entries debiting Cash and crediting Accounts Receivable. The total of these entries must agree with total remittances.

The *cashier* receives the money from the mail clerk and returns a signed copy of the remittance list to him as a receipt. The cashier prepares a deposit slip in duplicate and takes it and the money to the bank. The total of the deposit must agree with total remittances.

The *treasurer*, an officer who supervises the work of handling the money of the business, compares the duplicate deposit slip, receipted by the bank, with the total remittances listed by the mail clerk to be sure that all money has found its way into the bank.

The mail clerk has an opportunity to take money, but he cannot conceal the shortage because he has no access to the accounting records. If he fails to list a customer's payment, ultimately the customer's complaint is likely to lead to his detection. The accounts receivable and cash receipts bookkeepers can falsify records, but they have no access to money. The cashier can take money, but the shortage will be obvious when the treasurer compares the duplicate deposit slip with the mail clerk's remittance list.

Smaller businesses cannot make such an elaborate division of duties, but they can use many of the features described above even if only two employees handle cash and cash records. In both cases, two or more employees conspiring together can defeat the scheme of internal check. It is difficult to devise a system which cannot be defeated by such *collusion* of employees. Fortunately, most would-be embezzlers are reluctant to take someone else into their confidence.

(3) Physical safeguards should be used where they are justified to verify business activities and to protect business assets. Adding machines, cash registers, and other forms of mechanical equipment help to improve the efficiency as well as the accuracy with which records are kept. Safes and locked cages help to protect cash and other assets from unauthorized use. Forms used for authorizing or recording transactions of a given type, such as sales tickets or checks, should be serially numbered by the printer

and all numbers should be accounted for. The purpose is to prevent the falsification of records of sales, payments, and other types of transactions.

Internal check in operation

The preceding paragraphs have presented some representative features of a system of internal check, although by no means all possible features. The designer of the accounting system must decide what events are to be recorded; when, by whom, and how they are to be recorded; and what the flow of work and division of duties within the organization are to be. Internal check is built of the raw materials of the accounting system— the forms (basic documents, journals, ledgers, and reports); the duties or procedures carried out by people in preparing the forms; and mechanical devices. Larger organizations formally set forth their systems in manuals, which are useful in instructing new employees and in settling questions of procedure.

The system that is best on paper may fail in practice. Constant supervision is needed to insure that each system operates according to plan. Some supervision comes about automatically through the operation of the automatic checks, but more is needed. Many businesses have an *internal auditing* department whose duty it is to see that the accounting system operates accurately to carry out the plans and policies of managements. In addition, most businesses have a periodic independent audit made by a public accounting firm. One of the primary obligations of the auditor is to satisfy himself that the company's system of internal check is adequate, both in design and in practice.

The auditor or systems man should also be constantly alert for ways of improving the system of internal check by increasing its efficiency, incorporating better methods and equipment, and solving new problems.

Controlling cash receipts

The basic objective of cash receipts procedures and records is to make certain that all money actually collected for the business finds its way into the business treasury and that the facts of collection are accurately and promptly recorded. In accomplishing these ends, it is very important that collections be recorded immediately after receipt. This may be done either on a cash register or on some type of receipt-writing device which locks information as to the amounts of collections securely in the machine. Cash registers in common use print a receipt for the customer and also print, classify, and total information about collections on a tape which is locked in the machine.

The cash collections of each day should be deposited in total at the end of the day and no payments should be made from them. Prompt deposits reduce the risk of theft. Coupled with separation of receipts by days, they also discourage temporary "borrowing" by the cashier and make it easier to detect. Distinct separation of the duties of cash receiving and paying helps to insure that all payments are authorized by a responsible person and that fictitious payments are not used to conceal stolen receipts.

Each individual who handles cash receipts should have a specific responsibility for them. If two or more persons jointly operate a cash register, and the cash on hand at the end of the day is less than the recorded receipts, it is difficult if not impossible to pinpoint responsibility for the shortage. Each individual should have sole control over a cash register or of a locked drawer within a register.

In most businesses, mail remittances and cash sales account for the great bulk of cash receipts transactions. The need for controlling them is obvious. Often the following are more susceptible to mishandling because they occur infrequently: collections on notes, borrowings on bank loans, proceeds of the issuance of capital stock and bonds, collections of dividends and interest on investments, and receipts of proceeds of the sale of investments and other business assets not normally intended for sale.

The use of a specialized *Cash Receipts Journal* (described in Chapter 9) in which every collection of money is recorded provides internal check by assigning responsibility for journalizing cash collections to one person who does not have responsibility for the physical handling of cash.

Controlling cash disbursements

Accounting procedures for cash payments are intended to insure that business cash is disbursed only upon the approval of a responsible person, and only after another responsible person has assured him, on the basis of documentary evidence, that the payment is a proper one for goods or services which the business has received.

All cash payments except the very smallest should be made by check. Check payments are safer than payments in currency and coin because the payee can be named specifically and the payor need not keep large sums of currency on hand for making payments. In addition, the business can thus restrict authority for making payments to one or a very few officers or employees. Checks show specifically how much was paid and to whom, and the endorsements on cancelled checks are evidence that the payee received payment.

Often businesses safeguard their payments by requiring that *two* responsible persons sign each check. The *controller*, or chief accounting officer, signs to certify that the payment is proper. The *treasurer*, after determining that money is available to make the payment, then signs to direct the bank to pay out the company's money to the payee named in the check.

Many businesses have enough cash payment transactions to warrant the use of a special *Cash Disbursements Journal*, in which only checks issued are recorded. This journal provides internal check by permitting division of work, and it also localizes the responsibility for recording cash payments.

The treasurer or other company official who is responsible for the availability of sufficient cash should receive a daily report of the cash balance at the beginning of the day, a summary of cash receipts and payments during the day, and the balance at the end of the day. In addition to a cash forecast for the next month, he usually needs daily totals of payments to be made within the next week or so.

Petty cash

Payment by check helps to insure that all business disbursements are proper. However, the procedure for substantiating, approving, issuing, and recording check payments is rather costly and time-consuming. Many small payments, such as those for carfare of employees and postage due on incoming mail, are hardly worth the effort required to pay by check. For making such payments, businesses customarily set aside a fixed sum of currency and coin, called a *Petty Cash fund*. Payments are not made out of Petty Cash without proper approval, but they are handled in a simplified manner, which is described in Appendix 13-A.

Other cash accounts

In addition to a petty cash fund, a business usually needs to keep on hand several change funds of fixed amount. For example, it may be necessary to have $10 in coin on hand for each cash register at the beginning of each business day.

Very often payments of a particular type are so numerous that it is desirable to establish a checking account apart from the general bank account. Payroll and dividend payments are common examples. Such special accounts permit the treasurer to delegate authority for signing one type of check to an assistant while limiting the amount of payments that the assistant can make. Usually the treasurer transfers to the special account only enough to meet a single payroll or dividend payment.

Sometimes a business is required by contract to set money aside in a special bank account for a particular purpose. A *sinking fund* being accumulated to pay off the principal of Bonds Payable at maturity is an example. Usually such a fund is kept by a trustee and is not available to the business for making general payments. Other special funds are often set aside voluntarily, such as funds for constructing plant additions. Management policy requires that these bank accounts be separated from general cash and that they be devoted only to the purposes for which they were established.

Reconciling the bank accounts

Many of the provisions of the system of internal check are carried out as one employee of the business verifies the work of another. The accuracy and honesty with which business records are kept can also be partially determined by making comparisons with records prepared by persons outside of the firm. An example of such a verification is the *reconciliation* of the balance on deposit as shown by the depositor's books with that shown by the bank's statement of the depositor's account.

The relationship of the bank to the business is that of *debtor* to a creditor. The bank's record of its dealings with each depositor is a *liability* account, which normally has a credit balance. The bank satisfies this liability by paying money to persons whom the depositor designates. Checks are *orders* to the bank to make such payments.

The depositor keeps a record of his dealings with the bank in an asset account, usually called Cash in Bank. Actually, this is merely a special type of account receivable, but it merits a special designation because it represents money immediately available for making payments.

If there were no time lags between the collection of money by the customer and its deposit in the bank, and between the issuance of checks and their final payment by the bank, the customer's and bank's accounts of their mutual dealings would have balances *equal in amount* but of an *opposite nature*. That is, they would be *reciprocal* accounts. To illustrate:

Customer Kay's Books

A, Cash in Bank

19x1			19x1		
July 1	Receipts..............	4,000	July 2	Check #1 issued........	300
	Balance, 3,200		3	Check #2 issued....	500

Bank's Books

L, Customer Kay's Demand Deposit

19x1			19x1		
July 2	Check #1 paid.........	300	July 1	Deposit................	4,000
3	Check #2 paid.........	500		Balance, 3,200	

The ideal condition illustrated rarely exists in practice. There are usually time lags, and there are occasional errors in both the customer's and the bank's accounting records. When the depositor receives the bank's monthly statement of the account, he should compare it with his own records to determine what errors, if any, have been made on his books; what errors the bank has made; and what balance was actually on deposit in the bank subject to check at the end of the month.

A schedule which itemizes the results of this comparison is called a *bank reconciliation*. It is prepared in the following two parts:

Part 1—Depositor's account:

Debit balance at the end of the period, according to the customer's Cash account...	$4,000
Add debits to be made on the books for items as to which the Cash account is incorrect or incomplete, (such as notes collected by the bank).........	500
Total..	$4,500
Deduct credits to be made on the books for items as to which the Cash account is incorrect or incomplete (such as returned customer's checks)	$1,300
Cash balance available to the depositor at end of month.................	$3,200

Part 2—Bank's account:

Credit balance at the end of the period, according to the bank's Liability to Depositor account...	$5,100
Add credits to be made on the bank's books for items as to which its Depositor account is incorrect or incomplete (such as deposits in transit).........	300
Total..	$5,400
Deduct debits to be made on the bank's books for items as to which its Depositor account is incorrect or incomplete (such as checks which have not been presented to the bank for payment)............................	2,200
Deposit balance available to the depositor at end of month (must be the same as in Part 1)..	$3,200

This general form of reconciliation may be used when any debtor-creditor relationship exists, such as the Account Payable of a business to a supplier and the supplier's corresponding Account Receivable.

Appendix 13-B contains a detailed illustration of the procedure for making a bank reconciliation.

Cash in the statement of financial position

Chapter 5 pointed out that Cash includes only sums which are available readily and without restriction for payment of obligations which arise from the current operations of the business. Bank accounts which are restricted to the purchase of long-term assets or the payment of long-term debts are not Cash within this definition, nor are they even current assets. They are *funds*, and are classified under Investments. Bank accounts set aside for the payment of current liabilities, such as Dividends Payable and Wages Payable, are current assets.

Amounts of foreign currencies owned or receivable by the business may be reported as Cash if they are freely convertible into domestic money and if they are separately identified in the financial statements. Their amounts are converted into the domestic monetary unit by using the rate of exchange which is current at the end of the accounting period. If there are exchange restrictions on the conversion of such foreign balances into domestic money, the balances should not be reported as Cash, and often not even as current assets.

A negative, or credit, balance in a bank account is an *overdraft*. Usually such overdrafts are merely *technical*: that is, the bank shows a positive balance on deposit but checks in excess of this sum are outstanding. The overdraft is *actual* if the bank deposit account balance is negative. In either case, the Cash in Bank account on the depositor's books has a credit balance. If the company has no other bank accounts at the same bank, the credit balance should be shown among the current liabilities as *Bank Overdraft*. If other accounts at the same bank have debit balances greater than the overdraft, the excess of debit over credit balances may be shown as a current asset, *Cash in Bank*.

Summary

Earning an income is the most important objective of business, but cash is the lifeblood of business. Cash flow differs from income in that current cash receipts often represent revenue earned in an earlier or later accounting period, and current cash payments often represent expenses incurred in an earlier or later period.

In planning future cash payments and the sources of money for making them, management needs a *cash forecast*. While the timing and amounts of many receipts and payments are set by contracts previously made and the level of operating activity planned for the coming period, others can be postponed, altered, or avoided altogether. By comparing *cash available* from beginning balances and from operations with *cash needed* to make required payments, management can determine the amounts that will probably be available at different times for making *discretionary payments*, or the amounts of *cash deficiencies* that will have to be met from sources other than operations.

Internal check procedures for protecting cash and other assets should be designed for the purposes of *deterring* errors, dishonesty, and waste and of *detecting* them promptly if they do occur. Many of these procedures are based upon a division of duties which requires that one employee verify the accuracy of the work of another. Procedures for handling cash receipts are intended to insure that all money collected for the business actually finds its way into the business bank account. Cash payment safeguards are designed to permit disbursements only after a responsible person has determined from sufficient evidence that the payment is proper.

APPENDIX 13-A

Petty Cash Procedure

One individual should have sole responsibility for each petty cash fund. Such a fund can be established by issuing a business check payable to "Petty Cash" in an amount sufficient to make minor payments for a week or two. The effect on the accounts is:

(1)

A, Petty Cash.. 50
    A, Cash (or A, Cash in Bank)........................   50
    Established a petty cash fund of fixed amount for making small payments.

The custodian of the fund cashes the check and obtains $50 in currency and coin, which he should keep in a locked box or drawer. He should prepare a numbered petty cash ticket for each payment, giving the date, amount, nature of the payment, the account to be debited, and the signature of the person who receives the money. Invoices or other memoranda relating to the payment should be attached to the petty cash ticket. At any time the petty cash drawer should contain money plus paid tickets equal to its fixed balance.

The petty cash payment system involves a delay in journalizing payments. Journal entries to record payments out of Petty Cash are made when the fund is replenished, not when the payments are made. Ordinarily the fund is reimbursed for its payments when its money balance is low, but it should be reimbursed at the end of each accounting period regardless of the remaining amount of currency and coin. The accounts to be debited for the payments are incomplete until the entry for replenishment of the fund is recorded. The custodian summarizes the payment tickets according to the accounts debited. A reimbursement check is then prepared and recorded in the following manner:

(2)

OE, Communications Expense............................ 8
OE, Payroll Expense...................................... 17
OE, Office Supplies Expense.............................. 12
A, Merchandise Inventory................................. 9
OE, Cash Short and Over.................................. 1
    A, Cash in Bank.......................................   47
    Reimbursed the petty cash fund, which had a balance of $3 on hand.

The petty cash tickets and memoranda should be marked "Paid" to prevent their reuse.

In the preceding entry, Communications Expense includes payments for such things as collect telegrams and postage due; Payroll Expense includes carfare and supper money payments to employees; Office Supplies Expense is for minor items not bought through the usual purchasing procedure; and Merchandise Inventory is debited for small emergency purchases and for transportation charges paid on incoming merchandise. The *debit* to Cash Short and Over indicates that the currency and coin in the petty cash fund, plus paid tickets, totaled only $49. The shortage may have been due to an error in making change. An overage would be shown by a *credit* to Cash Short and Over. This account is an expense or a revenue, depending on whether it has a debit or credit balance.

The $50 balance in the Petty Cash ledger account is permanent. It is not reduced when cash is paid out of the petty cash fund, nor is it increased when the fund is replenished. It is debited only when the fund is established or increased, and credited when the fund is decreased or discontinued.

APPENDIX 13-B

Bank Reconciliation Procedure

The Novelty Company was organized on March 19, 19x1. It uses several special journals, including a Cash Receipts Journal and a Cash Disbursements Journal. Daily receipts are placed in a night depository at the close of business each day, and the deposit in the bank is formally completed the following day. All payments are made by check. The following records are condensed versions of the applicable journals and the Cash ledger account for March.

CASH RECEIPTS JOURNAL

Page 1

Date	Account Credited	Explanation	Cash Debit	Credit Amount
19x1				
Mar. 19	Capital Stock....................	Investment	5,000✓	5,000
21	Sales Revenue...................	Cash sales	200✓	200
22	Sales Revenue...................	Cash sales	300✓	300
23	Sales Revenue...................	Cash sales	500✓	500
25	Accounts Receivable.............	Collections	400 ⎫✓	400
25	Sales Revenue...................	Cash sales	250 ⎭	250
28	Notes Payable...................	Cash borrowed	2,000 ✗	2,000
29	Sales Revenue...................	Cash sales	450	450
30	Accounts Receivable.............	Collections	600✓	600
31	Other Revenue...................	Sale of scrap	50	50
31	Sales Revenue...................	Cash sales	700	700
31	Totals.......................		10,450	10,450
			(11)	

CASH DISBURSEMENTS JOURNAL   Page 1

Date	Check No.	Payee	Account Debited	Debit Amount	Cash Credit
19x1					
Mar. 19	1	X Wholesalers............	Mdse. Inventory	4,000✓	4,000
19	2	J Mfg. Co..............	Equipment	500✓	500
22	3	City of M...............	Prepaid taxes	100✓	100
22	4	I Realtors...............	Rent	400✓	400
25	5	L Ins. Co...............	Prepaid Insurance	200	200
28	6	Y Wholesalers...........	Accounts Payable	300✓	300
31	7	Paymaster..............	Payroll Expense	1,000✓	1,000
31	8	J Mfg. Co..............	Equipment	2,590	2,590
31	9	Y Wholesalers...........	Accounts Payable	200	200
31	10	Z Electric Co...........	Utilities Expense	50	50
31		Totals................		9,340	9,340
					(11)

A, Cash   #11

19x1		19x1
March 31 CR1 10,450		Mar. 31 CD1 9,340
Balance, 1,110		

To determine whether the Cash ledger account balance of $1,110 properly shows the amount available in the checking account, the cash increases, decreases, and balance according to the Novelty Company's books should be compared in detail with the corresponding items shown by the following bank statement.

THIRD NATIONAL BANK

Account of   The Novelty Company
                   111 East Adams St.
                   Cedar City, Kentucky

Checks (Debits)		Deposits (Credits)	Date	(Credit) Balance
		5,000✓	Mar. 21, 19x1	5,000
		200✓	Mar. 22, 19x1	5,200
4,000	100	300✓	Mar. 23, 19x1	1,400
400		500✓	Mar. 24, 19x1	1,500
500		650✓	Mar. 26, 19x1	1,650
180		1,980✗	Mar. 28, 19x1	3,450
300	1,000	600✓		
2 SC	40		Mar. 31, 19x1	2,708

Explanation of Symbols: SC—Service Charge
                         OD—Overdraft

The following items were included with the bank statements:

Cancelled checks
────────────────
#1	$4,000	#3	$100	#6	$300
2	500	4	400	7	1,000

A cancelled check for $180 signed by the Novel Manufacturing Company was also enclosed.

Debit memoranda
>   Mar. 31   Service charges for the month, $2.
>   31 $40 check of B. C. Dawes, a customer, included in the deposit of March 26, was returned marked "Insufficient funds."

Credit memorandum
>   Mar. 28   60-day, 6% note, $2,000, less $20 discount.

The bank reconciliation should be prepared by an employee who does not handle money or keep cash records, so that irregularities will be discovered. The reconciliation may be made in the following steps:

(1) *Compare payments made by the bank with payments shown in the cash disbursements journal.* Arranging the cancelled checks in numerical order facilitates this comparison. Amounts and names of payees on the cancelled checks should agree with the company's disbursement record, and the checks should be endorsed by the payees. Any discrepancies brought to light should be reported to the person who supervises cash record keeping. Check marks in the cash disbursements journal opposite each paid item show that this comparison has been made. Unchecked items are checks issued by the business but not paid by the bank. The most obvious explanation for them is that they are still in the hands of payees or in banking channels—that is, they are *outstanding checks*. They are out of the control of the issuing company and may be presented to the bank for payment at any time; therefore, they should be deducted from the bank's ending balance in order to arrive at true available cash. Outstanding checks in the illustration are:

#5, $200; #8, $2,590; #9, $200; and #10, $50.

The bank statements of later months should be examined to determine whether these checks have been paid and whether they were recorded properly in the company's cash records.

The $2 service charge deducted from the account by the bank is an actual payment that has been made, although it has not yet been recorded in the cash disbursements journal. It should be deducted on the company's books in arriving at the true balance on deposit.

The $40 "insufficient funds" check presents a special problem. Most companies treat incoming checks as Cash until they are proved otherwise. Banks accept such checks subject to their collection when presented to the payor's bank. The Novelty Company tentatively added $40 for Dawes' check to its Cash balance on March 25, and the bank tentatively added it to the deposit account balance on March 26. Both entries proved to be unjustified. The bank's debit of $40 on March 31 was a correction on its books, but a correction decreasing the Cash balance is still needed on the Novelty Company's books.

The bank erroneously deducted the $180 check of the *Novel Manufacturing Company* from the Novelty Company's account. Upon being notified, the bank will undoubtedly make a correction early in April. The $180 should be added to the bank balance, giving effect to this correction.

(2) *Compare deposits reported by the bank with receipts shown in the cash receipts journal.* Normally, a deposit should appear on the bank statement the day following collection, but there are exceptions on weekends and for special types of payments. Check marks should be made beside Cash debit and bank credit entries that are in agreement. Unchecked items in the cash receipts journal may be explained as follows:

The debit of $2,000 on March 28 should have been $1,980. The Novelty Company gave a note payable of $2,000 to the bank, but it included interest of $20 for the period of the loan. The company received only $1,980 cash; therefore, $20 should be deducted from the Cash balance on the company's books.

Collections of March 29, $450, should have appeared as a deposit on the bank statement on March 30. An investigation may reveal that the bank has credited the wrong depositor's account, that the deposit is still on the way to the bank, or that the money was not deposited. Here it is assumed that the first is the correct explanation, and that the $450 should be added to the bank balance pending a correction by the bank.

Collections of March 31, $750, would normally be recorded as a deposit on April 1, so it is natural that they should not appear on the bank statement. They may be added to the balance according to the bank on the assumption that the deposit will be completed on April 1. The person making the reconciliation should follow up this matter to be sure that the money actually did find its way to the bank.

(3) *List the points of difference brought to light by the foregoing comparisons in an orderly schedule* such as the following, which is designed to show the true balance on deposit.

THE NOVELTY COMPANY
Bank Reconciliation
March 31, 19x1

CASH LEDGER ACCOUNT

Debit balance, March 31, 19x1... $1,110
Additions (*debits*) for items as to which the Cash records are incorrect or
  incomplete:
  (Describe) .... None
  Total.. $1,110
Deductions (*credits*) for items as to which the Cash records are incorrect or
  incomplete:
  Bank service charge.. $ 2
  Insufficient funds check of B. C. Dawes...................... 40
  Interest on note payable of March 28........................ 20 $ 62
True debit balance of Cash in Bank, March 31........................... $1,048

BANK DEPOSIT ACCOUNT

Credit balance, March 31, 19x1... $2,708
Additions (*credits*) for items as to which the bank records are incorrect or
   incomplete:
Deposit of March 29 credited to wrong account................. $ 450
Deposit of March 31 in transit to bank....................... 750
Check of Novel Manufacturing Company erroneously debited to
   account... 180   1,380
   Total.. $4,088
Deductions (*debits*) for items as to which the bank records are incorrect or
   incomplete:
Outstanding checks:
   # 5.. $ 200
   8... 2,590
   9... 200
   10.. 50   3,040
True credit balance of deposit account, March 31........................ $1,048

Unless the final figures of the two halves of the bank reconciliation agree, the reconciliation is incomplete.

(4) *Make journal entries to correct the Cash balance on the books to the "true cash" figure.* All additions or deductions on the Cash Ledger Account part of the reconciliation require correcting entries. The following are needed in this case:

(1)

OE, Miscellaneous Financial Expense....................... 2
A, Accounts Receivable, Trade............................ 40
OE, Interest Expense..................................... 20
   A, Cash... 62
   To record corrections in the Cash account to arrive at the true
   balance on deposit on March 31.

The first debit is made on the assumption that bank charges are immaterial and do not warrant a separate expense account. The second assumes that B. C. Dawes' account is still collectible, even though the check he gave in payment of it was worthless. If the account is not collectible, it should be written off as uncollectible. The third debit is one of convenience. It is made under the assumption that the 60-day period of the note will expire and the full amount of interest will become an expense before the accounting period ends. If this is not the case, an additional entry should be made to show as a deduction from the face amount of the Note Payable and from Interest Expense the part of the discount applicable to the following accounting period.

(5) *Notify the bank of any corrections which it should make.* Information of this sort is found in the additions and deductions on the bank part of the reconciliation. No action is needed for deposits in transit and outstanding checks, since presumably they will arrive at the bank in the near future.

The person who prepares the bank reconciliation the next month should first determine that the proper disposition has been made of the reconciling items from March. Often checks remain outstanding for several months, and some of them are never presented for payment.

QUESTIONS AND PROBLEMS

13-1

REQUIRED:

a. Explain the difference between *revenue* and *cash receipts*.

b. Give examples of items that are revenue of a given period but not receipts of that period; items that are receipts but not revenue; and items that are both revenue and receipts.

13-2

REQUIRED:

a. Explain the difference between *expense* and *cash disbursements*.

b. Give examples of items that are expense of a given period but not disbursements of that period; items that are disbursements but not expense; and items that are both expense and disbursements.

13-3 As the company accountant, you have just presented financial statements to your president showing a net income of $30,000. "That can't be right!" exclaims the president, "The company has less cash than it had last year." He points to the following figures in the statement of financial position to support his contention: Cash, December 31, 19x1, $22,000; Cash, December 31, 19x2, $16,000.

REQUIRED:

What plausible explanations can you offer to the president?

13-4 A merchant complains to his accountant that the business does not have enough cash during the busy season, but has more than it needs in the slack season.

REQUIRED:

Explain why this may be true.

13-5

REQUIRED:

a. List three types of payments of a restaurant which are usually of a required nature.

b. List three types of payments which are usually *discretionary*.

c. List three sources of cash receipts other than operations.

13-6 The members of a church pledged $50,000 to its support in 19x1, and for 19x2, which is just about to begin, they have pledged $65,000. The finance committee has voted to increase salaries 10 per cent and wishes to make plans for buying a new organ.

REQUIRED:

How can the financial records of 19x1 be used in determining how much will be available for equipment in 19x2 and when it will be available?

13-7 Some bank accounts are considered as cash, while others are not.

REQUIRED:

a. Under what circumstances may bank accounts be classified as cash?

b. Describe two situations in which bank accounts should not be classified as cash.

13-8 The town of Millvale erected a toll bridge across a river which passed through the town. One councilman argued that, because of the limited amount of revenue expected from tolls, the town could only afford to have one employee at a time engaged in collecting them.

REQUIRED:

a. What weaknesses are there in this arrangement?

b. How could two employees be used to better advantage?

c. Describe how mechanical devices may be used to help solve such problems.

13-9 One of the most dramatic purposes of a system of internal check is to make fraud harder to commit and easier to detect. Other important purposes are sometimes overlooked.

REQUIRED:

a. What other purposes does a system of internal check have?

b. Does internal check apply to assets other than cash? To liabilities? Explain.

13-10 An auditor criticized the operation of the company's internal check because cash receipt forms were not prenumbered by the printer. The company prepared a receipt in duplicate for each collection at the central cashier's office, issuing the original to the payor and keeping the duplicate as evidence of cash collections.

REQUIRED:

a. What opportunity for irregularity was there in this situation?

b. How can prenumbering of forms be used to help insure the accuracy of records?

13-11 Cash registers, either key-driven or manually operated, should have locked-in information on the amounts of receipts.

REQUIRED:

Why should these amounts be inaccessible to the person operating the register?

13-12 Explaining the lack of safeguards over the operation of a petty cash fund, the manager of a store remarked, "After all, petty cash only amounts to $25, and it would not hurt us much to lose all of that."

REQUIRED:

What would you reply?

13-13 A store owner is trying to decide whether to buy a cash register which prints a small receipt for the customer or a less expensive model which does not print a receipt. He has expressed a preference for the latter on the ground that most people never look at the receipt.

REQUIRED:

a. What are the purposes of such receipts?

b. What advantages does the receipt-printing machine have over the other?

13-14 One of the first things an auditor does is determine the degree of adequacy of his client's system of internal check. The extent of his detailed examination of the client's records of transactions is based upon his findings regarding internal check.

REQUIRED:

Why do you suppose this is true?

13-15   The custodian of a $50 petty cash fund neglected to have it replenished on December 31, 19x1, because only $17 had been spent from the fund. Most of this expenditure was for emergency purchases of office supplies which had been used immediately. The fund was not replenished until January 18, 19x2, when total payments amounted to $49.

REQUIRED:

a. What errors were there in the 19x1 financial statements?

b. What errors were there in the 19x2 statements?

13-16

REQUIRED:

a. Does the mail clerk in Example 6 in this chapter have an opportunity to steal receipts? How?

b. If so, how would you prevent it?

13-17

REQUIRED:

a. How can a dishonest employee who writes checks and makes accounting entries embezzle money?

b. How can a dishonest employee who handles cash collections and makes accounting entries embezzle?

13-18   After recommending that his client install a cash register, an auditor was aghast to observe several employees ringing up sales on it. "Why, you might as well use a cigar box!" he exclaimed.

REQUIRED:

Why did he object?

13-19   Company *A* has its headquarters in the United States and has an important branch in a South American country. The accounts show that $1,200,-000 is on deposit in domestic banks and 2,000,000 pesos is on deposit in the country in which the branch is located.

REQUIRED:

How should these facts be shown in the statement of financial position?

13-20   The Walburn Company has three bank accounts. On April 30, 19x2, the end of its fiscal year, the balances according to the banks were in agreement with the balances according to the Walburn Company's ledger, except for outstanding checks. The details follow.

Account	Balance Per Bank	Outstanding Checks
General Account, Merchants Bank............	$18,200	$19,500
Payroll Account, National Bank.............	4,200	4,500
Dividend Account, National Bank...........	5,000	1,000

REQUIRED:

How should these facts be shown in the Walburn Company's April 30 statement of financial position?

13-21

REQUIRED:

Explain how the following can contribute to better internal control of cash within a business:

(1) Cash registers.
(2) Prenumbered slips for cash sales.
(3) A petty cash system.
(4) A separate payroll bank account.
(5) A cash forecast.
(6) A bank reconciliation.

13-22   A large corporation usually has an elaborate system of internal check, an internal auditing department, and annual audits by Certified Public Accountants. For these reasons, it is difficult for large misappropriations of cash to go undetected for long periods of time. On the other hand, small concerns often do not have sufficient capital or employees to provide for such effective measures of control.

REQUIRED:

a. Do the protective measures for large companies described above provide effectively for prevention of waste in the use of cash and other assets? Explain.
b. If your answer in (a) is "No," what measures would you recommend?
c. Describe some practical, inexpensive methods by which the proprietor of a small business can secure effective control of his cash receipts, his cash disbursements, and efficient use of his cash balance.

13-23   The Warren Company makes 25 per cent of its sales for cash and the remainder on account. In the past, losses from uncollectible accounts have averaged one per cent of sales on account. The company finds that usually about 60 per cent of charge sales are collected in the month following sale, 25 per cent in the second following month, and 14 per cent in the third following month.

Total actual sales in the preceding three months have been: October, 19x1, $40,000; November, $50,000; December, $70,000. January sales are expected to be $60,000.

REQUIRED:

a. Determine the expected net revenue from sales for January, 19x2.
b. Prepare a schedule of the expected cash collections from customers during January, 19x2.

13-24   The Parma Products Company sells goods at a gross margin of 25 per cent of sales price. The company pays for all of its merchandise on the tenth of the month following purchase and likes to maintain an inventory balance at the end of each month sufficient for the expected sales of the two following months. Because of an unexpected slump in sales for December, 19x1, excessive inventory has accumulated. The statement of financial position on December 31, 19x1, shows inventory of $53,000 and accounts payable for merchandise totaling $12,000. Budgeted sales for the first few months of 19x2 are:

January	$20,000	March	$30,000	May	$28,000
February	24,000	April	36,000	June	30,000

REQUIRED:

Prepare a schedule to estimate the following for each of the first three months of 19x2:

(1) Cost of goods sold expense;
(2) Required purchases of merchandise;
(3) Required cash payments for merchandise.

13-25 Marva Mfg. Co. debits all insurance premiums to an Unexpired Insurance account when the policy goes into effect. The credit is to Cash or Accounts Payable, depending upon whether the payment is made immediately or is delayed. All of its premiums are paid for a year in advance when the particular premium comes due. An analysis of payments for 19x1 shows the following:

Feb. 1.	$ 240
May 1.	1,200
Oct. 1.	900

It is expected that each of these policies will be renewed in 19x2 and that the annual premiums will be unchanged in amount.

REQUIRED:

Prepare an analysis showing:

(1) The amount of Unexpired Insurance on December 31, 19x1;
(2) The insurance expense and cash paid for insurance for each month of 19x2.

13-26

REQUIRED:

From the information below prepare a monthly cash budget for *AB* Trading Company for the three months ending March 31, 19x1.

AB Trading Company purchases merchandise on terms of 2/10, n/60, and regularly takes discounts on the tenth day after the invoice date. It may be assumed that one-third of the purchases of any month are due for discount and are paid for in the following month.

The company's sales terms are 2/10, n/30, E.O.M. It has been the company's experience that discounts on 80 per cent of billings have been allowed and that, of the remainder, one-half have been paid during the month following billing and the balance during the second following month.

The average rate of gross margin based on sales price is 25 per cent. Total sales for the company's fiscal year ending June 30, 19x1, have been estimated at 80,000 units, distributed monthly as follows:

July.	9%	October.	9%	January.	3%	April.	7%
August.	10%	November.	10%	February.	5%	May.	6%
September.	12%	December.	15%	March.	6%	June.	8%

To insure prompt delivery of merchandise, inventories are maintained during January and February at 6 per cent of the number of units estimated to be sold throughout the year, while during the rest of the year they are maintained at 10 per cent of that number. The inventories at December 31 and February 28 should be at the levels intended to be maintained during the respective ensuing seasons.

Total budgeted selling, administrative, and general expenses for the fiscal year ending June 30, 19x1, are estimated at $312,000, of which $120,000 are fixed expenses (inclusive of $24,000 annual depreciation). These fixed expenses are incurred uniformly throughout the year. The other selling, administrative, and general expenses vary with sales. In total, these expenses amount to $192,000, or 12 per cent of total sales for the year. Expenses are paid as incurred, without discounts.

It is assumed that at January 1, 19x1, merchandise inventory, at the 6 per cent level, will consist of 4,800 units, to cost $72,000, before discount, and the cash balance will be $112,000.

(Adapted from AICPA Examination in Accounting Practice—Part I, November 1948.)

13-27 The Parker Piano Sales Company sells a single type of piano for $600. On January 1, 19x2, the manager prepared the following 6-month sales forecast:

January...................	10 pianos	April......................	16 pianos
February.........	12 pianos	May......................	14 pianos
March....................	16 pianos	June.....................	12 pianos

All sales are made on terms of one-third down and the balance payable in four equal monthly installments.

The pianos cost $400 each, and all purchases are made on terms of n/30. The manager plans to provide for a beginning inventory equal to one-half of the month's forecasted sales. It is estimated that 8 pianos will be sold in July.

The following statement of financial position was prepared at the end of the preceding year:

PARKER PIANO SALES COMPANY
Statement of Financial Position
December 31, 19x1

ASSETS			EQUITIES		
Cash......................		$ 3,000	Liabilities:		
Accounts receivable:			Accounts payable...........		$ 2,500
Due in January......	$1,000		Notes payable..............		1,000
Due in February.....	1,200		Total liabilities..........		$ 3,500
Due in March.......	800				
Due in April........	600	3,600	Owners' equity:		
Notes receivable.............		500	Investment........	$10,000	
Inventory..............		2,000	Retained income....	6,500	16,500
Other assets.................		10,900			
Total assets.............		$20,000	Total equities............		$20,000

The notes receivable are due in March; all accounts payable are due in January; and the notes payable, which are non-interest-bearing, are to be paid in five equal monthly installments beginning in February.

Other monthly expenses are estimated to be as follows:

Nonvariable:
Rent..	$100	
Utilities...	50	
Salaries...	250	
Insurance.......................................	20	$420

Variable:
Transportation......	1% of sales
Sales commissions...	5% of sales
Free lessons........	$20 during the month of sale for each piano sold

The manager desires an ending cash balance of $1,000 each month.

REQUIRED:

a. Prepare a cash forecast for each of the 6 months.
b. Prepare a budgeted income statement for the 6-month period ending June 30, 19x2.

13-28   The Cash in Bank account in the Lowrey Company's ledger had a debit balance of $14,280 on November 30. The State Bank's statement of account on the same date showed a balance of $20,252. A comparison of payments shown by the books with those reported by the bank disclosed the following differences:

(1) The bank enclosed four debit memoranda for items not on the depositor's books. One was a $50 check of A. R. Bronson, a customer, given the Lowrey Company in payment of his account on November 26. The debit memo was marked "insufficient funds." Bronson, when contacted, promised to make the check good in December.

(2) Another check for $30 signed by James Brown and included in the deposit of November 27 was marked "no account in this name." The check had been cashed for Brown at the cashier's office. Investigation revealed that the address given by Brown was nonexistent, and his name was not in the telephone directory.

(3) Bank charges for collection and exchange on checks deposited were $3. The charge for printing blank checks delivered to the Lowrey Company during the month was $5.

(4) The Lowrey Company's check for $650 in payment of November rent was recorded in the cash disbursements journal as $560. The check was for the proper amount.

Differences between the book and bank cash receipt figures were:

(5) The Company had left a customer's note receivable for $1,000 with the bank for collection on November 27. A credit memo enclosed with the statement showed that the face of the note plus interest of $10 had been added to the account on November 29.

(6) The bank showed a deposit of $850 on November 17; the corresponding cash receipts journal entry for cash sales on November 16 was for $840. The Lowrey Company found that its cashier had added the items composing the sales total incorrectly.

(7) The cash receipts of November 30, $1,100, were placed in a night deposit box and were not credited by the bank until December 1.

(8) Checks issued by the Lowrey Company but not yet paid by the bank totaled $5,970. Of this amount, $300 represented checks issued in September and October.

(9) The bank statement showed a deposit of $260 on November 7 which upon investigation was discovered to belong to another depositor. There was no corresponding entry on the company's books.

REQUIRED:

a. Prepare a bank reconciliation for the Lowrey Company as of November 30, 19x1.

b. Record in journal form the entries necessary to correct the Lowrey Company's books.

13-29

REQUIRED:

Show in journal form all entries necessary to record Petty Cash transactions in April, 19x1.

April 1   A check for $50 was drawn to the order of "Petty Cash." The custodian cashed the check and placed the money in a metal box.

2   The custodian advanced $10 to a clerk for permanent use for cash register change, and took a receipt.

April 10 Several dozen petty cash tickets were summarized as follows:

Supplies expense... $11
Refunds to cash customers.................................   9
Postage due on letters.....................................   12
Collect telegrams.. 1.50
Supper money to employees.................................   4

> There were four $1 bills in the metal box. The Petty Cash custodian asked the treasurer to reimburse the fund. The latter decided that the fund should be increased to $80, and issued a single check to reimburse the fund and to increase it.

13-30

REQUIRED:

Show in general journal form all entries that should be made to reflect the operation of the Petty Cash fund.

Date
___
19x1
May 1 Established a Petty Cash fund of $25. Individual payments were to be limited to $3. The custodian of the fund cashed the check and placed the money in a locked drawer.
     2 Prepared Petty Cash ticket No. 1 for light bulbs, $1.50.
     3 Paid for postage on outgoing packages to customers, $2.50.
     4 Changed a $10 bill for a customer.
     5 Purchased a typewriter ribbon, $1.40.
     6 Gave a customer a $2 refund for a cash sale returned.
     7 Paid a boy $1 for delivering packages.
     8 Paid $3 for stamps for office use.
     9 Paid postage charges on incoming merchandise, $2.70.
    10 Contributed $2.50 to the Salvation Army.
    11 Paid $1.90 for nuts, screws, and bolts for repairs.
    12 Advanced an employee $1.30 bus fare for making several trips on company business.
    13 Paid $3 for minor items of merchandise for resale.
    14 The contents of the Petty Cash drawer consisted of a dollar bill, 4 quarters, a dime, and 10 pennies. The fund was reimbursed.

13-31

REQUIRED:

a. Prepare a bank reconciliation for the Carlo Corporation on January 31, 19x1, at the end of its first month of operations.

b. Show in general journal form the entries that are necessary to correct the Corporation's books.

CASH RECEIPTS JOURNAL, Page 1

19x1		Account Credited	Amount
Jan.	2	Capital Stock.....................................	10,000
	4	Sales...	500
	8	Accounts Receivable.............................	800
	12	Sales...	2,000
	20	Notes Payable....................................	5,000
	28	Sales...	1,560
	31	Accounts Receivable.............................	2,100
		Total...	21,960

CASH DISBURSEMENTS JOURNAL, Page 1

19x1	Check No.	Account Debited	Amount
Jan. 3	1	Equipment............................	6,000
5	2	Rent Expense........................	400
7	3	Mdse. Inventory.....................	3,000
9	4	Prepaid Insurance...................	500
12	5	Prepaid Taxes.......................	300
15	6	Mdse. Inventory.....................	5,000
21	7	Organization Cost...................	1,200
24	8	Supplies Expense....................	600
30	9	Utilities Expense....................	100
31	10	Salary Expense......................	2,000
		Total..............................	19,100

PEOPLES BANK

Account of Carlo Corporation

Debits		Credits	19x1	Balance
		10,000	1/2	10,000
6,000			1/4	4,000
10		500	1/5	4,490
400			1/7	4,090
		800	1/9	4,890
3,000			1/12	1,890
		1,900	1/13	3,790
300	500		1/16	2,990
80	5,000	4,950	1/20	2,860
1,200			1/25	1,660
		1,650	1/29	3,310
5			1/31	3,305

Enclosed with the bank statement were debit memoranda as follows:

1/5	$ 10	Printing checks.
1/20	80	Insufficient funds check of L. A. Wray included in deposit of 1/9.
1/31	5	Service charge for handling account.
1/13	100	Deposit slip total should have been $1,900, not $2,000 as shown.

There were credit memoranda for the following two items:

1/20	$4,950	Proceeds of $5,000, 60-day note to bank, less discount at 6%.
1/29	90	Deposit slip improperly added.

13-32

REQUIRED:

a. Prepare a bank reconciliation for the Acadia Company for March, 19x3.

b. Show in journal form the entries needed to correct the company's books at the end of March.

The Acadia Company prepared the following bank reconciliation on February 28, 19x3:

Balance of Cash ledger account, 2/28........................ $ 893

Add: Face, $2,000, and interest, $10, of customer's note collected
by bank...   2,010

$2,903

Deduct:
Bank service charges for February........................   3
Correct balance on deposit, 2/28.......................... $2,900
Balance of deposit account on bank's books, 2/28........... $3,040
Add: Deposit of 2/28 in transit............................   400
                                                             $3,440
Deduct outstanding checks:
    #117.. $ 90
    121...   150
    122...   300   540
Correct balance on deposit, 2/28.......................... $2,900

The following information was taken from the books of the Acadia Company at the end of March. The company's trial balance was out of balance.

Cash in Bank

19x3				19x3			
Mar.	1	Bal.	2,900	Mar. 31		CD5	19,300
	31		CR3 18,700				

CASH RECEIPTS JOURNAL, Page 3 (condensed)

19x3			
Mar.	5	Cash sales.....................................	3,000
	12	Cash sales.....................................	4,000
	19	Collections on account.........................	1,800
	26	Cash sales.....................................	7,000
	31	Collections on account.........................	3,900
		Total......................................	18,700

CASH DISBURSEMENTS JOURNAL, Page 5 (condensed)

19x3	Ck. No.		
Mar.	5	123..	1,000
	10	124..	2,000
	15	125..	4,500
	20	126..	3,800
	25	127..	3,000
	30	128..	5,000
		Total......................................	19,300

All check entries were matched by debits to Accounts Payable.

OLD STATE BANK
Statement of account with Acadia Company

Debits		Credits		Balance
			19x3	
			2/28	3,040
		400	3/1	3,440
300			3/2	3,140
		3,000	3/6	6,140
1,000			3/8	5,140
2,000	150	4,000	3/13	6,990
520	4,500	1,800	3/20	3,770
		7,100	3/27	10,870
5,000			3/31	5,870

A bank debit memorandum dated March 20 was for the principal, $500, and interest of a note owed it by the Acadia Company. The latter had authorized the bank to charge its account at the note's maturity.

The company incorrectly added the items composing the cash sales of March 26.

CASE 13-1. FAMILY FINANCE

You have just completed the following summary of your personal cash receipts and payments for 19x1:

Cash salary (after all deductions)........................		$7,200
Payments:		
Food............................	$2,000	
Mortgage on residence.........................	1,800	
Note payments on car........................	1,200	
Gasoline......................................	300	
Oil for heating house..........................	240	
Property taxes on house.......................	250	
Insurance on house...........................	200	
Insurance on car.............................	150	
Vacation......................................	300	
Entertainment................................	360	
Utilities......................................	300	
Other regular necessities.......................	480	7,580
Net deduction from bank balance...................		($ 380)

Your total bank balance on December 31, 19x1, was $150, just before depositing your December salary check.

Recognizing the need for protecting your family, you are planning to take out a life insurance policy which will require premium payments of $105 each quarter. Having experienced occasional financial pinches in the past, you would like to schedule these payments to start in either January, February, or March, depending on which will leave the largest minimum balance at the end of each month during the year. You like to keep at least $100 in the bank at all times to avoid a bank service charge of $2 a month which is made if the balance falls below $100.

For years your wife has wished for a dishwasher when the family finances would permit. You can buy one from a discount house for $250 cash, or from another source for $90 down and $90 a month for three months. If you buy the dishwasher, you would like to have it entirely paid for this year.

The following additional items relate to your expected receipts and payments:

(1) You have received a 10 per cent raise in take-home pay for 19x2, effective January 1. You are paid on the first day of each month for the preceding month.

(2) Food prices have been increasing at the rate of 5 per cent a year.

(3) The mortgage on the residence has several more years to run, but the last payment on the car note is due in July, 19x2.

(4) Heat is required during October, November, December, January, February, and March.

(5) The property taxes must be paid in October.

(6) The house insurance is due in April and the automobile insurance, in August.

(7) You usually take your vacation in August.

REQUIRED:

a. Prepare an analysis of the expected cash payments that you will be required to make in 19x2 and the cash that will be available from ordinary sources, using the following form:

(1) Use one column of a columnar analysis sheet for each month.
(2) Use major side headings for:

Required cash payments:
  Of fixed monthly amount (repeat only the total in months following
      January)
  Of irregular monthly amount
Total required payments
Monthly cash receipts
Monthly cash change:
  Increase
  Decrease
Cumulative available balance

b. Draw a chart showing the cumulative excess of probable receipts for 19x2 over
   probable disbursements.
c. When do you recommend that the insurance premiums be made payable?
d. When, if at all, do you recommend that the dishwasher be bought? How would
   you pay for it?
e. What suggestions can you make that would improve the timing of the cash
   payments during the year?

CASE 13-2. WALES AND YOUNG

Wales and Young operate a retail business as a partnership. Their financial
statements for 19x2 are shown below.

WALES AND YOUNG
Income Statement
For the Year Ended December 31, 19x2

Cash sales	$20,000	
Sales on account	80,000	
Total sales revenue		$100,000
Deduct loss from uncollectible accounts		1,200
Net sales revenue		$ 98,800
Deduct cost of goods sold		62,000
Gross margin		$ 36,800
Deduct operating expense:		
Variable:		
Salaries	$ 4,000	
Supplies	2,000	
Miscellaneous	1,000	7,000
		$ 29,800
Nonvariable:		
Advertising	$ 3,000	
Depreciation of equipment	2,400	
Insurance	1,200	
Rent	3,600	
Salaries	4,800	
Taxes	1,800	16,800
Net income from operations		$ 13,000
Deduct interest expense		600
Net income		$ 12,400

WALES AND YOUNG
Statement of Partners' Capitals
For the Year Ended December 31, 19x2

	Total	Wales	Young
Capital balance, January 1, 19x2	$13,400	$ 7,400	$ 6,000
Net income for the year	12,400	6,200	6,200
Totals	$25,800	$13,600	$12,200
Deduct drawings	9,000	4,200	4,800
Capital balance, December 31, 19x2	$16,800	$ 9,400	$ 7,400

WALES AND YOUNG
Statement of Financial Position
December 31, 19x2

ASSETS

Current Assets:			
Cash			$ 5,000
Accounts receivable:			
10% of October credit sales		$ 900	
40% of November credit sales		2,400	
100% of December credit sales		5,000	
Total		$ 8,300	
Deduct estimated uncollectibles		400	7,900
Merchandise inventory			8,000
Prepaid insurance			600
Total current assets			$21,500
Fixed Assets:			
Equipment		$24,000	
Deduct accumulated depreciation		9,600	
Total fixed assets			14,400
Total assets			$35,900

LIABILITIES

Current Liabilities:		
Accounts payable	$ 6,830	
Accrued taxes payable	150	
Notes payable to banks	12,000	
Accrued interest payable	120	$19,100

OWNERS' EQUITY

Wales, Capital	$ 9,400	
Young, Capital	7,400	
Total owners' equity		16,800
Total equities		$35,900

The partners expect their sales for each month of 19x3 to be about 20 per cent above the corresponding month of 19x2 as a result of improved economic conditions and community growth. The proportions of cash and credit sales and of uncollectible accounts are expected to remain the same. Sales for the first few months of 19x2 were as follows:

January	$10,000	April	$10,000
February	8,000	May	11,000
March	7,000	June	9,000

In the future it is hoped to maintain an inventory sufficient to fill the following two months' sales.

All accounts payable are to be paid in the month following the purchase. Merchandise, advertising, supplies, miscellaneous expense, and taxes require payment in the month following purchase or accrual. Salaries and rent are paid in the month in which they accrue. All insurance policies are due for renewal each July 1. All of the equipment was bought at one time 4 years ago. The partners plan to buy a new typewriter, which is expected to last for 5 years and to have no salvage value, for $240 cash at the end of January.

Interest on the bank loan accrues at the rate of 6 per cent per year and is payable quarterly. It was last paid on October 31, 19x2. The partners wish to pay as much as they can on the principal of the loan on January 31, in multiples of $100. They feel that the cash balance should not be reduced below $3,000. Each partner wishes to continue to make the same monthly withdrawal of cash for personal use.

REQUIRED:

a. Prepare the following for Wales and Young for January, 19x3:

(1) A budgeted Income Statement;
(2) A budgeted Statement of Financial Position at the end of the month;
(3) A Cash Forecast.

b. On the basis of the information in (*a*), what action would you advise the business to take with respect to its cash balance at the end of January?

c. Prepare the following for February, 19x3:

(1) A budgeted Income Statement;
(2) A budgeted Statement of Financial Position;
(3) A Cash Forecast.

d. What action would you recommend with respect to cash at the end of February?

Chapter 14

Measuring and Controlling Receivables

General nature

Accounts Receivable, Trade, are the claims of a business against its customers for goods and services sold to them in the ordinary course of operations. *Notes Receivable, Trade,* are formal written documents signed by customers which contain an unconditional written promise to pay to the business a stated amount of money, either on demand or at a determinable future time. Other classes of receivables which are frequently owned by businesses are *accrued receivables, claims receivable, dividends receivable,* and *advances* (to officers, employees, and other companies).

Chapter 5 discussed some of the general problems of classifying and measuring receivables. The present chapter deals with some of the more complex problems associated with measuring receivables and with some of the methods by which business management can plan and control the amount of business capital invested in receivables.

MEASURING ACCOUNTS RECEIVABLE, TRADE

General basis of measurement

The proper measure of Accounts Receivable, Trade, is the estimated amount collectible through ordinary business operations. Ordinarily the terms of sale specify no interest for accounts collectible in the very near future. As a practical matter, implied interest for the brief waiting period is usually so small that no attempt is made to estimate it.

Trade accounts receivable result from revenue transactions. They become assets when revenue is realized because of some definite event, such as the transferring of legal title of goods or the rendering of service to a customer. Each amount legally receivable should be recorded as an asset at the time a claim arises, so that the assets and the revenue of the business can be measured properly and so that timely collection efforts can be made.

In order to measure receivables at their cash value and to assign the appropriate amount of revenue to each time period, several types of deductions from the total amount of receivables legally owned are needed. These adjustments are for uncollectibles, returns, allowances, discounts, and reimbursable shipping charges. To fail to consider these items in financial statements prepared before the claims are settled would be to overstate both Sales Revenue and the asset, Accounts Receivable.

The amounts of these adjustments cannot be known exactly in advance, but that is no excuse for failing to make reasonable estimates. The seller's past experience, together with known changes in factors affecting allowances, returns, and losses, may be used as a basis for such estimates. Each estimate may be recorded by debiting an appropriately named *revenue deduction* account. The corresponding credit should be to an *asset valuation account* which is a deduction from Accounts Receivable, Trade.

Sales discounts

In the section "Deductions from Sales Revenue" in Chapter 7, two methods of accounting for sales discounts, the *net price method* and the *gross price method*, were described briefly. The following information related to the affairs of the Larson Company for December, 19x1, is used as a basis for comparing these two methods:

Sales for the month were $100,000, all subject to credit terms of 2/10 E.O.M., n/60. None of the accounts had been collected by December 31, the last day of the accounting period. The company's past experience showed that as a rule 80 per cent of sales were settled in cash within the discount period.

The net price method. Under this method, sales and accounts receivable are measured initially at the sales price minus the available discount, as follows:

(1a)

A, Accounts Receivable, Trade....................	98,000	
OE, Sales Revenue (19x1)....................		98,000
To record total credit sales for December at the sales price minus available discount.		

If no additional entry were made in 19x1, Accounts Receivable, Trade, would be shown as $98,000 in the December 31, 19x1, statement of financial position, and Sales Revenue would be shown as the same amount in the income statement. However, it is reasonable to predict, on the basis of customers' past behavior, that $98,400 will be collected on the accounts receivable which the business owns on December 31, 19x1. The following adjusting entry should be made on December 31 to show that $400 more than the net amount of receivables is expected to be collected:

(2a)

A, Accounts Receivable, Trade—Estimated Discounts Forfeited.................................	400	
OE, Revenue from Sales Discounts Forfeited (19x1)....................................		400
To record the estimated amount of sales discounts which will be forfeited by customers on accounts receivable outstanding on December 31, 19x1.		

The debit in this entry is an *addition (adjunct)* to the Accounts Receivable controlling account. It cannot be posted to the individual customers' accounts, because it is not known on December 31 which customers will fail to take the discount.

In the next year, 19x2, the entries would be as follows (assuming that customers' past payment habits continue):

(3a)

A, Cash..	78,400	
A, Accounts Receivable, Trade................		78,400
To record the collection of 80% of December's credit sales within the discount period.		

(4a)

A, Cash..	20,000	
A, Accounts Receivable, Trade................		19,600
A, Accounts Receivable, Trade—Estimated Discounts Forfeited.........................		400
To record the collection of 20% of December's credit sales, together with the forfeited discount, after the expiration of the discount period.		

The gross price method. Under this method, which is perhaps the more widely used in practice, the receivable and the revenue are recorded at the gross sales price at the time of the sale. The *discount actually taken* by the customer is recorded at the time he pays his account. The appropriate entries would be:

(1b)

A, Accounts Receivable, Trade....................	100,000	
OE, Sales Revenue (19x1)....................		100,000
To record total credit sales for December at the gross sales price.		

An adjusting entry must be made on December 31 to avoid *overstating* accounts receivable and revenue by the amount the business will not collect

—the \$1,600 discount which customers are expected to deduct in January. This entry is:

(2b)

OE, Sales Discounts Taken (19x1).................	1,600	
A, Accounts Receivable—Estimated Discounts Taken		1,600

To record the cash discounts expected to be taken in the future at 2% of the \$80,000 of accounts which are expected to be settled within the discount period.

The balance of Accounts Receivable—Estimated Discounts Taken is a *deduction* from (*contra* to) Accounts Receivable, Trade.

The entries in the following year would be:

(3b)

A, Cash..	78,400	
A, Accounts Receivable—Estimated Discounts Taken	1,600	
A, Accounts Receivable, Trade................		80,000

To record the collection of 80% of December's credit sales within the discount period.

(4b)

A, Cash..	20,000	
A, Accounts Receivable, Trade................		20,000

To record the collection of 20% of December's credit sales, together with the lost discount, after the expiration of the discount period.

Summary of the two methods. If proper adjustments are made at the end of the year of sale, the effect of the two sales discounts methods on the assets and income is the same, as shown below.

Partial Statement of Financial Position, December 31, 19x1

Net price method:

Current Assets:		
Accounts receivable, trade (net).............	\$98,000	
Add estimated discounts forfeited............	400	
Estimated collectible amount................		\$98,400

Gross price method:

Current Assets:		
Accounts receivable, trade (gross)...........	\$100,000	
Deduct estimated discounts taken............	1,600	
Estimated collectible amount..............		\$98,400

Partial Income Statement for Year Ended December 31, 19x1

Net price method:

Sales (net)...................................	\$ 98,000	

Nonoperating revenue:		
Sales discounts forfeited....................	400	

Gross price method:

Sales (gross).................................	\$100,000	
Deduct sales discounts taken.................	1,600	
Net sales...................................	\$ 98,400	

Variations of these principal methods are in use, but the total reported assets and income should be the same under any method.

Analysis of quality of accounts receivable

In addition to knowing the *amounts* of accounts receivable which are legally owed to a business, management and others wish to know the *quality* of the accounts: how much will eventually be collected on the accounts, how promptly it will be collected. Two general analyses which are used in appraising the quality of accounts receivable are the *age distribution* of the accounts and the *provision for estimated uncollectible accounts*.

Age distribution of accounts receivable

An analysis of accounts receivable according to the length of time each invoice has been owed is useful in estimating the amount of uncollectible accounts as well as in determining the effectiveness of management's credit and collection procedures. Each unpaid charge is classified as to age on a columnar analysis sheet like the following.

MADISON CORPORATION
Accounts Receivable Age Distribution
December 31, 19x2

Account Name	Total Balance	Age in Months				
		0–1	1–2	2–3	3–6	Over 6
Adams............	500	350	150			
Brown............	400					400
Carroll............	1,200	900	200	100		
Drake.............	200	200				
Totals..........	50,000	38,000	7,000	3,000	500	1,500
Per cent of total...	100%	76%	14%	6%	1%	3%

Summaries of this type of distribution, which frequently accompany statements of financial position, are especially useful to both management and creditors. Comparisons with age distributions of earlier periods enhance their usefulness. In general, increases in the percentage of accounts in the lower age classifications show an improvement in the quality of accounts and in credit and collection administration, while percentage increases in the older classes are unfavorable.

Estimating uncollectibles from age distribution

The age distribution may be used in estimating the amount of accounts receivable currently owed which the company can expect to become uncollectible. For this purpose, a company should maintain statistics of past experience comparing the amounts of accounts actually determined to be uncollectible with the totals of accounts receivable of each age group. As a rule, the probable percentage of loss from uncollectibility increases as accounts become older. A computation of expected losses for the Madison Corporation for 19x2 may be made as follows:

Age in Months	Accounts Receivable	Per cent of Expected Loss	Amount of Expected Loss
0–1	$38,000	0.2%	$ 76
1–2	7,000	1.0	70
2–3	3,000	5.0	150
3–6	500	25.0	125
Over 6	1,500	50.0	750
Totals	$50,000		$1,171

On the basis of this estimate, it would appear that $1,171 of the accounts receivable now on the books, regardless of when they originated, will become uncollectible. This is the balance that should be in the Accounts Receivable—Estimated Uncollectibles account after the adjusting entry has been made at the end of the period. If the credit balance in this account prior to the adjusting entry were $300 (a provision remaining from earlier periods), the appropriate entry would be:

(5a)

OE, Sales Revenue—Losses from Uncollectible Accounts
    (19x2)...   871
    A, Accounts Receivable, Trade—Estimated Uncollecti-
    bles..   871
    To increase the estimated uncollectibles provision to $1,171,
    the total of estimated uncollectibles.

The preparation of an age distribution is time-consuming. It is most practical for businesses whose accounts receivable consist of relatively few accounts which have only a few debit items each. When the accounts are few in number, however, percentages of past losses to total accounts in various age groups are a less reliable means of predicting future losses than if the accounts are numerous.

EXAMPLE 1:   A company follows the practice of making a final disposition of all unpaid account balances by the end of the year following the year of sale. Its total losses from uncollectible accounts for the past three years have been $300, and its three-year total of accounts receivable owed at the end of the years was $10,000, indicating an average loss of 3 per cent. At the end of the current year, its individual accounts receivable balances are as follows:

Customer A..	$1,200
Customer B..	400
Customer C..	700
Customer D..	1,700
Total..	$4,000

How should the estimated loss from uncollectibles be determined?

SOLUTION: There are so few accounts that the use of a loss percentage based on past-experience statistics would be unreliable. An expected loss of 3 per cent of accounts receivable of $4,000 would be $120; but if any account becomes uncollectible, it will probably be at least $400. In such a case, where the accounts are few in number, estimated uncollectibles can best be determined by appraising the quality of each customer's account individually.

Collection efforts may be improved by placing delinquent accounts in a separate ledger for special attention, or by marking them with a distinctive signal.

Estimating uncollectibles on the basis of credit sales

The section "Estimated Uncollectibles" in Chapter 5 described how to make an estimate of the amount of uncollectible accounts which will result from the current year's sales on account. This is done by using the average percentage of the actual uncollectible accounts to the credit sales of the year in which the sales were made. The estimated loss on the current year's sales determined by using this percentage is then *added to the balance* already in Accounts Receivable—Estimated Uncollectibles. The previous balance may apply to the uncollected accounts of prior years which are still carried in Accounts Receivable, Trade, or it may be a cumulative error which has not been corrected.

To illustrate this method, assume that the Madison Corporation wished to compare its results with those obtained under the percentage-of-receivables method. Its sales on account for the current year were $100,000 and its past actual losses from uncollectibles had averaged 1 per cent of sales on account. The entry would be:

(5b)

OE, Sales Revenue—Losses from Uncollectible Accounts (19x2)...	1,000
A, Accounts Receivable, Trade—Estimated Uncollectibles...	1,000

To add the expected loss on the current year's credit sales to the balance in Estimated Uncollectibles.

The balance in the account would then be:

A, Accounts Receivable, Trade—Estimated Uncollectibles

(Balance from prior year)	300
(Addition for this year) (5b)	1,000
Balance at end of year	1,300

This method is widely used in practice, but the cumulative balance tends to become excessive or deficient after several years unless periodic efforts are made to keep it reasonably related to the amount of uncollected accounts still on the books. In other words, the age-distribution method can be used to supplement the method of adding a percentage of sales on account to the balance in Accounts Receivable—Estimated Uncollectibles.

Writing off uncollectible accounts

The section "Writing Off Uncollectible Accounts" in Chapter 5 illustrated and explained the following type of entry, which would be made for writing off an account which was actually determined to be uncollectible in a later year:

19x3	(6)		
Jan. 30	A, Accounts Receivable—Estimated Uncollectibles..........	120	
	A, Accounts Receivable—Trade.....................		120
	To write off the uncollectible account of the Amco Corporation.		

The account, after several additional write-offs in 19x3 of specific accounts arising from 19x2 sales, would appear thus:

A, Accounts Receivable, Trade—Estimated Uncollectibles

(Actual)		(Estimate)	
19x3		19x2	
Jan. 30	120	Dec. 31 Balance	1,300
Feb. 7	200		
Dec. 11	80	Bal., 0	
18	900		
	1,300		

If all of the accounts from sales of 19x2 and prior years had been collected or written off, or were expected to be fully collectible at the end of 19x3, the 19x2 estimate in the illustration was perfect. This would be unusual in actual practice, although reasonably accurate estimates are common.

In reality, the details in the Estimated Uncollectibles account would be more complicated than in the illustration, because credits for estimated uncollectibles arising from the sales of later periods would be added to the account before the final disposition of balances from earlier periods had been made. Often several years elapse before a particular account receivable is collected or definitely determined to be uncollectible. For this reason, the balances in both Accounts Receivable, Trade and Accounts Receivable, Trade—Estimated Uncollectibles usually contain items relating to several different years. It is a good idea to keep supporting details which show the composition of these account balances by year of origin, as well as of the actual uncollectibles which have resulted from each year's credit sales. These statistics show trends in the amounts of uncollectibles as well as estimating errors of the past. They are useful in estimating future losses more accurately and in correcting the cumulative estimate in Accounts Receivable, Trade—Estimated Uncollectibles.

Correcting uncollectible account entries

Occasionally an account which has been written off as uncollectible is collected in a later period. The proper accounting treatment is to make an entry which is the opposite of the original write-off entry, and then to record the collection.

19x4	(7)		
Feb. 7	A, Accounts Receivable, Trade.............................	120	
	A, Accounts Receivable, Trade—Estimated Uncollectibles...		120
	To reverse the entry of Jan. 30, 19x3, writing off the Amco account.		
	(8)		
7	A, Cash...	120	
	A, Accounts Receivable, Trade.......................		120
	To record the collection of the Amco Corporation account.		

This seemingly roundabout procedure shows for credit reference purposes that the customer did finally pay his account.

The estimate of uncollectibles is nothing more than an educated guess and is rarely completely accurate. The accountant should watch the cumulative balance of the estimated uncollectibles account to see that it bears a realistic relationship to total accounts receivable. An excessive credit balance discloses that overestimates of uncollectibles have been made in prior years, while an inadequate credit balance or a debit balance indicates underestimates.

If an error in the estimate is immaterial in amount, it may be absorbed in the estimated uncollectibles of the period in which the difference is discovered.

EXAMPLE 2:   At the end of 19x3 all of the accounts receivable of earlier years had been disposed of, and there was a credit balance of $20 in Accounts Receivable—Estimated Uncollectibles. The estimated amount of uncollectibles applicable to credit sales of 19x3 was $3,000. The error for the prior year could be absorbed in the estimate of the current year by adding $2,980 ($3,000 minus $20) to the Estimated Uncollectibles account balance.

A material estimating error such as the following, however, should be shown as an extraneous item in the 19x3 income statement.

19x3   (9)
Dec. 31   OE, Correction of 19x1 Losses from Uncollectibles (19x3).... 4,100
              A, Accounts Receivable—Estimated Uncollectibles......   4,100
              To correct a substantial underestimate of uncollectibles re-
          sulting from 19x1 sales.

Other deductions from accounts receivable

Sales revenue and accounts receivable are also reduced by sales returns and allowances. Their amount should be debited to a special account, which is reported as a revenue deduction in the income statement, and credited to Accounts Receivable, Trade. When goods are returned, their unexpired cost should be debited to Merchandise Inventory and credited to Cost of Goods Sold Expense.

Proper matching of periodic revenues and expenses and proper measurement of the ending balance in the asset, Accounts Receivable, requires that an estimate be made at the end of the year to reflect the amount of the current year's sales which are likely to be returned in the following year. The amount of the expected return, based on past experience, should allow for probable damages to goods to be returned and transportation charges which the seller is likely to have to pay.

For convenience, immaterial amounts of estimated future sales returns may be combined with estimated future sales discounts in a year-end adjusting entry. The resulting amount is deducted from Accounts Receivable and from Sales Revenue as a single figure.

The following example shows how the net sales revenue of the Larson Company for December, 19x1, might be estimated.

EXAMPLE 3:   The Larson Company made sales of $100,000 in December, 19x1, all on credit terms of 2/10 E.O.M., n/60. None had been collected by December 31. The company's past experience showed that 80 per cent of sales were generally settled in cash within the discount period, 1 per cent were returned for credit in later months, and ½ of 1 per cent ultimately became uncollectible. How much revenue did the company realize from sales in December, and what was the collectible amount of the accounts receivable on December 31?

SOLUTION:

Per Cent of Sales	Gross Amount		Estimated Realizable Amount
80.0%	$ 80,000	To be collected within the discount period, minus 2% cash discount ($1,600)	$ 78,400
18.5%	$ 18,500	To be collected after the discount period.........................	18,500
1.0%	$ 1,000	To be returned...............	0
0.5%	$ 500	To be uncollectible.............	0
100.0%	$100,000	totals......................	$ 96,900

The accounting entries needed to reflect this information are explained in the preceding sections.

Special problems in reporting accounts receivable

In the absence of disclosure to the contrary, the reader of a statement of financial position may assume that the balance of Accounts Receivable, Trade, is owed to the company by its customers under its customary credit terms. Clarity of presentation requires that amounts receivable on installment accounts be stated separately according to the year of maturity. Such accounts are current assets if they conform to customary trade practices in the industry.

Businesses frequently sell, or *assign*, accounts receivable to financial institutions in exchange for their present value in cash. If the assignment is made *without recourse*, the purchaser of the accounts bears losses from uncollectibles. The seller records the receipt of cash, the applicable interest expense, and the reduction of accounts receivable owned.

If the assignment is *with recourse*, the seller has a potential, or *contingent, liability* to the financial institution. He must pay the account to the latter if the customer does not. A statement of financial position prepared while the company is still contingently liable should report the amount of the contingent liability in a footnote. Memorandum ledger accounts, whose balances do not appear in the body of the statements, may be used to keep information current as to the amount of the potential liability.

Accounts receivable may also be *pledged* as collateral for loans. In such cases the pledgor is obliged to collect the accounts in the usual way and either to pay their proceeds to the lender or to substitute new collateral for them. The pledging company should transfer the accounts to a special ledger so that the proceeds of their collection may be accounted for properly. It should show the face amount of pledged accounts in a footnote to its statement of financial position.

Detailed records of accounts receivable

The foregoing discussion has dealt with problems of recognizing and measuring Accounts Receivable, Trade, *in total*. A business must necessarily keep a record of the details of its transactions with *each customer*. Such detailed accounts are debited for the amount of sales on account and are credited for collections, returns, allowances, and uncollectibles. Even businesses of moderate size often have thousands of such customers' accounts, and it is important that procedures be employed which will maintain these accounts efficiently and accurately. Time-saving equipment is frequently used in keeping customers' records. Although the form of the detailed accounts varies with the needs and preferences of the individual business, the following general arrangement is common.

CUSTOMER'S NAME	John Doe
ADDRESS	8 Cedar St., City
CREDIT LIMIT	$100

Date		Explanation	Posting Reference	Debits	Credits	Balance
19x2						
Nov.	6	Sale	S 1107	82		82
Dec.	9	Cash	CR 18		20	62

Many types of bookkeeping machines print a balance after each posting, providing current information for ready reference.

Businesses which have more than a very few accounts receivable should keep them apart from the general ledger in a supporting ledger or file called a *subsidiary ledger*. The general ledger *controlling account*, Accounts Receivable, Trade, has a balance equaling the total balances of all customers' accounts in the detailed ledger. Posting procedures should insure that the total of all debits to individual accounts receivable is posted to the controlling account, and likewise the total of all credits. This double posting does not destroy the equality of debits and credits in the general ledger, because the customers' subsidiary accounts are not a part of the general ledger. They provide an independent check on the accuracy of the balance in the general ledger controlling account. Frequent comparisons, usually monthly, are needed to detect errors and to keep the total of individual accounts in the subsidiary ledger equal to the balance of the controlling account.

CONTROLLING ACCOUNTS RECEIVABLE, TRADE

Internal check of accounts receivable

The general objective of internal check procedures for accounts receivable is to insure that the business collects amounts owed by its customers promptly and fully, and that the collections are properly paid into the company's treasury. This requires measures to prevent fraud, errors, and inefficiency in debiting charge sales to customers' accounts and in recording subsequent deductions for collections, returns, allowances, and write-offs.

Detailed procedures for handling receivables are tailored to suit the individual business. If possible, however, separate employees should approve credit, ship the goods, bill the customers, receive cash, keep the customers' detailed accounts, and maintain the accounts receivable controlling account.

Responsibility for approving credit should be specifically assigned to one employee or department, preferably not to the sales department. In its zeal to increase sales, the sales department might be too lax in extending credit. The procedures should insure that credit is granted according to the company's policy, and only after proper investigation of the applicant's credit record.

Procedures for shipping goods and preparing sales invoices should provide the accounts receivable bookkeeper a prompt and accurate record of all sales. An individual other than the one who prepares the invoice should check the accuracy of the quantities, prices, computations, discounts, and shipping terms. Copies of sales invoices and collection memoranda should be routed to the accounts receivable subsidiary ledger bookkeeper for posting to the individual customers' accounts. The system of cross-checks is strengthened if information as to the total debits and credits for these types of transactions goes directly to the general ledger bookkeeper for posting to the accounts receivable controlling account independently of the information given to the subsidiary ledger bookkeeper.

Credits to customers' accounts for returns, allowances, and write-offs should be approved by an appropriate executive after he has determined that they are proper. An accounts receivable bookkeeper who has access to cash collections might otherwise pocket them and cover up by falsely recording returns or similar credits in the customers' accounts. A customer would never be the wiser: the books would show that his account was settled, and he would not be billed in the future.

An individual who has access to both accounts receivable records and cash collections can conceal temporary misappropriations of cash by *lapping*, or postponing credits to the customers' accounts.

EXAMPLE 4:   On March 1 a cashier-bookkeeper collected $20 from Customer *A* to apply on his account, but pocketed the money. On March 6, when he received a $25 remittance from *B*, he credited $20 to *A*'s subsidiary account receivable, and took $5 more for his own use. He continued this process thereafter, always being a few days behind in crediting each customer for his payment. The customers did not suspect the irregularity, because they were accustomed to a short time lag in posting to their individual accounts.

Lapping can be *detected* rather easily if cash collection and deposit records are compared carefully; it can be *prevented* if individuals who handle cash are not given access to the accounts.

There should be continuous follow-up efforts to collect accounts receivable, both those which have been written off as uncollectible and those which are considered good. Although the former have no balances on the books of the creditor, there is usually enough likelihood of collecting something to warrant keeping them in a special ledger and sending occasional reminders. The *customer* does not know that his account has been written off as uncollectible.

Frequent analytical reports of accounts receivable should be prepared for management review and action. Some of the more common types are described in the following pages.

Measuring past turnover rates

The *turnover rate* of any asset is intended to give a measure of the rate of change in that asset over a period of time. The general formula for computing the rate of turnover is:

$$\frac{\text{Change in Account during Time Period}}{\text{Typical Balance of the Account}} = \text{Number of Turnovers}$$

Measures of the turnover of Accounts Receivable, Trade, may be used to appraise the past performance of management as well as to plan for the future. Actual past accounts receivable turnover rates may be used to measure the effectiveness of the business in managing the amount of the investment in accounts receivable, which depends upon the functions of extending credit and collecting from the customers. In computing turnover, it is desirable to use an average balance of accounts receivable rather than the balance at a given time, because the former is likely to be more representative of the situation that exists during the accounting period.

EXAMPLE 5:   From the following condensed ledger account, compute the number of turnovers of Accounts Receivable, Trade, during 19x1:

A, Accounts Receivable, Trade

19x1				19x1		
Jan. 1	Balance............	45,000		Various		
Various				dates	Collections on account	190,000
dates	Sales on account.....	200,000		Dec. 31	Balance, 55,000	
		245,000				

$$\text{SOLUTION:} \quad \frac{\text{Change}}{\text{Typical Balance}} = \text{Number of Turnovers}$$

$$\frac{\text{Sales, \$200,000}}{\text{Average Balance, \$50,000}} = 4 \text{ turnovers}$$

The average balance used here is the arithmetic mean of the January 1 balance of $45,000 and the December 31 balance of $55,000.

The turnover of Accounts Receivable can be measured by comparing the typical balance with either the debit changes (sales on account) or the credit changes (collections). The former was chosen so that the turnover of Accounts Receivable could be compared with that of other assets whose changes are also related to the amount of sales.

The year-end balances may not be typical of those which exist during most of the year, in which case an average of the monthly balances would give a more useful turnover rate. Better still would be a turnover rate for each month, computed by dividing credit sales for the month by the average balance of Accounts Receivable during the month. These 12 monthly rates would reveal important seasonal variations in the rate of turnover, and, in comparison with the rates of prior years, they would show important trends.

Rapid changes in the balance of Accounts Receivable tend to distort the reliability of the turnover rate. So does the inclusion of accounts arising from several different classes of credit terms in one turnover computation. It would be meaningless, for example, to compute the average turnover of accounts receivable resulting partly from sales on 30-day open account and partly from installment sales on terms ranging up to 24 months. Separate turnover calculations should be made for each such class of receivables.

Using the turnover rates

A standard of comparison is needed to determine whether the turnover rate of 4, computed in Example 5, is *good* or *bad*. One such standard is the *rate for the preceding year*. If in this example the prior year's turnover rate had been 3.74, the current year's results would seem to indicate an improvement.

Another standard of comparison is the *planned*, or desired, *turnover rate*. If this had been 6 turnovers a year in Example 5, additional improvement is still needed. Action to improve turnover can be centered on the debit changes (sales on account), on the credit changes (collections), or on both. Such action might consist of the following:

(1) Changes in credit terms. Shorter terms result in a proportionately higher turnover rate.

(2) Changes in credit-granting policies. Less liberal extension of credit tends to result in a higher turnover rate.

(3) Action to improve customers' paying habits, to counteract such factors as economic downswings.

(4) Changes in effectiveness of collection efforts. Better follow-up efforts tend to cause a higher turnover rate.

Average collection period

A variation of the accounts receivable turnover rate which is in wide use is the *average collection period*. It is the reciprocal of (1 divided by) the number of turnovers.

EXAMPLE 6:   What is the average collection period in Example 5?
SOLUTION   (a):

$$\text{Average Collection Period} = \frac{1}{\text{Number of Turnovers}} = \frac{1}{4} \text{ year.}$$

Expressed in terms of days rather than years, this average collection period is $\frac{1}{4}$ of 365 days, or approximately 91 days.

SOLUTION (b):   The average collection period in years can also be computed thus:

$$\frac{\text{Average Balance of Accounts Receivable}}{\text{Credit Sales}} = \frac{\$50,000}{\$200,000} = \frac{1}{4} \text{ year}$$

The average collection period is often compared with the company's normal credit period. If the company's normal credit terms are *net 30 days*, the average collection period of 91 days indicates that, on the average, customers are taking about three times as long to pay their accounts as credit terms permit. It is also useful to compare one company's average collection period with that of others in the same industry.

Estimating future turnover rates

Actual accounts receivable turnover rates for recent past periods can be used in estimating the cash collections of future periods and future accounts receivable balances, if a reliable estimate of sales on account is available.

EXAMPLE 7:   The actual balance of Accounts Receivable, Trade, of a company on January 1, 19x2, is $50,000. Sales on account during the year are expected to be $300,000. The accounts receivable turnover rate in 19x1 was 5, and this rate is expected to continue in the coming year. How much cash can the company expect to collect on account in 19x2, and what will its December 31, 19x2, balance of Accounts Receivable probably be?

SOLUTION: $\dfrac{\text{Sales on Account}}{\text{Average Balance}} = \text{Number of Turnovers};$

therefore, $\dfrac{\text{Sales on Account}}{\text{Number of Turnovers}} = \text{Average Balance.}$

$$\frac{\$300,000}{5} = \$60,000 \text{ average balance}$$

$$\text{Average Balance} = \frac{\text{Beginning Balance} + \text{Ending Balance}}{2}$$

$$\$60,000 = \frac{\$50,000 + X}{2}$$

$$\tfrac{1}{2}X = \$35,000$$

$$X = \$70,000, \text{ the expected ending balance of Accounts Receivable}$$

$$\text{Ending Balance} = \text{Beginning Balance} + \text{Sales} - \text{Collections}$$

$$\$70,000 = \$50,000 + \$300,000 - \text{Collections}$$

$$\text{Collections} = \$350,000 - \$70,000$$

$$\text{Collections} = \$280,000$$

Any expected changes in the turnover rate should be considered in estimating future collections and asset balances.

Determining credit policy

Management needs data on the cost of extending credit as a guide in tightening or relaxing the credit it grants, in increasing or decreasing the service charges made for the extension of credit, and in improving the effectiveness of collections. The cost of granting credit, which may be accumulated in the accounts on a regular basis or analyzed in a special cost study, includes the following items:

(1) Direct expenses of running the credit department, such as salaries and supplies;

(2) A share of common expenses;

(3) The lost cost of merchandise, as well as transportation charges, which results from uncollectible accounts;

(4) Interest expense on money borrowed to finance the balance of Accounts Receivable.

If a business liberalizes its credit policy, it should attempt to match the resulting increased sales revenue with the applicable costs of granting credit. The credit liberalization is undesirable unless it results in an increased rate of income on the assets used by the business. On the other hand, a business should not tighten its credit terms to such an extent that its rate of net income is reduced.

MEASURING NOTES RECEIVABLE

General basis of measurement

Frequently notes receivable specify that the maker is to pay interest at a stated rate for the term of the note. Even if no interest is mentioned, it is often implicitly included in the maturity amount of the note.

Initially, notes receivable should be measured at their discounted value, which is their cash equivalent at the time of receipt. Immaterial amounts of discount applicable to non-interest-bearing notes are usually ignored in the measurement process. It is also customary to assume that the stated rate of interest is the appropriate one to use in the accounts. When a note receivable is actually transferred to someone else on a discount basis, the actual discount rate affects the amounts to be shown in the accounts. Illustrative entries for this situation appear in Appendix 14-A.

Financial institutions such as banks deal in a large number of promissory notes. Mercantile businesses often receive notes as a result of sales, in settlement of accounts receivable (often past-due), and in exchange for cash loans or advances. Notes which require installment payments are common when the unit selling price of merchandise is high.

Bills of exchange

Bills of exchange, or *drafts,* are formal written documents which are often used in settling accounts or loans. A draft is an *order* to pay, whereas a note is a *promise* to pay. The *drawer* of a draft, usually a creditor, orders the *drawee,* usually a customer, to pay a certain sum at a certain time. *Sight drafts* are often used to secure collection from a customer in another city before the goods are delivered to him. They are payable upon presentation, and the drawee must honor them by paying them before getting the *bill of lading,* which permits him to obtain the goods. The seller records the shipment as a sale on account and the collection of the sight draft as a credit to the customer's account.

At other times, the terms of sale require that the purchaser *accept,* or agree to pay, a time draft due at a specific future time. He does this by writing the word "Accepted," the date, and his signature on the face of the draft. Thereafter the effect of the accepted draft in the hands of the seller of goods is the same as that of a note receivable, and it may be recorded as a debit to the asset, Notes Receivable, Trade. A *trade acceptance,* evidencing the purchase and sale of goods, is generally easier for the owner to discount than is an ordinary note.

Recording receipt of notes

A business which receives a non-interest-bearing note makes this entry:

(10)

A, Notes Receivable, Trade......................	100	
A, Accounts Receivable, Trade.................		100
Received a 30-day non-interest-bearing note on account.		

If on another note the face amount includes interest, the proper entry is:

(11a)

A, Notes Receivable (Face)......................	1,060	
A, Notes Receivable—Unearned Discount........		60
A, Accounts Receivable......................		1,000
Received on account a non-interest-bearing note due in one year.		

In a statement of financial position prepared immediately after receipt of the note, the facts would appear thus:

```
Current Assets:
    Notes receivable, face amount.................... $1,060
    Deduct unearned discount........................     60
                                                      _____
                                                       $1,000
```

A common illustration of this situation is the practice of including interest and service charges in the face amount of installment notes receivable.

The discount is earned in proportion to the passage of time. If the accounting period ends 9 months after receipt of the note, the following entry should be made:

```
                         (12a)
A, Notes Receivable—Unearned Discount............    45
    OE, Interest Revenue...........................          45
    To record the accrual of 9 months' interest on $1,000
    at 6%.
```

Treatment in the statement of financial position at that time would be:

```
Notes receivable, face.............................. $1,060
Deduct unearned discount...........................      15
                                                      _____
                                                       $1,045
```

If the note were a 6 per cent interest-bearing note, the proper entries would be:

```
                         (11b)
A, Notes Receivable, Trade........................  1,000
    A, Accounts Receivable, Trade.................           1,000
    Received on account a 6% note due in one year.
```

```
                         (12b)
A, Accrued Interest Receivable....................     45
    OE, Interest Revenue..........................           45
    To record the accrual of 9 months' interest on $1,000
    at 6%.
```

The statement presentation would be as follows:

```
Notes receivable.................................. $1,000
Accrued interest receivable.......................     45
                                                    _____
                                                     $1,045
```

Internal check procedures for notes

The procedures for handling and recording notes receivable should insure that the business has an accurate account of notes received, that it uses adequate methods for safeguarding and collecting notes and interest, and that it authorizes and records properly the disposition of notes by sale or collection. Duties of employees should be so divided that each of the functions of recording, keeping custody of, and collecting or discounting notes is performed by a different individual.

A business which has frequent notes receivable transactions should establish a subsidiary notes receivable record to support the Notes Receivable general ledger controlling account. This detailed ledger may consist of a line on a page for each note, with columns provided for the following information:

Date of note	Name of endorser(s)
Face amount	Collateral
Interest rate	Amount of interest accrued
Date of transaction	Collections on principal
Term	Collections on interest
Due date	Disposition
Name of maker	

Installment notes receivable require numerous credits for collections. It is well to use a separate ledger page for each such note.

Summary

The proper measure of both Accounts Receivable, Trade, and Notes Receivable, Trade, is their current cash equivalent.

Matching of revenue deductions with the revenues of the appropriate period, as well as proper measurement of the asset, Accounts Receivable, Trade, require that estimates of future sales returns, allowances, discounts, and uncollectibles be deducted from the total amount of sales revenue and of accounts receivable legally owed the business. The preparation of an age distribution of accounts receivable is useful in evaluating the quality of accounts receivable and in estimating the amount of uncollectible accounts.

Analytical reports measuring the turnover rate of accounts receivable and its reciprocal, the average collection period, are useful to management in appraising the past performance of the business in extending credit and making collections as well as in forecasting the amounts of cash collections and accounts receivable of future periods.

APPENDIX 14-A

Discounted Notes Receivable

Most notes are *negotiable;* that is, they may be transferred to another owner in exchange for cash or in settlement of a debt. The original *payee* of the note transfers legal title by endorsing the note on the back. The *maker* of the note must then pay its face amount plus any interest specified to the *endorsee* when the latter presents the note for payment on its due date.

Endorsement without recourse

If the endorsement is *without recourse,* the endorser is not held responsible for paying the note if the maker fails to pay the final endorsee on the maturity date. A business which transfers a note without recourse records the transaction as an outright *sale* of the note. The two following entries record the receipt of a note by the Elson Co. and its subsequent transfer by endorsement without recourse.

(1)

Mar. 1	A, Notes Receivable........................ 1,000	
	OE, Sales Revenue.....................	1,000
	Received a 60-day, 6% note for $1,000 from Marks Co. in exchange for merchandise.	

(2a)

1	A, Cash................................... 1,000	
	A, Notes Receivable....................	1,000
	Immediately transferred the Marks note to a bank by endorsement without recourse. The bank paid face value for the note.	

Endorsement with recourse

If a note is transferred *with recourse,* the endorser is responsible for paying the note to the final endorsee at maturity if the maker fails to do so upon proper presentation. Even though the endorser has sold the note, he has a *contingent,* or potential, *liability* for paying it which he must show in his accounts and financial statements until the maturity of the note. At that time the contingent liability ceases to exist for one of the following reasons:

(1) The maker of the note pays the full amount owed to the final endorsee, and the endorser has *no further liability;* or

(2) The maker of the note fails to pay the amount owed to the final endorsee, and the endorser has an *actual liability* to pay the full amount owed on the note.

The following entry records the transfer of the Marks Co. note *with recourse:*

(2b)

Mar. 1	A. Cash................................... 1,000	
	L, Notes Receivable Discounted.........	1,000
	Transferred the Marks Co. note to a bank with recourse. The bank paid face value for the note.	

After this entry, the account balances on the endorser's books would be as follows:

A, Notes Receivable	L, Notes Receivable Discounted
Mar. 1 1,000	Mar. 1 1,000

The credit balance in Notes Receivable Discounted represents the endorser's *contingent liability* on the discounted note until its maturity. There is an equal balance in Notes Receivable, which represents a *contingent asset*. If the endorser is required to pay the maker's debt on the note at maturity, he will then have a claim against the maker for that amount.

Contingent assets and contingent liabilities should not be presented in the statement of financial position in the same manner as actual assets and liabilities because of the great uncertainty associated with them. Nevertheless, adequate disclosure to the reader of the financial statements requires that the amount of such contingencies be shown. The most common method is to omit both the contingent asset and the contingent liability amounts from the body of the statement, but to refer in the body of the statement to a footnote describing them. In a statement of financial position of the Elson Co. on March 31, after entry (2b), the facts would be shown as follows:

LIABILITIES

Current liabilities:		
Accounts payable	$14,000	
Accrued taxes payable	1,500	
Total current liabilities		$15,500
Contingent liabilities (See Note A)		
Total liabilities		$15,500
STOCKHOLDERS' EQUITY		
Capital stock, $100 par	$20,000	
Retained income	6,200	
Total stockholders' equity		26,200
Total equities		$41,700

Note A. The company was contingently liable on March 31 for notes receivable discounted amounting to $1,000.

Entries at maturity of note discounted with recourse

At the maturity of a note endorsed with recourse, the endorser is either relieved of liability or required to pay the amount which the maker fails to pay. In *either* case, the contingent asset and contingent liability should be removed from the books by the following entry:

(3)

Apr. 30 A, Notes Receivable Discounted	1,000	
A, Notes Receivable		1,000

To remove from the accounts the contingent liability and contingent asset on a note endorsed with recourse.

If the maker pays, or *honors*, the note upon presentation by the endorsee, the endorser has no further obligation. His accounts now show no balance relating to the endorsed note either in Notes Receivable or Notes Receivable Discounted.

If the maker fails to pay, or *dishonors*, the note, and the endorser is required to pay the maturity amount, the following *additional* entry would be needed on the endorser's books:

(4)

Apr. 30	A, Dishonored Note Receivable (or Accounts Receivable)............................. 1,010	
	A, Cash...........................	1,010

The contingent liability on an endorsed note became an actual liability when the maker, Marks Co., failed to pay the note to the bank. Paid the bank the entire amount owed on the Marks note, which included the face amount of $1,000 plus interest for 60 days at 6%, and charged the payment to a receivable from the Marks Co.

The endorser, the Elson Co., would then attempt to collect the $1,010 from the maker of the note. If this claim is of doubtful collectibility, the Elson Co. should consider it in estimating the amount of its uncollectible receivables.

Computing the proceeds of discounted notes

The amount which the endorser receives upon the transfer of a note is called the *proceeds* of the note. The amount of the proceeds is computed by deducting from the *maturity amount* of the note *discount* from the date of transfer to the maturity date. The following illustration shows how the proceeds of the Marks note would be computed if the Elson Co. discounted it at the bank on March 7 and the bank charged a discount rate of 6 per cent.

Maturity amount:	
Face amount.......................................	$1,000.00
Plus interest on the face amount for the entire term of the note (6% of $1,000 for 60 days)..................	10.00
Total maturity amount...........................	$1,010.00
Deduct discount:	
Discount at 6% on the maturity amount, $1,010, for the *remaining* term of the note, 54 days (March 7 to April 30)...	9.09
Proceeds...	$1,000.91

The *discount* is the endorsee's compensation for advancing money to the endorser and for waiting until the maturity date to be repaid. It is accounted for as *interest expense* by the business which pays it and *interest revenue* by the business which receives it.

Recording endorser's interest revenue or expense

Three parties are involved in a note which is discounted: the *maker*, the *endorser*, and the *endorsee*. The interest to be recorded in their accounts is determined as follows:

(1) *Maker. Records interest expense* for the full term of the note, from original date to maturity date. From his point of view, it does not matter whether the original payee or the endorsee has advanced the money; he has a liability on the note for its full term.

(2) *Endorsee. Records interest revenue* equal to the discount, which is applicable to the period from the date of transfer by endorsement to the maturity date.

(3) *Endorser. Records interest revenue* if the amount in (1) is greater than that in (2), or *interest expense* if (2) is greater.

In the computation of the proceeds illustrated in the preceding section, the *interest expense* of the Marks Co. will be $10, which is 6 per cent of the face amount of the note for the entire 60 days the company owes it. The *interest revenue* of the Elson Co. will be $0.91, the difference between the proceeds of the note, $1,000.91, and its face amount, $1,000. The *interest revenue* of the bank will be $9.09, the difference between the $1,010 which it will collect on the maturity date of the note and the $1,000.91 which it advanced to the Marks Co. at the time of transfer.

Summary:	Interest Expense	Interest Revenue
Maker............................	$10.00	
Endorser..........................		$ 0.91
Endorsee..........................		9.09
Totals.........................	$10.00	$10.00

The Elson Co. would record the transfer of the note as follows:

(2c)

Mar. 7 A, Cash..................................	1,000.91	
L, Notes Receivable Discounted.............		1,000.00
OE, Interest Revenue......................		.91

Transferred the Marks note by endorsement.
The proceeds were more than the face amount.

The endorser would earn a net revenue on the transaction if the discount rate used by the endorsee were *lower* than the interest rate on the note.

If the Elson Co. transferred the note shortly after its receipt, and if the endorsee used a discount rate *higher* than the interest rate on the note, the proceeds would be less than the face amount of the note. For example, if the bank used a discount rate of more than 6 per cent, the proceeds of the note might have been $995. In this case the Elson Co. would have *interest*

428 Measuring and Controlling Receivables [Ch. 14

expense of $5, the difference between the face amount of the note, $1,000, and the proceeds, $995. The bank would have interest revenue of $15, the difference between the maturity amount, $1,010, and the $995 advanced to the endorser.

Summary:	Interest Expense	Interest Revenue
Maker...	$10	
Endorser	5	
Endorsee		$15
Totals	$15	$15

The Elson Co., the endorser, would then make the following entry upon transferring the note:

(2d)

A, Cash	995	
OE, Interest Expense	5	
L, Notes Receivable Discounted		1,000

Transferred the Marks note by endorsement. The proceeds were less than the face amount.

Assigned accounts receivable

Businesses often sell, or *assign*, their accounts receivable to financial institutions in exchange for their present value in cash. If the assignment is *without recourse*, the entry would be as follows:

(5a)

A, Cash	980	
OE, Interest Expense	20	
A, Accounts Receivable, Trade		1,000

Assigned accounts receivable having a face amount of $1,000 to Commercial Factors. Received the cash proceeds, after a deduction of $20 for interest.

If the assignment is *with recourse*, the seller has a contingent liability to the financial institution if the customer does not pay the account. The following entry reflects this possible liability:

(5b)

A, Cash	985	
OE, Interest Expense	15	
L, Accounts Receivable, Trade—Assigned		1,000

Assigned accounts receivable having a face amount of $1,000 to Commercial Factors, with recourse. Received the proceeds after deduction of interest.

The interest charge is lower in the second case because the assignee is assuming less risk.

A statement of financial position prepared while the company is still contingently liable should show as a current asset only the difference between Accounts Receivable, Trade, and assigned accounts. The contingent liability should be disclosed in a footnote.

QUESTIONS AND PROBLEMS

14-1 "Accounting is based on realized changes which can be objectively measured. Recording a loss for accounts which are *expected* to become bad in the future violates this principle."

REQUIRED:

Evaluate this argument.

14-2 A company which has been in business for several years has never made any entries to record estimated cash discounts, returns, and allowances applicable to the year-end balances of accounts receivable. "It's a waste of time," says the head accountant, "because the charges applicable to the previous year's sales which are recorded in the current year will be offset by estimated charges applicable to this year which are not made at the end of the current year."

REQUIRED:

a. What weaknesses are there in this argument?
b. Illustrate the effect of ignoring estimated discounts, returns, and allowances on (1) the income statement and (2) the statement of financial position prepared at the end of 19x3. Use amounts of your own choice.

14-3 A college fraternity has an established schedule of charges for room rent, meals, and dues for its members. At the beginning of each month, the treasurer prepares a statement of charges for each member in duplicate, the original going to the member and the duplicate to the treasurer as the basis for making entries in the permanent records.

For each collection, the treasurer writes out a duplicate receipt, giving the original to the member and retaining the copy. Both statement and receipt forms are prenumbered by the printer.

REQUIRED:

a. What opportunities for error are there in this arrangement?
b. How could a dishonest treasurer obtain money improperly from this situation?
c. What system of cross-proofs and controls would you recommend to minimize the opportunity for fraud and error?

14-4 At the end of your company's accounting period, April 30, 19x2, you find the following balances in the ledger:

	Debit	Credit
Accounts Receivable, Trade	$18,000	
Accounts Receivable—Estimated Uncollectibles	300	

REQUIRED:

a. How did the Estimated Uncollectibles balance probably originate?
b. What action would you take to dispose of it?
c. Assuming such amounts as are needed, make appropriate journal entries as of April 30, 19x2.
d. Show how the accounts affected in (*c*) would appear in the financial statements.

14-5

REQUIRED:

Answer the following questions, using appropriate illustrations:
a. What effect does the write-off of a definitely uncollectible account arising from a sale in a prior year have on income in the year of write-off? On total assets?

b. What effect does the recovery of an account written off as uncollectible in a prior year have on income in the year of recovery? On total assets?

c. What effect does recording an estimate of uncollectible accounts have on income in the year in which the estimate is made? On total assets?

14-6 Mr. Peterson, the owner of a small business, stated, "I would much rather have a note receivable from a customer than an ordinary account, even if the note is non-interest-bearing."

REQUIRED:

a. Do you agree with Mr. Peterson? Explain.

b. Describe the procedure for accounting for a non-interest-bearing note from the time of its receipt until its collection two years later.

14-7 The Knox Corporation sold merchandise on account to the Moore Company on December 15, 19x1, and received payment in full on December 24. A few days later, the Moore Company returned a part of the shipment which had proved to be faulty, and the Knox Corporation issued a credit memorandum on December 31.

REQUIRED:

a. How would these facts affect the statement of financial position of the Knox Corporation on December 31, 19x1?

b. How would the statement of financial position of the Moore Company be affected?

14-8 Each of the following opinions is held by some accountants as to the proper location of Losses from Uncollectibles in the income statement:

(1) It is a deduction from sales revenue, as an amount never realized.

(2) It is a selling expense, associated with selling goods on credit.

(3) It is an administrative expense, because the credit manager approves the granting of credit.

(4) It is a financial expense, representing the cost of extending credit.

REQUIRED:

Evaluate the merits of each of these opinions, and state under what conditions, if any, you would consider each location proper.

14-9 The Metzger Company makes three or four purchases a month from O'Rourke Manufacturing Company. Adjustments are frequently necessary because of merchandise which is damaged in shipment, and occasional adjustments are necessary because the Metzger Company computes the amount of discounts improperly. Upon receiving the O'Rourke Manufacturing Company's statement each month, the Metzger Company bookkeeper compares it with his balance in the Accounts Payable subsidiary ledger. The two are almost never in agreement.

REQUIRED:

a. List the types of items that would probably cause differences between the customer's Account Payable balance and the seller's Account Receivable.

b. What procedure would you use to discover the points of difference between the two records?

14-10 On October 31, 19x1, the City Automobile Co. sold a new car to A. J. Gandy for $3,000. The car was carried in a perpetual inventory account at its cost of $2,400. Mr. Gandy made a cash down payment of $1,000 and signed a note promising to make 10 monthly payments of $210 on the last day of each month. The face amount of the note, $2,100, included interest and carrying charges, computed at ½ per cent a month of the original amount of the loan.

REQUIRED:

a. Give in journal form the entries to record the sale.
b. Record the collection of the monthly installments on November 30 and December 31.
c. Make the entry needed to state interest properly on December 31.
d. Show how the applicable items would appear in the December 31 statement of financial position.
e. Show how the applicable items would appear in the 19x1 income statement.

14-11 The following are selected transactions of the Rodman Co., which uses the net price method of recording sales and the perpetual inventory method.

REQUIRED:

Record the following transactions in general journal form.

Jan. 2—Sold merchandise on account to Bartow Sales Co., list price $1,000, less a quantity discount of 20 per cent. Payment terms were 2/10, n/30. The goods had cost $575.

9—Received a check in full settlement of the Bartow Sales Co. account.

10—Sold merchandise on account to Clarion, Inc., for an invoice price of $500, f.o.b. destination. Payment terms were 2/10, n/30. Cost of the goods was $300. The Rodman Co. paid transportation charges of $10 on the shipment.

12—Gave Clarion, Inc., an allowance of $100 because the merchandise shipped on Jan. 10 was faulty.

20—Received a check in full settlement of the Clarion account.

31—Estimated uncollectible accounts were expected to be 1 per cent of January's total credit sales of $40,000. (Assume that the sales entries have already been recorded.)

Feb. 2—M. J. Steele, a customer, was discharged in bankruptcy. There were no assets available for making payments to his creditors. On January 5 goods costing $150 had been sold to Mr. Steele for $300 on terms of 2/10, n/30. No payment had been received.

9—Efforts to locate A. R. Brynnan, a customer who owed $50 as a result of a January transaction, were fruitless.

Dec. 5—Received a check for $50 from A. R. Brynnan, together with a note of apology.

14-12 The McGregor Company uses the gross price method of recording sales, and at the end of each accounting period makes entries to reflect estimated returns, discounts, and uncollectibles. Before making these adjustments on December 31, 19x1, its account balances are as follows:

	Debit	Credit
Accounts receivable, trade	$55,000	
Sales revenue		$900,000
Sales returns and allowances	8,000	
Sales discounts	14,000	

All of the sales were on account. In the past, uncollectible accounts have averaged ½ per cent of sales. On December 31 specific accounts totaling $700 are known to be bad, but this fact has not yet been recorded.

On December 31 sales discounts of 2 per cent are still available on accounts of a gross amount of $35,000. It is expected that 90 per cent of these discounts will be taken.

Returns and allowances of an additional $3,000 of 19x1 sales are expected to be made early in 19x2. On the basis of past experience, it may be expected that the cost of the goods returned, less appropriate allowances for damage, will be $1,200.

REQUIRED:

a. Prepare journal entries to record the foregoing estimates.
b. Show how each item referred to will appear in the 19x1 income statement.
c. Illustrate the appropriate details of the December 31, 19x1 statement of financial position.

14-13   The Corvin Company has just begun operations in December, 19x1, and the accountant is trying to decide whether to use the net price method or the gross price method of recording sales. The company has decided to use the perpetual inventory method.

REQUIRED:

a. Record the following transactions in general journal form under the gross price method and the perpetual inventory method.
b. Show how accounts receivable, sales, and related accounts would appear in the financial statements at the end of 19x1.
c. Record the transactions under the net price method.
d. Show how the relevant accounts would appear in the financial statements.
e. Discuss the strong and weak points of each method.

Transactions:

Dec. 1—Sold merchandise on account to the AB Co., $800, terms 2/10, n/30. Cost of the merchandise was $480.

2—Sold merchandise on account to the CD Co., $600, terms 2/10, n/30, cost $360.

3—Sold merchandise on account to the EF Co., $400, terms 2/10, n/30, cost $240.

4—Allowed the CD Co. a price reduction of $50 to compensate for damaged goods.

5—Accepted one-fifth of the goods shipped to the EF Co. but returned by them for credit because they were not the style ordered. Allowed the EF Co. credit for $20 freight which they paid on the original shipment. Also paid freight of $11 in cash on the return shipment.

9—Collected the AB account in full.

10—Collected the CD account in full.

20—Collected the EF account in full.

23–31—Sold merchandise on account to various companies for $25,000, terms 2/10, n/30, cost $15,000.

31—Estimated that 80 per cent of the unpaid accounts would be collected within the discount period; 2 per cent would be returned undamaged; 1 per cent would result in uncollectible accounts; and the remainder would be collected slowly.

14-14   The following items summarizing the effect of selected transactions by quarters were taken from the ledger of the Feld Co.:

A, Accounts Receivable, Trade					OE, Sales Revenue		
19x3		19x3				19x3	
Jan. 1	16,000	Mar. 31	18,000			Mar. 31	15,000
Mar. 31	15,000	Jun. 30	17,000			Jun. 30	20,000
Jun. 30	20,000	Sep. 30	18,000			Sep. 30	22,000
Sep. 30	22,000	Dec. 31	24,000			Dec. 31	30,000
Dec. 31	30,000						

The Feld Co. makes all of its sales on credit on terms of net 30 days.

REQUIRED:

a. Compute the balance of Accounts Receivable at the end of each quarter.
b. Compute the number of Accounts Receivable turnovers for the year as a whole, using the average of the Accounts Receivable balances at the beginning and end of the year.
c. Compute the number of turnovers for the year, using the average of Accounts Receivable balances at the beginning of the year and at the end of each quarter.
d. Compute the number of turnovers during each quarter.
e. Explain what the results of your computations in (b), (c), and (d) mean.
f. Which computation seems to give more useful information? Why?

14-15 The following is a typical account taken from the Accounts Receivable subsidiary ledger of the Merrian Company:

Belmont Sales Co.

19x2		Ref.		Debits	Credits	Balance
Jan. 1	Balance....................					2,000
11	Collection	CR	2		1,600	400
Feb. 11	Collection..................	CR	4		400	0
Mar. 21	Sale.......................	S	9	600		600
Apr. 6	Sale.......................	S	11	300		900
May 12	Collection..................	CR	16		200	700
June 11	Collection..................	CR	18		200	500
Aug. 14	Collection..................	CR	21		200	300
Oct. 18	Sale...	S	25	500		800
29	Return.....................	RS	9		150	650
Nov. 2	Sale.......................	S	26	1,000		1,650
12	Collection..................	CR	23		400	1,250

The Merrian Company wishes an age distribution of its accounts receivable on December 31, 19x2, with the following age groups: Less than 1 month; 1–2 months; 2–3 months; 3–6 months; and over 6 months.

REQUIRED:

a. Determine the age of the Belmont Sales Co. balance according to the foregoing classification.
b. Assume that the total accounts in each classification were $45,000, $12,000, $4,000, $5,000, and $8,000, respectively. Show how you would use this information in estimating the amount of uncollectibles.
c. How might the age distribution be shown in a financial statement presented to a bank in support of a loan application?
d. How might the age distribution be used in making the cash forecast for the next year?
e. How might the age distribution be used in determining the effectiveness of the company in collecting its accounts?

14-16   The Madison Marker Co. computes an accounts receivable turnover rate by dividing the average of total accounts receivable at the beginning and end of each year into sales on account for the year. Data for 19x1 and 19x2 were:

	19x1		19x2	
Accounts receivable, trade, Jan. 1:				
30-day charge accounts.............	$ 40,000		$ 75,000	
Installment accounts...............	60,000		50,000	
Total..........................		$100,000		$125,000
Net sales on account:				
30-day charge accounts.............	$275,000		$360,000	
Installment sales..................	110,000		72,000	
Total..........................		$385,000		$432,000
Accounts receivable, trade, Dec. 31:				
30-day charge accounts.............	$ 75,000		$ 85,000	
Installment accounts...............	50,000		30,000	
Total..........................		$125,000		$115,000

The turnover rates as computed were 3.42 for 19x1 and 3.60 for 19x2.

REQUIRED:

a. Did the increase in turnover as computed indicate better or worse collection efficiency for 19x2?

b. Compute the turnovers as you think proper, and explain the meaning of your results.

c. Restate your results in (*b*) in terms of an average collection period, and explain the meaning of your results.

14-17   The following schedule appeared in the annual report of Federated Department Stores, Inc., for the fiscal year ended February 2, 1957.

ACCOUNTS RECEIVABLE	February 2, 1957	January 28, 1956
Due from customers:		
Thirty-day charge accounts...............	$ 39,606,844	$ 38,752,266
Deferred payment accounts...............	88,379,395	80,057,065
Other accounts receivable..................	5,694,307	3,828,047
	$133,680,546	$122,637,378
Less:		
Provision for possible future losses and deferred service charges..................	$ 8,495,597	$ 7,087,940
Accounts sold to banks without recourse (less Company's equity therein of $4,752,642 at February 2, 1957).....................	36,510,826	36,569,435
	$ 45,006,423	$ 43,657,375
Net.......................................	$ 88,674,123	$ 78,980,003

REQUIRED:

a. Explain the meaning of: (1) deferred payment accounts; (2) deferred service charges; (3) accounts sold to banks without recourse; (4) company's equity in (3).

b. Which of the items in the schedule may appropriately be included in Current Assets?

c. Using assumed amounts, illustrate the type of entries that would affect (1) deferred payment accounts, (2) provision for possible future losses, (3) provision for deferred service charges, (4) accounts sold to banks without recourse, and (5) the company's equity in (4).

d. The consolidated statement of income shows net retail sales (including sales of leased departments) of $601,491,511 for the 53 weeks ended February 2, 1957, and $537,722,365 for the 52 weeks ended January 28, 1956. What additional information would you need in order to determine the average age of accounts receivable on February 2, 1957?

14-18 The following are selected transactions of the Sabot Co., which uses the gross price method of recording sales and the periodic inventory method.

REQUIRED:

a. Record the transactions in general journal form.
b. Show how the resulting balances would appear in the September 30 statement of financial position.

Sept. 1—Sold merchandise on account, terms 2/10, n/30, for $1,000.

2—Assigned the accounts from the preceding sale to the *X* National Bank without recourse, receiving the proceeds of $980 in cash. The difference was an interest charge.

3—Sold merchandise for $2,000, terms sight draft attached to the bill of lading.

7—Collected the proceeds of the Sept. 3 sight draft, $1,995. The bank deducted a $5 collection fee.

8—Sold merchandise for $3,000, terms time draft due 60 days after acceptance and bearing interest at 6 per cent.

11—Received the customer's accepted draft dated September 10.

12—Received a non-interest-bearing note for $1,000, due in 60 days, for a sale made to the Carpet Co. today.

12—Discounted the Carpet Co. note at the *X* National Bank with recourse. The bank used a discount rate of 6 per cent.

18—Received a 6 per cent note for $4,000, due in 60 days, for a sale made to R. R. Godwin today.

30—Discounted the Godwin note at the *X* National Bank with recourse, at a discount rate of 6 per cent.

30—Made necessary adjusting entries to reflect the proper amount of interest for September.

Nov. 9—Collected the full amount of the draft dated September 10.

11—The *X* National Bank presented the Carpet Co. note due today to the Sabot Co. for payment as endorser. The note had been presented to the maker, who failed to pay. The Sabot Co. paid the principal, interest, and a $3 protest fee on the note.

18—Received a memorandum from the bank that Godwin had honored his note due yesterday.

CASE 14-1. THE WILLOW PRODUCTS COMPANY

The Willow Products Company was organized in 19x1. During that year, its sales on credit totaled $80,000, and on December 31, 19x1, accounts amounting to $14,000 were uncollected. Credit sales of 19x2 were $112,000, and accounts receivable on December 31, 19x2 were $18,000 (including $1,000 of 19x1 accounts). Losses from uncollectible accounts in the industry were 1 per cent of sales each year. During 19x2 the Willow Products Company determined that the following accounts resulting from 19x1 sales were definitely uncollectible:

L Co., $200; *M*, Inc., $140; *N* Mfg. Co., $300.

Just before preparing its financial statements at the end of 19x1, the Willow Products Company learned that Federal income tax rules permit taxpayers to use one of two methods of determining the deduction for uncollectible accounts:

Method 1. The taxpayer deducts only accounts that have definitely been determined to be uncollectible. No estimate of future uncollectibles is made.

Method 2. The taxpayer estimates uncollectibles that will result from past sales and records the estimate as an expense and an asset deduction.

There are two principal variations of Method 2: (a) The taxpayer adds to the asset-deduction account each year an amount determined by using a percentage of total sales, or of credit sales, for the year. This percentage is the estimated rate of loss based on the past experience of the particular business or of the industry. (b) The taxpayer determines what the balance should be in the asset-deduction account each year by appraising individual accounts, or by using an age distribution of accounts. An entry is then made to adjust the asset-deduction balance to the amount of total expected loss.

The Willow Products Company expects to continue its existing credit policy for the next year. It expects sales to increase about 20 per cent in 19x3 and about 10 per cent a year thereafter.

REQUIRED:

a. Record in general journal form the entries that the Willow Products Company would make in 19x1 and 19x2 under Method 1.
b. Record the entries that would be needed in 19x1 and 19x2 under Method 2.
c. What differences would there be in the income statements for both years under the two methods? In the statements of financial position?
d. What are the advantages and disadvantages of Method 1?
e. What are the advantages and disadvantages of each variation of Method 2?
f. Assuming that it is permissible for the company to use one method in its income tax return and another in its general-purpose financial statements, if desired, what method or combination of methods would you recommend that the Willow Products Company adopt? Why?

CASE 14-2. DANN SUPPLY CO.

Dann Supply Co., a retail store which had previously sold only for cash, began selling on credit as well in 19x8. At the end of the year, the store management wishes to appraise the results of its change in policy as a basis for deciding whether to continue to extend credit. Also under consideration is a plan to charge each customer interest at a monthly percentage of the unpaid balance during the month.

Comparative financial data for the Dann Supply Co. for 19x7 and 19x8 are shown below. There were no significant changes in policies or operating relationships, other than the credit policy, during 19x8. Changes in assets and equities from the beginning to the end of 19x7 were immaterial.

REQUIRED:

a. Using the available data, how would you determine whether selling on credit was profitable for 19x8?
b. What other financial costs and relationships, besides those shown, should be considered in deciding whether to continue the granting of credit?
c. What intangible factors have a bearing on the decision? Explain how they should be considered.

d. What additional factors should be evaluated before deciding whether to charge customers interest?

	19x7		19x8	
Sales......................................		$200,000		$300,000
Deduct loss from uncollectible accounts...		0		3,000
Net sales.................................		$200,000		$297,000
Cost of goods sold........................		120,000		180,000
Gross margin.............................		$ 80,000		$117,000
Variable operating expenses:				
Advertising...........................	$10,000		$15,000	
Sales supplies........................	4,000		6,000	
Office supplies........................	2,000		6,000	
Sales salaries........................	20,000		30,000	
Total variable expenses.............		36,000		57,000
Contribution to fixed expense............		$ 44,000		$ 60,000
Fixed expense:				
Depreciation of equipment............	$ 2,000		$ 2,500	
Sales salaries........................	10,000		10,000	
Credit manager's salary...............	0		6,000	
President's salary....................	10,000		10,000	
Rent.................................	12,000		12,000	
Total fixed expenses................		34,000		40,500
Net income before income tax...........		$ 10,000		$ 19,500
Assets:				
Cash.................................		$ 16,000		$ 23,600
Accounts receivable, trade.............			$20,000	
Deduct estimated uncollectibles......			2,000	18,000
Merchandise inventory.................		50,000		75,000
Equipment............................	$20,000		$25,000	
Deduct accumulated depreciation....	10,000	10,000	12,500	12,500
Total assets.....................		$ 76,000		$129,100
Liabilities:				
Accounts payable, trade...............		$ 10,000		$ 15,000

CASE 14-3. ALPHA PRODUCTS COMPANY

Alpha Products Company has a general ledger bookkeeper, an accounts receivable bookkeeper, and an accounts payable bookkeeper. A billing clerk types sales invoices for shipments to customers and then prepares an adding-machine tape of each day's shipments. Marked with the date and labeled as "sales on account," the tape is sent to the general ledger bookkeeper, who journalizes an entry for the total sales.

The original sales invoice is mailed directly to the customer and a copy is sent to the accounts receivable bookkeeper, who posts by hand directly from the invoice to a customers' subsidiary ledger.

Collections from customers go to a cashier, who makes a list showing the date, name of customer, and amount of each remittance. A copy of this list goes to the accounts receivable bookkeeper for posting to the subsidiary ledger. The general ledger bookkeeper makes a daily entry for the total collections.

The accounts receivable bookkeeper prepares monthly statements of account, which are then mailed to the customers. Special credits to customers' accounts for such items as returns, allowances, and uncollectibles are approved in writing by the credit manager. A copy is sent to the general and subsidiary ledger bookkeepers.

Once a year, a general ledger entry is made to bring the Accounts Receivable controlling account into agreement with the subsidiary ledger. At this time, the credit manager reviews each customer's account to judge whether it is uncollectible.

REQUIRED:

a. Do you see any easy opportunities for fraud in this arrangement? For error? For inefficiency?
b. What daily system of cross-checks would you recommend?
c. What types of monthly reports (if any) are needed?
d. Do you think that the annual entries to bring the controlling account into agreement with the subsidiary ledger will balance out over a period of years, with gains approximately equaling losses? Why?
e. How would you recommend that the problem of differences between the controlling account and the subsidiary ledger be solved?

CASE 14-4. GOLIATH MFG. CO.

The Goliath Mfg. Co. has followed the practice of estimating its uncollectible accounts each year on the basis of 1 per cent of sales on account. At the end of 19x3, the accountant feels that a supplementary analysis is needed to determine whether the company's experience for the past three years indicates that this rate is adequate, inadequate, or excessive.

The balances in the general ledger accounts on December 31, 19x3, are as follows:

	Debit	Credit
Accounts Receivable	$28,100	
Accounts Receivable—Estimated Uncollectibles...		$ 460
Losses from Uncollectible Accounts	1,050	
Sales Revenue		105,000

An analysis shows that the composition of the Accounts Receivable balance is as follows:

Accounts arising from sales in:
19x3... $26,600
19x2... 1,500
19x1...   0

Sales on account amounted to $91,000 in 19x1, $95,000 in 19x2, and $105,000 in 19x3.

Specific accounts determined to be uncollectible and written off have been as follows:

		Year Written Off		
Year of Sale:	Total	19x1	19x2	19x3
19x1	$ 900	$100	$500	$ 300
19x2	1,150		300	850
19x3	400			400
Totals	$2,450	$100	$800	$1,550

Collections of accounts have been as follows:

Year of Sale:	Total	Year Collected 19x1	19x2	19x3
19x1	$ 90,100	$75,550	$14,450	$ 100
19x2	92,350		76,000	16,350
19x3	78,000			78,000
Total	$260,450	$75,550	$90,450	$94,450

The credit manager and the accountant, after examining the unpaid accounts on December 31, 19x3, estimate that $450 of the 19x2 accounts and $1,100 of the 19x3 accounts still on the books on December 31, 19x3, will ultimately become uncollectible.

REQUIRED:

a. What entry or entries should be made to reflect these facts on December 31, 19x3? (*Suggestion:* Set up a T-account for the accounts receivable and another for estimated uncollectibles arising from each year's sales, and record all events in these accounts. Then form your conclusion by analyzing the balances.)

b. What relevant account balances should appear in the 19x3 financial statements?

c. Based upon the latest information available, what was the percentage of loss from uncollectibles for each of the past three years?

d. Sales on account were $100,000 in 19x4. Make the entry necessary to estimate uncollectibles on December 31, 19x4.

Chapter **15**

Measuring Inventory

The term *inventory* refers to items of
tangible personal property which are being held for sale in the ordinary
course of business, are being produced for sale, or are to be consumed in
the near future in producing goods or services for sale. Classes of goods for
sale, itemized in Chapter 6, include the *merchandise inventory* of a trading
concern and the *finished goods inventory* of a manufacturer. Goods being
produced are the *goods in process inventory* of a manufacturer, and con-
sumable items include *materials* and *supplies inventories*.[1]

Objectives of inventory accounting

The objectives of inventory accounting are to measure the periodic
income of a business, to determine its financial position, and to assist in
managing its assets efficiently and profitably.

In income measurement the expired costs of inventory items, such as
cost of goods sold, should be matched with the sales revenues to which they
apply. The *unexpired* costs of inventory—those which will benefit the
operations of future periods—are shown as assets in the statement of
financial position.

Records and reports of the physical quantities and costs of inventories,
including their balances, changes, and relationships, are essential to
managerial appraisal of past business performance and to planning and
control of future operations.

---

[1] AICPA Committee on Accounting Procedure, *Restatement and Revision of Accounting Research Bulletins* (*Accounting Research Bulletin No. 43*) (New York: The Institute, 1953), p. 27.

Matching costs with revenues

Chapter 6 explained how accountants attempt to determine periodic income by associating the expired costs of service benefits with the revenues which they helped to bring about. It emphasized that *economic*, rather than *physical*, association of costs with the related revenues was the essence of the matching process. Recognizing this limitation, however, it described how the process of matching is facilitated by tracing costs to *physical* items of inventory. Initially such costs are debited to asset accounts as *product* costs, to be transferred ultimately to expense in the period in which the goods are sold.

The starting point in determining the cost of an inventory unit is its invoice cost, after deducting trade, quantity, and cash discounts. To this net invoice cost should be added transportation, handling, and storage costs, excise and sales taxes, import duties, and other costs directly associated with obtaining the item.

An inventory item is often *transformed* before it is ready for sale. The transformation is intended to increase its salability and sales price. It may consist largely of aging, as in the case of cheese or liquor. Often the process of production, by means of which the original items of inventory change form and utility, is quite elaborate. As the product is transformed, so are the inventory costs. Inventory costs may be regrouped into several different asset categories before they are finally matched with revenue in the period of sale. The manufacturer, for example, transforms raw material inventory into goods in process inventory, and the latter into finished goods.

As a general rule, costs necessary to *prepare an inventory item for sale* are treated as product costs, while those necessary to *make the sale* (for example, advertising, sales commissions, and wrapping supplies) are treated as expenses of the period in which they are incurred.

Chapter 6 also pointed out that it is sometimes desirable and feasible to trace the expiration of inventory costs *directly* by means of the *perpetual inventory* method, while at other times the *indirect* approach, that of measuring the asset which remains by means of the *periodic inventory* method, is appropriate. Theoretically, these methods should give the same result, but for practical reasons they often do not. For example, the perpetual inventory will not record goods lost by theft until the loss is discovered, perhaps by periodic physical verification.

Criteria for evaluating methods of determining inventory cost

Although the components of inventory cost seem rather simple in theory, the practical difficulties of measuring them are often great. Measuring the items of cost which are associated with preparing inventory for sale often involves arbitrary assumptions as to the relationships of costs with particular units of product. For example, the total transportation cost of a shipment may be assumed to apply in equal amount to each unit in the shipment.

Even if the matter of tracing components of inventory cost to the physical items could be settled, there is a difficult problem of deciding which units have been sold when similar units have been acquired at different times and at different costs. This is essentially an *allocation* problem. It involves selecting an orderly method of assigning *expired* inventory costs to the current period as expense, and treating *unexpired* inventory costs as assets which are potential expenses of future accounting periods.

The process of allocating inventory costs to expense and to assets is an accounting problem, but it has an important bearing on many business decisions. Management often decides which alternative course of action to follow on the basis of information furnished by accounting, and for this reason it is important that the information be so prepared as to lead to sound decisions. The following criteria may be used in deciding which method of measuring inventory provides the most useful information for decision-making in a given instance:

(1) The method should help to provide a useful measure of income for the current period as a basis for appraising past performance. In doing so, it should match expired inventory costs with the revenues to which those costs are related.

(2) It should help to provide a useful measure of financial status at the end of the current period. The unexpired cost of inventory at any date is an asset, which is used in measuring the financial position of the business.

(3) It should help to provide a useful measure of the income of future accounting periods. The amount of inventory cost which is treated as an asset at the end of the current accounting period is postponed to future periods, in which it is available for use and is therefore a potential expense.

(4) It should furnish information useful to management in planning future operations. Important aspects of this requirement are its usefulness in measuring the past turnover rates of inventories, the rate of return on assets, and similar comparisons used in appraising past results and in planning for the future.

(5) It should be useful in promoting effective use and protection of the economic values represented by the inventory.

(6) It should be objective, orderly, and not subject to manipulation for the purpose of influencing the reported results artificially.

(7) It should be relatively simple to apply, and the time or difficulty involved in making inventory calculations should not outweigh the usefulness of the resulting information.

The important matter of the acceptability and desirability of the inventory method for the purpose of determining taxable income is discussed in

Chapter 24. With some notable exceptions, the inventory method used in measuring *business income* can differ from that used in measuring *taxable income*. The present chapter is concerned with the former measurement.

No method of measuring inventory fully achieves all of the objectives listed. The method that is appropriate in a given setting depends upon the nature of the business, the nature of the inventories, the relationships of acquisition cost and selling price, economic conditions and the extent of changes in them, the ability of the personnel who deal with inventory measurement, and the use to which the resulting information is to be put by management and others.

The importance of differences in results as between methods is relative. For example, the smaller the typical balance of inventory on hand in relation to the cost of goods sold during a period, the less is the relative difference in income determined by alternative inventory methods. Also, the smaller the usual inventory balance in relation to other assets, the less is the relative difference in financial position as determined by alternative methods of measuring inventory. Furthermore, if the differences in the acquisition costs of batches of a single class of inventory are relatively small, the differences in the results of inventory measurement methods tend to be small.

Basic illustration for comparing methods

What is the unexpired cost of the asset, inventory, and what is the amount of the expired cost, cost of goods sold expense, when various lots of a given class of inventory have been acquired at different times and at different unit costs? The following four basic methods of answering these questions are illustrated in the following sections, and their applicability to a given situation is evaluated on the basis of the criteria listed earlier:

(1) Specific-identification method.
(2) First-in, first-out (FIFO) method.
(3) Last-in, first-out (LIFO) method.
(4) Weighted-average method.

The following data from the records of the Emco Stores in 19x2 are used as the basis for illustrating each method.

19x2	Units	Unit Cost	Total Cost
Jan. 1 Inventory......................	100	$5.00	$ 500
Purchases:			
Mar. 17...........................	50	$5.30	$ 265
May 25............................	100	6.00	600
Jul. 10...........................	100	6.50	650
Oct. 1............................	50	6.60	330
Dec. 7............................	50	7.00	350
Total purchases..................	350		$2,195
Goods available for sale...............	450		$2,695

During 19x2 there were 300 units sold at various dates for total sales revenue of $2,400, and there were 150 unsold units in the final inventory.

In this series of illustrations it is assumed for simplicity that all purchases in 19x1, the first year of operations, were made at a unit cost of $5.00; therefore, the cost of the beginning inventory under any of the four methods was $500. Since the *cost of purchases* during a period is the same regardless of the method of deciding which units have been sold, the total cost of goods available for sale in 19x2 (beginning inventory plus purchases) in this illustration is the same under all four methods, $2,695. The problem, then, is to determine (1) how much of the cost of goods available for sale in 19x2 expired and became cost of goods sold expense and (2) how much of it was unexpired at the end of 19x2, representing the cost of the asset, inventory.

In 19x3 and later years, the cost of goods available for sale will differ under the four methods of determining inventory cost, because the beginning inventory will differ. The general approach described in the following sections will continue to be used, but the differences between the methods will be more complex.

Specific-identification method

One method of determining the cost of items in the ending inventory is to mark each article with its *specific* cost, usually in code. Determining the cost of the ending inventory then consists of adding up the marked costs of the specific unsold items.

Another method which produces similar results consists of keeping detailed cost records which specifically associate acquisition costs with particular units by the use of a serial number or some other means of identification. Under either this procedure or the preceding one, the ending inventory might be:

Dec. 31, 19x2, Inventory

	Units	Unit Cost	Total Cost
....	10	$5.00	$ 50
....	10	5.30	53
....	5	6.00	30
....	40	6.50	260
....	40	6.60	264
....	45	7.00	275
Total........................	150		$932

The cost of goods sold may be determined by subtracting the cost of the ending inventory from the cost of goods available for sale. The applicable part of the 19x2 income statement under the specific-identification method would be as follows:

	Units	Amounts
Sales revenue.............................	300	$2,400
Deduct cost of goods sold:		
Beginning inventory.................	100	$ 500
Add purchases......................	350	2,195
Goods available for sale...............	450	$2,695
Deduct ending inventory.......	150	932
Cost of goods sold.....................	300	1,763
Gross margin..............................		$ 637

It might seem at first that the specific identification method matches the expired cost of inventory items with revenue in a convincing way. Accounting seeks to match with revenues the costs which are economically related to them, however, and physical relationships may be misleading. If a unit of inventory bought at one date has the same economic service potential as one bought at another date, the items may be considered to be identical for purposes of measuring expired and unexpired costs even though the acquisition costs physically associated with each unit differ. The selection of specific items which are sold, and consequently of the specific items which remain in the ending inventory, may be purely accidental. Income and asset measurements based upon these results may be more misleading than helpful in appraising past performance and present status and in planning for the future.

The measurements produced by the specific-identification method may be erratic rather than orderly. The use of the method permits management to influence arbitrarily the amount of its income and of its assets by selecting an item, otherwise identical with its group, for sale purely on the basis of its specific cost.

The specific-identification method is simple to apply and is practical when only a relatively few inventory items are involved. However, it requires a great amount of detailed work when the items in inventory are numerous and of small unit value.

The specific-identification method is best suited to situations where differences other than cost, such as color, age, and condition, influence the selection of the particular item sold. When the units of a class are identical with each other, except for acquisition cost, a logical *assumed economic flow* of costs from asset to expense may be more objective and useful than an *identified physical flow*. The other three methods illustrated are based on assumed cost flows.

Types of assumed cost flows

Common types of assumed flows of cost are:

First-in, first-out (FIFO), which assumes that the first units acquired are the first units disposed of. As a result, the units on hand in the final inventory are from the most recent purchases.

Last-in, first-out (LIFO), which treats the *last* units acquired as being the first units disposed of. The ending inventory of a period is composed of units from the earliest acquisitions—beginning inventory, plus current acquisitions to the extent applicable.

Weighted average, which assumes that the costs of units acquired flow into a pool, where the cost of one unit cannot be distinguished from that of another. Items withdrawn for sale or use have a cost which is an average of the cost of each acquisition, weighted by the quantity acquired at that cost.

First-in, first-out (FIFO) method

The Emco Stores' inventory on December 31, 19x2, under the first-in, first-out assumption as to the flow of costs would be composed of the last 150 units bought, determined as follows:

Date of Acquisition	Units	Unit Cost	Total Cost
Dec. 7............................	50	$7.00	$ 350
Oct. 1............................	50	6.60	330
Jul. 10............................	50	6.50	325
Dec. 31 Inventory.................	150		$1,005

Cost of goods sold expense for 19x2 would be determined by subtracting the unexpired cost in the ending inventory, $1,005, from the cost of goods available for sale, $2,695. Its amount, $1,690, is composed of the 300 units which were bought *earliest,* as follows:

Date of Acquisition	Units	Unit Cost	Total Cost
Jan. 1 Inventory..................	100	$5.00	$ 500
Mar. 17............................	50	5.30	265
May 25............................	100	6.00	600
Jul. 10............................	50	6.50	325
Goods sold......................	300		$1,690

The FIFO method is often criticized for failing to match current acquisition costs of inventory with current revenues. In the illustration, acquisition costs were rising during 19x2, and perhaps selling prices were also increasing. Sales revenue for 19x2 includes the effect of the higher resale prices which were in effect during the latter part of the year, but cost of goods sold expense does not include the higher purchase costs under the FIFO method. The acquisition costs applicable to the latter part of 19x2 will be matched against the revenues of the early part of 19x3 because of FIFO's time lag in charging incurred costs against revenue. Its opponents point out that, in comparison with results obtained by matching with sales revenues the acquisition costs in effect at the time of the sale, FIFO produces the following distortions:

(1) When acquisition costs are rising, it understates cost of goods sold and overstates income, the ending asset balance, and retained income.

(2) When acquisition costs are falling, it overstates cost of goods sold and understates income, the ending asset balance, and retained income. FIFO's lag in treating costs as expired has a similar distorting effect on the income of future periods, as well as on the computation of inventory turnover rates.

The FIFO method generally results in an ending inventory balance more closely in line with current acquisition costs than do the other cost methods. For this reason, if plans regarding the future, such as setting prices, are based upon the balance of the asset, FIFO tends to promote better stewardship of the economic values of the inventory.

FIFO is objective since it results in an orderly chronological procession of costs in which the oldest expire first. It is largely free from manipulation to give a desired income figure. It is reasonably simple to apply, but it becomes cumbersome if there are many different acquisition costs for a given class of goods represented in the inventory at a single time.

FIFO is a suitable method of determining inventory cost when the turnover of goods is rapid, minimizing the time lag with which costs are charged against revenues. FIFO is also desirable when the types of items within a given inventory class change substantially during a period. It insures that the costs of the items no longer stocked are charged to expense and not retained as an asset. When management's policy is to set selling prices on the basis of FIFO cost, the method results in accurate matching of cost and revenue.

Last-in, first-out (LIFO) method

The ending inventory of Emco Stores for 19x2 under the last-in, first-out method would be as follows:

Date of Acquisition	Units	Unit Cost	Total Cost
Jan. 1 Inventory	100	$5.00	$500
Mar. 17	50	5.30	265
Dec. 31 Inventory	150		$765

Cost of goods sold expense would be determined by subtracting the cost of the ending inventory, $765, from the cost of goods available for sale, $2,695. Its amount, $1,930, would consist of the 300 units which were bought *last*, as follows:

Date of Acquisition	Units	Unit Cost	Total Cost
Dec. 7	50	$7.00	$ 350
Oct. 1	50	6.60	330
Jul. 10	100	6.50	650
May 25	100	6.00	600
Goods sold	300		$1,930

The principal argument in favor of LIFO is that it does a better job of matching current purchase costs against current sales revenues than do the other methods of allocating costs. However, the costs which it treats as expired are not those current at the time of the sale, but are the latest costs actually incurred. There may still be some time lag in matching costs with revenues if the matching is done on a perpetual inventory basis during the period. Quite often, however, LIFO is applied only at the end of the accounting period, and its effect may sometimes be to assign costs incurred *later* than the sale to the revenues from the sale.

LIFO may result in an *asset balance* that is substantially out of line with current costs if the quantity in the inventory remains stable or increases. If, for example, Emco Stores has an inventory of 150 units of Article A 30 years later when current purchase costs are $20 a unit, the LIFO ending inventory would still be $765, using unit costs of $5.00 and $5.30 incurred in 19x1 and 19x2. Use of this figure in making business decisions would be improper, because the current cost of the inventory at that time would be $3,000.

Under LIFO the asset, inventory, is unreliable to a varying extent. The longer the method has been in use and the greater the relative cost changes which have occurred during that period, the greater is the difference between the LIFO asset cost and current costs. Using the LIFO asset amount will distort the rate of inventory turnover, the rate of return on assets, and other ratios resulting from the comparison of assets with each other or with equities.

If the quantity in inventory decreases after remaining stable or increasing for a long period, LIFO may result in a *poorer matching* of costs and revenues than do other cost methods. This is true because the costs of inventory items acquired many years earlier will be treated as a part of the cost of goods sold in the current period, in addition to the costs of items acquired in the current period.

LIFO also permits manipulation of reported profit figures. Suppose that a company using LIFO finds early in December that its net income for the year to date is greater than it wishes to be publicized. If prices are rising, the company can purchase some items at the current higher prices and charge them, by the LIFO method, to cost of goods sold expense for the year, even though not a one of them has physically been sold. Conversely, a similar purchase at lower current prices can be used to bolster a sagging net income figure.

LIFO is probably no more difficult to apply in its basic form than is FIFO, although some very complex variations of LIFO are used by businesses.

When prices are rising and inventory quantities are stable or increasing, LIFO results in a lower taxable net income for the current period than do other cost methods. The advantages and limitations of this effect are discussed in Chapter 24.

LIFO is most suitable for those businesses in which the typical inventory balance is substantial in relation to total assets or to sales (that is, when the inventory turnover is slow). It is also appropriate when the product is relatively free from changes in nature or style and when changes in acquisition costs are rather quickly followed by changes in selling prices. It tends to be undesirable when there are relatively large upswings and downswings in the quantity of inventory on hand from time to time.

Weighted-average method

Many variations are used in computing inventory cost by the weighted-average method, differing in the frequency with which new averages are determined and the extent to which old balances are used in computing the average. Common variations in the method require that weighted averages be recomputed each time there is an acquisition at a unit cost different from the previous average cost; once a month; once a year; or at any other desired interval. The costs averaged, under the variation used, may be only those of the purchases for a given period of time, or they may include the beginning balance as well as purchases.

In the following illustration, a weighted-average cost is computed at the end of the year from the combined cost of the beginning inventory and purchases. It is used as the unit cost of items in the ending inventory and in cost of goods sold expense for the period.

Date of Acquisition	Units	Unit Cost	Total Cost
Jan. 1 Inventory	100	$5.00	$ 500
Mar. 17	50	5.30	265
May 25	100	6.00	600
Jul. 10	100	6.50	650
Oct. 1	50	6.60	330
Dec. 7	50	7.00	350
Total available	450		$2,695

$$\text{Weighted-Average Unit Cost} = \frac{\text{Total Cost}}{\text{Number of Units}} = \frac{\$2,695}{450} = \$5.989$$

The cost of the ending inventory on December 31, 19x2, is $898.35, determined by multiplying the number of units in the ending inventory, 150, by the weighted-average unit cost, $5.989.

The cost of goods sold for 19x2 is $1,796.65. It is determined by subtracting the ending inventory, $898.35, from the cost of goods available for sale, $2,695.00. Approximately the same result could be obtained by multiplying the number of units sold, 300, by the average cost per unit, $5.989. This method should not be used, however, where the unit cost has been rounded. Because of rounding, the sum of the ending inventory and the cost of goods sold determined by multiplying quantities by unit costs differs slightly from the cost of goods available for sale.

The weighted-average method tends to give an inventory cost which is between those resulting from FIFO and LIFO. It may have more or less of a time lag in matching current costs with current revenues than does FIFO, depending upon the length of the inventory turnover period in relation to the frequency with which new averages are computed. Its expired costs tend to be less current than those computed under LIFO.

Over a series of periods in which there are both price rises and price declines, the weighted-average method tends to produce smaller fluctuations in the computed amount of income between periods than does FIFO but larger fluctuations than does LIFO.

The degree of distortion in turnover rates and rates of return caused by the weighted-average method depends to a great extent upon how frequently new averages are computed and upon whether the current acquisitions are large in relation to the beginning balance.

The weighted-average method is generally objective, orderly, and free from manipulation. When there are many types of articles in the inventory, or when acquisition costs change frequently, the method requires a large number of computations. Sometimes, too, unit costs must be carried to three or four decimal places to yield the necessary degree of accuracy in computing totals. The method is perhaps best suited to those situations in which inventory is composed of a large number of relatively low-cost units which are replaced infrequently.

The weighted-average method is often criticized because, if it is applied strictly as illustrated above, the average unit costs are influenced to some extent by all costs previously experienced. An unusually large purchase at an abnormal price will have a lasting effect on future calculations of inventory and cost of goods sold. To combat this objection and to give a more current measure of costs, the *moving-average* method may be used.

Under one variation of the moving-average method, a weighted unit cost of all purchases during the preceding 12 months is computed. This unit cost is used during a month to compute the cost of goods sold during that month. At the end of the month, a new average unit cost is computed, using the purchases of the most recent 12 months. At the end of January, 19x2, for example, January purchases would be substituted in the average calculation for those of January, 19x1. At the end of February, 19x2, a new moving average would be computed by using all acquisition costs from March, 19x1, through February, 19x2.

A strong point of both the weighted- and moving-average methods is that they assign equal costs to items in the ending inventory which presumably have equal economic significance. Specific identification, FIFO, and LIFO do not usually do this.

Comparison of the results of the cost methods

The following are the results produced for Emco Stores in 19x2 by the four inventory cost methods just described.

	Specific Identification	FIFO	LIFO	Weighted Average
Sales revenue	$2,400	$2,400	$2,400	$2,400.00
Cost of goods sold expense	1,763	1,690	1,930	1,796.65
Gross margin	$ 637	$ 710	$ 470	$ 603.35
Asset, ending inventory	$ 932	$1,005	$ 765	$ 898.35

In later years the beginning inventories will not be the same under the various methods, because the ending inventory of the preceding year depends upon the inventory method used. Whether one particular cost method will give a higher or lower gross margin than another depends upon the direction of price movements and the increase or decrease in the physical quantity in inventory during the year. The four following illustrations show the effect of combinations of some of the possibilities which might occur in 19x3:

(1) Prices rise and the ending-inventory quantity increases;
(2) Prices rise and the ending-inventory quantity declines;
(3) Prices fall and the ending-inventory quantity increases;
(4) Prices fall and the ending-inventory quantity declines.

The comparative results of methods will also depend upon the relative amount of price changes during a period and the extent of the change in the inventory balance. The illustrations given do not cover all possible variations. The results under the specific-identification method are not shown, because they would behave in an irregular, unpredictable manner.

(1) *Prices rise and ending-inventory quantity increases.* In this illustration, it is assumed that 400 units are bought in 19x3 at $8.00 a unit, and that 300 units are sold for a total of $3,000.

	Units	FIFO		LIFO		Weighted Average	
Sales revenue	300	$3,000		$3,000		$3,000.00	
Cost of goods sold:							
Beginning inventory	150	$1,005		$ 765		$ 898.35	
Add purchases	400	3,200		3,200		3,200.00	
Goods available	550	$4,205		$3,965		$4,098.35	
Ending inventory	250	2,000		1,565		1,863.00	
Cost of goods sold	300		2,205		2,400		2,235.35
Gross margin			$ 795		$ 600		$ 764.65

The ending inventories were computed as follows:

FIFO: 250 units @ $8.00 = $2,000

LIFO: 100 units @ 5.00 = $ 500
       50 units @ 5.30 =   265
      100 units @ 8.00 =   800
Total 250 units   = $1,565

Average: $\frac{\text{Cost of Goods Available, \$4,098.35}}{\text{Number of Units Available, 550}}$ = Average Unit Cost, $7.452

250 × $7.452 = Ending Inventory, $1,863

(2) Prices rise and ending-inventory quantity declines. In this illustration, it is assumed that 200 units are bought in 19x3 at $8.00 a unit, and that 300 units are sold for a total of $3,000.

	Units	FIFO	LIFO	Weighted Average
Sales revenue........	300	$3,000	$3,000	$3,000.00
Cost of goods sold:				
Beginning inventory............	150	$1,005	$ 765	$ 898.35
Add purchases.....	200	1,600	1,600	1,600.00
Goods available....	350	$2,605	$2,365	$2,498.35
Ending inventory..	50	400	250	356.90
Cost of goods sold	300	2,205	2,115	2,141.45
Gross margin........		$ 795	$ 885	$ 858.55

The ending inventories were computed as follows:

FIFO: 50 units @ $8.00 = $400

LIFO: 50 units @ $5.00 = $250

Average: $\dfrac{\text{Cost of Goods Available, \$2,498.35}}{\text{Number of Units Available, 350}}$ = Average Unit Cost, $7.138

50 × $7.138 = Ending Inventory, $356.90

(3) Prices fall and ending-inventory quantity increases. In this illustration, it is assumed that 400 units are bought in 19x3 at $4.00 a unit, and that 300 units are sold for a total of $1,500.

	Units	FIFO	LIFO	Weighted Average
Sales revenue........	300	$1,500	$1,500	$1,500.00
Cost of goods sold:				
Beginning inventory............	150	$1,005	$ 765	$ 898.35
Add purchases.....	400	1,600	1,600	1,600.00
Goods available....	550	$2,605	$2,365	$2,498.35
Ending inventory..	250	1,000	1,165	1,135.50
Cost of goods sold	300	1,605	1,200	1,362.85
Gross margin (loss)...		($ 105)	$ 300	$ 137.15

The ending inventories were computed as follows:

FIFO: 250 units @ $4.00 = $1,000

LIFO: 100 units @ $5.00 = $ 500
50 units @ 5.30 = 265
100 units @ 4.00 = 400
Total 250 units = $1,165

Average: $\dfrac{\text{Cost of Goods Available, \$2,498.35}}{\text{Number of Units Available, 550}}$ = Average Unit Cost, $4.542

250 × $4.542 = Ending Inventory, $1,135.50

(4) Prices fall and ending-inventory quantity declines. In this illustration, it is assumed that 200 units are bought in 19x3 at $4.00 a unit, and that 300 units are sold for a total of $1,500.

	Units	FIFO	LIFO	Weighted Average
Sales revenue........	300	$1,500	$1,500	$1,500.00
Cost of goods sold:				
Beginning inventory...........	150	$1,005	$ 765	$ 898.35
Add purchases.....	200	800	800	800.00
Goods available....	350	$1,805	$1,565	$1,698.35
Ending inventory..	50	200	250	242.60
Cost of goods sold	300	1,605	1,315	1,455.75
Gross margin (loss)...		($ 105)	$ 185	$ 54.25

The ending inventories were computed as follows:

$$\text{FIFO: 50 units @ } \$4.00 = \$200$$

$$\text{LIFO: 50 units @ } \$5.00 = \$250$$

$$\text{Average: } \frac{\text{Cost of Goods Available, } \$1{,}698.35}{\text{Number of Units Available, } 350} = \text{Average Unit Cost, } \$4.852$$

$$50 \times \$4.852 = \text{Ending Inventory, } \$242.60$$

Effect of inventory methods on decisions

In the preceding illustrations, it has been assumed that the only financial elements which are changed as a result of the selection of one inventory method or another are those which are affected by the allocation of a given amount of acquisition costs between accounting periods:

(1) Cost of goods sold expense of the current period;
(2) Asset inventory at the end of the current period;
(3) Cost of goods sold and asset inventory in the future.

Actually, many other elements may change as a result of the selection of a particular inventory method. Management uses the income and asset information, which has been influenced by the inventory method, to decide what quantity of goods to buy, when to buy them, how much to pay for them, and what prices to sell them for. To the extent that the inventory method is unrealistic, it can lead management to unwise decisions in these matters.

The choice of an inventory method also affects the rate of flow of cash into and out of the business through its effect on purchase and sales decisions and its effect on the amount of income tax to be paid.

Recoverable cost of inventory

The inventory methods just described have shown four different ways of assigning the acquisition costs of inventory items to cost of goods sold expense and to the ending balance in the asset inventory. The justification for carrying *any* amount of cost forward as an asset is the expectation that the business will receive a future service benefit from it at least equal to its cost. There are many occasions in business when such future benefit cannot reasonably be expected.

EXAMPLE 1:   A business purchased two identical units, designated as Unit 1 and Unit 2, for $6 each in 19x1. Unit 1 was sold for $10 in 19x1 and Unit 2 is in the inventory, unsold, at the end of the year. The cost of the unit sold, $6, is an expense which should be matched against the revenue from its sale, $10, in 19x1. If it is expected that Unit 2 can be sold in 19x2 for $10 or more, its full original cost of $6 may appropriately be shown in the 19x1 ending inventory as an asset. Unit 2 should not be stated in the inventory at more than $6, because to do so would be to count revenue that has not yet been realized by sale.

EXAMPLE 2:   If, on the other hand, Unit 2 had been damaged prior to December 31, 19x1, and its expected resale price in 19x2 is less than $6, would it be proper to carry the original cost of $6 forward as an asset in the ending inventory?
Most businessmen and accountants would say "No," contending that the unsold unit has lost part of its economic significance.

There is substantial disagreement among accountants as to just what represents a decline in the economic significance of an inventory item sufficient to warrant reducing its amount in the asset account. This matter is covered by the accounting concept of *recoverable cost*, which means that the unexpired cost carried forward as ending inventory should not be greater than an amount which can properly be charged against the revenues expected in the future when the inventory items are used or sold.

The AICPA opinion: lower of cost or market

The view of the American Institute of Certified Public Accountants, a professional organization composed mostly of accounting practitioners, is stated in the following quotation:

When there is evidence that the utility of goods, in their disposal in the ordinary course of business, will be less than cost, whether due to physical deterioration, obsolescence, changes in price levels, or other causes, the difference should be recognized as a loss of the current period. This is generally accomplished by stating such goods at a lower level commonly designated as market.[2]

---

[2] *Ibid.*, p. 30.

The principle of measurement described above is carried out by using the *lower of cost or market* (L/CM) method to determine the amount of the ending inventory. *Market* as used here basically refers to the amount that it would cost at the end of the period to *replace* the inventory item, either by purchase or by manufacture. It relates to prices in the market in which the business *buys*, rather than in the market in which it sells. In determining the market replacement cost of purchased items, it is appropriate to use unit market prices quoted at the date of the inventory by the company's customary sources of supply for the quantities which it usually buys. If the market replacement cost of an item is *less* than its original cost, this is *tentative* evidence that the original cost of the item cannot be recovered. If market is *higher* than cost, the original cost is recoverable and should be used in measuring the item in the ending inventory. To use a market higher than cost in measuring the asset would be to anticipate revenue that has not yet been realized.

The fact that the market replacement cost of the item is less than cost is only *tentative* evidence that cost cannot be recovered. To make a *final* decision as to whether cost can be recovered, *upper and lower limits* are applied to the amount of market which is to be compared with cost.

The *upper limit* of the amount which may be used as the market value of an inventory item is its *net realizable value*—its estimated resale price in the ordinary course of business, less reasonably predictable costs of completing and selling it. If it were carried at a higher figure, a loss on its sale, which can reasonably be predicted now, would be postponed until the following accounting period.

The *lower limit* of market is *net realizable value, reduced by a normal profit margin* on the item. To measure an item in the inventory at a replacement cost lower than this figure would be to record a *loss* in the period in which the replacement cost declined and a *greater income than normal* in the following period when the item was sold.

EXAMPLE 3: A company has one of each of the following items in its ending inventory on December 31, 19x1. At what amount should each be stated under the lower-of-cost-or-market method?

Item	Original Cost	Replacement Cost December 31, 19x1	Net Realizable Value	Normal Profit Margin
A	$60	$54	$70	$10
B	60	54	60	9
C	60	54	50	8
D	60	54	80	11

Item	Replacement Cost	Upper Limit	Lower Limit	Market	Original Cost	Lower of Cost or Market
A	$54	$70	$60	$60	$60	$60
B	54	60	51	54	60	54
C	54	50	42	50	60	50
D	54	80	69	69	60	60

The reasoning behind the rule as applied to these items is discussed in Appendix 15-A.

To summarize, *market* means replacement cost, but not more than net realizable value and not less than net realizable value reduced by a normal profit margin. Market is then compared with the original cost of the item, as determined by the specific-identification, FIFO, or weighted-average method, and the lower of the two is used in measuring the asset, inventory, at the end of the period. The resulting inventory amount might more appropriately be called "the lower of cost or remaining useful cost."

The comparison of original cost and market may be made for individual items in the inventory, for classes of items, or for the inventory as a whole, depending upon which seems more appropriate for the particular business.

Although LIFO is a method of determining inventory cost, it does not seem appropriate to use it in conjunction with the lower-of-cost-or-market method of measuring inventory. The purpose of the L/CM method is to charge the lost cost of inventory items to the period in which the loss occurs rather than to the succeeding period when the items are sold. Under LIFO, usually little of the inventory balance carried forward is charged to expense in the succeeding period. Use of the two methods in combination would result in carrying forward for an indefinite time an unrealistically low asset balance.

The AAA view of recoverable inventory cost

The American Accounting Association, a professional organization composed principally of educators, has a different opinion regarding proper inventory measurement, stated as follows:

> The residual cost should be carried forward in the balance sheet for assignment in future periods except when it is evident that the cost of an item of inventory cannot be recovered, whether from damage, deterioration, obsolescence, style change, oversupply, reduction in price levels, or other cause. In such event the inventory item should be stated at the amount of sales proceeds less direct expense of the completion and disposal.[3]

The view of the AAA differs from that of the AICPA as to whether or not an inventory item which has declined in significance should be written down far enough to permit a normal profit margin to be recorded in the later period of sale. The AAA thinks that it should not, and would record no loss in the current period unless the net realizable value (without reduction for a normal profit margin) is expected to be less than cost.

---

[3] American Accounting Association, Committee on Concepts and Standards, *Accounting Concepts and Standards Underlying Corporate Financial Statements* (1948 Revision).

EXAMPLE 4: The inventory amounts determined by the AAA method, using the facts in Example 3, would be as follows:

Item	Original Cost	Net Realizable Value	Lower of Cost or Realizable Value
A............	$60	$70	$60
B............	60	60	60
C............	60	50	50
D............	60	80	60

The two methods differ in the inventory valuation of Item B. The AICPA lower-of-cost-or-market method would result in showing a loss of $6 on the item in 19x1, and a gain of $6 in 19x2 if expectations materialized. The AAA method would show no loss in 19x1, and neither gain nor loss in 19x2, when the cost is expected to be recovered exactly.

Recording reductions of inventory to market

When it is necessary to write down the amount of the asset, inventory, from original cost to market, the account debited should be as follows:

(1) *Cost of Goods Sold Expense*, or some similar expense, if the decline in cost contributed something to the revenue of the current period. This would be true in the case of obsolescence of an item which was acquired in order to offer a complete assortment of styles, or of the damage of an item which was used as a sample. Cost of Goods Sold Expense might also be debited for immaterial amounts of write-downs due to other causes.

(2) *Loss in Recoverable Cost of Inventory*, or some similar loss account shown separately from Cost of Goods Sold Expense, when the amount of the write-down is material or unusual.

Special problems in measuring inventories

In certain unusual situations, it is proper to measure inventories at a figure *higher* than cost. For precious metals, such as gold and silver, the government has established a fixed market price at which it stands ready to accept any quantity offered. The definiteness of the sale and of the selling price meet the test of realization, and such metals which are on hand in a refined state may be measured at their selling price, less the expected cost of marketing them.

Net selling price as a method of measuring inventory is applicable only if the item meets the following tests:

(1) Its cost cannot be determined;
(2) It can be sold immediately at a quoted market price; and
(3) Any unit of it is interchangeable with any other unit.

It is sometimes difficult to determine just what items should be included in the ending inventory. Use of the exact quantity of goods on hand is not always proper, because the legal title to some of them may have already passed to the customer. In addition, incoming items in transit at the end of the period should be included in ending inventory if title to them has already passed to the business. Careful attention is needed at the end of the accounting period and for a short time thereafter to insure that such items are excluded from, or included in, the inventory, whichever is proper.

Goods on hand which are held on consignment for sale for another business should not be included in inventory. On the other hand, goods which belong to the business but which are consigned to others for sale should be included as a part of the inventory. Memorandum records of goods on both incoming and outgoing consignments provide useful information in determining just what items should, and what should not, be included in inventory.

Disclosure of inventories in financial statements

Because there are so many different methods commonly used for determining the amount of the asset, inventory, and at the same time for determining the expired cost of inventory during the current period, it is essential that financial statements disclose clearly which method the company is using. This may be done parenthetically beside the item in the body of the statements or in a footnote to the statements by a phrase such as the following:

Inventories, at lower of FIFO cost or market........... $1,635,000

When the LIFO method is in use, it is desirable that the statement reader be informed of the approximate inventory amount under another method which better reflects the cost current at the date of the statement of financial position. Such additional information permits the reader to make more realistic comparisons which involve the use of the ending inventory amount.

If substantial quantities of goods are consigned to others, their amount should be disclosed separately from other inventories because of the greater degree of risk which attaches to them.

Summary

Inventory, which is composed of tangible personal property being produced or held for sale or use in the ordinary course of business, should be measured at its unexpired cost—the amount which is expected to be *recoverable* in future operations. Inventory costs properly include all expenditures reasonably required on the item up to the point when it is ready for sale.

When various lots of inventoriable items of a single type have been acquired at different unit costs, there is a problem of deciding which costs apply to the units on hand in the ending inventory. This problem may be resolved by *specifically identifying* costs with units on hand, or by using such assumed flows of cost as *first-in, first-out (FIFO)*, *weighted average*, or *last-in, first-out (LIFO)*. If there has been a decline in the *recoverable cost* of some of the items in the inventory, the decline can be measured by the use of the *lower-of-cost-or-market method* of the AICPA or the *lower-of-cost-or-net-realizable-value method* of the AAA. The inventory method selected should be the one which best meets the needs of the particular company. Each method can be evaluated by these general criteria:

(1) Will it give useful information?
(2) Will it permit a proper appraisal of management performance?
(3) Will it lead to the right action?

The specific criteria listed in the chapter should also be used in selecting an inventory method.

APPENDIX 15-A

Application of Lower of Cost or Market

The following illustrations, which were presented in condensed form in the chapter, are expanded to show the reasoning behind the lower-of-cost-or-market inventory method.

Item A: Decline in replacement cost; original cost fully recoverable

The business bought two units of Item A at $60 each in December and sold one for $100 during the month. The wholesale market price has declined, and on December 31, 19x1, the unsold item could be replaced for a cost of only $54. The wholesale price change has not been passed on to the consumer. The business expects that the item can be sold in January, 19x2, for $100, and that the cost of selling it will be $30. The company's net income margin on the item is normally 10 per cent of selling price, or $10. The original cost of the unsold item, $60, is fully recoverable at the end of 19x1, according to the following summary of expected results in 19x2:

Expected sales price..	$100
Deduct cost of selling..	30
Net realizable value..	$ 70
Deduct normal income margin................................	10
Net realizable value less normal income margin................	$ 60

According to the L/CM rule, market cannot be less than $60. This amount is the same as original cost, $60, and is the proper measurement of the ending inventory.

Item B: Decline in replacement cost; reduction in normal income

The facts are the same as for Item A, except that the selling price in 19x2 is expected to be $90. The 10 per cent normal income margin will amount to $9.

Expected sales price	$90
Deduct cost of selling	30
Net realizable value	$60
Deduct normal income margin	9
Net realizable value less normal income margin	$51

The replacement cost, $54, falls between the lower market limit of $51 and the upper limit of $60. *Market* is thus $54, and, since it is lower than original cost, $60, market is used in measuring the ending inventory.

In this case $6, the difference between the item's original cost of $60 and its market of $54, is treated as an expense of 19x1. The income on this item in 19x2 will probably be $6 ($90 sales − $54 cost of goods sold − $30 selling costs). This is less than the normal income of $9.

Item C: Decline in replacement cost; no income expected

The facts are the same as for Item A, except that the expected selling price in 19x2 is $80 and the normal income margin is $8.

Expected sales price	$80
Deduct cost of selling	30
Net realizable value	$50
Deduct normal income margin	8
Net realizable value less normal income margin	$42

Because the replacement cost, $54, is higher than the upper market limit of $50, market is $50. Since cost is $60, market is used in measuring the ending inventory.

A loss of $10 in the recoverable cost of the unsold item is recorded in 19x1, reducing the asset inventory. In 19x2 there will probably be net income of zero ($80 sales − $50 cost of goods sold − $30 selling costs) on the item. The loss is recorded in 19x1 when it becomes evident that it will occur, rather than being postponed until 19x2.

Item D: Decline in replacement cost; abnormal income expected

The facts are the same as for Item A, except that the expected resale price is $110 and the normal income on the item is $11.

Expected sales price.......................................	$110
Deduct cost of selling......................................	30
Net realizable value.......................................	$ 80
Deduct normal income margin..............................	11
Net realizable value less normal income margin...............	$ 69

Replacement cost of $54 in this case is lower than the lower limit of market, $69; therefore, market is $69. The cost of $60, which is lower than market, is used in measuring the inventory. If events turn out as expected, there will be an income of $20 on Item D in 19x2, $9 more than normal.

SUMMARY OF L/CM CASES

	Item A	Item B	Item C	Item D
(a) Replacement cost........................	$ 54	$54	$54	$ 54
(b) Upper limit—net realizable value...........	70	60	50	80
(c) Lower limit—net realizable value less normal income..............................	60	51	42	69
(d) Market, (a), but not more than (b) nor less than (c)...............................	$ 60	$54	$50	$ 69
(e) Cost.....................................	60	60	60	60
(f) Inventory amount [lower of (d) or (e)]......	$ 60	$54	$50	$ 60
Expected 19x2 Results				
Sales revenue.........................	$100	$90	$80	$110
Cost of goods sold.....................	60	54	50	60
Gross margin..........................	$ 40	$36	$30	$ 50
Cost of selling........................	30	30	30	30
Net income, 19x2......................	$ 10	$ 6	$ 0	$ 20
Inventory loss, 19x1...................	$ 0	($ 6)	($10)	$ 0

Objections to lower of cost or market

Chapter 15 discussed the objection of the AAA to the lower-of-cost-or-market method on the ground that it sometimes permits *income* to be recognized on an item in the year of its sale by recording a *loss* in a prior year. The results for Item B illustrate this point.

A comparison of the results for Item C and Item D reveals another weakness of the lower-of-cost-or-market method. For Item C, it shows a loss of $10 resulting from a price decline in the year prior to sale; for Item D, the additional gain from increased selling prices is not recognized until the period of the actual sale. Critics argue that it is inconsistent thus to anticipate losses but not to anticipate gains.

A further charge of inconsistency of L/CM is based on the argument that often in the inventory at a particular date some items are measured on the basis of market while others are stated at cost.

L/CM is also criticized because it is complicated.

It is well to understand the purposes and weaknesses of the L/CM method because, in spite of its shortcomings, it is used by a large majority of businesses in measuring a part or all of their inventories.

QUESTIONS AND PROBLEMS

15-1 Inventories are sometimes described as *product costs*, as distinguished from *period costs*.

REQUIRED:

a. Explain the difference between period costs and product costs, stating how each is used in measuring the income for a period and the financial status at a given time.
b. Give an example of each type of cost in the accounts of (1) a retailer and (2) a manufacturer.

15-2 "Inventory costs properly include all expenditures reasonably required on the item up to the point when it is ready for sale."

REQUIRED:

a. Give three examples of types of cost which could be included in the inventory of a retailer under this rule, and explain why each is a proper element of the cost of an asset.
b. Give three examples of costs which are associated with selling goods which should not be included in the asset, inventory, and explain why they should be excluded.
c. Explain how the concept of recoverable cost of inventory is related to the term "expenditures *reasonably* required" in the quoted rule.

15-3

REQUIRED:

Give an illustration of how the concept of recoverable cost might be applied to an asset other than inventory.

15-4 On December 31, 19x1, the end of the first year of operations, the management of a company is trying to decide whether to use the FIFO or the LIFO method in measuring the inventory. It finds that the LIFO method would produce the higher asset amount.

REQUIRED:

a. Which method would produce the higher cost of goods sold?
b. Which method would produce the higher net income for 19x1?
c. Which method would produce the higher cost of goods available for sale?
d. In what direction have prices been moving during the year? Explain.

15-5 In 19x2 the company described in Problem 15-4 increased the quantity in its inventory. The unit cost of goods bought during 19x2 increased steadily.

REQUIRED:

a. Under what circumstances would LIFO result in a greater income for 19x2? Illustrate.
b. Under what circumstances would FIFO result in a greater income for 19x2? Illustrate.

15-6 The purchasing agent of your company contracted to buy some goods, which were delivered in December at a contract price of $10,000. Soon afterward, and before the goods were sold, he discovered that by shopping around he could have obtained goods of identical quality for $9,000.

REQUIRED:

Discuss the proper accounting treatment of this situation.

15-7 A corporation which uses the calendar year as its accounting period changed its method of determining inventory effective January 1, 19x2. In the 19x1 statements, the ending inventory was costed by the FIFO method, while the December 31, 19x2, inventory was determined by the LIFO method.

REQUIRED:

a. Discuss the implications of this change with respect to persons who read the corporation's 19x2 financial statements.
b. What items in the 19x2 financial statements would be affected by the change?
c. Using figures of your own choice, show exactly how you would explain the effect of the change to the reader of the financial statements.

15-8

REQUIRED:

Criticize each of the following statements:

a. "I know exactly the cost of my ending inventory," says a retailer, "because I have the original cost of each item marked on it in code."
b. "FIFO is the only method we can use to determine inventory cost," says the retail grocer. "We must move our old stock first, or our loss from deterioration would be exorbitant."
c. "Average cost is the only inventory method open to us," argues the grain elevator operator. "After we have stored the grain, it is impossible to distinguish one shipment from another."
d. "Cost of goods sold should be charged with the replacement cost of each item sold. You haven't made a profit until you have replaced the inventory item. LIFO is the only acceptable method, because it charges replacement costs to cost of goods sold."

15-9

REQUIRED:

a. Determine the proper amount to include in December 31, 19x1, inventory for Article K under the lower cost or market (L/CM) method.
b. If the expected results materialize in 19x2, how would they be shown in condensed income statement form?
c. Can you justify the use of L/CM in this situation? How?

Units on hand December 31, 19x1	400
Unit cost	$15
Customary selling price	$25
Unit replacement cost, December 31, 19x1	$13
Expected selling price in 19x2	$22
Expected direct costs of sale in 19x2	$ 6

Customary income margin is 10 per cent of selling price.

15-10 The Ybor Company uses lower of FIFO cost or market in measuring its ending inventory.

REQUIRED:

From the following data, determine its ending inventory on December 31, 19x3:

Inventory, 12/31/19x2	1,000 units @ $33
19x3 purchases:	
Jan. 18	500 units @ 34
Mar. 20	500 units @ 35
Jul. 1	500 units @ 35
Sept. 5	500 units @ 36
Dec. 19	500 units @ 37

During 19x3, 2,400 units were sold for a total of $120,000 cash. A physical inventory taken on December 31, 19x3, revealed that 1,060 units were on hand. The manufacturer from whom the Ybor Company usually made its purchases quoted a price of $38 in lots of 500 units on December 31. Expected resale price in 19x4 was $55 a unit; expected cost of selling, $15 a unit; and normal income margin, $5.50 a unit.

15-11. The Berg Corporation began business on January 1, 19x4. Information about its inventories under different valuation methods is shown below.

REQUIRED:

Using this information, you are to choose the phrase which most accurately completes each of the numbered statements. Select the letter of the best answer, and present a computation or explanation to support your choice.

	\multicolumn{4}{c}{Inventory Measurement}
Date	LIFO Cost	FIFO Cost	Market	Lower of Cost or Market
Dec. 31, 19x4	$10,200	$10,000	$ 9,600	$ 8,900
Dec. 31, 19x5	9,100	9,000	8,800	8,500
Dec. 31, 19x6	10,300	11,000	12,000	10,900

(1) The inventory basis which would show the highest net income for 19x4 is: (a) LIFO cost; (b) FIFO cost; (c) market; (d) lower of cost or market.

(2) The inventory basis which would show the highest net income for 19x5 is: (a) LIFO cost; (b) FIFO cost; (c) market; (d) lower of cost or market.

(3) The inventory basis which would show the lowest net income for the three years combined is: (a) LIFO cost; (b) FIFO cost; (c) market; (d) lower of cost or market.

(4) For the year 19x5, how much higher or lower would profits be on the FIFO cost basis than on the lower-of-cost-or-market basis? (a) $400 higher; (b) $400 lower; (c) $600 higher; (d) $600 lower; (e) $1,000 higher; (f) $1,000 lower; (g) $1,400 higher; (h) $1,400 lower.

(5) On the basis of the information given, it appears that the movement of prices for the items in the inventory was: (a) up in 19x4 and down in 19x6; (b) up in both 19x4 and 19x6; (c) down in 19x4 and up in 19x6; (d) down in both 19x4 and 19x6.

(Adapted from AICPA Examination in Theory of Accounts, November, 1956)

15-12 The Artho Company, organized in 19x1 to sell a single product, is attempting to decide for practical purposes which elements of cost to include in inventory as product costs and which to treat as period costs. The following data were taken from its records for 19x1.

Sales revenue.	$220,000
Invoice cost of purchases (all on terms of net 30 days, and all at the same unit cost).	210,000
Freight, express, and postage on incoming shipments.	14,700
Invoice cost of purchases returned for credit.	10,000
Transportation charges on returned purchases.	700
Transportation charges on sales.	11,000
Cost of operating the receiving department.	8,400
Cost of operating the stores department.	16,800
Cost of operating the shipping department.	10,500
Advertising.	13,200
Sales commissions (paid when goods are shipped).	21,000
General administration.	11,850

Ending inventory was 40% of goods remaining after purchase returns.

REQUIRED:

a. State which of the amounts should in theory be treated as a part of inventory cost.

b. Describe the chief practical difficulties involved in following this theoretical treatment for particular items.

c. Prepare an income statement for 19x1 showing in detail the components of cost of goods sold, using the theoretical classification which you recommended in (a). (Ignore income tax.)

d. Prepare an alternative income statement treating all costs other than invoice cost as period costs.

e. Comment on the comparative effects of (c) and (d) on 19x1 income and on the December 31, 19x1, financial position.

f. State in general terms what the comparative effects of the methods used in (c) and (d) would be upon the income and the financial position in 19x2.

15-13 The following situations deal with the choice of an appropriate inventory method.

REQUIRED:

For each situation, state (1) on the basis of the data given, what method you would use for measuring ending inventory, and why; and (2) what additional information you would need before arriving at a final conclusion as to the appropriate method.

a. A grocer has annual sales of about $1,000,000. His average inventory is usually about $80,000, his total current assets are about $120,000, and his total assets are about $140,000. His net income for the past few years has ranged from $8,000 to $13,000. During recent years, purchase prices have risen about 1 per cent a year on the average, and sale prices have followed suit promptly.

b. A ladies' dress shop has annual sales of about $100,000. Its average inventory is usually about $15,000, its total current assets are about $40,000, and its total assets are about $55,000. Its net income during the past few years has ranged from $2,500 to $5,000. Frequent markdowns are necessary because of style changes and shopwear.

c. A textile manufacturer has annual sales of about $2,000,000. The principal raw material usually constitutes about 60 per cent of the final cost of manufacturing the product, and in recent years it has not been uncommon for the price of the raw material to increase or decrease as much as 15 per cent in a single year. The other costs of production are rather stable, and the company has had difficulty passing price increases on to its customers because of competition from other types of textiles. The average cost of the principal raw material on hand in raw materials, work in process, and finished goods inventories is usually about $70,000. Total current assets usually average about $150,000 and total assets, about $300,000. Income in the past few years has ranged from a loss of $20,000 to a net income of $50,000.

d. A public accounting firm finds it necessary to keep a variety of stationery and forms on hand. The gross revenue of the firm is usually about $100,000. The principal expense is salaries, which average about $40,000. Office supplies used during a year usually amount to about $2,000. At any given time, the amount of supplies on hand is about one-fourth of the annual usage. The total net income of the partners of the firm is usually about $45,000. Total assets average about $10,000, of which about half is composed of receivables from clients.

15-14   At the end of 19x1, its first year of operations, a company had 300 units of a class of merchandise on hand, each of which had been purchased at a cost of $10. During 19x2 it made the following purchases:

Mar. 17	200 units @ $9
May 25	100 units @ 8
Aug. 14	100 units @ 7
Oct. 3	300 units @ 6
Dec. 5	200 units @ 5

A physical count on December 31, 19x2, showed that there were 400 units on hand.

REQUIRED:

Compute the December 31, 19x2, inventory under each of the following methods:

a. FIFO.
b. LIFO.
c. Weighted average.

15-15   The Montague Company, seeking to introduce its product into new territories, adopted the practice of consigning some of its goods to retailers. These retailers were to send the proceeds of sales, less a commission of 25 per cent of the sales price, to the Montague Company immediately after the sales were made. In 19x1 the company purchased goods costing $80,000 for cash and sold half of them outright to its regular customers for $65,000 cash. It paid operating expenses of $18,000 in cash during the year.

The company also shipped goods costing $30,000 to various retailers on consignment, paying in cash $3,000 freight on the shipments. By the end of the year, the retailers had reported sales of two-thirds of the goods for a total sales price of $40,000. The Montague Company had collected cash for the sales price, minus the sales commission.

REQUIRED:

a. Show how the pertinent facts from the preceding information would be disclosed in the income statement of the Montague Company for 19x1.
b. Give in detail the company's presentation of inventory in the December 31, 19x1, statement of financial position.

15-16   Karlsen Corporation, which measures its inventory at the lower of average cost or market, had the following results at the end of its fiscal year, April 30, 19x4:

	Item A	Item B	Item C	Item D
Number of units..........................	2,000	20	100	10
Average unit cost..........................	$4.00	$ 8.50	$2.00	$75.50
Replacement cost, 4/30/x4.................	4.50	7.50	1.80	60.00
Expected net realizable value................	5.50	10.00	1.90	80.00
Expected net realization value minus a normal income margin..........................	4.40	8.00	1.40	70.00

REQUIRED:

Prepare an orderly schedule to show (1) the market inventory valuation of each type of item on April 30, under the AICPA method, (2) the amount at which each class of item would be measured in the April 30 inventory, and (3) the total inventory of Karlsen Corporation on April 30.

CASE 15-1. RIDDLEVILLE MFG. CO.

Early in January, 19x2, Mr. Sims, president of Riddleville Mfg. Co., was reviewing the operating results of the company for 19x1. The company accountant, Mr. Newman, had furnished him the following condensed information:

Sales (20,000 units)...................................		$100,000
Deduct cost of goods sold:		
Inventory, January 1, 19x1 (25,000 units)......	$ 75,000	
Add cost of goods manufactured (40,000 units)	160,000	
Cost of goods available for sale.............	$235,000	
Deduct inventory, December 31, 19x1 (FIFO)..	175,000	
Cost of goods sold................................		60,000
Gross margin...		$ 40,000
Deduct other operating expenses:		
Expenses variable with sales..................	$ 10,000	
Fixed expenses...............................	27,000	37,000
Net income before income tax...........................		$ 3,000
Deduct Federal income tax (30%).......................		900
Net income..		$ 2,100

The inventory consisted solely of finished goods, as was customary in the business.

Mr. Sims was very disappointed at the poor showing, particularly since the total assets used in the business averaged about $70,000. He asked the accountant to prepare an analysis of the net income on each unit so that he could plan corrective action for the future. The resulting analysis, in condensed form, was as follows:

Selling price per unit, 19x1...............................		$5.00
Cost per unit:		
Manufacturing cost...............................	$4.00	
Variable expense...................................	.50	
Average fixed expense ($27,000 divided by 20,000 units)	1.35	5.85
Net loss per unit, at current cost..........................		($0.85)

Mr. Newman pointed out that in this special analysis he had used the current unit manufacturing cost of $4.00, rather than the $3.00 cost per unit from the beginning inventory which had been treated as cost of goods sold in the income statement. He thought this figure would be more useful to Mr. Sims in planning for 19x2.

Mr. Sims reviewed the company's production costs carefully, and in 19x2 inaugurated an extensive campaign to increase production efficiency. As a result, unit costs of production in 19x2 were $3.00. He was also able to reduce the costs of operating the general office by $2,000. Because of the cost economies, Riddleville Mfg. Co. held its selling price at $5.00 a unit in spite of a rising trend of prices in the industry. As a result, sales volume went up to 25,000 units in 19x2.

Mr. Sims was very pleased with the results in 19x2 and made the following computation before he received the annual financial statements from Mr. Newman:

Selling price per unit, 19x2		$5.00
Cost per unit:		
Manufacturing cost	$3.00	
Variable expense	.50	
Average fixed expense ($25,000 divided by 25,000 units)	1.00	4.50
Net income per unit, before income tax		$0.50
Federal income tax per unit		0.15
Net income per unit		$0.35

Multiplying the $0.35 net income per unit by the 25,000 units sold, Mr. Sims estimated that the net income of the company for 19x2 was $8,750.

Three days later, when Mr. Newman presented an income statement showing a substantial net loss, Mr. Sims was visibly shaken. He verified the accuracy of the quantities and other data in his calculation, and found that they were in agreement with those of Mr. Newman except for cost of goods sold and beginning and ending inventories. When he challenged the accuracy of those amounts, Mr. Newman replied, "They have been computed correctly under generally accepted accounting principles." Mr. Sims exploded.

REQUIRED:

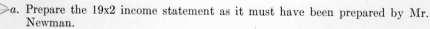
a. Prepare the 19x2 income statement as it must have been prepared by Mr. Newman.

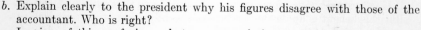
b. Explain clearly to the president why his figures disagree with those of the accountant. Who is right?

c. In view of this confusion, what recommendations would you make for the future?

CASE 15-2. THE BARRETT DRESS SHOP

The Barrett Dress Shop makes all of its purchases on terms of 3 per cent 10 days E.O.M. During December, 19x1, its first month of operations, it made purchases on account having an invoice cost of $20,000, before considering discount. Merchandise having an invoice cost of $5,000 was sold for $8,000 cash in December. None of the purchase invoices were paid in December.

Mr. Spears, the shop's bookkeeper, made the following type of entry at the time of each purchase:

A, Merchandise Inventory	100	
L, Accounts Payable		100
Purchased merchandise on account, list price $100, terms 3/10 E.O.M.		

Contending that a discount is not earned until the bill is paid, he planned to make the following type of entry at the time each invoice was paid:

```
  L, Accounts Payable.....................................  100
     A, Cash.................................................       97
     OE, Purchase Discount Revenue.....................        3
```

The shop used a perpetual inventory system.

The Barrett Dress Shop paid for all of its December, 19x1, purchases before January 10, 19x2. In January its total purchases on account were $30,000 at list price, all on terms of 3/10 E.O.M. Goods having an invoice cost of $9,000 were sold to customers for $15,000 cash.

REQUIRED:

a. Show how these facts would appear in journal entries and in financial statements for December, 19x1, under Mr. Spears' method.

b. Show how the journal entries and financial statements would appear for January, 19x2, under Mr. Spears' method.

c. Show how the facts for both months would appear under the method which you have previously been taught to use.

d. What advantages and disadvantages do you see in Mr. Spears' method for presenting the results in December? In January?

e. What method would you recommend that the company use? Why?

CASE 15-3. LIQUIDATION OF LIFO INVENTORY

Part I. Some Steel Users Seek to Avoid a Strike-Caused Tax Detriment

The following item is reprinted from the "Tax Report" column of the *Wall Street Journal* of October, 14, 1959, p. 1:

"Under the 'last-in, first-out' method of valuing inventories for tax purposes, materials used up in production are figured at current replacement costs, rather than actual earlier purchase costs. In times of rising prices, this 'LIFO' system boosts reported production costs and thus cuts taxable profits. But this benefit is applicable only to an inventory whose physical quantity equals or exceeds that of a year earlier. If the inventory is smaller, a taxable profit must be reported on that part of the inventory which has been sold or used up and not replaced. This extra profit is the excess of the sale value over original cost.

"Even with early resumption of steel output, many steel users may be unable to rebuild their strike-riddled stocks by the end of the year to the level that existed at the end of 1958. To avoid tax on any 'profit' resulting from such liquidation, some 'LIFO' firms have moved up the closing dates of their fiscal years to the end of last June or July, when inventories were still up. Under the law, a corporation may change its annual accounting period without prior approval of the Revenue Service if, among other things, it hasn't made such a switch within the prior ten years.

"Companies making such an automatic change must file a return for the 'short' year no later than two and a half months after its close. In the case of a July 31 year-end, the deadline is tomorrow.

*   *   *

"OTHER COMPANIES look to Congress for possible relief.

"These are firms that are unable or don't want to change fiscal years. They pump for a law change to revive a war-time provision excusing tax on any involuntary liquidation 'profit.' Such a clause was last in effect during the Korean War period and has expired.

"House Ways and Means Committee sources say it's possible the question of providing for involuntary inventory liquidations resulting from long strikes may be brought up at the group's tax hearings next month. Treasury officials say, however, they don't have any indication yet that the problem will still exist by the end of the year."

Part II. An Illustration of LIFO Liquidation

A business which had been using the LIFO method for costing its inventory for more than 20 years had a 19x2 beginning inventory of 10,000 units at a cost of $5 a unit. In 19x2 the employees of the company's principal supplier engaged in a prolonged strike. Sales of 20,000 units for a total of $1,000,000 were filled partly by making purchases of 12,000 units in 19x2 at $30 a unit and partly by reducing the ending inventory to 2,000 units. A partial income statement for 19x1 had shown the following results:

Sales (25,000 units)..................................... $1,200,000
Deduct cost of goods sold............................   720,000
Gross margin.. $ 480,000

REQUIRED:

a. Apart from the effect of LIFO in this case on the income of the company which is subject to income tax in 19x2, how would you suggest that the company report its 19x2 affairs in its income statement and statement of financial position? Why?

b. What are the implications of your suggestion in (a) for the general-purpose financial statements of the company in future years?

c. Does this situation invalidate the use of the LIFO inventory method in reporting business results? If not, what modification of LIFO would be appropriate in such cases?

d. Comment on the desirability of changing a company's fiscal period to cope with such a difficulty, in connection with general-purpose financial reports.

CASE 15-4. BERNADOT, INC.

Bernadot, Inc., has determined its inventory by FIFO cost for the years 19x1, 19x2, and 19x3. Now, at the beginning of 19x4, it wishes to consider changing to one of the three following methods, each computed at the end of the year:

(1) LIFO cost;
(2) Weighted-average cost;
(3) Average of current year's purchase costs.

The following data were taken from the records:

	19x1		19x2		19x3	
	Quantity	Amount	Quantity	Amount	Quantity	Amount
Sales.............	1,500	$50,000	2,000	$100,000	2,500	$100,000
Beginning inventory..........	0		1,000	?	1,500	?
Purchases in chronological order:						
....	1,500	30,000	1,000	30,000	500	15,500
....	1,000	25,000	1,000	32,500	1,000	25,000
....			500	17,000	1,000	20,000

There were no inventory shortages during any of the years.

REQUIRED:

a. For the present method and for each of the proposed methods, set up a columnar schedule to show, for 19x1, 19x2, 19x3, and total of the three years, the following items: (1) sales; (2) cost of goods sold, and its components, beginning inventory, purchases, and ending inventory; (3) amount of gross margin; and (4) per cent of gross margin to sales.

b. Construct a graph or graphs showing, for each of the four inventory methods: (1) average selling price of each unit for each year and (2) average unit cost of goods sold for each year.

c. Draw such conclusions as you can as to the effect of each method on income and ending asset balances (1) when prices are rising and (2) when prices are declining.

d. What are the strong and weak points of each method under the circumstances of this case?

e. What would be the probable effect of the adoption of each of the methods on the readers of the company's financial statements?

f. Which method would you recommend that Bernadot, Inc., use in the future? Why?

CASE 15-5. BIG ESSEX AGENCY

Your company, the Big Essex Agency, sells new and used cars and has a service department. At statement date, April 30, 1956, the used car inventory consisted of four cars.

	Used Car Number			
	1	2	3	4
Allowed on trade-in	$1,700	$2,400	$1,000	$1,400
Over-allowance (1)	300	300	200	200
Service Department charges for work on car (2)	60	—	40	160
National Auto Dealers Association estimate of market value (at retail):				
At time of trade-in	1,600	2,200	875	1,200
At audit date	1,550	2,200	850	1,150
Probable sale price if sold during May 1956 (3)	1,600	2,150	825	1,300

Note (1). During the year, new cars were being sold at less than list where no trade-in was involved. The amounts in this line represent the discount that would have been allowed on the new car sold had that new car been sold for cash with no trade-in.

Note (2). The service department makes necessary repairs on used cars traded in and bills the used car department at cost plus a 33⅓ per cent mark-up. The amounts in this line are the bills from the service department.

Note (3). With the exception of cars 2 and 4, which are still on hand, the used cars were sold for cash during the first week of May, 1956, at the amounts shown on this line.

REQUIRED:

Discuss the various factors which should be considered in assigning a value to the inventory of used cars. Indicate the computations needed to arrive at an acceptable inventory value for each car as at April 30, 1956. (Adapted from AICPA Examination in Theory of Accounts, May, 1956.)

Chapter 16

Planning and Controlling Inventory

The preceding chapter treated inventory as though it were a homogeneous asset which could be measured and controlled in a single way. Actually, in most businesses it is not. Included in the total inventory of many businesses are items that are dissimilar in economic as well as in physical characteristics. The need for certain classes of inventory items may be declining while the need for others is growing; some selling prices and costs may be rising while others are falling; and the physical characteristics of different classes of inventory may require diverse methods of physical handling, storing, recordkeeping, and measuring in terms of money.

Objective of inventory planning

The objective of inventory planning is to try to maintain the investment in inventories at the lowest amount which is sufficient to meet the production, sales, and financial requirements of the enterprise. The inventory must be adequate to maintain an efficient level of operations and to meet, within reason, the needs of customers. However, it must not be greater than is necessary to meet these requirements because of the interest cost, and sometimes the lack of availability of capital for investment in inventory; the cost of handling and storing excessive quantities of inventory; the dangers of adverse price changes and obsolescence; and the increased exposure to physical deterioration.

This chapter explains some of the problems which are associated with planning the investment in inventories and suggests approaches to solving them. It outlines some of the most widely accepted methods of setting standards of performance for controlling inventory, together with ways of appraising actual performance.

The loss from a combination of the causes listed, and often from a single one of them alone, may far exceed losses to the business as a result of fraud.

EXAMPLE 1:   A business with total assets of $100,000 had an average inventory balance of $40,000. A careful study revealed methods of reducing this inventory to $20,000 while continuing to serve the customers' needs adequately. The company was able to reduce its annual interest cost for borrowing money to finance the inventory balance by $1,200. The savings in reduced handling and storage costs and reduced exposure to damage, obsolescence, and price declines were much greater.

Perpetual inventory records as a basis for control

As an aid to efficiency in planning, purchasing, and controlling the size of inventory balances, many businesses find it desirable to keep detailed perpetual inventory records of each item or major class of items. Such records provide current information about the receipts, issues, and balances on hand of each inventory class.

The following are some of the advantages of perpetual inventory records:

(1) They provide current information about quantities on hand, so that orders can be placed at appropriate times.

(2) They provide a starting point in planning the size and timing of future orders by furnishing a record of the number of units of each inventory item actually issued during a past period of time.

(3) They give information needed in preparing financial statements quickly, without the necessity of taking a physical inventory.

(4) They furnish for control purposes a record of the inventory quantities that *should be* on hand. The subsidiary inventory ledger balances, when compared with the results of a periodic physical count, give information about the extent of inventory shortages, overages, and clerical errors in the procedures of receiving and issuing inventory items and of keeping records.

The simplest of such perpetual inventory subsidiary accounts are kept in terms of *quantities only*, along the lines shown in the illustration at the top of page 474.

Inventory cards kept in terms of quantities only have the advantages of simplicity and relatively low clerical cost. However, they also have certain limitations. Since the quantities of different types of articles are not stated in the common denominator of money cost, the balances of the

PERPETUAL INVENTORY CARD (Quantities only)

Description of item	Z	Standard order quantity	300
Location Aisle 4, Shelf 6		Order point	150
Unit of measure Pound			

Date	Receipts	Issues		Balance
		Amount	Quarterly Total	
19x2				
1/1....................				340
1/9....................		40		300
2/5....................		60		240
2/20...................		50		190
3/7....................		60		130
3/15...................	300			430
3/21...................		40	250	390
4/1–6/30*.............	300		310	380
7/1–9/30*.............	300		390	290
10/1–12/31*..........	300		370	220
Yearly Totals..........	1,200		1,320	

* Details omitted to condense illustration.

various subsidiary accounts cannot be combined. As a result, it is difficult to provide reports which show the investment in major classes of inventory. It is also impossible to prove the balances of the detailed quantity records with the general ledger account, Inventory, which is stated in terms of money.

PERPETUAL INVENTORY CARD (Quantities and costs)

Description of item	Y	Standard order quantity	144
Location Aisle 4, Shelves 9–12		Order point	96
Unit of measure Number			

Date	Ref.	Receipts		Issues		Balance on Hand		
		Quantity	Total Cost	Quantity	Total Cost	Quantity	Total Cost	Unit Cost
19x2								
1/ 1						160	800.00	5.00
1/ 9	M831			10	50.00	150	750.00	5.00
1/30	M882			70	350.00	80	400.00	5.00
2/ 8	P 26	144	720.00			224	1,120.00	5.00

Detailed inventory accounts expressed in terms of *dollars of cost* as well as quantities provide a useful means of planning the financial requirements of the inventory, appraising over-all performance in managing inventories, and checking upon the accuracy of inventory accounting. Such records are more detailed and present more complex problems than do records of quantities alone. They are practical only in those situations where the quantities of individual items handled or their unit costs are large enough to warrant the cost of the clerical work of keeping records.

The basic types of information shown in the table at the bottom of page 474 are usually found in detailed inventory cards which show costs.

In addition to quantity and cost data, it is sometimes useful to maintain on the subsidiary inventory cards information on *quantities ordered, quantities reserved* for special use so that they will be available when needed, and *customary sources of supply.*

Planning physical quantities

Planning the needed *additions* to inventory by purchase or manufacture, setting the proper levels for *inventory balances,* and planning *issues or sales* of inventory items should ordinarily be done first in terms of physical quantities of each inventory class. The expected quantities required and the necessary acquisitions of each inventory class may be computed as follows:

	Units
Planned inventory at the end of the current period............	100
Add expected sales (or issues) during the period................	50
Total units required.......................................	150
Deduct units in beginning inventory.........................	55
Total units to be acquired during the period.................	95

The section "Setting standards for inventory balances" later in this chapter discusses some of the considerations which are important in planning the future level of each class of inventory.

If there is a substantial time lag between the placing and filling of orders, or between the beginning and end of the manufacturing process, it is very important that acquisitions be carefully planned well in advance so that they will arrive when needed. Formal accounting entries, expressed in terms of debits and credits, are not made at the time orders are placed for future delivery. Assets and equities are not affected until the title to the items actually passes. However, it is essential that a business have an accurate memorandum record of outstanding orders by classes of inventory to aid in the proper scheduling of future orders and deliveries and to avoid duplicate orders. These memoranda may contain the following types of information:

	Units
Quantity on order at the beginning of the period..............	105
Add orders placed during the current period..................	100
Total...	205
Deduct orders filled during the current period................	95
Quantity on order at the end of the period...................	110

The information may be expanded to include money amounts, and also the quantities scheduled for delivery in each future period.

Converting units to money costs

Planning in terms of physical units as illustrated above may be impractical if the variety of inventory classes is very large. Whether or not this is true, however, the physical quantities of inventory items to be purchased should be converted into the common denominator of money costs to facilitate planning the means of financing them. The cost of planned inventory acquisitions will appear as an important component of the cash forecast and of other parts of the financial budget.

Controlling the amount of the money investment in inventory and taking steps to improve its profitability likewise require cost data. Total future inventory requirements in dollars can be determined by multiplying the quantity of each class of inventory by its unit cost and then adding together the resulting costs.

Timing acquisitions

It is important to determine the total amounts of various classes of inventory required during an entire accounting period, but that is not enough. The *right quantities* must also be on hand at the *right time*. There must be a delicate balance between too little and too much.

If the quantities on hand are *insufficient*, there may be costly delays or shutdowns while the company is waiting for an emergency order to be filled. Placing special orders for items of merchandise or raw material often entails excessive cost. Special runs of items which the company manufactures may require costly set-up time, uneconomical production runs, and overtime premiums for employees. Sales orders may be lost because a particular item desired by a customer is not in stock and cannot be obtained soon enough to fill his need.

At the other extreme, inventory can become *too large*. A policy of having everything in stock that might ever possibly be needed, or of having excessive quantities on reserve, ties up capital needlessly and causes unnecessary costs associated with storage and handling, warehouse space, insurance, deterioration of inventory, risk from price fluctuations, and interest on investment in inventory.

Action to control the balance of inventory on hand may consist of measures to control the *withdrawals* from inventory or measures to control inventory *additions*. In connection with the former, a great deal can often be done by special promotions to stimulate sales in what would otherwise be an off season or by efforts to level seasonal peaks and dips in quantities of materials used. However, most companies find that more can be done to control inventory balances by *efficient timing of purchases*.

Two guides which are often used in improving the timing of purchases are an *order point* and a *standard order quantity* for each type of inventory.

Order point

The *order point* is the *minimum level* which the balance of an inventory item should be allowed to reach before a replenishing order is placed. The order point should be set at a balance which will be sufficient, with a margin of safety, to meet expected requirements for withdrawal from inventory until the ordered items arrive.

The order point should be determined by estimating how much of the inventory item will be used in the *future period* after the order is placed and before it is filled. The time required for filling the order will depend upon the time necessary to place the order and the time the supplier needs to fill and ship it. The dependability of the sources of supply and variations in the rate of usage from time to time will determine what margin of safety should be included in the minimum balance.

EXAMPLE 2:   The normal usage of material X is 900 pounds a month. The time needed to place an order and to have it filled by the supplier is ordinarily 10 days, although occasionally the required time has been as much as 12 days. What should the order point be?

SOLUTION: Management feels that a margin of safety of 5-days' supply is needed, and therefore sets the order point at 15-days' supply, or 450 pounds. If a replenishing order is placed when the quantity on hand reaches this point, if the order requires 10 days to be filled, and if the rate of usage is normal, there will be 150 pounds (the margin of safety) on hand when the items arrive.

Balance when order was placed........................ 450 pounds
Deduct usage during 10 days (⅓ of 900 pounds)........ 300   "
Balance when order is filled........................... 150   "

Order points should be reviewed at frequent intervals and should be revised if changes in conditions warrant. The rate of usage of a given class of inventory may change from time to time, as may the time required to place and fill an order. If the order points are not revised, dangerous shortages or excessive inventory accumulations may result.

Standard order quantity

The *standard order quantity* for each type of inventory is the size of order that should be placed to keep the total costs related to inventory at a minimum. It is determined by trying to *minimize the total* of two types of costs which move in opposite directions:

(1) *Costs of ordering*, which tend to be relatively fixed in amount for each order that is placed and which therefore vary in total in proportion to the number of separate orders placed to acquire a given quantity.

(2) *Costs of maintaining an inventory balance*, which consist of storage, insurance, deterioration, risk from price fluctuations, and interest on investment.

The more numerous the orders placed to fill the estimated inventory requirements of a time period, the greater will be the total cost of ordering. At the same time, however, each order will be for a smaller quantity, and therefore the maximum quantity on hand just after an order is filled will be lower as more frequent orders are placed. As a result, the average inventory balance on hand during the period will be lower and so will the cost of carrying the inventory.

The following illustration shows how the standard order quantity would be computed for item W, whose expected usage is 100 pounds a month (1,200 pounds a year), spaced evenly throughout the year. The desired margin of safety is 50 pounds. The fixed costs required to process each order are $5, and the costs of insurance, storage, and interest on the investment in inventory total $0.10 per pound of item W per year.

INVENTORY COSTS FOR ORDERS OF VARIOUS QUANTITIES OF ITEM W

Number of Orders Each Year	Size of Each Order (Pounds)	Average Inventory Balance (Pounds)	Cost of Maintaining Inventory ($0.10 per pound)	Cost of Ordering ($5 per Order)	Total Cost
1	1,200	650	$65.00	$ 5.00	$70.00
2	600	350	35.00	10.00	45.00
3	400	250	25.00	15.00	40.00
4	300	200	20.00	20.00	40.00
5	240	170	17.00	25.00	42.00
6	200	150	15.00	30.00	45.00
12	100	100	10.00	60.00	70.00

The average inventory balance that will exist for any frequency of orders during the year is determined as follows:

$$\frac{\text{Minimum Balance} + \text{Maximum Balance}}{2}$$

The *minimum* balance would be the *margin of safety*—50 pounds in each case—and would be reached just before the replenishing shipment arrived. The *maximum* balance in any case would be the *margin of safety plus the number of units in the order*. It would be reached just after the shipment arrived.

EXAMPLE 3: The average inventory balance if one order is placed during the year is computed as follows:

$$\frac{\text{Minimum Balance, 50 pounds} + \text{Maximum Balance, 1,250 pounds}}{2} = 650 \text{ pounds}$$

According to the table, combined costs of ordering and carrying an inventory balance are at a minimum, $40, when the requirements for the year are met by placing 3 orders of 400 pounds each, or 4 orders of 300 pounds each.

A lower total cost can be found by interpolating between these two order sizes and computing what the average costs per year would be if orders were placed for 350 units at a time. If orders of this size were placed, the results would be as follows:

Number of orders each year:

$$\frac{1,200 \text{ pounds usage}}{350 \text{ pounds per order}} = 3.43 \text{ orders}$$

Average inventory balance:

$$\frac{\text{Minimum, 50 pounds} + \text{Maximum, 400 pounds}}{2} = 225 \text{ pounds}$$

Cost of maintaining inventory: 225 pounds @ $0.10 =	$22.50
Cost of ordering: 3.43 orders @ $5.00 =	17.15
Total cost: $22.50 + $17.15 =	$39.65

In actual situations there are other factors which complicate the determination of the minimum total cost associated with ordering and owning inventory. Examples related to the purchase of merchandise and materials are quantity discounts and costs of handling. Changing conditions, such as upward or downward trends in usage, changes in costs, and changes in supply conditions, should also be taken into consideration.

In the case of manufactured inventories, determination of the optimum size of the production order is more complicated still. Elaborate formulas have been developed for computing the optimum order size. Additional items that have to be considered are the amount of set-up costs in relation to the size of the production batch; the availability of labor and facilities at various times; and the behavior of manufacturing overhead costs. The size of the standard order in manufacturing is often determined by striking a balance between the objective of minimizing average production costs by maintaining a stable level of production and that of minimizing the costs of carrying the inventory balance.

Like order points, standard order quantities become outdated. Both should be used as guides only and not as substitutes for good judgment.

Setting standards for inventory balances

The standards by which the efficiency of the business in managing its inventory are to be judged may be expressed in one of several forms:

(1) *Planned inventory balance* at a certain future date, usually the end of the budget period. The balance may be in terms of *quantities* of each type of inventory, *costs* of inventory classes, or *number of days' supply* represented by the balance. The desired balance at a future date, however it is described, should be based upon the requirements of later periods and upon a consideration of the costs of acquiring and maintaining inventory.

(2) *Planned average inventory balance during the planning period.* This is generally expressed as an average quantity or an average cost.

(3) *Planned inventory turnover rate.* This is an application of the general formula for computing the turnover of an asset. The formula is:

$$\frac{\text{Change in Inventory During Period}}{\text{Typical Inventory Balance}} = \text{Number of Turnovers}$$

The change and balance may both be expressed in terms of *physical quantities* or they may both be expressed in terms of *money costs*. It is customary to use the quantity or cost of inventory *issued* as a measure of the change during the period. Another variation commonly used in connection with inventories of merchandise and finished goods is to use *sales* (units issued at selling price) as a measure of the inventory change.

The selection of one of these methods of measuring inventory performance for use in a given business would depend largely upon the preferences of management. Occasionally, however, one method is more reliable than another in a given case—often because it is subject to less distortion. Illustrations of such situations appear later in this chapter and in the problem material.

Regardless of which method is used in setting a standard, it is often difficult to determine the *amount* of a desirable standard. How many turnovers should there be during a year or how many days' supply should be on hand at the end of the year? The results actually achieved in the past are often used as a standard against which to compare future results. They are subject to the limitation that they may represent inefficient performance; standards based upon efficient conditions are more desirable.

Number of days' supply in inventory

One way of determining whether an inventory balance at a given time is adequate, inadequate, or excessive is to compare its amount with the expected needs in the future.

EXAMPLE 4:   The balance of item V on hand on January 1, 19x2, was 330 pounds. Issues in the future are expected to average 90 pounds a month, or 3 pounds a day. The inventory balance represents 110 days' supply (330 pounds on hand ÷ 3 pounds needed a day).

The desirable standard in terms of days' supply should be set by considering the expected future issues of the particular inventory; the reliability of the sources of supply; and the time required to secure replacement. The actual balance at a given time should be compared with the standard set in advance, and this comparison should be followed by such explanations and action as are necessary.

Inventory turnover rate

The average inventory balance on hand is not discussed separately as a standard of performance because it is used in computing the *number of inventory turnovers*. The *actual* inventory turnover rate, when compared with a desired standard which has been set in advance, gives valuable clues as to whether the quantity of the item on hand is appropriate, as well as whether the item is moving at a satisfactory rate.

Inventory turnover rates are more meaningful when computed separately for each of various classes of inventory items which are similar in behavior. The use of physical quantities instead of costs eliminates the distorting effect of changes in unit costs which have taken place during the period. The costs which are reflected in the change in the inventory account (equaling Cost of Goods Sold) and those which are used in determining the average balance should be comparable.

The following illustration shows how an inventory turnover rate may be computed by using physical quantities.

ANNUAL INVENTORY TURNOVER RATES OF ITEM Z

Date	Balance	Computation of Average of Year-end Balances	Computation of Average of Quarter-end Balances
19x2			
1/ 1.....	340	340	340
3/31.....	390		390
6/30.....	380		380
9/30.....	290		290
12/31.....	220	220	220
Totals..............................		560	1,620
Divided by number of items...........		2	5
Equals average balance................		280	324
Quantity issued......................		1,320	1,320
Divided by average balance............		280	324
Equals number of turnovers...........		4.71 times	4.07 times

The turnover rate computed by using the quarterly balances is more reliable than that which uses the annual balances because it is more representative of the conditions which prevailed throughout the year. The computation of *separate turnover rates for each quarter* would indicate still better the changes in conditions which occurred during the year, because rates of movement may change substantially during such a long period. The quarterly turnover rates would be computed by dividing the usage for each quarter by the average of the beginning and ending balances for the quarter, as follows:

QUARTERLY INVENTORY TURNOVER RATES OF ITEM Z

19x2 Quarter	Average Balance	Quantity Issued	Number of Quarterly Turnovers	Annual Turnover Rate
First...........	365	250	0.68	2.74
Second........	385	310	0.81	3.22
Third..........	335	390	1.16	4.63
Fourth........	255	370	1.45	5.80

The quarterly rates show that the rate of turnover has changed substantially during the year and that it has improved each quarter. The last column translates the quarterly turnover rate into an annual rate by multiplying the quantity issued by 4. It permits easier comparison with the average annual turnover rates of 4.71 and 4.07 computed in the previous table. If an investigation shows that the causes of the increase in the quarterly turnover rate are not seasonal, there has been a definite improvement during the year.

Dollar costs of inventories should be used rather than physical quantities in determining *how effectively the business has employed its assets*. The turnover of the investment in inventory should be computed thus:

$$\frac{\text{Cost of goods sold during period, \$240,000}}{\text{Average inventory at cost, \$60,000}}$$
$$= 4 \text{ turnovers of inventory investment during the period.}$$

Dollar cost of *materials used* could be compared similarly with the average cost of *materials on hand*. If the turnover is to be meaningful, both the numerator and the denominator should be measured on a consistent basis. They are consistent when both are stated at current cost and when both are stated at current selling price. Some inventory methods, particularly LIFO when the asset balance is stated at costs of a time in the distant past, distort the reliability of the turnover rate.

Inventory control when types of items change

The illustrated methods of controlling the investment in inventories by giving particular attention to economical acquisition quantities and appropriate inventory balances are suitable for staple inventory items.

It is possible to predict the future requirements for such items with some assurance. These standards are of little use, however, in situations where the types of articles handled change rapidly. This condition is true of many items which are stocked by the typical variety or department store.

Often such stores purchase special items which will be salable for only a short time. The buyer of each department is usually given considerable latitude in deciding what types of items to feature and how much of each to buy. Planning and control of such classes of inventories by means of order points and standard order quantities expressed in units is practically meaningless. Still, some limit must be placed upon the total cost of the departmental buyer's *investment in inventory at any time;* otherwise, the store might find that it had tied up all of its resources in inventory. Such control is often exercised by placing a monetary limit upon the total of the investment in inventory and purchase orders which the departmental buyer may have outstanding at any time.

Retail inventory method

A method which is frequently used by department stores and others for determining how the persons responsible for inventory have discharged their accountability is the *retail inventory method*. It is a means of measuring as well as of controlling the investment in inventory at any given time. It is based on the following general formula:

(A) Beginning inventory, stated at selling price............ xxx
     Plus purchases during the period, at selling price....... xxx
       Equals total goods to be accounted for.................. xxxx
(B) Sales.. xxx
     Plus ending inventory, stated at selling price.......... xxx
       Equals total goods accounted for....................... xxxx

The total goods accounted for in part (B) must equal the accountability established in part (A).

In addition to determining the extent to which the responsible person has discharged his responsibility for inventory, the retail inventory method provides a quick means of converting the ending inventory, stated at retail selling price, to its equivalent *cost*.

The retail inventory method requires that records be kept of the *total additions to goods available for sale* in terms of both *cost* and *retail* selling price. The following is a summary of such information:

EXAMPLE 5:

19x2	Cost	Retail
Beginning inventory...........................	$12,400	$ 20,000
Add purchases for the year....................	49,600	80,000
Total goods available for sale.................	$62,000	$100,000

Each item of merchandise is tagged with its selling price. At the end of the year $100,000, the total goods available at retail, must be accounted for as being in 19x2 sales revenue or as being on hand in the December 31, 19x2, inventory, measured at retail.

EXAMPLE 6: If sales revenue for 19x2 was $75,000 in Example 5, a physical count on December 31, 19x2, should disclose goods on hand priced to sell at $25,000. If the physical count at retail is only $24,000, there is a shortage of $1,000, measured at retail. It may represent an actual shortage, errors in the inventory, or errors in the records of purchases or sales.

The ending inventory stated at retail cannot be used as the amount of the asset in the statement of financial position because it contains an element of unrealized income equal to the mark-up of the selling price over the cost of the goods. The inventory amount may be converted to cost by using the ratio of cost of goods available for sale to the total retail price of goods available for sale.

EXAMPLE 7: In Example 5, total cost is $62,000 and total retail is $100,000, a ratio of .62, or 62 per cent. The *cost* of the ending inventory is then determined to be 62 per cent of $25,000, or $15,500. If there is a shortage at retail of $1,000, the loss of $620 (62% of $1,000) should be deducted from the computed inventory of $15,500.

The foregoing computation assumes that the ratio of cost to retail for goods in the ending inventory is the same as for all goods handled during the period. Ending inventory is distorted to the extent that this assumption is not true. For this reason, separate retail inventory calculations should be made of each class of goods which has a significantly different rate of mark-up.

There are many more elements involved in the retail inventory method. A summary record must be kept of all *additions to inventory*, both at cost and at retail. Examples would be purchases and transfers from other departments. Purchase returns involve a *reduction* of goods available for sale, stated at both cost and at selling price.

Transportation on purchases should ordinarily be considered an addition to cost. It may sometimes appear in the accounts as a separate item, in which case there is no corresponding addition to the accountability for goods at retail. The accountability was increased when the goods were received: transportation is merely an additional cost of the same goods.

Records are also needed of changes in retail price which result from additional mark-ups and mark-downs of selling prices of goods in stock. These records are necessary to keep the summary of accountability in agreement with the retail prices of unsold goods as shown by the price tags on individual articles.

The following calculation illustrates some of these complications.

EXAMPLE 8:

19x2	Cost	Retail
Beginning inventory...........................	$ 6,000	$10,000
Add purchases for the year....................	26,000	39,000
Additional mark-ups of retail..................	—	1,000
Ratio of cost to retail, 64%..................	$32,000	$50,000
Deduct mark-downs of retail...................	—	(2,500)
Goods available for sale.......................	$32,000	$47,500
Deduct sales..................................	? (a)	39,500
Ending inventory to be accounted for...........	? (b)	$ 8,000
Physical ending inventory.....................		$ 8,000

The ending inventory priced at retail, $8,000, is converted to cost by multiplying it by the cost-to-retail ratio, 64 per cent. The result is $5,120, the answer to question (b) above. The cost of goods sold in question (a), $26,880, can be determined by subtracting the computed cost of ending inventory from the cost of goods available for sale ($32,000 − $5,120).

The cost ratio of 64 per cent was determined by comparing the cost of goods available for sale with their retail *without considering markdowns*. The result is intended to give an ending inventory which approximates the results of the *lower-of-cost-or-market method*. Under L/CM it would presumably be necessary to measure marked-down goods at market, and this ratio gives an approximation of that result.

The results of *average cost* can be approximated under the retail method by using the ratio of cost of goods available, $32,000, to their selling price, *considering both mark-ups and mark-downs*, $47,500. *LIFO retail* is a much more complex method, beyond the scope of this text.

Financial statements can be prepared quickly under the retail inventory method, without taking a physical inventory, by using sales data and the summary records of cost and retail. This computation is also desirable in determining how much insurance coverage is currently needed on the inventory. The method simplifies physical inventory-taking, reveals the extent of inventory shortages, and helps in controlling the amount of income by giving current information about the realized rate of gross margin.

The retail inventory principle for establishing the accountability of an individual for merchandise and sales receipts can also be applied to individual employees, departments, branches, and divisions of a company.

The gross margin inventory method

Another method which is frequently used in estimating the cost of the ending inventory and in determining how responsible persons have discharged their accountability for inventory is the *gross margin method*. It is simpler to apply than the retail method but sometimes less accurate.

Given the sales revenue, the cost of the beginning inventory and inventory additions for the current period, and the percentage of gross margin to sales, the ending inventory at cost can be estimated.

EXAMPLE 9:

	Amounts	Per Cent of Sales
Sales, 19x2..	$50,000	100%
Deduct cost of goods sold:		
Beginning inventory.................... $10,000		
Purchases......................... 38,000		
Cost of goods available................	$48,000	
Deduct ending inventory................	?	
Cost of goods sold.............................	?	?
Gross margin.......................................	?	30%

What is the cost of the ending inventory?

SOLUTION: If the gross margin applicable to 19x2 sales is 30 per cent of sales, it is $15,000. Cost of goods sold, therefore, is 70 per cent of sales, or $35,000. To complete the calculation:

Cost of goods available for sale...........................	$48,000
Deduct estimated cost of goods sold (70% of $50,000 sales)..	35,000
Estimated cost of ending inventory.......................	$13,000

The estimated rate of gross margin is usually based upon the company's past experience. Changed relationships of costs and selling prices of each class of merchandise, or changes in sales mix during the current period, will distort the validity of the inventory calculation. Similarly, errors in sales, beginning inventory, or purchases will cause the computed ending inventory to be unreliable.

The gross margin method does not require that detailed current records be kept of costs and selling prices and of mark-ups and mark-downs in selling prices. It can be used to give a quick approximation of what the ending inventory *should be* if a physical inventory is not possible or desirable or if the reported ending inventory is thought to be inaccurate.

Sometimes the gross margin method is used in a slightly different way to estimate *what sales revenue should have been*, when it is suspected that the reported sales figure is inaccurate.

EXAMPLE 10:   The top management of a business suspects that the manager of a department has been understating the sales of the department and pocketing the difference. The costs of the beginning inventory, purchases, and ending inventory are known, and the percentage of cost of goods sold to sales has consistently been 60 per cent in the past. There is no reason to think that it should have changed in the current year. How can management determine whether sales have been falsified?

SOLUTION:

Beginning inventory, at cost..............................	$15,000
Add purchases..	50,000
Cost of goods available for sale...........................	$65,000
Deduct ending inventory, at cost........................	35,000
Cost of goods sold.......................................	$30,000

Estimated Sales:

$$\frac{\text{Cost of Goods Sold, \$30,000}}{\text{Past Ratio of Cost of Goods Sold to Sales, 60\%}} = \$50,000$$

Estimated sales for the period........................... $50,000
Deduct reported sales.................................... 45,000
Shortage in reported sales............................... $ 5,000

The estimated amount of sales is accurate only if the past ratio of cost of goods sold to selling price has continued during the current period.

Internal check of inventories

One of the principal means of preventing errors, fraud, and waste in handling inventories is assigning to different individuals the responsibilities for ordering, receiving, testing, paying for, keeping custody of, issuing, and maintaining records of inventory. Internal check procedures for handling inventories should be designed to insure that the business *receives* the proper kind and quality of goods in the right quantity at the right time and at the best price; that the goods are *stored* with due attention to protection from damage, obsolescence, and theft as well as to accessibility and ease of handling for later use; that cash *payment* is made for purchases only upon sufficient evidence that the goods were properly ordered and received and that the amount of the payment is correct; and that there is no waste or fraud in the *use* or *sale* of the inventory items.

Means of detecting the more subtle form of waste which is occasioned by maintaining excessive inventory balances were described earlier in this chapter.

The system of internal check for inventories should provide a method of charging each individual who receives goods with *accountability* for them. Each individual who releases goods on proper authority should have a receipt discharging his accountability. The system should be completed by determining that the goods in the custody of the responsible individual are equal to the remainder of his accountability.

Additions to accountability may be evidenced by *purchase invoices and receiving reports*. Issues may be substantiated by *requisitions*. Balances on hand may be recorded in individual *subsidiary accounts*. Periodically, perhaps once a month, the agreement of the total of the subsidiary account balances with the general ledger inventory account should be proved. At least once a year the accuracy of the individual perpetual inventory records should be determined by taking a physical count of the inventory.

Summary

The objective of inventory planning and control is to maintain the investment in inventories at the lowest amount which is consistent with the available capital of the business and its requirements for future issues. The use of standard order quantities and order points aids in timing the acquisitions of inventory items to achieve this result. Comparison of actual inventory balances and inventory turnover rates with predetermined standards, and necessary action to correct any deviations, help to keep the investment in inventory at an efficient level.

The retail inventory method, the gross margin method, and subsidiary inventory ledgers are all means of improving the control exercised over inventories. All provide inventory information for preparing financial statements and for related purposes without the necessity of taking a physical count. All furnish a means of estimating discrepancies between inventories that *should be* on hand and inventories that actually *are* on hand at a given time.

Careful separation of the functions of ordering, receiving, storing, and using inventory and the keeping of detailed and controlling inventory accounts help to promote effective internal check of inventories.

QUESTIONS AND PROBLEMS

16-1 Determining what the proper level of inventory should be at a given time requires a delicate balance between opposing tendencies. The sales manager likes to have a complete assortment of merchandise on hand and to be able to fill customers' orders promptly. The production manager wishes to have a quantity of raw materials on hand sufficient to avoid work stoppages when the rate of usage suddenly changes or when there are delays in obtaining materials. The treasurer wishes to keep the investment in inventories at a minimum so as to minimize the necessity for borrowing funds to finance inventories and to maximize the rate of return on the company's investment.

REQUIRED:

a. To what general extent should each of these limitations be considering in setting company policies regarding inventory?
b. Describe some of the principal objective methods which can be used to help keep the investment in inventory under control, and explain how they may be used by management.

16-2 The home office of a business in Dallas ships finished goods to its branch in Amarillo for sale by the latter. The invoice covering each shipment is priced at retail selling price, although the company as a whole uses average cost in its financial statements. One such shipment was made on December 8, 19x1. The home office completed the manufacture of 1,000 identical units at a total cost of $4,000 and immediately shipped the entire amount to Amarillo, paying transportation of $0.50 a unit in cash. During December the branch sold 200 units for cash at $8.00 each.

REQUIRED:

a. Record the entries on the books of the home office and on the books of the branch, using the procedure followed by the company.

b. What special problems does this procedure create in the preparation of financial statements? Show in journal form how you would solve them.

c. What are the purposes and the advantages of this accounting procedure? The disadvantages?

16-3 Some companies keep perpetual inventory records in terms of quantities only; other keep them in terms of quantities and costs; and still others do not keep perpetual inventory records at all.

REQUIRED:

a. What purposes are served by maintaining perpetual inventories in terms of quantities only?

b. What are the weaknesses of such a system?

c. What additional purposes are served by the use of perpetual inventory costs as well as quantities?

d. Describe some of the disadvantages of the method in (*c*).

e. Outline the general conditions under which you would recommend that a business (1) keep perpetual quantity inventory records only, (2) keep perpetual quantity and cost records, or (3) keep no perpetual inventory records.

16-4 "We keep a perpetual record of our inventories, and as a result we avoid disrupting our work and spending countless hours at the end of the year by taking a physical inventory."

REQUIRED:

a. How, if at all, does the maintenance of a perpetual inventory system lessen the hours involved in taking physical inventory?

b. How can it be used to avoid disrupting work?

c. What purposes other than determining the cost of goods on hand does the process of taking a physical inventory serve?

d. Do you agree with the procedure described? Explain.

16-5 The standard order quantity is the order size which results in keeping at a minimum the combined cost of ordering and maintaining an inventory balance.

REQUIRED:

a. List as many types of cost as you can which vary closely with the frequency of orders placed during an accounting period.

b. List as many types of cost as you can which vary closely with the balance of inventory on hand.

c. Would you recommend that all of the costs listed in (*a*) and (*b*) be included as a part of the inventory cost for purposes of preparing financial statements? Explain.

d. Is the use of different cost classifications for planning and for income determination appropriate in connection with inventory management? Why?

16-6 The following data taken from the inventory record for material K for 19x1 is considered to be typical of expected future conditions. All figures represent quantities.

Month	Purchases	Issues	Month	Purchases	Issues
January.............	300	100	July...............	280	200
February..........		120	August............		200
March.............	380	140	September.........	160	160
April..............		160	October...........		120
May...............	400	180	November..........	220	80
June...............		200	December..........		80

The beginning inventory balance consisted of 250 units.

REQUIRED:

a. Set up a perpetual inventory card showing purchases, issues, and ending balance for each month.

b. Determine the inventory turnover rate for the year as a whole.

c. How many days' supply of material K are on hand on December 31?

d. What are the limitations of the computation in (b), and how would you suggest that they be overcome?

e. What are the limitations of the computation in (c), and how would you over-come them?

16-7

REQUIRED:

a. Using the following data, compute the inventory turnover rate for the year, using (1) quantities only; (2) FIFO cost; (3) LIFO cost.

b. For what purposes may the turnover rates be used?

c. Which method(s) in your opinion best serve these purposes? Why?

	Units	Unit Cost
Inventory, Jan. 1, 19x2..........................	2,000	$4.00
Purchases in 19x2:		
Feb. 6.....................................	2,000	3.50
Mar. 9.....................................	1,000	3.40
Jun. 16.....................................	1,000	3.20
Oct. 27.....................................	1,000	3.00
Inventory, Dec. 31, 19x2........................	2,600	?

16-8   Thurston Products, Inc., has total assets of $120,000, of which 40 per cent is represented by inventory consisting of the following major classes:

Class	Balance, 12/31/x3	Expected Cost of Sales, 19x4
1....................	$10,000	$12,000
2....................	18,000	30,000
3....................	6,000	15,000
4....................	14,000	30,000

After a careful survey, the company management believes that inventory turn-over rates for the classes should be as follows:

Class 1....... 2.0   Class 2....... 2.5   Class 3....... 3.0   Class 4....... 2.0

The present ratio of income before income tax to average assets is 8 per cent.

REQUIRED:

a. How many months' supply of inventory is represented by the balance of each class of goods on hand on December 31, 19x3?

b. What average inventory quantities should be maintained to achieve the standard turnover rates?

c. Judged by the standards in (b), what is the excess investment in inventory on December 31?

d. If the costs associated with maintaining an inventory balance, other than return on investment, are 10 per cent of the inventory cost, how much could be saved a year by maintaining inventories at the standard level?

e. What would be the rate of return before tax on assets if the standard turnover rates were maintained for an entire year?

f. If Thurston Products, Inc., adjusts its balance of each class of goods to the new level as quickly as possible, what would be the turnover rate for each class of goods during 19x4?

16-9 Raybow Company uses about 500 pounds of material M in its manufacturing process each month. The supplier of M usually fills orders within 2 months from the date they are placed. Raybow Company likes to keep a minimum of 1 month's supply of M on hand at all times in case orders require longer to be filled, and its balance has reached that minimum at the beginning of the current year.

The costs which tend to be constant for each order placed, including such items as labor, supplies, and postage, total $9 per order. Insurance premiums are 1 per cent of the average cost of inventory a year, and storage costs are approximately $0.02 per pound per year. Loss from obsolescence has been about 2 per cent of the average inventory balance in recent years. The invoice cost of material M is $2 per pound.

REQUIRED:

a. Determine the order point for material M.

b. Set up a table to determine the standard order quantity.

c. Describe some of the limitations of the results which you obtained in (*b*).

d. If the average usage increases to 600 pounds a month, the invoice cost increases to $3 a unit, and the time required to fill an order decreases to 1½ months, what revisions would you make?

16-10 It has been suggested that the totals of the perpetual inventory records be proved with the general ledger controlling account frequently, and that a physical check of the accuracy of the inventory records be made at least once a year.

REQUIRED:

a. What would cause the balance of the inventory controlling account to be larger than the sum of the balances in the subsidiary ledger? Smaller?

b. How would you dispose of the differences in (*a*)?

c. What would cause the balance of a perpetual inventory card to be larger than the quantity shown by the physical inventory? Smaller?

d. How would you dispose of the differences in (*c*)?

16-11 Standard Stores has a small retail branch in a remote mining community. It is impractical for the company's internal auditors to reach the branch often. In the past year they discovered that the former manager failed to report the full amount of goods sold, pocketing the amount of the understatement. Most of the merchandise which is sold by the branch consists of items of low unit value, and it is shipped from one of Standard Stores' regional warehouses.

REQUIRED:

a. Describe how the retail method might be used to improve the internal check in this situation.

b. How could the gross margin method be used as a measure of control?

c. Which method would you recommend in this case? Why?

16-12   M. K. Morello's store burned down on April 15, 19x4. Fortunately, Mr. Morello's records were in a fireproof safe. A careful analysis of the merchandise revealed that goods which had an original cost of $2,000 were not damaged by the fire; goods which had an original cost of $7,000 had a salvage value of $1,000; and all other merchandise was a total loss.

The accounting records showed the following information:

	1/1–4/15, 19x4	19x3	19x2
Sales on account...................	$12,000	$41,000	$37,000
Cash sales..........................	9,000	40,000	33,000
Sales returns.......................	1,000	4,000	3,000
Purchases on account...............	15,000	51,800	46,800
Beginning inventory (cost)..........	13,000	14,000	12,000
Ending inventory (cost).............	?	13,000	14,000
Operating expenses.................	4,000	19,000	18,000

REQUIRED:

a. Determine what the April 15, 19x4, inventory probably would have been at cost, if it had not been damaged by the fire.
b. Determine the amount of the loss from the fire.
c. What are the limitations of the computation in (*a*)?
d. Assuming that no insurance was carried on the inventory, how would you recommend that the facts in (*a*) and (*b*) be shown in financial statements for the period 1/1–4/15, 19x4?
e. What would your accounting treatment be if the loss was fully covered by insurance?

16-13   The quantities of item R used during the past year, 19x1, were as follows:

January........... 2,000	May.............. 2,800	September......... 1,800
February.......... 3,000	June.............. 2,400	October........... 2,600
March............. 3,000	July.............. 1,600	November......... 2,800
April............. 3,500	August........... 1,200	December......... 3,000

It is expected that the total usage in 19x2 will be 10 per cent higher, but that the seasonal pattern of usage will continue. It is difficult to obtain item R other than by purchasing 1,000 units at a time. The storekeeper sends a requisition to the purchasing department just as soon as the quantity on hand reaches the predetermined order point. It takes the order one day to reach the purchasing department, and it requires the purchasing department from 3 to 7 days to receive quotations and place the order. Usually the orders are mailed to the supplier, requiring from 1 to 3 days in transit. Depending upon the current market conditions, the supplier may require from 10 to 16 days to process the order, and shipment requires from 4 to 6 days. Receiving and testing together require from 1 to 3 days.

REQUIRED:

a. What minimum balance would you recommend that the company keep on hand as a margin of safety at all times?
b. What quantity would you suggest that the company use as an order point?
c. If your order point is adopted, prepare a schedule showing the expected receipts, issues, and balance on hand at the end of each month of 19x2.
d. Does the use of your order point seem desirable in this situation? Explain. If not, what recommendation would you make?

16-14 Omar Stores uses the retail inventory method. The following data relate to Departments 1 and 2 for 19x3.

	Department 1		Department 2	
	Cost	Retail	Cost	Retail
Sales.....................................		$45,000		$110,000
Purchases................................	$40,000	50,000	$60,000	100,000
Purchase returns.........................	2,000	2,500	1,200	2,000
Sales returns.............................		500		1,000
Additional mark-ups.....................		1,000		5,000
Mark-downs..............................		4,000		2,000
Inventory, Jan. 1, 19x3.................	9,000	12,000	23,000	40,000

REQUIRED:

a. Compute the December 31, 19x3, inventory at retail for each department.
b. Convert the ending inventory from retail to approximate lower of cost or market using a single cost ratio for the store as a whole (both departments combined). Carry your cost ratio to the nearest third decimal place (nearest tenth of a per cent).
c. Convert the ending inventory from retail to approximate lower of cost or market using a separate cost ratio for each department.
d. Which method, (b) or (c), do you recommend? Why?

16-15 Department C of a small department store had an inventory of $5,000 at retail on January 1, 19x4. The ratio of cost to retail in this inventory was 60 per cent. During 19x4 the department purchased merchandise having an invoice cost of $25,000 on terms of 2/10, n/30. Transportation costs on the purchases were $2,500. The merchandise purchased was originally marked to sell for a total of $40,000.

During 19x4 prices of goods which had originally been marked to sell for $9,000 were increased to $12,000. Other goods which had been priced at $8,000 were reduced to $6,000. Merchandise which had cost $1,300 and which was priced to sell at $2,000 was transferred to Department K, on authority of the store manager.

Department C's total sales during 19x4 were $36,000, and sales returns were $2,000. A physical count of the inventory taken on December 31, 19x4, showed goods on hand at retail amounting to $7,812.

REQUIRED:

a. Determine what the ending inventory should have been at retail.
b. Convert the ending inventory to approximate lower of cost or market for use in the financial statements. Carry any ratios to the nearest third decimal place (nearest tenth of a per cent).
c. Explain the probable origin of any discrepancies in the ending inventory and make recommendations for disposing of them.

CASE 16-1. ALLSWELL COMPANY

Allswell Company sells three classes of goods, A, B, and C. The following information was taken from the company's records in 19x3.

	A	B	C
Sales revenue.........................	$20,000	$50,000	$10,000
Beginning inventory at cost............	4,000	6,000	5,000
Ending inventory at cost...............	6,000	4,000	6,000
Cost of goods sold....................	12,000	40,000	5,500

The company expects to sell goods costing $66,000 for a total of $100,000 in 19x4 and would like to maintain an average inventory level of 3 months' supply. The sales revenue of 19x4 is expected to be derived 20 per cent from Product A, 40 per cent from Product B, and 40 per cent from Product C, spaced evenly throughout the year. The ratio of cost to selling price is expected to remain the same as in 19x3.

REQUIRED:

a. Compute the inventory turnover rate for the company as a whole.
b. Compute the inventory turnover rate for each department separately.
c. Evaluate your results in (a) and (b).
d. What additional information do you need in order to determine whether the inventory turnover is satisfactory?
e. Is the standard which the company has set for its inventory balance an appropriate one? Explain.
f. How would you set more meaningful standard inventory levels for the company?

CASE 16-2. GENERAL ELECTRIC COMPANY

The following items are quoted from the 1953 annual report of General Electric Company, through the courtesy of the company:

"Ratio of Inventories to sales

"Inventories of both consumer goods and heavy apparatus lines increased somewhat during the year. Inventories related to the manufacture of defense materials declined.

"Inventories after reserves at the end of 1953 were $641 million, compared with $623 million at the end of 1952, an increase of $18 million, or 3%.

"One measure of the success of inventory management is the ratio of inventories to sales, with a lower ratio almost always being more desirable.

"The chart below compares this ratio for the last fifteen years. At the end of 1953, net inventories were 20.5% of 1953 sales, compared with 23.7% a year earlier."

YEAR-END INVENTORIES AS A PERCENTAGE OF NET SALES BILLED

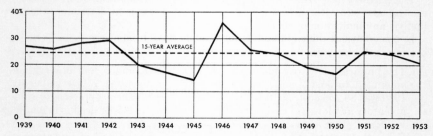

" . . . The Company's sales were a record $3,128,127,000 in 1953, up 19% over 1952 sales of $2,623,888,000.

"Sales increased in all major product areas. Leading increases were in the Appliance and Electronics Group, up 31%, and in the Defense Products Group, up 28% over 1952. Export sales of International General Electric Company were the highest in its history, representing an increase of 17% over 1952. New foreign orders were, however, somewhat lower than the 1953 level of shipments.

"During the last quarter of the year, sales of defense materials declined to some extent from earlier levels. Total sales for the Company during the final quarter were, however, at an annual rate of more than $3.1 billion."

The following item is quoted from the notes to the financial statements:

"Note 4. *Inventories* were verified by physical count during the latter part of the year. With the exception of tungsten stocks, inventories were carried, in accordance with long-established practice, at the lower of cost (exclusive of certain indirect manufacturing expenses) or market values of individual items or groups of items on a first-in, first-out basis, less reserves which (a) make provision for possible losses on inactive and excess stocks; (b) have the effect of accounting for the inventory of copper substantially in accordance with the base stock principle; and (c) eliminate unrealized inter-company profits. The tungsten metal stocks were valued on a 'last-in, first-out' basis."

REQUIRED:

a. Explain what you consider to be the purpose of the inventory "reserves" which are described in these quotations. Show in journal form how they would be accounted for.
b. How can you justify the use of the LIFO method for tungsten stocks when other methods are being used for other inventories?
c. Do you agree that a lower ratio of inventory to sales is almost always desirable? Explain.
d. What are the advantages and disadvantages of the manner in which the company has measured the success of inventory management?

CASE 16-3. F AND T

F and *T* are partners in the operation of a retail store. They are concerned about the apparent discrepancy between their income and their volume of sales. Although they maintain incomplete accounting records, their experience in the business suggests to them that there is possible theft or larceny on the part of their staff.

The partners have asked you, in connection with your initial audit (covering the calendar year 19x1), to apply such tests as you can to determine whether there is any indication of shortage.

In the course of your investigation, you obtain the following facts having a bearing on the problem:

(1) The physical inventory taken December 31, 19x1, under your observation, amounted to $4,442 cost, $4,171 market. The inventory of December 31, 19x0 was $6,256 cost, $6,013 market. It has been the firm's practice to value inventory at "lower of cost or market," treating any loss or decline in market value as "other expense."
(2) Using the treatment of "loss or decline in market value" of inventory as mentioned in (1) above, the average gross profit in recent periods has been 35 per cent of net sales. The partners inform you that this per cent seems reasonable and that they expected the same result for 19x1, since their mark-up per cent was approximately the same as in the past.
(3) The December 31, 19x0 balance sheet shows accounts receivable of $2,057. Notes payable to banks and trade accounts payable were combined on the December 31, 19x0 balance sheet. They totaled $9,622. The firm records accounts payable at the net figure, as cash discounts are seldom missed.

Purchases have been shown net in past income statements. Sales discounts have been treated as deductions from sales in the past.

(4) During 19x1 accounts were written off in the amount of $216, and an account for $148 written off in 19x0 was collected and recorded as a regular collection on account.

(5) Unpaid sales slips show that customers owed $3,246 on December 31, 19x1.

(6) Unpaid invoices indicate that the firm owed trade creditors $5,027 at the end of 19x1. Records of notes outstanding indicate that $3,000 was owed to banks on December 31, 19x1.

(7) Sales returns amounted to $95 and purchase returns amounted to $272.

(8) Of the items in the cash records, the following are pertinent:

From customers (after $272 discounts)	$49,851
From bank loan (net of 60-day, 6% discount)	2,970
Disbursements:	
To trade creditors (after $916 cash discounts)	38,970
To banks on loans	4,000
To customers for returned goods	72

REQUIRED:

Compute the amount by which the physical inventory is short, assuming that the gross profit rate of 35 per cent is reasonable. (Suggestion: Set up T-accounts or a transaction work sheet to record all of the transactions of the year.)

(Adapted from AICPA Examination in Accounting Practice, November, 1952.)

CASE 16-4. ABC CORPORATION

The *ABC* Corporation, which began operations in 19x1, manufactures one product, Gimco. At the present time, the major portion of the corporation's output is used by four large companies. The principal ingredient used in the manufacturing process is X13, which is purchased and stored in tanks on the company premises. Management of the *ABC* Corporation is faced with the problem of large variations in quantities of inventories on hand because of seasonal fluctuations in sales orders, which cause changes in production schedules. Once X13 has been put into production, the process must be completed promptly; therefore, the company does not have any inventory in process.

The following schedules show the amount of X13 purchased and put into production and the amount of Gimco produced and sold during the past three years.

	Purchases of X13 (Thousands of barrels)			Amount of X13 Put into Production (Thousands of barrels)		
	19x1	19x2	19x3	19x1	19x2	19x3
J	120	150	140	80	190	160
F	340	200	350	250	180	300
M	410	310	430	460	335	450
A	450	340	480	500	360	490
M	220	280	300	200	225	300
J	150	100	150	130	135	120
J	75	120	140	90	100	140
A	50	80	100	40	90	100
S	250	300	240	280	320	290
O	300	330	280	325	280	250
N	330	280	310	270	300	290
D	170	200	190	160	215	185

	Production of Gimco			Sales of Gimco		
	(Thousands of pounds)			(Thousands of pounds)		
	19x1	19x2	19x3	19x1	19x2	19x3
J	7,200	17,000	14,400	6,100	18,000	18,600
F	22,500	16,400	27,200	21,000	17,100	28,000
M	41,000	30,000	41,600	38,000	28,000	42,500
A	45,000	32,200	44,900	47,000	34,500	41,600
M	18,000	20,200	27,000	19,500	17,000	28,000
J	11,500	12,200	10,700	12,000	14,100	12,400
J	8,100	9,100	12,500	7,500	10,000	13,000
A	3,500	8,000	8,900	2,500	6,500	9,900
S	24,900	29,300	26,000	24,700	27,000	25,400
O	29,100	25,200	22,500	28,000	24,000	21,700
N	24,300	27,000	26,100	26,800	25,400	27,100
D	15,500	19,300	16,700	14,000	19,200	17,900

Acquisition cost of X13 during 19x1 was $60 per barrel during the first six months. There was a 10 per cent increase in the cost per barrel in each of the following six-month periods. Gimco was retailing for $1.55 per pound in December of 19x1, $1.70 per pound in 19x2, and $1.65 per pound in 19x3. Its cost was $1.00 per pound in 19x1, $0.95 per pound in 19x2, and $1.05 per pound in 19x3.

The ABC Corporation uses the first-in, first-out method for costing its ending inventory. A physical inventory is taken at the end of each fiscal year. Total assets, exclusive of inventory, were $12,300,000 in 19x1, $17,600,000 in 19x2, and $15,100,000 in 19x3. The management of the ABC Corporation is of the opinion that the company should adopt the last-in, first-out method for costing its ending inventory.

REQUIRED:

a. The management of the ABC Corporation wishes to know whether you consider it advisable for it to change from FIFO to LIFO. Write a report explaining how the method operates, the principal advantages and disadvantages of each method as applied to this particular situation, and a general summary of what the results might have been if ABC had used the LIFO method during the past three years.
b. If management decides to use the LIFO method, do you think the present beginning and ending dates used for the accounting period are the most appropriate ones? Explain.

Chapter 17

Accounting for Manufacturing Inventories

Earlier chapters have explained how the accountant seeks to measure the periodic income of a business by matching its expired costs with the related revenues. The matching process is facilitated by treating some types of costs—referred to as *period costs*—as expenses of the accounting period in which they are incurred, and others—referred to as *product costs*—as expenses of the period in which the physical unit to which they apply is sold.

The illustrations used previously have dealt chiefly with accounting for the product costs, or *inventories*, of *trading concerns* (wholesalers and retailers). The basic principles which underlie accounting for *manufacturing inventories* are the same, but they are discussed in this separate chapter because of the complex practical accounting problems of manufacturing enterprises.

Production costs and distribution costs

Production costs are those costs which are associated with the manufacture of physical units of output. They include all costs reasonably incurred in *preparing* an item for sale, as contrasted with *distribution costs*, which are associated with *making* the sale.

Production cost accounting consists of recording, classifying, summarizing, and interpreting the costs incurred in manufacturing units of product. In the production process, the physical nature of the inventory items is *transformed*. Accounting attempts to associate the related costs with the physical items; therefore, the production costs are also transformed in the accounting records.

Distribution costs are assigned directly to expense accounts in the accounting period in which they expire, without being accumulated in inventory accounts.

Uses of unit production costs

The uses to which unit costs of manufactured products may be put are of two general types:

(1) Measuring financial results; and
(2) Planning and controlling business operations.

The *expired* unit costs of products have an effect upon the amount of the *income* of the business through their effect on *cost of goods sold expense*. The *unexpired* unit product costs help to determine the *financial position* of the business at any time, through their effect on *goods in process* and *finished goods inventories*.

In spite of their importance in financial measurement, unit production costs are generally more useful as aids to management in controlling operations and planning for the future in the following connections:

(1) Appraising the performance of responsible managers of parts of the organization;

(2) Comparing the cost of manufacturing a unit of product and of each of its important components with a standard of efficiency, and taking corrective measures which such comparison indicates to be worth while;

(3) Seeking better ways of performing an operation or a service, or of making a product, as a result of knowing unit costs;

(4) Where selling prices are largely independent of costs, determining upon which products to concentrate manufacturing and selling efforts;

(5) Where selling prices or bids are based largely upon costs, determining what the prices should be in order to maximize income;

(6) Estimating various components of the operating and financial budgets of future periods.

Inventory accounts of manufacturers

Inventories, as defined in Chapter 6, are expendable physical items which a business acquires for sale to its customers, for use in manufacturing its products, or for consumption in carrying on its activities. The inventory of a trading concern is described as *Merchandise Inventory*, while the inventories of manufacturers consist of *Finished Goods, Goods in Process*, and *Materials and Supplies*. Production costs are accumulated in the asset account, *Goods in Process Inventory*, awaiting the completion of the product. Upon completion, the costs are transferred to *Finished Goods Inventory*, to be reassigned to *Cost of Goods Sold Expense* when the articles are sold.

The general basis for measuring all inventories is *acquisition cost*— the sum of the expenditures made directly or indirectly in bringing the inventories to their existing condition and location. Usually the acquisition costs of the *merchandise inventory* of a trading concern may be more readily associated with physical units in the inventory than may the *production costs* of the manufacturer.

After the costs of manufacturing each unit have been determined, the problems of accounting for *finished goods inventories* are largely the same as those of accounting for *merchandise inventories*, described in Chapters 15 and 16. The flow of costs of manufacturing inventories, like those of merchandise inventories, may be measured by *specific identification* or by an assumed flow such as *FIFO, LIFO*, or *weighted average*. It is sometimes appropriate to use one method for measuring one class of the manufacturer's inventory and other methods for other classes.

Periodic and perpetual inventory methods

The inventories of manufacturers may be measured by either the *periodic* or the *perpetual* inventory method, although the latter is usually preferable. The periodic inventory method is most appropriate when the inventory amounts are relatively small and the inventory components are simple.

In most manufacturing processes, the relationship of many important types of production costs to specific items of product is indirect and complex. As a result, it is frequently quite difficult to use the *periodic inventory* method to determine the costs of units in various stages of completion (goods in process inventory) and the costs of units manufactured (finished goods) at various times under changing conditions. If a periodic inventory system is used, the cost per unit is the average cost of all units completed since the last periodic inventory was taken. It is necessary to estimate the stage of completion of work in process in order to obtain an average unit cost, and the results so obtained are sometimes subject to a wide margin of error.

Under the conditions just described, it is preferable to use a *perpetual inventory* record to accumulate the costs of units in the process of manufacture, unless the cost of doing so is excessive. A perpetual inventory system permits the computation of average unit costs more frequently and provides more current information relating to the trends of unit costs for the use of production, accounting, and other management groups.

In almost any case, the perpetual inventory method permits better control over the inventories by means of safeguards of the receiving, storing, and issuing functions.

Cost centers

If production costs are to be controlled effectively, it is essential that they be accounted for along the lines of *responsibility* of the management personnel, following the principles outlined in Chapter 12.

A *cost center* is a unit of activity within the organization, assigned as the responsibility of a single individual, for which information about expired costs is collected. A single individual may be responsible for several cost centers, but the responsibility for a single center should not be divided.

EXAMPLE 1: In a given factory, all costs of operating a single large machine are accumulated. The *foreman* in charge of the group of employees who operate the machine is assigned responsibility for controlling the operating costs of the machine.

EXAMPLE 2: In the same factory, the costs of operating the factory Personnel Department are collected. The *personnel manager* is responsible for controlling them.

Costs of operating a given cost center may be reassigned immediately as a part of the cost of the products which the center helps to produce, or they may be reassigned to other cost centers before ultimately being treated as a part of the cost of the manufactured product.

Direct and indirect production costs

In arriving at the final result, which is the unit cost of a *completed manufactured product*, it is often necessary for the accountant to trace production costs through many complex stages. The routes by which costs flow through the accounts to the units of product may be *direct* or *indirect*.

As explained in Chapter 12, a *direct* financial element (cost, revenue, asset, or equity) is one which can be traced convincingly to the unit of activity in question, and a *common*, or *indirect*, financial element is one which cannot be so traced. The units of activity to which *production costs* may be traced are:

(1) Factory service departments;
(2) Factory production departments;
(3) Units of product.

It is the prevailing business practice to attempt to assign all factory costs to units of product. The assignment may be made *directly* to the unit of product when the cost expires in its initial form, or the assignment may be made *indirectly* to the unit of product by one of two routes:

(1) *Directly* to a production department and *indirectly* to the unit of product.

EXAMPLE 3:   The machine in Example 1 is used in the manufacture of a single type of product. Each month an equal share of the cost of operating the machine cost center is assigned to each complete unit of product on which the machine was used during the month.

(2) *Directly* to a service department, then *indirectly* to a production department, and finally *indirectly* to the unit of product.

EXAMPLE 4:   The costs of the Personnel Department in Example 2 are reassigned to the production departments, including the machine cost center in Example 1, in proportion to the number of full-time employees in each. The cost of each unit of product thus includes a part of the cost of operating the Personnel Department. The costs of other factory service departments are treated in a similar manner.

Whether an item of cost is *direct* or *indirect* depends upon whether it is traceable without question to the unit of activity—department or product—under consideration.

Basic elements of manufactured product cost

The accounts of most manufacturers recognize three main elements of production cost:

(1) *Direct materials*. Those physical items used in manufacturing which can be traced convincingly to the unit of product without incurring clerical effort out of proportion to the usefulness of the resulting cost information.
(2) *Direct labor*. The wages of workers which it is possible and practical to trace to the unit of product.
(3) *Manufacturing overhead*. All manufacturing costs other than direct materials and direct labor.

The components of *direct materials* are similar to each other in that they can be traced to the units of product. They are also similar in their physical characteristics and in the general nature of the methods used to acquire, store, and use them.

The components of *direct labor* are also homogeneous in their traceability to the product and in the methods used to acquire, use, and control the services of workers.

Manufacturing overhead consists of a heterogeneous mixture of service benefits which have one principal feature in common: their lack of traceability to individual units of product. A few of the many types of manufacturing costs which are included in manufacturing overhead are the following:

Indirect labor. Factory wages which it is impossible or impractical to trace to units of product. An example is maintenance labor.

Indirect materials. Items used in manufacturing which it is impossible or impractical to trace to units of product. An example is oil for lubricating machines.

Factory maintenance

Factory insurance

Factory taxes

Factory heat, light, and power

Depreciation of machinery

Depreciation of factory building

ACCOUNTING FOR HISTORICAL COSTS

Production cost accounting systems may be described as *historical cost* or *predetermined cost* systems. The former collect information dealing only with costs actually incurred, while the latter set up in advance cost standards with which actual costs may be compared.

There are two basic methods of assigning costs of manufacture, whether historical or standard costs, to individual products: *job order* (or *production order*) and *process*. They are described and illustrated in the following sections.

Methods of assigning costs to units: job order and process

In a *job order cost system*, the accounting records of production costs are identified with *specific physical units of product*. It must be possible to distinguish each unit, or each group of units, from other units at all times during production. The job order method has been widely used to record the costs of a single item, such as a machine or a building, or a group of similar items which are being manufactured under the specifications of a customer. It is also sometimes used when a product is manufactured for stock in definite batches or lots. A detailed cost record is maintained for each physical job or lot which is produced. As materials and labor are used on the physical units, their cost is added to the cumulative job order cost records for those specific units. Manufacturing overhead applicable to the physical units is also recorded on the appropriate detailed cost record.

A *process cost system* identifies costs with the total output of a productive *operation*, or *series of closely related productive operations*, over a *period of time*. This method is suitable when one unit of product cannot be distinguished from other units of product, and when production is largely continuous. It is well adapted to the needs of refineries and chemical plants. The process cost method develops an *average cost* of all units produced during a given time period, such as a day, week, or month, computed as follows:

$$\frac{\text{Total Manufacturing Costs of the Process for the Period}}{\text{Number of Units Produced}}$$
$$= \text{Average Cost of Unit Produced in the Process during the Period}$$

Separate average unit costs can be computed for materials, labor, and overhead and for the principal components of each. Under the process cost system, it is important to keep a record of the manufacturing costs attributable to a process during a time period and of the quantity of production during the same period.

Illustration of job order cost accounting procedure

The Calla Machine Company builds machines according to the specifications of its customers. On December 31, 19x1, the balances of its factory inventory accounts were as follows:

A, Materials Inventory	$24,000
A, Goods in Process Inventory	8,000
A, Finished Goods Inventory	0

The company uses a job order cost system to accumulate the cost of each machine manufactured. The balance in the Goods in Process Inventory consisted of the following costs incurred in November and December, 19x1, on Job No. 115, which was not yet complete:

Direct materials	$3,500
Direct labor	3,000
Manufacturing overhead	1,500
Total cost to date	$8,000

The following journal entries record the transactions of January, 19x2 which are closely related to manufacturing operations. Other entries are omitted.

(1)

A, Materials Inventory............................	15,000	
L, Accounts Payable...........................		15,000

Total materials purchased during the month.

(2)

A, Goods in Process Inventory......................	17,000	
A, Materials Inventory........................		17,000

Total materials used on jobs, as follows:

Job No. 115...........................	$3,000
Job No. 116 (new)....................	8,000
Job No. 117 (new)....................	6,000

(3)

A, Goods in Process Inventory......................	14,000	
A, Manufacturing Overhead Clearing Account........	3,000	
OE, Sales Salaries Expense.........................	2,000	
OE, Administrative Salaries Expense................	1,000	
L, Accrued Salaries Payable....................		20,000

To record total pay earned by employees during
January. Details of the factory payroll were as
follows:

Directly traceable to jobs:

Job No. 115...........................	$ 1,500
Job No. 116...........................	8,000
Job No. 117...........................	4,500
Total debit to Goods in Process.......	$14,000

Not directly traceable to jobs:

Factory supervision...................	$ 1,200
Factory maintenance salaries...........	1,800
Total debit to Manufacturing Overhead Clearing Account.........	$ 3,000

In the preceding entry, the amounts of sales and administrative
salaries, which are *period costs*, are debited immediately to expense
accounts. Those factory costs which can be traced *directly* to jobs are
debited to the *Goods in Process Inventory* account. Those factory costs
which *cannot be traced directly* to specific jobs are collected in a *Manufacturing Overhead Clearing Account*, where they will be combined with
other items of manufacturing overhead cost incurred during the period.
At the end of the period they will be reassigned to specific jobs and to
Goods in Process Inventory, and the balance of the Manufacturing Overhead Clearing Account will become zero (will be *cleared*).

(4)

A, Manufacturing Overhead Clearing Account........	500	
A, Materials Inventory........................		500

Indirect materials used (those not traceable to
specific jobs) for lubrication, cleaning, and maintenance.

(5)

A, Manufacturing Overhead Clearing Account........	200	
A, Unexpired Insurance........................		200

Expiration of insurance premiums applicable to the factory.

(6)

A, Manufacturing Overhead Clearing Account........	3,300	
L, Accounts Payable		3,300

Amounts owed for January factory overhead costs such as rent, repair services, and utilities.

(7)

A, Goods in Process Inventory......................	7,000	
A, Manufacturing Overhead Clearing Account....		7,000

The indirect manufacturing costs were reassigned to jobs in proportion to the direct labor costs of each. Total manufacturing overhead was 50 per cent of direct labor cost for January ($7,000/$14,000); therefore, the January overhead of each job was considered to be 50 per cent of its direct labor cost. The results are:

Job No. 115........... 50% of $1,500 = $ 750
Job No. 116........... 50% of 8,000 = 4,000
Job No. 117........... 50% of 4,500 = 2,250

(8)

A, Finished Goods Inventory.......................	33,250	
A, Goods in Process Inventory..................		33,250

Job Nos. 115 and 116 were completed, with total costs as follows:

	Job No. 115	Job No. 116
Direct materials........	$ 6,500	$ 8,000
Direct labor.............	4,500	8,000
Manufacturing overhead .	2,250	4,000
Totals...............	$13,250	$20,000

(9a)

A, Accounts Receivable...........................	30,000	
OE, Sales Revenue............................		30,000

Job No. 116 was shipped to the customer.

(9b)

OE, Cost of Goods Sold Expense...................	20,000	
A, Finished Goods Inventory...................		20,000

The cost of producing Job 116 was matched with the revenue from its sale.

Posting the transactions of the Calla Machine Company to the general ledger accounts related to factory operations produces the results shown in Figure 15.

The detailed job order cost records in the Goods in Process subsidiary ledger would contain the following information:

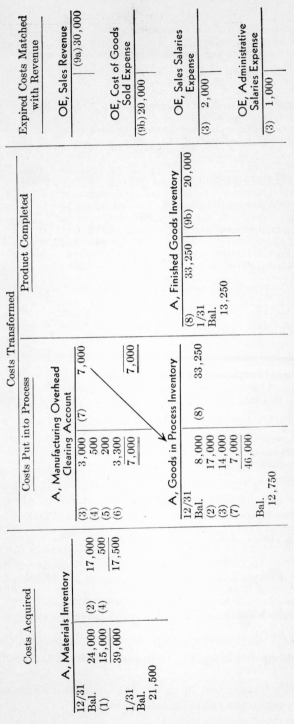

Fig. 15. Flow of Costs in a Manufacturing Enterprise Using a Job Order Cost System.

Goods in Process—Job No. 115

Date	Reference	Materials	Labor	Overhead	Credits	Debit Balance
		Debits				Debit
19x1						
Dec. 31	Balance	3,500	3,000	1,500		8,000
19x2						
Jan.	(2)	3,000				11,000
	(3)		1,500			12,500
	(7)			750		13,250
	(8)				13,250	0

Goods in Process—Job No. 116

Date	Reference	Materials	Labor	Overhead	Credits	Debit Balance
		Debits				Debit
19x2						
Jan.	(2)	8,000				8,000
	(3)		8,000			16,000
	(7)			4,000		20,000
	(8)				20,000	0

Goods in Process—Job No. 117

Date	Reference	Materials	Labor	Overhead	Credits	Debit Balance
		Debits				Debit
19x2						
Jan.	(2)	6,000				6,000
	(3)		4,500			10,500
	(7)			2,250		12,750

Financial statements of a manufacturer

The principal differences between the statement of financial position of a manufacturing business and that of a merchandising business are in the *inventory* accounts, which appear under "Current Assets." The manufacturer's statement will list Finished Goods Inventory, Goods in Process Inventory, and Materials and Supplies Inventory, while the merchandiser's statement will show only Merchandise Inventory.

There should be no difference between the statement of retained income of a manufacturer and that of a merchandiser, and there should also be no difference between their income statements if cost of goods sold expense is shown as a single amount. It is customary for manufacturing businesses to prepare a separate statement or schedule showing the components of the cost of goods sold, such as the following:

CALLA MACHINE COMPANY
Schedule of Cost of Goods Sold For the Month Ended January 31, 19x2

Direct materials...............................		$17,000
Direct labor....................................		14,000
Manufacturing overhead:		
Indirect materials.....................	$ 500	
Indirect labor.........................	3,000	
Factory insurance.....................	200	
Factory rent, repairs, and utilities........	3,300	
Total manufacturing overhead...............		7,000

Total manufacturing cost added this period.................	$38,000
Add beginning goods in process inventory..................	8,000
Total...	$46,000
Deduct ending goods in process inventory..................	12,750
Cost of goods completed this period.....................	$33,250
Add beginning finished goods inventory...................	0
Cost of goods available for sale.........................	$33,250
Deduct ending finished goods inventory...................	13,250
Cost of goods sold (to Income Statement)................	$20,000

The information contained in the schedule was obtained by analyzing the components of the general ledger accounts which relate to manufacturing costs.

Limitations of the job order cost system

The foregoing illustration was intentionally simple, and for that reason it failed to show some of the shortcomings of the job order system of assigning production costs to units of product. Some of the system's principal limitations are the following:

(1) It requires detailed records of the materials issued and the labor hours worked on each job. If the jobs in process at a given time are numerous, the time required to collect this information can be extensive.

(2) It combines in a single total the costs incurred on a job over several periods and thereby hides important trends in production efficiency.

(3) It delays collecting information on the overhead cost of a job until the *end* of the accounting period, when the actual amounts of the various components of overhead cost of the period are known. For jobs which are completed *during* the period, this information is not timely enough to permit management to improve productive efficiency or to change selling prices.

(4) It allocates *actual* overhead to individual jobs manufactured. When rates of productive activity change, this practice leads to confusing and often meaningless fluctuations in the unit costs of similar jobs produced at different times. Many components of manufacturing overhead, such as depreciation, rent, taxes, and insurance, tend to vary more with the passage of time than with the volume of production. As a result, the overhead component assigned to each unit of product will be relatively *high* in periods of *low* production and *low* in periods of *high* production.

Accounts required in a process cost accounting system

A manufacturing company which uses a *process cost* accounting system, like one which uses a job order system, maintains inventory accounts for finished goods, goods in process, and materials and supplies. Of the general ledger accounts of the two systems, only *goods in process inventory* accounts are likely to be different. The following variations are common under process cost systems:

(1) A single goods in process inventory account is used. This is appropriate when there is only one production process.

(2) A separate goods in process inventory account is used for each element of cost: *Goods in Process—Materials, Goods in Process—Labor,* and *Goods in Process—Manufacturing Overhead.* This variation is useful when there is one production process but separate unit costs are desired for each element of cost.

(3) A goods in process inventory account is used for each process of a factory with more than one process. Each account parallels the responsibility of the manager in charge of the process.

(4) A separate goods in process account is used for each element of each process.

At the end of each time period for which unit costs are to be computed, a *cost of production report* is prepared. It summarizes the total manufacturing costs incurred according to elements, the physical number of units produced, and the cost of each element for each unit of manufactured product.

Illustration of process cost accounting procedure

The Burson Chemical Company manufactures a single product, *Burmical,* by using one productive process. Liquid and solid raw materials are mixed together, cooked in vats for 4 days, and then transferred to bulk storage tanks awaiting shipment to customers. The company computes the average cost of manufacturing a gallon of Burmical once a month.

At the beginning of April, 19x1, the vats were empty. During April 24,000 gallons of Burmical were completed and transferred to the storage tanks. On April 30 the vats contained 4,000 gallons of mixture including all of the necessary raw materials, which had been placed in the vats at the beginning of April 29. No further loss from evaporation was expected. Labor is incurred evenly throughout the productive process.

The balances in the relevant general ledger accounts on April 30, representing costs incurred during the month, were:

	Debit
Goods in Process Inventory—Materials	$56,000
Goods in Process Inventory—Labor	10,400
Goods in Process Inventory—Manufacturing Overhead	13,000

The following formula is used to compute the average cost of each element for each unit of manufactured product:

$$\frac{\text{Total Cost Incurred during the Period}}{\text{Number of Units Produced}} = \text{Unit Cost}$$

In computing the cost of each element in a unit of output, the *number of units completed as to that element* should be used as the denominator. Units completed as to an element of cost and units only partially completed must be expressed in a common denominator before being divided into the total cost incurred. The common denominator used is *equivalent whole units produced.*

EXAMPLE 5:   A cost of $10 was incurred in manufacturing 4 units which were complete and 3 units which were one-third complete. What was the cost of manufacturing a complete unit?

SOLUTION: The partially finished units are each equivalent to one-third of a completed unit. The number of equivalent whole units produced is computed as follows:

$$4 + \tfrac{1}{3}(3) = 5$$

The cost of manufacturing a complete unit is $10/5, or $2.

The following summary shows the computation of unit costs for the Burson Chemical Company for April, 19x1:

BURSON CHEMICAL COMPANY
Cost of Production Report
For the Month Ended April 30, 19x1

| | Units | | | | | |
Cost Element	Complete	In Process	Fraction Completed	Equivalent Whole Units	Total Cost	Unit Cost
Materials.....	24,000	4,000	All	28,000	$56,000	$2.00
Labor.........	24,000	4,000	½	26,000	10,400	0.40
Manufacturing Overhead...	24,000	4,000	½	26,000	13,000	0.50
Totals....					$79,400	$2.90

The average cost of manufacturing a gallon of Burmical, $2.90, could *not* have been computed by dividing the total cost, $79,400, by the 28,000 gallons on which work was performed during the period. A unit in process should not be assigned the same amount of cost as a unit finished and transferred to the storage tanks, because, although it has had all the necessary material added to it, it has had only half of the necessary amount of labor and manufacturing overhead.

The only journal entry needed on April 30 is one to record the transfer of costs from goods in process to finished goods, as follows:

(10)

A, Finished Goods Inventory....................... 69,600
    A, Goods in Process Inventory—Materials.......   48,000
    A, Goods in Process Inventory—Labor..........   9,600
    A, Goods in Process Inventory—Mfg. Overhead..   12,000
    To transfer the cost of 24,000 gallons completed at
    $2.90 each to Finished Goods Inventory.

After this entry has been posted, the balances remaining in the Goods in Process Inventory accounts will be as follows:

Goods in Process—Materials..... $8,000 (4,000 units $\times$ $2.00)
Goods in Process—Labor........   800 (4,000 units $\times$ $\frac{1}{2}$ $\times$ $0.40)
Goods in Process—Mfg. Overhead 1,000 (4,000 units $\times$ $\frac{1}{2}$ $\times$ $0.50)

Management use of historical cost information

Information about the historical costs of units of product can be used by management in appraising manufacturing efficiency, in setting future prices, and in determining which products to produce under an existing price structure.

Some basis for comparison is needed in appraising productive efficiency. The unit costs of the current period may be compared with the unit costs of the same type of product in *past periods;* they may be compared with unit costs which were *expected*, or estimated in advance, for the current period; or they may be compared with *predetermined standards* which have been set up after a study of what the quantities and prices of factors of production used should be under efficient operating conditions. The next section is devoted to the use of such predetermined costs.

ACCOUNTING FOR PREDETERMINED COSTS

Behavior of production costs

In most manufacturing enterprises, the cost of direct materials tends to *vary* closely with the number of units produced, and so does the cost of direct labor. Some of the items that compose *manufacturing overhead* also vary with the quantity of production. The amounts of most of them, however, tend to vary with the passage of time and to be *nonvariable* with the volume of production. Examples of such nonvariable manufacturing overhead items are depreciation, rent, and salaries of supervisory employees. If such nonvariable costs are divided by the number of units produced to arrive at a manufacturing overhead cost per unit of product, the resulting unit costs tend to fluctuate with the volume of activity.

EXAMPLE 6: A manufacturer of one product finds that its variable costs of direct materials and direct labor tend to be about $4 and $6 per unit, respectively, while manufacturing overhead is approximately constant at $20,000 per month. In January it manufactured 1,000 units, and in February, 10,000 units. What were total and unit costs by elements for each month?

SOLUTION:

	Total Costs	Units Produced	Cost per Unit
January:			
Direct materials...................	$ 4,000	1,000	$ 4.00
Direct labor......................	6,000	1,000	6.00
Manufacturing overhead...........	20,000	1,000	20.00
Totals........................	$ 30,000	1,000	$30.00
February:			
Direct materials...................	$ 40,000	10,000	$ 4.00
Direct labor......................	60,000	10,000	6.00
Manufacturing overhead...........	20,000	10,000	2.00
Totals........................	$120,000	10,000	$12.00

The difference between the total cost of manufacturing a unit in January, $30.00, and that of manufacturing a unit in February, $12.00, is due solely to the fact that the same cost of manufacturing overhead was distributed over fewer units in January. Production was not less efficient in January, nor will customers pay more for the product of January than for that of February simply because it has a higher overhead cost per unit. For these reasons, the widely varying unit overhead costs when volume of production fluctuates are of limited usefulness.

Predetermined manufacturing overhead rate

One method of smoothing out seasonal fluctuations in the average amount of nonvariable manufacturing overhead per unit of manufactured product is to divide the amount of overhead for the year by the number of units produced during the year. If actual data are used for this purpose, cost information will be delayed too long to be of much use to management. The use of a *predetermined overhead* rate, based upon estimated cost and production data for the year, provides management with timely information that is usually accurate enough to be useful.

EXAMPLE 7: The manufacturer in Example 6 decided to use a predetermined rate to smooth out seasonal fluctuations in unit overhead costs, as well as to provide timely information on total unit production costs. The rate was computed as follows:

$$\frac{\text{Estimated Manufacturing Overhead for the Year, \$240,000}}{\text{Estimated Units to Be Produced during the Year, 80,000}}$$
$$= \text{Average Overhead per Unit, \$3.00}$$

The predetermined overhead rate would be used in computing the cost of units manufactured during the year and in making journal entries transferring costs from Manufacturing Overhead Clearing Account to Goods in Process Inventory. The following is an example.

(11)

A, Goods in Process Inventory...................... 3,000
    A, Manufacturing Overhead Clearing Account....   3,000
    To record the estimated overhead costs for 1,000
    units actually manufactured in January, at a pre-
    determined rate of $3 per unit.

During the month, actual overhead costs are accumulated in the clearing account by entries such as the following:

(12)

A, Manufacturing Overhead Clearing Account........ 19,700
    L, Accounts Payable...........................   15,000
    A, Prepaid Expense............................   1,000
    A, Materials and Supplies Inventory.....   3,700
    To record actual overhead for January.

After posting these entries, the items in the clearing account would be:

A, Manufacturing Overhead Clearing Account	

19x1
Jan. (Actual overhead)
     (12)................. 19,700
 	
    Balance, 16,700.
	19x1
	Jan. (Overhead transferred to
	    Goods in Process at pre-
	    determined rate) (11)... 3,000

Analyzing the manufacturing overhead variance

The difference between the actual manufacturing overhead and the overhead computed by using the predetermined rate is called the *overhead variance*. In this illustration there is a *debit* variance of $16,700. Analysis of the causes of such variances helps management to decide upon the action necessary to correct inefficient operating conditions and to plan more accurately for the future. The total variance can be broken down into a *volume variance* and an *efficiency variance*, according to the method illustrated in Chapter 12 for analyzing the difference between the actual results and the budgeted results of a merchandising company. The analysis is as follows:

Actual manufacturing overhead for January................ $19,700
Minus overhead transferred to Goods in Process............   3,000
Total debit variance to be analyzed........................ $16,700
Volume variance:
   Estimated overhead for the month.............. $20,000
   Minus overhead transferred to Goods in Process..   3,000
   Debit variance caused by producing at less than the
     expected average volume for the year................. $17,000

Budget variance:
Actual manufacturing overhead for the month.... $19,700
Minus estimated overhead for the month......... 20,000
Credit variance caused by difference of actual fixed
    overhead from the budget........................... ($ 300)
Net debit total of variances analyzed..................... $16,700

The $17,000 volume variance was *expected*. If actual volume is as planned during the year, 80,000 units, the net total of the twelve monthly debit and credit volume variances will be zero.

The $300 credit *budget* variance was *unexpected*. It may have consisted of differences between the actual and the budgeted amounts of many individual components of manufacturing overhead, some differences being debits and others being credits. It might actually represent a *saving* by management on one or a number of components of overhead cost items. For example, insurance policies may have been acquired at lower rates than those anticipated in the budget.

If a detailed component of the budget variance is caused by an error in budgeting, knowledge of its cause should result in more accurate budgeting in the future. If it is caused by increased operating efficiency, knowledge of the cause can lead to savings elsewhere. If it is caused by operating *inefficiency*, management should seek the cause or causes and take the necessary corrective measures.

Bases for allocating predetermined overhead to products

The two preceding sections have illustrated a situation in which the business manufactured a single product, in which case it was feasible to assign manufacturing overhead in equal amounts to each unit of product, using the predetermined rate.

In most actual manufacturing operations, there are a number of different types of products being manufactured. Total number of units produced is *not* a common denominator which can be divided into total overhead cost in arriving at a cost per unit produced. Instead, overhead costs must be assigned to units of product on the basis of some factor which is common to all units. The factor selected should be one with which the overhead cost varies, so that each unit of product will be assigned the amount of overhead for which it is responsible.

Most factory overhead components tend to vary with the passage of time; therefore, units of time are ordinarily a suitable factor to use in assigning overhead to units of product. Variations of this factor are the *number of labor hours* or *machine hours* spent on each unit of product.

EXAMPLE 8: The management of a manufacturing company thought that jobs produced were responsible for manufacturing overhead approximately in proportion to the number of labor hours worked on each job. The budget estimate for 19x2 was as follows:

Estimated Manufacturing Overhead, $500,000
  Estimated Direct Labor Hours, 100,000
                        = Manufacturing Overhead per Direct Labor Hour, $5

During 19x2, 12 direct labor hours were worked on Job No. 401, and it was assigned manufacturing overhead of $60 (12 hours times the predetermined rate of $5 per hour). Overhead allocated to Job No. 402 was $80, determined by multiplying the 16 actual hours spent on the job by $5.

When a significant part of the manufacturing overhead is variable, or when substantial parts are thought to vary in proportion to different factors, one basis may be used for assigning a part of the overhead to units of product and another allocation basis may be used for the remainder.

Standard costs: nature and purposes

The purposes and basic methods of *standard costs* are similar to those of predetermined factory overhead rates, but standard costs are much more useful. They are standards of efficiency with which actual results can be compared. The following are some of their advantages:

(1) They give management timely signals of the existence of non-standard results in the unit costs of manufacturing;

(2) They help management pinpoint the causes of departure of costs from the desired level;

(3) They simplify the details of accounting by permitting many detailed records to be maintained in terms of quantities only, since the standard cost of a given component of cost is the same for each unit of the manufactured product.

The starting point in a standard cost system is an itemization of the costs which are considered to be desirable for *one* unit of manufactured product. The details of the standard cost for a unit of product show the standard costs for each cost element, and these in turn are subdivided into *price* and *quantity* components. The following is an example.

STANDARD COST SHEET for 1 gallon of Product KM			
	Quantity	Price	Cost
Direct material Y.....................	1.5 gallons	$2.00	$ 3.00
Direct labor...........................	2.0 hours	2.50	5.00
Manufacturing overhead...............	1 unit of product	2.00	2.00
Total..........................			$10.00

Accounting for standard costs

Under one standard cost system, the inventory accounts—Materials, Goods in Process, and Finished Goods—are debited and credited with amounts determined by multiplying the *actual quantities* received or issued by the standard cost per unit. The product is a total standard cost for the element of cost in question. The total actual cost incurred for each element is compared with the standard cost, and the differences, or *variances*, are analyzed into *price variances* and *quantity variances*. Other variations of standard cost accounting procedure are also in common use.

The following are the actual results of the manufacturer of Product KM for the month of March, 19x3. For simplicity, it is assumed that there were no inventories on hand at the beginning of the period, and that all units started during the month were completed.

Materials Y purchased: 5,000 gallons at $1.90......... $9,500
Materials Y used to produce 2,000 gallons of Product
   KM... 3,200 gallons
Direct labor: 3,700 hours at $2.70................... $9,990
Actual overhead.................................. $4,000

The journal entries to summarize these results are as follows:

(13)

A, Materials Inventory (5,000 gallons at $2.00)........ 10,000
   L, Accounts Payable (5,000 gallons at $1.90)......   9,500
   OE, Materials Price Variance (5,000 gallons at
     $0.10).....................................   500
To debit Materials Inventory for the standard cost of items bought; to credit a liability for their actual cost; and to record a credit (favorable) price variance for the saving based upon the standard unit price.

(14)

A, Goods in Process Inventory (3,000 gallons at $2).... 6,000
OE, Materials Quantity Variance (200 gallons at $2)...   400
   A, Materials Inventory (3,200 gallons at $2).......   6,400
To debit Goods in Process for the standard material cost of manufacturing 2,000 gallons of product; to record an unfavorable variance for the excess quantity used; and to reduce Materials Inventory by the actual quantity of materials used, priced at standard.

(15)

A, Goods in Process Inventory (4,000 hours at $2.50).... 10,000
OE, Labor Price Variance (3,700 hours at $0.20).......   740
   OE, Labor Quantity Variance (300 hours at $2.50).   750
   L, Accrued Payroll (3,700 hours at $2.70).........   9,990
To debit Goods in Process for the standard labor cost of manufacturing 2,000 gallons of product; to record an unfavorable price variance for the rate paid labor above standard; to record the favorable variance resulting from hours saved as compared with standard; and to record the liability for the actual labor cost.

(16)

A, Manufacturing Overhead Clearing Account......... 4,000
    Various individual assets and liabilities............   4,000
To record the actual manufacturing overhead cost incurred.

(17)

A, Goods in Process Inventory (2,000 units at $2)...... 4,000
    OE, Manufacturing Overhead Clearing Account....   4,000
To transfer overhead to Goods in Process at the standard rate of $2 per gallon of product for each of the 2,000 gallons manufactured.

The figures in the illustration have been designed so that there would be no manufacturing overhead variance. In reality, manufacturing overhead variance analysis is quite complex. It proceeds along the lines explained in the earlier section, "Analyzing the manufacturing overhead variance."

Reporting and using variance information

The preceding types of variances, which have been developed in the accounts by means of the standard cost accounting system, and their supporting details (price and quantity variances for each principal type of material and for each major labor operation) should be reported to the individual managers who are responsible for those phases of production.

The next step consists of determining the cause of each variance. The cost accountant may be able to explain some of the variances, especially those caused by budgeting errors. The manager who is responsible for the activity which resulted in the variance should be asked to explain the reasons for variances of significant amount. The purchasing manager, for example, should be called upon to explain materials price variances. It may be that they were caused by hand-to-mouth buying; or that a price change was unavoidable; or that the production department caused the excess price by setting unnecessarily tight material specifications.

The variances should be divided into *controllable* and *noncontrollable* groups. The responsible manager should take proper steps to prevent the recurrence of controllable unfavorable variances, and to extend elsewhere the opportunities for cost savings brought to light by favorable variances.

DIRECT COSTING

Earlier sections of this chapter have discussed the components of production costs and the means of accounting for them under traditional concepts and procedures. The approach described may be referred to as *full costing*, or *absorption costing*, whereby all elements of manufacturing cost—direct materials, direct labor, and direct and indirect overhead—are accumulated as a part of the asset, inventory, as *product costs*.

Illustration of absorption costing

In recent years absorption costing has been challenged by many who feel that it gives misleading and often useless results. One of the defects which they point out is the fact, mentioned earlier, that the share of fixed overhead assigned to each unit of product is greater in periods of slack activity. The high production costs of units produced in such periods are often carried forward to be deducted as cost of goods sold expense in succeeding periods in which the current average production costs are lower. This may result in the confusing phenomenon of the *net income of a period being lower* than that of the preceding period while at the same time *production efficiency and the volume of sales are higher*. The following illustration emphasizes this result.

C MANUFACTURING COMPANY
Income Statement (Absorption Costing)
For the Year Ended December 31

	19x2 (1,000 units produced; 1,200 units sold)		19x1 (1,500 units produced; 1,000 units sold)	
Sales.......................		$600,000		$500,000
Deduct cost of goods sold expense:				
Production cost incurred:				
Direct materials..............	$100,000		$150,000	
Direct labor..................	110,000		180,000	
Nonvariable factory overhead...	240,000		240,000	
Total.....................	$450,000		$570,000	
Add beginning finished goods inventory......................	190,000		0	
Cost of goods available for sale....	$640,000		$570,000	
Deduct ending finished goods inventory....................	135,000		190,000	
Cost of goods sold expense......		505,000		380,000
Gross margin....................		$ 95,000		$120,000
Deduct distribution costs:				
Variable......................	$ 60,000		$ 50,000	
Nonvariable..................	30,000	90,000	30,000	80,000
Net income before income tax.......		$ 5,000		$ 40,000

The average unit production costs for the two years were as follows:

	19x2	19x1
Direct materials..........................	$100	$100
Direct labor.............................	110	120
Nonvariable factory overhead..............	240	160
Total.................................	$450	$380

Labor efficiency increased in 19x2, with the result that the cost of direct labor in a unit of product decreased from $120 to $110. However, this was more than offset by an increase of $80 per unit in factory overhead, caused by allocating the same total amount of overhead to the smaller number of units produced in 19x2. The quantity of sales also increased 20 per cent in 19x2, while the selling price per unit remained unchanged. In spite of this and the improvement in efficiency, net income before tax *decreased* from $40,000 to $5,000. This result was caused by charging more nonvariable manufacturing costs to expense in 19x2, the year of *high sales but low production*, than in 19x1, the year of *high production but low sales*. The amounts charged were:

	19x2	19x1
Nonvariable factory overhead charged to cost of goods sold expense:		
1,000 units produced and sold at $160........		$160,000
500 units produced in 19x1, sold in 19x2, at $160....................................	$ 80,000	
700 units produced and sold at $240........	168,000	
Totals...............................	$248,000	$160,000

Illustration of direct costing

Direct costing is a procedure by which only *variable* manufacturing costs are treated as *product costs*, while *nonvariable* manufacturing costs are treated as costs of the *period* in which they are incurred. The revised income statements of the C Manufacturing Company using the direct costing method would be as follows:

C MANUFACTURING COMPANY
Income Statement (Direct Costing)
For the Years Ended December 31

	19x2 (1,000 units produced; 1,200 units sold)		19x1 (1,500 units produced; 1,000 units sold)	
Sales...........................		$600,000		$500,000
Deduct direct cost of goods sold:				
Production costs incurred:				
Direct materials..............	$100,000		$150,000	
Direct labor..................	110,000		180,000	
Total.....................	$210,000		$330,000	
Add beginning finished goods inventory......................	110,000		0	
Cost of goods available for sale....	$320,000		$330,000	
Deduct ending finished goods inventory....................	63,000		110,000	
Cost of goods sold expense......		257,000		220,000
Manufacturing margin............		$343,000		$280,000
Deduct variable distribution costs...		60,000		50,000
Contribution to nonvariable expenses and income....................		$283,000		$230,000
Deduct period costs:				
Nonvariable production costs.....	$240,000		$240,000	
Nonvariable distribution costs.....	30,000	270,000	30,000	270,000
Net income (loss) before income tax .		$ 13,000		($ 40,000)

Direct costing shows a larger income in 19x2, when the sales and production efficiency improved. The income in 19x1 under the direct costing method, a loss of $40,000, is $80,000 less than the net income under the absorption costing method. This is exactly equal to the amount of nonvariable manufacturing cost ($\frac{1}{3}$ of $240,000) which is added to an asset, ending inventory, at the end of 19x1 under the absorption costing method. The net income in 19x2 is $8,000 higher than under the absorption costing method, because $80,000 less is added to cost of goods sold through the beginning inventory, and $72,000 less is subtracted from cost of goods sold through the ending inventory.

The cumulative retained income for a period of years will be higher under the absorption costing method by the amount of the nonvariable manufacturing cost which is included in the inventory at the end of the period.

The income statement under the direct costing method resembles the statement of marginal income for a merchandising company illustrated in Chapter 11. Both emphasize the *contribution to nonvariable expenses and income*, which is the excess of revenue over *direct costs* (*variable costs* would be a more accurate term).

The direct costing income statement differs from the absorption costing statement in a more fundamental way than in the arrangement of the items, however. The nonvariable production costs are *not added to inventory*, but are treated as *expenses of the period* in which they are incurred. Advocates of direct costing contend that these costs are not *costs of producing*, but costs of having the *capacity to produce*.

Proponents of direct costing stress the following advantages of the method:

(1) The net income for a period tends to move in the same direction as sales and is not affected by changes in the amounts of nonvariable production costs absorbed in inventory when levels of production and inventory change.

(2) It emphasizes the *contribution* to nonvariable overhead and income of various segments of business and thus facilitates management decisions as to which products to sell and how to price them.

On the other hand, direct costing fails to assign full costs of production to units of product. If a business establishes its selling prices on the basis of direct costs alone, it will not recover all of its costs in the long run.

A desirable compromise between the two points of view is one whereby direct costing statements are prepared for internal use and the statements prepared for outsiders are adjusted to an absorption costing basis by assigning an appropriate share of nonvariable factory overhead to inventory.

Unit costs of distribution and service

The actual costs of manufacturing units of products and of their direct material, direct labor, and factory overhead components form a *continuous* part of the accounting records of the manufacturer. So do the predetermined standard costs which are used as a basis against which to measure deviations from planned production costs.

It is frequently desirable to measure the actual unit costs of *distribution* and *service* and to compare them with predetermined standards. These unit costs are useful to management in revealing the existence of *variances* from efficient conditions. They do not form a part of inventory asset accounts and as a rule they are not recorded on a continuing basis like that used for production costs. Instead, such unit costs are often determined in special *cost studies* which sample the costs of distribution and service activities at convenient time intervals.

Unit costs of distribution and service can be computed only if it is possible to measure the activity in terms of a homogeneous physical unit and to trace the total costs which apply to it for the period whose results are being measured.

Summary

Following the general rule that all costs reasonably incurred up to the point where an item is ready for sale are proper additions to the asset, inventory, costs of manufacturing are treated as product costs. Production costs are assigned to individual units of product by identifying them with the total production of a *process* for a period of time or by tracing them to a *job* which is physically segregated during production. The principal elements of manufacturing costs are direct materials, direct labor, and factory overhead.

Predetermined rates are often used to assign factory overhead to individual units of product in order to smooth out the effect of fluctuations in the level of production. A further refinement is the use of predetermined standard costs against which actual costs are compared. The variances of actual costs from standard illustrate the use of the management principle of exception; they denote where operations have deviated from the planned standards of efficiency and provide a basis for corrective action.

Direct, or variable, costing is a device for drawing management attention to the contribution margins of products and for leveling out the periodic assignment of nonvariable production costs to income.

Unit costs may be measuerd for distribution and service activities. Unlike production costs, however, they are not usually a permanent part of the accounts but are derived from special cost studies.

QUESTIONS AND PROBLEMS

17-1   A large retailer buys some types of merchandise in bulk and packages it in smaller quantities for resale.

REQUIRED:

a. Using assumed amounts, show how you would account for the acquisition, packaging, and sale of the merchandise.
b. How does this situation resemble the inventory accounting of a manufacturer? How does it differ?

17-2   The costs of a manufacturer may be classified into two broad groups, *production costs* and *distribution costs*.

REQUIRED:

a. List three specific types of production costs.
b. List three specific types of distribution costs.

17-3   "Production costs are . . . transformed in the accounting records."

REQUIRED:

a. Explain the difference between *cost transformation* and *cost expiration*.
b. Use journal entries to show how a manufacturer would account for each.

17-4   "Distribution costs are assigned directly to expense accounts in the accounting period in which they expire."

REQUIRED:

a. Does this statement imply that distribution costs are less important than production costs?   Explain.
b. How can this accounting treatment be justified?

17-5

REQUIRED:

a. Give three examples of factory production departments.
b. Give three examples of factory service departments.
c. Give three examples of departments of a manufacturing business which are neither (a) nor (b).
d. Explain how cost information can be used to evaluate the performance of each of the three types of departments: production, service, and other.

17-6

REQUIRED:

a. Illustrate a type of situation in which selling prices are based largely upon production costs.
b. Illustrate a type of situation in which selling prices of a manufactured product are largely independent of production costs.
c. Is information about unit production costs useful in (b)? Explain.

17-7

REQUIRED:

Would it be appropriate to establish *cost centers* for nonmanufacturing businesses? Explain.

17-8

REQUIRED:

Which method of accumulating costs of product, job order or process, do you think would be more appropriate for:

(1) A book publisher?
(2) A paper manufacturer?
(3) A driveway construction company?
(4) A manufacturer of military airplanes?
(5) A cement manufacturer?
(6) A brick kiln?

17-9   The use of the job order cost system is not appropriate unless it is possible to identify the manufactured product at all times.

REQUIRED:

a. In what ways does the job order method resemble the specific identification method of accounting for merchandise inventory?
b. How do the two methods differ?

17-10   "The job order cost system merges many dissimilar costs and hides important trends in unit costs."

REQUIRED:

a. Explain why this is true.
b. How would you suggest that this limitation be overcome?

17-11

REQUIRED:

Give an example of each of the following in determining the unit costs of publishing a book:

(1) Direct materials.
(2) Indirect materials.
(3) Direct labor.
(4) Indirect labor.
(5) Manufacturing overhead.

17-12

REQUIRED:

a. What is the purpose of the Manufacturing Overhead Clearing Account?
b. How would you classify it in the financial statements?

17-13   One of the limitations of the historical job order system described in this chapter is that it allocates *actual* overhead to jobs.

REQUIRED:

a. Why is this a shortcoming of the job order system?
b. How would you suggest that it be remedied?

17-14

REQUIRED:

a. Which is likely to have more general ledger inventory accounts, a job order cost system or a process cost system?   Explain.
b. Which is likely to have more subsidiary ledger accounts?   Explain.
c. Which is likely to require more clerical effort?   Why?

17-15

REQUIRED:

Describe carefully how production costs are associated with individual physical units of product under (1) a job order cost system and (2) a process cost system.

17-16

REQUIRED:

a. In what way does the use of a predetermined rate for assigning overhead to units of production resemble the operation of a standard cost system?
b. In what way do the two differ?

17-17   Perhaps the most important purpose of a standard cost system consists of the investigation and action taken by management on the basis of reported variances.

REQUIRED:

What disposition would you recommend in the accounting records for each of the following variances? All are substantial in amount.

a. A debit materials quantity variance caused by unrealistic product specifications.
b. A debit materials price variance caused by unexpected price changes which seem likely to continue.
c. A labor quantity variance caused by the use of inexperienced labor.
d. A labor quantity variance caused by a shortage of materials.
e. A labor price variance caused by signing a new labor contract at higher rates.
f. A credit balance in the factory overhead volume variance at the end of the year resulting from operations considerably above the normal rate.
g. A debit balance in the factory overhead budget variance account due to careless budgeting.

17-18

REQUIRED:

a. Which will report a larger net income for the first year of operations in a given case, direct costing or absorption costing?
b. Which will report a larger net income for a year other than the first? Explain.
c. Which will report a larger total net income for a series of years, beginning with the founding of the business? Explain.

17-19   For simplicity, the illustrations of direct costing in this chapter treated all factory overhead as nonvariable and used the FIFO inventory assumption.

REQUIRED:

a. How would variable factory overhead be accounted for under direct costing? Illustrate.
b. Can direct costing be used with other inventory methods than FIFO? Explain.

17-20   The Beecham Machine Company manufactures large construction machinery to the specifications of its customers. On March 31, 19x1, its inventories were the following:

Materials and Supplies Inventory.......................... $17,000
Goods in Process Inventory............................... 8,500
Finished Goods Inventory................................. 10,000

The company used an actual cost system, assigning factory overhead to individual jobs at the end of each month in proportion to the direct labor cost of each job during the month.

On March 31 the Goods in Process Inventory consisted of partly finished Job No. 55, on which the following costs had been incurred in previous months: direct labor, $3,000; factory overhead, $2,100; and direct materials, $3,400. Finished Goods Inventory was represented entirely by Job No. 57.

The following events occurred during March:

(1) Purchased materials on account for $12,000.
(2) Payroll for the month accrued in the amount of $15,000. Of this amount, $1,000 was on Job No. 55, $3,000 was on Job No. 58, and $6,000 was on Job No. 59. In addition, factory supervisory salaries were $2,000, salesmen's salaries were $1,200, and general administrative salaries were $1,800.
(3) Issued materials and supplies as follows:

Job No. 55	$1,600
Job No. 58	7,000
Job No. 59	4,000
Factory supplies	1,500
Shipping supplies	300

(4) Shipped completed Job No. 57 to the customer and billed him for the selling price of $16,000.
(5) Other costs incurred during the month were as follows:

Advertising	$ 500
Factory depreciation	1,000
Factory insurance	800
Factory taxes	700

(6) Completed Job No. 55 and transferred it to the finished goods storeroom awaiting shipment.

REQUIRED:

a. Journalize the necessary entries for March.
b. Post transactions to the general ledger and to the Goods in Process subsidiary ledger.
c. Prepare an income statement for the month.
d. Do you think the job order cost system is suitable in this situation? If not, what would you recommend?
e. How can you justify the method used for assigning factory overhead to jobs?
f. What are the disadvantages of the method used for allocating factory overhead?

17-21   The Mathews Mfg. Co. uses a job order system for assigning manufacturing costs to individual units of product. It has decided to change from a system of allocating actual factory overhead costs to jobs at the end of each month to a predetermined system of allocating overhead. Most of the factory overhead does not vary with the volume of production, but with the passage of time. At the beginning of 19x3 the following estimates are made of the production costs for the coming year:

Direct materials	$500,000
Direct labor	600,000
Factory overhead	900,000

During January, 19x3, direct materials actually used were $26,000 and direct labor was $30,000. Actual factory overhead for the month, determined during the first week of February when all bills for January had been received, amounted to $73,000. The production volume for the year is still expected to be as estimated at the beginning of the year.

REQUIRED:

a. What basis would you recommend for assigning a predetermined amount of overhead to jobs produced during the year? Why?
b. Compute the predetermined overhead rate.
c. Record in journal form the assignment of factory overhead to Job No. 101, which was begun on January 5 and completed on January 14 with a direct labor cost of $200 and a direct materials cost of $500.
d. Record summary journal entries for total manufacturing costs incurred in January.
e. Prepare an analysis explaining the balance in the Factory Overhead Clearing Account at the end of January. What disposition would you make of it?

17-22 The Tell Chemical Company manufactures its product in one continuous productive process. Raw material is added at the beginning of the productive process. A careful record is kept of all material withdrawn from the storeroom each month, all labor costs incurred, and all manufacturing overhead. The quantity of finished product transferred to stock, measured in pounds, is weighed on a large scale.

The following data relate to production for the month of May, 19x2:

(1) There were no units in process at the beginning of the month.
(2) During May 14,500 pounds of raw material were issued to the production department from the storeroom. At the end of the month, 500 pounds of material were unused, but in good condition, on the production floor. Each pound of material had cost $5.
(3) Direct labor cost for May was $18,000; sales salaries were $3,000; and general salaries were $2,000.
(4) Factory overhead costs amounted to $13,500; selling overhead, to $2,500; and general overhead, to $5,000.
(5) During May 8,000 pounds of product were transferred to finished stock.
(6) At the end of May 2,000 pounds of semi-finished product were still in the process of production. All necessary material had been added, and all of the shrinkage which normally occurred during the production process had already taken place. Half of the necessary labor and factory overhead cost had been incurred on the goods in process.

REQUIRED:

a. Prepare a unit cost of production report for May.
b. Journalize entries necessary to record the foregoing data for May.
c. Post the entries to T-accounts.
d. How can the unit cost figures computed in (a) be used by the Tell Chemical Company?
e. What are the shortcomings of the unit cost figures in (a), and how would you recommend that they be improved?

17-23 The Monson Gadget Co. has been manufacturing product X for a number of years. On the basis of its past experience, together with a careful study by production engineers, it estimates that the cost per unit of product X under efficient operating conditions should be as follows:

Standard Cost per Unit of X

Materials:
  4 pounds @ $2.00 per pound.......................... $ 8.00
Labor:
  2 hours @ $3.00 per hour............................   6.00
Factory overhead:
  2 hours @ $1.50 per hour............................   3.00
      Total.. $17.00

The factory overhead rate was based upon the assumption that 20,000 hours would be worked during a normal month.

During November, 19x1, actual production figures were as follows:

Quantity of product X produced.................... 10,000 units
Quantity of materials used........................ 40,500 pounds
Labor hours worked................................ 20,000 hours
Cost per pound of materials....................... $2.10
Cost per hour of labor............................ $2.75
Actual factory overhead........................... $32,000

REQUIRED:

a. Prepare a table showing for each element of cost (1) the total actual cost of production during the month, (2) the total standard cost for the month, and (3) the total variance for the month, identified as a debit or a credit.
b. Analyze the total variance for each element of cost into its main components.
c. Whom within the factory would you ask for an explanation of the cause of each of the variances in (b)?
d. List several possible causes of each of the variances, and explain what disposition you would make of the matter in each case.

17-24 At the end of December, 19x5, you find the following accounts in the general ledger of a manufacturing company which uses a standard cost system:

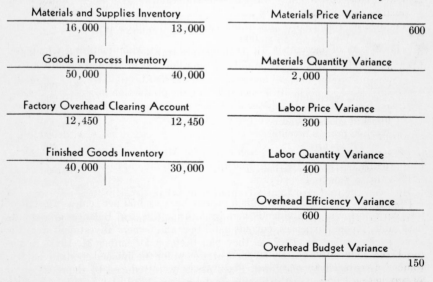

Materials and Supplies Inventory		Materials Price Variance	
16,000	13,000		600

Goods in Process Inventory		Materials Quantity Variance	
50,000	40,000	2,000	

Factory Overhead Clearing Account		Labor Price Variance	
12,450	12,450	300	

Finished Goods Inventory		Labor Quantity Variance	
40,000	30,000	400	

Overhead Efficiency Variance	
600	

Overhead Budget Variance	
	150

There were no inventories on hand at the beginning of the month.

REQUIRED:

a. Reconstruct in journal form summary entries needed to record the production costs for the month.

b. Give an analysis of the elements of cost comprising the Finished Goods Inventory balance at the end of the month.

c. How would you recommend that management use the information on variances?

17-25   The Colos Products Company wishes a comparison of the results of direct costing and absorption costing, using the data taken from its records for the past three years. Average unit costs of production are to be computed separately for each year, and the FIFO method is to be used in assigning product costs of different years to sales revenue. There are no ending goods in process inventories. The following figures are available:

	19x1	19x2	19x3
Quantities:			
Beginning finished goods inventory...............	0	4,000	2,000
Current production.............................	5,000	2,000	4,000
Sales...	1,000	4,000	4,000
Costs and revenues:			
Sales...	$50,000	$200,000	$200,000
Direct materials................................	75,000	30,000	60,000
Direct labor....................................	50,000	20,000	40,000
Nonvariable factory overhead....................	60,000	60,000	60,000
Variable selling and administrative costs...........	2,500	10,000	10,000
Nonvariable selling and administrative costs........	4,000	4,000	4,000

REQUIRED:

a. Prepare an income statement for each of the years under the absorption costing method.

b. What weaknesses are there in the results determined in (*a*)?

c. Prepare an income statement for each of the years under direct costing.

d. What weaknesses are there in the results determined in (*c*)?

e. What method do you suggest that the company follow? Why?

17-26   As of December 31, 19x1, the Bobbett Manufacturing Company, with owners' investment of $30,000, had the following assets and liabilities:

Cash...	$ 5,000
Accounts receivable.....................................	10,000
Raw materials inventory.................................	4,000
Finished goods inventory................................	6,000
Work in process inventory...............................	2,000
Prepaid expenses.......................................	500
Fixed assets...	40,000
Accumulated depreciation...............................	10,000
Current liabilities......................................	17,500

During the year 19x2, the retained income increased 50 per cent as a result of the year's business. No dividends were paid during the year. Balances of accounts receivable, prepaid expenses, current liabilities, and owners' investment were the same on December 31, 19x2, as they had been on December 31, 19x1. Inventories were reduced by exactly 50 per cent, except for the finished goods inventory, which was reduced by one-third. Fixed assets were reduced by depreciation of $4,000, charged three-fourths to manufacturing overhead cost and one-fourth to general expense. Sales were made at 50 per cent above the cost of goods sold, which was $40,000. Direct labor cost was $9,000 and manufacturing overhead, in addition to depreciation, was 50 per cent of labor cost. Total general and selling expenses amounted to 15 per cent and 10 per cent, respectively, of gross sales.

REQUIRED:

a. Prepare a statement of financial position as of December 31, 19x2.
b. Prepare an income statement for the year 19x2.
c. Support the formal statements with a work sheet or T-accounts.

(Adapted from AICPA Examination in Accounting Practice—Part I, May, 1950.)

CASE 17-1. RYLE COMPANY POWER PLANT

Ryle Company, a medium-sized manufacturing company, maintains its own power plant to serve its three production departments, A, B, and C. It has been assigning actual power costs to the departments at the end of each month in proportion to the number of kilowatt hours used by each during the month.

In April, 19x3, Mr. Walker, manager of Production Department A, has called upon the company's controller to explain why, although his department used fewer kilowatt hours in April than in March, it has been charged a larger amount for power cost for April. During the course of the discussion, the following information is examined:

	Total	Department A	Department B	Department C
March results:				
Kilowatt hours used...	250,000	100,000	30,000	120,000
Per cent of total hours.	100%	40%	12%	48%
Power cost assigned...	$5,000	$2,000	$ 600	$2,400
April results:				
Kilowatt hours used...	150,000	75,000	45,000	30,000
Per cent of total hours.	100%	50%	30%	20%
Power cost assigned...	$4,200	$2,100	$1,260	$ 840

Mr. Barnum, the controller, points out that the power department has a large amount of fixed costs which continue regardless of the level of output. "All power costs must be charged to some department," he says. "We have to have enough capacity to serve your peak requirements, and that costs each department something. Your department used a greater share of the output of the power plant for April than for March, and therefore it must bear a higher amount of power costs."

"It just doesn't make sense to me," replies Mr. Walker, "that we have to pay more for using less. We ought to be charged at a flat rate of so much per kilowatt hour every month."

REQUIRED:

a. Is there any merit in Mr. Walker's point of view? Explain.
b. Estimate the amount of the power department costs which are fixed.
c. Outline a system which can be used to measure the efficiency of the power department, and at the same time to charge the production departments fairly for the use of power.

CASE 17-2. THE MADISON MACHINE COMPANY

The Madison Machine Company, which operates a job order cost system, wishes to use a predetermined rate for assigning factory overhead to individual jobs. In the past, some items of factory overhead have tended to vary closely with the number of direct labor hours worked, while others have remained constant. The estimated amounts for 19x2 are as follows:

Direct materials......................	$1,200,000	
Direct labor..........................	1,000,000	(500,000 hours)
Factory overhead:		
Supervision................	$ 18,000	
Indirect labor.............	180,000	
Indirect materials.........	150,000	
Depreciation...............	120,000	
Rent.......................	60,000	
Insurance..................	30,000	
Property taxes.............	24,000	
Utilities..................	48,000	
Total............................	630,000	

The controller is considering two possibilities: (1) using a single predetermined factory overhead rate, and (2) using two rates simultaneously, one for the variable component of factory overhead and one for the fixed component.

At any given time, there are approximately 10 jobs in process, and about 100 jobs are completed each year. The proportion of labor time of highly paid hourly workers is about the same on all jobs.

The month of lowest activity usually accounts for about 5 per cent of the year's production, while the peak month accounts for about 20 per cent.

REQUIRED:

a. If a single rate is used to assign overhead to jobs, what should it be?
b. Assuming that all costs behave exactly as expected during 19x2, prepare T-accounts showing the debits and credits to Factory Overhead Clearing Account in the months of lowest and highest production.
c. What rates would you recommend if dual rates are used?
d. Determine the effect of dual rates on the Factory Overhead Clearing Account in the months of lowest and highest production.
e. What other factors should be considered in deciding what rate or rates to use?
f. What rate or rates do you recommend that the company use? Why?

CASE 17-3. WONDER FILM CO.

The Wonder Film Co. produces educational films which it sells to schools and other educational organizations. Its salaried employees consist of the Director, Mr. Marion; a secretary-bookkeeper; a script writer; and 5 employees who spend varying amounts of their time in filming, editing, and other phases of the film production process.

Most of the movies are produced under contract, with the total selling price being determined in advance. In these cases the purchaser receives all rights to the film, including the negatives. Occasionally other films which are considered to have more general appeal are produced for sale by the Wonder Film Co., and additional prints are made as demand warrants.

Although the production time varies according to the length of the film, the complexity of production requirements, the weather, the company's work load, and other factors, practically all movies are in process during at least three months. Some require as much as nine months.

The Wonder Film Co. is operated for the purpose of earning an income for its owners, although it has suffered substantial losses in recent years. Mr. Marion believes that one of the principal reasons for the unprofitable operations has been a lack of accurate cost information for the purpose of income measurement after contracts are completed; for setting reasonable bid prices on new contracts; and for controlling costs while films are in the process of production.

The company's assets and equities consisted of the following on December 31, 19x1:

WONDER FILM CO.
Statement of Financial Position
December 31, 19x1

ASSETS

Cash...		$ 2,000
Accounts receivable...........................		800
Inventory of unused film and bulbs...............		1,500
Office equipment—cost...................	$ 3,000	
Less accumulated depreciation..........	900	2,100
Production equipment—cost..............	$36,000	
Less accumulated depreciation..........	10,800	25,200
Inventory of completed films.....................		2,000
Inventory of films in process....................		30,000
Total assets.......................................		$63,600

LIABILITIES

Accounts payable..............................		$ 1,300
Advances on film contracts.....................		18,000
Total liabilities.......................................		$19,300

STOCKHOLDERS' EQUITY

Capital stock, $100 par, 5,000 shares authorized, issued, and outstanding........................		$50,000
Less deficit....................................		(5,700)
Total stockholders' equity............................		44,300
Total equities.......................................		$63,600

All of the assets except the inventories of films in process and completed films are considered to be stated accurately, but the method of measuring these items properly has been a matter of some concern to Mr. Marion. In the past, all production costs which could be directly traced to each contract have been added to the appropriate Inventory of Films in Process subsidiary account. Comparatively little difficulty has been experienced in tracing such costs as film, bulbs, and similar items directly to individual contracts. The salaries of the script writer and of each of the five production employees have been assigned to contracts at the end of each month, in proportion to the time spent by each employee on each job.

The estimated lives of the office equipment and production equipment, 10 years in each case, are considered to be accurate. Depreciation of production equipment is allocated to each job in proportion to the number of hours spent on that job during the month. Mr. Marion feels that the treatment of depreciation does not require any immediate attention because of its relatively small amount.

The salaries of Mr. Marion and the secretary-bookkeeper are treated as expenses of the month when incurred, as are miscellaneous costs of running the office.

Revenue is recorded during the month when a contract is completed, at which time the accumulated cost of production is charged to expense.

The following data relating to November and December, 19x1, are representative of the conditions which the company faces:

	November	December
Office expense:		
Director's salary............................	$ 800	$ 800
Secretary-bookkeeper's salary.................	300	300
Depreciation of office equipment..............	25	25
Other office expense........................	140	190
Total office expense.......................	$ 1,265	$1,315
Direct production costs:		
Films, bulbs, and other direct costs:		
Film No. 27...............................	$ 500	$ 0
Film No. 43...............................	1,200	3,000
Film No. 44...............................	4,100	1,000
Total.....................................	5,800	4,000
Salaries of production employees:		
Script writer................................	$ 480	$ 480
Production employee A.......................	480	480
Production employee B.......................	640	640
Production employee C.......................	640	640
Production employee D.......................	800	800
Production employee E.......................	800	800
Total.....................................	3,840	3,840
Depreciation of production equipment...........	300	300
Productions completed:		
Film No. 27—contract price..................	12,000	
—total production cost............	13,100	
Miscellaneous revenue........................	300	500
New contracts signed:		
Film No. 44—contract price..................	15,000	
Film No. 45—contract price..................		8,000
Advances previously received on Film No. 27.....	10,000	
Advances received on Film No. 44...............	1,000	7,000

Advances of $10,000 were received on Film No. 43 in October. In an average 30-day month, each employee works 160 hours. The time of each employee during November and December was spent as follows:

	Hours Worked				
	Production			Vacation	In Office,
	Film 27	Film 43	Film 44	or Sick Leave	Unassigned
November:					
Script writer..........		40	120		
A....................	40		80		40
B....................		140		20	
C....................		140			20
D....................			130	10	20
E....................			120		40
December:					
Script writer..........			60	80	20
A....................			120	40	
B....................		120		40	
C....................		100		40	20
D....................			80	80	
E....................		120		40	

Mr. Marion does not feel that the present method of assigning salary cost to films in process is proper. He also thinks the cost of running the office should be allocated to the individual jobs.

REQUIRED:

a. Show in journal form the entries needed to record the signing of the contract for Film No. 44 and the receipt of the advances in November and December.

b. Give the journal entries needed when Job No. 27 was completed in November.

c. Prepare detailed records for each contract, showing the following: (1) contract price, (2) advances on contract price, (3) November costs incurred, including direct and allocated salaries, and (4) December costs incurred, including direct and allocated salaries.

d. Prepare income statements for November and December, using the company's present methods.

e. Comment on the propriety of the basis the company uses for recording revenue realization.

f. Evaluate the method used for allocating salaries to films in process.

g. What changes in accounting would you recommend to help the company solve its problems?

MEASURING, PLANNING, AND CONTROLLING LONG-TERM ASSETS AND EQUITIES

Chapter 18

Accounting for Long-Term Unexpired Costs

Chapter 6 described *long-term unexpired costs* as consisting of the following principal classes:

(1) *Physical assets*, such as land, buildings, and equipment, which are expected to render long-term services to the business through *use* rather than consumption or sale;

(2) *Natural resources*, such as timber tracts, oil wells, and mines, which are held for *consumption* or *sale* over a long period, and whose physical quantity is reduced as the resources are extracted; and

(3) *Intangibles*, such as patents and goodwill, which are expected to yield long-term benefits to the business in the form of *rights*.

The chapter stated the general components of the *acquisition cost* of such assets: all costs which are reasonably incurred in obtaining the asset and preparing it for use in the business. It also described the general nature of the accounting process of *cost amortization* (called *depreciation* when applied to physical assets, *depletion* when applied to natural resources, and *amortization* when applied to intangibles). It illustrated the simplest method of computing and recording depreciation—the *straight-line method*.

The present chapter explores in detail some of the more complex problems involved in determining the acquisition costs of long-lived assets; the merits of alternative methods of measuring cost amortization; the method of accounting for the disposal of long-lived assets; and special problems of report presentation and interpretation.

Capital and revenue expenditures

One of the fundamental problems of accounting for long-term unexpired costs is that of deciding what types of items such costs include. This is the problem of distinguishing between *capital expenditures* and *revenue expenditures*. An *expenditure* consists of making a payment, or incurring a liability to make a payment, for an asset or an expense.

Costs which are incurred with the expectation that they will benefit business operations in future accounting periods as well as in the current period are called *capital expenditures*. They are debited initially to asset accounts and are later allocated equitably to the accounting periods which they benefit.

Costs incurred for the benefit of the current period only are called *revenue expenditures;* they are debited directly to expense accounts and are therefore matched against the revenue of the period in which they are incurred.

A business should make a careful distinction between capital and revenue expenditures. If a revenue charge is improperly treated as a capital expenditure, the result is to *understate expense* (and overstate income) of the period in which it is incurred and to *overstate the assets* at the end of that period. The same error also *overstates expense*, with a consequent understatement of income, in the *future* accounting periods to which the cost is allocated. Debiting a capital expenditure incorrectly to current-period expense creates errors of the opposite nature.

Types of expenditures that are considered to be capital in nature are: *additions*, which consist of new fixed asset units; *improvements*, which increase the probable useful life, capacity, efficiency, or operating economy of an existing asset unit; and *replacements*, which involve a substitution of a new asset for part or all of an existing asset. Ordinary *maintenance and repair* expenditures, made for the purpose of keeping the asset operating as originally planned, are treated as revenue expenditures.

Often it is difficult, if not impossible, to tell for sure whether a particular expenditure will benefit future periods. The business should follow a *consistent policy*, preferably stated in an accounting manual, in classifying each type of expenditure. *Materiality* also has an important bearing on the capital-revenue classification. For practical purposes, most companies establish a minimum cost below which expenditure items are charged to current expense regardless of the length of their expected useful lives.

EXAMPLE 1: A company followed a policy of treating all individual expenditures costing less than $10 as expense, even though the resulting benefit was expected to last for several years. The officers felt that the clerical cost of accounting for such items as long-term assets would be excessive.

DEPRECIATION

Objectives

The allocation of the cost of a long-lived asset (a *capital expenditure*) to the individual accounting periods of its useful life should accomplish two basic objectives:

(1) It should reflect the cost of the benefit which the *current period* receives from the use of the asset; and

(2) It should result in carrying forward as an asset at the end of the current period only that part of the original cost which corresponds to service benefits expected from the asset in *future periods*.

Criteria for judging depreciation methods

As in the case of inventory, a wide variety of methods have been developed for measuring *depreciation*, the portion of the cost of Plant and Equipment which expires each period. Like inventory methods, depreciation methods should be evaluated in comparison with each other according to the following general criteria:

(1) Which method provides more useful information?

(2) Which method provides a better appraisal of management performance?

(3) Which method is more likely to lead to the proper action?

More specific criteria by which alternative depreciation methods may be judged are the following:

(1) The method should provide a useful measure of income for the current period as a basis for appraising past performance. It should match the long-term asset costs which expire during each period with the periodic revenues to which those costs are related.

(2) It should help to provide a useful measure of financial status at the end of the current period. The unexpired cost of plant and equipment, which is used in measuring the financial position of the business, is the difference between the original cost and the total amount of accumulated depreciation on the asset. Plant and equipment are acquired for use rather than for sale; therefore, the amounts for which they could be sold at various dates during their useful lives are not relevant to measuring the unexpired cost which applies to their future service benefits.

(3) The method should help to provide a useful measure of the income

of future accounting periods. The undepreciated cost of an asset at the end of the current accounting period is postponed to future periods, in which it is subject to expiration.

(4) It should furnish information useful to management in planning future operations. An important application is its effect on the past and planned rate of return on assets. Depreciation has a dual effect on this measure: its amount for the current period is a *deduction in computing income;* and the unexpired amount of the asset which the method shows as being related to the future is one of the *assets upon which the rate of return is computed.*[1]

(5) It should be useful in promoting effective use and protection of the economic values represented by the depreciable asset. The policy of distinguishing between capital and revenue expenditures is also very important in this connection.

(6) It should be objective, orderly, and not subject to manipulation for the purpose of influencing reported results artificially.

(7) It should be relatively simple and inexpensive to apply.

The effect of the depreciation method upon the periodic amount of income tax expense is also a critically important matter which, because of its complexity, is discussed along with other income tax matters in Chapter 24. It is not unusual for a business to use one method of depreciation in computing its taxable income and another in measuring its business income.

The depreciation method that is most appropriate in a given situation depends upon the nature of the business, the characteristics of the depreciable assets, the length of life of the assets and the degree of change that occurs therein, the ability of the personnel who keep the records, and the use to which the resulting information is to be put.

All of the depreciation methods which are described in this chapter are *cost methods*—that is, they allocate the original cost of the long-lived asset to the periods which are benefited by its services. All such historical-cost methods are subject in greater or lesser degree to distortion as compared with the *current costs* of similar assets. The distortion tends to be greater the more significant the amount of the assets, the longer their useful lives, and the greater the price changes during this term. The last-named factor receives further attention in Chapter 26.

The materiality of the difference in the effect of various methods of computing depreciation upon the measurement of income and financial status depends upon (1) the amount of depreciation relative to other ex-

[1] For this and other reasons, some companies use the *original cost*, with no deduction for accumulated depreciation, in arriving at the asset total used in computing the rate of return.

penses and to revenue and (2) the amount of depreciable assets in relation to total assets. The differences resulting from alternative depreciation methods tend to be great because of the long life of many depreciable
assets. Cumulative differences between methods can become significant
over long periods.

Different depreciation methods have a tendency to result in greater
differences in income and assets than do different inventory methods.
One important reason for this is that fixed assets have a much longer
life than merchandise assets—usually several years, while that of inventory items is several weeks or months. The chances are far greater that
material changes in internal and external conditions affecting the usefulness of the asset will occur over the longer period.

A second cause contributing to the failure of depreciation methods to
meet the foregoing criteria is the difficulty of matching the cost of the
asset's service with the resulting revenue. Merchandise inventory can
be *physically identified* with a single sale. Each item of plant and equipment, however, usually represents a bundle of services of unknown number and unknown individual significance, available for use rather than
for direct sale, and to be used for a long and indefinite future time.

Estimating useful life

The principal differences among depreciation methods are (1) the units
in which they express the estimated useful life of the asset and (2) the
manner in which they determine what fraction of the useful life expires
during each accounting period. Under each method, the formula for determining the periodic depreciation for the entire life of the asset is set
up in advance. In general terms, the formula is:

$$\text{Annual Depreciation } (D) = \frac{\text{Cost } (C) - \text{Net Salvage Value } (S)}{\text{Units of Estimated Life } (n)}$$

The units in which the length of an asset's life is expressed may be
calendar years, units of service or output, or a combination of the two.

The amount of the cost of a long-lived asset to be allocated to any
accounting period is proportionate to the fraction of the asset's useful
life which expires during that accounting period.

EXAMPLE 2:   A delivery truck with a cost of $3,000 is expected to have
a useful life of 4 years and a salvage value of $600. The total cost which will
expire during its useful life is $2,400 (cost, $3,000 − scrap, $600). If one-fourth
of the useful life of the delivery truck expires in 19x1, one-fourth of the $2,400
total cost which will expire, or $600, is debited to 19x1 expense.

In estimating the *total useful life* of an asset, it is well to consider the
general factors which cause the useful life of assets to terminate, as well

as the extent to which those factors will affect the operations of that particular asset. The general causes are *ordinary wear and tear, inadequacy, obsolescence,* and *casualties.*

Ordinary wear and tear results from actual use of the asset as well as from the action of the elements over time. The effect of wear and tear on the length of an asset's useful life depends upon the intensity of use, the extent of exposure to the elements, and the company's maintenance policy. In some cases, idleness of an asset hastens its economic death.

Long before an asset is physically worn out, its useful life may end because it is *inadequate* to fill the company's needs. Inadequacy may result from the gradual growth of the business or from changes in management's plans. On the other hand, it may be caused by sudden changes in conditions in the company or in the industry.

Obsolescence is the effect of technological progress on existing assets. *Normal obsolescence* usually occurs slowly and is predictable with some accuracy, while *extraordinary obsolescence* is caused by unexpected changes or radical innovations.

Casualties result from sudden and unexpected natural phenomena, or from accidents. The effect of gross misuse of an asset is similar to that of a casualty.

In estimating the future service life of a particular asset, a business should include the effects of ordinary wear and tear, predictable inadequacy, and normal obsolescence. It is not feasible to estimate in advance the effect of extraordinary inadequacy or obsolescence and casualties on the probable useful life of an asset. Although the risk of loss from many types of casualties can be covered by insurance, the effects of these three unpredictable factors are accounted for when they actually occur.

The extent to which the predictable factors affect useful life vary from one type of asset to another. Some types of assets are subject to little technological change; wear and tear are the most important determinants of their useful life. For others, wear and tear have little effect on the economic life of the asset. The particular conditions affecting each asset should be considered in estimating its total useful life and the fraction of its life which expires in each accounting period. These characteristics are very important in selecting the appropriate depreciation method from those described below.

Sudden changes in operating conditions or in the economic environment may dictate that a part of the cost of an asset be shown as a loss in the period of the change.

EXAMPLE 3:   A machine with an original cost of $10,000, an estimated life of 10 years, and no estimated scrap value is being depreciated at the annual rate of $1,000. Its sudden obsolescence in 19x6, the sixth year of its life, might require the recognition of a loss of $4,000 of its potential benefit to future years in addition to the $1,000 normal depreciation for the current year.

The straight-line method of depreciation

The simplest, and probably the most widely used, method of computing periodic depreciation is the *straight-line method*. Under it, the estimated life of the asset is expressed in calendar years and an equal amount of depreciation is assigned to each *full year of use*. If the asset is in use for only part of an accounting period, only the appropriate fraction of a full year's straight-line depreciation should be charged to depreciation expense for the period.

Most businesses apply simplifying conventions in computing depreciation for the year of an asset's acquisition or disposal. One common rule considers that all changes in the asset account occur at the *middle of the year*.

EXAMPLE 4:   If the delivery truck in Example 2 were acquired on April 17, 19x1, by a company which used the calendar year as its accounting period, application of the mid-year convention would result in charging one-half of a year's depreciation, $300, to 19x1 expense.

EXAMPLE 5:   If the same truck were sold on November 3, 19x4, the same convention would result in assigning one-half of a year's depreciation, $300, to 19x4, the year of disposal.

A similar convention assumes that all changes occur at the *middle of the month*. Other methods compute depreciation to the *nearest full month* or *full year* of use. The convention in use should be applied consistently. If asset acquisitions and disposals are spaced fairly evenly over time, the results of these conventions will be reasonably accurate.

The *annual rate of depreciation* under the straight-line method is determined by the formula:

$$\frac{\text{Annual Depreciation}}{\text{Original Cost}} = \text{Annual Rate of Depreciation}$$

EXAMPLE 6:   The annual depreciation rate of the delivery truck in Example 2 is $600/$3,000, or 20 per cent of the original cost.

The straight-line depreciation method is objective and systematic, but perhaps its outstanding virtue is its simplicity. It results in charging each full year of the asset's life with an equal amount of expired cost, without regard to the amount of service actually rendered by the asset during each year.

The straight-line method is appropriate when the service benefits received from an asset are approximately equal each year of its life. This is true of some assets which continue to be used approximately the same amount each year without notable changes in operating efficiency. It is also true when the most important service of an asset is its *availability*, not its *use*. Availability may be the most important measure of the service of a stand-by machine. A strong case may also be made for the straight-line method when the length of an asset's useful life depends more on obsolescence than on physical use.

An asset's service benefits to each accounting period of its life may be conceived of as *units of physical use*, such as number of miles driven or number of running hours, rather than as availability for use. The service benefits may also be thought of as *contributions to revenue*, or *cost reductions* resulting from the asset, although such benefits are usually difficult or impossible to trace. By these standards, the use of the straight-line method, expressing useful life in years, is improper for many common types of assets whose operating efficiency declines and whose operating costs increase with age.

Production methods of depreciation

Because of the limitations of the straight-line method, in which depreciation is considered to depend upon the passage of time, several depreciation methods have been designed to attempt to charge accounting periods with expired cost in proportion to the *use* of long-lived assets. These methods are referred to as *production methods* of depreciation.

One common form of the production method expresses the useful life of the fixed asset in units of *operating activity*, such as the number of hours a machine is operated or the number of miles a truck is driven.

EXAMPLE 7:   The delivery truck in Example 2 is expected to have a useful operating life of 48,000 miles. Its depreciation per mile is computed as follows:

$$D = \frac{C - S}{n} = \frac{\$3,000 - \$600}{48,000 \text{ miles}} = \$0.05 \text{ per mile}$$

If the truck was driven 14,000 miles in 19x1, depreciation expense for 19x1 would be $700 ($0.05 × 14,000). Depreciation in 19x2 would be $550 if mileage driven in that year was 11,000.

Methods of this type are feasible when the life of an asset depends almost entirely upon use, and when both the total useful life and the part of life expiring each year can be measured in terms of a standard unit of activity. Other forms of the production method state useful life in terms of *units of product* made by the asset, or in *revenue dollars* resulting from the product. It is usually difficult or impossible to estimate accurately the output of a long-lived asset in terms of units of product or revenue. Furthermore, *all* productive factors of a business, not just fixed assets, contribute to the earning of revenue, and the individual contribution of each factor cannot be identified.

Aside from the difficulties described, production methods of depreciation are relatively simple and objective. They are appropriate for assets whose useful life depends largely upon physical use.

Depreciation methods resulting in declining periodic charges

The annual service benefits derived from many types of long-lived assets decline as the assets become older. In addition, the usefulness of an asset can be predicted more accurately for its earlier years than for its later years. For these and other reasons, many businesses use methods which allocate greater amounts of depreciation expense to the earlier periods of an asset's life. Some of these methods are arbitrary means of measuring declining benefits which result from the use of the asset. Two of them are described in the following paragraphs: (1) *the uniform-rate-on-declining-balance* method (also referred to as the "declining-balance method") and (2) *the sum-of-the-years'-digits*-method (also referred to as the "SYD method").

The uniform-rate-on-declining-balance depreciation method

The uniform-rate-on-declining-balance method is designed to result in decreasing annual amounts of depreciation expense. The depreciation of each year is determined by multiplying the *unexpired cost* (not the original cost) of the asset at the beginning of the year by a *uniform percentage*.

The resulting depreciation charges under the method resemble the declining periodic amounts of interest which are computed at a constant interest rate on a principal balance which declines as a part of it is repaid each period.

A depreciation rate which will reduce the unexpired cost of an asset (its original cost minus accumulated depreciation) to salvage value during its expected life can be computed by a complex formula. A simpler and more widely used expedient is to use a uniform percentage which is *double the reciprocal of the estimated life*, or:

$$\text{Uniform Rate} = 2\left(\frac{1}{\text{Estimated Life}}\right)$$

EXAMPLE 8:   For the delivery truck in Example 2, whose estimated life is 4 years, the uniform annual depreciation rate is computed as follows:

$$2(\tfrac{1}{4}) = 50\%.$$

The resulting amounts each year would be:

End of Year	Year's Depreciation	Accumulated Depreciation	Original Cost	Unexpired Cost
0...............			$3,000	$3,000
19x1...............	$1,500	$1,500	3,000	1,500
19x2...............	750	2,250	3,000	750
19x3...............	150*	2,400	3,000	600
19x4...............	0*	2,400	3,000	600

* Depreciation computed by continuing to multiply the unexpired cost by the uniform percentage, 50%, would have been $375 in 19x3 and $187.50 in 19x4. However, depreciation of an asset is no longer recorded after its unexpired cost equals its expected salvage value.

In some cases the use of the uniform-rate method will leave an unexpired cost *greater* than the expected salvage value at the end of an asset's estimated life. In such a case, additional depreciation should be taken to reduce the unexpired cost to the salvage value. The income tax rules, upon which this method is based, permit the taxpayer to change from the uniform-rate method to the straight-line method at any time, to avoid leaving such an undepreciated balance at the end of an asset's life.

The sum-of-the-years'-digits depreciation method

Another method of computing depreciation which results in a declining amount of depreciation expense each year of an asset's useful life is the *sum-of-the-years'-digits* method. It assigns depreciation to each accounting period in proportion to the number of years of an asset's useful life which remain at the beginning of the current year. The formula is:

$$\text{Year's Depreciation} = \frac{\text{Number of Years Remaining}}{\text{Total of Digits of Years of Life}} (\text{Cost} - \text{Salvage})$$

EXAMPLE 9:   For the delivery truck in Example 2, the first year's depreciation is computed as follows:

$$\frac{4}{(1 + 2 + 3 + 4)} (\$3,000 - \$600) = \frac{4}{10} (\$2,400) = \$960$$

In succeeding years the numerator of the fraction is 3, 2, and 1, respectively. The resulting amounts each year would be:

End of Year	Year's Depreciation	Accumulated Depreciation	Original Cost	Unexpired Cost
0...............			$3,000	$3,000
19x1...............	$960	$ 960	3,000	2,040
19x2...............	720	1,680	3,000	1,320
19x3...............	480	2,160	3,000	840
19x4...............	240	2,400	3,000	600

Evaluation of the declining annual depreciation methods

Both the uniform-rate-on-declining-balance method and the sum-of-the-years'-digits method are objective, and both are fairly simple to apply (though more complex than the straight-line method). These methods are most appropriate for assets whose service benefits decline with age. Whether the rate of decline is more similar to that produced by the uniform-rate method or the SYD method, or whether it resembles neither, depends upon the characteristics of the particular asset in question.

Both methods are widely used for income-tax purposes, for reasons discussed in Chapter 24.

Comparison of results of depreciation methods

The following tables summarize the results of the four depreciation methods as applied to the delivery truck described in Example 2.

	19x1	19x2	19x3	19x4	Total
Annual depreciation:					
Straight-line............................	$ 600	$ 600	$ 600	$ 600	$2,400
Production (mileage)................	700	550	500	650	2,400
Uniform-rate-on-declining-balance....	1,500	750	150	0	2,400
Sum-of-the-years'-digits.............	960	720	480	240	2,400

	Beginning of Year				End of
	19x1	19x2	19x3	19x4	19x4
Unexpired cost:					
Straight-line............................	$3,000	$2,400	$1,800	$1,200	$ 600
Production (mileage)................	3,000	2,300	1,750	1,250	600
Uniform-rate-on-declining-balance...	3,000	1,500	750	600	600
Sum-of-the-years'-digits.............	3,000	2,040	1,320	840	600

Percentage of annual depreciation to original cost:	19x1	19x2	19x3	19x4
Straight-line............................	20.0%	20.0%	20.0%	20.0%
Production (mileage)................	23.3	18.3	16.7	21.7
Uniform-rate-on-declining-balance...	50.0	25.0	5.0	0.0
Sum-of-the-years'-digits.............	32.0	24.0	16.0	8.0

Percentage of annual depreciation to unexpired cost at beginning of year:	19x1	19x2	19x3	19x4
Straight-line............................	20.0%	25.0%	33.3%	50.0%
Production (mileage)................	23.3	23.9	28.6	52.0
Uniform-rate-on-declining-balance...	50.0	50.0	20.0	0.0
Sum-of-the-years'-digits.............	32.0	35.3	36.4	28.6

The differences in the results of these three methods will vary when applied in other situations, depending upon the length of life, the salvage value of the asset, and the number of service units produced in each period. The general results of the methods may be summarized as follows:

(1) The *straight-line* method produces a *constant amount* of annual depreciation, which is a constant percentage of the original cost but an increasing percentage of the unexpired cost of the asset.

(2) The *production* method results in an amount of annual depreciation which fluctuates with changes in the volume of services produced by the asset.

(3) The *uniform-rate-on-declining-balance* method yields a declining annual amount of depreciation, decreasing more sharply the shorter the estimated life. The percentage of depreciation to the original cost declines each year, but the percentage of annual depreciation to unexpired cost at the beginning of each year is constant until the balance reaches the scrap value.

(4) The *sum-of-the-years'-digits* method yields an annual depreciation charge which is a declining percentage of the original cost, the rate of decline being greater for short-lived assets.

Recording sales of plant and equipment

When a depreciable asset is disposed of, two accounting entries are necessary: the first should record depreciation expense for the time since the last adjustment was made, and the second should clear from the records the original cost and the accumulated depreciation on the asset up to the date of disposal.

EXAMPLE 10:   A piece of equipment which had been acquired at the beginning of 19x1 for $1,000, and which had an estimated life of 5 years and an estimated net salvage value of zero, was sold for $240 cash on April 1, 19x5. Depreciation had last been recorded on December 31, 19x4, and the relevant account balances just prior to recording the sale were:

A, Equipment		A, Equipment—Accumulated Depreciation	
1/1/19x1 1,000		12/31/19x1	200
		12/31/19x2	200
		12/31/19x3	200
		12/31/19x4	200
		Balance, 800	

What entries were needed at the time of sale?

SOLUTION: The entry to record depreciation for the period from January 1 to April 1, 19x5, would be:

(a)

OE, Depreciation Expense (19x5)......................	50	
A, Equipment—Accumulated Depreciation.........		50
Depreciation for ¼ year.		

After this entry had been posted, the accounts would show that the unexpired cost of the equipment on April 1 was $150 ($1,000 original cost minus $850 accumulated depreciation). The equipment was sold for a gain of $90 (sales price, $240, minus unexpired cost, $150). The entry for sale should be:

(b)

```
A, Cash.............................................    240
A, Equipment—Accumulated Depreciation.............    850
    A, Equipment..................................           1,000
    OE, Gain on Disposal of Equipment.............              90
    To record sale of equipment having an unexpired cost
    of $150 for $240 cash.
```

Any costs incurred in removing retired depreciable assets reduce the gain (or increase the loss) resulting from the sale.

Recording trades of plant and equipment

The acquisition of a new asset by trading an old asset, or an old asset plus cash, consists of two distinct elements: a retirement of the old asset, and an acquisition of the new. Often the stated trade-in allowances are unrealistic; if so, they should be disregarded in measuring the acquisition cost of the new asset. The new asset should be recorded at *cost*—the sum of the *cash* paid and the *fair market value* of the asset given up. If the latter cannot be determined readily, the new asset should be recorded at its own fair market value as the best evidence of its cost.

EXAMPLE 11: A business traded a piece of equipment with an original cost of $2,000 and accumulated depreciation to date of $1,600 for another piece of equipment which had a list price of $3,000. The payment for the new equipment consisted of a trade-in allowance of $700 on the old equipment plus $2,300 cash. The old equipment could have been sold for $500 cash. What are the proper entries to record the exchange?

SOLUTION: The business received an *overallowance* of $200 on the old equipment, in effect reducing the price of the new equipment to $2,800. Both the trade-in allowance and the unexpired cost of the old asset are irrelevant in determining the acquisition cost of the new. The proper entry is:

(a)

```
A, Equipment (new)................................  2,800
A, Equipment—Accumulated Depreciation (old)........  1,600
    A, Equipment (old)............................           2,000
    OE, Gain on Disposal of Equipment.............             100
    A, Cash.......................................           2,300
    To record acquisition of new equipment for $2,300 cash
    plus old equipment with a current market value of $500;
    to remove the original cost and accumulated depre-
    ciation on the old equipment from the books; and to
    reflect a gain of $100, the difference between the amount
    realized on the old equipment, $500, and its unexpired
    cost, $400.
```

Depreciation for individual items or for groups

Many businesses maintain some or all of their records dealing with depreciable assets in terms of *individual items*. A card or other detailed record would show for each item the original cost, later additions to cost, estimated life, estimated salvage value, depreciation for each period, and accumulated depreciation. Earlier illustrations have dealt with accounting for such individual depreciable units.

A *composite depreciation rate* is one which is based upon the average life of a number of units. The units in the composite group may be similar to each other in *form* or in *function*.

A depreciation rate which is applied to a group of depreciable assets that are similar to each other in *form*, such as a number of identical machines, is called a *group depreciation rate*. The depreciation rate used is based on the *weighted-average estimated life* of all of the units in the group. It is to be expected that within a group some items will have shorter useful lives, and others will have longer lives, than the average of the group. When an asset that is a part of such a group is retired, it is considered to be fully depreciated, even if its retirement occurs earlier than the end of the estimated average life of the group.

EXAMPLE 12:   In 19x1 a business acquired 100 identical machines, each with a cost of $60 and an estimated salvage value of zero. The weighted-average estimated life of the group is 3 years. The company follows the policy of recording half a year's depreciation in the year an asset is acquired and half a year's depreciation in the year of its disposal.

One machine was destroyed by accident in 19x2. What would the appropriate entries be in 19x1 and 19x2?

SOLUTION:

(a)

OE, Depreciation Expense (19x1).....................	1,000	
A, Machinery—Accumulated Depreciation.........		1,000

Depreciation for 19x1 was ½ of a full year's depreciation of $2,000 (cost, $6,000/estimated life, 3 years).

(b)

OE, Depreciation Expense (19x2).....................	1,990	
A, Machinery—Accumulated Depreciation.........		1,990

Depreciation for 19x2 was as follows:

⅓ of cost of 99 machines used all year (⅓ of $5,940)...............................	$1,980
⅙ of cost (6 months' depreciation) of 1 machine retired during the year..........	10
Total..................................	$1,990

(c)

A, Machinery—Accumulated Depreciation.............	60	
A, Machinery....................................		60

To remove from the records cost and accumulated depreciation on retired machine.

Just as the machine in entry (c) had an actual life of one year, or less than the expected 3-year average life of the 100 machines, others can be expected to last 2 years, and still others 3, 4, and 5 years. *Neither gain nor loss is recorded* on assets which are retired earlier than the expiration of the average life. On the other hand, annual depreciation on the cost of assets still in use after the end of the average life of the group is continued on the basis of $\frac{1}{3}$ of their original cost. If the estimates of useful life and salvage value are perfect, the related asset and accumulated depreciation accounts will be exactly balanced out when the last unit is retired.

The group method of depreciation is often simpler to apply than the unit method, particularly for assets of relatively small unit cost. The group method avoids the necessity of making entries for gains or losses on the retirement of individual components of a group, unless it becomes evident that the predicted life of the group is incorrect. However, if the average is substantially incorrect, revisions are very complex.

The group method tends to match expired costs with revenues better than does the unit method, because it assigns depreciation in proportion to the *number of asset units in use during each period.* If an estimated life of 3 years were used for the 100 identical machines in Example 12 on an individual-item depreciation basis, a *loss* of $40 would be assigned to the second year when one unit was retired after one year. *No depreciation* would be assigned to years after the third, even though some of the individual units were still in use.

A composite depreciation rate for a group of assets which are *dissimilar in form* but *related in function* might be applied to a building as a whole. The roof, the floors, the heating plant, and the lighting equipment are likely to have different useful lives, and it may be expected that one or more of them will have to be replaced before the useful life of the building as a whole terminates. One approach is to use a *composite depreciation rate* for the entire building. When individual items are replaced, they are considered to be fully depreciated unless there is strong evidence that their lives have been different from the estimate made in determining the composite rate for the building. An alternative method is to keep *separate records* of the cost and estimated lives of each of the major segments of such a composite asset and to depreciate each separately.

Unless careful revisions are made, the use of such a composite rate can lead to large errors when the proportion of some items to the total changes, when the costs of some replacement components change at a different rate from the costs of others, and when errors are made in the estimated lives of the components when computing the composite rate. For these reasons, composite depreciation rates for dissimilar assets should be used cautiously.

Partial replacements

Replacing a part of an asset rather than the whole often gives rise to difficult accounting problems. Usually the accounting treatment is governed by the *materiality* of the replacement. If it is *small* and of a type which is likely to recur frequently during the life of the asset, the cost of the replacement is treated as expense at the time of replacement. A case in point is the replacement of a spark plug in a motor. If the replacement is a *major* one which has the effect of increasing the service benefits to be expected from the asset, it should be treated as a retirement of the old asset and an acquisition of a new one. An example is the replacement of a truck motor by a more powerful and durable one. The cost and accumulated depreciation of the part being replaced should be estimated and removed from the accounts, and the cost of the new part should be debited to the asset account.

Often it is difficult to estimate the balances which apply to the parts being replaced. A partial solution to this problem is the practice of keeping separate detailed asset records of each major part of an asset which is likely to be replaced before the life of the whole asset ends. This procedure could easily be carried to an extreme. Furthermore, the accumulated cost of an asset which has practically been rebuilt piece by piece is likely to be excessive in comparison with the cost of such an asset acquired as a unit.

Revision of depreciation rates

The estimated remaining useful lives of depreciable assets should be reviewed frequently for the purpose of making appropriate revisions. Two general methods are used in making entries to revise depreciation rates:

(1) The remaining unexpired cost of the asset is assigned to the periods of the asset's estimated life, as revised, which remain after the date of the revision.

(2) A retroactive correction is made so that the depreciation of each past and future period will be based on the revised estimate of the asset's total life.

EXAMPLE 13:   A machine with a cost of $10,000, a salvage value of zero, and an estimated life of 10 years, was acquired at the beginning of 19x1. At the beginning of 19x3, the third year of its life, it becomes evident to management that the remaining useful life will be 4 years, not 8. Balances in the accounts before revision are:

	Debit	Credit
A, Equipment......................................	10,000	
A, Equipment—Accumulated Depreciation...........		2,000

How should the revision of the estimated remaining life of the machine be accounted for?

FIRST SOLUTION: Under the first method, revised depreciation in the future will be $2,000 a year ($8,000 unexpired cost divided by 4 years of remaining life). Past depreciation has been recorded at $1,000 a year.

SECOND SOLUTION: Under the second method, depreciation for the current year and each of the three future years will be $1,667 (rounded to the nearest dollar), determined by dividing the original cost, $10,000, by the revised estimate of total life, 6 years. Future depreciation of $6,667 plus the $2,000 of depreciation already recorded will amount to only $8,667. The difference of $1,333 is additional depreciation applicable to the past two years, based on the revised estimated life. It should be recorded as follows:

OE, Correction of Prior Years' Depreciation............ 1,333
   A, Equipment—Accumulated Depreciation.........   1,333
   To bring accumulated depreciation for past years up to
   ⅓ of the machine's cost (for 2 years expired out of 6).

The account debited is shown as an extraneous item in the income statement of 19x3, the year in which the correction is made.

If the original estimate of the useful life of the asset had been made carefully and later changes in circumstances required that the estimate be revised, the first solution would seem to be preferable. The second method, that of making a retroactive correction, would be warranted only if there had been a material error in the past. Hindsight is more accurate than foresight, but little is to be gained by constant minor revisions after the resulting information has already been used by management to interpret the financial status and progress of the business.

Depletion of natural resources

Natural resources include physical assets such as mineral deposits, oil and gas resources, and timber, which yield their service benefits by use or sale after being extracted from the basic deposit or tract. A *physical reduction* in the quantity of the deposit occurs as the resource is exploited, although in some cases the reduction is offset by growth (*accretion*) or development of additional deposits. The extracted resources are accounted for in the same manner as inventory.

The acquisition cost of a natural resource includes its purchase cost plus the cost of development incurred until the asset begins producing. Development costs can easily be excessive; in fact, unproductive explorations such as dry wells are a common feature of extractive industries. Such costs should be accumulated as an asset until the production stage is reached or until it becomes clear that the asset will not be productive. In the first case, the asset cost is then systematically amortized over its expected useful life; in the second, it is charged promptly to a loss account.

The periodic amortization of the cost of a natural resource is called *depletion*. The *unit of production* method is appropriate because of the nature of the operation. Depletion for each unit extracted is determined as follows:

$$\text{Depletion per Unit } (D) = \frac{\text{Acquisition Cost } (C) - \text{Residual Value } (S)}{\text{Estimated Life in Production Units } (n)}$$

EXAMPLE 14:   A lumber company acquired a timber tract for $10,500 and incurred costs of $500 in developing the tract. The tract is estimated to contain 500,000 (500 M) board feet of timber, and it is expected that the cut-over land can be sold for $1,000 after the timber has been cut. Depletion per thousand board feet is computed as follows:

$$D = \frac{C\ (\$10{,}500 \text{ plus } \$500) - S\ (\$1{,}000)}{n\ (500 \text{ M feet})} = \frac{\$10{,}000}{500} = \$20 \text{ per M feet}$$

If 90 M feet of timber were cut in 19x1, the entry for depletion for the year would be:

```
A, Inventory.......................................  1,800
     A, Timber Tract—Accumulated Depletion.........          1,800
     To record depletion for 90 M feet of timber at $20 per
     M feet.
```

The cost of depletion is treated as a cost of producing the inventory item, along with labor and overhead costs. Inventory costs are transferred to expense as *cost of goods sold* at the time the lumber is sold.

Amortization of goodwill

Goodwill is a long-lived *intangible* asset which represents the ability of a business to earn more than a normal rate of return on its tangible assets. It is recorded only when an entire going business, or a substantial share of ownership in a going business, is purchased. Like other assets, it should be recorded initially at its *cost.*

Often when new owners purchase a business or a substantial equity therein, the buyers and sellers mutually agree on the price of goodwill. The purchaser should debit *Goodwill* for this cost. Sometimes, in lump-sum purchases of businesses, no price is specified for goodwill or for any other individual asset. In such a case the buyer may need to have the tangible assets appraised individually. Each tangible asset is then assigned a cost equal to its appraised value. If the sum of the appraised values of tangible assets is *less* than the total cost of the business, the difference may be treated as the cost of goodwill. If the appraised values of the tangible assets exceed the total cost of the business, presumably there is no goodwill, and the total cost of the business should be allocated to the tangible assets in proportion to their appraised values.

If the factors which are thought to contribute to the abnormal earning power of a business are expected to have a limited life, a portion of the cost of goodwill should be transferred periodically to the expired cost account, *Amortization of Goodwill.* Clues to the length of the period for which this superior earning power is expected to continue may sometimes be found in the negotiations between the buyer and the seller. If so, that period is the proper estimated life of goodwill to be used in measuring the periodic amortization.

REPORTING AND INTERPRETING LONG-TERM UNEXPIRED COSTS

Knowledge of how much of the cost of long-lived assets has expired during the current and past accounting periods and how much applies to the future is useful to management and outsiders in appraising the past performance of the business and its future prospects. The internal-check procedures and detailed records used in accounting for long-lived assets help to increase the accuracy of this information and to promote the safety and proper use of the assets. Accounting data are also often useful as a starting point for management decisions relating to the retention or replacement of long-lived assets. The remainder of this chapter deals with the matters of *reporting, analysis,* and *internal check* as they are related to long-term unexpired costs.

General-purpose reporting requirements

Statements of financial position prepared for general use should classify long-lived assets according to their major types, such as land, buildings, land improvements, equipment, natural resources, patents, copyrights, trade marks, franchises, leaseholds, leasehold improvements, goodwill, and organization costs, which were defined in Chapter 6. The amounts of accumulated amortization should be reported separately for each major type of asset.

Construction work in progress and other property not being used in operations, such as *idle plant* or *plant held for future development*, should also be disclosed as separate amounts. They represent sums invested in assets but not now producing revenue. The statement analyst is interested in knowing what part of the total assets are not now in use, and he wishes to compare revenues and income with only the assets which were used in producing them.

The amount of *fully depreciated assets which are still in use*, if material in amount, should also be reported separately. An asset is fully depreciated for accounting purposes when its cost minus accumulated depreciation is equal to its estimated salvage value. For example:

Machine—cost...	$5,000
Deduct accumulated depreciation..........................	5,000
Unexpired cost..	$ 0

The asset may have an additional useful life; if so, depreciation expense of past periods has been overstated. No further depreciation may be recorded in future periods, however (unless a retroactive adjustment is warranted); and as a result, the expense of future periods in which the fully depreciated asset is used will be understated. Information about the cost of fully depreciated assets still in use helps the statement reader form an opinion about the propriety of the depreciation rates used. He can then make a mental adjustment of the results reported in the financial statements in appraising the past results and future potential of the business.

The financial statements should also disclose the *basis of measuring* long-lived assets. In most cases this is *cost,* although in rare instances *appraised values* are used. Interpretation of the data is further aided by a statement of the method of determining periodic depreciation and the policy of distinguishing between capital and revenue expenditures. If there are significant liens, such as mortgages, against the property, their amounts should be stated.

Supporting schedules which show for a series of years the amounts of additions, deductions, and balances of the major types of long-lived assets and their related accumulated amortization accounts are desirable.

Comparison of depreciation with cost

The information about long-term assets that is presented in the typical general-purpose report is often inadequate to permit more than a superficial analysis. It is frequently seriously distorted because the long-lived assets have been acquired over a long period of time at different price levels. Subject to these limitations, the following comparisons dealing with long-lived asset balances are often worth while.

The percentage of *accumulated depreciation to cost* gives some indication of the age of the plant. Assume the following balances:

	Company *A*		Company *B*	
Plant and equipment—cost......	$100,000	100%	$100,000	100%
Accumulated depreciation.......	20,000	20%	70,000	70%
Unexpired cost.................	$ 80,000	80%	$ 30,000	30%

If the companies have used reasonable estimated lives and the same depreciation method, the figures indicate that the plant of Company *B* is much older. In the not-too-distant future, substantial outlays will probably be needed for replacements. Furthermore, the operating expenses for repairs and maintenance of Company *B* during the next few years are likely to be greater than those of Company *A* because of the age of the plant.

A comparison of the percentage of *annual depreciation expense to the cost of assets* with the corresponding percentages of similar companies which use the same depreciation method and whose assets are approximately the same age provides some indication of whether the company's periodic depreciation charges are excessive or inadequate.

Evidence of deferred maintenance

In some industries there should be a stable relationship between the periodic expense for *maintenance of fixed assets* and *periodic revenues*. If maintenance is normally 5 per cent of sales revenue and Company *A*'s maintenance of 19x5 is only 3 per cent, it may be that the company is letting its fixed assets deteriorate. Such *deferred maintenance* will require more than normal expenditures for maintenance in some future year or will shorten the useful life of the asset. In the latter case, the depreciation expense of the current year and perhaps of future years should be increased.

Turnover of long-lived assets

The plant and equipment turnover rate (sales revenue divided by average balance of plant and equipment) is an indication of how intensively plant and equipment were worked during the period. This comparison is of greatest importance for businesses, such as public utilities, which derive most of their revenue from the use of their plant and equipment. The turnover rate for a telephone company might be computed as follows:

$$\text{Operating revenues} \dots \dots \dots \dots \dots \quad \frac{\$30,000,000}{\$100,000,000} = .3 \text{ turnover}$$
$$\text{Telephone plant} \dots \dots \dots \dots \dots \dots$$

As in the case of other asset turnovers, action to improve the turnover rate may be directed toward increasing revenue or toward reducing the asset balance in relation to the amount of revenue. Usually a longer period of time is required to effect changes of the latter type for long-lived assets than is true of such short-lived assets as receivables and inventories.

Internal check

The objectives of internal-check procedures for long-lived assets are to insure that such assets are acquired, used, and disposed of according to company policy. The company's policy for distinguishing capital from revenue expenditures and its procedures for initiating and approving requests for asset additions and disposals should be spelled out in a manual. Responsibility for approving asset changes and for keeping custody of the assets should be assigned to specific individuals. The records and reports of long-lived assets should show how the responsibility was discharged.

Some of the major considerations involved in planning capital asset additions are discussed in detail in Chapter 22. The individual who approves requests for acquisitions should determine that their nature conforms with the plans of the business, that their timing is appropriate, and that their cost is proper and within the company's means. Major additions such as long-term construction projects require continual authorization of expenditures as work progresses.

Because individuals should not establish their own accountability for assets, persons other than those who have physical custody of assets should keep accounting records of the asset changes and balances. Subsidiary, or detailed, records of long-lived assets are essential. Some of their uses are:

(1) They assist in the preparation of financial statements by giving information as to periodic depreciation expense, cost of assets in use, and accumulated depreciation.

(2) They promote accuracy in estimating future useful lives of assets on the basis of an analysis of past histories of similar individual assets.

(3) They provide information regarding the operating performance of various types of individual assets which is useful to management in evaluating the desirability of replacing assets or in selecting particular types of assets for additions and replacements.

At regular intervals, the physical assets themselves should be compared with the records by someone other than the custodian. The aim of this comparison is more than to determine that all assets which should be on hand are accounted for; it also insures a regular examination of the physical condition of each asset. Periodically, too, the totals of the subsidiary records should be compared with the three general ledger accounts for which they provide detailed information: Plant and Equipment (cost), Plant and Equipment—Accumulated Depreciation, and Depreciation Expense.

Summary

Capital expenditures, which are expected to benefit the business in more than one accounting period, are debited to asset accounts and amortized systematically over their useful lives. The cost which expires each period is called *depreciation* when applied to plant and equipment, *depletion* for natural resources, and *amortization* for intangible assets. Various alternative methods have been developed for assigning to accounting periods the cost of the benefits received from capital expenditures. The *straight-line* method allocates expired cost to periods in proportion to the lapse of time; the *production* methods allocate expired cost in proportion to some unit of activity; and the *declining-balance* methods, in proportion to the unexpired cost of the asset. In selecting an appropriate method, the business should consider the extent to which the method properly reflects the service benefits received from the asset in each past, current, and future accounting period.

Financial reports should disclose the amounts of each significant class of long-lived asset, the basis of measurement, the principal changes during the period, and the method of amortization. The internal-check procedures and subsidiary records should be designed to insure that the acquisition, use, and disposal of long-lived assets are in accordance with the best interests of the business. Detailed records may be used to collect information that is helpful in controlling assets and in evaluating alternative assets which are being considered as additions or replacements.

QUESTIONS AND PROBLEMS

18-1

REQUIRED:

Classify the following expenditures on a delivery truck as *capital* or *revenue* expenditures. Explain your answer in each case.

a. Invoice cost of truck.
b. Annual license.
c. Collision insurance.
d. Replacing spark plugs.
e. Replacing worn-out battery.
f. Replacing worn-out motor.

g. Washing.
h. Gasoline.
i. Repainting.
j. Repairing dented fender.
k. Painting owner's name on side.

18-2 *L* Department Store and *M* Department Store buy identical delivery trucks (except for exterior painting) on the same day.

REQUIRED:

a. Will the estimated life of each truck be the same?
b. How should the stores go about determining the estimated life of their trucks?
c. Should the companies use the same depreciation method? Explain.

18-3 Sometimes in past decades business managements would prepare income statements showing "Net income before depreciation," and then subtract depreciation as a final figure. Often the amount charged to depreciation depended upon whether the year was a good or a bad one in terms of profits. The latter policy was justified on the ground that the good years were able to bear a larger amount of depreciation expense than the bad ones.

REQUIRED:

Comment carefully on the implications of the statement presentation and depreciation policy described above.

18-4 The chief engineer of a manufacturing firm suggested in a conference of the company's executives that the accountants should speed up depreciation on the machinery in Department 3 because *improvements are making those machines obsolete very rapidly, and we want to have a depreciation fund big enough to cover their replacement.*

REQUIRED:

Discuss fully the accounting concept of depreciation and the effect on a business concern of the depreciation recorded for fixed assets, paying particular attention to the issues raised by the chief engineer. (AICPA Examination in Theory of Accounts, November, 1956.)

18-5 "Expenditures during 1958 for additional and replacement facilities were $1,780,000, as compared with charges of about $1,520,000 for depreciation and amortization of buildings, machinery and equipment. In addition to the provision for depreciation and amortization, approximately $1,253,000 was charged against earnings in 1958 for the acquisition of jigs, tools, dies and fixtures, in accordance with the Corporation's policy of writing off against earnings the full costs of such assets immediately upon their acquisition." (From the 1958 annual report of Stewart-Warner Corporation, manufacturer of automotive equipment and chemicals.)

REQUIRED:

a. Under what circumstances would the company's policy of expensing the costs of jigs, tools, dies, and fixtures seem to be acceptable?
b. What possible weaknesses can you see in this policy?
c. If you disagree with the company's policy, what alternative would you recommend?

18-6 Upon reading the financial statements of a company, a stockholder objected to the following item:

Automotive equipment	$20,000	
Deduct accumulated depreciation	4,000	$16,000

"I am sure that we could not get more than $12,000 on the market for this equipment," he said.

REQUIRED:

a. Prepare a suitable reply to the stockholder.
b. To what extent should market values of equipment be considered in measuring depreciation?
c. Can you justify assigning a different weight to market values in measuring the unexpired cost of depreciable assets from that used in measuring inventory? Explain.

18-7 Your company showed the following balance relating to a 4-year-old machine which was originally expected to have a useful life of 10 years.

Machine—cost	$20,000	
Deduct accumulated depreciation	8,000	$12,000

An employee doubted the accuracy of this information, stating that the machine was still operating at peak efficiency. "There hasn't actually been any depreciation," he said.

REQUIRED:

a. What would be your reply to the employee?
b. How would your answer differ if the employee had stated that the machine was operating at less than 50 per cent of its original efficiency?

18-8 At the beginning of 19x3, your company developed two patents on articles which it expects to manufacture. Patent A, costing $8,500, was associated with manufacturing a staple product which is expected to be in demand indefinitely. Patent B, costing $5,100, is associated with making a novelty item which is expected to be in demand only a few months or a year. The legal life of each patent is 17 years from the beginning of 19x3.

REQUIRED:

a. Make the entries necessary to reflect these facts in 19x3.

b. State how the relevant accounts will appear in the statement of financial position on December 31, 19x3.

18-9 The 1958 annual report of Inland Steel Company and subsidiary companies shows the following item:

	1958	1957
"Property, Plant and Equipment—at cost (see page 9):		
Operating properties..............	$722,584,776	$636,512,180
Properties not used in operations...	6,592,045	6,318,401
	$729,176,821	$642,830,581
Depreciation, amortization and depletion.......................	284,928,169	263,841,385
	$444,248,652	$378,989,196"

REQUIRED:

a. Why is the distinction made between operating and nonoperating properties?

b. In what other places, if any, should this distinction be shown in the financial statements?

c. Should depreciation be recorded on properties not used in operations? If so, how should it be measured?

18-10 A company has a number of fully depreciated tangible fixed assets which are still used in the business.

REQUIRED:

a. Discuss the possible reasons why this should happen.

b. Comment on the significance of the continued use of these fully depreciated assets.

c. In the past, these fully depreciated assets and their accumulated depreciation have been merged with other fixed assets and related depreciation on the balance sheet. Discuss the propriety of this accounting treatment, including a discussion of other possible treatments and the circumstances in which they would be appropriate. (Adapted from AICPA Examination in Theory of Accounts, May, 1955.)

18-11 A corporation which does not have a subsidiary ledger for plant recorded the construction of a new factory building by the following entry:

Factory building....................................... $xx
Cash... $xx

After reviewing contracts and cost data, the corporation's public accountant recommended that the company use the following classifications in future accounting for the building.

Building foundation.. $xx
Framing and sheathing...................................... xx
Outside finish... xx
Roof... xx
Interior finish.. xx
Partitions... xx
Acoustical ceiling... xx
Electric wiring.. xx
Electric fixtures.. xx
Furnace.. xx
Boiler xx
Plumbing system.. xx

What might be the advantages (or disadvantages) of following the recommendation? Discuss fully from the standpoint of the effect of the recommendation on maintenance, depreciation, and retirement. (AICPA Examination in Theory of Accounts, November, 1955.)

18-12   The owner of a machine wishes to compare the results of alternative depreciation methods before deciding which method to select. The machine had an installed cost of $12,000 on January 7, 19x1. Actual operations began on January 12. The company has followed the policy of considering that all depreciable acquisitions before the 16th day of any month were made on the first of the month, and that all additions acquired from the 16th through the last of the month were acquired on the first of the following month.

Technological changes in machines of this type have been gradual in the past and are expected to continue to be so in the future. It is estimated that the useful life of the machine will be 6 years, after which it will bring a scrap value of $500. This amount is expected to be almost completely offset by the cost of dismantling and moving the machine.

REQUIRED:

a. Prepare a table showing the depreciation for each year of the machine's life, and its unexpired cost at the end of each year, using the following methods:

(1) Straight-line.
(2) Uniform-rate-on-declining-balance.
(3) Sum-of-the-years'-digits.

b. What other factors should the owner consider in selecting a depreciation method, and how would they affect his decision?
c. If the owner wished to consider the production method, what additional information would he need, and how should it be used in making the decision?

18-13   Your company purchased a car for its executives on July 1, 19x1, at a cost of $5,000. The car was expected to have a useful life of 3 years and a salvage value of $1,400. On December 31, 19x3, your company traded the old car for a new one which had a list price of $7,000. The dealer agreed to accept the old car and cash of $4,500 in full payment of the new car. The old car was appraised at $2,000 on the day of the trade.

REQUIRED:

a. Set up T-accounts showing the balances related to the old car at the end of 19x3, just prior to the trade.
b. Journalize all entries necessary to record the trade and post them to your T-accounts.
c. Journalize the entry to record depreciation for 19x4.

18-14   The Kappa Mining Company purchased for $50,000 a tract of land thought to contain a substantial mineral deposit. The purchase was completed on July 7, 19x1. Legal fees connected with the purchase, $1,000, were paid on August 1, 19x1. During the next few months, Kappa did extensive exploratory work to locate commercial deposits of ore, paying a total of $9,000 for supplies and labor for this purpose. On the basis of this work it was estimated that 190,000 tons of ore could be mined, and that the land could be disposed of for $3,000 at the conclusion of mining operations. Actual tons mined were 10,000 in 19x2 and 50,000 in 19x3.

Other production costs amounted to $4,000 in 19x2 and $20,000 in 19x3, and administrative costs were $5,000 in each year. There were no sales in 19x2, but 48,000 tons were sold in 19x3 at $1 a ton.

REQUIRED:

a. State how the facts would appear in the financial statements prepared at the end of 19x1.

b. Journalize all entries required by the information given for events of 19x1, 19x2, and 19x3.

c. Prepare an income statement and a statement of financial position for 19x2.

d. Prepare an income statement and a statement of financial position for 19x3.

18-15 According to its 19x1 annual report, the McClellan Petroleum Company amortizes the cost of each property producing oil or gas by annual charges for depletion in the proportion which the production for the year bears to the estimated recovery of oil or gas, calculated separately for each property unit. The annual depreciation charge applicable to equipment used on productive wells is computed separately for each property, in the same manner as depletion. The depreciation charge on all other equipment is computed on the straight-line method, at annual rates commensurate with the estimated useful life of each of the various kinds of equipment in use.

REQUIRED:

a. Using assumed figures, illustrate how the method of amortizing the cost of producing property is applied.

b. Does the method in (a) seem appropriate? Explain.

c. Assume that a piece of equipment used on one of the wells was acquired at the beginning of 19x2 at a cost of $10,000. It was expected to be useful during the extraction of 200,000 barrels of oil or to become obsolete at the end of 10 years. In either case its net salvage value was expected to be zero. During 19x2 oil extracted from the well totaled 40,000 barrels.

   Make the necessary journal entries to record these facts, using the Company's method.

d. Does the method illustrated in (c) seem appropriate? Explain.

18-16 Your company acquired a piece of equipment for $6,000 at the beginning of 19x1. It has been depreciated on the basis of an estimated life of 5 years and an estimated salvage value of zero. Just prior to making the annual depreciation entry for 19x4, it becomes evident that the equipment will last until the end of 19x8.

REQUIRED:

a. Make the necessary journal entries to reflect these facts in 19x4.

b. What objections can be made to the method used in (a)?

c. What substitute method can be used, and what are its strong and weak points?

18-17 Several individuals acquired the business of the Parnassus Corporation for a total cash payment of $150,000. The business was to be continued at the same location and under the same name; only the ownership and management were to be different. The assets were appraised at the following amounts:

Accounts receivable, trade	$30,000
Merchandise inventory	40,000
Prepaid expenses	5,000
Land	15,000
Buildings	75,000
Equipment	35,000

The new owners wished to open a new set of accounting records for the business.

REQUIRED:

a. Journalize the entry or entries needed to record the opening of the business under the new ownership.

b. Show what your entry to record the opening would have been if the cost of the business had been $250,000.

18-18 On January 2, 19x1, the Wills Manufacturing Company acquired a machine at a cost of $10,000. Its estimated useful life was 10 years and its estimated salvage value was zero. Rapid developments in technology in the latter part of 19x6 resulted in the availability of a new machine that was vastly superior to the old. Management of the Wills Manufacturing Company planned to use the old machine for one additional year (to the end of 19x7), when it was expected that it could be sold for $500 more than the cost of dismantling.

REQUIRED:

a. Set up T-accounts showing the account balances resulting after depreciation entries for 19x5.

b. Journalize and post the necessary entries for 19x6.

c. State how the facts would appear in the 19x6 financial statements.

d. Journalize the entries for 19x7, showing the sale of the old machine for $500 cash on December 31, 19x7.

18-19 *ABC* Corporation purchased a machine in 1955, trading in an older machine of a similar type. The old machine was acquired in 1942 at a cost of $77,250. Both old and new machines had an estimated 20-year life and no net salvage value. *ABC* Corporation takes ½ year of depreciation in years of acquisition and disposal.

The terms of the purchase provided for a trade-in allowance of $25,000 and called for a cash payment of $125,000 or 12 monthly payments of $11,000 each. *ABC* chose to accept the latter alternative. Other expenses incurred in connection with the exchange were as follows:

Payroll payments:	
Removal of old machine	$ 800
Repairs to factory floor	700
Installation of new machine	900
Invoices received:	
Sales engineer who supervised installation, 40 hours at $10.00	400
Hotel, meals, travel, etc., for sales engineer	200
Freight in—new machine	1,100
Freight out—old machine	1,000

REQUIRED:

a. Prepare entries to reflect the exchange on the books of *ABC*.

b. Compute depreciation on the new machine for the years 1955, 1956, and 1957, showing all computations clearly labeled:

   (1) On the straight-line method.

   (2) On the declining-balance method at twice the straight-line rate.

(Adapted from AICPA Examination in Accounting Practice, November, 1955.)

18-20 A small manufacturing company owned one factory building in 1949 with a net depreciated cost of $90,000. Machinery and equipment was carried at $120,000. Because of expanding business in 1950, it built a new building at a cost of $150,000 and installed $210,000 worth of equipment in it. In the period from 1950 to the end of 1953, it put some new equipment into the old building and continued to operate both plants. Depreciation has been computed on a straight-line basis.

In 1954 the company's owners shut down the old plant because of lack of orders. They propose that they should quit taking depreciation on the old building and machinery. They suggest that, while the old plant is useful, it is not in use and is not wearing out. They also suggest that to take depreciation on it increases their cost, overvalues inventory, and places them in a poor competitive position to bid for business, since their costs are high.

REQUIRED:

You are to give a full discussion of their proposal and of their arguments. (AICPA Examination in Theory of Accounts, May, 1954.)

18-21   The Valley Manufacturing Company was incorporated on January 2, 1956 but was unable to begin manufacturing activities until July 1, 1956 because new factory facilities were not completed until that date.

The Land and Building account at December 31, 1956 was as follows:

Date	Item	Amount
1956		
Jan. 31	Land and building..............................	$ 98,000
Feb. 28	Cost of removal of building.....................	1,500
May 1	Partial payment of new construction.............	35,000
May 1	Legal fees paid.................................	2,000
June 1	Second payment on new construction............	30,000
June 1	Insurance premium.............................	1,800
June 1	Special tax assessment.........................	2,500
June 30	General expenses...............................	12,000
July 1	Final payment on new construction..............	35,000
Dec. 31	Asset write-up to appraised value...............	12,500
		$230,300
Dec. 31	Depreciation—1956 at 1%......................	2,300
	Account balance..............................	$228,000

The following additional information is to be considered:

(1) Cost of removal of old buildings amounted to $1,500, with the demolition company retaining all materials of the building.

(2) Legal fees covered the following:

Cost of organization.......................................	$ 500
Examination of title covering purchase of land...............	1,000
Legal work in connection with construction contract..........	500
	$2,000

(3) Insurance premium covered premiums for the 3-year term beginning May 1, 1956.

(4) General expenses covered the following for the period from January 2, 1956 to June 30, 1956:

President's salary..	$ 6,000
Plant superintendent's salary, covering supervision on new building..	5,000
Office salaries...	1,000
	$12,000

(5) The special tax assessment covered street improvements.

(6) Because of a general increase in construction costs after the company entered into the building contract, the board of directors increased the value of the building $12,500, believing that such increase was justified to reflect current market at the time the building was completed. Retained Income was credited for this amount.

(7) Estimated life of building—50 years. Write-off for 1956—1 per cent of asset value (1 per cent of $230,000, or $2,300).

REQUIRED:

a. List in detail the items that should be included in the land, building, and accumulated depreciation accounts.

b. Explain the reason for each change you made from the company's classification or measurement.

c. Show the proper presentation of these items in the December 31, 1956 statement of financial position.

(Adapted from AICPA Examination in Accounting Practice, November, 1957.)

18-22   Millvale Company uses a large number of units of a small type of equipment, and for a number of years it has kept careful records of the service life of each item. The summary of this past experience per hundred units is as follows:

Years of Useful Life	Number of Units with Each Life Length	Number of Service-Years
1	10	10
2	20	40
3	40	120
4	20	80
5	10	50
Totals	100	300

Dividing the total number of service-years of all units, 300, by the number of units, 100, it has arrived at an average life of 3 years per unit.

At the beginning of January, 19x1, 100 units were acquired at a cost of $50 per unit. The actual retirements of these units by years was as follows:

19x1	9 units	19x4	19 units
19x2	21 units	19x5	7 units
19x3	42 units	19x6	2 units

For simplicity, you may assume that retirements occurred at the end of the year, and that no unit had any salvage value.

REQUIRED:

a. Record in journal form the entries for 19x1 and 19x2, using the *group* method of depreciation.

b. Prepare a table showing the balances in the Equipment, Equipment—Accumulated Depreciation, and Depreciation Expense accounts at the end of each of the two years.

c. Prepare in journal form the entries for 19x1 and 19x2 under the *item* method of depreciation.

d. Prepare a table showing the balances of all affected accounts at the end of each of the two years.

e. Contrast the results of the two methods in this situation.

f. What was the average life of this group of assets?

CASE 18-1. XX AIRLINES

XX Airlines maintains separate accounts for the cost of the fuselage and the cost of the motor of each plane, finding that typically a body will outlive several motors. The management is studying past records with a view to selecting an appropriate depreciation method for future use. The case of Motor 101 is typical:

Cost..	$20,000
Estimated salvage value..................................	2,000
Estimated flying hours...................................	1,200
Average flying hours a year..............................	400

(Distributed 500 hours to the first, 400 to the second, and 300 to the third year.)

REQUIRED:

a. Set up a table comparing annual depreciation and annual unexpired cost balances for Motor 101 under:

   (1) The straight-line method;
   (2) The sum-of-the-years'-digits method;
   (3) The flying-hours method.

b. On the basis of the information given, which method would you advise *XX* Airlines to adopt for future use for the motor? For the body? Why?

c. What other information would have a bearing on the selection of an appropriate depreciation method?

CASE 18-2. W. R. GRACE & CO.

The following excerpt is from the W. R. Grace & Co. 1956 Annual Report:

"Among the developments of 1956 was our decision to participate in a petroleum exploration venture in Libya. Under an agreement with a wholly-owned subsidiary of Texas Gulf Producing Company, your Company has agreed to provide 75%, or up to $7,500,000, of the exploration expenses on extensive oil concessions in the United Kingdom of Libya. If commercial oil reserves are discovered, Grace may elect to provide 49% of the funds required for development of the productive areas and would then be entitled to the equivalent of 49% of the net profit. As part of the agreement, W. R. Grace & Co. also purchased 50,000 shares of the common stock of Texas Gulf Producing Company.

"The first exploratory well, near Benghazi, was sunk to 9,500 feet but was non-productive and was abandoned in January of this year. Drilling has begun on a second exploratory well. The Suez crisis has heightened interest in Libya on the part of other oil firms, many of which are now accelerating their exploratory activities."

In its 1956 Consolidated Balance Sheet, the company lists the following items under Other Assets:

Investment in Texas Gulf Producing Company, at cost (market value, $2,015,000)...........................	$2,225,000
Investment in Libyan oil project—Note 7................	892,637

The Statement of Consolidated Income contains a deduction of $1,211,106 for "Exploratory expenditures—Libyan oil project."

REQUIRED:

a. Summarize the general accounting principles which apply to this situation.
b. What accounting treatment has the company followed with respect to the exploratory well? Does it seem to be justified?
c. What is the justification for showing the investment in Texas Gulf Producing Company at cost even though the market value has declined?

CASE 18-3. WARNER BROS. PICTURES, INC.

The following excerpts from the financial statements for 1951 and 1952 relate to the depreciation policy of Warner Bros. Pictures, Inc.

"The charges for amortization and depreciation of fixed assets are based, except for minor variations, on established rates as shown below which are applied on the straight-line method to the gross book value of assets:

Buildings............................	2½ to 10% per annum
Equipment...........................	10%* to 33⅓% per annum
Improvements........................	10% to 33⅓% per annum
Leasehold improvements...............	Over life of lease

* Effective September 1, 1952 the rate will be changed to 7%.

"Maintenance and repairs are charged directly to profit and loss, except for maintenance and repairs relating to production activities which are charged to costs.

"Renewals of assets not fully depreciated are charged directly to profit and loss; renewals of assets fully depreciated or written off are capitalized. Expenditures for betterments, unless of a minor nature, are generally capitalized.

"When assets become fully depreciated or amortized the relative reserves are applied to the respective asset accounts. Generally, when properties are retired, or otherwise disposed of, before becoming fully depreciated or amortized, the related assets and reserves are removed from the accounts and the resulting profits or losses are credited or charged directly to profit and loss."

REQUIRED:

a. Explain what is meant by "gross book value of assets."
b. Does the procedure for accounting for maintenance and repairs relating to production activities seem sound? Why?
c. Using assumed figures, illustrate how a renewal of an asset not fully depreciated would be recorded under this policy.
d. Illustrate the accounting for a renewal of an asset which was fully depreciated.
e. Comment upon the company's policies of accounting for depreciable assets.

CASE 18-4. ROSS MACHINE CO.

The Ross Machine Co. completed the manufacture of a machine on January 2, 19x1, for a total cost of $50,000. The machine was expected to have a useful life of 5 years and a net salvage value of zero. The company immediately leased the machine to a customer for a monthly rental of $1,250. It estimated that its expenses on the machine during the period of the lease would be:

Year	Property Taxes and Insurance	Repairs
19x1.....................................	$1,500	$ 0
19x2.....................................	1,250	750
19x3.....................................	1,000	1,500
19x4.....................................	750	2,250
19x5.....................................	500	3,000

The expenses of each year would be incurred evenly throughout the year.

REQUIRED:

a. Prepare a table showing for each year the revenue, expenses, net income before income tax, the average balance of the machine's unexpired cost during the year, and the per cent of net income before tax to the average balance of the machine's cost under each of the following methods:

   (1) The straight-line method;
   (2) The uniform-rate-on-diminishing-balance method.

b. What conclusions can you draw about the appropriateness of each of the depreciation methods in this instance?

c. What further information would you wish before recommending a depreciation method to the management of the Ross Machine Co.?

Chapter 19

Accounting for Liabilities

Definition and method of measurement

Chapter 2 defined liabilities as follows:

Liabilities are the equities of the creditors of the entity. As a rule, they require the payment of a specific amount of money to a particular party at a definite future time, although occasionally the amount of money to be paid is indefinite or they may be settled by some means other than money, the identity of the creditor is not yet known, or the due date is uncertain.

Chapter 7 explained that, on the basis of the general methods used to measure them, liabilities may be classified as:

(1) *Monetary liabilities*, which are the claims of outsiders against the business, to be paid in money or money equivalent; and

(2) *Deferred credits to income*, which result from past transactions and are to be treated either as revenues or as reductions of expenses in measuring future income.

Chapter 7 also explained the purposes and general methods of classifying liabilities, and listed the more common types of liability accounts.

The present chapter will explore in more detail the characteristics which determine whether a particular item is a liability; some of the more difficult problems involved in accounting for liabilities; and some of the principal methods used by management in controlling the amounts of liabilities and in scheduling their payment.

Characteristics of a liability

In the past there has been a tendency to think of an *accounting liability* as the equivalent of a *legal debt*, which is an enforceable obligation to pay a certain sum of money at a fixed or determinable future time. This point of view is reflected in the first part of the liability definition presented earlier.

In the recent development of accounting, increasing emphasis upon the measurement of income has led to including in the accounting definition of liabilities some items which do not fit into the legal definition of *enforceable claims*. Instead, many items now considered to be liabilities are credit balances which must be carried forward at the end of an accounting period to permit a *proper matching of revenue and expense* in future periods. The logical place in which to show these items is the liability section of the statement of financial position.

Moonitz[1] lists four characteristics of the present-day liability:

(1) It involves a *future payment* of money, or an equivalent which is acceptable to the recipient.

(2) It results from a *past transaction* of the business with an outside entity.

(3) Its *amount must be definite*, or be subject to close estimation.

(4) Both the *debit and credit* effect must be considered (that is, if a liability is to be recorded, the corresponding asset, expense, loss, or income distribution must also be recorded).

These characteristics clearly apply to accounts payable, notes payable, dividends payable, accrued payables, liabilities as an agent, and bonds payable. The extent to which they apply to the less clear-cut cases of estimated liabilities, deferred credits to income, and contingent liabilities is discussed in later sections of this chapter.

Interest and discount

The interest which accrues day by day during the term of a note payable is a liability in that it *results from* a past transaction, the borrowing of money, goods, or services, and meets the other tests of a liability.

Lenders commonly provide for their interest on loans by using one of two plans:

(1) Accepting an *interest-bearing note*, which requires the borrower to pay at maturity the face amount of the note plus interest at a specified percentage of the face amount for each time period.

(2) Accepting a *non-interest-bearing note*, which includes in the face amount of the note compensation for waiting. Each payment of a part of the face amount of the note includes a payment for interest. This method

---

[1] Maurice Moonitz, "The Changing Concept of Liabilities," *The Journal of Accountancy*, May, 1960, p. 44.

of computing interest is referred to as *discounting* a note. Two common variations of computing the amount of the discount (or interest) are:

(a) The *true discount* method, in which the discount is the specified percentage of the *sum originally advanced;* and

(b) The *bank discount* method, in which the discount is the specified percentage of the *maturity* value, which includes both the sum originally advanced and interest (or discount) for the waiting period.

Chapter 7 illustrated the basic methods of computing simple interest and of recording related transactions and accruals. Appendix 19-A shows how to compute the amounts of true discount and bank discount, and how to record discounted notes in the accounts.

ACCOUNTING FOR BONDS PAYABLE

Nature, classification, and statement presentation

Bonds, which were described briefly in Chapter 7, are written certificates of indebtedness, usually held by a number of persons as evidence of a long-term debt.

The *account title* used for bonds payable should disclose the general nature of the security upon which they rest. If specific assets are pledged to secure a liability, both the asset and the liability captions should reveal this fact. It is also important to show the rate of interest applicable to the bonds and their maturity date in the statement of financial position.

EXAMPLE 1:   The following title indicates that payment of the bonds is secured by a pledge of property:

5% First mortgage bonds due in 1970.................. $1,000,000

EXAMPLE 2:   The following title shows that the bonds are unsecured, depending upon the general credit of the company; that, in the event of liquidation of the business, they would rank after claims of other creditors in priority of payment; and that they are due *serially* over several years:

6% Subordinated debentures due in 1965–68............ $3,000,000

A footnote to the statement of financial position, or a supporting schedule, should report how much of the face amount becomes due each year.

Other important terms of the bonds which might influence the decision of a financial statement reader should also be disclosed. For example, bond agreements often restrict the borrower's payment of dividends during the life of the bond issue to the amount of income earned after the bonds were issued, or permit dividends only if the amount of current assets or net working capital exceeds a specified amount. Sometimes these restrictions require the use of long footnotes.

In addition, the statement of financial position should disclose the face amount of bonds which the company has been authorized to issue but has not issued at the date of the statement. Such bonds represent an important potential additional liability of the company, as well as a potential source of additional funds.

Recording authorization of bonds payable

The fact that a corporation has complied with the necessary legal requirements for issuing bonds payable, including authorization by the stockholders, may be shown by a memorandum such as the following:

L, 4% Bonds Payable Due January 1, 19x6
(Issuance of face amount of $100,000 authorized Jan. 1, 19x1)

Some accountants prefer to record the memorandum in double-entry form, debiting a liability contra-account called Bonds Payable—Unissued and crediting a liability account, Bonds Payable—Authorized, for the face amount of the bonds. Prior to the issuance of the bonds, the net balance of these two liability accounts combined is zero. The form of memorandum illustrated above seems simpler, yet is adequate.

Bonds issued at par

Most bond contracts provide that the borrower will make a periodic cash payment called "interest," computed at a specified percentage of the face amount, or *par*, of the bonds. This periodic payment is interest *in name only*, unless the amount of money received by the borrower upon issuance of the bonds is equal to their *par*. Lenders will pay par for bonds when the current *market* interest rate on other bonds of equivalent terms and risk is equal to the *nominal* interest rate specified in the bond contract.

The following entry records the issuance of bonds at par.

(1)

19x1			
Jan. 1	A, Cash................................	60,000	
	L, 4% Bonds Payable Due 19x6.........		60,000
	Issued at par bonds of a face amount of $60,000.		

Periodic interest payments

Bonds may be in *registered* form or *coupon* form with respect to the payment of periodic nominal interest. If they are *registered*, interest checks are mailed to the persons who are the owners according to the records.

Coupon bonds contain a certificate, or coupon, for each periodic interest payment. The owner of the bond collects his interest by clipping the coupon and presenting it for payment.

Corporate bonds usually provide for semiannual payments of interest. If the bond issue in the preceding illustration provided for semiannual interest payments on January 1 and July 1 (J and J), and the company closed its books for 19x1 on December 31, the appropriate entries would be:

(2)

```
19x1
July  1   OE, Bond Interest Expense................   1,200
              A, Cash............................              1,200
          To record the payment of bond interest on
          $60,000 for 6 months at 4 per cent per
          annum.
```

(3)

```
Dec. 31   OE, Bond Interest Expense................   1,200
              L, Accrued Interest Payable...........              1,200
          To record the accrual of bond interest on
          $60,000 for 6 months at 4 per cent.
```

The presentation in the statement of financial position at the end of the first year would be:

LIABILITIES

```
Current Liabilities:
   Accrued interest payable..............................   $ 1,200
Long-term Liabilities:
   4% Bonds payable due in 19x6:
      Authorized, $100,000; issued and outstanding...........   $60,000
```

For convenience, the bond issuer usually pays a full 6 months' interest to the bond owner on each interest payment date. If bonds change hands between interest dates, the seller collects the amount of the interest he has earned since the last interest payment date from the buyer at the time of sale. The following entry records the *issuance* of bonds between interest dates.

(4)

```
19x2
Mar. 1   A, Cash...................................   30,200
             OE, Bond Interest Expense.............              200
             L, 4% Bonds Payable Due 19x6.........           30,000
         Issued bonds of a face amount of $30,000 at
         par and accrued interest for 2 months at
         4 per cent.
```

The $200 which the issuer collects for interest is an *advance refund* of interest which the buyer will collect on the next semiannual interest payment date but *will not have earned*. The *credit* to Bond Interest Expense in the preceding entry will be *offset* against (deducted from) the debit to the account for the semiannual interest paid, as follows:

OE, Bond Interest Expense

19x2			19x2		
July 1	(6 months' interest paid		Mar. 1	(Advance refund of	
	on $30,000 par).........	600		2 months' interest)	200
	Balance, 400.				

The balance in the account, $400, represents the interest expense which accrued on the $30,000 of bonds payable during the 4 months they were actually outstanding.

Bonds issued at a discount

Bonds sell at a discount below their face amount when their periodic *nominal interest rate* is *lower* than the *market rate* of interest for alternative investments of equal risk. The true interest for the term of the bonds is computed by subtracting the amount received when the bonds were issued from the total payments made by the borrower over their life.

EXAMPLE 3:   A company issued 4 per cent, 2-year bonds of $100,000 par at an effective interest rate of 5 per cent. The proceeds of issue were $98,141. Interest was payable annually on December 31. What was the total interest cost for the life of the bonds, and what was the annual interest cost?

SOLUTION:

Total payments over life of bonds:		
Nominal annual "interest" payments, 2 × $4,000.....	$ 8,000.00	
Face amount paid at maturity......................	100,000.00	
Total payments.................................	$108,000.00	
Deduct proceeds of issue............................	98,141.00	
Total effective interest cost for 2 years.................	$ 9,859.00	
Average effective annual interest cost, $9,859/2.........	4,929.50	

The entries to record the issuance of the bonds in Example 3 at a discount and to reflect the payment of interest during the first year would be:

(5)

19x1			
Jan. 1	A, Cash..........................	98,141.00	
	L, Bonds Payable—Discount........	1,859.00	
	L, 4% Bonds Payable Due in		
	19x2—Face.................		100,000.00
	Issued bonds due in 2 years, nominal interest rate 4%, at an effective rate of 5%.		

(6)

19x1			
Dec. 31	OE, Bond Interest Expense.........	4,929.50	
	L, Bonds Payable—Discount...		929.50
	A, Cash.....................		4,000.00
	Interest expense of $4,929.50 accrued during the first year. Of this amount, $4,000 was paid in cash and the rest was to be paid as a part of the face amount of the bonds at maturity.		

The accounting process which allocates the bond discount as additional periodic interest expense during the life of the bonds and at the same time increases the balance of the liability is called *accumulating the discount* (or, sometimes, *amortizing the discount*). The *straight-line* method of accumulating discount assigns equal amounts to each year of the term of the bonds.

Bonds Payable—Discount is a *contra-liability* account. In a statement of financial position prepared at the end of 19x1, its remaining debit balance should be deducted from the credit balance of Bonds Payable—Face to show the amount of the liability, as follows:

> Long-term Liabilities:
> 4% Bonds payable due in 19x2—face..... $100,000.00
> Deduct applicable discount..............   929.50
> Total liability on bonds........................... $99,070.50

This method of presentation shows the amount of the liability on a *going-concern* basis of measurement at the date of the statement. The amount to be paid eventually is the face amount of the liability, but that amount is not the proper total of the liability on December 31, 19x1, because the face amount is due one year in the future.

It is sometimes contended that the balance of Bonds Payable—Discount is an asset, to be classified as a Deferred Charge to Income. It seems more logical to treat it as a liability valuation account, because, although it does have a debit balance, it does not represent a prepayment for future service benefits.

Bonds issued at a premium

Bonds sell at a *premium* over their face amount when their *nominal interest rate* is *greater* than the *effective rate* of interest for alternative investments of equal risk. Again, the true interest cost is the excess of the total receipts over the total payments during the life of the bonds.

EXAMPLE 4:   A borrower issued $100,000 face amount of 10-year, 6 per cent bonds for a total of $107,721. Interest was payable annually on December 31. What was the total interest cost over the life of the bonds, and what was the annual interest cost?

SOLUTION:

> Total payments over life of bonds:
> Nominal annual "interest" payments, 10 × $6,000.. $ 60,000.00
> Face amount paid at maturity...................   100,000.00
> Total payments............................... $160,000.00
> Deduct proceeds of issue...........................   107,721.00
> Total effective interest cost for 10 years.............. $ 52,279.00
> Average effective annual interest cost, $52,279/10.....   5,227.90

The entries to record the facts of Example 4 during the first year would be as follows:

```
19x1                            (7)
Jan.  1  A, Cash.....................................  107,721.00
            L, 6% Bonds Payable Due in 19x0—Face...              100,000.00
    ⟶    L, Bonds Payable—Premium.........  ....                    7,721.00
            Issued bonds due in 10 years, nominal interest
            rate 6%, at a premium.
                                (8)
Dec. 31  OE, Bond Interest Expense....................    5,227.90
            L, Bonds Payable—Premium...................      772.10
               A, Cash.................................                6,000.00
            Interest expense of $5,227.90 accrued. Paid
            $6,000, which includes the accrued expense as
            well as a return of $772.10 of the original prin-
            cipal of the loan.
```

At the end of the first year, the appropriate presentation in the statement of financial position would be:

```
Long-term Liabilities:
   6% Bonds Payable due in 19x0—face... $100,000.00
   Add unamortized premium.............   6,948.90
      Total liability on bonds....  ....................  $106,948.90
```

The accounting process of treating a part of the bond premium as a reduction of interest expense each year and as an equal reduction of the liability for bonds is called *amortization* of the premium. At any time the bond liability should be shown in the statement of financial position at its face amount plus the unamortized premium which is applicable to future years (the same as the original issue price *minus* the premium which has been amortized in *past* years). The liability account balance gradually declines and equals the face amount of the bonds at maturity.

Bond issue costs

Costs of issuing bonds include those associated with printing the certificates, securing necessary professional advice, and the marketing of the bonds to prospective lenders by underwriters or others. They are long-term unexpired costs similar to organization costs, except that the period of benefit—the life of the bond issue—is reasonably definite.

Bond issue costs should be assigned to periodic expense in the same way as bond discount. Because of their different nature, however, the two should not be combined unless their amounts are immaterial.

Retirement of bonds payable

Entries at the *maturity date* to record the retirement of bonds payable are the same whether the bonds were originally issued at par, at a premium, or at a discount: debit the liability, Bonds Payable—Face, for the par of the bonds, and credit Cash for the same amount. At maturity the entire issuance premium or discount will have been assigned to the interest expense of past periods.

The issuer of bonds sometimes retires them *earlier* than their maturity date, either by purchasing them in the market or by redeeming them at a price stated in the contract. When bonds are retired before maturity, there may be a *gain* or *loss* upon retirement, measured by the difference between the consideration paid to retire the bonds and the amount at which the bond liability is currently carried on the books. If the consideration paid is *greater than the book value* of the liability, there is a *loss;* if the consideration is *less than book value*, there is a *gain.*

EXAMPLE 5:   On January 1, 19x1, 5-year bonds payable of $100,000 par value were issued at $102,000. What would be the gain or loss on retirement if the issuer repurchased the bonds and cancelled them on December 31, 19x3, paying (*a*) par, (*b*) 103 per cent of par, (*c*) 99 per cent of par?

SOLUTION:

	(*a*)	(*b*)	(*c*)
Repurchase price	$100,000	$103,000	$ 99,000
Deduct book value:			
Par	$100,000		
Add unamortized premium	800		
Total book value	100,800	100,800	100,800
Gain on retirement	$ 800		$ 1,800
Loss on retirement		($ 2,200)	

The entries necessary to record the retirement of bonds before maturity are:

(1) Record the accumulation of discount or amortization of premium up to the date of retirement;

(2) Remove the two accounts showing the current amount of the liability—face and premium or discount—from the books; record the payment of cash; and record the gain or loss.

The following entry reflects the facts of Example 5(*b*), assuming that an entry to record the $400 premium amortization for the third year has already been made:

19x3	(9)		
Dec. 31	L, Bonds Payable Due in 19x6—Face	100,000	
	L, Bonds Payable—Premium	800	
	OE, Loss on Retirement of Bonds	2,200	
	A, Cash		103,000
	To record the retirement of bonds which were carried on the books at $100,800 for $103,000, a loss of $2,200.		

Material gains and losses on bond retirements should be reported as *extraneous items* in the income statement.

Accounting for serial bonds

The foregoing illustrations have dealt with *term* bonds, which are due at a single future date. The same general principles apply to issues of *serial* bonds, portions of whose face amounts fall due at more than one date. When an issue of bonds maturing at several different dates is issued at a single lump-sum price, the premium or discount is allocated to each series in proportion to the face amount of the series, weighted by the number of years it will be outstanding.

EXAMPLE 6: A company issued bonds of $200,000 par, $100,000 to be paid at the end of 2 years and $100,000 to be paid at the end of 3 years. The total issue price was $202,000. How much of the premium applied to each series, and how much should be amortized each year?

SOLUTION:

	Par	Years Outstanding	Dollar-Years	Fraction of Total
2-year series........	$100,000 ×	2	$200,000	$\frac{2}{5}$
3-year series........	100,000 ×	3	300,000	$\frac{3}{5}$
			$500,000	

	Amortization of Bond Premium			
	Total	Year 1	Year 2	Year 3
2-year series....................	$ 800	$400	$400	
3-year series....................	1,200	400	400	$400
Total.........................	$2,000	$800	$800	$400

The method illustrated assigns bond premium to each year in proportion to the *bonds outstanding* during that year. This is proper, because bond premium is an *adjustment of interest*, and interest accrues in proportion to the amount of the debt outstanding during the period.

Accounting for bond investments

Bonds held as *temporary investments*, as pointed out in Chapter 5, are accounted for on the basis of *cost*, except that they are reduced to market if a decline in the latter seems to be permanent.

Bonds held as *long-term investments*, as explained in Chapter 6, are measured on the basis of their *amortized cost*. *Premiums* paid when the bonds are acquired are treated as periodic *reductions of interest revenue* over the term of the investment, and *discounts* are treated as *additional interest revenue*. The investor's entries to account for long-term bond investments and related interest parallel those of the bond issuer, with one difference. It is customary for the investor to record his investment in a single account, including par plus the premium applicable to future periods, or par minus discount.

ACCOUNTING FOR OTHER LIABILITIES

Estimated liabilities

Estimated liabilities meet the same basic tests as other liabilities but differ from them in the *degree of accuracy* with which their amounts can be determined. Liabilities such as accounts, notes, bonds, and dividends payable can be measured precisely, or almost so, while the amounts of *estimated* liabilities are subject to a wider margin of error.

Examples of liabilities which frequently require estimates are Warranties Payable, Liability for Pensions, and Corporate Income Tax Payable.

Warranties payable

Businesses often sell products with a *warranty* under which they promise to replace or repair defective products or parts, or to service the product, during a stated time period. Proper matching of revenue and expense requires that an estimate of the costs to be incurred under the warranty agreement be made and recorded in the period of sale by debiting an expense and crediting Warranties Payable.

In the period in which the products are sold, it is not known how many customers will take advantage of the warranty contract, who they will be, and what the cost of fulfilling the warranty will be. Still, it is usually possible for the seller to make a reasonably accurate estimate of the cost and the related liability on the basis of past-experience statistics.

Warranties Payable are *current liabilities* if the term of the warranty does not exceed a year or an operating cycle; otherwise, a part of the liability should be classified as a *long-term liability*.

Actual costs incurred under the warranty contract should be debited to Warranties Payable.

Liability under pension plan

Often one of the most complex estimated liabilities is the *liability under the company's pension plan*.

If the business is required only to make a certain periodic payment to a pension trust fund and its responsibility for pensions ends there, the accounting treatment is relatively simple. The *expense* applicable to the period is the amount which the company is obligated to pay as a result of the activities of that period, and the *liability* at the end of the period is the amount owed but not yet paid to the pension fund. Frequently pension plans administered by outside agencies require that the employer pay an amount based on the past services of employees prior to the adoption of the pension plan. Such past-service costs apply to a current and future benefit—the services expected of the employees—and should be allocated to expense of the current and future periods.

Quite often the pension plan requires the employer to pay periodic benefits of a fixed amount for a definite or determinable time. In such cases, the estimated cost and related liability under the pension plan should be accrued as an *additional cost of employee compensation* which is to be paid at a later date. The entry to record the total employee compensation accrual for a period might be:

```
19x1                         (10)
Jan. 31   OE, Wages and Salaries Expense............ 50,000
          OE, Pension Expense...................... 10,000
                L, Accrued Payroll...................         50,000
                L, Liability for Pensions..............        10,000
          Accrual of employees' compensation, con-
          sisting of $50,000 to be paid to them cur-
          rently and an estimated $10,000 payable in
          the form of future pensions.
```

Perhaps the most difficult part of accounting for pension liabilities is estimating their amount. The total cost of a pension plan over its entire life may be estimated as follows:

```
Total payments expected to be made to employees covered by
  the plan................................................. xxx
Deduct:
  Contributions to be made by employees.................. xx
  Interest to be earned on accumulated funds.............. xx   xx
Estimated net cost to the employer......................... xxx
```

Major factors which must be considered in estimating total pension payments to employees are:

(1) The number of employees expected to retire under the plan. This will be the present number of employees, reduced by those who are expected to resign or die before retirement.

(2) The benefits which employees are expected to receive in each period. This amount will be based upon the terms of the pension contract, which may require that the benefits be reduced by the amount the employees receive from Federal Old Age and Survivors Insurance.

(3) The number of periods for which retired employees are expected to receive pensions.

Life expectancy tables and past employee turnover statistics of the business may be used as a starting point in estimating these items.

The estimated interest to be received will depend upon the timing of the payments into the pension fund and the rates which can be earned upon invested funds.

The financial statements should report the chief requirements of the pension or retirement plan. Practice regarding presentation of the accumulated liability under pension plans is quite diverse.

Corporate income taxes payable

Taxes payable on the income of a corporation should be classified as a current liability. Frequently the amount cannot be determined precisely because (1) the exact meaning of certain tax rules has not yet been established, or (2) the extent to which the taxing authorities will allow borderline deductions or exclude borderline revenue items is not known. The business should make the best estimate of the income tax applicable to the current period which is possible under the circumstances. When amounts of refunds or additional taxes become known in later years, an asset or a liability, whichever is appropriate, should be reported in the statement of financial position. The income statement effect of the correction should, if material, be shown as an extraneous item.

Differences between *income subject to income tax* under the tax laws and the most *logical and useful measure of income* as determined by accountants and businessmen have become more and more substantial in recent years. These differences give rise to perplexing accounting problems. Good judgment may dictate that an item of revenue or expense be reported in the general-purpose financial statements at an earlier or later period than it is reported as a determinant of taxable income. When such differences are material, many accountants feel that revenues and expenses are not properly matched unless the income tax in the current income statement is the amount which would have been payable on the before-tax income shown in the general-purpose income statement. This treatment will result in carrying in the statement of financial position, in addition to the amount of income taxes legally owed, a debit representing a *future reduction of*, or a credit representing a *future addition to*, income taxes. This complex matter is discussed further in Chapter 24.

Deferred revenues

Advances by customers for goods or services to be delivered in the future are often called *deferred revenues*. They are *liabilities*, differing from monetary liabilities only in that they will probably be settled by delivering goods or rendering services rather than by paying money.

Examples of deferred revenues are Customers' Deposits, Rent Collected in Advance, Unearned Interest, Unearned Subscriptions, and Unearned Service Fees. Such accounts should be classified as *Current* or *Long-term Liabilities*, depending upon when they will probably be earned. When the event occurs which justifies the recognition of revenue, the following type of entry should be made:

(11)

L, Unearned Subscriptions........................... 5,000		
OE, Subscription Revenue........................		5,000

Earned revenue by delivering magazines under subscription contracts sold in earlier periods.

Contingent liabilities

Kohler[2] defines a *contingent liability* as follows:

"An obligation, relating to a past transaction or other event, that may arise in consequence of a future event now deemed possible but not probable. If probable, the obligation is not contingent but real (ordinarily, a current liability), and recognition in the accounts is required, notwithstanding that its amount must be estimated in whole or in part. The possibility of a future loss, as from a fire, not linked with a past event, does not give rise to a contingent liability."

He lists the following, among others, as sources of contingent liabilities:

(1) A lawsuit resulting from breach of contract, patent infringement, personal or property damages, or antitrust-law violation.

(2) A commitment to buy goods when prices are fluctuating, that may have to be settled without delivery of the goods.

(3) A guaranty of securities or other obligations. Examples are *notes receivable discounted* and *accounts receivable assigned*, the entries and statement presentation for which were illustrated in Appendix 14-A.

(4) Product guaranties, where experience is not available to permit a reasonable estimate.

(5) Proposed additional income tax assessments for past periods which the taxpayer has not agreed to.

(6) Possible additional compensation to employees in connection with a labor dispute.[3]

Contingent liabilities are not entered in the accounts, except occasionally in memorandum form. The statement of financial position usually contains a footnote describing the general nature of the contingency. It is often impractical to estimate the amount of the liability which may arise.

---

[2] Eric L. Kohler, *A Dictionary for Accountants*, 2nd ed. (Englewood Cliffs, N. J.: Prentice-Hall, Inc., 1957), p. 120.

[3] *Idem.*

Reporting liabilities under long-term leases

Although long-term leases meet all four of the characteristics of liabilities listed earlier, it has not been customary for the lessee to report a liability for future rental payments. This practice may be justified on the ground that the payments made in each future period will be in exact proportion to the benefits received.

The AICPA[4] recommends that substantial fixed rentals due in the future be disclosed in financial statements. The details concerning long-term leases which should be reported in the financial statements or accompanying footnotes are: (1) the annual rentals to be paid and the term for which they are payable, and (2) other important obligations assumed in connection with the lease. This information should be given as long as the amounts are material. In addition, the details of important sale-and-leaseback transactions should be disclosed in the year in which the transaction originates.

PLANNING AND CONTROLLING LIABILITIES

General purposes of planning

Every business is faced with the problem of obtaining the assets which are necessary for carrying on its operations. *Liabilities* are an important *source* of these business assets.

Some of the important factors which management must consider in planning the liabilities of the business are:

(1) The *availability* of different types of credit, including *whether* credit is available at all, *when* it will be available, and the *amount*.

(2) The *terms* under which credit may be obtained, including such factors as *interest cost*, the *length of time* for which the credit is to be granted, the *amounts and timing of periodic repayments*, the nature of the *security* required, and the *restrictions* upon the management of the borrower.

(3) The *suitability* of the particular type of credit to the borrower, including the costs and the risks to which it will subject him.

(4) The *sources of repayment*, including the nature of the sources and the amounts that will become available at different times.

---

[4] AICPA Committee on Accounting Procedure, *Accounting Research Bulletin No. 43* (New York: The Institute, 1953), p. 126.

Selecting the particular types of credit instruments and tailoring their provisions to the needs of the business are problems of *financial management*. The following sections suggest ways in which accounting information can be used in solving these problems.

Budgeting borrowings and repayments

Chapter 12 explained how the planned sources of the assets of the business, forming the *financial budget*, are related to the *operating budget* of revenues and expenses for the next period. Chapter 13 showed how closely the *cash budget*, or forecast, is related to the operating plans of the business and its expected nonoperating sources and uses of cash. Knowledge of the excess of cash expected to become available from operations over required payments is an aid to management in scheduling payments of existing liabilities during the coming budget period. Similarly, a deficiency of cash available as compared with required payments indicates to management that additional funds are needed from some source, perhaps from borrowing.

In addition to using an operating budget and a cash forecast to estimate how much the payments on liabilities in the coming period will be and when they will need to be made, management can use them to *plan* the timing of maturities under new liability contracts, such as seasonal loans for working capital.

Chapter 22 explains how a *capital budget* may be used to plan acquisitions of long-lived assets. As a source of assets, liabilities are an important part of this budget. A *long-range cash forecast* aids management in deciding when the business will need to obtain funds from borrowing and from other sources to finance its planned asset acquisitions and other requirements. It also indicates when cash will become available to repay the sums borrowed. The long-range forecast need not be so detailed as the cash forecast for the coming year because its amounts are subject to a much wider margin of error.

Scheduling repayments of a loan may sometimes be accomplished by estimating the periodic amounts of net cash receipts that will become available from the project to be financed. Maturities of principal are then geared to the available cash. This approach is satisfactory if the schedule of payments on existing liabilities is in balance with expected cash receipts. If it is out of balance, the use of the complete cash forecast described earlier is much safer.

Knowledge of the major debt service requirements of each future year, such as those shown in the accompanying schedule, facilitates planning for liabilities.

BETA PRODUCTS CORP.
Schedule of Debt Service Requirements
For the Years 19x2–19x5

Description:	19x2	19x3	19x4	19x5
Principal Maturities (All Dec. 31):				
6% Serial bonds of 19x2–x4...........	$100,000	$100,000	$100,000	
5% Term bonds of 19x3...............		400,000		
6% Mortgage note of 19x5............				$200,000
6% Serial bonds of 19x4–x5..........			150,000	100,000
Total principal requirements........	$100,000	$500,000	$250,000	$300,000
Interest Maturities:				
6% Serial bonds of 19x2–x4	$ 18,000	$ 12,000	$ 6,000	
5% Term bonds of 19x3...............	20,000	20,000		
6% Mortgage note of 19x5............	12,000	12,000	12,000	$ 12,000
6% Serial bonds of 19x4–x5...........	15,000	15,000	15,000	6,000
Total interest requirements..........	$ 65,000	$ 59,000	$ 33,000	$ 18,000
Total debt service requirements.........	$165,000	$559,000	$283,000	$318,000

A year-by-year comparison of total debt service requirements with expected receipts may indicate that no additional principal maturities should be scheduled for 19x3, and that slightly more should be scheduled for 19x4 than for 19x5.

An aid to efficient management of the *payment* of liabilities is the maintenance of a *tickler file*, in which invoices, notes, or other evidences of liabilities are filed according to *due date*. The treasurer can determine from this file how much is to be paid on any given date, and can make arrangements to have the necessary cash available then for payment. Such a file is also an aid in making such payments on time, thus avoiding penalties and lost discounts.

Controlling payments: the voucher system

Medium-sized and large businesses usually find it necessary to install formal procedures for providing *internal check* in paying their liabilities. It is usually impossible for a single individual to maintain effective controls for insuring that every liability paid by the business is a proper one. A system designed to provide such controls by permitting payments only upon proper authorization is called a *payment voucher system* (or a *voucher system*).

Besides its major function of helping to insure that only proper payments are made, a well designed voucher system has the following additional advantages:

(1) It facilitates bookkeeping for the incurrence and payment of liabilities;

(2) It facilitates prompt payment of liabilities;

(3) It provides information as to the amounts and due dates of liabilities;

(4) It accumulates detailed evidence in support of payments.

Under the voucher system, *all payments* are made by *check*, and only after an approved *voucher* has been prepared as evidence that the payment is proper. Often the check is a copy of, or an attachment to, the voucher which *authorizes* the payment.

Responsibilities for particular stages of the approval and payment process are assigned to many different individuals. At the end of the process, the *treasurer*, after receiving a voucher signed by the *controller* certifying that the payment is justified, signs a check ordering the bank to make the payment. Many supporting documents, each prepared and approved by a different responsible employee, usually accompany the voucher. Some of these documents and their functions are:

(1) A *purchase requisition*, prepared by a production or stores department, indicates that the ordered items were needed.

(2) A *purchase order*, prepared by the purchasing department, requests that the supplier ship the goods under specified terms.

(3) A *receiving report* shows how many items were received and in what condition.

(4) A seller's *invoice*, verified as to terms and computations, shows prices and quantities of the items purchased.

A more complete description of the process of approving the payment for a purchase appears in Appendix 19-B.

The documents which support the authorization for payment are usually enclosed in a serially numbered *voucher jacket*, the outside of which indicates the names of the accounts to be debited and credited for the purchase, and the appropriate amounts.

The individual vouchers are often journalized in a *voucher register*, a special journal with money columns for Vouchers Payable, Credit, and for debits to accounts which are frequently debited. The individual vouchers are then filed according to due date until the time for payment, when they are presented to the person who is to sign the check. Then they are transferred to a paid voucher file.

Analysis of liability balances

Management, stockholders, and creditors are all interested in the present and continuing ability of the company to pay its liabilities as they come due. A cash budget is an excellent means of estimating the amount of money which will be available to meet debt requirements in the future. Some businesses do not prepare cash budgets, however, and even if they are prepared, they are generally not available for the use of stockholders and creditors.

Substitute measures for analyzing the liabilities of the business which are sometimes used are the *number of times fixed charges are earned* and the *ratio of liabilities to total equities.*

Fixed charges are the amount of periodic interest expense on borrowed funds. The formula for computing the number of times they are earned is:

$$\frac{\text{Net Income before Interest and Income Taxes}}{\text{Periodic Interest}}$$

$$= \text{Number of Times Fixed Charges Earned}$$

The earnings should be sufficient to provide for the payment of the interest charges in good years as well as bad, with an ample margin of safety. A stable ratio of income to fixed charges is more desirable than a fluctuating ratio of about the same amount, since the former denotes more dependable earnings.

The interpretation and limitations of the ratio of liabilities to total equities are discussed in Chapter 25.

Summary

Liabilities involve future payments of fairly definite amounts which result from past transactions with outside entities.

A major problem in accounting for Bonds Payable is that of assigning portions of the issuance premium or discount to each period as adjustments of interest expense. The balance of the premium or discount applicable to future periods should be deducted from the face amount of the bonds to reflect the present balance of the liability.

Warranties Payable, Liability for Pensions, Corporation Income Tax Payable, and similar liabilities usually cannot be estimated as accurately as can other common types of liabilities because of the many complex factors which affect their amounts. Nevertheless, proper matching of revenue and expense requires that careful estimates of their amounts be made.

Cash budgets for the coming period and capital budgets for the long-range future are useful in estimating the sums that the business will need to borrow in future periods and the times at which they can be repaid. Schedules of debt service requirements are also helpful in this regard.

A voucher system is a useful means of controlling the payment of liabilities, of estimating the cash needs of the future, and of facilitating the recording of liability transactions.

APPENDIX 19-A

Discounted Notes Payable

Computation of discount

Computing true discount. True discount may be computed by the same formula as that used for simple interest if the initial sum borrowed is known. Often, however, the maturity value (which includes the initial sum plus interest) and the rate of interest are known but the principal borrowed is unknown. It may be determined by the formula,

$$S = S_n - S(i)(n),$$

where S is the initial sum borrowed, or principal;

    S_n is the maturity value, including interest;

    i is the interest (or *true discount*) rate per time period; and

    n is the number of time periods.

EXAMPLE 1:   A company borrows money from a bank for one year and gives in exchange a non-interest-bearing promissory note for $1,060, which includes principal plus true discount at the rate of 6 per cent of the initial amount per year. (a) What is the sum borrowed? (b) What is the interest cost?

SOLUTION: (a) $S = S_n - S(i)(n)$
            $S = \$1,060 - S(.06)(1)$
            $S = \$1,060 - .06S$
      $1.06S = \$1,060$
            $S = \$1,060/1.06 = \$1,000$, the sum borrowed
    (b) $I = S_n - S$
          $I = \$1,060 - \$1,000 = \$60$, the interest cost

Computing bank discount. In the case of *bank discount*, the maturity value and the rate of discount are usually known, while the initial sum is unknown. Here, however, the stated rate is multiplied by the *maturity value* rather than by the principal sum. The formula for determining the initial sum is:

$$S = S_n - S_n(d)(n),$$

where S is the initial sum borrowed;

    S_n is the face, or maturity amount of the note;

    d is the discount rate per time period; and

    n is the number of time periods.

EXAMPLE 2:   An individual borrows money from a bank for one year and gives in exchange a non-interest-bearing note for $1,063.83. The bank computes its discount at the rate of six per cent of the face amount of the note per year, deducts this from the face amount, and lends the difference to the borrower in cash. What amount does the borrower receive?

SOLUTION:

$$S = S_n - S_n(d)(n)$$
$$S = \$1{,}063.83 - \$1{,}063.83(.06)(1)$$
$$S = \$1{,}063.83 - \$63.83$$
$$S = \$1{,}000$$

The amount of the discount in this case is \$63.83.

Example 1 showed that true discount at 6 per cent on a 1-year loan of \$1,000 would be \$60. By basing the charge for interest on the *face* amount of the note, which includes principal and interest, the bank-discounting process results in a true interest charge of more than 6 per cent of the amount of the loan.

EXAMPLE 3:   What is the true interest rate in Example 2?

SOLUTION:

$$i = \frac{I \text{ (total interest cost)}}{S \text{ (initial sum borrowed)}}$$

$$i = \frac{\$63.83}{\$1{,}000}$$

$i = 6.383\%$, the true interest rate.

Recording discounted notes payable

The following entries show how the facts of Example 1 would be recorded.

19x1	(1)		
Oct. 1	A, Cash....................................	1,000	
	L, Notes Payable—Discount................	60	
	L, Notes Payable to Bank—Face.........		1,060
	Borrowed money on a one-year, non-interest-bearing note. The amount borrowed was computed by using a true discount rate of 6 per cent.		

The account L, Notes Payable—Discount, is a deduction from (*contra* to) the liability for the face amount of the note. Together these accounts show the actual amount owed on the note, including accrued interest, at any time. If a statement of financial position were prepared on October 1, the facts would be shown as follows:

LIABILITIES

Notes payable to banks—face......................		\$1,060
Deduct applicable discount.........................		60
Total liability on notes....................................		\$1,000

The following entry would be necessary at the end of the year:

```
19x1                             (2)
Dec. 31   OE, Interest Expense.....................        15
             L, Notes Payable—Discount...........                15
             To record the interest applicable to
             three months of 19x1, and to increase
             liabilities by the same amount.
```

In the 19x1 income statement, Interest Expense would be shown as $15. The presentation in the December 31 statement of financial position would be:

LIABILITIES

Notes payable to banks—face......................	$1,060
Deduct applicable discount.......................	45
Total liability on notes..........................	$1,015

The total liability was increased by *reducing* the liability *contra-account*, L, Notes Payable—Discount.

The total of the liabilities for the face amount of the note and accrued interest at any date under the *true discount* method should be the same as for an interest-bearing note which carries the same rate. It is equal to the sum borrowed, $1,000, plus interest that has accrued for the three months to date, $15. The method of recording and presenting the interest accrual under the *bank discount* procedure would be similar, except that the total amount of discount and the periodic accrual would be slightly higher.

APPENDIX 19-B

Procedure for Approving a Purchase Voucher

The following is a list of the various individuals or departments who help to verify the propriety of a purchase, together with their duties respecting it. Each business is likely to have variations to suit its own needs, some simpler and some more complex than the procedure illustrated.

A. Operating department head or storekeeper who requests the goods
   1. After determining that goods are needed, sends a written *purchase requisition* to the purchasing department, requesting an appropriate quantity.
B. Purchasing department
   2. Determines that the requisition is proper as to the authority of the person signing it, the amount requested, and other details.
   3. Prepares a *purchase order* requesting the outside supplier from whom the best terms are available to furnish goods.

4. Notifies operating department that order has been placed.
5. Notifies receiving department when to expect the goods.

C. *Receiving department*

6. Determines that goods received were actually ordered by comparing them with a copy of *purchase order*.
7. Counts or otherwise determines that the quantity received is correct.
8. Determines whether quality and condition are proper.
9. Sends a *receiving report* to purchasing department.
10. Sends goods, together with a copy of the receiving report, to the storeroom.

B. *Purchasing department*

11. Compares the seller's *invoice* for the goods with the *receiving report* as to accuracy of quantities ordered, billed, and received.
12. Determines that prices and other items on the invoice are in agreement with the purchase order.
13. Follows up on any delayed shipments, shortages, or damages.

A. *Operating department or storeroom*

14. Accepts goods from receiving department, signing a copy of the receiving report as evidence of accountability.

D. *Inventory subsidiary ledger bookkeeper*

15. Receives a copy of the purchase invoice and enters on the subsidiary ledger card for each type of inventory the quantity received and, under some systems, the unit and total cost.

E. *Accounts payable clerk*

16. Determines that all prior documents—purchase order, invoice, receiving report—are in order.
17. Checks accuracy of mathematical calculations, such as quantities multiplied by unit prices, discounts, and totals.
18. Prepares a *voucher*, or authorization for payment. Enters on the voucher the name and number of the general ledger account to be debited.
19. Sends the voucher and supporting documents to the controller. The latter signs to attest that all documents are in order and then sends the voucher-check to the treasurer, who signs to authorize payment.

QUESTIONS AND PROBLEMS

19-1 Many items which are now considered to be liabilities do not fit into the strict legal definition of a liability or *debt*.

REQUIRED:
Give as many examples of such types of liabilities as you can, and explain why each should be considered as a liability in the financial statements.

19-2 "Whether or not a particular item is accounted for as a liability depends upon whether it involves a *probable*, as distinguished from a *possible*, future payment."

REQUIRED:

a. Is this statement correct?
b. Give an example of an item that will *probably* require a future payment, and illustrate how you would account for it.
c. Illustrate an item that will *possibly*, but not probably, involve a future payment.

19-3   Advances by customers, rent collected in advance, and similar items will probably *not* require future payments.

REQUIRED:

How can you justify accounting for them as liabilities?

19-4   The payee of a note receives his compensation for letting someone else use his assets in the form of either *interest* or *discount*.

A certain individual wishes to borrow exactly $2,000 for one year.

REQUIRED:

a. Compare the true interest cost to the borrower if the lender's compensation is in the form of (1) interest; (2) true discount; (3) bank discount.
b. For each of the three methods of compensation in (a), prepare the following from the point of view of the borrower:
   (1) Entry at date of loan.
   (2) Entry at end of accounting period 9 months later.
   (3) Appropriate sections of financial statements at end of accounting period.
   (4) Entry for payment of note one year later.

19-5   The owner-manager of a small business which employs a bookkeeper-cashier and three sales clerks is visiting the business of a friend, who is manager of a retail establishment with 10 times as many employees. He is especially impressed with the safeguards provided by the latter's payment voucher system, and wonders if he should not install such a system.

REQUIRED:

a. What features of a payment voucher system would be appropriate for the use of the small business?
b. What would be the disadvantages of such a system?
c. What action would you recommend that the owner-manager of the small business take?

19-6   One advantage claimed for a payment voucher system is that it eliminates posting to individual accounts payable subsidiary ledger accounts for each creditor.

REQUIRED:

a. What is the subsidiary accounts payable record, if any, under a payment voucher system?
b. Is the elimination of a detailed record for each creditor an advantage? If not, what modification of the voucher system would you suggest?

19-7   "A bond which sells at a premium is a better bond than one which sells at a discount."

REQUIRED:

Comment on the validity of this statement, including a careful explanation of the nature of bond premium and bond discount.

19-8 A business was authorized to issue $500,000 of 10-year, 6 per cent debenture bonds payable on June 30, 19x1. Interest was payable semiannually on each June 30 and December 31.

REQUIRED:

a. Journalize the following transactions for 19x1:
   (1) Issuance of $300,000 of the bonds at 102 per cent of par on June 30, 19x1.
   (2) Accrual and payment of interest for 19x1.
b. Show how the relevant items would appear in the statement of financial position for (1) December 31, 19x1 and (2) December 31, 19x2.
c. Journalize all entries that are needed on June 30, 19x0, 10 years later, when the bonds are retired.

19-9 On December 31, 19x1, 12 years after the issuance of its bonds, a corporation's adjusted trial balance shows the following accounts:

    5% Bonds Payable, due 12/31/x9—Par.................. $150,000
    Bonds Payable—Premium..............................   1,800

Interest is payable annually on December 31. Periodic amortization has been made properly under the straight-line method.

REQUIRED:

a. At what percentage of par were the bonds originally issued?
b. Journalize all entries related to the bonds in 19x2.
c. Show how the items affected would appear in the 19x2 statement of financial position.

19-10 The Magnum Corporation was authorized on December 20, 19x1, to issue $200,000 of 5-year, 5 per cent mortgage bonds payable. Semiannual interest payment dates were January 1 and July 1. All of the bonds were issued at 97 per cent of par on January 1, 19x2.

On December 31, 19x2, the Magnum Corporation wished to use some of its idle cash to reduce its indebtedness. Accordingly, it purchased in the open market and immediately retired its own bonds having a par value of $20,000, paying 101 per cent of par.

REQUIRED:

a. Journalize the entries for:

   (1) Issuance of the bonds.
   (2) Payment and accrual of interest during 19x2.
   (3) Retirement of the bonds on December 31, 19x2.

b. Show how all relevant items would appear in the income statement and statement of financial position prepared at the end of 19x2.

19-11 On July 1, 19x1, the Ethan Company issued $1,000,000 of bonds payable to finance the construction of a plant. Expecting that it would require two years for the plant to get into production and an additional year for it to reach its peak level of activity, the company arranged for serial bonds, bearing interest at 5 per cent, to be retired on June 30 of each year as follows:

19x4	$100,000	19x7	$200,000
19x5	200,000	19x8	300,000
19x6	200,000		

The company's fiscal year ends on June 30.

REQUIRED:

a. Prepare a schedule showing the cash payments required to service the debt for each of the years ending June 30, 19x2, through June 30, 19x8.
b. Assuming that the bonds were issued at a total discount of $30,000, prepare a schedule showing the interest expense of each year.
c. Show how the facts would appear in the statement of financial position of June 30, 19x2.

19-12 On July 1, 19x1, an investor purchases at 103 per cent of par a $1,000 par bond which matures on June 30, 19x4, and which pays interest at 6 per cent of par each June 30.

REQUIRED:

a. What total amount of interest will the investor earn if he holds the bond to maturity?
b. Draw up a table with the following headings and fill in the correct amounts, using the straight-line method of amortization.

End of Year	Cash Collected	Interest Earned	Investment Recovered	Investment Balance
0	$	$	$	$
1				
2				
3				

c. Present in journal form all entries needed in connection with the investment, assuming that the investor's fiscal year ends June 30.

19-13 On January 1, 19x1, Company A purchases, at 88 per cent of their par value, bonds of the X Company which have a face amount of $10,000. The bonds pay interest of 4 per cent annually and mature on January 1, 19x6. Company A expects to hold the bonds to maturity.

On the same day, Company B also buys $10,000 par value of X Company bonds at 88. B expects to resell the bonds in a few months to finance a plant expansion. On December 31, 19x1, the quoted selling price of the bonds is 86, but neither company has sold its holdings.

REQUIRED:

a. Give Company A's journal entries for 19x1.
b. Give Company B's journal entries for 19x1.
c. Show how each company would present the facts in its December 31, 19x1, statement of financial position.

19-14 The following items often appear in the "Equities" section of statements of financial position:

(1) Estimated Federal income taxes payable
(2) Product guarantees

(3) Sundry accrued items
(4) Dividends payable on preferred stock
(5) Accrued bonuses to officers and employees
(6) Pensions payable
(7) Serial bonds payable

REQUIRED:

For each of the items listed explain:

a. What it means.
b. How the amount is measured.
c. What account is debited when the equity originates.
d. How it should be classified in the statement of financial position.

19-15   The following are excerpts from the statement of financial position of the Horner Company:

"Notes receivable (See Note 1)......................... $100,000"
  . . .

"Note 1. The company is contingently liable to the Merchants and Farmers Bank for $50,000 of notes receivable discounted for which payment is not yet due."

REQUIRED:

a. Explain the meaning of these two items.
b. Do you think that this method of disclosure presents the financial position of the company fairly? Explain.
c. Making any assumptions which you desire, rewrite the footnote to give more adequate disclosure.

19-16   The following items appear on the statements of financial position of Companies A and B:

Company A

Fixed Assets:

Buildings (cost).............................	$500,000	
Less accumulated depreciation...	200,000	
	$300,000	
Less 6%, 20-year bonds payable, for which the building is pledged as security..............	160,000	
Net unpledged fixed assets....................		$140,000

Company B

Fixed Assets:

Equity in machinery (Note 1)................	$ 15,000
  . . .

Note 1. Three years ago Company B entered an agreement whereby machinery which has a cash price of $50,000 can be leased for four years at an annual rental of $5,000. At the end of the fourth year, Company B has the option of purchasing the machinery and applying the previous rental payments to the purchase price. The company plans to exercise the purchase option.

REQUIRED:

a. Evaluate the statement presentation made by each company.
b. If the machinery of Company B has an estimated useful life of 10 years, and if an annual rental of $4,000 is charged on similar machines by other companies, what changes in the statement presentation of the two companies would you recommend? Why?

19-17   In an examination of the Marco Corporation as of December 31, 19x4, you discover the following situations, for which no entries have been made in the accounting records.

(1) The Marco Corporation has guaranteed the payment of interest on the 10-year, first-mortgage bonds of the Newart Company, an affiliate. Outstanding bonds of the Newart Company amount to $150,000, with interest payable at 5 per cent per annum, due June 1 and December 1 of each year. The bonds were issued by the Newart Company on December 1, 19x2, and all interest payments have been met by that company with the exception of the payment due December 1, 19x4. The Marco Corporation states that it will pay the defaulted interest to the bondholders on January 15, 19x5.
(2) During 19x4 the Marco Corporation was named as a defendant in a suit for damages by the Dalton Company for breach of contract. An adverse decision to the Marco Corporation was rendered, and the Dalton Company was awarded $40,000 damages. At the time that the financial statements were being prepared, the case was under appeal to a higher court.

REQUIRED:

What *entries* would you recommend and what *disclosures*, if any, would you make of these situations in the financial statements for December 31, 19x4? (Adapted from AICPA Examination in Auditing, May 19, 1955.)

19-18   The annual report of Family Finance Corporation for the year ended June 30, 1952 contained the following items:

	June 30	
	1952	1951
"CURRENT LIABILITIES		
Federal and State taxes on income (Note 3)............	$5,037,634	$2,740,033"

. . .

From Income Statement:

"Provision for Federal and State Taxes on Income

(Including Federal excess profits tax: 1952, $253,308;		
1951, $189,305) (Note 3).........................	$3,894,710	$2,740,498"

Note 3 read as follows:

"3. In June 1952, subsidiaries of the Company received notices of determinations by the Commissioner of Internal Revenue of deficiencies in Federal taxes on income for the fiscal years 1944 to 1949, inclusive, in the aggregate amount of $2,810,000 resulting mainly from the disallowance of certain deductions for inter-company interest. The subsidiaries intend to litigate such determinations; and the Company intends to file claims for refund of Federal taxes on income in the aggregate amount of $1,670,000 in respect of the same years, to which it has been advised by Counsel that it would be entitled if the determinations should be sustained. If the determinations were sustained in full, subsidiaries of the Company might become liable for additional Federal taxes on income for the fiscal years 1950 to 1952, inclusive, in the estimated aggregate amount of $2,790,000; in which event the Company has been advised by Counsel that it would be entitled to refunds of Federal taxes on income for such years in the estimated aggregate amount of $2,270,000. The net amount of interest applicable to the deficiencies for the years 1944 to 1949, inclusive, and to the possible additional taxes for the years 1950 to 1952, inclusive, after giving effect to interest on the above-mentioned refunds for such years, would amount to approximately $560,000 to June 30, 1952. The Company is unable to predict the outcome of the litigation and no provision has been made for such taxes or interest in the accompanying financial statements."

REQUIRED:

a. What entry does the company make to record the income tax applicable to the current year?
b. What entry does it make to record the payment of taxes?
c. Why do the amounts for income taxes in the income statement and statement of financial position differ?
d. What entries have been made for the items described in Note 3?
e. Do you agree with the company's accounting treatment of the items in Note 3? Why?

19-19 The annual report of Colonial Stores, Incorporated, for the fiscal year 1953, showed the following items, among others:

	December 26, 1953	December 27, 1952
Property, plant and equipment, at cost...	$19,636,634	$17,339,862
Less accumulated allowances for depreciation and amortization............	7,936,409	6,804,107
	$11,700,225	$10,535,755
Total assets..........................	$43,134,002	$37,378,280
Total stockholders' equity..............	$18,525,585	$17,653,499
Net profit............................	$ 2,623,860	$ 2,302,281

It also contained the following two footnotes:

"(5) LEASED PREMISES:

"At December 26, 1953, the company was lessee of warehouse, store and other properties under 437 leases, of which 260 have terms extending beyond three years from that date. The rentals for the year 1954 under the 260 leases expiring after 1956, including those referred to in the following paragraph, aggregate $2,023,044 plus, in some instances, real estate taxes and other expenses, or increased amounts based on percentages of sales; approximately 58% of such aggregate relates to leases expiring within ten years and the balance to leases expiring in from ten to twenty-seven years.

"Upon the completion of construction and lease-back arrangements during the year ended December 26, 1953, the company sold for $4,595,880 (approximate cost) one warehouse and four store properties. Such properties were leased back to the company by the purchasers for initial periods of ten to twenty-eight years; the rentals for the year 1954 under such leases aggregate $309,040 plus, in most instances, real estate taxes and other expenses.

"(6) EMPLOYEE RETIREMENT PLAN:

"Under the trusted retirement plan for employees (including officers) in effect at December 26, 1953, the unfunded cost of past service and early retirement benefits payable entirely by the company over a remaining period of fourteen and one-half years is estimated on an actuarial basis to approximate $1,346,000. The statement of profit and loss for the year ended December 26, 1953 includes charges amounting to $731,157 representing the company's contribution to the plan for the year; of such amount, $165,938 is in respect of past services and $565,219 relates to current services.

"While the company expects to continue the plan indefinitely, the right to modify, amend or terminate it has been reserved. In the event of termination, the entire amount theretofore contributed under the plan must be applied to the payment of benefits to participants or their beneficiaries."

REQUIRED:

a. What is the purpose of Note 5? How does it affect the income and financial position of the company?
b. What is the purpose of Note 6? How does it affect the income and financial position of the company?
c. Do you agree with the company's accounting treatment of the items in the two footnotes? Explain.

19-20 The Trumb Radio Corporation manufactures television tubes and sells them with a 6 months' guarantee under which defective tubes will be replaced without a charge. On December 31, 19x3, the estimated liability for product warranty had a balance of $510,000. By June 30, 19x4, this liability had been reduced to $80,250 by charges for estimated net cost of tubes returned which had been sold in 19x3.

The company started out in 19x4 expecting 8 per cent of the dollar volume of sales to be returned. However, owing to the introduction of new models during the year, this estimated percentage of returns was increased to 10 per cent on May 1. It is assumed that no tubes sold during a given month are returned in that month. Each tube is stamped with a date at the time of sale so that the warranty may be properly administered. The following table of percentages indicates the likely pattern of sales returns during the 6-month period of the warranty, starting with the month following the sale of tubes.

Month Following Sale	Percentage of Total Return Expected
First	20
Second	30
Third	20
Fourth through sixth—10% each month	30
Total	100

Gross sales of tubes were as follows for the first six months of 19x4:

Month	Amount
January	$3,600,000
February	3,300,000
March	4,100,000
April	2,850,000
May	2,000,000
June	1,800,000

The company's warranty also covers the payment of freight cost on defective tubes returned and on new tubes sent out as replacements. This freight cost runs approximately 10 per cent of the sales price of the tubes returned. The manufacturing cost of the tubes is roughly 80 per cent of the sales price, and the salvage of returned tubes averages 15 per cent of their sales price. Returned tubes on hand at December 31, 19x3, were thus valued in inventory at 15 per cent of their original sales price.

REQUIRED:

a. Prepare a schedule to compute the proper balance of the estimated liability for warranty account on June 30, 19x4.

b. Journalize the necessary adjusting entry.

(Adapted from AICPA Examination in Accounting Practice.)

CASE 19-1. ARMOUR AND COMPANY

The following items appeared in the Consolidated Statement of Financial Position of Armour and Company:

	Oct. 31, 1959	Nov. 1, 1958
"Current liabilities:		
Long term debt and subordinated long term debt payable within one year (notes 4 and 5).........	$ 7,122,707	$ 3,633,246

. . .

"Long term debt (note 4):

First Mortgage Twenty-Five Year 2¾% Sinking Fund Bonds, Series F, due July 1, 1971..........	$40,000,000	$42,500,000
First Mortgage 3% Sinking Fund Bonds, Series G, due July 1, 1971.............................	9,966,000	10,206,000
3½% Sinking Fund Debentures, due September 1, 1968...	24,000,000	26,000,000
Purchase Money Notes, payments due in installments to 1968...............................	10,480,240	1,006,977
	$84,446,240	$79,712,977
Subordinated long term debt (note 5):		
3½% Cumulative Income Debentures (Subordinated), due November 1, 1972..................	$14,670,000	$16,954,000
5% Cumulative Income Subordinated Debentures, due November 1, 1984.......................	58,223,700	58,463,520
	$72,893,700	$75,417,520"

. . .

"Notes to financial statements:

. . .

"*4. Long term debt*

"Long term debt maturities and sinking fund requirements for the fiscal year 1960 aggregate $7,363,887. Of this amount $2,765,000 has been anticipated and paid in advance; the balance of $4,598,887 has been deducted from long term debt and included in current liabilities at October 31, 1959. The amount payable in 1961 will be $8,079,677, in 1962 $9,080,369, in 1963 $9,081,093, and in 1964 $9,056,845.

"*5. Subordinated long term debt*

"Subordinated long term debt sinking fund requirements for the 1960 fiscal year aggregate $2,523,820, of which $2,284,000 is applicable to the 3½% income debentures and $239,820 to the 5% income debentures. This amount has been deducted from subordinated long term debt and included in current liabilities as at October 31, 1959. Since the computation of sinking fund requirements is based on formulae relating principally to annual earnings, such requirements for 1961 and subsequent years are not presently determinable.

"fifty-two weeks ended	Oct. 31, 1959	Nov. 1, 1958
Income		
Sales, including service revenues............	$1,869,801,148	$1,850,438,524
Other income............................	2,493,659	2,363,393
Total income........................	1,872,294,807	1,852,801,917
Costs		
Cost of products, supplies and services......	1,694,809,997	1,691,932,881
Selling and administrative expenses........	108,612,052	111,710,808
Depreciation.............................	12,884,625	12,546,838
Contributions to employes' pension funds....	7,030,558	6,613,707
Interest expense:		
Current debt..........................	344,436	1,220,853
Long term debt........................	5,977,046	6,207,319
Miscellaneous deductions...................	1,283,341	583,650
Taxes (other than income taxes)............	14,069,948	12,866,411
Provision for Federal income taxes (note 2)..	13,085,000	3,501,000
Provision for other income taxes............	131,073	58,908
Total costs...........................	1,858,228,076	1,847,242,375"

REQUIRED:

a. Explain the meaning of the following terms as they are used in connection with the Armour statements:

   (1) Sinking Fund Bonds   (4) Cumulative Income Debentures
   (2) Series F   (5) Subordinated
   (3) Purchase Money Notes

b. Explain and evaluate the company's statement classification of the various items.

c. Explain the probable purpose of issuing subordinated debentures.

d. Compute and interpret the *number of times fixed charges were earned* by the company for the years ending in 1959 and 1958.

CASE 19-2. TRACY STONE

Learning that Mr. Stafford, the owner of the Quick Launderette near the State University campus, was anxious to sell his business, Tracy Stone arranged an interview to discuss the possibility of purchasing it.

During the course of the meeting, Tracy learned that Mr. Stafford rented the laundry building for $100 a month under a 10-year lease, which still had 7 years to run. He owned outright all of the equipment, which included 10 one-year-old combination washer-dryers and several chairs, tables, and metal clothes containers. Each of the washer-dryers could be expected to last for an additional four years. Other equipment included an office desk, a metal file cabinet, and a water fountain, all of which belonged to Mr. Stafford.

Tracy asked Mr. Stafford to quote a price for the business. Mr. Stafford replied that he would take $4,000 cash for all of the assets of the business, provided that Tracy would assume his obligation on the lease. Being short of cash, Tracy asked what installment terms Mr. Stafford would accept. After careful consideration, the latter offered to sell the business to Tracy in exchange for a promissory note of $4,800, to be paid off in 24 installments due at the rate of $200 at the end of each month.

After further discussion, Tracy signed a contract to purchase the business under the terms stated. The effective date of the note was June 30, 19x1, and the equipment title was to be transferred upon payment of the last installment.

At the end of each month, Tracy made an entry in his books debiting Depreciation of Laundry Equipment $200 and crediting Cash. He also recorded the cash receipts and payments associated with operating the laundry.

One year later he found it necessary to approach the Citizens Bank for a loan to finance the purchase of additional equipment. Asked for a statement of financial position, he informed the banker that he owned practically no assets, because he would not obtain title to the launderette until he had made the final payment on the installment note. "All I could include on a financial statement would be the $1,200 which I have in the bank, $100 worth of supplies, and the $2,400 balance which I owe on the note to Mr. Stafford," he said.

Upon request, he prepared the following income statement for the first year's operations and submitted it to the banker:

Laundry receipts......................................		$7,000
Less expenses:		
Rent..	$1,200	
Depreciation of equipment......................	2,400	
Utilities.......................................	440	
Licenses and property taxes....................	50	
Supplies purchased............................	400	
Miscellaneous.................................	300	4,790
Net income.....................................		$2,210

REQUIRED:

a. As the banker, evaluate the financial information which Mr. Stone has presented to you.

b. Using the information available, reconstruct the financial statements in accordance with good accounting principles.

c. What additional information would you wish before extending a loan on the basis of the revised financial statements?

CASE 19-3. LONNER MANUFACTURING CO.

The Lonner Manufacturing Co. wishes to expand its productive capacity by buying additional equipment which it could purchase for $2,000,000 cash. It estimates that one year will be required to get the equipment installed and to build up demand to the point where the machinery is operating at approximately full capacity. Additional net annual cash receipts which can be expected from the increased production, over and above payments for materials, labor, other added costs of manufacturing, and all other items, are as follows:

Year	Expected Net Receipts
19x1..	$ 300,000
19x2..	400,000
19x3–19x0..................................	500,000 per year
Total.....................................	$4,700,000

The Lonner management feels that these estimates are subject to a margin of error of no more than 10 per cent in either direction.

The equipment has an estimated useful life of 10 years, and the straight-line method of depreciation is considered to be applicable.

The manufacturer of the equipment is willing to sell the equipment to Lonner Manufacturing Co. under one of two general plans:

(1) The entire principal is to be repaid within 6 years. Principal installments and interest are to be paid at the end of each year. Interest is computed at the rate of 5 per cent of the principal balance at the beginning of the year.

(2) An immediate down payment of $200,000 is to be paid, and the remainder is to be paid within 5 years. Interest is computed at the rate of 4 per cent of the principal balance at the beginning of the year, and both principal installments and interest are to be paid at the end of each year.

The manufacturer has expressed a willingness to tailor the schedule of principal maturities to suit the circumstances of the Lonner Manufacturing Co., and has asked the latter's treasurer to propose a repayment schedule under each of the plans. Principal repayments must be in multiples of $10,000.

REQUIRED:

a. Prepare a schedule of proposed repayments for each of the plans, explaining the reasoning behind any decisions you make.
b. Evaluate your proposal from the point of view of the manufacturer.
c. Which plan would the manufacturer prefer? Why?
d. Which plan would the Lonner Manufacturing Co. prefer? Why?

Chapter 20

Accounting for Owners' Equity

Chapter 7 pointed out that the principal variations in the owners' equity accounts as between individual businesses result from differences in legal requirements. The legal form of business organization—proprietorship, partnership, or corporation—is the basic cause of variations in owners' equity accounts. Beyond this, however, other differences in the owners' equity accounts of businesses arise from the provisions of the law of the particular state in which the business is organized, from distinct classes of owners' equity, and from special features of a particular class of owners' equity which result from legal requirements or from the preferences of the business.

The major part of this chapter is devoted to owners' equity accounting for corporations, which is generally more complex than accounting for proprietorships and partnerships. The principal sources of the owners' equity of a corporation are *owners' investment* and *retained income*.

CORPORATE OWNERS' EQUITY

Capital stock and its status

In exchange for his investment, each of the owners of a corporation receives a *share or shares of capital stock* as evidence of his ownership interest. If a corporation has only one class of capital stock, each share represents an equal ownership interest. The percentage of the total owner's equity which is owned by a given individual may be computed by dividing the number of shares he owns by the number of shares owned by all stockholders.

In determining the number of ownership shares of a corporation for various purposes, it is necessary to know the number of shares in each status: *authorized, unissued, issued,* in the *treasury,* and *outstanding.*

(1) *Authorized* capital stock is the total number of shares, or the total dollar amount of stock, which the corporation's articles of incorporation permit it to issue. It is common for the number of shares authorized to be substantially larger than the number needed initially, to facilitate later expansion.

(2) *Unissued* capital stock is that part which has not yet been issued.

(3) *Issued* capital stock is that part of the stock which the corporation has given to owners in exchange for money, claims to money, or some other consideration.

(4) *Treasury* stock is stock which has once been issued in exchange for full payment but which the issuing corporation has reacquired. It is available to be reissued or cancelled.

(5) *Outstanding* capital stock is that part of the stock which is owned by the public. Unissued or treasury shares held by the corporation itself are not outstanding.

The relationship of these terms to each other is illustrated in the following example.

EXAMPLE 1: When a corporation was organized, it was authorized to issue 10,000 shares of a single class of capital stock. During the past few years it has issued 6,000 shares but has later reacquired 1,000 of them, which it hopes to reissue at a later date. The status of its capital stock is as follows:

Authorized.....................................	10,000 shares
− Unissued.....................................	4,000 shares
= Issued..	6,000 shares
− In treasury..................................	1,000 shares
= Outstanding.................................	5,000 shares

An individual stockholder who owns 50 shares owns 1 per cent (50/5,000) of the total owners' equity in the corporation.

Rights of stockholders

The rights of the stockholders of a corporation are of the following main types:

(1) To *manage* the corporation. They do so by electing a board of directors, which in turn elects officers of the corporation.

(2) To share in *distributions of assets* by the corporation *out of income* when the board of directors declares such a distribution, or *out of capital* when the corporation is partially or completely liquidated.

(3) To *approve or prevent changes* in the charter and bylaws of the corporation and changes in the rights associated with the existing property

of the corporation. One principal right of this type is the *pre-emptive right*, which permits the stockholder to acquire shares of new issues of stock in proportion to his present ownership interest in the corporation. The purpose of this right is to permit him to maintain his proportionate ownership interest when the owners' equity of the corporation is to be increased by additional issues of stock.

If there is but one class of capital stock, each share carries equal rights. Often, however, stockholders waive some of their rights by contract. This is especially true when more than one class of stock is issued. For example, one class of stockholders may surrender its rights to manage the corporation in exchange for a right to receive greater assurance of income distributions than another class of stock has.

Paid-in capital

The accounts which comprise the owners' equity of a corporation are of two types: (1) *paid-in*, or contributed, *capital* and (2) *retained income*.

"Paid-in capital," according to the American Accounting Association,[1] "is measured by the cash, or the fair market value of other assets or services, contributed by stockholders *or* by persons acting in a capacity other than that of stockholders or creditors, *or* by the amount of liabilities discharged upon the transfer of an equity from a creditor to a stockholder status."

The purpose of this distinction is to permit those interested to tell how much of its net assets a business has derived from *contributions*, either from owners or from others, and how much it has *earned*.

Capital paid in by stockholders

The principal source of corporate paid-in capital is the amount contributed by stockholders in connection with the following types of events:

(1) Original investment, in exchange for stock certificates.
(2) Additional assessments upon outstanding shares.
(3) Gains or losses made by the corporation from the purchase and subsequent resale of its outstanding shares.
(4) Forfeiture of partial payments on stock subscriptions.
(5) Conversion of liabilities into stockholders' equity.
(6) Donations by stockholders.

---

[1] American Accounting Association, Committee on Concepts and Standards, *Accounting Concepts and Standards Underlying Corporate Financial Statements* (Columbus, O.: The Association, 1948).

The only other significant source of corporate paid-in capital is the donation of long-lived property by individuals and institutions other than stockholders.

The following sections examine some of the accounting problems which are associated with recognizing, classifying, and measuring paid-in capital.

Par, no-par, and low-par value stock

In the early history of American corporations, all shares of capital stock were assigned a *par*, or *face* amount, frequently of $100 per share, which was printed on the stock certificate. Often the state law required that the issue price of a share of stock be at least par. If this were the case, creditors of the corporation were assured that the corporation had received at least this consideration for the stock, which would serve as a cushion of residual equity to absorb losses and help protect the interests of creditors.

Many people misunderstood the significance of the par value, and assumed that the *worth* of a share of stock on the market was always at least its par value. This, of course, was not true; the market value of a share of stock at any time depends upon the estimate made by present and potential owners of its *future prospects* of earnings and dividends. Furthermore, stock was often *watered;* that is, non-cash property and services received in exchange for capital stock were often recorded in the corporation's accounts at the par value of the stock, which was sometimes far in excess of the economic significance of the consideration received.

These abuses led, around the second decade of the twentieth century, to the popularity of *no-par* stock, which was not assigned any face amount. One purpose of no-par stock was to emphasize that the nature of a share of stock was an interest in an indefinite equity, whatever that might be worth, and not a claim to a specific amount of money. The absence of a face amount for the stock was intended to put the would-be purchaser on guard to estimate its worth on the basis of the rights which its ownership conveyed. But in levying taxes, particularly taxes on the transfer of stock, states later treated such no-par stock as though it had a par value of $100 a share. Such taxes became excessively burdensome for shares of stock which were worth only a few dollars on the market.

In recent years many corporations have shifted to the use of *low-par* stock—stock which has a nominal par value far below its market value. It is quite common, for example, for a share of stock of $1 par to sell on the market for scores or even hundreds of dollars.

Earlier chapters have, for convenience, credited the entire proceeds of the issuance of capital stock to OE, Capital Stock. If the sole purpose of owners' equity accounts were to show the economic *sources* of owners' equity, this approach would be satisfactory. Actually, however, state laws differ as to the amount of the proceeds of capital stock which represents a permanent part of the capital of the corporation. In some jurisdictions the law, and in others a resolution of the board of directors, determines how much of the proceeds of stock issuance becomes a part of the corporation's *stated*, or *legal, capital*—the amount which must remain invested as a cushion of protection for the creditors.

Issuance of par-value stock

It is usually satisfactory to record the *authorization* of an issue of capital stock by means of a memorandum notation in the capital stock account.

There is no difficulty in recording the issuance of stock if the consideration received by the corporation is exactly equal to the par value of the stock. In such a case assets (or sometimes liabilities or expense) are debited and Capital Stock is credited for the amount of the consideration.

When the consideration exceeds the par value of the stock, it is customary to credit the excess to a *premium* account, as illustrated below.

(1)

A, Cash	105,000	
OE, Capital Stock—Par		100,000
OE, Capital Stock—Premium		5,000

The corporation issued 1,000 shares of its $100-par value stock for $105 a share.

If legal requirements permit, it would seem sensible to credit the entire $105,000 proceeds to Capital Stock. The premium is from the same source —stockholders' investment—as the par value.

Many states forbid the issuance of par-value stock for less than par. If it is done, however, the deficiency should be debited to a *discount* account.

(2)

A, Cash	99,000	
OE, Capital Stock—Discount	1,000	
OE, Capital Stock—Par		100,000

Issued 1,000 shares of $100-par value stock for $99 a share.

Stock issued by a corporation at a discount is not fully paid. In the event the corporation is unable to pay its debts in full, the individual who purchased stock from the corporation at a discount may be required to pay in the amount of the discount. Because of this contingency, Capital Stock—Discount should be carried as a permanent account on the corporation's records.

It should be emphasized that this contingent liability applies only to a stockholder who acquires the stock *directly* from the corporation at a discount or one who later buys it from him knowing that it was originally issued at a discount. There is no such contingent liability if a stockholder who paid the corporation par or more for his stock later sells it to another individual for less than par. The second transaction is a private one between the two individuals; the price at which the stock changes hands is not shown on the corporation's books.

The presentation in the statement of financial position of the facts in transactions (1) and (2), together with other assumed facts, would be as follows:

STOCKHOLDERS' EQUITY

Capital stock, $100 par value per share:
  Authorized, 4,000 shares; issued and outstand-
    ing, 2,000 shares.......................... $200,000
Add premium on capital stock..................   5,000
                                           $205,000
Deduct discount on capital stock.............. (1,000)
    Total paid-in capital................................. $204,000
Retained income.......................................   71,400
    Total stockholders' equity.......................... $275,400

Adequate disclosure requires showing the nature of each class of capital stock; the amount of its par value (or the fact that it has no par value); its principal features; and the number of shares authorized, issued, in the treasury, and outstanding. For clarity of presentation, it is recommended that the total amount *paid in* by the stockholders be shown.

Issuance of no-par stock

The laws of some states provide that only a part of the proceeds of no-par stock must become a part of the legal capital of the corporation. In some cases the law provides a legal *minimum stated capital* below which shares cannot be issued. Sometimes the board of directors is permitted to assign to stated capital a part of the proceeds of shares in excess of the legal minimum. This declared amount or *stated value* of no-par stock may even be the entire proceeds. The last approach seems to reflect the economic realities more adequately than either of the first two.

Entries using stated value. The following entries are based on the assumption that the stock issued in entries (1) and (2) had no par value, that the minimum legal capital was $20 a share, and that the board of directors ordered that this amount be credited to Capital Stock.

(3a)

A, Cash....................................... 105,000
    OE, Capital Stock—Stated Value.............   20,000
    OE, Paid in-Capital in Excess of Stated Value..   85,000
    Issued 1,000 shares of no-par stock for $105 a share.
    The stated value of $20 a share was credited to
    Capital Stock.

The account "Paid-in Capital in Excess of Stated Value" is similar in nature to Capital Stock—Premium. By definition, however, premium applies only to par-value stock.

(4a)

A, Cash...	99,000	
OE, Capital Stock—Stated Value............		20,000
OE, Paid-in Capital in Excess of Stated Value..		79,000
Issued 1,000 shares of no-par stock, stated value $20 a share, for $99 a share.		

The presentation in the statement of financial position would be as follows:

STOCKHOLDERS' EQUITY

Capital stock, no-par value, stated value $20 per share:		
Authorized, 4,000 shares; issued and outstanding, 2,000 shares.........................	$ 40,000	
Add paid-in capital in excess of stated value.....	164,000	
Total paid-in capital................................		$204,000
Retained income......................................		71,400
Total stockholders' equity...........................		$275,400

Entries crediting capital stock for entire proceeds. If, in accordance with the law, the board of directors orders that the full amount of the proceeds of no-par stock be credited to the Capital Stock account, the entries would be as follows:

(3b)

A, Cash...	105,000	
OE, Capital Stock, No-Par Value............		105,000
Issued 1,000 shares of no-par stock for $105 a share.		

(4b)

A, Cash...	99,000	
OE, Capital Stock, No-Par Value............		99,000
Issued 1,000 shares of no-par stock for $99 a share.		

In the statement of financial position, the entire proceeds of $204,000 would be shown under the caption "Capital stock, no-par value, stated value $20 per share."

The titles used to record the issuance of low-par stock are the same as those for par stock, but the portion of the proceeds credited to Capital Stock would be unrealistically small, as in the case of no-par stock. The statement presentation is especially misleading if, as was formerly the custom, the proceeds in excess of the par or stated value are described as "Capital Surplus."

Accounting for stock subscriptions

If the individuals who buy the shares of a corporation's stock pay for it immediately upon subscription, the appropriate entries would be like those illustrated in entries (1) through (4). If, however, the subscriber is to pay for his subscription over a period of time, the following types of entries would be needed:

(5)

19x1

Mar. 1 A, Subscriptions Receivable.............. 10,000
                OE, Capital Stock Subscribed........   10,000
              An individual subscribed for 100 shares of
              $100-par value stock at par.

In a statement of financial position prepared at the end of 19x1, the balance of Subscriptions Receivable would be shown under Current Assets or under Investments and Other Assets, depending upon whether it is expected to be collected in the near or distant future. Capital Stock Subscribed, with a notation of the number of shares involved, would be shown as a component of capital stock immediately below the amount representing capital stock issued.

(6)

19x2

Mar. 6 A, Cash.............................. 10,000
                A, Subscriptions Receivable..........   10,000
              Collected the balance due on the subscrip-
              tion.

(7)

Mar. 6 OE, Capital Stock Subscribed............ 10,000
                OE, Capital Stock—Par..............   10,000
              Issued shares of stock to the subscriber.

Different classes of stock

Often corporations have two or more classes of capital stock, each with different rights as to participation in management, participation in distributions from income or capital, and as to other matters. Generally, one of these classes of stock is called *preferred* stock and the other, *common* stock.

The owners of preferred shares receive rights which are superior in some respects to those of the common stockholders, usually in exchange for relinquishing other rights. If preferred stock is *preferred as to dividends*, the rate of the priority which attaches to each share must be stated. The dividend preference of par-value stock is stated as a *per cent of par*, for example:

STOCKHOLDERS' EQUITY

6 per cent preferred stock, $10 par value per share:
Authorized, issued, and outstanding, 1,000 shares $10,000
Premium on preferred stock................................   500
Total paid-in capital, preferred..................................... $ 10,500
Common stock, no-par value, stated value $1 per share:
Authorized, 50,000 shares; issued and outstanding, 12,000
shares...   86,300
Total paid-in capital.. .. $ 96,800
Retained income   11,100
Total stockholders' equity...................................... $107,900

In a given year, each holder of one preferred share in the illustration must receive a dividend of $0.60 a share (6 per cent of $10)—a total of $600 for preferred stockholders as a class—before the common stockholders may receive any dividend. This does not mean that the preferred dividend *must* be paid, however. Any class of stockholders has a right to receive a dividend only if it is *declared* by the board of directors. The board will declare a dividend only if it is legal, feasible, and desirable to do so. If no dividend is declared on the preferred stock in a given year, however, no dividend can be paid to the common stockholders in that year.

The dividend preference rate of no-par preferred stock is expressed in terms of dollars of dividends per share, such as "$3.50 preferred stock, no-par value."

If preferred stock is *preferred as to assets in liquidation*, the preferred stockholders must receive the stated amount upon the termination of the business before the common stockholders receive anything. Sometimes, but not always, the preference per share upon liquidation is based upon the price at which the preferred stock was originally issued.

Cumulative preferred stock

Preferred dividend rights may be *noncumulative*, in which case a dividend not paid in a given year is not carried forward to future years as a prior claim. They may be *cumulative*, meaning that a dividend not paid in one year is carried forward as an additional priority of preferred stockholders in future income distributions.

EXAMPLE 2:   A corporation had outstanding 1,000 shares of 6 per cent cumulative preferred stock of $100 par value and 3,000 shares of $100-par value common stock. In its first year, 19x1, it did not declare a dividend. In 19x2 it wishes to distribute a total of $27,000 in dividends. How much must be distributed to a holder of one share of each class of stock, and how much to each class in total?

SOLUTION:

Order of Priority	Total	Per Share
Preferred stock (1,000 shares, $100,000 par):		
6 per cent dividend in arrears................	$ 6,000	$6
6 per cent current preference.................	6,000	6
Total.....................................	$12,000	$12
Common stock (3,000 shares, $300,000 par):		
Remainder................................	15,000	5
Total distributed........................	$27,000	

The preferred dividend rights are sometimes *cumulative only to the extent earned* during a given year.

Occasionally preferred stock has a right to *participate* with the common stock in additional dividends beyond the preference rate. The participation may be limited or unlimited.

A separate set of accounts, such as the following, is needed for each class of stock:

> Capital Stock, Preferred—Par
> Capital Stock, Preferred—Premium
> Subscriptions Receivable—Preferred
> Capital Stock Subscribed—Preferred
> Capital Stock, Common—Par
> Capital Stock, Common—Premium
> Subscriptions Receivable—Common
> Capital Stock Subscribed—Common

Reacquisition of capital stock

Capital stock is a means by which a corporation obtains permanent *capital*. Most state laws limit the extent to which a corporation can reacquire its own shares from its stockholders, frequently providing that only net assets (equaling owners' equity) in excess of *legal capital* are available for this purpose. If there were not some such restriction, a corporation in financial difficulty, with insufficient assets to pay its creditor's claims and its stockholders' original investments in full, might give preference to the stockholders by repurchasing some of their stock before the corporation was liquidated.

Some of the main purposes for which a corporation is permitted to reacquire its own shares are for use in employee stock-purchase plans and in settlement of claims which might otherwise result in a loss. It is also usually permissible for stockholders to *donate* some or all of their shares to the corporation, for this does not reduce the corporation's assets.

When *treasury stock* (reacquired stock that was fully paid when originally issued) is purchased, an asset is credited. The account which is debited in this transaction is not an asset, but rather a *reduction of owners' equity*. It represents a *disinvestment* in, rather than a future service potential to, the business. Two widely accepted methods of accounting for treasury stock are discussed in the following sections.

Accounting for treasury stock as a retirement

The American Accounting Association advocates treating the amount paid by a corporation for its own capital stock as a *reduction of paid-in capital* up to the amount per share represented by the reacquired shares, whether they may be reissued or not. If the payment for the reacquired shares exceeds the appropriate reduction of paid-in capital, the excess is treated as a *distribution of retained income.* The accounting for the later reissue of these shares should be the same as for stock issued for the first time.[2]

The following condensed information will be used as a basis for illustrating the two methods of accounting for treasury stock.

STOCKHOLDERS' EQUITY (BEFORE REACQUISITION OF STOCK)

Capital stock, $100 par value per share:

Authorized, issued, and outstanding, 1,000 shares		$100,000
Add premium on stock		5,000
Total paid-in capital		$105,000
Retained income		20,000
Total stockholders' equity		$125,000

The corporation acquired 10 shares for later reissue under an employee stock-purchase plan, paying $112 a share. Early in the next accounting period, these shares were reissued to employees for $108 per share. The entries and statement presentation of these facts under the AAA recommendation would be:

(8a)

OE, Treasury Stock—Par	1,000	
OE, Treasury Stock—Premium	50	
OE, Retained Income	70	
A, Cash		1,120

Reacquired 10 shares of the corporation's own stock for $112 a share. Reduced paid-in capital (consisting of the par and premium originally received for the stock) by $105 a share, and treated $7 a share as a distribution of retained income.

STOCKHOLDERS' EQUITY (AFTER REACQUISITION OF STOCK)

Capital stock, $100 par value per share:

Authorized and issued, 1,000 shares		$100,000	
Deduct in treasury, 10 shares		1,000	
Outstanding, 990 shares			$ 99,000
Add premium on capital stock		$ 5,000	
Less amount applicable to treasury stock		50	
Applicable to outstanding shares			4,950
Total paid-in capital on outstanding stock			$103,950
Retained income			19,930
Total stockholders' equity			$123,880

(9a)

A, Cash	1,080	
OE, Treasury Stock—Par		1,000
OE, Treasury Stock—Premium		50
OE, Paid-in Capital on Reissuance of Treasury Stock		30

To record reissuance of shares for $108 a share; removal of applicable amounts representing a reduction of original paid-in capital (par and original premium); and receipt of additional premium of $3 a share.

---

[2] *Idem.*

The Stockholders' Equity section of the statement of financial position will be the same as before the stock was reacquired, except that paid-in capital will be $5,030 ($30 more) and Retained Income will be $19,930 ($70 less).

Accounting for treasury stock as an incomplete transaction

Another widely used method of accounting for the reacquisition of stock is to treat it as an incomplete transaction, awaiting later reissuance of the stock. When the stock is reacquired, Treasury Stock is debited for its *cost*. In the statement of financial position, this cost is shown as a deduction from total stockholders' equity, without allocation to par, premium, and retained income. The treatment is illustrated below.

(8b)

OE, Treasury Stock (cost)	1,120	
A, Cash		1,120

Reacquired 10 shares of the corporation's own stock for $112 a share.

STOCKHOLDERS' EQUITY (AFTER REACQUISITION OF STOCK)

Capital stock, $100 par value per share:

Authorized and issued, 1,000 shares	$100,000

(Of these, 10 shares are in the treasury and 990 are outstanding.)

Add premium on capital stock	5,000
Total paid-in capital on issued stock	$105,000
Retained income	20,000
Total stockholders' equity on issued stock	$125,000
Deduct cost of 10 shares of treasury stock	1,120
Total stockholders' equity on outstanding stock	$123,880

Note that the *total* stockholders' equity is the same as under the preceding method, but that the details are different.

(9b)

A, Cash	1,080	
OE, Retained Income	40	
OE, Treasury Stock (cost)		1,120

To record the proceeds of reissuing 10 shares of treasury stock for $108 a share, and to show the excess of cost of reacquisition over the proceeds of reissuance ($112 − $108 per share, a total of $40) as a distribution of retained income.

Under the *cost* method, all items of stockholders' equity except Retained Income will be the same after the stock was reissued as before it was reacquired. Retained Income will be $40 less. Any excess of the reissuance price over the cost of treasury stock would be shown as a credit to OE, Paid-in Capital on Reissuance of Treasury Stock.

Other paid-in capital accounts

In addition to the accounts described in detail in earlier sections, other important sources of paid-in capital should be designated by such account titles as "Paid-in Capital—Stock Assessment," "Paid-in Capital—Land Donation," and "Paid-in Capital—Forfeited Stock Subscriptions."

Components of retained income

The principal sources of additions to Retained Income are the operations and related activities of the business; investments; and gains realized from the sale of long-lived assets or favorable settlement of liabilities. Losses from these sources are deducted from Retained Income. A corporation does not realize income by issuing, reacquiring, or reissuing its own capital stock, although occasionally such transactions result in *distributions of income*.

Chapter 8 listed the following types of items which, if material in amount, should be excluded from income under the *current operating performance* concept of income:

(1) Charges or credits of a nonrecurring nature which are specifically related to the operations of prior years;

(2) Charges or credits resulting from unusual sales of items not normally held for sale;

(3) Losses of a nonrecurring nature from hazards which are not usually insured against.

In addition, the following should not be used in measuring income under this approach:

(4) Material amounts of unamortized bond premium or discount which are written off when an issue of bonds is *refunded* (replaced by another issue) prior to its maturity.

All of the preceding types of items would be reported as components of the income of the current period under the *all-inclusive* approach. Under the *current operating performance* point of view, however, they would be shown as debits or credits *directly to Retained Income*, in addition to the reported income for the period.

Under either point of view, these extraordinary items should be clearly labeled in the financial statements. *Income distributions* must be shown as direct reductions of Retained Income in the statement of retained income under both methods.

Restrictions of retained income

Retained income represents a source of a part of assets in total, not of any specific assets. It also sometimes represents (with many important exceptions) the amount *legally* available for dividends.

Often *restrictions* upon the use of retained income as a basis for declaring dividends result from legal requirements, from contractual obligations, or from management policy.

A common legal provision which restricts the availability of retained income for dividends provides that total distributions to stockholders (acquisitions of treasury stock plus dividends out of income) cannot exceed retained income. In states where this law applies, the following entry should be made when treasury stock is acquired, in addition to entry (8a) or (8b) illustrated earlier:

```
OE, Retained Income...............................  1,120
    OE, Retained Income Restricted for Cost of Treasury
       Stock........................................           1,120
    To show a restriction of Retained Income equal to the
    cost of treasury stock.
```

In the statement of financial position this restriction, under the *cost method* of recording treasury stock, would be shown as follows:

```
           STOCKHOLDERS' EQUITY (AFTER REACQUISITION OF STOCK)
Capital stock, $100 par value per share:
  Authorized and issued, 1,000 shares....................  $100,000
    (Of these, 10 shares are in the treasury and 990 are out-
      standing.)
  Add premium on capital stock...........................     5,000
    Total paid-in capital on issued stock.................  $105,000
Retained income:
  Restricted for cost of treasury stock.......... $ 1,120
  Unrestricted.............................        18,800
    Total retained income.................................    20,000
    Total stockholders' equity on issued stock...........  $125,000
  Deduct cost of 10 shares of treasury stock..............     1,120
    Total stockholders' equity on outstanding stock.......  $123,880
```

The restriction means that, of the total of $20,000 of retained income, $1,120 is *not available for dividends* as long as the corporation holds the treasury stock. When it is reissued, the restriction is removed by the following entry, which is made in addition to entry (9a) or (9b):

```
OE, Retained Income Restricted for Cost of Treasury
    Stock......................................... 1,120
    OE, Retained Income...............................           1,120
    To remove restriction equal to cost of treasury stock
    upon reissuance of the stock.
```

Occasionally bond indentures and other liability contracts require the borrower to make periodic transfers to an account such as OE, Retained Income Restricted for Bond Retirement. The purpose of this restriction is to help insure that the borrower will retain in the business assets equal to the restriction, for the purpose of making payments on the debt. It is doubtful whether this restriction accomplishes its purpose effectively unless a *fund* for the payment of the debt is accumulated at the same time.

More commonly, loan agreements limit the dividend payments of the borrower but do not require that a formal entry be made for the restriction. In such a case, footnote disclosure of the nature of the restriction, illustrated in some of the problems at the end of this chapter, is adequate.

Restrictions, also called *appropriations* or *reserves*, of retained income are also sometimes used to explain management's reasons for reinvesting the related assets in the business. The American Accounting Association opposes this practice for the following reason:

> Appropriations of retained income which purport to reflect managerial policies relative to earnings retention are ineffective, and frequently misleading, unless all retained income which has in fact been committed to operating capital is earmarked. Partial appropriation fosters the implication that retained earnings not earmarked are available for distribution or dividends.[3]

The AAA recommends the increased use of footnotes and the president's letter to stockholders as devices for explaining management's earnings retention policy.

Neither the establishment nor the removal of a restriction on retained income affects the amount of income. Similarly, neither has any effect upon the *total* of retained income, restricted and unrestricted, which must be shown in the statement of financial position.

Stock dividends

The board of directors' declaration of a dividend payable in cash or other property reduces the amount of retained income (and of total stockholders' equity) immediately and increases the liability, Dividends Payable. The later payment of such a dividend reduces the liability and reduces Cash or some other asset. The final result is an equal decrease in the corporation's assets and its stockholders' equity. The individual stockholders receive a valuable asset from the corporation.

A *stock dividend*, while similar in name to an *asset dividend*, serves a quite different purpose. Rather than reducing the total of assets retained for corporate use and reducing retained income, it denotes that assets have been *permanently reinvested* in the business. The stock distribution

---

[3] AAA Concepts and Standards Committee, *Reserves and Retained Income, Supplementary Statement No. 1* (Columbus, O.: The Association, 1950).

does not reduce the total assets of the corporation and does not increase
the assets of the individual stockholders. Its only effect is to change the
composition (but not the total) *of stockholders' equity*, by reducing Retained
Income and increasing Capital Stock (and perhaps other paid-in capital
accounts).

If the corporation described earlier in this chapter issued 100 shares of
capital stock as a dividend after the reissuance of treasury stock, its entry
would be as follows:

(10)

OE, Retained Income..........................	10,500	
Capital Stock—Par..........................		10,000
Capital Stock—Premium.....................		500

To record the issuance of a 10 per cent stock dividend
and the transfer of $105 a share from Retained In-
come to paid-in capital accounts.

The determination of the amount to be transferred from Retained
Income to paid-in capital for each share of stock issued as a dividend is
a complex matter, beyond the scope of this text. The preceding entry is
made on the assumption that each dividend share is to be assigned the
same amount of paid-in capital as that received for each old share, $105.

For each 10 shares that he previously owned, a stockholder will receive
1 additional share as a dividend. The effect on Stockholder A, who owned
10 shares before the stock distribution, is as follows:

	Before Stock Dividend	After Stock Dividend
Total stockholders' equity:		
Capital stock—par..................	$100,000	$110,000
Capital stock—premium..............	5,000	5,500
Total paid-in capital..............	$105,000	$115,500
Retained income....................	19,960	9,460
Total stockholders' equity..........	$124,960	$124,960
Divide by number of shares outstanding..	1,000	1,100
Stockholders' equity per share...........	$ 124.96	$ 113.60
Multiply by number of shares owned by A	× 10	× 11
Equity of Stockholder A................	$ 1,249.60	$ 1,249.60

The total equity of each stockholder is no greater after the stock dividend than before; the same equity is represented by more shares of stock.

Some factors may cause the *market value* of Stockholder A's stock (as
distinct from his share of the corporation's *book equity*) to increase as a
result of the stock dividend. One such factor is that the shares may be more
readily marketable, since they would tend to command a slightly lower
price per share than before. The increased marketability might cause the
11 shares A owned after the dividend to have a slightly higher total market value than the 10 shares he owned before the dividend.

The issuance of a stock dividend sometimes implies that management
plans to increase the *total cash dividend* paid by the corporation to stock-

holders in the future. If the previous cash dividend rate were $10 a share for each of the 1,000 shares, the total annual dividend payment amounted to $10,000, of which Stockholder A received $100. Continuation of this same dividend rate per share in the future would require the company to pay a total dividend of $11,000 ($10 times 1,100 shares), of which Stockholder A would receive $110 ($10 times 11 shares). If such an increased total dividend is anticipated, the market value of the stock in total will probably rise. One of the most important determinants of the market value of a share of stock is the amount of its expected future dividends.

In deciding whether or not to issue a stock dividend, management should consider its implication of higher total cash dividends in the future, and decide whether or not it wishes to undertake to pay them.

Stock split-ups

The increased marketability of shares is desirable to management because it tends to spread the ownership of the stock among more people and to improve the corporation's sources of capital. However, a *stock split* —the issuance of more than one new share to *replace* one old share—accomplishes the same purpose without requiring a transfer from Retained Income to paid-in capital.

EXAMPLE 3:   A corporation had 1,000 shares of $100-par value stock outstanding in the hands of 50 owners. The current market value of the stock was about $160 a share. Wishing to broaden its ownership, the corporation declared a 2-for-1 stock split, issuing 2,000 shares of $50-par value stock to replace the $100-par value stock. The immediate effect should be to reduce the market value of a new share to about $80, but the ultimate effect should probably be to increase the marketability of the stock and to increase the number of individual stockholders.

The entry for the stock split-up would be:

```
OE, Capital Stock—$100 Par.................... 100,000
   OE, Capital Stock—$50 par.................          100,000
   To record the issuance of 2,000 shares of $50 par
   to replace 1,000 shares of $100 par.
```

Management planning for stockholders' equity

Tailoring the detailed provisions of capital stock contracts to the needs and circumstances of the particular business is one of the major problems of financial administration.

In deciding upon particular features of various classes of stock, as well as of bonds, the corporate management should project the financial requirements which the security will place upon the business. It should then compare these requirements with the funds which are expected to be available to service them.

EXAMPLE 4:   A corporation is planning to issue 1,000 shares of $100-par value 6 per cent preferred stock. It is contemplating a provision requiring the retirement of 10 per cent of the stock each year, starting with the third year. Management should compare the total annual requirements for dividends and stock retirement with the amounts which will probably become available for those purposes. Although preferred dividends do not constitute a fixed obligation *legally*, economically there is strong pressure on the company to pay them regularly. If it does not do so, its future attempts to secure capital will be severely handicapped.

The restrictions of security contracts upon management action should not be so narrow as to hamper effective business operations. Sometimes arbitrary limitations upon management action become unreasonable when conditions change.

The security provisions should also be flexible. From time to time changes occur in general economic conditions and in the affairs of the particular issuer. Existing contracts should provide means for modifying their terms in case of hardship; new contracts should reflect current market conditions and should provide for sufficient flexibility to adapt to subsequent developments.

Management performance as to stockholders' equity

The board of directors and the officers of a corporation are responsible to the stockholders for their performance in managing the business. The basic purpose of the corporation is to maximize the long-range return to the stockholders. If there is more than one class of stock, management is usually elected by, and is primarily responsive to the wishes of, the residual stockholders. The better the terms that financial management can obtain from preferred stockholders and creditors, the greater is the advantage which accrues to common stockholders.

Each share of common stock outstanding at a given time has the same rights as each other share; therefore, management has an equal responsibility to each owner of one share. From time to time, however, the corporation finds it necessary to issue additional shares of stock in order to obtain capital. Whether or not the existing stockholders exercise their pre-emptive right to acquire their proportionate parts of new issues, management has an obligation to the present generation of stockholders to protect their interests when issuing additional stock. Proper accounting and careful analysis of accounting reports aid management in fulfilling this obligation.

One of the most useful methods of appraising management's stewardship of the corporate assets, analysis of the *rate of return* and its various components, was discussed in Chapter 10. Rates of return computed on the basis of stockholders' equity should include *all* components of such equity: capital stock, other paid-in capital items, and both restricted and unrestricted retained income. It is just as important for management to administer soundly and use profitably the assets derived from income as the assets obtained from the direct investment of stockholders.

ACCOUNTING FOR PARTNERSHIP OWNERS' EQUITY

According to Chapter 7, the owners' equity accounts of a partnership generally include a *Capital* account for each partner, consisting of his direct investments in the partnership and his share of its retained income, and a *Drawing* account for each partner, representing the reduction of his equity by withdrawals during each accounting period.

The remainder of this chapter describes some of the important features of the partnership contract which affect accounting requirements.

The partnership agreement

A partnership may be formed by an oral agreement between the partners, or even by an implied agreement, but a carefully drawn *written* agreement which specifies the rights and obligations of each of the partners is highly desirable. The following are some of the principal points which should be covered in the agreement:

(1) The name, location, and nature of the business.

(2) The effective date of the agreement and its duration.

(3) The amount of capital to be contributed by each partner, the time of contribution, and the method of measuring non-cash investments.

(4) The rights, together with any limitations thereon, and the obligations of each partner.

(5) The method for determining the compensation of each partner.

(6) The amounts, timing, and limitations on partners' drawings.

(7) Provisions for determining the amount of a partner's equity and for settling it in the event of his death.

(8) Provisions for voluntary withdrawal of a partner.

(9) Method of settling disputes among the partners.

The advice of a competent lawyer and of a competent accountant is needed in drawing up the details of a partnership agreement.

Management considerations in organizing a partnership

Some types of businesses which are jointly owned by more than one person are required to be organized as partnerships because it is not in the public interest to limit the liability of the owners. Examples are the professions of medicine, law, and accountancy.

When the owners of a business have selected the partnership form of organization, either through necessity or because of financial or income tax reasons, they should plan the articles of the partnership agreement so that they will not hinder effective management. Unless the partnership agreement expressly provides for the manner of allocating authority and responsibility, each partner shares equally in them. To avoid such an unworkable arrangement, a managing partner should usually be designated and the extent of his authority and responsibility should be outlined.

Provisions for sharing income and for sharing assets upon the withdrawal of an existing partner or upon the admission of an additional partner should be drawn up with a view to facilitating the management process.

Factors relating to partners' shares of income

The individual partners usually contribute one or more of the following to the partnership:

(1) *Capital*, in the form of cash or other property.

(2) *Labor*, including time spent in performing management functions as well as other duties.

(3) *Risk-bearing*, including the possibility of loss greater than the capital invested. Often some of the partners have their risk of loss *limited* to their investment in the partnership; however, there must be at least one *general* partner who has unlimited liability to the creditors of the partnership.

In the absence of a specific agreement, the law provides that both partnership profits and losses will be shared equally by the partners. If they intend to share income other than equally, the partners should state in the partnership agreement the method by which each partner is to be compensated for his capital, his labor, and his assumption of risk. The compensation for capital may be in the form of a specified rate of *interest* on the amounts invested; the compensation for labor, perhaps as a *salary allowance*, should be in proportion to the amount of time devoted by the partner as well as his ability; and the compensation for risk should be in proportion to the relative risk borne by each partner.

The formula agreed upon for dividing net income also applies to net losses unless the partners specify to the contrary. Before making an income-sharing arrangement, the partners should compute the shares that each would receive under the contemplated method of division at various levels of net income and net loss. They may then wish to provide for one method of sharing income if there is a net income or a net income above a certain minimum, and another method if there is a net loss or a small net income.

Examples of partnership income-sharing plans

In accounting for shares of partnership income, there are two general problems: (1) computing the amount of each partner's share and (2) recording and reporting the division of income.

The following are basic types of plans which are used for sharing partnership income. The possible variations and combinations of provisions are almost limitless.

Basic data for illustrations. Varn and Weldon, partners, had the following balances in their accounts on December 31, 19x1, after closing all revenue and expense accounts to Income Summary:

Varn, Capital

19x1			19x1		
July 1		2,000	Jan. 1	Balance	12,000

Weldon, Capital

			19x1		
			Jan. 1	Balance	4,000
			Oct. 1		2,000

Income Summary (19x1)

			19x1		
			Dec. 31		8,000

Salaries allowed to partners. The partnership agreement provided that Varn, who spent half of his time in the business, would receive a salary allowance of $2,500, and Weldon, who spent full time, would receive a salary of $5,000. The remainder of income after allowing salaries was to be divided equally. The division for 19x1 would be as follows:

	Income Shares of Varn	Weldon	Total Available
Partnership net income..............			$8,000
Salaries to partners..................	$2,500	$5,000	(7,500)
Remainder...........................			$ 500
Equal shares to partners..............	250	250	(500)
Income of each partner...............	$2,750	$5,250	

If there were a net loss of $2,000 before distributions to partners, the same partnership agreement would result in the following division:

	Income Shares of		Total
	Varn	Weldon	Available
Partnership net loss................			($2,000)
Salaries to partners................	$2,500	$5,000	(7,500)
Remainder........................			($9,500)
Equal shares to partners............	($4,750)	($4,750)	9,500
Income (loss) of each partner........	($2,250)	$ 250	

Interest allowed on partners' capitals. If the partnership agreement of Varn and Weldon allowed each partner interest at 6 per cent of his invested capital, with the remainder to be divided equally, it should specify how to determine the invested capital. If there are substantial changes in the amount of a partner's capital balance during the year, it would not be equitable to compute interest on either the capital balance at the beginning or at the end of the year. Instead, interest should be computed on each partner's balance for the time it was invested, as follows:

	Capital Balance	Term (Fraction of Year)	Annual Rate	Interest Allowance
Varn				
1/1 to 6/30.............	$12,000	1/2	.06	$360
7/1 to 12/31.............	10,000	1/2	.06	300
Total................				$660
Weldon				
1/1 to 9/30.............	$ 4,000	3/4	.06	$180
10/1 to 12/31...........	6,000	1/4	.06	90
				$270

If income were $8,000 before allowing partners' interest, the distribution to partners would be as follows:

	Income Shares of		Total
	Varn	Weldon	Available
Partnership net income...............			$8,000
Interest to partners..................	$ 660	$ 270	(930)
Remainder...........................			$7,070
Equal shares to partners.............	3,535	3,535	(7,070)
Income of each partner..............	$4,195	$3,805	

Entries to record partners' income shares

Unless special accounts are desired in the financial statements to show the details of each partner's compensation, the total share of each partner can be recorded by the following type of entry:

(11)

```
OE, Income Summary (19x1)........................ 8,000
     OE, Varn, Capital.............................          4,195
     OE, Weldon, Capital...........................          3,805
     To record the total share of income credited to each
     partner.
```

Because the partnership is not a legal entity apart from its owners, a partner's compensation for capital, labor, or risk, is considered to be a *distribution* of income, rather than an expense to be deducted in computing income. In spite of this, the partners and others who read the partnership's financial statements may be able to appraise the business results more effectively, and make more valid comparisons with other businesses, if the allowances for partners' services are shown in the operating statement. If this type of presentation is desired, a separate account may be used to show the components of each partner's share of net income. These accounts would be closed to Income Summary.

Dissolution of partnerships

The assets and equities of a partnership, like those of any other business, are measured on a *going-concern* basis, not a *liquidating* basis. When a partnership does terminate, however, the steps in the accounting process are:

(1) Record the disposal of assets by crediting the assets for their book amounts, debiting Cash for the amount received, and debiting Loss on Realization or crediting Gain on Realization for the difference.

(2) Divide the net gain or loss on realization between the partners according to their income-sharing arrangement, and record it in their capital accounts.

(3) Close each partner's drawing account to his capital account.

(4) Record the payment of the liabilities in the order of their legal priority.

(5) Record the payment to the partners of the balances in their individual capital accounts resulting after entries (2) and (3) have been recorded.

The amount remaining after the liabilities of the business are paid off is not a *gain* or *loss;* it is an amount of *capital,* consisting of each partner's original investment, minus his withdrawals, and plus or minus his share of partnership gains or losses. The balance remaining in each partner's capital account is the amount that he should be paid upon liquidation.

The same general order of priority is used in settling the equities of corporations upon liquidation: (1) creditors; (2) preferred stockholders whose stock is preferred as to assets on liquidation; and (3) common stockholders.

Summary

The owners' equity accounts of a corporation should identify the major components of capital paid in by stockholders and by others. Although

economically the amount paid in by stockholders in exchange for shares
is derived from owners' investment, state laws and variations in types of
stock contracts may dictate that the components of the investment be
recorded in two or more accounts. Acquisitions of shares of treasury stock
represent a disinvestment in the corporation. Restrictions upon the availability of retained income for dividends which result from legal or contractual requirements or from management policy may be disclosed by
footnotes, unless a formal transfer to a restricted retained income account
is required. Stock dividends are accounted for as a transfer of owners'
equity from retained income to paid-in capital. All components of stockholders' equity should be considered when measuring management's performance by the rate of return on stockholders' equity.

The partnership agreement should spell out the partners' wishes on
important financial matters, such as the nature of each partner's capital
contribution and the manner of determining his compensation. Invested
capital, labor, and risk-bearing should be considered in arriving at a
formula for dividing partnership income among the partners.

QUESTIONS AND PROBLEMS

20-1

REQUIRED:

a. If you were planning to form a partnership with two other people, what are
some of the features you would wish to have included in the partnership
agreement?

b. In order for a partnership agreement to be valid, does it have to be in writing?
Explain.

c. If there is no formal partnership agreement and there is disagreement among
the partners as to the method of dividing partnership income, what position
does the law take if the disagreement is taken into court?

20-2   Don Layton and Sam Drake have organized a business to manufacture
a new product, Drims. Layton is furnishing $50,000 cash to finance the operations,
but is not planning to participate in the management of the business. Drake will
devote full time to supervising the operations of the business. The two men have
decided to form a partnership and wish to provide a fair and practical method for
distributing the partnership net income or net loss.

REQUIRED:

a. What provisions for sharing the partnership income would you suggest? Why?

b. Present the prospective partners a series of illustrations showing the results of
your suggested plan if the partnership operating results are (1) moderately
good, (2) very good, (3) moderately bad, and (4) very bad.

20-3   Mr. Shields is general manager of the *ABC* Company and draws a
salary of $15,000 per year. He owns one-third of the net assets of the business.

REQUIRED:

a. How would the salary of Mr. Shields be treated on the income statement if the
ABC Company were incorporated?

b. How would the salary be treated on the income statement if the *ABC* Company were a partnership?

c. Why is a difference between your answers in (*a*) and (*b*) justified?

20-4   "It is not worthwhile for the owners of a small business to incorporate because of the red tape and expense involved."

REQUIRED:

Do you agree with this statement? Explain.

20-5   "As long as a partnership is limited to a small number of partners, it is a desirable form of business organization. When the business has a large number of owners, it is better to incorporate."

REQUIRED:

Comment on the reasonableness of this statement.

20-6   The word "par" is often used in describing both stocks and bonds.

REQUIRED:

a. Does it mean the same thing in both cases? Explain.

b. How is the par value treated in accounting for each of these security classes?

20-7   The word "value" is used in many different terms which describe capital stock.

REQUIRED:

Explain how the following terms differ in meaning, and how, if at all, they are treated in the accounting records:

a. Market value
b. Book value
c. Par value
d. No-par value
e. Stated value
f. Liquidating value

20-8

REQUIRED:

a. Explain the differences between the nature and purposes of stock with a high par value, stock without par value, and stock with only a nominal par value.

b. Show in comparative form the journal entries needed to record the authorization and issuance of 1,000 shares of each type of stock in (*a*) for $105 cash per share. Assume any additional facts that are required.

c. Illustrate how you would present each type of stock in a statement of financial position prepared after the issuance in (*b*).

20-9   A corporation was authorized to issue 10,000 shares of capital stock with a par value of $50 per share. Early in the corporation's life 4,000 shares were issued for cash at par, and somewhat later 3,000 additional shares were issued for cash at $70 a share.

REQUIRED:

a. Show how you would present these facts in a statement of financial position.

b. Cannon owns 70 shares which he bought at the time of the corporation's formation, and Drake owns 70 shares for which he has paid $70 a share. Which stockholder has the greater share in the company? Explain.

c. How can you explain Drake's willingness to pay more for the stock than did Cannon?

d. If Drake sold all of his stock to Evans for $4,200, what entry should the corporation make?

20-10 A corporation originally issued its entire 1,000 shares of authorized stock for the par value of $20 a share. Some years later the corporation reacquired 100 shares for $18 a share, and in the same accounting period reissued them for $24 a share.

REQUIRED:

a. What valid business reason might the corporation have had for trading in its own stock?
b. How much income did the corporation make on trading in its stock? Explain.
c. Show how these facts would appear in the financial statements (1) after the stock had been repurchased but before it had been reissued (2) after it had been reissued.
d. How does "treasury stock" differ legally from "unissued stock"? How do the two differ economically?

20-11 Mrs. Sloaner was planning to invest $50,000 and was considering several stocks which had been recommended to her. Included in this group was *B* Company Common Stock and *C* Company Preferred Stock. Mrs. Sloaner requested the meaning of "preferred" in the description of the *C* Company stock and was told that it meant that the stock was preferred as to dividends. "Obviously, then, I should purchase the *C* Company stock and not the *B* Company stock," remarked Mrs. Sloaner.

REQUIRED:

Was Mrs. Sloaner correct in her conclusion? Explain.

20-12 The Marion Corporation presents the following information regarding its capital stock on December 31, 19x2:

	Number of Shares		
	Authorized	Issued	In Treasury
7 per cent cumulative preferred stock, par $100 per share......	1,000	800	0
Common stock without par value, stated value $1 per share......	200,000	150,000	10,000

No dividend was paid on the preferred stock in 19x1.

REQUIRED:

a. How many shares of each class of stock are unissued? Outstanding?
b. The board of directors would like to declare a dividend so that the common stockholders will receive 20¢ a share, and asks you how much cash would be required. Prepare a table, with supporting computations, showing the total amount of dividend that would be necessary for each class of stockholders.
c. If the board of directors declares the dividend on December 31, 19x2, payable on January 15 to stockholders of record on January 6, what entries should it make:

(1) On December 31?
(2) On January 6?
(3) On January 15?

20-13 Mr. Frank was overheard to remark: "The Rator Company, in which I own 1,000 shares of stock of $100 par, has just declared a 10 per cent stock dividend. This amounts to $10,000, and added to the $1,000 dividend check which

I received earlier this year, it means that I have earned an 11 per cent return on my $100,000 investment in the company this year."

REQUIRED:

a. Is Mr. Frank's calculation correct? Explain.
b. What entries should the corporation make to record the issuance of the stock dividend? (Assume any needed facts.) The cash dividend?
c. What entries should Mr. Frank make to record receipt of the dividend stock? The cash dividend?

20-14   The Newington Mfg. Co. presented the following condensed statement of financial position on December 31, 19x1:

ASSETS		LIABILITIES	
Cash	$100,000	Accounts payable	$ 75,000
Various other assets	400,000		
		STOCKHOLDERS' EQUITY	
		Capital stock, without par value:	
		Authorized, issued, and outstanding, 10,000 shares	300,000
		Retained income	125,000
Total assets	$500,000	Total equities	$500,000

REQUIRED:

State what the effect of each of the following events would be on (1) total assets, (2) total liabilities, and (3) total equities.

a. Declaration of a $50,000 dividend payable in cash at a later date.
b. Receipt of 100 shares of the company's own stock in settlement of an account receivable for $3,000.
c. Issuance of 1,000 shares of stock as a dividend in the stated amount of $30,000.
d. Approval of a charter amendment authorizing the issuance of 5,000 additional shares of stock.
e. Receipt of subscriptions to 2,000 shares of stock at $40 a share. The collection of the subscriptions and the issuance of stock were both to occur at a later date.
f. Receipt of a building site worth $50,000 from the City of Dellaville as an inducement to locate a plant there.
g. Sale of old equipment, carried on the books at a cost of $180,000 minus accumulated depreciation of $100,000, for $100,000 cash.
h. Receipt of a stock dividend of 1,000 shares from the Argot Corporation. The Newington Mfg. Co. had previously owned 2,000 shares, for which it had paid a total of $20,000 some years earlier. The Argot stock was quoted on the market at $20 a share immediately after the dividend.
i. A creditor to whom the company owed $5,000 agreed to accept 100 shares of Newington stock in full settlement of the debt.
j. The cash dividend declared in (a) was paid.
k. Collected the stock subscriptions in (e) and issued the stock.
l. Reissued the 100 shares in (b) for $2,800 cash.

20-15

REQUIRED:

a. Using the information in 20-14, record each event in journal form.
b. Prepare the resulting statement of financial position. If any needed information is missing, make appropriate assumptions.

20-16 On December 31, 19x1, the Marlow Company presented the following Stockholder's Equity section in its statement of financial position:

Capital stock, (1,000 shares of $100 par value authorized, of which 200 are unissued and 100 are in the treasury)......	$ 80,000
Premium on common stock.............................	8,000
Retained income.......................................	75,000
	$163,000
Less treasury stock (cost).............................	24,000
Total stockholders' equity.....................	$139,000

REQUIRED:

a. At what average price was each share of the capital stock issued?
b. At what average price was each share of the treasury stock purchased?
c. Present the Stockholders' Equity section in better form and explain any changes which you make.
d. Assuming that the Marlow Company later sold 50 shares of the treasury stock for $90 a share, draft the journal entries to record the sale.

20-17 The Adar Company has purchased 1,000 shares of treasury stock for $50,000. The laws of the state in which the company is incorporated limit total distributions to stockholders, whether in the form of dividends or treasury stock acquisitions, to the amount of retained income. The equity section of the company appears as follows:

STOCKHOLDERS' EQUITY

Capital stock, $100 par value: 10,000 shares authorized, of which 5,000 shares have been issued and 1,000 are in the treasury.		$500,000
Retained income:		
Restricted because of the purchase of treasury stock.........	$ 50,000	
Unrestricted..	260,000	310,000
		$810,000
Deduct treasury stock (cost)...............................		50,000
Total stockholders' equity.................................		$760,000

REQUIRED:

a. Do you agree with the presentation of the Stockholders' Equity section by the Adar Company? Explain.
b. Why does treasury stock appear *three times* in the Stockholders' Equity section?
c. Prepare the Stockholders' Equity section if an acceptable alternative method had been used for recording the purchase of the treasury stock.
d. Record the entry for the reissuance of 200 of the treasury shares for $120 cash per share, using the cost method of accounting for treasury stock.
e. Restate the Stockholders' Equity section to include the results of (d).

20-18 The capital accounts of Watson Bros. at December 31, 19x1, were as follows: Arthur, $50,000; Barry, $25,000; and Charles, $75,000. The net income of the business for the year ended December 31, 19x1, was $60,000.

REQUIRED:

How would this income be distributed to the partners under each of the following agreements:

a. The net income is to be distributed in proportion to the partners' capital balances.
b. There is no partnership agreement.

c. Each partner is to be allowed 6 per cent interest on his capital balance, and the remainder is to be divided equally.

d. Arthur is to be allowed a salary of $20,000; Barry, a salary of $15,000; and Charles, a salary of $10,000. Each partner is also to be allowed 6 per cent interest on his capital balance, and the remainder is to be divided equally.

20-19

REQUIRED:

a. What would your answer have been in each of the situations in 20-18 if the net income for 19x1 had been $9,000?

b. Under what circumstances would each of the four methods of distributing the partnership income be desirable?

CASE 20-1. LANE, JENKINS, AND SIMS

Lane, Jenkins, and Sims, a retail business, has been in existence for 10 years. Its statement of financial position for last year appears below.

LANE, JENKINS, AND SIMS
Statement of Financial Position
June 30, 19x1

ASSETS

Current Assets:			
Cash....................................		$10,000	
Trade accounts receivable.............	$22,000		
Less estimated uncollectibles.........	600	21,400	
Notes receivable.........................		500	
Merchandise inventory...................		82,000	$113,900
Investments:			
U. S. Government securities..............			5,000
Fixed:			
Land.....................................		$ 5,000	
Building...............................	$50,000		
Less accumulated depreciation.......	10,000	40,000	
Equipment............................	$20,000		
Less accumulated depreciation.......	2,000	18,000	63,000
Total assets..................................			$181,900

LIABILITIES AND OWNERS' EQUITY

Current Liabilities:		
Accounts payable...........................	$ 5,900	
Notes payable..............................	16,000	$ 21,900
Owners Equity:		
Lane, Capital.............................	$64,000	
Jenkins, Capital..........................	16,000	
Sims, Capital.............................	80,000	160,000
Total equities..................................		$181,900

In the original partnership agreement Mr. Lane was to receive 50 per cent of the partnership income.

Early in 19x2, Mr. Sims suggested that because of the constant increase in prices and the large amount of money tied up in inventory the company should adopt the LIFO inventory method. He presented a schedule which he had drawn up showing that the use of LIFO by the company in the previous year would have resulted in an ending inventory figure of $57,000. According to him, the company had reported $25,000 of "paper profits," which required increased income taxes for each of the partners. Mr. Jenkins readily agreed with Mr. Sims that this seemed to be a wise move, and indicated that he was ready to vote for the change. Mr. Lane, who was considering retiring from the partnership at the end of 19x2, asked for a week to think over the proposal. The two other partners agreed.

REQUIRED:

a. What points should Mr. Lane consider before giving his decision on the proposal?

b. What conditions should Mr. Lane require his partners to accept before agreeing to the proposal?

CASE 20-2. JONES, SIMPSON, AND THOMPSON

At the end of 19x1, Amos Jones, Thomas Simpson, and Durward Thompson were considering a plan to organize a partnership to carry on a retail business. Jones, who was already in business alone, offered to furnish his net assets other than cash as his share of the capital contribution. He suggested that the other two each contribute $50,000 in the form of cash, to be used in increasing the working capital of the business and expanding its facilities. Each would have a one-third interest in partnership assets and income. Jones' accountant had prepared the following statement:

AMOS JONES
Statement of Financial Position
December 31, 19x1

ASSETS			LIABILITIES		
Current assets:			Current liabilities:		
Cash..............	$ 5,000		Accounts payable...	$ 2,500	
Accounts receivable.	3,000		Notes payable......	10,000	
Inventory..........	10,000		Total...................		$12,500
Prepaid expenses....	500				
Total current assets.......		$18,500			
			OWNER'S EQUITY		
Fixed assets:					
Land..............		5,000			
Building...........	$30,000		Jones, Capital.................		30,000
Accumulated					
depreciation....	15,000	15,000			
Equipment.........	$10,000				
Accumulated					
depreciation....	6,000	4,000			
Total fixed assets........		$24,000			
Total assets..............		$42,500	Total equities.................		$42,500

Shortly before the end of the year Mr. Jones had been offered $50,000 for his equity in the business.

Jones, Simpson, and Thompson met to discuss the proper treatment of Jones' assets and equities if the partnership were formed. They agreed that the accounts receivable were 90 per cent collectible; that the prepaid expenses would be of no value to the new business; and that it would cost $9,000 to replace the inventory. They also agreed that the equipment would have to be replaced in the very near future. An equipment company offered a trade-in allowance of $1,000 if all of the equipment were traded in on new items of a similar nature.

To determine the value of the land and building, the three decided to have them appraised by three local real estate dealers. There was considerable variation in the estimates of the dealers: Dealer *A* appraised the real estate at $57,000; Dealer *B*, at $52,000; and Dealer *C*, at $50,000. Both of the latter dealers, however, were of the opinion that the real estate was located in a rapidly growing area and that future prospects for an increase in the real estate value were good.

It was understood that the partnership would assume the liabilities of Mr. Jones' business.

Having concluded that Mr. Jones' proposal was reasonable, the three men signed a partnership agreement, to take effect on January 1, 19x2. Each made the required investment. Actual business operations of the partnership were to begin on January 2, because January 1 was a holiday.

On the way to work on January 2 Mr. Jones died of a heart attack. His lawyer immediately informed Simpson and Thompson that it would be necessary to liquidate the business to provide funds to support Mrs. Jones. During the next two months the business assets other than cash were sold or collected, bringing in a total of $70,000 in cash. The only cash payments consisted of $3,000 for the costs of liquidation. No liabilities had been paid.

On February 26, Mr. Simpson and Mr. Thompson met with their lawyers and the lawyer representing the late Mr. Jones to discuss the final settlement of the business.

REQUIRED:

a. Record in journal form the entries necessary to record the formation of the partnership on January 1.
b. Prepare a statement of financial position as of the date of Mr. Jones' death.
c. Record in summary form the events of January and February.
d. Prepare a statement of financial position as of February 26.
e. How should the business cash be divided on February 26, and in what order of priority?
f. How, in general, would the outcome have differed if the business had been organized as a corporation?

CASE 20-3. COLONIAL STORES INCORPORATED

In March, 1953, Colonial Stores Incorporated distributed 134,192 shares to common stockholders in accordance with a resolution of the Board of Directors. The result of this distribution was to increase the number of outstanding shares by 20%, from 670,960 to 805,152 shares, by the issuance of one additional share for each five shares previously held.

The following excerpts from the company's annual report for the fiscal year 1953 provide further details about changes in stockholders' equity during the year.

	Dec. 26, 1953	Dec. 27, 1952
"Stockholders' equity:		
Cumulative preferred stock of $50 par value per share (note 1):		
Authorized 100,000 shares (issuable in series)		
Outstanding:		
4% series: 1953, 51,000 shares; 1952, 51,600 shares	$ 2,550,000	$ 2,580,000
5% series: 1953, 36,136 shares; 1952, 36,773 shares	1,806,800	1,838,650
Common stock of $2.50 par value per share:		
Authorized 1,000,000 shares (note 2)		
Outstanding: 1953, 805,152 shares; 1952, 669,789 shares	2,012,880	1,674,473
Capital in excess of par value of capital stock	2,241,060	1,825,384
Earnings retained and invested in the business (exclusive of amounts capitalized)—(note 3)	9,914,845	9,734,992
Total	18,525,585	17,653,499

Statements of Capital

Fiscal Year ended December 26, 1953
(with comparative figures for the fiscal year ended December 27, 1952)

in Excess of Par Value of
Capital Stock and Earnings Retained

	Fiscal Year Ended	
	December 26, 1953	December 27, 1952
Capital in Excess of Par Value of Capital Stock		
Balance at beginning of year	$ 1,825,384	$ 1,783,969
Add:		
Net excess of par value over cost of cumulative preferred stock retired through sinking funds (4% series: 600 shares in 1953, 1,200 shares in 1952; 5% series: 637 shares in 1953, 740 shares in 1952)	4,228	.5,477
Excess of market value over par value of common stock issued to certain executive employees upon exercise of options (1,405* shares in 1953; 1,380* shares in 1952)—(note 2)	38,643	35,938
Amount transferred from earnings retained and invested in the business in connection with common stock distribution (note 4)	372,805	—
Balance at end of year	$ 2,241,060	$ 1,825,384
Earnings Retained and Invested in the Business		
Balance at beginning of year	9,734,992	8,968,338
Net profit for the year	2,623,860	2,302,281
	12,358,852	11,270,619
Deduct:		
Cash dividends paid:		
Cumulative preferred stock:		
4% series ($2.00 per share)	101,537	103,263
5% series ($2.50 per share)	90,977	92,786
Common stock ($1.92* per share in 1953; $1.67* per share in 1952)	1,543,208	1,339,578
	1,735,722	1,535,627
Amount transferred to capital accounts in connection with common stock distribution (note 4)	708,285	
	2,444,007	1,535,627
Balance at end of year	$ 9,914,845	$ 9,734,992

See notes 1 to 6, inclusive, below.

Adjusted to reflect distribution in 1953 to common stockholders of one additional share for each five shares previously held.

"NOTES TO FINANCIAL STATEMENTS

(1) PREFERRED STOCK:

(a) Holders of the preferred stock are entitled to preference in the event of liquidation to the extent of par value plus accrued dividends and, if such liquidation (or redemption) be voluntary, maximum premiums of $2.00 per share.

(b) The company is obligated to set aside sinking funds in specified amounts for the redemption of the preferred stock, which may be called for this purpose at par value plus accrued dividends and maximum premiums of $1.00 per share. At December 26, 1953, the sinking funds were comprised of 600 shares of the 4% series purchased for retirement at a cost of $24,954, and unexpended cash, $8,284. Maximum payments to the sinking funds required during the year 1954 aggregate $103,989, which is after deducting unexpended cash in the amount of $4,626 held in the 4% series sinking fund at December 26, 1953.

(2) OPTIONS TO PURCHASE COMMON STOCK:

Pursuant to authorization by the Board of Directors, options were granted in 1950 to certain executive employees of the company to purchase an aggregate of 19,800* shares of the authorized but unissued common stock of the company at $25.21* per share. Such options were exercisable when granted; they expire on December 31, 1960 or at such earlier dates as the optionees cease to be employees of the company. The quoted market value of the common stock at the date the options were granted was $29.58* per share.

During the year 1953, options relating to 1,405* shares were exercised (option price: $25.21* per share, aggregate $35,423; quoted market value at date exercised: $29.58* per share, aggregate $41,571). The excess ($4.37* per share, aggregate $6,148) of the quoted market value of such shares at the date the options were granted over the option price is included among the operating expenses of the year.

At December 26, 1953, unexpired options relating to 15,431* shares had not been exercised (option price: $25.21* per share, aggregate $389,016; quoted market value at date granted: $29.58* per share, aggregate $456,449).

(*Adjusted to reflect distribution in 1953 to common stockholders of one additional share for each five shares previously held.)

(3) EARNINGS RETAINED AND INVESTED IN THE BUSINESS:

The provisions of the 3⅜% unsecured promissory note and the terms of issuance of the preferred stock impose certain limitations on the financial activities of the company, including restrictions as to the payment of cash dividends on common stock and the purchase or retirement of its capital stock, if such action would impair the specified ratios of current assets to current liabilities, working capital, or undistributed earnings beyond stated limits. Under the most restrictive provisions, which are contained in the 3⅜% note, the earnings retained and invested in the business at December 26, 1953 are restricted to the extent of $6,790,963 as to the payment of cash dividends on common stock.

(4) COMMON STOCK DISTRIBUTION:

Pursuant to resolution of the Board of Directors to increase by 20% the number of outstanding shares of common stock of the company, 134,192 shares were distributed to common stockholders of record as of March 6, 1953. The resolution authorized the appropriation to the capital accounts of the company of earnings retained and invested in the business to the extent of the sum of the par value of the shares distributed ($2.50 per share, aggregate $335,480) and 20% of the amount, immediately prior to the distribution, of the capital in excess of par value of capital stock ($2.78 per share, aggregate $372,805)."

REQUIRED:

a. Record in summary form the entries needed to show the changes in the stockholders' equity during the year.
b. Comment on the company's account terminology and method of statement presentation.
c. What were the probable purposes and major effects of the stock dividend?
d. What were the purposes and general accounting treatment of the sinking funds for preferred stock?
e. What were the purposes and general accounting treatment of the options to purchase common stock?
f. What entry is required to reflect the information in footnote (3)?
g. Itemize the amounts that the company will probably need to pay out in cash in the next year to service its stockholders' equity requirements, assuming that its present policies are continued.

Chapter 21

Long-Range Planning:
Compound Interest
Fundamentals

Business decisions deal with action to be taken in the future. In making decisions, management should consider the comparative effects of alternative courses of action on future income. Thus, the important amounts in making business decisions are *expected future amounts*. Accounting figures about the past, nevertheless, are often the most reliable starting point available to management in estimating future amounts.

There are usually important differences in the expected income from alternative business plans. These differences may be

(1) In the amount of expected income;
(2) In the timing of its receipt; or
(3) In the degree of uncertainty that the income will materialize at all, or that its actual amount will deviate from the expected amount.

This chapter and the next one present a framework for comparing business alternatives which differ in one or more of these respects. The present chapter shows how comparisons are made when the amount and timing of future income are reasonably certain. Chapter 22 illustrates some modifications of the basic method of comparison that are appropriate when future income is uncertain, and also some approximate methods that are often used as practical expedients.

Period planning versus project planning

The chief measure of the performance of a business as a whole during a *period* of time is the *income* it earns during that period, measured by the excess of revenues over expenses. Income is composed of a cross-section of many different segments of business activity which are taking place during the same span of time. The revenue of a period includes amounts earned during that period, whether they are collected in cash in the current period, in an earlier period, or in a later period. Similarly, expense is the cost of service benefits which expire during the current period. The cash payment for these expired costs may be made in the current, a past, or a future time period.

Most of the actions of business management are directed toward maintaining or improving the income of the business. Each action, however, applies to a specific phase of business activity, such as buying an insurance contract or a machine, hiring an employee or increasing his wages, or changing the selling price of a product. Each business action which is important enough to justify separate planning may be called a *project*. The plan is for the entire life of the project, which may last for several accounting periods. *Period planning*, on the other hand, focuses attention on all of the financial events which are expected to occur during a given time interval, such as a year. It is illustrated in Chapter 12, "The Operating Budget."

Projects which warrant individual planning may involve carrying out existing activities in different ways, adding new activities, abandoning old ones, or substituting new ones for old. They may or may not require the use of additional funds. In selecting each such course of action, management should compare its total effects on the business during its entire life with the effects of alternative decisions. Selecting the alternatives which are likely to provide the greatest income should help management to maximize the long-run income of the business as a whole.

METHODS OF MAKING COMPARISONS

Importance of cash flow in project planning

Many projects, such as special sales of merchandise, are begun and completed in the same accounting period. Thus, the period's revenue and cash receipts from the project are the same, and the period's expense for the project equals its cash payments. For such short-lived projects, the importance of differences in timing of receipts and payments is often negligible.

Other projects, such as the acquisition and use of a store building or a machine, affect many accounting periods. In such projects there may be significant differences in the timing of revenue and cash receipts, or of expense and cash disbursements.

EXAMPLE 1:   A machine with a cost of $10,000 and a useful life of 10 years is acquired and completely paid for in the first year. The cash payment resulting from this action is $10,000 the first year and zero each of the remaining nine years, but depreciation expense (under the straight-line method of depreciation) is $1,000 each year.

Substantial differences in the total income of the business may result from differences in the timing of receipts and payments from alternative long-range plans. This is true because money can be put to other productive uses, earning a return, just as soon as it becomes available. The plan which will result in earlier cash receipts or later cash payments has an advantage in timing. The effect of differences in the timing of cash flow should be considered in evaluating plans which will require more than a year for completion. Such comparisons require an elementary understanding of the mathematics of compound interest, the subject of the next part of this chapter.

Although individual projects should be *planned* on the basis of their expected cash flow, their actual *operation* should be accounted for on the accrual basis—revenue being recorded as it is earned and expense as it is incurred. The accrual basis matches effort (expense) with the related accomplishment (revenue) for each time period.

Methods of comparing cash flows

Comparisons of two or more different courses of business action should be made in terms which allow for differences in the timing of their respective receipts and payments. The estimated results of each alternative may be stated as

(1) Its cash equivalent at a common *future time* (its accumulated amount at compound interest); or

(2) Its cash equivalent at the *present time* (its present value). A variation of the first method is often used for projects which require an initial investment of funds. This variation expresses the earnings over the project's life as an *average rate of return* on the investment.

The future value of a sum of money

The amount to which a sum of money plus its earnings will accumulate by a given future date may be described as its *future value*. If, for example,

$100 deposited in a savings account will earn 4 per cent interest a year, its future value one year from the date of the deposit is $104 (the $100 initial investment plus the earnings of $4). Comparisons of the future values of alternative plans should be based upon an equal lapse of time.

EXAMPLE 2:   Should a company deposit $100,000 of idle cash in a savings account in Bank A, which pays interest once a year at the rate of 4 per cent of the beginning balance, or in Bank B, which pays 2 per cent interest every six months? The risk that each bank will fail to pay principal or interest is the same.

SOLUTION: Compare the future values of the two plans after one year.

	Deposit in Bank A	Deposit in Bank B
Original deposit..............................	$100,000	$100,000
Interest credited at end of first six months.....	0	2,000
Deposit balance during second six months.....	$100,000	$102,000
Interest credited at end of year..............	4,000	2,040
Deposit balance at end of year..............	$104,000	$104,040

The future value of a deposit in Bank B is $40 greater than a deposit in Bank A at the end of one year, therefore it is the better alternative. This advantage results from a difference in the timing of the interest receipts: the $2,000 interest received in Bank B at the end of the first six months is reinvested to earn interest of $40 (2 per cent of $2,000) during the second six months.

Compound interest and rate of return

Interest is said to be *compounded* when its amount for a given period is computed on the original principal plus the amount of interest earned in earlier periods. Business alternatives often differ as to the frequency of compoundings. In Example 2, Bank A's interest rate was 4 per cent a year, *compounded annually;* Bank B's rate was 4 per cent a year, *compounded semiannually* (or 2 per cent a half-year). Usually a quoted interest rate is an annual rate unless some other period is specified. Likewise, annual compoundings are usually implied unless there is a statement to the contrary.

When *rates of return* are used to compare long-term plans, they are ordinarily based upon annual compoundings, although tables for other compounding periods are available. The rate of return may be computed as follows:

$$\frac{\text{Annual earnings}}{\text{Investment balance}} = \text{Rate of return.}$$

In the preceding example, the rate of return in Bank A is established by contract at 4 per cent a year, while the return in Bank B is equivalent to a rate of 4.04 per cent compounded annually ($4,040 earnings for the year divided by $100,000 beginning investment balance).

Determining future value by formula and tables

The amount to which a sum of money will accumulate at compound interest after a given lapse of time may be computed by the formula

$$S_n = S(1 + i)^n,$$

where S_n is the future value of the accumulation;

S is the original sum of money;

i is the earnings rate for each compounding period; and

n is the number of compounding periods.

EXAMPLE 3:   Use the formula to compute the balance on deposit in Bank B at the end of one year.

SOLUTION: $S_n = \$100,000(1 + .02)^2$

$= \$100,000(1.02)(1.02)$

$= \$100,000(1.0404)$

$= \$104,040$

The future value formula is equally applicable in determining the amount of money that is to be received in the future on an investment and the amount that is to be paid on a debt.

Because compound interest calculations are needed frequently in business, printed tables are available which show the *ratios* of the future accumulation to the original sum for various rates of compound interest and various numbers of time periods. These ratios are called the *amount of $1 at compound interest* (a). Such a table would show that the ratio of the accumulated balance in Bank B (Example 2) to the original sum after one year would be 1.0404. This is the amount of $1 at compound interest at a rate of 2 per cent for two periods. Multiplying the sum originally deposited, S, by this ratio of future dollars to present dollars gives the amount to which the deposit will accumulate at the end of a year, $104,040 ($100,000 × 1.0404 = $104,040).

The present value of a sum of money

The preceding sections have shown how alternative plans may be compared on the basis of the amounts to which their resulting cash flows will accumulate at the end of a given number of periods. Most people, however, are accustomed to comparing values in terms of today's dollar. For this reason it is usually desirable to measure the future cash flow associated with each alternative in terms of its equivalent in today's dollars. This *present value* (often called *discounted value*) is especially useful in trying to decide whether a long-lived asset is worth the price asked for it today. The present value method also helps to compare plans which are expected to result in irregular cash flows or which do not require any initial investment of money.

EXAMPLE 4:   How much can a business afford to pay today for a savings certificate which can be redeemed for $100,000 a year from now, if the best alternative use of money at equal risk will earn 4 per cent a year, compounded annually?

In this illustration the future value of the investment at the end of one year is known; it is the present value which is to be computed. This may be done by formula or by tables, as explained in the following sections.

Determining present value by formula

The mathematical relationship between the present value of a sum and its future value is the same whether the present value or the future value is used as the base for comparison. That is, p, the ratio of the present sum to each dollar of the future accumulation, is the reciprocal of (1 divided by) a, the ratio of the future accumulation to each dollar of the present sum. Symbolically, $p = \dfrac{1}{a}$, and $a = \dfrac{1}{p}$. If p is known, a can be determined, and *vice versa*.

The present value of a sum to be received or paid at a future time may be computed by the formula

$$S = S_n \left(\frac{1}{1+i}\right)^n,$$

where S is the present value of the cash flow;

S_n is the future sum of money;

i is the earnings rate for each compounding period; and

n is the number of compounding periods.

The following illustration shows how this formula may be applied in Example 4.

SOLUTION TO EXAMPLE 4:

$$S = S_n \left(\frac{1}{1+i}\right)^n$$

$$S = \$100,000 \left(\frac{1}{1.04}\right)$$

$$S = \$100,000 \,(.96154)$$

$$S = \$\ 96,154, \text{ the present value of } \$100,000$$
$$\text{to be received one period later.}$$

Conclusion: If the savings certificate is now for sale for less than $96,154, the business would be better off to buy it. If its price is higher, the business should invest in the best alternative, which will pay $100,000 at the end of the year for $96,154 invested now.

Proof of Computation:

Present value of certificate............................. $ 96,154
Interest received at the end of the year, 4% of $96,154.....   3,846
Future value at the end of one year..................... $100,000

Present value computations are just as appropriate for the seller of an asset as for the buyer, and just as appropriate for the borrower of money as for the lender.

Determining present value from tables

A table which shows today's value, p, of each $1 to be received or paid in the future, for various rates of interest and time periods appears in Appendix 21-A. Multiplying the ratio of the present value, p, to each future dollar by the known number of dollars accumulated in the future, S_n, gives S, the present value of the future sum.

EXAMPLE 5:   A business is considering making an investment in a non-interest-bearing bond which promises to pay the face amount of $100,000 at the end of two years. Alternative investments of equal risk yield an annual rate of return of 4 per cent. How much is the bond worth now?

SOLUTION: 1. Find the number of periods for which interest is compounded (2) and the rate for each compounding period (4%).

2. Find the column for the applicable interest rate (4%) in Appendix 21-A.

3. Find the figure in this column on the line for the proper number of periods (2).

Periods	4% Interest Rate
1	.96154
2	.92456
3	.88900

4. Multiply the ratio at this point (.92456), p, by S_n, the sum to be received in the future ($100,000). The product, S, is $92,456, the amount that the bond is worth at present at a rate of 4 per cent.

Proof of Computation:

Present value of bond................................. $ 92,456
Interest for first year, 4%...........................   3,698*
Future value at the end of one year................... $ 96,154
Interest for second year, 4%..........................   3,846*
Future value at the end of two years.................. $100,000

    (* Note: Amounts are rounded to the nearest dollar.)

Determining rate of return from present value tables

Present value tables may be used to determine the rate of return on a given investment if the future accumulation and the number of periods are known. This may be done by:

(1) Computing the ratio of the present sum to the future accumulation, p; and

(2) Following the line for the given number of periods to the interest rate column in which this ratio is located. The interest rate at the top of the column is the rate of return on the investment.

EXAMPLE 6:   If a business invests $675.56 in a non-interest-bearing bond now, it will receive $1,000 at the end of 10 years. What is the rate of return?

SOLUTION: 1. Divide S by S_n to get the ratio for p.

$$\frac{\$675.56}{\$1,000} = .67556$$

2. On the line for 10 years in Appendix 21-A, find the interest rate column in which this ratio is located. It is in the 4 per cent column; therefore, the rate of return is 4 per cent.

Future value of a series of equal payments or receipts

Preceding sections have shown how to find the amount of a future accumulation of money when the initial sum, the elapsed time, and the rate of interest are known. This general method might be used for a *series* of future payments. This would involve computing the accumulation on each sum from the date of its receipt to a common future date, and then adding the individual accumulations. This procedure becomes tedious, however, when there are many periodic payments. If the periodic payments are equal, a short-cut formula or a table may be used to compute the future value of the entire series.

A series of such equal periodic payments is called an *annuity*, and each of the periodic payments is called a *rent*. The ratio of the future accumulation to the amount of the periodic rent is called the *amount of an annuity of $1*, frequently designated as A. It is multiplied by the amount of the periodic rent, R, to give the total future accumulation, S_n.

EXAMPLE 7:   A business is planning to build a plant addition in two years. It expects to accumulate the needed funds by depositing $10,000 at the end of each year in a savings bank which pays 5 per cent interest compounded annually. How much will be available for the plant expansion at the end of two years?

SOLUTION: $S_n = R(A) = \$10,000(2.05) = \$20,500$

The ratio 2.05 is derived from a table showing the amount of an annuity of $1 for various periods. It is the A ratio for 2 periods at 5 per cent.

Present value of a series of equal payments or receipts

A plan which involves a series of payments, like one with a single payment, can often be evaluated more readily if its results are expressed in terms of their equivalent in today's dollars. This might be done by multiplying each payment by the ratio of the present value of $1, p, for the appropriate period, and adding the products. However, tables of the *present value of an annuity of $1*, often called P, give a single ratio which expresses the current equivalent of each dollar of the future periodic payments. Appendix 21-B contains a table of P ratios. The P ratio, multiplied by the amount of the periodic payments, R, gives S, the present value of the series of payments.

EXAMPLE 8:   A business is considering investing in a savings bond due in two years. The bond contract promises to pay the lender $40 at the end of the first year, $40 at the end of the second, and the face amount, or *par*, of $1,000 at the end of the second year. How much can the business afford to pay for the bond today if its best alternative use of money at equal risk will earn 5 per cent a year, compounded annually?

FIRST SOLUTION: 1. The periodic payments of $40, the nominal interest on the bond, constitute an annuity. Multiply $40 by the present value of an annuity of $1 for 2 periods at 5 per cent, determined from Appendix 21-B.

2. Multiply the face amount by p, the present value of $1 due at the end of two periods at 5 per cent.

3. Add the products.

Computation:

Present value of rents	$ 40 × 1.85941 =	$ 74.38
Present value of face amount	$1,000 × 0.90703 =	907.03
Present value of savings bond		$981.41

Conclusion: If the price of the bond is less than $981.41, the business would gain by buying it. If it is more, the business should select the alternative investment, which pays a 5 per cent return.

Proof of Computation:

Initial investment		$ 981.41
Earnings first year at 5%		49.07
Total accumulation at end of first year		$1,030.48
Cash collected at end of first year		− 40.00
Balance invested during second year		$ 990.48
Earnings second year at 5%		49.52
Total accumulation at end of second year		$1,040.00
Cash collected at end of second year:		
Face	$1,000.00	
Nominal interest	40.00	−1,040.00
Investment balance at end of second year		$ .00

SECOND SOLUTION: Use a table of bond values, which expresses as a single ratio the relationship of the present value of all receipts on the bond—interest coupons as well as face—to each $1,000 of the bond's face amount.

Nominal and effective interest rates; bond discount

It is common practice to say that a bond such as that in Example 8 pays interest of 4 per cent a year, expressing the relationship of the periodic payments ($40) to the face of the bond ($1,000). This periodic payment is interest in name only, however. The real, or *effective*, interest for the life of the bond is the difference between the amount originally lent and the total amounts collected by the lender, computed as follows:

```
Receipts during life of bond:
    Nominal annual "interest" payments, 2 × $40.........  $    80.00
    Face amount at maturity...........................      1,000.00
        Total receipts................................     $1,080.00
Deduct initial payment................................        981.41
Total effective interest for two years................  $    98.59
```

The most accurate method of measuring the interest earned on the bond each year is the compound interest method. In the "Proof of Computation" in Example 8 this method shows that the effective interest is $49.07 the first year and $49.52 the second year.

Recording bond interest under effective interest method

The entries to reflect the bond investment in Example 8 and the periodic interest earned on it under the effective-interest method are shown below.

```
                              (1)
A, Long-term Investment.....................   981.41
    A, Cash................................              981.41
    Purchased a $1,000 bond due in two years and
    bearing a nominal interest rate of 4%, at an effec-
    tive rate of 5%.
                              (2)
A, Cash.....................................    40.00
A, Long-term Investment.....................     9.07
    OE, Interest Revenue....................               49.07
    Earned $49.07 interest the first year, computed
    by multiplying the previous balance in the in-
    vestment account, $981.41, by 5%. Collected
    $40 of the interest in cash and added the re-
    mainder to the balance of the investment account
    as a part of the face amount to be collected at
    maturity.
                              (3)
A, Cash.....................................    40.00
A, Long-term Investment.....................     9.52
    OE, Interest Revenue....................               49.52
    Earned $49.52 interest the second year, com-
    puted by multiplying the previous balance in
    the investment account, $990.48 (original cost,
    $981.41, plus first year's discount accumulation,
    $9.07), by 5%. Collected $40 of the interest in
    cash and added the remainder to the investment
    account.
                              (4)
A, Cash..................................... 1,000.00
    A, Long-term Investment.................            1,000.00
    Collected the face amount of the bond at maturity.
```

The entries under this method should be compared with those illustrated in Chapter 19, under which the discount is assigned in equal amounts to each time period. The method used in that chapter is called the *straight-line method* of accumulating discount. In the preceding illustration, it would have treated the average annual amount of interest ($98.59/2, or $49.29½) as the amount of interest earned each year. The differences in the results produced by the effective-interest and straight-line methods are usually immaterial, and the latter is usually preferred because it is simpler to apply.

Under either of the two methods of accumulating discount, the effective amount of interest earned each year is more than the $40 nominal interest which is collected in cash. The difference between the $981.41 purchase price of the bond and the $1,000 face amount of the bond is *additional interest* which is earned partly each year but is collected in cash at the maturity of the bond. This additional interest, $18.59 in the illustration, is called *bond discount*. Bonds sell at a discount from their face amounts when the *nominal* interest rate (4 per cent in this case) is *less* than the rate which investors can earn on alternative investments of equal risk (5 per cent here).

Bonds sell at a *premium* when the nominal interest rate is *more* than the rate which investors can earn on alternative investments of equal risk.

The methods of accounting for bonds which are issued at a discount and at a premium are illustrated in Chapter 19, "Accounting for Liabilities."

Summary

Compound interest tables have many business applications. The purpose of the present chapter has been to explain their derivation and basic uses, which may be summarized as follows:

1. Amount of $1, *a*:

PROBLEM: To what future sum, S_n, will a given amount invested or owed now, S, accumulate at compound interest?

SOLUTION: $S_n = S(a)$

2. Present value of $1, *p*:

PROBLEM: What sum, S, should be invested now to accumulate a given fund, S_n, in the future; or what sum, S, should be paid now to settle a given debt, S_n, due in the future?

SOLUTION: $S = S_n(p)$

APPENDIX 21-A
Present Value of $1 at Compound Interest

(p)

Number of Periods	1%	2%	3%	4%	5%	6%	8%	10%	12%	14%	16%	18%	20%	25%
1	0.99010	0.98039	0.97087	0.96154	0.95238	0.94340	0.926	0.909	0.893	0.877	0.862	0.847	0.833	0.800
2	0.98030	0.96117	0.94260	0.92456	0.90703	0.89000	0.857	0.826	0.797	0.769	0.743	0.718	0.694	0.640
3	0.97059	0.94232	0.91514	0.88900	0.86384	0.83962	0.794	0.751	0.712	0.675	0.641	0.609	0.579	0.512
4	0.96098	0.92385	0.88849	0.85480	0.82270	0.79209	0.735	0.683	0.636	0.592	0.552	0.516	0.482	0.410
5	0.95147	0.90573	0.86261	0.82193	0.78353	0.74726	0.681	0.621	0.567	0.519	0.476	0.437	0.402	0.328
6	0.94205	0.88797	0.83748	0.79031	0.74622	0.70496	0.630	0.564	0.507	0.456	0.410	0.370	0.335	0.262
7	0.93272	0.87056	0.81309	0.75992	0.71068	0.66506	0.583	0.513	0.452	0.400	0.354	0.314	0.279	0.210
8	0.92348	0.85349	0.78941	0.73069	0.67684	0.62741	0.540	0.467	0.404	0.351	0.305	0.266	0.233	0.168
9	0.91434	0.83676	0.76642	0.70259	0.64461	0.59190	0.500	0.424	0.361	0.308	0.263	0.225	0.194	0.134
10	0.90529	0.82035	0.74409	0.67556	0.61391	0.55839	0.463	0.386	0.322	0.270	0.227	0.191	0.162	0.107
11	0.89632	0.80426	0.72242	0.64958	0.58468	0.52679	0.429	0.350	0.287	0.237	0.195	0.162	0.135	0.086
12	0.88745	0.78849	0.70138	0.62460	0.55684	0.49697	0.397	0.319	0.257	0.208	0.168	0.137	0.112	0.069
13	0.87866	0.77303	0.68095	0.60057	0.53032	0.46884	0.368	0.290	0.229	0.182	0.145	0.116	0.093	0.055
14	0.86996	0.75789	0.66112	0.57748	0.50507	0.44230	0.340	0.263	0.205	0.160	0.125	0.099	0.078	0.044
15	0.86135	0.74301	0.64186	0.55526	0.48102	0.41727	0.315	0.239	0.183	0.140	0.108	0.084	0.065	0.035
16	0.85282	0.72845	0.62317	0.53391	0.45811	0.39365	0.292	0.218	0.163	0.123	0.093	0.071	0.054	0.028
17	0.84438	0.71416	0.60502	0.51337	0.43630	0.37136	0.270	0.198	0.146	0.108	0.080	0.060	0.045	0.023
18	0.83602	0.70016	0.58739	0.49363	0.41552	0.35034	0.250	0.180	0.130	0.095	0.069	0.051	0.038	0.018
19	0.82774	0.68643	0.57029	0.47464	0.39573	0.33051	0.232	0.164	0.116	0.083	0.060	0.043	0.031	0.014
20	0.81954	0.67297	0.55368	0.45639	0.37689	0.31180	0.215	0.149	0.104	0.073	0.051	0.037	0.026	0.012

Ratios for the Present Value of $1 and for the Present Value of an Annuity of $1 for rates up to 6% in Appendix 21-A and Appendix 21-B were based upon tables appearing in *Accountants' Handbook*, Fourth Edition, edited by Rufus Wixon and Walter G. Kell. Copyright 1956, The Ronald Press Company, Chapter 29, pp. 58-59 and 68-69. Ratios for rates higher than 6% are reprinted by permission from Robert N. Anthony, *Management Accounting, Text and Cases* (Homewood, Illinois: Richard D. Irwin, Inc., 1956), pp. 495-496.

It is felt that the greater accuracy of five decimal places is needed for the lower rates, which are frequently used in bond and interest problems. The higher rates are generally used in problems dealing with estimated rates of return, where rounding to three decimal places seems appropriate.

APPENDIX 21-B
Present Value of an Annuity of $1 at Compound Interest

(P)

Number of Periods	1%	2%	3%	4%	5%	6%	8%	10%	12%	14%	16%	18%	20%	25%
1	0.99010	0.98039	0.97087	0.96154	0.95238	0.94340	0.926	0.909	0.893	0.877	0.862	0.847	0.833	0.800
2	1.97040	1.94156	1.91347	1.88610	1.85941	1.83339	1.783	1.736	1.690	1.647	1.605	1.566	1.528	1.440
3	2.94099	2.88388	2.82861	2.77509	2.72325	2.67301	2.577	2.487	2.402	2.322	2.246	2.174	2.106	1.952
4	3.90197	3.80773	3.71710	3.62990	3.54595	3.46511	3.312	3.170	3.037	2.914	2.798	2.690	2.589	2.362
5	4.85343	4.71346	4.57971	4.45182	4.32948	4.21236	3.993	3.791	3.605	3.433	3.274	3.127	2.991	2.689
6	5.79548	5.60143	5.41719	5.24214	5.07569	4.91732	4.623	4.355	4.111	3.889	3.685	3.498	3.326	2.951
7	6.72819	6.47199	6.23028	6.00205	5.78637	5.58238	5.206	4.868	4.564	4.288	4.039	3.812	3.605	3.161
8	7.65168	7.32548	7.01969	6.73274	6.46321	6.20979	5.747	5.335	4.968	4.639	4.344	4.078	3.837	3.329
9	8.56602	8.16224	7.78611	7.43533	7.10782	6.80169	6.247	5.759	5.325	4.946	4.607	4.303	4.031	3.463
10	9.47130	8.98259	8.53020	8.11090	7.72173	7.36009	6.710	6.145	5.650	5.216	4.833	4.494	4.192	3.571
11	10.36763	9.78685	9.25262	8.76048	8.30641	7.88687	7.139	6.495	5.988	5.453	5.029	4.656	4.327	3.656
12	11.25508	10.57534	9.95400	9.38507	8.86325	8.38384	7.536	6.814	6.194	5.660	5.197	4.793	4.439	3.725
13	12.13374	11.34837	10.63496	9.98565	9.39357	8.85268	7.904	7.103	6.424	5.842	5.342	4.910	4.533	3.780
14	13.00370	12.10625	11.29607	10.56312	9.89864	9.29498	8.244	7.367	6.628	6.002	5.468	5.008	4.611	3.824
15	13.86505	12.84926	11.93794	11.11839	10.37966	9.71225	8.559	7.606	6.811	6.142	5.575	5.092	4.675	3.859
16	14.71787	13.57771	12.56110	11.65230	10.83777	10.10590	8.851	7.824	6.974	6.265	5.669	5.162	4.730	3.887
17	15.56225	14.29187	13.16612	12.16567	11.27407	10.47726	9.122	8.022	7.120	6.373	5.749	5.222	4.775	3.910
18	16.39827	14.99203	13.75351	12.65930	11.68959	10.82760	9.372	8.201	7.250	6.467	5.818	5.273	4.812	3.928
19	17.22601	15.67846	14.32380	13.13394	12.08532	11.15812	9.604	8.365	7.366	6.550	5.877	5.316	4.844	3.942
20	18.04555	16.35143	14.87747	13.59033	12.46221	11.46992	9.818	8.514	7.469	6.623	5.929	5.353	4.870	3.954

Source: See note on preceding page.

3. Amount of an annuity of $1, A:

PROBLEM (a):   To what future sum, S_n, will a series of equal periodic investments, R, accumulate at compound interest; or to what future sum, S_n, will a debt owed in a given series of equal periodic payments, R, accumulate?

SOLUTION (a): $S_n = R(A)$

PROBLEM (b):   What equal periodic installment, R, should be invested to accumulate a given future sum, S_n, at compound interest; or what equal installment, R, should be paid to settle a future debt of a given amount, S_n?

SOLUTION (b): $R = \dfrac{S_n}{A}$

4. Present value of an annuity of $1, P:

PROBLEM (a):   What sum, S, should be paid now in exchange for a right to receive a series of equal periodic payments of a given amount, R, in the future; or what sum, S, paid now would settle a debt due in a series of equal future periodic payments, R?

SOLUTION (a): $S = R(P)$

PROBLEM (b):   What equal periodic receipt, R, is necessary to justify the investment of a given sum now, S, at compound interest; or what periodic payment, R, should be made to settle a debt of a given amount now due?

SOLUTION (b): $R = \dfrac{S}{P}$

This chapter has compared plans which are expected to result in definite, regular amounts of future cash receipts and payments, and has illustrated the methods of accounting for some of these plans. The certainty of the results of the plans illustrated, such as the bond investments, is more apparent than real. Although the sums to be paid are definite amounts fixed by contract, there is a chance that the borrower may be unable or unwilling to live up to the terms of the contract.

Chapter 22 deals with project planning when the amounts of expected receipts and payments for alternative plans are irregular or uncertain. It also illustrates approximate methods of comparison which are simpler to apply than the compound interest method and which often yield satisfactory results.

QUESTIONS AND PROBLEMS

21-1   This chapter has illustrated some business situations in which a knowledge of the basic mathematics of compound interest is useful. Actually, the application of these computations in business is much broader.

REQUIRED:

List all of the types of business problems you can in which compound interest mathematics helps one to arrive at a solution.

21-2

a. The ratio of the future value of an accumulation to each dollar invested now is 2.19112. How much must be invested now for each dollar accumulated at the end of the investment's term?

b. Each $0.83676 invested now will accumulate to $1.00 at the end of a period of years. What will be the ratio of the accumulation at the end of the term to each dollar invested now?

21-3

REQUIRED:

For each of the following situations, state (1) which table in the appendices should be used, (2) the number of time periods, (3) the interest rate, and (4) the result.

a. A credit union pays its depositors at the annual rate of 4 per cent, compounded quarterly. At the end of three years, what will be the total accumulation on an initial deposit of $1,000?

b. Using the facts in (*a*), how much must be deposited now to accumulate a balance of $1,000 in three years?

c. A man owes a non-interest-bearing note with a face amount of $600, which is due in four years. How much must he pay now to settle the debt if the lender requires an annual rate of return of 6 per cent, compounded semiannually?

d. On March 31, 19x1, a business issues bonds of a face amount of $1,000 each, which includes interest to the maturity date, March 31, 19x6. Other businesses of equal risk are able to issue at par 5-year bonds which pay interest every 6 months, at an annual rate of 6 per cent. What price should the business expect to receive for each bond?

e. A widow wishes to purchase an annuity contract under which she will receive cash payments of $4,000 a year at the end of each of the next 10 years. If the current rate of interest for such investments is 4 per cent, how much will the contract cost?

21-4   Under a bond contract, the lender usually has the right to receive equal periodic payments of nominal interest, as well as the face amount of the bond at maturity date. For example, the investor in a 10-year, 6 per cent, $1,000 bond with annual interest payments expects to receive $60 at the end of each year and an additional $1,000 at the end of the tenth year.

REQUIRED:

If the best comparable alternative investment pays a 6 per cent return, determine at the date of purchase of the bond:

a. The value of each dollar of the first year's interest;

b. The value of each dollar of the ninth year's interest;

c. The value of each dollar of the face amount;

d. The total value of the face amount;

e. The total value of the interest payments;

f. The total value of the bond contract.

21-5   Federal Government financing makes wide use of discount bonds, by which the lender collects all of his interest at maturity. Assume that Series Z bonds will pay the lender a face amount of $100 at the end of 5 years for each $82.03 invested now.

REQUIRED:

a. Using the compound interest tables, determine to what semiannual interest rate this is equivalent.

b. Record the investor's entries for the first full year, assuming that the investment is made on the first day of an accounting period.

c. Show how the investment would be presented in a statement of financial position at the end of one year.

21-6   It is a common practice for banks to lend money on notes which include in their face interest to maturity, computed on the face amount. For example, Bank *A* takes a note of $1,000 in exchange for a 1-year loan, deducts interest at 6 per cent of the face amount, and gives the borrower the proceeds of $940 in cash.

REQUIRED:

a. What interest rate is Bank *A* actually charging?

b. Show in journal form the borrower's entries (1) on the date of the loan and (2) at the end of his accounting period 3 months later.

c. Show in journal form the bank's entries (1) on the date of the loan and (2) at the end of its accounting period 9 months later.

21-7   A manufacturer offers a purchaser of a machine his choice of paying $4,200 cash or making 5 payments of $900 each, the first due immediately and the remainder at 6-month intervals.

REQUIRED:

a. If the purchaser can borrow the money needed to buy the machine at the rate of 8 per cent a year, compounded semiannually, should he do so?

b. What is the highest interest rate in (*a*) which the purchaser should consider paying, rather than choosing the manufacturer's credit plan?

c. Show in journal form all entries made by the purchaser during the first year if he buys the machine on the first day of his accounting period and the machine has an expected useful life of 10 years, (1) if he pays cash and (2) if he takes advantage of the manufacturer's credit terms.

21-8   Several individuals incorporated a small business venture and received common stock in exchange for cash and other property which they invested in the corporation. Needing additional capital, they issued 50 shares of 8 per cent cumulative preferred stock, par $100, to an outsider at par. The preferred stock contract gave the corporation an option to call the stock for redemption at 105 per cent of par at any time after 5 years from date of issuance.

The annual preferred dividend requirements sharply reduced the earnings available for the common shareholders. At the end of the second year, they voted to make the preferred stockholder an offer for the immediate purchase of his stock.

REQUIRED:

a. Using compound interest tables, compute the average rate of return that the preferred stockholder would earn if the stock were redeemed at the end of 5 years.

b. Compute the minimum offer which is likely to be attractive to him at the end of the second year.

c. What other factors should the preferred stockholder consider before deciding whether to accept the offer in (*b*)?

d. What other factors should the common stockholders consider before deciding whether to make the offer?

e. Show in journal form the corporation's entry if the stock is redeemed at the end of the fifth year.

21-9   On March 1, 19x1, an investor is considering buying a $10,000 bond of the *XYZ* Company which was originally issued for a 20-year period and which matures on March 1, 19x9. Nominal interest is paid each March 1 at the rate of 4 per cent of par. Newly issued bonds of similar quality and term yield a return of 6 per cent of the investment.

REQUIRED:

a. What is the maximum amount which the investor would be willing to pay for the *XYZ* bond?
b. If he buys it for this maximum amount, what would his entries be during the accounting period ending December 31, 19x1?
c. How would all of the related items appear in his 19x1 financial statements?

21-10

REQUIRED:

a. Compute the price of a $1,000 bond due in 3 years which pays nominal interest of 4 per cent annually. Similar bonds pay annual interest of 3 per cent.
b. Prepare a table showing the annual interest, the annual amortization, and the bond balance under (1) the compound interest method of amortization and (2) the straight-line method of amortization.

21-11   The owner of a business is trying to decide how to finance the purchase of a store building. Lender *A* will take a 10-year mortgage note requiring annual interest payments of 6 per cent of the face amount of the note, $9,400. Lender *B* quotes a 5 per cent interest rate on a 10-year note for $10,000 face amount, from which it will deduct a discount of 6 per cent.

REQUIRED:

Present computations needed to compare these two proposals.

21-12   A bride and bridegroom of a few months have found the house of their dreams. Its cost is $20,000, and it can be financed by a $2,000 down payment and a 20-year mortgage loan bearing interest at 6 per cent. The bridegroom has been advised not to spend more than 20 per cent of his annual income, after income tax, for housing, and he would like to know whether his salary is large enough to justify purchasing this house. For simplicity, assume in your computations that salary receipts and mortgage payments both occur at the end of each year.

REQUIRED:

a. Compute the annual salary, after taxes, which the bridegroom must earn in order to afford this house on 20 per cent of this salary.
b. What must his income before tax be, assuming that the first $6,000 of his taxable income is subject to a 20 per cent tax and the next $4,000 to a 22 per cent tax? (For the present, ignore the effect on income tax of deductible interest payments.)

21-13   The *J* Realty Company has leased a building to a tenant for 5 years under an agreement which requires the payment of an annual rental of $3,000 at the end of each year. At the beginning of the second year, the *J* Realty Company offers the tenant an opportunity to make an immediate payment of $9,500 in lieu of the remaining rentals. The tenant's treasurer estimates that his company can earn 10 per cent a year, compounded semiannually, if it does not make the advance payment.

REQUIRED:

a. Should the tenant accept the offer? Give computations to support your conclusion.

b. What entries should *J* Realty Company make in the second year if (1) the tenant makes the advance payment and (2) if the tenant does not make the advance payment?

c. How would the facts related to (*b*)(1) and (*b*)(2) appear in the landlord's financial statements for the second year?

d. What conditions probably induced the *J* Realty Company to make the offer?

21-14   The Utica Corporation planned late in 19x1 to issue 10-year bonds to finance some capital additions. In December arrangements were made to issue bonds of $200,000 face amount, paying coupon interest of 6 per cent annually on December 31. On December 17 the corporation paid printing costs connected with the issue, $600. On December 21 it received a bill for legal fees in connection with the issue, $1,200, which it did not pay until February 1, 19x2.

Late in December, 19x1, market interest rates took a sharp turn downward, and the Utica Corporation decided to delay the issue, scheduled for December 31, to take advantage of possible lower interest rates. Accordingly, the bonds were issued on December 31, 19x2 at a price which resulted in a net interest cost of 5 per cent, excluding costs of issuance.

REQUIRED:

a. What journal entries should Utica make in 19x1?

b. How should the facts be presented in its 19x1 statement of financial position?

c. What price did it receive when the bonds were issued?

d. Make all journal entries needed by the issuer in 19x3.

e. Illustrate how the affected items would appear in the 19x3 income statement and statement of financial position.

CASE 21-1. THE NORTHERN STATES POWER COMPANY

The Northern States Power Company, a Minnesota corporation, planned in the spring of 1958 to ask for proposals for the purchase of $30,000,000 of its First Mortgage Bonds, Series due July 1, 1988. The company intended to use $18,944,-400 of the proceeds from the sale of these new bonds to refund the $18,000,000 of its 5 per cent First Mortgage Bonds, Series due August 1, 1987, which were outstanding at that time. The balance of the proceeds of the new bonds were to be added to the company's general funds and used to help finance $43.9 million of additions and improvements to its utility properties. It was anticipated that expenses of the new issue to be paid by the company would be $140,000.

The First Mortgage 5s of 1987 had been offered to the public at 100 on August 14, 1957, by a group composed of Blyth & Co., Inc., The First Boston Corp., and associates. The proceeds to the company amounted to $17,866,800, or 99.26 per cent of face value. The purpose of the issue had been to repay bank loans of $5,000,000 for property additions and improvements, to pay off long-term debt and bank loans in connection with the acquisition of the Wisconsin Hydro Electric Company properties, and to defray costs incurred under the company's construction program.

The 1987 issue was secured by the same mortgage which was applicable to all of the company's first mortgage bonds. The bonds were dated August 1, 1957; their maturity date was August 1, 1987; and their interest was payable semiannually on February 1 and August 1. The bonds were callable as a whole or in part on at least 30 days' notice at any time to each July 31, inclusive, at the following prices:

1958	105.00	1963	104.14
1959	104.83		
1960	104.66		
1961	104.49	1986	100.18
1962	104.32	1987	100.00

(Redemption prices for 1964–1985 are omitted.)

During 1957 this issue ranged in price on the New York Stock Exchange from 103½ to 104. During approximately the first half of 1958, price ranges of the company's bond issues were as follows:

	Low	High
First Mortgage 2¾s of 1975	86½	91½
First Mortgage 3¼s of 1982	91	91
First Mortgage 3⅛s of 1984	85½	87
First Mortgage 4⅛s of 1986	101½	104
First Mortgage 5s of 1987	104¾	107¼

On July 9, 1958, a group headed by Merrill Lynch, Pierce, Fenner & Smith; Kidder, Peabody & Co.; and White, Weld & Co., of New York, offered the $30,000,000 1988 Series of First Mortgage 4s to the public at a price of 100. The net proceeds to the Northern States Power Company were 99.39 per cent of face value. The issue was quickly subscribed by purchasers. During the remainder of 1958, its price on the bond market ranged from 95 to 98.

The entire issue of the First Mortgage 5s of 1987 was retired at 104.83 and accrued interest on August 15, 1958, at the offices of Harris Trust & Savings Bank, Chicago, and Schroder Trust Co., New York.

Exhibits 1, 2, and 3 contain selected items from the financial statements of the Northern States Power Company and its subsidiaries for the years ended December 31, 1956, 1957, and 1958.

NORTHERN STATES POWER COMPANY (MINNESOTA)   Exhibit 1
and Subsidiary Companies, Consolidated
Condensed Balance Sheets, December 31

	1958		1957	
	(Thousands of Dollars)			
ASSETS				
Utility plant—at original cost	$600,348		$561,841	
Reserves for depreciation and amortization	124,009		114,236	
		$476,339		$447,605
Investments—at cost or less		2,832		2,633
Current assets		42,380		51,983
Deferred charges:				
Unamortized debt discount and expense	$ 719		$ 652	
Miscellaneous deferred charges	1,506	2,225	1,862	2,514
Capital stock expense (not being amortized)		1,483		1,493
Total assets		$525,259		$506,228
LIABILITIES				
Common stock	$ 71,402		$ 71,326	
Premium on common stock	36,805		36,575	
Earned surplus	41,110	$149,317	37,469	$145,370
Cumulative preferred stock (all series)		90,311		90,311
Minority interests in subsidiaries		516		816

First mortgage bonds:
Northern States Power Company
(Minnesota):

Series due 1974, 2¾%............	$ 5,000		$ 5,000
Series due 1975, 2¾%............	75,000		75,000
Series due 1978, 3%..............	10,000		10,000
Series due 1979, 2¾%............	15,000		15,000
Series due 1982, 3¼%............	21,500		21,500
Series due 1984, 3⅛%............	20,000		20,000
Series due 1986, 4¼%............	15,000		15,000
Series due 1987, 5%..............	30,000		18,000
Northern States Power Company (Wisconsin)—(less current sinking fund requirement shown as current liability) (all series)...............	35,620	227,120	36,010	215,510
Current liabilities		45,937		43,067
Unamortized premium on debt.........		381		398
Other deferred credits.................		668		867
Contributions in aid of construction....		3,132		2,958
Accumulated deferred taxes on income.		7,877		6,931
Total liabilities		$525,259		$506,228

NORTHERN STATES POWER COMPANY (MINNESOTA)   Exhibit 2
and Subsidiary Companies, Consolidated
Condensed Statements of Earned Surplus

	Year Ended December 31		
	1958	1957	1956
	(Thousands of Dollars)		
Balance at beginning of period......................	$37,469	$34,365	$30,756
Add—Net income for the period....................	22,076	21,162	20,471
	$59,545	$55,527	$51,227
Deduct:			
Cash dividends on preferred......................	$ 3,558	$ 3,558	$ 3,482
Cash dividends on common......................	14,273	12,720	12,681
Write-off of balance at December 31, 1957 of unamortized debt discount and expense of refunded issues		1,560†	
Other deductions.................................	604*	220	699
	$18,435	$18,058	$16,862
Balance at end of period.........................	$41,110	$37,469	$34,365

* Includes write-off of premiums and unamortized debt discount and expense, less related income taxes, applicable to bonds redeemed, $536,011.

† The balance at December 31, 1957, of unamortized debt discount and expense on refunded issues amounting to $1,560,546 was charged off to surplus.

NORTHERN STATES POWER COMPANY (MINNESOTA)   Exhibit 3
and Subsidiary Companies, Consolidated
Condensed Summary of Earnings

	Year Ended December 31		
	1958	1957	1956
	(Thousands of Dollars)		
Operating revenues.........................	$154,787	$147,918	$139,300
Operating revenue deductions.................	125,827	120,466	113,528
Net operating income......................	$ 28,960	$ 27,452	$ 25,772
Other income................................	138	543	276
Gross income..............................	$ 29,098	$ 27,995	$ 26,048

	Year Ended December 31		
	1958	1957	1956
	(Thousands of Dollars)		
Income deductions:			
Interest on long-term debt....................	$ 7,088	$ 6,175	$ 5,149
Amortization of debt discount and expense:			
On refunded issues........................		551	551
Outstanding issues, less premium...........	12	4	
Interest charged to construction (credit).....	(526)	(466)	(753)
Other income deductions...................	448	569	630
Total income deductions.............. ..	$ 7,022	$ 6,833	$ 5,577
Net income................................	$ 22,076	$ 21,162	$ 20,471
Ratio of earnings to fixed charges*.............		7.68	8.60

* Note from preliminary prospectus dated May 29, 1958, describing the First Mortgage Bonds, Series of 1988:

Earnings consist of consolidated net income shown above, to which have been added Federal, State, and deferred taxes based on income, and fixed charges. Fixed charges consist of interest on long-term debt, interest on notes payable to banks, amortization of debt discount and expense and premium on outstanding issues, and preferred stock dividend requirements of a consolidated subsidiary. Rental payments under long-term leases are not considered material. Adjusted to give effect to the issuance by the Company of the new bonds bearing interest at an assumed rate of 3¾% per annum and to the retirement of $18,000,000 principal amount of First Mortgage Bonds, Series due August 1, 1987, 5% preferred stock of the Wisconsin Company, and bank loans, the earnings ratio for the year ended December 31, 1957 would be 6.76. A change of ⅛ of 1% from the assumed 3¾% interest rate would change this ratio approximately .035.†

Technical Note

(Excerpts from American Institute of Certified Public Accountants, Committee on Accounting Procedure, *Accounting Research Bulletin No. 43*, pp. 130–132.)

"Discussion of the treatment of unamortized discount, issue cost, and redemption premium on bonds refunded (hereinafter referred to as unamortized discount) has revolved mainly about three methods of disposing of the unamortized balance:

(a) A direct write-off to income or earned surplus,
(b) Amortization over the remainder of the original life of the issue retired, or
(c) Amortization over the life of the new issue.

Each of these methods has had support in court decisions, in determinations by regulatory agencies, and in accounting literature.
. . .

"It is acceptable accounting to write off unamortized discount in full in the year of refunding. This treatment is based on the view that the unamortized bond discount represents in effect the cost of the privilege of terminating a borrowing contract which has become disadvantageous and hence comes under the accounting doctrine that a loss or expense should be recognized as such not later than the time when the series of transactions giving rise to it is completed.
. . .

---

† (*Sources: Moody's Public Utility Manual*, 1958 and 1959; *Commercial and Financial Chronicle*; Prospectus, Northern States Power Company (a Minnesota corporation) $30,000,000 First Mortgage Bonds, Series due July 1, 1988); Northern States Power Company Annual Report, 1957.)

"The second alternative, distributing the charge over the remainder of the original life of the bonds refunded, has strong support in accounting theory. Its chief merit lies in the fact that it results in reflection of the refinancing expense as a direct charge under the appropriate head in a series of income accounts related to the term of the original borrowing contract.

"This method is based on the accounting doctrine that when a cost is incurred the benefits of which may reasonably be expected to be realized over a period in the future, it should be charged against income over such period. In behalf of this method, it is argued that the unamortized bond discount represents the cost of making a more advantageous arrangement for the unexpired term of the old agreement. In other words, such discount is regarded as the cost of an option included in the borrowing contract to enable a corporation to anticipate the maturity of its obligations if it finds it possible to refund them at a lower cost, either as the result of a favorable change in interest rates or as the result of its own improved credit. Continuing this line of reasoning, it is argued that the cost of money over the entire period of the original issue is affected by the terms of the original contract, and that if the cost of anticipating maturity is incurred, it is only because it is advantageous to do so; if the saving over the unexpired term of the old bonds will exceed the amount of unamortized discount to be disposed of, such discount should properly be spread over that unexpired term as a proper element of the cost of borrowed money.

"This method should be regarded as preferable. It conforms more closely than any other method to current accounting opinion.

. . .

"The third alternative, amortization over the life of the new issue, runs counter to generally accepted accounting principles. It cannot be justified on the ground that cost may be spread over the period during which the benefit therefrom may be presumed to accrue. Clearly discernible benefits from a refunding accrue only for the period during which the new issue is replacing the previously outstanding issue. To determine whether any benefit will accrue to an issuing corporation for the period during which the new issue is to be outstanding after the maturity date of the old issue would require an ability to foresee interest rates to be in effect during that period. Since such foresight is plainly impossible, there is no ground for assuming a benefit will result during that period. Moreover, the method does not possess any marked practical advantages in comparison with the second alternative. On the contrary, it results in an understatement of the annual cost of money after refunding and during the remainder of the term of the old issue, and consequently might tend to encourage consummation of transactions which are not, when properly viewed, advantageous. Furthermore, not only is there a lack of logical relationship between the amount of unamortized discount on the *old* issue and the term of the *new* issue, but also it is unconservative from both the balance-sheet and the income standpoints to carry forward part of the unamortized discount over the longer period. The committee considers the argument that the expense of retiring the old issue is a part of the cost of the new transaction to be untenable. In view of the above considerations the committee's conclusion is that this method is not acceptable."

For Federal income tax purposes, the unamortized discount on an issue of bonds retired for cash must be deducted as a loss in the year in which retirement takes place.

REQUIRED:

a. Why did the company plan to retire the 1987 bonds less than a year from date of their issuance?

b. Using information which was available to the management of the company in May, 1958, prepare an analysis comparing the future effect on the company (1) if the 1987 bonds are refunded and (2) if they are not refunded. You may assume that the effective rate of all income taxes on the company is 50 per cent of net income before income tax.

c. What other action related to the 1987 issue should the company have considered?

d. Was the refunding issue a success? Explain.

e. Show in journal form all entries on the company's books:

   (1) To record the issue in 1957 of the 1987 series.
   (2) To summarize 1957 interest and amortization on this series.
   (3) To record the retirement of the series in 1958.
   (4) To record the issue in 1958 of the 1988 series.
   (5) To summarize 1958 interest and amortization on this series.

Where alternative methods of recording are widely accepted, state why you selected the method you used.

f. Explain the probable justification for the charge to retained income of $1,560,-546 in 1957.

Long-Range Planning:
Comparing Alternatives

The preceding chapter showed how the fundamentals of compound interest mathematics may be used to compare alternative courses of business action when the amounts and timing of the future receipts and payments associated with each alternative are known. Bonds and similar financial contracts which promise to pay specific sums of money at definite future times were used for illustration. A particular financial contract was selected on the basis of a comparison of its *outlay cost* with the *present value of its stream of future receipts,* discounted at the interest rate that could be earned on the best alternative investment of equal risk.

Comparison of long-range business alternatives by the present-value method has several practical limitations. First, the illustrations in the last chapter assumed that the future payments under each plan were certain, while actually they depend upon the credit of the promisor and the course of future economic events. Second, each plan was accepted or rejected after comparing it with a single best alternative. In most business decisions there are many alternatives, and it is awkward to try to compare them on the basis of their present values. Third, the interest rate used in computing the present value of a plan was the rate earned on the best alternative of equal risk. In reality, however, one of business management's major problems is to *recognize what the relevant alternatives are* in a given situation, and then to select the best. The rate of return on this best course of action is not given information, but must be determined.

Most of the investments made by business are *real* rather than *financial.* That is, they are commitments of funds for an indefinitely long term to specific assets, such as land, buildings, equipment, and permanent working capital, instead of investments in securities such as bonds and stocks. They involve *expected* rather than *promised* future receipts. The amounts, timing, and degree of uncertainty associated with the cash flow from such investments are all indefinite. This chapter outlines appropriate methods of selecting long-range plans in view of these uncertainties. It also proposes a general approach to planning and administering a budget of the capital additions which the enterprise needs during the next year and during the long term.

Types of plans which require no capital investment

When the alternative plans which are being compared require no additional capital investment, the plan chosen should be the one with the greatest present value. The present value of each plan may be estimated by discounting its expected future stream of net cash receipts at a rate which reflects the relative risks associated with the project. Examples of such alternatives are whether to change selling prices; whether to change marketing channels; whether to purchase a component part of the finished product or continue to make it with facilities already owned; and whether to rearrange the flow of work. Often there are capital costs associated with such plans, but it is difficult to measure them.

Types of plans which require capital investment

Examples of alternative solutions to a business problem, only one of which requires an additional capital outlay, are decisions whether to replace equipment or plant prior to the end of their useful lives or to continue using the existing ones, and whether to lease or to buy equipment or real estate.

Examples of alternatives all of which require additional capital are choices between several possible new machines or new plant locations.

There may be many possible alternative courses of action to supply a given business need—the decision may be not merely whether to replace an asset at all, but also which of several possible replacements to select. Usually, some of the possibilities may be quickly eliminated from serious consideration. The detailed analysis can then be confined to the few best contenders.

Need for a long-range capital additions budget

Capital budgeting consists of planning the nature, cost, and timing of the acquisition of long-lived assets and the means of financing them. A business should plan its additions of long-lived assets well in advance for several reasons. First, because their cost is often large, management should know the amount of funds needed for capital assets in time to make arrangements for obtaining them. Second, long-lived assets tie up funds in specific assets for a long period of time. Usually many years elapse before the cost of fixed assets is completely recovered through operating revenues. Third, the risk of loss on such assets is great, because major changes in the economy and in the internal operating conditions of the enterprise can occur during their long lives. Fourth, the investment in such assets is often inflexible, a *sunk cost* that must be recovered by use because it can be recovered only partially, or not at all, by sale. Finally, the selection of specific long-lived assets has a far-reaching effect on the productive capacity of the business, the nature of its products, and the amount of its operating expenses.

A business should plan in general terms the long-lived assets which will be needed to achieve its sales and income goals for the next 5, 10, or 15 years. Such planning will help to avoid the extremes of inadequate capacity, with consequent loss of sales revenue, and excess capacity, with consequent unproductive assets. The long-range capital additions budget is necessarily tentative because changes in demand, competition, technology, and costs can be predicted only in broad outline for the distant future. The plan must be flexible, too; capital expenditures can usually be postponed if necessary.

The responsibility for co-ordinating the capital additions budget should rest with top management. Supporting details about specific requirements should be supplied by the intermediate and lower levels of management which will be responsible for the actual execution of the plans.

Rationing capital to specific projects

Usually the requirements for capital additions which confront a business are greater than the funds available to finance them, and it is necessary to ration funds to projects on the basis of their relative desirability. One of the most important factors bearing on the desirability of plans is the comparative effect of each on the rate of return which the company earns on its assets. Intangible, or qualitative, considerations, such as the effect of a course of action on company prestige or on employee morale, also often have an important influence on capital investment decisions. It is usually advisable to make a careful, objective appraisal of alternatives by outlining the advantages and disadvantages of each, expressing them, where possible, in terms of dollars of expected cost and revenue. Then if the final choice is dictated by an intangible factor, at least management can see the cost of such a decision.

In some cases, a business has no choice but to make a capital outlay, regardless of its rate of return. A roof blown off by a windstorm, for example, should be replaced at once. The cost of the alternative, not replacing it, in damage to merchandise and equipment would be prohibitive. On the other hand, some proposed uses of capital may be rejected immediately because they will never pay for themselves in increased income. Between these two clear-cut extremes are a variety of possible capital expenditures which promise a wide range of profitability. Some are optional or postponable; some are merely different ways of filling an important current need. It is to this wide band of borderline cases that the method of analysis in this chapter applies.

Ranking projects as to rate of return

To the extent that proposed capital additions may be compared on the basis of quantitative factors, it is useful to rank each according to the expected rate of return on the investment it requires. This ranking often follows a preliminary comparison in which the best of several ways to accomplish each given purpose has been selected, also largely on the basis of rate of return on the investment. Assume that computations give the following results:

Project	Expected Cost	Expected Annual Return
A	$20,000	22%
B	30,000	20%
C	50,000	18%
D	50,000	17%

If the company's cash forecast plus an estimate of funds available from outside sources indicates that only $50,000 can be spent for capital outlay in the coming year, Projects A and B should be selected (assuming that profitable reinvestment opportunities will be available at their termination). Their combined $50,000 investment will probably increase the annual income of the business by $10,400 ($4,400 plus $6,000), while the next best alternative, Project C, would bring in only $9,000.

There is a lower limit beyond which the ranking process should not be carried. One suggested minimum, below which projects will be rejected, is the *expected average cost of capital* to the business in the future. This is estimated by considering the net return which creditors and stockholders will probably require in order to continue supplying funds to the business. Another minimum is the *desired future rate of return* of the business. However, there is no substitute for judgment in evaluating the risks associated with alternative courses of action. Some projects involving a high degree of uncertainty should be rejected even though their expected rates of return are well above these minimum rates. Other projects whose cash flow is practically assured may occasionally be accepted even though their rates of return are below these limits.

If in management's judgment the expected rates of return on all alternative projects are very low, management should consider (1) postponing all capital expenditures until a later time, when prospects may appear better; or (2) using the available funds for dividends to stockholders so that they may put them to more profitable use elsewhere.

MEASURING THE RATE OF RETURN

Formula for time-adjusted rate of return

To determine the expected rate of return on a capital investment, allowing for differences in the timing of resulting cash receipts and payments, it is necessary to estimate carefully:

(1) The initial net cost of the investment, S;
(2) The amount of net cash receipts, R, for each future period; and
(3) The estimated useful life of the investment, n.

The problem then is to find the unknown rate of return which, when used to discount the known stream of expected future receipts from the investment, will equate this stream to the known initial cost of the investment. This computation requires the use of tables of P, the present value of an annuity of $1, and substitution in the formula

$$S = R(P).$$

The calculation is easier if the formula is rearranged thus:

$$P = \frac{S}{R}.$$

The expected rate of return can then be found by the following steps:

(1) Substitute the amounts of S and R in the equation and divide to find the required P ratio;
(2) Then, in tables of the present value of an annuity of $1, such as that in Appendix 21-B, read across the line for the number of periods of the asset's useful life to the interest rate column in which the computed P ratio is located. It is unlikely that the exact P ratio will appear, but an approximation is satisfactory for most business purposes. This rate is the expected rate of return on the investment.

EXAMPLE 1:   A machine which costs $7,360 is expected to reduce operating costs $1,000 a year for 10 years. What rate of return will it yield?

SOLUTION:
$$P = \frac{S}{R} = \frac{\$7,360}{\$1,000}$$
$$P = 7.360.$$

In the table of the present value of an annuity of $1 in Appendix 21-B, this exact ratio is on the line for 10 years and in the 6% column; therefore, the expected rate of return on the investment is 6%.

Note that the formula used above is the same as that used in determining the rate of return on a bond in Chapter 21. The difference is that here the net annual receipts and estimated useful life are much more uncertain.

Measuring initial net cost of the investment

The first step in computing the rate of return on an investment in a long-lived asset is to determine the net additional cash payment, S, which it requires at the beginning of its life. This net initial cost of an asset consists of the outlay for its purchase, transportation, installation, and preparation for first use. If the asset is a replacement, the cash received as the salvage value of the old asset is subtracted from the gross outlay for the new asset to measure the net investment.

EXAMPLE 2(a):   At the end of 19x4, Company X is trying to decide whether to continue to use an old machine for its estimated remaining useful life of 5 years or to replace it immediately with a new one. The facts about the two machines are as follows:

	Old Machine	New Machine
Original cost............................	$9,000	$10,000
Accumulated depreciation................	4,000	0
Salvage value, 12/31/x4..................	3,000	
Expected salvage value, 12/31/x9.........	0	0
The productive capacity of the two machines is equal.		

What is the net initial cost of the new machine (S)?

SOLUTION: If the business purchases the new machine, it will sell the old one for $3,000 cash, and then pay a total of $10,000 for the new one. The net cash payment will be only the difference, $7,000; this is the net initial cost of the new machine.

A word of caution is in order. The $5,000 unexpired cost, or *book value*, of the old machine (its original cost of $9,000 minus accumulated depreciation of $4,000) should be ignored in computing the difference in the capital cost of the two alternatives. It is a *sunk cost*, representing a cash payment made at some time in the past. This historical fact cannot be changed by future action. Only future cash flows, which *can* be affected by the choice now being made, are relevant in comparing the effects of alternative courses of action on the future income of the business. The old machine can be used for the next 5 years without an additional investment, or it can be sold now for $3,000. If it is not sold now, the business sacrifices a chance to receive $3,000 cash. This immediate salvage value measures the capital cost of continuing to use the old machine.

Estimating differential future receipts

The second step in comparing the profitability of two or more courses of action is to estimate R, the difference in future periodic net receipts which can be expected under the alternatives. Expected differences in net receipts may be the result of *cost savings* of one plan as compared with alternative plans; they may arise from its *additional revenue;* or they may result from a favorable combination of the two.

It cannot be emphasized too strongly that the appropriate payments and receipts for comparing alternative plans are *expected future payments and receipts.* Records of past payments and receipts may give valuable clues as to probable future amounts, especially for the course of action now being followed or for one similar to it. However, estimates of future results must allow for expected future changes in prices and in internal and external operating conditions.

Only the operating receipts and payments which are expected to be changed under any of the plans need be listed in making a comparison of the expected receipts of alternatives. The objective is to determine whether *differences in receipts* resulting from each alternative justify their respective *differences in investment.*

EXAMPLE 2(b):   The expected annual operating costs of the two machines described in Example 2(a) are shown below. Expected revenues are omitted, because the two machines have equal productive capacity.

	Expected Annual Operating Costs	
	Old Machine	New Machine
Operator's wages....................	$4,000	$2,600
Scrap materials......................	1,000	400
Repairs.............................	200	50
Maintenance........................	400	300
Property tax........................	120	320
Insurance..........................	100	400
Totals............................	$5,820	$4,070

It is assumed that these operating costs are expected to be the same for each future year, and that differences in the timing of the receipt of the various services and payment for them are negligible.

What will be the annual differential net receipts, R, if the old machine is replaced?

SOLUTION:

	New Machine's Expected Differential Net Receipts	
	Costs Saved	Costs Added
Operator's wages....................................	$1,400	
Scrap materials......................................	600	
Repairs...	150	
Maintenance..	100	
Property tax..		$200
Insurance...		300
Totals...	$2,250	$500
Deduct costs added.................................	500	
Net annual operating saving of new machine, before income tax......................................	$1,750	

Some analysts prefer to list all of the costs of each alternative, whether or not they are different, as a reminder to consider all possible points of difference between the plans.

Computing the rate of return

EXAMPLE 2(c): The illustrated asset replacement problem may be summarized as follows: the new machine will require an additional initial cash outlay of $7,000; it is expected to reduce cash payments for operating costs by $1,750 a year for the next 5 years, a total of $8,750. Does the expected future saving justify the additional asset investment?

SOLUTION:
$$P = \frac{S}{R} = \frac{\$7,000}{\$1,750}$$
$$P = 4.000$$

The table of the present value of an annuity of $1 in Appendix 21-B shows the following:

Years	6%	8%	10%
5..................................	4.21236	3.993	3.791

The expected rate of return on the investment in the new machine is slightly less than 8 per cent. The exact indicated rate could be determined by interpolating between 8 per cent and 6 per cent in the table, but this refinement is unwarranted. The estimated future savings, their timing, and their duration are by nature rough approximations; therefore, it seems desirable to round the estimated rate of return to the nearest whole per cent.

Conclusion: If the average cost of capital for the company is less than 8 per cent and the risk associated with this type of investment is not considered to be unusual, the company should replace the machine.

Special problems in estimating the rate of return

Example 2 illustrated the computation of an investment's estimated rate of return under simple assumptions. It was designed merely to show

how to apply the basic mechanics of the method. The following paragraphs explain briefly how to deal with some more complicated factors which are encountered in actual practice.

(a) *Unequal annual differential receipts.* If the variations in the annual receipts expected from a capital investment are relatively small, a satisfactory approximation of the rate of return may be calculated by using the average annual receipts. If the annual variations are significant, the following trial-and-error method should be used:

(1) Multiply the receipts of each year by the present value of $1 for the number of time periods from the present to that particular year, using a trial interest rate;

(2) The products, representing the present value of each annual receipt, added together should equal the net initial investment.

Usually several interest rates must be tried before the correct one is found. An illustration of the trial-and-error method may be found in the *Accountant's Handbook.*[1]

(b) *Substantial salvage value at end of life.* A substantial salvage value expected to be realized at the end of an asset's life may be treated as a cash receipt of the last year. This plan will probably cause the expected annual receipts to be unequal, in which case the trial-and-error method outlined in (a) is appropriate.

(c) *Investments with lives of different length.* The rates of return on capital investments which are mutually exclusive should be compared for the same time period. If it is a question of buying Machine *A*, which has an estimated useful life of 10 years, or Machine *B*, with an estimated life of 12 years, the comparison should be made for a 10-year period. The expected salvage value of Machine *B* at the end of 10 years, if substantial, can be treated as a receipt of the tenth year.

(d) *Investments with varying degrees of uncertainty.* When there is a strong chance that an investment will result in receipts materially below or above its most probable receipts, three computations of its rate of return may be helpful: one using the *most likely* annual receipts; another using the *highest probable* annual receipts; and a third using the *lowest probable* annual receipts. This range of probable annual rates of return helps management allow for the uncertainty of the investment in evaluating its desirability. Sometimes the possible loss associated with a particular investment is so great that, even though the chance of its occurring is slight, the investment should be rejected because of its potential danger to the business.

EXAMPLE 3:   Management feels that the most likely saving from the purchase of the new machine in Example 2 is $1,750, but that the average annual

---

[1] Rufus Wixon and Walter G. Kell, eds., *Accountant's Handbook*, 4th ed. (New York: The Ronald Press Company, 1957), Chap. 9, pp. 81 and 82.

saving may be as much as $2,500 or as little as $1,500. What is the most probable rate of return, and what is the range of expected rates?

SOLUTION:
$$P = \frac{S}{R} = \frac{\$7,000}{\$2,500}$$
$$P = 2.800$$

P tables for 5 years show a ratio of 2.864 for 22 per cent and 2.745 for 24 per cent, so that the indicated *highest* probable rate of return is about 23 per cent.

$$P = \frac{\$7,000}{\$1,500}$$
$$P = 4.667$$

P tables for 5 years show a ratio of 4.452 for 4 per cent and 4.713 for 2 per cent, so that the *lowest* probable rate of return is slightly more than 2 per cent.

Summary: The most likely rate of return on the new machine is 8 per cent (see Example 2(c)), but the rate may be as low as 2 per cent or as high as 23 per cent.

Another approach is to group together for consideration investments which are thought to have a similar degree of uncertainty. A different minimum acceptable rate of return is then set for investments in each group.

Rate of return after income tax

When the alternatives being compared do not require any initial capital investment, their relative desirability can be determined just as well by using expected net annual receipts before income tax as by using receipts after tax. Although the after-tax receipts will be reduced by income tax at the rate applicable to the business, the receipts from each alternative will be reduced in the same proportion.

When the alternatives do require an initial capital investment which is subject to amortization for income tax purposes (for example, depreciable equipment), the timing of taxable income by periods will differ from the timing of net cash receipts by periods. This is true because periodic *cost amortization* does not require a cash payment; rather, it is the *purchase* of the depreciable asset that requires cash. Amortization of an asset's cost does affect cash flow indirectly, however, through its effect on the amount of periodic income tax. Because the tax rates applicable to a business are often quite high, the desirability of investments which are subject to amortization should be compared on the basis of their after-tax rates of return. The method of making such after-tax comparisons is described in Chapter 24, "Planning and Accounting for Income Taxes."

The use of accelerated depreciation for income tax purposes usually increases the rate of return which a business can earn on a new investment, especially if accelerated depreciation is permissible for the new asset but not for the old. The effect of the accelerated depreciation methods, which are described in Chapter 24, is to increase the net cash receipts of the early years by decreasing tax payments, and to decrease the receipts of the later years. A stream of declining annual receipts has a greater present value (and yields a greater rate of return) than a uniform stream which totals the same amount for a given period of years.

APPROXIMATE METHODS OF COMPARING PLANS

The payoff period method

One commonly used method of evaluating alternative capital expenditures is to determine the *payoff period* of each—the length of time it will probably require the additional cash receipts from its operations to equal its additional capital investment. The formula for computing the payoff period is:

$$\frac{\text{Differential capital investment } (S)}{\text{Differential annual net receipts } (R)} = \text{Payoff period } (n).$$

Note that this is the same ratio which is computed as a first step in determining the time-adjusted rate of return.

EXAMPLE 4:   Using the data of Example 2, the payoff period of the new machine would be computed thus:

$$\frac{S}{R} = \frac{\$7,000}{\$1,750} = 4 \text{ years.}$$

Conclusion: This machine replacement would get the nod over a competitor for capital funds which had a similar risk but a payoff period of 5 years.

Some companies have established arbitrary maximum acceptable payoff periods for accepting or rejecting investments in assets of various types. The riskier the investment, the shorter is the maximum acceptable payoff period.

The payoff period method is simple but crude. It does not give any weight to differences in the useful lives of the competing assets beyond the ends of their payoff periods. Applying it strictly would result in selecting Machine A with a payoff period of 5 years and a useful life of 6 years over Machine B with a payoff period of 6 years and a useful life of 10 years, although the latter would give the business a higher rate of return on the capital employed.

The payoff period method is perhaps best suited to situations where it is imperative that the cash outlay for new assets be recovered as rapidly as possible, or where their risk of obsolescence within a very few years is great. For the first use, it is inferior to a cash budget, because it does not reflect differences in annual receipts. Perhaps the method should be used only to test plans quickly to see whether they merit more refined analysis. If an investment's payoff period is longer than its estimated useful life, it should obviously be rejected. If its payoff period is short in comparison with that of other projects, it warrants further investigation.

Rate of return unadjusted for time differences

A second approximate method computes the expected annual rate of return on a capital investment for its entire useful life, but without allowing for differences in the timing of cash receipts and payments. The formula is:

$$\frac{\text{Additional annual income}}{\text{Average additional investment}} = \text{Unadjusted rate of return.}$$

The additional annual income may be before or after considering income tax, although the latter is preferable. The additional annual income before tax is computed by subtracting an *annual allowance for the recovery of the additional investment* (amortization) from the annual operating saving. The average additional investment is determined by adding the additional initial investment to the additional ending salvage value, and dividing the sum by 2.

The following illustration shows the computation of the unadjusted rate of return before tax on Company X's proposed new machine.

EXAMPLE 5:

Annual operating saving (from Example 2(b))............................. $1,750
Deduct annual capital recovery allowance ($7,000 additional investment
   divided by estimated life of 5 years)................................. 1,400
Additional annual income before tax..................................... $ 350
Additional initial investment.. $7,000
Add expected salvage value... 0
   Total... $7,000
Average additional investment = $7,000/2.............................. $3,500

Unadjusted rate of return before tax $= \dfrac{\$350}{\$3,500} = 10\%.$

The principal weakness of the unadjusted rate of return method is that it ignores differences in timing. It values a dollar of savings to be realized 10 or 15 years in the future just as highly as a dollar expected next year, thus overstating the computed rate of return. While the unadjusted rate in Example 5 is 10 per cent, it would be 8 per cent if allowances were made for differences in the timing of receipts.

USING THE CAPITAL BUDGET

The annual capital additions budget

The capital additions budget for the next year should include the proposed outlays for the *specific* long-lived assets which the business plans to acquire during that period, classified by areas of responsibility, together with the means of financing them. Example 6 shows a part of such a budget which applies to a single department of the business.

EXAMPLE 6:

MODERN PRODUCTS COMPANY
Shipping Department
Capital Additions Budget
Year Ending December 31, 19x2

L. Watt, Manager

| | | Expected | | Expected | |
| | | Starting | Completion | Monthly Payments | |
Item	Total Cost	Date	Date	January	February
Plant:					
Platform..............	$ 4,000	1/15/x2	4/1/x2	$1,500	$1,800
Rail siding.............	7,000	2/1	5/1		2,500
	$11,000				
Equipment:					
Scales.................	$ 500		6/1		
Truck.................	3,500		1/5	3,500	
	$ 4,000				
Grand Total.............	$15,000			$5,000	$4,300

The form should, of course, be extended to include cash requirements for each month of the year.

Some assets in next year's budget will be acquired to replace others which have worn out or become outmoded; others will be needed to facilitate expected additional sales or to reduce operating costs; still others will be needed to carry out new activities. Many of these investments will have been selected on the basis of an evaluation of their potential rates of return, together with qualitative considerations. All of them should be consistent with the long-range capital budget.

The *cash forecast* for the coming year should include an estimate of the outlay for each capital addition which is large enough to justify individual planning. It should also contain lump-sum provisions for estimated minor capital expenditures which individually are too small to warrant separate planning.

Administering the capital budget

Responsibility for originating a request to purchase a long-lived asset in most cases rests with the department head who will be responsible for its use. He may have the capacity to authorize small capital additions without further approval, but larger projects require careful screening at higher levels of management.

Mere inclusion of a capital-addition item in the annual budget is not an authorization to purchase it. Careful control requires that specific approval be obtained before each order is placed, based upon a consideration of the current availability of funds and of changes in asset requirements. The desirability of major projects is thus examined three times: first, in a broad way in the long-range budget; second, in the annual budget; and third, at the time the order is placed.

Frequent reports on the status of spending in comparison with the capital budget should be made to those who are in a position to control the amount of expenditures, particularly for projects which require a long time to complete. Where possible each budget allowance should be based on a desirable standard of cost for the acquisition. The following is an illustration of such a report.

EXAMPLE 7:

MODERN PRODUCTS COMPANY
Shipping Department
Capital Additions Report
Month Ending February 28, 19x2

L. Watt, Manager

Item	Budget Allowance	Actual Cost This Month	Actual Cost To Date	Estimated Total Cost	Estimated Under (Over) Budget	Explanation
Plant:						
Platform....	$ 4,000	$1,602	$2,105	$ 3,900	$100	
Rail siding...	7,000	2,880	2,880	7,400	(400)	Increased
Total.....	11,000					rail costs.
Equipment:						
Scales.......	$ 500	0	0	500	—	
Truck.......	3,500	3,490	3,490*	3,490*	10	
Grand total....	$15,000	$7,972	$8,475	$15,290	($290)	

* Completed project.

Supplementary data should include the expected completion date of projects and comments on factors which have caused delays or major changes in costs. The recipient of the report should require further investigation, when needed, of the causes of departures from budget allowances. He should then initiate steps to bring the costs into line. A further means of focusing attention on deviations from the plan is to require special approval for each expenditure in excess of the original authorization.

Appraising the performance of investments

If management is to apply the lessons of past experience in improving income, it must evaluate the performance of capital additions after they have been acquired. Even if capital investments have been selected on the basis of a rigorous analysis of their expected profitability, follow-through is needed to assure that the expectations are fulfilled. Periodic comparisons, at least on a test basis, should be made to determine how well the actual performance of an asset measures up to expectations. If actual results are below the estimates, action should be initiated to improve them. When the fault lies in inaccurate estimating, efforts should be made to improve future estimates of acquisition costs, useful lives, and operating savings.

Summary

Comparisons of the desirability of business projects should be based on the expected behavior of many factors in the *future*. Some of these factors can be expressed in the common denominator of dollars of *differential costs* or *differential revenues* of the projects; others cannot. The use of a formal outline for estimating the effects of alternatives, however, helps to make comparisons objective and to bring the relevant factors into view. The outline should consist roughly of the following steps:

(1) Recognizing a business need and the alternative ways of filling it;
(2) Estimating and weighing the quantitative factors relating to each alternative;
(3) Weighing the qualitative factors;
(4) Reaching a decision, even if some of the information is not so complete as desired.

In spite of the apparent precision of the methods used in estimating the relative future profitability of alternatives, the reader must remember that the comparisons are *merely estimates*. Furthermore, the many factors bearing on a decision which cannot be expressed in terms of dollar costs must not be overlooked. Finally, planning alone will not bring about increased income. *Action* must be taken to bring performance into line with the plans when the plans are sound, and to improve planning when they are not.

QUESTIONS AND PROBLEMS

22-1   In controlling the acquisition of long-lived assets most companies subject each project to analysis at least three different times. What are these occasions, and why is each analysis desirable?

22-2 Many companies have very thorough procedures for authorizing the acquisition of new long-lived assets, but less adequate procedures for authorizing their disposal.

REQUIRED:

a. What possibilities of fraud, error, or waste are associated with the retirement of movable equipment?

b. How would you recommend that these weaknesses be eliminated or minimized?

22-3 ". . . the selection of specific long-lived assets has a far-reaching effect on the productive capacity of the business . . . and the amount of its operating expenses."

REQUIRED:

Give examples of costs which will be largely fixed as a result of a business' decision to purchase a particular type of air-conditioning equipment for its sales and office building.

22-4 In 19x1 a company finds that the prospective rates of return on capital additions are substantially less than they have been in recent years.

REQUIRED:

State the likely reasons for this change, and give management advice which is appropriate in each case.

22-5 A manufacturing company is contemplating adding a newly developed line which will require an investment which is substantial in relation to its present assets. According to all indications, the line will be well received; however, little of the capital can be recovered if the product turns out to be a failure.

REQUIRED:

Outline the type of analysis which you would present to management to take these factors into consideration.

22-6 In preparing your company's capital budget for the coming year, you find that some projects will apparently yield very stable and highly predictable results; others will be more irregular and uncertain; and still others will be characterized by a very high degree of uncertainty.

REQUIRED:

State how you would allow for these differences in uncertainty in presenting comparisons of the projects to the board of directors for final decision.

22-7 In comparing the desirability of Project X with Project Y, a company's treasurer arrives at the following results:

	Project X	Project Y
Additional capital outlay.....................	$20,000	$21,000
Estimated useful life........................	5 years	10 years
Estimated net annual operating saving.........	$ 5,000	$ 3,000

REQUIRED:

a. Compute the time-adjusted rate of return on each project.

b. The company has noted a decline in the prospective and actual rates of return on its capital additions during the past few years. In view of this fact, which project would you advise the company to select? Explain.

22-8 "The unexpired cost of the asset to be replaced should be ignored in computing the difference in the capital cost of the old and new assets."

Early in 19x3, management is considering replacing Machine 1, which had an original cost of $7,000 and has accumulated depreciation of $4,500 on the basis of a 10-year life, with Machine 2. The latter has a cash cost of $12,000 without trade-in, or $10,000 if Machine 1 is traded. Machine 2 has an expected life of 10 years; Machine 1 could conceivably be used for 5 more years.

REQUIRED:

a. Prepare journal entries for 19x3 and 19x4, assuming that Machine 1 is replaced.
b. Prepare entries for 19x3 and 19x4, assuming that Machine 1 is retained.
c. Present comparative income statements (partial) for the 5-year period affected by the decision, and state whether you think this comparison proves or disproves the quotation.

22-9   The process of comparing alternative long-lived asset acquisitions is very complex and time-consuming. Businesses often have many alternative ways of performing a given job, and there may be hundreds of jobs within a business for which capital expenditures should be considered.

REQUIRED:

a. To what extent would you recommend that differential comparisons of the type illustrated in this chapter be made for these alternatives?
b. In situations for which you do not think such differential comparisons are appropriate, how would you suggest that the business make capital expenditure decisions?

22-10   The British Government issues perpetual bonds, called *Consols*, which promise the holder a periodic nominal interest payment. The bonds never mature.

REQUIRED:

a. Assume that a hypothetical Consol gives the owner the right to receive a cash payment of $100 at the end of each year. What is it worth if investments of similar risk are yielding an annual rate of return of 4%?
b. What conditions would cause the value of the Consol to change? Illustrate.

22-11

REQUIRED:

Using tables where needed, make the following computations.

a. An additional investment of $5,000 is expected to result in annual operating savings of $400 for 20 years. What is its time-adjusted rate of return?
b. The payoff period of an investment of $8,000, which has an estimated useful life of 15 years, is expected to be 11.1 years.

(1) What is the expected annual operating saving?
(2) What is the time-adjusted rate of return?

c. What maximum price can a company afford to pay for an asset which will probably yield an annual additional net revenue of $300 for 5 years, if the company's best alternative use of capital will pay a rate of return of 8 per cent?
d. How much can a company afford to pay for each dollar of annual operating savings expected from an investment estimated to have a useful life of 10 years, if the company's alternative investments of similar risk are yielding a return of 10 per cent?
e. A capital outlay which is expected to yield a rate of return of 6 per cent has a cash payoff period of 10.1 years. What is the estimated useful life of the investment?

22-12

a. Why might the prospective rate of return on a given investment be different for a company at different times?
b. Why might it be different for different companies at the same time?
c. Why might one company select a machine and another reject it, both on the basis of its estimated time-adjusted rate of return?

22-13 The Yarmouth Company estimates that it will have $50,000 available for capital expenditures during 19x3. Of this amount, $20,000 is to be reserved for emergency projects and projects which cannot be postponed. The company uses the payoff period as the basis for determining the most desirable capital expenditures. The following additions are being considered for 19x3:

Project Number	Additional Capital Investment	Expected Annual Income	Estimated Life in Years
101	$10,000	$2,500	5
102	10,000	3,000	4
103	8,000	1,600	7
104	8,000	2,000	4
105	4,000	500	15
106	2,000	500	6
107	2,000	1,000	2
108	5,000	500	20
109	5,000	1,250	3
110	10,000	1,250	15

REQUIRED:

a. Rank the projects in the order of their desirability under the payoff period method.
b. Assuming that none of the proposed additions will have any salvage value at the end of their useful lives, determine the time-adjusted rate of return on each (estimated to the nearest whole per cent).
c. Explain any glaring inconsistencies between your results in (a) and (b).
d. What additional data should be obtained before preparing the final capital additions budget? How should they be used?
e. Submit your recommended capital additions budget for 19x3.

22-14 A real estate company owns two identical business buildings, each of which is leased for the next 5 years. The terms of each lease are as follows:

(1) The tenant of Building No. 1 has agreed to pay annual rent of $1,000 at the end of each year.

(2) The tenant of Building No. 2 has agreed to pay a minimum annual rental of $800 at the end of each year, and an additional amount equal to 1 per cent of the sum by which its sales exceed $100,000. During the last three years, respectively, the tenant has paid rentals of $1,020, $900, and $1,080.

It may be assumed that the annual operating costs are $200 for each building. Each has a resale value of $3,000 now, and is expected to have no salvage value at the end of five years.

REQUIRED:

a. Compare the expected rates of return on the two buildings.
b. What other factors should be considered before deciding which asset is likely to provide the better return?

22-15 The following are examples of general problems that are often encountered in comparing the desirability of alternative uses of capital. Explain how you would handle each item in making such a comparison.

a. Machine A is expected to have a useful life of 5 more years; Machine B, a candidate to replace it, has an expected useful life of 10 years.

b. Machine C is expected to result in greatest additional annual receipts in the early years of its life; Machine D, its competitor, is expected to result in greatest additional annual receipts in the late years of its life.

c. Machine E is expected to result in additional receipts of a stable annual amount throughout its life; Machine F, being considered as an alternative to it, may result in very high additional receipts or no additional receipts at all.

d. Machine G has an unamortized cost of $8,000. If it is replaced by Machine H it can be sold for only $2,000. Machine H can be purchased outright for $20,000.

e. Machine I has an operating capacity of 9,000 units of product a year; Machine J, a proposed replacement, has a capacity of 25,000 units a year.

f. If Machine K is purchased to do work that is now done chiefly by hand, it will replace 5 men who now earn $4,000 a year each. The company's policy is to assign men displaced by technological improvements to other jobs in the business.

22-16 In a meeting on March 11, 19x1, the board of directors of Z Company authorized the construction of a new warehouse for the company at a total cost of $400,000. It was expected that the project would be begun on April 1, 19x1, and be completed by April 30, 19x3. Construction work was to be done by the company's own employees.

Construction was actually begun on May 1, 19x1. On December 31, 19x2, the following information was collected:

Costs incurred through December 31, 19x1.......................... $151,200
Costs incurred in 19x2...   217,800
Unfilled orders for materials on 12/31/19x2..........................   11,000
Estimated percentage of total cost incurred through 12/31/19x2........   80%
Estimated percentage of total construction time elapsed through
    12/31/19x2...   75%

REQUIRED:

a. Arranging the information in orderly form, prepare a report of the status of the construction project for the board of directors as of December 31, 19x2.

b. What additional information do you think should be included in the report?

c. Illustrate how the facts would appear in the statement of financial position on December 31, 19x2.

CASE 22-1. CAROLINA EQUIPMENT COMPANY

In making its decisions on capital investment proposals which are expected to cost more than $5,000 and to last more than two years, the Carolina Equipment Company uses the time-adjusted rate of return method. The company reviews each such accepted investment shortly after installation and again at the end of one year of operation, in order to find out whether the asset is operating according to plan.

In 19x1 the company was considering whether to install a group of labor-saving machines which were expected to cost $15,000, to have a useful life of 5 years, and to reduce labor requirements by 3,000 man-hours a year at an average cost of $2 an hour. The machines were expected to require power at a cost of $400 a year, insurance and property taxes at 3 per cent of their book value at the beginning of each year, and maintenance costs increasing gradually from $300 in the first year to $700 in the fifth. The machines were expected to have no net salvage value at the end of their lives and were to be depreciated by the straight-line method.

Estimating that the rate of return on this investment would be 2 per cent above its minimum for outlays of this type, the company purchased the equipment early in 19x2.

At the end of 19x2, the subsidiary records for equipment showed the following regarding these machines.

1/17/19x2	Invoice cost...............................	$14,000
	Transportation in...........................	400
	Installation.................................	300

The company had an unusually difficult time putting the machines into operating order and charged $600, which it considered as excessive installation cost, to 19x2 expense. Maintenance for the year was $390, insurance $150, and power $420. No property taxes were assessed on the machines, since the company did not own them on January 1. It was estimated that the machines had actually saved 2,600 man-hours, but a new union contract went into effect July 1, 19x2, increasing the wage rate to $2.40 per hour. The deficiency in man-hours saved resulted largely from the excessive break-in period.

REQUIRED:

a. Compute the rate of return which the company expected on this investment in 19x1.
b. Prepare an analysis comparing the actual results for 19x2 with the expected results.
c. Make such explanatory comments as you think are necessary to evaluate the actual results of this investment.
d. Make, and justify, a revised estimate of the rate of return on the investment on the basis of all information which you have at the end of 19x2.

CASE 22-2. ACE PUBLISHING COMPANY

Ace Publishing Company is in the business of publishing and printing guide books and directories. The board of directors has engaged you to make a cost study to determine whether the company is economically justified in continuing to print, as well as publish, its books and directories. You obtain the following information from the company's cost accounting records for the preceding fiscal year:

	Departments			
	Publishing	Printing	Shipping	Total
Salaries and wages.................	$275,000	$150,000	$25,000	$ 450,000
Telephone and telegraph............	12,000	3,700	300	16,000
Materials and supplies..............	50,000	250,000	10,000	310,000
Occupancy costs....................	75,000	80,000	10,000	165,000
General and administrative.........	40,000	30,000	4,000	74,000
Depreciation.......................	5,000	40,000	5,000	50,000
	$457,000	$553,700	$54,300	$1,065,000

Additional data:

1. A review of personnel requirements indicates that, if printing is discontinued, the publishing department will need one additional clerk at $4,000 per year to handle correspondence with the printer. Two layout men and a proofreader will be required at an aggregate annual cost of $17,000; other personnel in the printing department can be released. One mailing clerk, at $3,000, will be retained; others in the shipping department can be released. Employees whose employment was being terminated would immediately receive, on the average, three months' termination pay. The termination pay would be amortized over a 5-year period.

2. Long-distance telephone and telegraph charges are identified and distributed to the responsible department. The remainder of the telephone bill, representing basic service at a cost of $4,000, was allocated in the ratio of 10 to publishing, 5 to printing, and 1 to shipping. The discontinuance of printing is not expected to have a material effect on the basic service cost.

3. Shipping supplies consist of cartons, envelopes, and stamps. It is estimated that the cost of envelopes and stamps for mailing material to an outside printer would be $5,000 per year.

4. If printing is discontinued, the company would retain its present building, but would sublet a portion of the space at an annual rental of $50,000. Taxes, insurance, heat, light, and other occupancy costs would not be significantly affected.

5. One cost clerk would not be required ($5,000 per year) if printing is discontinued. Other general and administrative personnel would be retained.

6. Included in administrative expenses is interest expense on a 5 per cent mortgage loan of $500,000.

7. Printing and shipping-room machinery and equipment having a net book value of $300,000 can be sold without gain or loss. These funds in excess of termination pay would be invested in marketable securities earning 5 per cent.

8. The company has received a proposal for a 5-year contract from an outside printer, under which the volume of work done last year would be printed at a cost of $550,000 per year.

9. Assume continued volume and prices at last year's level.

REQUIRED:

Prepare a statement setting forth in comparative form the costs of operation of the printing and shipping departments under the present arrangement and under an arrangement in which inside printing is discontinued. Summarize the net saving or extra cost in case printing is discontinued.

(AICPA Examination in Accounting Practice.)

CASE 22-3. MORGAN MANUFACTURING COMPANY

At the end of 19x1 Morgan Manufacturing Company is trying to evaluate the relative desirability of acquiring Machine B or Machine C to replace Machine A, which is worn out. The machine selected will be used to make the company's entire output of Product No. 1, a staple article which the company sells for $1 a unit. The following information was taken from the accounting records for 19x1.

Sales, 4,000 units at $1
Units produced, 4,000
Material cost, 13,200 pounds at 15¢
Operator's labor cost, 500 hours at $2
Depreciation on Machine A, $1,000

Building rent and maintenance allocated to Machine A on the basis of floor space occupied, $300

Property taxes and insurance, $100

Other variable costs, $0.05 per unit of product.

Machine A had an original cost of $10,000, and its accumulated depreciation at the end of 19x1 is $8,500. Its trade-in allowance on either Machine B or Machine C will be $1,000.

The following estimated data relate to Machines B and C.

	Machine B	Machine C
List price...	$9,000	$12,000
Estimated useful life...................................	10 years	10 years
Productive capacity, in units per year...................	6,000	10,000
Estimated salvage value................................	0	0
Material usage per unit of product......................	3 pounds	3.5 pounds
Cost of material per pound.............................	.14	.14
Operator's labor time in hours per unit of product.........	.10 hour	.04 hour
Operator's wage rate per hour..........................	$ 2.20	$ 2.50
Building rent and maintenance allocated to machine on basis of floor space occupied...............................	$ 300	$ 400
Other variable costs per unit of product.................	$ 0.05	$ 0.05
Shipping cost of machine...............................	$ 400	$ 600
Installation cost of machine............................	$ 200	$ 200
Machine insurance and property taxes...................	$ 270	$ 360
Fringe labor costs as a percentage of labor cost............	20%	20%

The machine chosen will be operated by an employee who tends a group of similar machines. Machine C is semi-automatic, and, although it will require the attention of a more skilled operator than will Machine B, it will require less of the operator's time. Machine C will cause a higher rate of scrap material, indicated by its greater usage of material per unit of product. A greater share of the building rent and maintenance cost will be allocated to Machine C because it requires more space; however, unused space is now readily available.

The sales manager expects that sales of Product No. 1 will average 5,000 units per year for the next few years.

REQUIRED:

a. Prepare condensed estimated income statements for 19x2, (1) assuming that Machine B is purchased and (2) assuming that Machine C is purchased.

b. Compute the unadjusted rate of return on each machine.

c. Compare the two machines on the basis of their time-adjusted rates of return.

d. Has the company selected the right alternatives for consideration? Explain.

e. List and evaluate other factors which you think are important in reaching a decision.

f. State your decision, supporting it by appropriate justification.

CASE 22-4. THE ELDORADO SALES COMPANY

In December, 19x4, Mr. William Certa, general sales manager of The Eldorado Sales Company, was deeply involved in planning his recommendations for the 19x5 operating and capital additions budgets for the sales division. One particularly knotty problem dealt with the amount required for operating expenses for salesmen's automobiles; another, with the amount of capital that would be required to finance needed automobile replacements and the source of obtaining it.

The company employed two regional sales managers, each of whom supervised the work of four traveling salesmen. For a number of years, the company had furnished automobiles to the salesmen and regional sales managers. Recently, however, profit margins had become very thin because of competitive conditions, and the operating costs for the automobiles had increased. Furthermore, the company's needs for funds for financing working capital and other items were greater than the available supply. As a result, Mr. James Glammon, the company's controller, had asked Mr. Certa to review the policy of furnishing automobiles very carefully and to submit an analysis of alternatives for consideration by the president and the board of directors.

The company used medium-priced automobiles for the salesmen and had followed a policy of keeping them in good operating condition and good appearance. It computed depreciation under the straight-line method at 25 per cent a year, and replaced automobiles when they had been driven 60,000 miles or were 3 years old, whichever occurred first. In this way the company had attempted to avoid major repair bills.

In the past, there had been a tendency for maintenance costs to become excessive, and the company required that work be done through authorized dealers for the make of car involved. Repair bills were submitted to Mr. Certa's office, where detailed records were kept of the mileage and maintenance costs for each car.

Lately Mr. Certa had found that he was spending more and more of his time trying to keep maintenance costs within reasonable bounds, trying to eliminate the use of the cars for personal purposes, listening to salesmen's complaints that their cars were too cheap or out of date, and listening to the sales managers' reports of abuse of the company's automobiles. Complaints of this type were interfering with his more important tasks of planning ways to increase sales volume and increase margins.

The following data were taken from the individual records of each automobile for 19x4.

Automobile	Cost	Accumulated Depreciation to 12/31/19x4	Estimated miles in 19x4	Estimated total miles end of 19x4
1	$ 2,800	$ 2,100	12,000	32,000
2	2,400	1,800	21,000	58,000
3	2,400	1,800	24,000	61,000
4	2,400	1,800	21,000	55,000
5	2,600	1,300	16,000	35,000
6	3,200	1,600	7,000	11,000
7	2,600	975	23,000	34,000
8	2,600	975	22,000	35,000
9	2,600	650	19,000	19,000
10	2,600	650	17,000	17,000
Totals	$26,200	$13,650	182,000	357,000

In past years the company had found very little variation between the book value of the old automobiles at the time they were traded in and the trade-in allowances received for them.

Automobiles Nos. 1 and 6 were assigned to the regional sales managers; the rest, to the salesmen under their supervision. The company's policy has been to purchase slightly larger and more luxurious cars for the sales managers. At the end of 19x4, current replacement cost for a car of the type furnished the managers was $3,400, and for a car of the salesmen's type, $2,700.

Cost records kept by Mr. Certa's office for the past 5 years showed the following average variable operating costs per mile:

Gas..	2.10¢
Oil and lubrication.......................................	.30
Tires and tubes..	.35
Maintenance...	.30
Total..	3.05¢

In estimating costs for 19x5, Mr. Certa thought that an upward adjustment of 5 per cent should be made to allow for increased prices.

Other expenses per year for each car were:

Liability insurance.......................................	$130
Wash...	18
Licenses and tax...	20
Anti-freeze and miscellaneous............................	15
Depreciation (average for 19x4)..........................	655
Total..	$838

These costs were reasonably representative of costs current at the end of 19x4.

Mr. Certa had investigated the possibility of leasing all of the salesmen's cars under a plan whereby the Eldorado Sales Company would pay a fixed monthly rental per car, which would include all expenses of operation except gasoline and oil, washing, garaging, and liability insurance. The leasing company would assume the responsibility of keeping cars in good condition and would pay for regular oil changes, lubrication, tires and tubes, repairs, and anti-freeze. One company had quoted a flat monthly rate of $110 a month for a salesman's car of the type now used by the company, and $120 a month for a sales manager's car. The lease would run for a period of 18 months.

Mr. Certa thought that leasing would have a great potential advantage in freeing the company's funds for other needs. He also hoped to release some of his time and that of an office clerk from many of the details of keeping and analyzing the automobile operating reports. One of his business acquaintances who used a leasing plan stated, however, that his salesmen were somewhat dissatisfied with the limited choice of models which they were allowed under his leasing plan.

One of the regional sales managers, Mr. French, suggested that Mr. Certa consider the possibility of allowing the salesmen to furnish their own cars and of reimbursing them for mileage traveled on company business. Mr. French described the following plan that had been in effect in a company for which he had previously worked.

Salesmen were classified into two groups for purposes of automobile expense reimbursement.

Group 1 consisted of those who drove less than 12,000 miles a year. The company paid them 10 cents a mile for the first 2,000 miles traveled in a year, and 8 cents a mile for additional mileage up to 12,000. Each man paid for his own liability insurance as well as all other operating costs.

Group 2 consisted of employees who drove more than 12,000 miles a year. The company paid each salesman a fixed monthly allowance of $50 to cover depreciation, registration, washing, and similar expenses, and 3 cents a mile to cover gasoline, oil, tires, grease, and similar running expenses.

"Of course," said Mr. French, "that was several years ago, and the rates may not reflect current costs. Nevertheless, I think the plan was most successful from the point of view of the company and the salesman."

Mr. Certa had reservations about this plan, because he had heard complaints from several of his friends about inadequate allowances for car operation in the face of mounting costs. He also remembered an occasion many years earlier when he had been unable to accept a job because he did not have the funds to buy his own car. Still, the possibility of eliminating the headaches of keeping records of operating costs and trying to eliminate abuses appealed to him.

REQUIRED:

a. List the principal alternatives, and their principal variations, that should be considered by Mr. Certa. Outline the advantages and disadvantages of each.

b. Make a rate-of-return comparison of the three principal alternatives: (1) company-owned, (2) salesman-owned, and (3) leased automobiles. Explain the reasons for any assumptions you make.

c. What plan should Mr. Certa recommend?

(Source: Background information adapted from *Automobile Plans for Salesmen*, Studies in Business Policy, No. 76, National Industrial Conference Board, Inc., 1955. All facts and figures in this case are hypothetical.)

Chapter 23

Estimating the Value of a Business

Occasions for making an estimate

A person who is contemplating selling his business, or a large share in it, and a person who is thinking of buying a business are both interested in making a careful estimate of what it is worth. Their points of view are quite different, of course; the seller will attempt to justify as high a selling price as he can, and the purchaser will attempt to get the lowest possible price.

Estimates of the value of a business are also often important when the business is being reorganized, refinanced, or combined with other businesses by means of a merger or a consolidation; when it is attempting to arrange for a substantial amount of borrowing; when it must be appraised for the purpose of paying income, estate, or property taxes; and, in the case of a regulated public utility, when the fairness of the rates that it charges is being reviewed by the regulatory body.

The approach used in estimating the value of a business depends to some extent on the purpose for which the valuation is being made. The estimated worth of a business used in determining whether its rates are fair to its customers as well as to its owners may differ somewhat from its estimated worth to a purchaser. The approach used in this chapter is that of a buyer or seller of a business.

Limitations of historical cost

Business accounting for general purposes is based upon objective information which is derived from completed transactions. Monetary assets, such as cash and receivables, are measured by their realizable values, but the other assets of a business are customarily measured by their unexpired cost. If cost is suitable as a basis for measurement in the day-to-day accounting of a business, why is it unsuitable when a business is being appraised for the purpose of sale?

A purchaser of any asset is interested in it because of its potential usefulness to him in the future. If he is negotiating for the purchase of land which the seller originally bought for $3,000 twenty years ago, he still expects to pay a price which reflects the present market price of similar land—whether it is $1,000 or $1,000,000. Moreover, the seller will miss opportunities for maximizing his income (or minimizing his losses) if he treats historical cost, or the unexpired part of it, as the measure of value for purposes of sale.

EXAMPLE 1:   A company owns a machine which cost $10,000 six years ago, and on which it has accumulated depreciation of $6,000 in its accounting records. Because of recent rapid technological developments, the machine is useless to the company. It can be sold now for $500; if it is not sold now, it may be worthless within a year. What is the machine worth?

SOLUTION: The machine is worth $500 on the market. Its value in use to the company is zero. Even though its sale would require that a book loss of $3,500 be recorded, this is the best alternative open to the owner.

The reader should not conclude that recorded cost is useless as a guide in making business decisions, such as the price to ask or offer for a business. Although the significant values of assets for this purpose are current values, often there is no readily quoted market price for specialized assets. Their value depends upon their future contribution to the income of the business in the form of an excess of revenues over costs. Although actual past costs and revenues shown in the accounting records mean nothing in themselves, they are often the most useful starting point in estimating what future costs and revenues will be. They show what has happened and, with due allowance for known changes in conditions, give a much more reliable estimate of what the future will bring than do mere guesses.

Framework for estimating the value of a business

The general approach which has been presented in earlier chapters for estimating the rate of return or the present value of a single asset may also be used in estimating the rate of return or the value of an entire business. To its owners, a business is an asset held for the purpose of earning a return on the capital invested. If the current cost of a business, S, is known and a reasonable estimate can be made of its estimated stream of future net income, R, the anticipated rate of return on the investment can be determined. As explained in the preceding chapter, the steps in this calculation are:

(1) Determine the ratio of the present value of the asset to its future rents by substituting in the formula $P = \dfrac{S}{R}$; then,

(2) Using the table of the present value of an annuity in Appendix 21-B, follow the line for the appropriate number of periods to the interest rate column in which the computed P ratio is located. This rate is the estimated rate of return on the investment.

In most instances the present value of the business, S, will be the unknown. Given the estimated stream of future net income and the desired rate of return, the present value of the business can be estimated by using the formula in its form $S = R(P)$. The ratio for P is found in the tables at the intersection of the line for the estimated life and the column for the desired rate of return.

EXAMPLE 2:   A business is expected to earn net income of $5,000 for each of the next 10 years. Businesses of comparable risk generally earn a rate of return of 6 per cent of the capital sum invested. What is the business worth now?
 SOLUTION: $S = R(P) = \$5,000(7.360) = \$36,800.$

The reader should not be deceived by the apparent simplicity and exactness of the foregoing computations of the present value and expected rate of return of a business. Actually, the various components of the computation are usually so indefinite that they are a matter of bargaining between the seller of a business and the prospective buyer. The framework of the analysis is appropriate, however, and its use should give each of the parties an objective basis upon which to make his judgments. Later sections of this chapter offer suggestions for estimating the components of the analysis.

Liquidating value, replacement cost, and discounted earnings

The owner of a business generally would not sell it as an operating unit for less than he could receive for its various parts sold individually. For this reason, if the assets are readily salable, their *total liquidating value sets a lower limit to the value of the business*. If the value of the business in operation appears to be less than its liquidating value, and if this condition seems likely to persist, the owners should seriously consider liquidating it for whatever its assets will bring. As a practical matter, the liquidating value of specialized assets is usually far below their probable value in use. An extreme example is that of the roadbed of a railway, which cannot be moved elsewhere. It has value solely if it is used in its present location and if it will make a contribution to the future income of the business as a whole. The same is often true of intangibles such as organization costs, technical know-how, and patents.

At the other extreme, even though a business is very profitable, a buyer will not be willing to pay more for it than he would have to pay to duplicate its earning power. *Replacement cost* of the business as a whole, often estimated on the basis of what would have to be paid for a business of similar risk and earning power, therefore *sets the upper limit of value of the business entity.*

Between the break-up value as a minimum and replacement cost as a maximum there is a wide zone in which it is appropriate to estimate the value of a business by *discounting its expected stream of future earnings.*

Estimating the value of perpetuities

An investment which is expected to yield an income for an indefinitely long period is a *perpetuity*. The capital sum representing its present value will never be exhausted. Its present value, S, may be estimated by the formula

$$S = \frac{R}{i}$$

where R is the expected annual income and i is the rate of return which can be earned on investments of comparable risk.

EXAMPLE 3:   The income from an asset has been $1,000 for centuries, and seems likely to continue for centuries more. The best alternative investment of similar risk yields a rate of return of 5% a year. What is the asset worth?

SOLUTION: $S = \frac{R}{i} = \frac{\$1,000}{.05} = \$20,000.$

If the purchaser pays $20,000, his annual rate of return will be 5% ($1,000/$20,000) and his capital investment will continue to have a value indefinitely.

The computation of the present value of a perpetuity is appropriate in estimating the value of common or preferred stocks which are expected to continue to earn a fairly uniform annual return for a long period of time. In each case the owner expects a stream of income to continue while his capital remains approximately intact. Of course, these securities will not be expected to pay a return forever, but their income in distant future years has little effect on present-value computations.

EXAMPLE 4:   If the $1,000 annual return in Example 3 is expected to continue for only 50 years, the asset is worth $18,256, computed as follows:

$$S = R(P) = \$1,000(18.256) = \$18,256.$$

This value is not materially different from the present value of a perpetuity, $20,000, especially considering the degree of uncertainty associated with predicting amounts of income in the distant future and applicable interest rates. The present value of the $1,000 income for the fiftieth year is only $87(0.087 × $1,000), and more distant rents decline proportionately in present value.

The point of this illustration is that, when the income from an investment is expected to continue for a fairly long time, satisfactory estimates of present value may often be obtained by using the very simple formula for a perpetuity.

Estimating the value of a limited-term income stream

It is difficult to predict accurately what the revenue and expense of a business will be in the next year, and far more difficult to predict what they will be 10, 15, or 20 years in the future. For this reason some analysts, in estimating the present value of a business, view its income stream as an annuity which will last for a rather short span of time. Furthermore, the length of the venture's probable life is often so uncertain that they use a high rate of discount in estimating its present value.

EXAMPLE 5:   A business is expected to earn net income of $5,000 for each of the next 10 years. Businesses of comparable risk earn a rate of return of 6% of the capital sum invested. What is the business worth now?

SOLUTION: $S = R(P) = \$5,000(7.360) = \$36,800.$

The present value of a *perpetuity* of $5,000 would amount to $36,800 if an interest rate of approximately 13.6 per cent were used

$$\left(i = \frac{R}{S} = \frac{\$5,000}{\$36,800} = .136, \text{ or } 13.6 \text{ per cent}\right).$$

Steps in estimating the value of a business

The following are the important steps in estimating the value of a business enterprise:

(1) *Estimate future revenues and expenses.* It would be appropriate to use the cash receipts and payments for revenue and expense items, rather than accruals, if the former could be estimated accurately. However, accruals are usually a satisfactory substitute when estimating the value of an entire business. During the term for which the results of the business are being estimated, it will probably be necessary to make cash outlays to maintain the productive facilities represented by depreciable assets.

The pattern of revenue and expense should be estimated by years, if this can be done with any reliability. Usually, however, an expected average of revenues and expenses for future years which considers fluctuations above and below the typical figure is more reliable than estimates of the individual figures for each year.

Records of past revenues and operating costs may give very valuable clues to amounts to be expected in the future, but due allowance must be made for expected changes in prices, quantities, and mix of all of the components of revenue and expense. A good starting point is a series of income statements of the business for the past few years. A series of years is more appropriate than a single year because it is more likely to include the effects of cyclical upswings and downswings which have occurred in the past and which may be expected to recur, in some measure, in the future. The period should not be so long that it will be greatly affected by factors, within the business or external to it, which are no longer at work.

(2) *Estimate the length of time for which the expected income will continue.* Usually this term is highly indefinite, but it has been shown earlier that the expected income of years in the far-distant future has little influence on the resulting present value.

(3) *Determine the normal rate of return for the industry.* The appropriate rate for estimating the value of a business is the rate which is needed to attract capital into the industry in the future. Information bearing on this rate can be obtained from published statistical summaries, such as that of Roy A. Foulke, Vice President of Dun & Bradstreet, in his *Practical Financial Statement Analysis*.[1] Such summaries often give industry rates of return based upon stockholders' equity, or upon stockholders' equity invested in tangible assets. The reader may wish to construct his own average rate of return for the industry from information gathered in published financial reports or compendiums such as *Moody's Manual of Investments* and *Standard and Poor's Standard Corporation Records*. By computing his own averages, he obtains more assurance that the data he includes in the rate of return are comparable to those of the company he is analyzing.

Other information bearing on the capital-attracting rate of return can be obtained from the trend of prices of recent issues of capital stock and bonds of similar companies.

Many variations of the method of computing the rate of return are in common use, and the analyst must be careful to use a rate that is applicable to businesses that are comparable to the business whose value he is estimating. Some of the common variations of the rate of return are:

---

[1] Roy A. Foulke, *Practical Financial Statement Analysis*, 4th ed. (New York: McGraw-Hill Book Company, Inc., 1957), pp. 641–653.

   a. Rate of return on owners' equity after deducting income tax;

   b. Rate of return on owners' equity before tax;

   c. Rate of return on long-term capital (owners' equity plus long-term liabilities) before interest and tax;

   d. Rate of return on all assets (or, what is the same thing, on all equities) after tax;

   e. Rate of return on all assets before tax.

The extended illustration in this chapter uses a before-tax rate of return based upon all assets used in the business, in order to remove the effect of different sources of financing and different effective tax rates as between businesses. The prospective purchaser of the business may wish to obtain a different proportion of his funds from creditors than does the seller, and the tax rates applicable to his business may not be the same as those applicable to the seller's business.

The rates of return for different companies computed by using historical income and asset amounts taken from accounting records will be distorted to a varying extent because of the effect of price level changes.

(4) *Compute the estimated value of the business by the formula* $S = P(R)$, using tables of the present value of an annuity of $1 (Appendix 21-B). It may be useful to compute a range of values, determined by using the minimum and maximum probable figures for annual income, its expected duration, and the normal rate of return for the industry.

An alternative approach is to compute the present value of the most dependable segment of the income stream at a rate which reflects its relatively low risk, and to add to it the present value of the more uncertain part of income, measured by using a higher discount rate.

(5) *Compare the present value of the income stream with the total market value of the specific individual assets.* Replacement costs and liquidating values may be useful in arriving at values for individual assets.

This general approach to estimating the value of a business may be used by the seller as well as the buyer. Because many of the factors in the computation are subjective, however, it is unlikely that both will arrive at the same estimate of the present value of the business. The final sales price will undoubtedly be determined by negotiation.

Illustration of estimation process

Early in 19x6, Warren and Milton Hart are interested in purchasing the Kindeman Company, Inc., a retail store which sells one principal product. They would retain all of its employees and continue its principal policies. Upon request they are given the following condensed financial statements.

KINDEMAN COMPANY, INC.
Statement of Financial Position
December 31, 19x5

ASSETS			LIABILITIES	
Cash........................		$ 5,200	Accounts payable.............	$21,000
Accounts receivable...	$25,000		Notes payable to banks........	10,000
Less estimated un-			Witholding taxes payable......	500
collectibles.......	1,500	23,500	Corporate income tax payable..	3,000
Merchandise inventory			Total liabilities...........	$34,500
(LIFO)....................		45,000		
Prepaid expenses.............		2,100	STOCKHOLDERS' EQUITY	
Equipment—cost.....	30,000		Capital stock.................	$20,000
Less accumulated			Retained income..............	34,800
depreciation......	18,000	12,000	Total stockholders' equity .	$54,800
Organization costs............		1,500		
Total assets..............		$89,300	Total equities..........	$89,300

KINDEMAN COMPANY, INC.
Combined Statement of Income and Retained Income

	Years Ended December 31				
	19x5	19x4	19x3	19x2	19x1
	(in Thousands of Dollars)				
Sales.............................	$350	$321	$290	$319	$301
Deduct cost of goods sold...........	210	190	175	191	181
Gross margin......................	$140	$131	$115	$128	$120
Operating expense:					
Sales salaries.....................	$ 35	$ 33	$ 30	$ 32	$ 30
Office salaries....................	5	4	4	4	4
Officers' salaries.................	27	25	25	25	25
Building rent.....................	6	6	6	6	6
Depreciation.....................	3	3	3	3	2
Other selling expense.............	15	14	12	13	12
Other administrative expense......	8	8	8	8	8
Total operating expense.........	$ 99	$ 93	$ 88	$ 91	$ 87
Net operating income...............	$ 41	$ 38	$ 27	$ 37	$ 33
Other income:					
Gain on sale of land..............				10	
Gain on sale of equipment........	1	2			
Total........................	$ 42	$ 40	$ 27	$ 47	$ 33
Other expense:					
Interest.........................	1				1
Loss from windstorm.............			5		
Net income before tax.............	$ 41	$ 40	$ 22	$ 47	$ 32
Deduct Federal income tax..	16	15	7	19	11
Net income.......................	$ 25	$ 25	$ 15	$ 28	$ 21
Deduct dividends paid..............	20	15	20	15	15
Net addition to retained income.....	$ 5	$ 10	($ 5)	$ 13	$ 6
Retained income, January 1.........	30	20	25	12	6
Retained income, December 31......	$ 35	$ 30	$ 20	$ 25	$ 12

(1) *Estimate of future revenue and expense.* The prospective buyers recall that 19x3 was a recession year. Including it, they find that average sales have been $316,000 for the past five years. They expect the volume of sales to increase slightly in the next few years, and use an estimated figure of $330,000 for their projection of sales revenue.

Cost of goods sold is expected to continue to be approximately 60 per cent of sales. Sales salaries and other selling expense are expected to remain at about the same proportions of sales.

Office salaries and other administrative expense are expected to average $5,000 and $9,000, respectively, in the near future.

The equipment could be sold for about $16,000. It is expected to have a remaining life of 4 years.

The business acquired land as a prospective building site in 19x1, but abandoned plans to build and sold the land at a gain in 19x2. No similar gain is anticipated in the near future. The gains on sale of equipment were due principally to inadequate depreciation recorded in 19x1 and 19x2.

The Kindeman Company's lease on its building will expire within a month. The landlord has offered to renew it for 10 years at an annual rental of $8,000.

The Harts estimate that fair salaries for the officers of the corporation would be $30,000 a year, based on salaries paid by other companies for comparable positions.

The loss from windstorm in 19x3 resulted from the company's negligence in replacing an insurance policy which it had cancelled.

The annual loss from estimated uncollectibles has been classified as "other administrative expense." The Harts, after careful analysis of the open accounts, estimate that accounts totaling $2,500 are uncollectible.

The physical quantity of the inventory has remained virtually unchanged since the beginning of 19x1, when its amount under the LIFO method was stated at $44,000. The inventory at December 31, 19x5, would cost approximately $60,000 to replace.

The prepaid expenses, mostly supplies, are stated at current cost. The organization costs will be of no value unless the purchaser continues to operate under the charter of the Kindeman Company, Inc.

The prospective buyers summarized their expectations of the typical future income of the business for the next few years as shown at the top of page 694.

The $4,000 figure for depreciation requires further explanation. As emphasized earlier, depreciation does not involve a cash payment; it is merely amortization of a cost which has been incurred earlier. In evaluating the stream of future benefits from a single asset in Chapter 22, depreciation was not deducted. This was proper because the life of each asset was treated as a separate, complete venture for the purpose of comparing it with other assets. In evaluating a business which is expected to

KINDEMAN RETAIL BUSINESS
Statement of Estimated Average Income
for the Years Beginning 19x6

Sales...		$330,000
Deduct estimated cost of goods sold, 60% of sales.....................		198,000
Estimated gross margin.......................................		$132,000
Deduct estimated operating expense:		
Sales salaries, 10% of sales...............................	$33,000	
Other selling expense, 4.3% of sales.......................	14,190	
Office salaries...	5,000	
Other administrative expense, including $200 additional uncol-lectibles per year ($1,000/5)...........................	9,200	
Officers' salaries..	30,000	
Building rent..	8,000	
Depreciation (or average replacement).....................	4,000	
Total estimated operating expense.....................		103,390
Estimated net operating income.......................		$ 28,610

continue indefinitely, however, as is the typical case in this chapter, it is appropriate to assume that the productive power of depreciable assets will be replaced in some fashion more or less continuously. Thus, it is proper to use the $4,000 in the preceding calculation if it is interpreted as an average outlay to replace various items of equipment over the next 10 years.

(2) *Estimate of duration of income.* Demand for the type of goods which the Kindeman Company sells has been relatively stable for many years and seems likely to continue so. The Harts arbitrarily select a period of 10 years as an estimate of its duration. They feel that customers' preference for trading with the business, as well as other intangible factors which have contributed to its profitability, can be expected to continue for at least that long.

(3) *Estimate of the normal rate of return.* A careful study of the results of comparable businesses for several years indicates that the rate of income, before deducting interest and income taxes, can be expected to average about 15 per cent of all assets for the next few years.

(4) *Computation of estimated present value.*

$$S = P(R) = 5.0188(\$28,610) = \$143,588.$$

(5) *Comparison of present value with total market value of individual assets.* The Harts summarized their estimate of the current values of the individual assets as follows:

Cash..	$ 5,200
Accounts receivable...........................	22,500
Merchandise inventory.........................	60,000
Prepaid expenses..............................	2,100
Equipment....................................	16,000
Total assets..............................	$105,800

If the Harts purchase the assets for $144,000—a round sum based upon the estimated present value of the stream of earnings in Step (4)—the purchase price would be $38,200 more than the total current value of the specific, identifiable assets. This excess is presumably paid for *goodwill*, which is the present value of the expected earnings of a business in excess of the normal rate of return for the industry.

It should be emphasized that the $144,000 estimated value has no unique significance. It is merely an approximation based on many subjective estimates, and it is likely to have a wide range of error. It will give the purchaser some guidance in deciding how much to offer for the business, but the final price will result from bargaining between the buyer and the seller.

Recording the purchase of a business

The purchase of a going business by new owners is a proper occasion for changing the basis of measuring its assets. The assets are transferred from one accounting entity to another, and their price is objectively determined by means of a completed transaction between parties dealing at arm's length. As in the illustration of the Kindeman Company, the purchase price of the individual assets paid by the new owners is often different from the amount at which they were recorded on the seller's books. The new entity, however, should measure the assets at their cost to it.

It should be emphasized that it is *not* proper for a business to restate the basis on which its assets are recorded merely as the result of an appraisal or an offer for purchase. Only if the sale is completed is there a change in the basis of accountability.

The acquisition of a business by others may take many different forms, some of which are discussed in the next section. Continuing the illustration of the Kindeman Company, the following journal entries reflect the acquisition of its assets and the assumption of its liabilities by the Hart Corporation, with the latter paying cash for the amount of the net assets. The entries are based on the assumption that the buyer and seller agreed on a valuation of $144,000 for the assets.

(1)

```
A, Cash........................................... 120,000
    OE, Capital Stock...........................          120,000
    The newly-formed Hart Corporation issued capital
    stock to Warren and Milton Hart in exchange for
    cash.
```

In entry (2) Accounts Receivable is debited for the amount legally owed, and Accounts Receivable—Estimated Uncollectibles is credited for the doubtful accounts, on the assumption that none of the specific accounts can be definitely identified as uncollectible.

(2)

A, Cash	5,200	
A, Accounts Receivable	25,000	
A, Merchandise Inventory	60,000	
A, Prepaid Expenses	2,100	
A, Equipment	16,000	
A, Goodwill	38,200	
A, Accounts Receivable—Estimated Uncollectibles		2,500
L, Account Payable to Kindeman Co., Inc.		144,000

Acquired the assets of the Kindeman Co., Inc., at their estimated current values.

(3)

L, Account Payable to Kindeman Co., Inc.	34,500	
L, Accounts Payable		21,000
L, Notes Payable to Banks		10,000
L, Withholding Taxes Payable		500
L, Corporate Income Tax Payable		3,000

Assumed the liabilities of the Kindeman Co., Inc., reducing the amount owed it.

(4)

L, Account Payable to Kindeman Co., Inc.	109,500	
A, Cash		109,500

Paid the Kindeman Co., Inc., the net amount owed for the equity in its business.

Purchase versus pooling of interests

Often two existing businesses are combined to be operated as one. In some cases the combined businesses are continued under the legal structure of one of the existing businesses (a *merger*); in other cases, a new corporation is formed to operate the combined business (a *consolidation*). The owners of the previously existing businesses sometimes receive shares in the combined business in exchange for their previous equities; sometimes they receive promissory notes or bonds; and occasionally they are paid in cash.

The difficult accounting question when businesses combine depends not upon what is the legal form of the combination, but upon whether or not the ownership of the combined business is substantially the same as that of the previously separate businesses. If substantially all of the equity interests in the predecessor companies continue in the surviving company, the combination is a *pooling of interests*. If a substantial part of the ownership of the acquired company is eliminated, the combination is a *purchase*. A purchase, as in the case of the Kindeman Company, is a proper occasion for restating the assets at the price paid for them in the combination of the businesses. None of the retained income of the purchased business should be carried over to the combined business. In a pooling of interests, however, the assets of the resulting company, as well as its retained income, should continue to be carried at the amounts shown on the books of the predecessor companies.

Summary

When a business is to be reorganized, refinanced, or sold, its present value may be estimated by the general method described in the two preceding chapters. The steps in the process consist of:

(1) Estimating the future revenue and expense, using records of the past as a point of departure but taking expected changes into consideration;

(2) Estimating the length of time for which the expected income will continue;

(3) Determining the normal rate of return for the industry;

(4) Computing the estimated present value of the business by the formula $S = P(R)$, making use of the estimates in (1), (2), and (3);

(5) Comparing the present value of the income stream with the total current value of the specific individual assets.

If a business changes hands in what amounts to a substantial change of ownership, its assets should be restated on the basis of their current values. If the ownership of the new business is substantially the same as that of the old (a pooling of interests), the assets should continue to be carried on the basis of unexpired cost or other measure of accountability used on the books of the predecessor companies.

QUESTIONS AND PROBLEMS

23-1 Although it is often appropriate for an owner to estimate the value of his business as a whole, it is rarely appropriate for him to record this value.

REQUIRED:

a. When is it appropriate to record the appraised value?

b. Why is it inappropriate to record it on other occasions?

23-2 An investor bought 100 shares of the Catalyst Corporation in 19x1 at $30 a share. In 19x4 the market quotation for the stock hovered around $18 a share. "I'm going to hold on to this stock," said the investor. "I can't afford to take a $1,200 loss."

REQUIRED:

Was the investor's decision proper? Explain.

23-3 A group which is examining the income statements of the *RST* Company for the past five years, with a view to purchasing the company, finds a number of items listed under the heading "Extraneous Gains and Losses." Some of the items are relatively large, but few of them appear in the income statements of more than one year.

REQUIRED:

a. List several representative types of gains and losses which might be classified under this caption.

b. For each item in (a), state how the purchasers should treat it in estimating the value of the business.

23-4 What factors other than dollar amounts should be considered when the average annual net income is being determined for a series of years, as a basis for estimating future net income?

23-5 Mr. Stan Framlin, president of the Emco Corporation, states that the average annual net income of the corporation for the past 5 years has been $22,000. The corporation has total assets on its statement of financial position amounting to $100,000. According to a recent financial publication the average return for a company of this type is 10 per cent. Mr. Framlin argues that this is positive proof of the existence of goodwill because his company is earning 22 per cent on its assets.

REQUIRED:

Comment on the validity of Mr. Framlin's statement.

23-6 The statement of financial position of the Jemo Corporation showed total assets of $1,250,000. The Maylo Corporation has offered to purchase the business for $1,600,000. The president of Maylo Corporation has concluded that his company is paying $350,000 for goodwill.

REQUIRED:

a. Is the president correct in his conclusion?
b. If you were asked to determine whether goodwill existed, how would you go about computing its amount?

23-7 Several years ago an individual purchased for a cost of $10,000 a perpetual bond which paid an annual return of $500. The bond was transferable to others.

REQUIRED:

a. If the interest rate which can currently be earned on very long-term investments of comparable risk is 4 per cent, what is the bond worth?
b. If it were sold for the amount you computed in (a) just after the owner had collected the annual interest, what would the entry be?

23-8 The *LMNO* Company's accounts show total assets of $103,200. A would-be buyer of the business makes a firm offer of $125,000 for the total assets.

REQUIRED:

a. Why might the value of the assets to the buyer be different from the amount at which they are stated on the seller's books?
b. What might lead the seller to decline the offer?
c. If the seller does decline the offer, how should he disclose it in his accounts and financial statements?

23-9 *R* Company, Inc., has been in existence for 30 years, during most of which time it earned a substantial rate of return. It has suffered net losses for the last 3 consecutive years.

REQUIRED:

a. Under what circumstances might other interests wish to buy this business?
b. How should they proceed to estimate its value?
c. Assume that the total assets are recorded at $300,000 on the seller's books, and that the buyer makes an offer of $250,000 for them, which the buyer accepts. How should these facts be recorded (1) on the books of the seller; (2) on the books of the buyer?

23-10 An individual who wishes to buy a business estimates that its annual income will be $5,000 for a long time in the future. Based upon data for comparable businesses, he thinks that a normal rate of return is 10 per cent.

REQUIRED:

a. Estimate the value of this business as an annuity for 15 years;
b. Estimate its value as an annuity for 20 years;
c. Estimate its value as a perpetuity.

23-11   J. T. Tolleson, a young lawyer, is thinking of buying the legal practice of A. T. Mitchell, who wishes to retire. Mr. Mitchell lists the following assets devoted to his practice:

Cash	$2,600
Office supplies	300
Law library	1,000
Office furniture and equipment	3,000

Mr. Mitchell reports fees earned averaging $30,000 for the past few years, out of which he has paid operating expenses of $7,000.

REQUIRED:

a. To what extent should Mr. Tolleson consider the rate of return on assets in estimating the value of the practice?
b. How would you recommend that he determine the amount of the offer he is willing to make for the practice?

23-12

REQUIRED:

a. Select three companies in a single industry for which you can obtain published financial information. Compile the following information for each company for each of the 3 most recent years:

  (1) Net income before interest and income tax;
  (2) Average total assets in use during the year;
  (3) Percentage of net income before interest and tax to total assets;
  (4) Average percentage of net income before interest and tax to assets for the industry.

b. List and comment upon any specific items which you think limit the usefulness of your result in (*a*)(4) for estimating the normal rate of return for the industry.

23-13   The Ocean View Motel is located on one of the most traveled tourist routes in Florida. It has been owned and operated for 5 years by an elderly couple, Mr. and Mrs. Kingslow. Realizing that they will not be physically able to care for the property in the future, the couple has offered the property for sale. You are interested in buying the property and ask them to quote you a price.

The couple has kept no formal accounting records, but Mr. Kingslow informs you that he paid $40,000 for the property and that annual receipts from rent have averaged $10,000. He states that after deducting the cost of taxes, utilities, repairs, supplies, and the services of one maid, his average annual net income has been $4,000 for the time he has owned the property. You have verified these figures by an examination of receipts, invoices, and paid checks.

Mr. Kingslow emphasizes the fact that he has earned 10 per cent on his investment and that he has built up tremendous goodwill through the years because of his courtesy and interest in his guests. He states that he is making a financial sacrifice when he offers you the property for $30,000.

REQUIRED:

a. Is $30,000 a bargain price for the property?
b. What factors other than the cost might influence your decision as to whether to purchase the property?

23-14 The stockholders of the Jay Corporation, a manufacturer, and those of the Kay Company, which supplies its principal raw material, see an opportunity to improve operating efficiency and increase the stability of earnings by combining the two businesses. The stockholders' equity of the Jay Corporation consists of $250,000 of $100 par value capital stock and retained income of $150,000. That of the Kay Company is composed of $25,000 of $10 par value capital stock and $75,000 of retained income.

The two groups agree to change the name of the Kay Company to the Jay-Kay Company; to recall its par value stock and issue no-par stock in exchange; and to operate the combined company under its charter, as amended. This is done, and the previous stockholders of the Kay Company receive 12,500 shares of no-par stock in exchange for their $10 par stock. In recognition of the superior earning power of their company, the stockholders of the Jay Corporation receive 55,000 shares of the no-par stock of the Jay-Kay Company.

REQUIRED:

a. Assuming any amounts you wish for the assets and liabilities of each company, record the preceding events in journal form on the books of the Jay-Kay Company.
b. Should the assets of the Jay-Kay Company be recorded on the basis of current market values or of unamortized cost? Explain.
c. What does the balance of Retained Income of the combined company represent immediately after these transactions?

23-15 A group composed of K, L, and M is preparing to make an offer for the purchase of the Merline Company. On the basis of a careful projection, they estimate that the revenue of the company will range between $2,000,000 and $3,000,000 for the next 10 years, with the average about $2,500,000. They antici-pate that operating expenses, other than asset amortization, will range from $1,800,000 to $2,200,000 a year, with $2,000,000 the probable average. Similar businesses yield a rate of return before income tax of 10 per cent of assets.

The book values and appraised sale values of the Merline Company's assets are as follows:

	Book Value	Appraised Value
Cash.....................................	$ 120,000	$ 120,000
Receivables.............................	190,000	188,000
Inventories.............................	220,000	229,000
Fixed assets—gross......................	1,500,000	2,100,000
Accumulated depreciation.............. (	500,000) (	700,000)
Fixed assets—net.......................	1,000,000	1,400,000
Current liabilities......................	160,000	163,000
Capital stock...........................	500,000	
Retained income.......................	870,000	

The average annual amortization rate is 12 per cent of the cost of the assets, and that rate seems appropriate for the future.

REQUIRED:

a. Present an analysis of the estimated value of the business to K, L, and M.
b. Journalize entries necessary if K, L, and M organize the Sormer Corporation, contributing $2,500,000 cash in exchange for its capital stock. The Sormer Corporation immediately acquires the assets and assumes the liabilities of the Merline Company for $2,400,000 cash.

23-16 On May 1, 19x3, the Karvin Corporation acquired the business of Peterson, Inc., giving in exchange $75,000 cash and a 6 per cent promissory note for $20,000, due in 5 equal annual installments.

The following condensed information was taken from the statements of the two companies on April 30, 19x3, just prior to the change.

Debits	Karvin Corporation	Peterson, Inc.
Cash........................	$75,000	$ 6,500
Accounts receivable.................		35,000
Merchandise inventory...............		53,000
Plant and equipment—cost...........		80,000
Total.................	$75,000	$174,500

Credits		
Accumulated depreciation.............		$ 40,000
Accounts payable....................		32,000
Capital stock.......................	$75,000	95,000
Retained income....................		7,500
Total.................	$75,000	$174,500

In negotiating for the purchase Arthur Karvin, on behalf of himself, his wife, and his son, had successfully contended that the inventory was worth only $50,500 and the plant and equipment, $35,000. Both seller and buyer agreed that the book values of the other items were reasonable.

Immediately after the transfer of the business, Mr. Karvin asked his bookkeeper to prepare a financial statement as a basis for requesting a bank loan. The following was the result:

KARVIN CORPORATION
Balance Sheet
May 1, 19x3

ASSETS		LIABILITIES	
Cash........................	$ 6,500	Accounts payable............	$ 32,000
Accounts receivable..........	35,000	Notes payable...............	20,000
Merchandise inventory.......	53,000	Reserve for depreciation......	40,000
Plant and equipment.........	80,000	Capital stock................	75,000
		Earned surplus..............	7,500
	$174,500		$174,500

REQUIRED:

a. Prepare an appropriate financial statement for submission to the bank.

b. Explain the reason for any changes you make in amounts.

CASE 23-1. J. L. DEE

J. L. Dee has been operating a small but successful manufacturing enterprise as a sole proprietorship for 10 years. Early in 19x4 he is thinking of retiring and is looking for a buyer for his business.

A group of three individuals is exploring the possibility of making an offer for the purchase of the business. They would form a corporation to take over all of its assets and assume its liabilities. Arthur Carey, one of the group, would be president and chairman of the board of directors, and the other two would participate in management through occasional meetings of the board of directors.

The group has engaged you to make a study of the future potential of the business. You obtain the following statements from Mr. Dee.

J. L. DEE
Balance Sheet

	December 31		
ASSETS	19x1	19x2	19x3
Cash............................	$ 10,000	$ 19,800	$ 26,600
Accounts receivable................	30,000	37,500	42,000
Less reserve for bad debts........(	1,500) (	2,000) (	2,000)
Prepaid expenses...................	5,000	4,500	5,500
Inventories:			
Finished goods (FIFO)...........	48,000	50,200	52,400
Raw materials (LIFO)...........	15,000	15,000	15,000
Land............................	12,000	12,000	12,000
Buildings........................	100,000	100,000	100,000
Less reserve for depreciation......(	32,000) (	36,000) (	40,000)
Equipment.......................	108,000	114,000	126,000
Less reserve for depreciation......(	44,000) (	53,500) (	64,000)
Total assets..................	$250,500	$261,500	$273,500
LIABILITIES			
Accounts payable..................	$ 42,000	$ 45,000	$ 47,000
Employees' withholding taxes.......	2,000	1,800	2,300
Capital..........................	206,500	214,700	224,200
Total liabilities...............	$250,500	$261,500	$273,500

J. L. DEE
Statement of Profit and Loss

	For the Years Ended December 31		
	19x1	19x2	19x3
Sales..........................	$405,000	$380,000	$430,000
Cost of goods sold:			
Direct materials.................	$ 81,000	$ 76,000	$ 86,000
Direct labor....................	117,450	110,200	124,700
Factory overhead	90,500	88,000	93,000
Total......................	$288,950	$274,200	$303,700
Gross profit......................	$116,050	$105,800	$126,300
Operating expense:			
Selling expense..................	$ 30,000	$ 33,000	$ 36,000
Administrative expense*.........	17,000	18,000	19,000
Total......................	$ 47,000	$ 51,000	$ 55,000
Net profit.......................	$ 69,050	$ 54,800	$ 71,300

* Does not include a salary for Mr. Dee.

J. L. DEE
Statement of Capital

	For the Years Ended December 31		
	19x1	19x2	19x3
Capital, January 1.................	$182,450	$206,500	$214,700
Add net income...................	69,050	54,800	71,300
	$251,500	$261,300	$286,000
Deduct withdrawals...............	45,000	46,600	61,800
Capital, December 31..............	$206,500	$214,700	$224,200

Mr. Dee does not receive a formal salary from the business. The amount of his withdrawals is governed by the availability of funds in the business and his own personal requirements, especially for income tax. Mr. Carey would be paid an annual salary of $15,000, and the other two owners would receive $2,000 a year each as directors' fees.

Your investigation shows that other businesses in the same line earn an average rate of return, after deducting reasonable allowances for management compensation but before deducting interest and income taxes, of 15 per cent of their average total assets.

A careful examination of the assets of the business leads you to believe that cash and prepaid expenses are properly stated. The probable losses from accounts receivable are likely to be $2,000 larger than Mr. Dee has provided for, chiefly because of a more lenient credit policy which he initiated in 19x3.

The finished goods inventory contains shopworn goods which are stated at $500 more than their net realizable value, and other goods whose cost on the FIFO basis is $2,000 lower than the current replacement cost, owing to an extraordinary price increase in the latter part of 19x3.

The buildings, as well as equipment with an original cost of $60,000, were acquired when prices for such items were approximately 50 per cent of current prices for similar assets. Other equipment acquisitions, all made in the last 3 years, represent approximate current cost. The estimated life used in depreciating the building is considered appropriate. Mr. Dee's policy has been to depreciate equipment on the basis of an estimated life of 12 years, a full year's depreciation being taken in the year of acquisition. You find that this estimated life is reasonable.

The land is currently appraised at $15,000.

Mr. Dee's bookkeeper failed to reflect earned but unpaid salesmen's salaries in the accounts at the end of 19x1, 19x2, and 19x3. These amounts were $2,000, $1,600, and $2,200, respectively.

The current cost of the raw materials owned is $25,000. There has been an even rate of increase in material prices during the last ten years.

REQUIRED:

a. Submit a detailed estimate of the value of the business to the prospective buyers. Include detailed schedules, supported by reasons for any assumptions you may make.

b. Assuming that the business is bought for your price in (a), make journal entries to record this fact on the books of the new corporation.

Chapter **24**

Planning and Accounting for
Income Taxes

Earlier chapters have attempted to present a logical discussion of the methods used by businesses in measuring their financial status at any given time and their progress toward their income objectives. They have explained briefly that the income tax on corporations is a *business expense* which must be deducted in computing the corporation's periodic income earned for its stockholders, and that the unpaid balance of income taxes is a *liability* which must be shown in a description of the corporation's financial position. When questions of differences in the methods of determining the components of *taxable income* and *business income* have arisen, the reader has been referred to this chapter for a fuller explanation. This has been done because the objectives of measuring the two are significantly different, as are the forces which have helped to develop their rules of measurement. It is felt that the reader should have a thorough understanding of the theory and practice of measuring business income for general purposes before considering the sometimes confusing differences between income tax laws and business accounting methods.

Different objectives of income taxation and business accounting

Chapter 1 described business accounting as

. . . a language for communicating the financial facts about an enterprise or activity to those who have an interest in interpreting and using those facts. It

704

is a means of analyzing and controlling enterprise operations and of planning future action. In order to be useful it must be adapted to the particular needs of each enterprise. These needs arise from the financial information requirements of the various individuals and groups who are affected directly by enterprise operations.

The principal purpose of income taxation is to raise revenue to finance the activities of the government. Taxing authorities think of income as a measure of the taxpayer's *ability to pay* for the support of those activities. This purpose significantly influences Congress when it is enacting laws to define the components of taxable income and the progressive rates of Federal income tax. It also has a significant effect upon the Treasury Department in formulating regulations to aid in interpreting the laws and upon the Internal Revenue Service in enforcing the tax laws and regulations. It is equally important to the legislators and the tax enforcement officials of those states which have state income tax laws.

Other purposes of income taxation also help to shape the specific provisions of income tax laws and regulations. Congress occasionally grants special tax benefits to groups or industries in order to promote the national welfare. One example is the special tax benefits given to the petroleum and other extractive industries to encourage the development of productive wells and mines. Another example is the permission given businesses to deduct rapidly from their periodic taxable income the cost of their facilities which are certified to be necessary for national defense.

Income taxation has also been used consciously in recent decades in attempts to stimulate national economic activity in times of recessions and to brake runaway booms. This has been done chiefly by varying tax rates and the amounts of certain deductions from taxable income.

Because of the different objectives of measuring them, it is likely that the business income and the taxable income of a given business will often be materially different. Moreover, judicial interpretations have further compounded these differences. What is true in one jurisdiction is sometimes not true in another.

Importance of income taxes in business decisions

Even though the income reported in the general financial statements of a corporation may differ from that reported in its income tax return, income taxes can by no means be ignored in making business decisions.

If the business is organized as a *corporation*, it is considered to be a separate legal person subject to income tax. In recent years the income tax rates applicable to most types of business corporations have been 30 per cent of the first $25,000 of taxable income and 52 per cent of all taxable income over $25,000. In times of war, *excess profits taxes* have increased the rate of tax applicable to some parts of corporate income to more than 80 per cent.

A business which is organized as an individual proprietorship or a partnership is not subject to income tax as an entity. Instead, the general tax rules treat the shares of income *earned* by the owners of such businesses, whether distributed to them or not, as taxable to them as individuals. Income tax rates applicable to individuals have been changed frequently, but in recent years they have ranged from 20 per cent on income in the lowest brackets to more than 90 per cent on income in the highest brackets.

The major part of corporate income which is redistributed to stockholders is subject to *double taxation:* once as taxable income of the business corporation which earns it, and a second time as taxable *dividend income* of the stockholder. Certain credits and exclusions which apply to stockholders help to reduce the amount of dividends subject to the second tax.

Even though a particular business is not now earning a large taxable income, its potential income tax expense in the future may be substantial. Some decisions relating to the form of business organization, the types of transactions in which it engages, the form of its transactions, and the manner in which it reports them for tax purposes will have a significant influence on the *amount* of its income tax burden in the future as well as in the current year. They also have an important bearing on the *timing* of the payment of taxes as between years, even in cases where the total dollar income tax effect of alternatives is the same over a series of years.

Good management requires that the responsible persons plan the transactions of a business and the manner of reporting them for tax purposes in such a way as to *maximize* the amount and rate of *income after income taxes.* If revenue and all other expense items are unchanged by the amount of current income taxes, decisions should be made so as to minimize the burden of taxes on the business in the long run, considering both the total amount and the timing of taxes. The businessman and his tax adviser should use every legal means at their disposal to accomplish these objectives.

Effect of taxation on business form

The corporation, as stated earlier, is subject to income tax as a taxable entity, while the income of a business organized as a proprietorship or partnership is considered to be the taxable income of the individual owners, whether it is distributed to them or not.

Reasonable amounts of salaries of stockholders who are also corporation officers are treated as expenses of the corporation before arriving at its net income subject to income tax. In a partnership or proprietorship, on the other hand, the tax law makes no distinction between the parts of income which the owner earns as salary, as payment for the use of capital, and as compensation for risk.

EXAMPLE 1:   *A* and *B* are trying to decide whether to organize their business as a partnership or as a corporation. Each plans to invest $25,000, and each feels that $8,000 a year is reasonable compensation for his services. They expect that the revenue of the business will be $100,000 and that operating expenses other than owners' salaries will be $70,000. All net income will be distributed to the individual owners in cash. The following is a comparison of the income tax status of the two forms of organization.

		Corporation		Partnership
Financial Results of the Business:				
Sales.....................................		$100,000		$100,000
Deduct expenses:				
Officers' salaries..................	$16,000		$ 0	
Other expenses..................	70,000	86,000	70,000	70,000
Net income before income tax...............		$ 14,000		
Deduct corporate income tax (at 30 per cent).		4,200		
Net income.............................		$ 9,800		$ 30,000
Deduct income distributed to owners.........		9,800		30,000
Increase in owners' equity of the business.....		$ 0		$ 0

		Corporation		Partnership
Income and Tax Payments of Each Owner:				
Officer's salary...........................		$8,000		
Dividends................................		4,900		
Share of partnership income:				
Salary..................................				$8,000
Remainder, shared equally..............				7,000
Total taxable income of each owner.......		$12,900		$15,000
Assumed individual income tax:				
Exemptions and deductions........	$3,400			
Taxable at 20%..................	4,000	$ 800		$ 800
Taxable at 22%..................	4,000	880		880
Taxable at 26% (after deducting dividend exclusion of $100, which assumes joint stock ownership by married couple)................	1,400	364		
Taxable at 26%..................	3,600			936
Deduct tax credit of 4% of taxable dividends of $4,800.............		(192)		
Total tax of each owner.........		1,852		2,616
Disposable income of each owner...........		$11,048		$12,384
Disposable income of both owners..........		22,096		24,768

Caution should be used in interpreting Example 1. It does *not* prove that the partnership form always has an income tax advantage over the corporate form, or even that it has an advantage in this case. It merely illustrates the procedure for making the comparison. The results will be different if the business is expected to suffer losses during its early years, or if it is expected to earn income which will be taxable at the 52 per cent rate. The income tax of each of the individual owners will depend upon the amount of his income from other sources, the number of his personal exemptions, and the amount of his personal deductions. Because of large amounts of taxable income from other sources, the owners may find that their taxable income from a partnership would be taxed at rates higher than the 52 per cent maximum rate applicable to corporations.

In the example, too, it was assumed that the business did not grow, but that all earnings were distributed. The relative desirability of the two forms of organization changes when the growth of a business is to be financed by retained income. In the corporate form, earnings retained in the business are not taxable to the individual stockholders as dividend income. However, the tax laws limit the extent to which corporations can retain income by providing that a penalty can be assessed on "unreasonable accumulations" of retained income. The total income of a partnership is taxable to the partners whether they wish to reinvest it in the business or not. If their income is subject to high tax rates and they must withdraw from the partnership the cash needed to pay their taxes, the business organized as a partnership may not be able to grow as rapidly as it would if organized as a corporation.

There are many more complicated features of the income tax law which the owners of a business should consider in deciding upon its form of organization. Also, under certain conditions corporations may elect to be taxed as partnerships, and partnerships may elect to be taxed as corporations.

In addition to the income tax status of each form of organization, the owners should consider advantages and disadvantages not related to taxation, such as the duration of the life of the business, the extent to which owners are personally liable for business debts, the ease with which ownership interests may be transferred, the ease and flexibility with which the business can be managed, and the legal and other costs involved.

Effect of taxation on business size

Besides influencing the *form* of the business organization, income tax often has an important effect on the *size* of the business. The possibility of a penalty upon the unreasonable accumulation of retained income has already been mentioned. In addition, owners sometimes find it worth while to organize divisions of their business as separate corporations if there are sound business reasons for doing so, in order that more of the total business income will be taxed at lower rates.

EXAMPLE 2:   The owners of a business which is expected to earn a net income before tax of $125,000 a year are considering whether to form a single corporation or 5 separate corporations of equal size. They estimate the income tax effects as follows:

	1 Corporation	Each of 5 Corporations
Net income subject to income tax.........	$125,000	$25,000
Income tax:		
30 per cent on first $25,000.............	$ 7,500	$ 7,500
52 per cent on all over $25,000.........	52,000	0
Income tax of each corporation.........	$ 59,500	$ 7,500
Total tax of 5 corporations.............		37,500
Tax saving of 5 corporations...........		22,000

If the expected tax saving exceeds the additional organization and management costs which separate corporations entail, the owners will probably find it worth while to organize separate corporations. In order to be able to offset a net loss of one corporation against the net income of the others in computing taxable income, however, the group must file a *consolidated income tax return* and pay a 2 per cent higher rate of income tax. Once a group of corporations elects to file a consolidated income tax return, it is generally required to continue to do so in the future. It should be emphasized, too, that tax benefits from the organization of multiple corporations are likely to be disallowed unless there are good reasons, other than tax ones, for the use of several corporations.

Tax saving by means of long-term capital gains

Where there is a choice, it is generally more advantageous for a business to receive income in the form of *long-term capital gains* than in the form of *ordinary income*. Capital gains result from the *sale of capital assets*, or from the *exchange* of one capital asset for another of a different type. *Capital assets* include all business property, with the following major exceptions:

(1) Inventory items which are held for sale to customers in the ordinary course of business;

(2) Real estate and depreciable business property which are used in the business; and

(3) Accounts or notes receivable acquired in the course of business in exchange for goods or services sold.

A *long-term capital gain* results from the sale of a capital asset which the business has held for more than six months. If a business has but one capital transaction during the year, and that transaction results in a gain, the gain is taxed at one of the following rates:

(1) If the business is a corporation, the maximum tax rate on the gain is 25 per cent.

(2) If the business is unincorporated, its owners include only half of

their share of the long-term gain in taxable income. The rate of tax is limited to 50 per cent of the *taxable* amount of the long-term gain (which is the same as 25 per cent of the total amount of the gain).

All of the capital gains and losses of a taxpayer, short-term as well as long-term, must be considered together. The excess of *net long-term capital gains* from all transactions combined over *net short-term capital losses* is taxed in the same way as a single long-term capital gain. *Net short-term capital gains* are taxed at the same rates as ordinary income.

Although real estate and depreciable property used in the business are not capital assets, *gains* on the sale of such property are treated as capital gains and *losses* are deductible in full in computing taxable income.

In planning a *single* sale or exchange of a capital asset, management should generally try to have a gain on the asset qualify as a *long-term capital gain*, which is taxable at a reduced rate. The objective of tax planning is to minimize the *total burden* of taxes, however, and the effect of ordinary income and ordinary losses on the total income tax of the business for the current period and for other periods must also be considered.

Planning the *timing* of a number of capital asset transactions is more complicated. If a capital gain and loss occur in the same year, they partially or wholly offset each other. It may be advantageous, particularly for individual taxpayers, to time a capital gain transaction so that it will occur in one year and will be taxed at a reduced rate, and to time a capital loss so that it will occur in a different year and can be partially or wholly offset against ordinary income subject to tax.

Business owners as individuals may be able to reduce their taxes by arranging for their income from the business to be taxed as a long-term capital gain rather than as ordinary income. For example, it may be desirable and feasible for a stockholder to receive his gain from the growth of a corporation as a long-term capital gain when he sells the stock rather than as annual dividends.

EXAMPLE 3:   An individual is planning to invest $100,000 in a corporation for 5 years. He thinks that, if he receives his compensation in the form of dividends of $10,000 a year, the stock can be sold for $100,000 at the end of 5 years. On the other hand, if the corporation uses its income to finance growth for the 5-year period, the stock will probably sell for $150,000 at the end of 5 years. What will the tax effect of each alternative be if the individual's other income is such that additional annual income will be taxed at about 50 per cent?

SOLUTION: This individual's tax on his annual dividends will be approximately 50 per cent of $10,000, or $5,000 a year. After paying income tax, his net receipts from the corporation will be $5,000 a year for 5 years. The tax on the long-term capital gain will be 25 per cent of $50,000, or $12,500, paid at the end of 5 years. Under this alternative, his net receipts will be $37,500 at the end of the fifth year. This solution does not evaluate the effect of differences in the timing of receipts and payments from the point of view of either the individual or the corporation.

Computing after-tax rate of return on investment

Chapter 22 described the following method of computing the expected rate of return on an investment before considering income tax:

(1) Determine P, the ratio of the additional investment required (S) to the expected differential net receipts in each future year (R);

(2) Using a table of the present value of an annuity of $1 (Appendix 21-B), locate the approximate rate of return by following the line for the investment's estimated life to the interest rate column in which the computed P ratio appears.

When the initial capital investment is subject to amortization for income tax purposes, the periodic net receipts differ from income subject to tax. The tax paid, in turn, affects the periodic net receipts. Example 4 shows the method for computing the *rate of return after tax* on an investment, using the same basic data as that in Examples 2(a), 2(b), and 2(c) of Chapter 22.

EXAMPLE 4: Company X is trying to decide whether to use an old machine for its estimated remaining life of 5 years or to replace it with a new one which has a net initial cost of $7,000, an expected net annual operating saving before income tax of $1,750, and therefore an estimated before-tax rate of return of slightly less than 8 per cent. To simplify the analysis, it is assumed that the new machine will also have a useful life of 5 years. What is the estimated rate of return on the investment *after income tax?*

SOLUTION:

	New Machine's Expected Differential	
	Taxable Income	Net Receipts
New machine's net annual operating saving before income tax	+$1,750	+$1,750
Deduct *additional* annual depreciation on new machine for tax purposes, using straight-line method:		
Depreciation on new machine (⅕ of tax cost, $12,000,* minus salvage, 0)........... $2,400		
Depreciation on old machine (⅕ of remaining cost, $5,000, minus salvage, 0). 1,000	− 1,400	
Differential taxable income	+$ 350	
Deduct income tax at 52 per cent	− 182	− 182
Differential income after tax	+$ 168	
Differential cash receipts after tax		+$1,568

$P = \dfrac{S}{R} = \dfrac{\$7,000}{\$1,568} = 4.464$. Appendix 21-B shows that the approximate after-tax rate of return is slightly more than 4 per cent.

---

* Income tax law does not recognize a gain or a loss when similar productive assets are exchanged. Hence, the cost of the new machine for tax purposes will be the unexpired cost of the old machine, $5,000, plus the $7,000 additional outlay for the new.

Tax saving in choice of financing methods

The principal external sources of funds for long-term investment in the business are the issuance of bonds, preferred stock, and common stock, and many variations of each type of security.

The interest paid to bondholders is a deductible business expense for the purpose of computing business income subject to tax, but dividends paid to preferred and common stockholders are not deductions from the corporation's taxable income. The effect of the use of bonds is to reduce the net cost of borrowed capital to the corporation by the amount of the tax reduction which the corporation receives for the interest expense.

EXAMPLE 5:   A corporation which needs $1,000,000 of additional capital is considering raising the sum by issuing either 5 per cent bonds or 7 per cent preferred stock. The corporation expects that its net income before deducting interest and income tax will be approximately $175,000 a year in the future. What are the comparative costs of each method of financing, after considering income taxes?

	5% Bonds	7% Preferred Stock
Net income before interest and tax..............	$175,000	$175,000
Deduct bond interest expense....................	50,000	
Net income subject to income tax................	$125,000	$175,000
Deduct Federal income tax (30 per cent of first $25,000 plus 52 per cent of income over $25,000).	59,500	85,500
Net income.....................................	$ 65,500	$ 89,500
Deduct dividends on preferred stock.............		70,000
Net income to common stockholders..............	$ 65,500	$ 19,500

The net cost of funds obtained by borrowing is 2.4 per cent (5 per cent of the funds borrowed minus income tax at 52 per cent of 5 per cent of the sum borrowed), while the net cost of preferred stock is 7 per cent.

The tax deductibility of interest has sometimes caused businesses to ignore considerations of financial safety in choosing between bonds and stocks. The business risk associated with bonds is greater because they require fixed payments of interest and principal. If earnings decline, these fixed requirements may cause the business financial difficulty. At the same time, the tax advantage also declines. If there is no income before interest and tax, there is no tax reduction associated with the interest. In such a case, the net interest cost in Example 5 would be 5 per cent, not 2.4 per cent.

TAX SAVING BY CHOICE OF ACCOUNTING METHODS

In addition to opportunities which most businesses have for reducing their income tax burden by planning the form and nature of business transactions, there are also a number of *choices of accounting methods* by which businesses may attempt to *minimize* or *postpone* their taxes. The corporate or individual taxpayer should choose its methods of reporting transactions for tax purposes very carefully. In many cases, changes of method are permitted only if the Treasury Department gives permission, and taxpayers are not permitted to change back and forth in such a way as to "have their cake and eat it, too."

Circumstances in which tax postponement is desirable

Many of the elections which a taxpayer is permitted to make in reporting taxable income deal largely with the *timing* of taxable revenue or deductible expenses. As compared with Method X of reporting taxable income, Method Y results in the *postponement of taxable income* because it permits the taxpayer to *report revenue later* or *deduct expenses earlier*.

EXAMPLE 6:   A taxpayer is trying to decide which of two methods to use in reporting a tax deduction: Method X, which will result in a tax deduction of \$10,000 in 19x1 and zero in 19x2; or Method Y, which will result in a tax deduction of zero in 19x1 and \$10,000 in 19x2. Other taxable income for each of the two years is expected to be \$40,000. What effect on taxable income will each method have?

SOLUTION:

	19x1	19x2	Total for Two Years
Method X:			
Other taxable income..................	\$40,000	\$40,000	\$80,000
Deduction in question................	10,000	0	10,000
Taxable income.....................	\$30,000	\$40,000	\$70,000
Method Y:			
Other taxable income..................	\$40,000	\$40,000	\$80,000
Deduction in question................	0	10,000	10,000
Taxable income.....................	\$40,000	\$30,000	\$70,000

Method X will postpone \$10,000 of taxable income from the first year to the second.

Postponement of taxable income to a later year lessens the burden of income taxes on the business if:

(1) The tax rate applicable to the income in question is lower in the second year than in the first;

(2) The applicable tax rate is expected to be the same for both years, and the business can earn a return during the second year on the funds not paid out in taxes at the end of the first year;

(3) The business can earn more on the funds not paid out than the increase in the tax applicable to the item.

EXAMPLE 7:   If the taxpayer in Example 6 would have to pay income tax of 52 per cent on the $10,000 in question in 19x1 but expects the applicable tax rate in 19x2 to be 30 per cent, Method X would result in a total tax saving of $2,200 for the 2-year period.

EXAMPLE 8:   If the taxpayer in Example 6 expects the applicable tax rate to be 52 per cent in both 19x1 and 19x2, Method X will not reduce total income tax. However, if the taxpayer can earn 6 per cent on the $5,200 *not* paid out in taxes at the end of the first year under Method X as compared with Method Y, it will have $312 more before taxes and $149.76 more after taxes at the end of 19x2 by using tax Method X.

EXAMPLE 9:   The taxpayer in Example 6 will be better off to postpone the item of taxable income to 19x2 if it can earn 6 per cent on its money during 19x2, unless the applicable tax rate increases to about 53.5 per cent.

The following sections describe some of the alternative methods which a taxpayer may elect to change the *timing* of taxable income. A method which results in an *indefinite postponement* of taxable income may usually be considered to provide a tax saving.

Cash versus accrual basis of accounting

This textbook has presented the basic principles and chief uses of the *accrual basis* of accounting, under which *income* is defined as the difference between *revenue earned* and *expenses and losses incurred*. Under income tax law, a business is permitted to use the *cash basis* of measuring income unless inventories are a substantial factor in its operations. Under this tax reporting method, items of revenue are included in taxable income in the period in which they are collected and expenses are deducted in the period in which they are paid. The taxpayer must allocate long-term unexpired costs, such as depreciable assets, to the tax periods in which the assets are used.

Under the cash basis of reporting taxable income, the taxpayer can influence the amount of taxable income to some extent by changing the timing of revenue collections or expense payments.

Even if the taxpayer uses the *accrual basis* of reporting taxable income, the tax rules generally provide that revenue items collected in advance, such as rentals, are taxable even if the taxpayer has not earned them. This provision is in conflict with the requirements of good accounting, which treat only *earned* amounts as revenue.

Under the accrual basis of reporting for income tax purposes, the taxpayer is usually not permitted to deduct expenses until all factors which affect their amount have occurred. Most of the "estimated expenses" for product warranties and similar items, which are proper deductions in computing business income, cannot be deducted in the tax return until the period in which payments for them are actually made.

Installment sales method

A taxpayer may elect to treat as taxable income only that part of the sales price of installment sales which it has *collected* during the accounting period. Under the rules of financial accounting, on the other hand, the entire sales price is generally considered to be realized revenue at the time of the sale. A deduction from sales revenue can be estimated for the uncollectible accounts and collection costs which are expected to occur in later accounting periods.

Percentage-of-completion and completed-contract methods

In reporting income from long-term contracts, the taxpayer is permitted to use either the *percentage-of-completion method* or the *completed-contract method*. Under the former, income is reported in each period in the same proportion as costs incurred on the contract during the period bear to the estimated total costs of the entire contract.

The taxpayer may postpone reporting taxable income to the period in which the contract is completed. If the contract extends over several years, reporting the entire amount of income in a single year may result in higher total taxes than spreading it over several years, particularly if the taxpayer is an individual. His income in the year of completion of the contract may be taxed at much higher rates than would apply to smaller amounts of income reported in several different years.

Deductions from accounts receivable

A taxpayer on the accrual basis of reporting taxable income may deduct an estimated amount of uncollectible accounts (the recommended method for financial accounting), or he may wait and deduct uncollectible accounts in the period in which they are definitely determined to be worthless. The total taxable income over a period of years is less under the former method if at the end of the period the business expects any accounts at all to become uncollectible. Consequently, this method can usually be expected to result in the postponement of income tax for an indefinite period.

Under income tax rules, present regulations permit the taxpayer to deduct cash discounts on sales and similar revenue deductions only when they have actually been taken by the customer. An advance estimate is not acceptable.

Inventory method

Tax rules generally permit the taxpayer to use any inventory method which is acceptable under good accounting principles. The taxpayer must use an inventory method consistently, and often must obtain permission to change methods.

There is a considerable difference of opinion as to what components should be included in determining the cost of an inventory item, particularly of an item which has been manufactured. The status of direct costing as an acceptable method for income tax purposes is very doubtful.

The lower-of-cost-or-market method may be used as an inventory method unless the LIFO (last-in, first-out) cost method is in use.

LIFO has received attention chiefly as a method for postponing income taxes indefinitely. The time at which it is adopted, the expected movement of acquisition costs of goods in the future, and the extent to which ending inventory balances are likely to decline are important factors in estimating whether LIFO will result in tax benefits. If future costs are expected to rise substantially and future inventory balances are expected to remain constant or to increase, LIFO will probably postpone income taxes indefinitely. In times of declining prices, however, LIFO will result in higher income taxes than the FIFO or average cost methods of measuring inventory. Furthermore, if a part of inventory which has been assigned a low unit cost on a LIFO basis is liquidated during a period of high income, the method may result in higher taxes than would an alternative method.

If a business elects to use LIFO in its income tax returns, it must also use the method in reporting to its stockholders and creditors. This is one case in which the tax law dictates the accounting method which is to be used in general-purpose financial reports.

Depreciation method

The Internal Revenue Code of 1954 permitted taxpayers to use any one of several *accelerated depreciation* methods for new property with an estimated useful life of 3 years or more acquired after 1953. The best-known of these methods, the *uniform-rate-on-declining-balance method* and the *sum-of-the-years'-digits method,* were described and illustrated in Chapter 18. In addition, the taxpayer can use any other consistent method of depreciation which does not accumulate a greater amount of depreciation during the first two-thirds of the property's life than would be accumulated under the declining-balance method at twice the straight-line rate.[1]

---

[1] *Internal Revenue Code* of 1954, Sec. 167(b).

The taxpayer may elect to use an accelerated depreciation method for one asset or group of assets and not for others. He may use one method for assets acquired in one year and another method for those acquired in later years.

The declining-balance method tends to provide greatest tax benefit for an asset whose estimated useful life is short. The information in Examples 2 and 8 of Chapter 18 is presented below, together with the effect of income taxes, for the purpose of comparing the results of the declining-balance method with those of the straight-line method.

EXAMPLE 10: A taxpayer has just acquired a new machine with a cost of $3,000, an estimated useful life of 4 years, and an estimated salvage value of $600. It expects its taxable income during the next few years to be subject to corporate income tax at 30 per cent. What are the comparative effects of the straight-line and declining-balance methods of depreciation on its net income and net cash receipts if it uses the same method in both its general-purpose financial statements and its income tax returns?

SOLUTION:

	19x1	19x2	19x3	19x4	All 4 Years
Straight-line depreciation........	$ 600	$600	$600	$600	$2,400
Declining-balance depreciation...	1,500	750	150	0	2,400
Difference in taxable income under declining-balance method	−$ 900	−$150	+$450	+$600	$ 0
Difference in income tax........	− 270	− 45	+ 135	+ 180	0
Difference in net income after income tax.................	− 630	− 105	+ 315	+ 420	0
Difference in net cash receipts by years (equaling tax postponed).	+ 270	+ 45	− 135	− 180	0
Cumulative difference in net cash receipts under declining-balance method....................	+ 270	+ 315	+ 180	0	0

As a result of the postponement of taxes under the declining-balance depreciation method, the taxpayer has the use of $270 more money in the first year than it would have under the straight-line method, $315 more in the second year, and $180 more in the third. If any return at all can be earned on these funds, the taxpayer will be better off using the declining-balance method.

The sum-of-the-years'-digits method also results in a smaller charge for depreciation for each succeeding year of an asset's useful life and therefore tends to postpone the payment of income taxes. It can result in reducing the unexpired cost of an asset to zero at the end of its estimated useful life, while the declining-balance method cannot.

Because of the rapid reduction of the unexpired cost of an asset for tax purposes during the early years of its life, it is possible that occasional sales of such assets before the ends of their expected lives will result in long-term capital gains.

Other important choices of accounting methods

A taxpayer who has an emergency facility which has been properly certified may elect to deduct the certified portion of its cost over a period of 60 months instead of over its entire useful life. This privilege has been granted principally in wartime, and its application is now very limited.

Expenditures incurred for the purpose of exploring a deposit of a mineral up to $100,000 a year or $400,000 in all may be deducted in the year in which they are incurred or may be treated as deductions in the periods in which the mineral is sold.

If a corporation wishes, it may deduct organization costs incurred after 1953 over a period of not less than 60 months. From the standpoint of financial accounting, such costs are considered to be an asset with a benefit for the life of the corporation.

The taxpayer also has a choice of deferring or not deferring the deduction of research and experimental costs which are of the nature of current expenses as distinct from capital expenditures.

OTHER DIFFERENCES BETWEEN FINANCIAL AND TAXABLE INCOME

In addition to the differences caused by election of accounting methods, the income of businesses as reported in their general-purpose financial statements may differ from that reported in their income tax returns because of (1) the nontaxability of some exchanges, (2) gains on the involuntary conversion of property, (3) the special deductions allowed for percentage depletion, and (4) the carrying back and forward to other years of business casualty losses and operating losses.

Nontaxable exchanges

When a taxpayer exchanges property, other than inventory, which it holds for productive use in its business or for investment for property of a like kind to be held for the same purpose, it has neither a taxable gain nor a deductible loss. According to recognized accounting principles, there may be a gain or loss on such an exchange, measured by the difference between the unexpired book cost of the asset parted with and its fair market value at the date of the exchange.

EXAMPLE 11: A taxpayer traded a machine with an original cost of $10,000 and accumulated depreciation of $4,000 for a smaller machine. On the date of the trade the old machine could have been sold for $5,000. What is the amount of the gain or loss for tax purposes?

SOLUTION: Since property held for productive use in the business is being traded for like property to be held for the same purpose, there is neither a taxable gain nor a deductible loss. The exchange has the following effect, for tax purposes:

Income Tax Method:

A, Machine (new)......................................	6,000	
A, Machine—Accumulated Depreciation (old).........	4,000	
A, Machine (old)................................		10,000
To record the trade of an old machine for a new one with no effect on taxable income.		

The tax cost of the new machine, which is used for computing depreciation on future tax returns, is $6,000.

Financial Accounting Method:

A, Machine (new)......................................	5,000	
A, Machine—Accumulated Depreciation (old).........	4,000	
OE, Loss on Exchange of Machine...................	1,000	
A, Machine (old)...............................		10,000
To record the trade of an old machine for a new one at a loss of $1,000.		

The cost of the new machine to be used in computing depreciation for financial accounting purposes in the future is $5,000.

Under the income tax method of recording tax-free exchanges, the gain or loss on an asset which is no longer owned is carried forward to future periods as an addition to or reduction from the cost of the new asset.

Gains on involuntary conversions

When a taxpayer receives cash for an asset which has been condemned for public use, or when he receives the insurance proceeds for an asset which has been destroyed by a casualty, in effect he has sold the asset against his will. Tax rules provide that he may elect not to report the gain at the time of the involuntary conversion if he uses all of the cash received to replace the asset. His cost of the new asset for tax purposes is the same as that of the asset converted. Losses on such involuntary conversions may be deducted in full at the time they are incurred.

Percentage depletion

A taxpayer may elect to compute the depletion on a natural resource by the method described in Chapter 18, dividing the cost of the resource by the estimated total number of units to be extracted, and then multiplying this rate of depletion per unit by the number of units extracted during each period. On the other hand, he may elect to deduct, in lieu of depletion based on cost, an allowed percentage of the gross income obtained from the property. This *percentage depletion* may be deducted for income tax purposes even when the total previous deductions for depletion have exceeded the original cost of the asset.

Loss carrybacks and carryforwards

In recognition of the fact that an undue hardship would often be worked on businesses by taxing at a high rate their net income of one year, with no offsetting refund in succeeding loss years, the income tax provisions permit a form of averaging the periodic taxable income of a business over a series of years. This is especially beneficial to new businesses, which often operate at a loss during their early years. It also helps to stabilize the results of businesses over cyclical economic swings.

Under the law currently in effect, a net tax loss of 19x4 may be carried back first to be offset against a net taxable income of 19x1. Any remaining loss may then be offset against the net income of 19x2, 19x3, 19x5, 19x6, 19x7, 19x8, and 19x9, in that order. The taxpayer may be entitled to refunds of taxes paid in earlier years, and the loss carryforwards will reduce the amount of income tax that it would otherwise pay on the basis of net income earned in later years.

EFFECT OF DIFFERENCES BETWEEN ACCOUNTING AND INCOME TAX METHODS

Influence of taxation on accounting methods

Earlier sections of this chapter have pointed out that, although financial accounting and income tax reporting have different objectives, the income tax is a significant business expense which must be considered in planning the form of the business, the nature and timing of its transactions, and the method of accounting for those transactions.

Because of the many differences between the income tax rules and the generally accepted financial methods of accounting for items of revenue and expense, business income usually differs in some respects from taxable income. These differences may be *permanent*, caused by the fact that items of business revenue are not subject to income tax, or that items of business expense are not deductible at all. They may be *temporary*, caused by the fact that the tax provisions require the business to report an item of revenue or expense earlier or later than do accepted accounting principles.

In some cases, a business is not permitted under the tax law to use a method in reporting its taxable income if it does not use the same method in its financial statements. In other cases, the differences between the amounts of income reported for income tax and for financial accounting purposes are immaterial, and the tax method is adopted for both purposes to avoid additional accounting work.

Often, however, the method which it is desirable for a business to use in minimizing its income taxes does not properly reflect the income which is to be used by management, stockholders, creditors, and others as a measure of its financial progress. If the differences involved are material, the business should adhere to the accepted method of accounting in its general-purpose financial statements.

Matching income tax expense with business income

Material differences between the income reported in the income tax return for a period and that reported in the income statement pose a vexing problem. Some accountants contend that income tax is not an expense, but rather a *distribution of income* to the government, paralleling the distribution of dividends to stockholders. Accordingly, the proper amount of income tax to be shown as a deduction from business income in any period is the amount *actually owed* on the basis of the taxable income reported for that period.

Another group of accountants maintains that income tax is an expense which should be *allocated to accounting periods*, like other expenses. The amount to be reported as income tax expense for a given period is the amount of tax that has been paid in the past, or is likely to be paid in the future, on the business income reported in the current period. The amount of income tax expense in the income statement may differ from the amount of income tax to be paid on the current year's *taxable income* for the following reasons:

(1) Income tax has been *postponed* by
   (a) Reporting revenue in the financial statements earlier than in the tax return, or
   (b) Reporting an expense deduction in the financial statements later than in the tax return.
(2) Income tax has been *prepaid* by
   (a) Reporting revenue in the income tax return earlier than in the financial statements, or
   (b) Reporting an expense deduction in the income tax return later than in the financial statements.

The second group of accountants argues that the readers of financial statements will be misled unless the amount of income tax expense reported is based on the amount of income shown in the statements.

Illustration of methods of accounting for income taxes

The following illustration shows the accounting treatment of income taxes under the two methods.

In 19x1 Company *T* has acquired at a cost of $90,000 a machine with an expected useful life of 3 years and an estimated salvage value of zero. The company has elected the sum-of-the-years'-digits method for computing depreciation in its income tax return, but feels that the straight-line method is more appropriate in its financial statements because the asset's services will be equal in each year. Total revenue is expected to be $100,000 and expenses other than depreciation are expected to be $20,000 for each of the three years.

	Comparison of Income Tax Returns		
	19x1	19x2	19x3
Revenue..	$100,000	$100,000	$100,000
Deduct expenses:			
SYD depreciation.........................	$ 45,000	$ 30,000	$ 15,000
Other expenses............................	20,000	20,000	20,000
Total expenses.........................	$ 65,000	$ 50,000	$ 35,000
Taxable income.............................	$ 35,000	$ 50,000	$ 65,000
Computation of income tax:			
30 per cent of $25,000......................	$ 7,500	$ 7,500	$ 7,500
52 per cent of remainder....................	5,200	13,000	20,800
Total income tax.........................	$ 12,700	$ 20,500	$ 28,300

The income tax which would be payable each year if Company *T* used the straight-line method of depreciation for tax purposes would be $20,500. The use of the sum-of-the-years'-digits method postpones the payment of $7,800 of income tax from the first year to the third. The tax payable in the second year would be the same under either depreciation method in this illustration.

	Comparison of Income Statements		
	19x1	19x2	19x3
Income Tax Treated as Income Distribution:			
Net income (before income tax)...............	$50,000	$50,000	$50,000
Deduct income tax...........................	12,700	20,500	28,300
Net income for stockholders..................	$37,300	$29,500	$21,700
Income Tax Treated as Expense:			
Net income before income tax.................	$50,000	$50,000	$50,000
Deduct income tax expense...................	20,500	20,500	20,500
Net income..................................	$29,500	$29,500	$29,500

The *total* income for the three years is the same under both methods. Under the second method, the income tax is smaller in the first year, and larger in the third, by the amount of income tax which is *postponed* from the first to the third year.

If income tax is treated as an income distribution, the current liability for Corporate Federal Income Tax Payable is credited for the amount of income tax shown in the income tax return and the income statement.

If income tax is treated as an expense to be allocated to periods, the following entry is necessary in the first year:

(1)

OE, Income Tax Expense..........................	20,500	
L, Corporate Federal Income Tax Payable.......		12,700
L, Corporate Federal Income Tax Postponed.....		7,800

To record the expense for income tax applicable to income reported in the income statement for 19x1, and to set up liabilities for the income tax currently payable and for that postponed to a future year.

I disagree with this Acct.

Corporate Federal Income Tax Postponed would be classified as a long-term liability at the end of 19x1. The opponents of this method argue that it is not a liability at all, because this amount of tax is not now owed and may never be owed by the corporation. The corporation may not pay an income tax in the future if its operations are unprofitable.

In 19x3 the following entry is needed:

(2)

OE, Income Tax Expense..........................	20,500	
L, Corporate Federal Income Tax Postponed.........	7,800	
L, Corporate Federal Income Tax Payable.......		28,300

To record the liability for income tax currently payable, including that postponed from 19x1.

Treatment of other income taxes

Because of the diversity of state and foreign income tax provisions, this chapter has dealt only with the provisions of the Federal income tax laws. The principles applicable to planning for and accounting for other income taxes are the same as for Federal income taxes, although the latter are usually more material.

Summary

The objectives of income taxation are to provide revenue for the support of governmental activities and to promote or discourage particular business activities, according to the judgment of the legislative body. General-purpose accounting is designed to report the financial progress and status of a business to managers, stockholders, creditors, and others who have a direct interest in its affairs. Because of these differences in purpose, there are many differences between the determinants of *taxable income* and those of *business income*.

A business should plan to maximize its rate and amount of income in the long run. Income tax is a significant factor to be considered in planning alternative courses of action. Income tax provisions may have an important effect on the way in which the business is organized; on the types, form, and timing of the transactions in which it engages; and on the manner in which it accounts for these transactions in its income tax returns.

Income tax rules do not follow a completely unified theory of income measurement. For this reason they should not be permitted to dictate the methods which the business uses in its general-purpose financial reports. However, where there are substantial differences between the income reported for income tax purposes and that reported in the financial statements, the effect of such differences on the periodic amounts reported as income tax expense should be disclosed.

QUESTIONS AND PROBLEMS

24-1 "Both the income tax return and the financial statements are designed to report the *income* of a business for a period of time. Since they are designed to accomplish the same purpose, they should follow the same method. Uniformity of method can best be achieved by law; therefore, accounting methods of reporting should follow the requirements of the income tax laws."

REQUIRED:

a. Discuss the validity of this statement, giving reasons if you disagree with any part of it.

b. Is uniformity in the methods of measuring business income desirable? Is it feasible? Explain.

24-2 For income tax purposes, many items of revenue collected in advance are fully taxable in the period in which they are received. For general accounting purposes, however, they are treated as additions to income only to the extent that they are earned.

REQUIRED:

a. How can the income tax treatment be justified?

b. How can the financial accounting treatment be justified?

c. How would you reconcile these opposing viewpoints?

24-3 "How can you expect the income tax laws to agree with generally accepted accounting requirements if accountants can't even agree among themselves? Look at all of the different methods which accountants use for measuring inventory: LIFO, FIFO, specific identification, average cost, and lower-of-cost-or-market. And differences in depreciation methods are just as numerous."

REQUIRED:

To what extent do you think differences in accounting methods could be justified even if there were no income tax?

24-4 "A corporation is subject to double taxation; therefore, it will pay the owners of a business to organize it as a partnership."

REQUIRED:

a. Illustrate what is meant by "double taxation."

b. How can double taxation be avoided in the corporate form of business?

c. If double taxation cannot be avoided in a given case, will the partnership form result in lower income tax than the corporate form? Explain.

d. If the partnership form of organization seems likely to minimize the income tax burden on the business and the individual owners combined, would you recommend that it be used for the business? Why?

24-5 "The tax burden of a business can be minimized by proper timing of its taxable revenue and deductible expenses."

REQUIRED:

a. Under what circumstances will it be advantageous for a business to use straight-line depreciation for its principal depreciable asset on its income tax return?

b. Under what circumstances should the business use one of the accelerated depreciation methods for the asset in (a)?

24-6 Three individuals are planning to form a business which they expect to grow rapidly. Each will invest all of his personal capital in the business, and the three agree that most of the business income will be retained for expansion. Because of the risk involved, it is unlikely that outside capital can be obtained in significant amounts for many years.

REQUIRED:

a. What are the advantages and disadvantages, both as to tax and in general, of the corporate form of organization in a situation of this sort?

b. What are the advantages and disadvantages of the partnership form of organization?

24-7 The promoters of a business enterprise are considering the relative desirability of forming three corporations instead of one.

REQUIRED:

a. What income tax advantages do the promoters hope to achieve by forming three corporations?

b. What adverse income tax factors must they consider?

c. What are some other important advantages and disadvantages of the multiple corporations as opposed to the single corporation?

24-8 A business acquired an automobile 3 years ago at a cost of $4,000 and has deducted depreciation of 20 per cent a year in its income tax returns. Now it is planning to dispose of the old automobile and to acquire a new one which will cost a total of $5,000. A new car dealer has offered a trade-in allowance of $1,500 on the old car. Another dealer has offered to pay $1,300 in cash for it.

REQUIRED:

a. Under what circumstances would the business be better off to *trade in* the old car on the new one?

b. Under what circumstances should it *sell* the old car and buy the new one?

c. Show the necessary journal entries for the trade in (a):

  (1) Under the income tax method;
  (2) Under the financial accounting method.

d. Show the necessary journal entries for the sale in (b):

  (1) Under the income tax method;
  (2) Under the financial accounting method.

e. How would your answers to (a) and (b) differ if the trade-in allowance and the resale price on the old car were each $500 higher?

24-9 During 19x4 a corporation had the following sales of property:

(1) Preferred stock of another company acquired in 19x1 for $3,000 was sold for $5,000.

(2) A shipment of unusual goods which had been acquired in December, 19x3, for $5,000 was sold in July, 19x4, for $6,200.

(3) A machine which had cost $10,000 6 years earlier, and on which depreciation of $6,000 had been accumulated, was sold for $5,500.

(4) A block of capital stock of another company which the corporation had acquired in January, 19x4, for $8,000, was sold in June, 19x4, for $6,000.

(5) The other business transactions during 19x4 resulted in total taxable revenue of $10,000 and deductible expenses of $4,000.

REQUIRED:

a. Which of the preceding items resulted in long-term capital gains or losses?

b. Which of the items resulted in short-term capital gains or losses?

c. What was the excess of net long-term capital gains over net short-term capital losses for the year?

d. What was the amount of ordinary income for the year?

e. Which transactions might have been timed more advantageously? Explain.

24-10 A corporation is trying to decide whether to raise $500,000 of additional capital by issuing 6 per cent bonds payable due in 10 years or 5 per cent cumulative preferred stock. Its annual net income available for the payment of a return to the bondholders or preferred stockholders, before deduction of income tax, is expected to be $75,000.

REQUIRED:

a. Prepare a table comparing the effect of the issuance of bonds and preferred stock on the amount of return available to common stockholders:

(1) If the expected income materializes;

(2) If the net income before interest, dividends, and income tax is only $10,000.

b. What other factors should the corporation consider before reaching a decision?

24-11 "Loss carrybacks and carryforwards are in effect an averaging of periodic income for income tax purposes. The income tax paid in one year is only tentative; it is subject to downward revision in later years if the business later suffers reverses."

REQUIRED:

a. Assume that the applicable income tax rate is 40 per cent, and that net losses may be carried back 3 years and then forward 5 years to be offset in full against taxable income. Using the following annual taxable income data, compute the amount of tax liability originally owed by a business at the time its tax returns were filed for 19x1, 19x2, 19x3, and 19x4:

19x1	$10,000 net income
19x2	10,000 net income
19x3	30,000 net income
19x4	(25,000) net loss

b. What was the amount of income tax as finally determined for each of the three years?

c. How do the carryback and carryforward provisions help to stabilize economic activity?

d. How do they encourage the formation of new businesses and the making of additional capital investments by existing businesses?

24-12 The Sandel Company was organized in 19x2. It followed the practice of waiting until an account receivable was definitely determined to be uncollectible before writing it off for both financial accounting and income tax reporting purposes. On the basis of its accumulated experience, together with additional losses expected on accounts not yet collected, it now feels that an estimated loss of 1 per cent of the sales on account for each year is reasonable.

The Sandel Company presents the following information for the past 4 years:

Year	Sales on Account	Accounts Written Off During Year
19x2	$ 80,000	$ 100
19x3	130,000	1,000
19x4	150,000	1,200
19x5	135,000	1,500

REQUIRED:

a. What was the effect of the company's policy of writing off accounts on specific items in its financial statements for each of the 4 years and at the end of 19x5?
b. Has the company's policy been a good one from the standpoint of its income tax expense? Explain.
c. If the company changes its accounting policy for general accounting purposes at the end of 19x5, after all necessary entries under the old policy have been made, state what the specific effect would be on its statement of financial position for December 31, 19x5.

24-13 The Madden Construction Company, Inc., is engaged in the construction of bridges. During the past three years, its activities have been as follows:

	19x1	19x2	19x3
Contract let on Bridge No. 1, contract price	$400,000		
Costs incurred on Bridge No. 1	70,000	$210,000	$ 70,000
Contract let on Bridge No. 2, contract price	$500,000		
Costs incurred on Bridge No. 2	200,000	100,000	100,000
Contract let on Bridge No. 3, contract price		900,000	
Costs incurred on Bridge No. 3		360,000	270,000

Bridge Nos. 1 and 2 were completed in 19x3. It is anticipated that Bridge No. 3 will be completed in 19x4, and that it will require additional costs of $180,000.

REQUIRED:

a. Compute the taxable income and the annual income tax of the company for 19x1, 19x2, and 19x3 under the completed-contracts method.
b. Compute the taxable income and the annual income tax of the company for the three years under the percentage-of-completion method.

24-14 The Kingland Corporation, manufacturer of heavy equipment, purchased machinery for $720,000 on June 30, 19x1. The company received a certificate of necessity from the Federal government which allowed it to write off the cost of the machinery over a period of 60 months for income tax purposes. The company estimated the useful life of the machinery to be 15 years and elected to use this life in calculating the depreciation shown in its financial statements to stockholders. Net income of the corporation for the year ended December 31, 19x1, before considering depreciation charges, was $250,000.

REQUIRED:

a. Determine the net income after Federal income taxes if the income tax is considered to be

(1) A distribution of income;
(2) An expense.

b. Prepare the accounting entries which should be made if the income tax is considered to be

(1) A distribution of income;
(2) An expense.

c. If the company follows one method for income tax purposes and another for its financial statements, will it be taking depreciation twice in future years? Explain.

d. Explain the accounting theory supporting each method of handling Federal income taxes.

24-15   It has been suggested by some that plant and equipment would be replaced more quickly if depreciation rates for income tax and accounting purposes were substantially increased. As a result, business operations would receive the benefit of more modern and more efficient plant facilities.

REQUIRED:

Discuss the merits of this proposition.

(AICPA Examination in Theory of Accounts, May, 1957.)

24-16   Your client, *ABC* Company, is contemplating changing its method of computing depreciation for Federal income tax purposes for the calendar year 1958 from a straight-line method to the "sum-of-the-years'-digits" method. However, the company has not decided whether it will record on the books the increased depreciation provision. The company provides you with the following data:

Net taxable income before provision for depreciation.....	$1,000,000
Provision for depreciation:	
Straight-line method................................	200,000
Sum-of-the-years'-digits method.....................	300,000
Amount of income taxes (not yet recorded):	
Based on $700,000...................................	358,500
Based on $800,000...................................	410,500

REQUIRED:

a. If the sum-of-the-years'-digits method for computing depreciation is claimed for Federal income tax purposes but straight-line depreciation has been recorded and will remain unchanged on the books:

(1) Give the journal entries, if any, relating to income taxes which should be recorded on the books.
(2) Prepare the notes to financial statements, if any, which would be needed.

b. If the sum-of-the years' digits method for computing depreciation is claimed for tax purposes and has been recorded on the books:

(1) Give the journal entries, if any, relating to income taxes which should be recorded on the books.
(2) Prepare the notes to financial statements, if any, which would be needed.

(Adapted from AICPA Examination in Auditing, May, 1959.)

24-17 Refer to Problem 22-7.

REQUIRED:

a. Compute the time-adjusted rate of return on each project after allowing for Federal income tax.

b. In what way does consideration of income tax affect the decision reached in Problem 22-7?

24-18 Refer to Problem 22-13.

REQUIRED:

a. Assuming that none of the proposed additions will have any salvage value at the end of their useful lives, determine the time-adjusted rate of return on each *after income tax.* Estimate the rate to the nearest whole per cent.

b. Submit your recommended capital additions budget for 19x3 on the basis of your answer in (*a*).

c. Explain the reasons for any differences between the capital additions budget after considering income tax and that which was prepared in Problem 22-13.

CASE 24-1. PLEMSON COMPANY

In 19x8 the amount of depreciation charged in the accounts of Plemson Company was $90,000 and the amount of depreciation deducted for income tax purposes was $150,000. The difference resulted from the use of accelerated depreciation in the tax return and straight-line depreciation in the financial records. The income tax return shows that the company must pay $346,000 in income taxes to the Federal government on 19x8 taxable income. If the same method had been used for income tax purposes as was used in the accounts of the company, the income tax would have been $31,200 more. The management of the company realizes that, in effect, there has been a postponement of income taxes because of the use of two different depreciation methods.

Four accountants were asked how to make the entry for income tax expense on the books of the company. Their answers were as follows:

Accountant 1:

OE, Income Tax Expense.........................	346,000	
L, Federal Income Tax Payable................		346,000

He proposed that the Federal income tax payable be shown on the statement of financial position as a current liability.

Accountant 2:

OE, Income Tax Expense.........................	377,200	
L, Federal Income Tax Payable..............		346,000
L, Deferred Income Tax Payable..............		31,200

He claimed that the Federal income tax payable should be shown as a current liability and the deferred income tax, as a long-term liability.

Accountant 3:

He agreed with the entry of Accountant No. 2, but contended that the deferred income tax should be shown as a restriction of retained income.

Accountant 4:

OE, Depreciation Expense........................	121,200	
A, Machinery—Accumulated Depreciation.....		121,200
OE, Income Tax Expense.........................	346,000	
L, Federal Income Tax Payable..............		346,000

REQUIRED:

Which accountant do you think is right, and why?

CASE 24 2. MR. FLOWERS

Mr. Flowers, who is operating a small manufacturing business, did not keep adequate records during 1956 to determine his taxable income or to prepare an acceptable balance sheet. He has furnished you with the following schedules of his assets and liabilities at December 31, 1955 and December 31, 1956 and has asked you to determine his taxable business income for the year and to make adjustments needed for a balance sheet as of December 31, 1956.

INVENTORY OF ASSETS AND LIABILITIES

	December 31, 1955	December 31, 1956
Cash	$ 5,000	$ 3,100
Accounts receivable	22,100	17,600
Notes receivable	6,000	8,500
Inventories—Raw materials	6,000	10,000
Inventories—Manufactured products	22,000	24,000
Fixed assets	105,000	112,000
Allowance for depreciation	(77,000)	(83,500)
Investments	36,700	24,900
	$125,800	$116,600
Accounts payable	$ 21,000	$ 14,500
Notes payable	—	10,000
Flowers, capital	104,800	92,100
	$125,800	$116,600

From inquiry and examination of available records you determine the following additional information:

(1) The cash figures given are the amounts appearing as the balances on his bank statement at each of the balance sheet dates. By reviewing subsequent bank statements and cancelled checks you find the following:

    (a) A deposit of $1,000 made on December 31, 1955 was not recorded by the bank until January 3, 1956. Four checks totaling $900 dated prior to December 31, 1955 were returned by the bank in January, 1956.

    (b) A deposit was entered by the bank on December 31, 1956 in the amount of $4,000 which was a collection from Jones & Jones on a sight draft. Mr. Flowers did not receive notice of the collection until January 5, 1957.

    (c) Outstanding checks at December 31, 1956 were found to total $450.

(2) The following is a trial balance of accounts receivable at December 31, 1956:

Accounts Receivable

Ace Sales Co	$ 6,000
Ajax Construction Co	3,000
Jones & Jones	4,000
Williamson & Sons	2,500
Blue Mt. Construction Co	2,100
	$17,600

An account receivable from M.B.A. Construction Co. totaling $4,500 has not been included in accounts receivable because full collection was doubtful. Prior to the time you start work you find that $3,700 of this receivable was collected in full settlement of the account.

(3) Notes receivable are from customers and are considered collectible.

(4) The inventories of manufactured products are stated at sales price at the inventory date. The average margin on sales was 40 per cent at December 31, 1955 and 39.5 per cent at December 31, 1956. Raw materials are stated at cost.

(5) The receivable from Ace Sales Co. contains $2,000 of merchandise shipped on consignment on December 26, 1956 and billed at regular sales price.

(6) In reviewing fixed assets it was found that in 1956 a machine purchased in 1935 at a cost of $4,000 was sold for $2,000 and the proceeds credited to the asset account. It was also determined that depreciation rates in prior years were not consistently applied each year. The asset acquisitions are set forth in the following schedule with proper depreciation rates. Depreciation for one-half year is recorded in year of acquisition and disposition and no consideration is given to salvage value.

December 31, 1955:	Year Acquired	Cost	Depreciation Rate
Machinery and equipment.......	1935	$ 20,000	5%
	1939	16,000	5%
	1940	69,000	5%
Total 12/31/55.............		$105,000	

Purchased in 1956:			
Machinery....................		$ 9,000	$6\frac{2}{3}$%

In addition to the sale mentioned above it is found that a machine purchased in 1939 for $6,000 was traded in on the machine purchased in 1956. An allowance of $3,000 for the old machine was received on the new machine which listed for $12,000.

(7) In reviewing stock transactions you find the following stock was owned at December 31, 1955 and December 31, 1956:

Stock	Shares	Par Value	December 31, 1955	December 31, 1956
ABC Company.....................	100	$100	$10,000	$10,000
Columbia Mfg. Co..................	200	50	10,000	
New York Exporting Co............	167	100	16,700	
Jones & Jones Company............	149	100		14,900
			$36,700	$24,900

(a) Fifty shares of ABC Company stock was acquired at par value in 1950 In 1952 a 100 per cent stock dividend was received.

(b) The Columbia Mfg. Co. stock was purchased for $11,000 in 1952 and was sold for $9,500 in 1956.

(c) The New York Exporting Co. stock was purchased for $17,000 in January, 1953 and sold in 1956 for $20,000.

(d) The Jones & Jones Company stock was purchased in October, 1956 for $22,500.

(8) An account payable to Steel Supply Co. in the amount of $1,800 has been carried in accounts payable since June, 1955. This was found to have been paid in November of 1955. An account payable to Peter Steel Fabricating

Co. for $900 was included in the December 31, 1956 trial balance of accounts payable. The material covered by this invoice was not received until January 25, 1957 and was not included in the inventory at December 31, 1956.

(9) The note payable covers a loan which was obtained for purchase of a home for the proprietor's daughter who was married in 1956.

(10) The following expenditures other than those commented on were made during the year 1956:

    (a) Payments on 1955 income tax—$3,100.

    (b) Payments on 1956 estimated tax—$6,000.

    (c) An automobile costing $3,000 was purchased for Mrs. Flowers and charged to delivery expense on the books.

    (d) Household and other personal expenditures amounted to $14,900 for the year and were all paid out of a separate bank account into which withdrawals from the business had been deposited in this amount.

REQUIRED:

a. Record the transactions of Mr. Flowers for 1956 in journal entries and post them to T-accounts (or as an alternative, use a transaction work sheet).

b. Prepare financial statements for Mr. Flowers.

c. Explain specifically which items require special treatment on Mr. Flowers' income tax return for the year, and what the nature of the income tax presentation is.

(Adapted from AICPA Examination in Accounting Practice, May 16, 1957.)

CASE 24-3. NIDER MACHINE COMPANY

On January 5, 19x1, the Nider Machine Company began operations as a machine rental service. On the same date it acquired 4 machines at a cost of $10,000 each. The machines are expected to have a useful life of 4 years each, and to have no salvage value.

At the end of 19x1 management is trying to decide whether to use the sum-of-the-years'-digits or the straight-line method of depreciation for income tax purposes. Taxable income before deducting depreciation for 19x1 is $10,000. The officers of the company feel that as demand for machine rentals increases and as the company's operations become more efficient, taxable income before depreciation will be about $20,000 in 19x2, $30,000 in 19x3, and $40,000 in 19x4. They anticipate that the machines will have to be replaced in kind at the end of 19x4 and that an additional machine will be needed at the end of 19x4 and at the end of each of the succeeding 3 years to serve new customers. They also estimate that each additional machine above the original 4 machines will add $5,000 to annual net income, before deducting depreciation and income tax.

Management expects the income tax rates to remain at 30 per cent of the first $25,000 of taxable income, and 52 per cent of income in excess of $25,000. It also thinks that it will be able to utilize fully the amounts of any tax loss carrybacks or carryforwards.

REQUIRED:

a. Prepare tables to compare the income tax effects of the two depreciation methods for the years 19x1 through 19x8.

b. Which method, or combination of methods, do you recommend that the company adopt? Support your answer with any additional computations needed.

c. What important factors other than income tax should be considered in making this decision?

PART 4

APPRAISAL OF BUSINESS
AND ACCOUNTING

Chapter **25**

except 744-752

External Appraisal of
Business Results

Chapter 10 pointed out how those who
are concerned with the future of a business may use accounting information for appraising its past results, preliminary to formulating their plans
of action. The principal groups who make such appraisals are *management,* who make them as a basis for deciding upon actions needed in operating the business, and *investors* and *creditors,* who make them as a basis
for deciding whether to invest in or lend to the business.

Chapter 10 presented some general methods of making comparisons
which are applicable to both of these principal groups, but emphasized
the types of comparison which are useful to management. Management
generally has more information at its disposal relating to the past operations and future plans of the business than do investor and creditor
groups, facilitating some of the detailed types of budgets and analyses
which were presented in Part 2, "Measuring, Planning, and Controlling
Income and Working Capital."

It should not be inferred that investors and creditors are not interested
in the types of comparisons which were presented in those chapters.
They are interested in a different way, not as those who are directly
charged with the management of the business, but as those whose capital
is being entrusted to others who will carry on the active management of
the enterprise. Furthermore, they often do not have the information
available for making, or their commitments are not large enough to warrant the time spent in making, the detailed plans and analyses of business
affairs which are suitable for management.

The present chapter stresses the types of appraisals of the past results
of a business which are useful to those who do not have full information
on internal operations and plans at their disposal, or who must content

themselves with rougher approximations of business performance and prospects.

General methods and standards of comparison

Investors and creditors, as well as the financial analysts who often provide them with information, find the computation of relationships and averages, comparative financial statements and graphs, and analyses of composition and change useful in formulating their decisions. They are interested primarily in comparisons of the following types:

(1) Comparison of a financial element with another element of the same company for the same accounting period.

(2) Comparison with the corresponding balance or relationship of the same company for an earlier accounting period.

(3) Comparison with the corresponding balance or relationship of another company for the same accounting period.

Lacking *internal* standards of comparison, such as the planned amount of a given financial category or the desirable level of achievement, they emphasize *external* standards, particularly those for representative businesses in the same industry. In interpreting these comparisons, the analyst must be careful to remember their limitations. He needs to know something of the real business events which are back of the figures—the ability of the management and the physical and economic conditions of the business. He also needs to remember that the comparisons represent past results only, and imperfectly at that. They are not strictly comparable with the past results of other businesses, even in the same line of endeavor, because of different characteristics. It is especially important that he remember that it is the *future* results that are the important ones, and that the imperfect information about the past is useful only to the extent that it provides a helpful guide for projecting future results.

With these limitations in mind, the analyst may find the detailed measures for appraising the operating results of a business suggested in Chapter 10—the rate of income on stockholders' equity, the earnings per share of stock, the effect of leverage on the return to stockholders, and the rate of income on total assets—quite useful. No particular modifications of these measures are necessary from the point of view of the investor or the creditor, except that these groups should be certain that the measures were compiled in a manner consistent with that used for other companies with which they are making comparisons.

The relationships which are computed, even if reliable, do not constitute the end result of financial analysis. The person making the analysis uses them as a guide only, and must also consider qualitative factors within the business itself, within the industry, and within the economy as a whole, in making his decision whether to invest in, or lend to, the business.

Importance of liquidity, solvency, and profitability

Creditors and potential creditors of a business are chiefly interested in the answer to the question:

Will the business be able to pay its liabilities as they come due, both in the near and distant future, and will it have enough working capital and facilities left to carry on normal operations?

This question deals with the *solvency* of the business, also often called *liquidity* when referring to the ability of a business to meet its obligations in the *near future*. The *liquidity* of the business can be determined to a large extent by the soundness of the items which appear as *current assets* in its statement of financial position on a given date, and the rapidity of their probable conversion into cash. Liquidity is more complex than that, however, even when used to measure the ability to pay a short-term debt. The soundness of the assets may change quickly, or other requirements for their use may intervene before the due date of the liability. More importantly, most creditors anticipate a continuing relationship with a customer. It is true that the given extension of credit may be merely for 30 or 60 days, but when the current claim is settled, the customer will probably soon apply for additional credit.

The continuing liquidity of a business, or its *long-range solvency* from the point of view of a long-term creditor or investor, depends upon the soundness of the *financial structure* of the business and its *profitability*. A sound financial structure is one which has a proper balance between various types of long- and short-term liabilities and owners' equity. The requirements for payment of both principal and periodic interest to creditors and dividends to stockholders should be well within the ability of the business.

Profitability, the income-earning ability of a business, is also of importance to creditors. Although their claims are usually fixed in amount, the existence of a healthy margin of income over and above debt service requirements helps to insure them that their payments of interest and principal will be made when due.

Profitability is of primary interest to stockholders, particularly common stockholders, because the amount of their investment income depends to a large extent upon the amount of business income. Liquidity and solvency are also important to them, however. These qualities help to determine whether the business can obtain the outside capital which it needs on reasonable terms, and whether it can survive in the long run to meet its fixed obligations, with an adequate amount of income remaining for the residual owners.

Liquidity and solvency are partly a matter of existing financial position, but they are more a matter of the *flow of events*—of income and liquid assets—over a future period of time. Later sections of this chapter deal with specific methods of analyzing the liquidity of a business at a given time and its continuing liquidity or solvency over a period of time.

MEASURES OF LIQUIDITY

As pointed out earlier, the *liquidity*, or short-range solvency, of a business cannot be determined without giving some consideration to its *long-term solvency*. Its *income-earning ability* has an important influence on both of these conditions. Still, there are some quantitative measures which are more directly related to determining the liquidity of a business than of measuring its long-term solvency and profitability. The following sections describe the meaning, purposes, and limitations of some of the more common measures.

Basis for illustration

Chapter 10 presented the case of Sound Center, Inc., as a basis for illustrating methods of appraising the operating results of the company. The owners of the business, who had become increasingly dissatisfied with the amount of its annual income, had met as the board of directors to study the financial results of the past two years and to decide upon a course of action.

SOUND CENTER, INC.
Income Statement

	For the Years Ended	
	December 31, 19x3	December 31, 19x2
Net sales revenue	$150,000	$120,000
Deduct cost of goods sold expense	100,500	80,400
Gross margin on sales	$ 49,500	$ 39,600
Deduct operating expense:		
Advertising	$ 3,900	$ 2,000
Commissions on sales	6,000	4,800
Depreciation	1,000	1,000
Insurance	2,000	2,000
Rent	6,000	6,000
Salary, manager	8,000	8,000
Salaries, other	13,860	12,360
Supplies	1,740	1,500
Taxes (other than income tax)	1,900	1,840
Miscellaneous	2,100	1,980
Total operating expense	$ 46,500	$ 41,480
Income (loss) before Federal income tax	$ 3,000	($ 1,880)
Corporate Federal income tax expense	900	0
Net income (loss) (to Statement of Retained Income)	$ 2,100	($ 1,880)

SOUND CENTER, INC.
Statement of Retained Income

	For the Years Ended	
	December 31, 19x3	December 31, 19x2
Retained income at beginning of year..................	$ 28,300	$30,930
Add net income, or deduct net loss for the year (from Income Statement)..............................	2,100	(1,880)
	$ 30,400	$29,050
Deduct dividends........	1,500	750
Retained income at end of year (to Statement of Financial Position)................................	$ 28,900	$28,300

SOUND CENTER, INC.
Statement of Financial Position

	December 31	
ASSETS	19x3	19x2
Current Assets:		
Cash..	$ 5,000	$ 6,000
Accounts receivable, trade.........................	36,500	34,600
Deduct estimated uncollectibles.................(	3,000)	(2,800)
Merchandise inventory............................	51,000	49,000
Prepaid expenses.................................	4,000	4,200
Total current assets...........................	$ 93,500	$91,000
Fixed Assets:		
Equipment (cost)...............................	$ 14,000	$11,500
Deduct accumulated depreciation.................(	5,500)	(4,500)
Total fixed assets..	$ 8,500	$ 7,000
Total assets...............................	$102,000	$98,000
LIABILITIES		
Current Liabilities:		
Notes payable to banks...........................	$ 5,000	$ 4,500
Accounts payable, trade...	25,600	24,500
Corporate Federal income tax payable..............	900	800
Accrued liabilities...............................	2,100	2,200
Total current liabilities.......................	$ 33,600	$32,000
Long-Term Liabilities:		
Long-term notes payable..........................	9,500	7,700
Total liabilities..............................	$ 43,100	$39,700
STOCKHOLDERS' EQUITY		
Capital stock, $50 par, 600 shares....................	$ 30,000	$30,000
Retained income (from Statement of Retained Income)	28,900	28,300
Total stockholders' equity.....................	$ 58,900	$58,300
Total equities...............................	$102,000	$98,000

As a result of that meeting, the owners and management decided upon an expansion policy which would require an additional investment in the form of cash, receivables, and inventories. Mr. Farley, the manager, has approached the First City Bank for a short-term loan to help finance this expansion. He has furnished the company's comparative financial statements for the two preceding years, which are reproduced here, to Mr. Keyes, the vice-president of the bank, for analysis.

Amount of net working capital

Chapter 8 defined the meaning of *current assets* and *current liabilities* and of the difference between them, *net working capital*. The amount of net working capital is the margin of current assets which remains, after deducting the amounts required for the payment of liabilities which come due in the near future, for meeting the operating requirements of the business during the next year or the next operating cycle (whichever is longer).

EXAMPLE 1:   Mr. Keyes, the bank vice-president, computes the net working capital of Sound Center, Inc., for the two years as follows:

	December 31, 19x3	December 31, 19x2
Total current assets......................	$93,500	$91,000
Deduct total current liabilities............	33,600	32,000
Net working capital...................	$59,900	$59,000

In making his computation, Mr. Keyes does not use the totals of current assets and current liabilities presented by the company without further scrutiny. Being interested in the bank's *margin of safety* if it makes the loan, he must be sure that the working capital is not *overstated* by an *overstatement* of current assets or an *understatement* of current liabilities. He scans the items which compose each category and attempts to determine whether their classification as current and their amounts seem to be proper. He can make this analysis more confidently if the statements are accompanied by the opinion of an independent Certified Public Accountant.

In this particular case, Mr. Keyes would conclude that the working capital changed only slightly, with the direction of the increase being favorable. He needs to form an opinion, however, as to whether this merely represents the continuation of an unfavorable situation. If the amount of net working capital was inadequate in 19x2, it is probably still inadequate at the end of 19x3. To make this judgment, he needs a standard of comparison for estimating its adequacy.

Current ratio

The *amount* of net working capital is of less assistance in measuring the liquidity of a business than the *relationship* of total working capital to the amount required. A measure of this relationship is the *current ratio*, which is computed as follows:

$$\text{Current Ratio} = \frac{\text{Current Assets}}{\text{Current Liabilities}}$$

EXAMPLE 2:   The current ratio for Sound Center, Inc., at the ends of the two years would be:

	December 31, 19x3	December 31, 19x2
Total current assets.....................	$93,500	$91,000
Divided by total current liabilities........	$33,600	$32,000
Equals current ratio....................	2.78	2.84

Again, the change in the current ratio is slight, but it is a decrease. Unless the ratio was higher than needed in 19x2, this shows a slight worsening. The analyst might compare the ratio of Sound Center, Inc., with ratios of other similar businesses to determine whether it is in line with those of the stronger companies in its field. The comparison is of limited value unless the other companies have very similar characteristics and follow similar accounting policies, particularly in the measurement of accounts receivable and inventories.

To know whether the net working capital or the current ratio of a business is sufficient one needs to consider the *particular operating conditions* of that business. How much working capital the business needs depends upon the amount of payments it will have to make during its next operating cycle. The current ratio should be interpreted according to the line of business in which the company is engaged, any peculiarities it may have, and the general economic conditions of the time. The current ratio is used in an attempt to predict whether available resources in the near *future* will be on hand in sufficient quantities and at sufficient times to pay the liabilities as they mature. It gives only an approximation, and is subject to a margin of error to the extent that the assets will be collected, or the liabilities will mature, at irregular intervals.

The amounts of current assets and current liabilities in the statement of financial position may not be representative of their typical amounts during the next accounting period. In fact, if the business is using a *natural year* as its accounting period, the balances of current assets and current liabilities at the end of the year are probably *not typical* of the balances which exist during most of the year. Even if these difficulties can be overcome, the current ratio must be supported by additional analysis in determining short-term solvency. Arbitrary ratios are far inferior to a cash budget for estimating the needs of the business for the coming period, and even the cash budget is imperfect. Exercise of judgment cannot be avoided in deciding whether the firm's current position is sound, for there is no standard current ratio which is satisfactory in all circumstances.

Quick ratio

Most retail businesses complete several operating cycles within a year, which means that the dividing line between their current and non-current assets and liabilities is twelve months. Although they may expect to collect enough assets during the next year to pay current debts, irregularity in the rate of either collections or payments may cause temporary financial embarrassment. Thus, even if the current ratio is satisfactory, the degree of liquidity of assets may not be.

EXAMPLE 3: A particular business has a high current ratio, but a large part of its current assets consist of slow-moving inventory. Although it will probably be in sound current condition at the end of the year, it may run into temporary difficulty in meeting its debts during the year. Inventory cannot be used for paying rent or salaries.

For the reason illustrated, it is usually desirable to supplement the current ratio with a computation of the *quick*, or *acid-test*, *ratio*, which shows the relationship to current liabilities of the total assets which will quickly be converted into cash. Its formula is:

Quick Ratio

$$= \frac{\text{Cash} + \text{Short-Term Receivables} + \text{Temporary Investments}}{\text{Total Current Liabilities}}$$

The *quick assets* consist of *cash*, *receivables*, and *temporary investments*. Inventories are excluded, because they must first be sold and then the resulting accounts receivable must be collected before cash is available for making payments. Prepaid expenses are also omitted from quick assets, as are any receivables which the business does not expect to collect in the very near future.

EXAMPLE 4: The quick ratio of Sound Center, Inc., for the two years is computed as follows:

	December 31, 19x3	December 31, 19x2
Cash.................................	$ 5,000	$ 6,000
Plus estimated collectible accounts receivable..........................	33,500	31,800
Total quick assets....................	$38,500	$37,800
Divided by total current liabilities........	$33,600	$32,000
Equals quick ratio.....................	1.15	1.18

The computation means that at the end of 19x3, Sound Center, Inc., had $1.15 of highly liquid assets for each dollar of liabilities then owed which were to be paid during the next year. Apparently the business will be able to meet its debts as they come due, even if most of the liabilities are due in the very near future.

The quick ratio is somewhat lower than it was the previous year, and coupled with the slight decline in the current ratio, the indication is that Sound Center,

Inc., is not in as strong a current position as it was. The banker still needs to determine whether its liquid position is now, and is likely to continue to be, sound enough to warrant making the requested loan.

Composition of assets

Working capital may appear to be adequate in amount and sufficiently liquid on the basis of the three preceding computations, but it may still lack the proper *balance* between components. One way of attempting to judge whether the balance is proper is to determine the *percentage of each asset to total assets*. This measure of asset composition is then compared with that of the same company at earlier dates and with that of similar companies at the same date.

EXAMPLE 5:   The percentage composition of the assets of Sound Center, Inc., was as follows:

	December 31, 19x3		December 31, 19x2	
	Amount	Per Cent	Amount	Per Cent
Current Assets:				
Cash............................	$ 5,000	4.9%	$ 6,000	6.1%
Accounts receivable, net.............	33,500	32.9	31,800	32.5
Merchandise inventory...............	51,000	50.0	49,000	50.0
Prepaid expenses...................	4,000	3.9	4,200	4.3
Total current assets..............	$ 93,500	91.7%	$91,000	92.9%
Fixed Assets:				
Equipment (unexpired cost)..........	$ 8,500	8.3%	$ 7,000	7.1%
Total assets.....................	$102,000	100.0%	$98,000	100.0%

The percentages of each asset to the total, and of each current asset to total current assets, tell something about the composition of assets, but these measures should be used with caution. One asset, such as cash, may appear to be the desirable percentage of total assets, while in truth both cash and total assets are too small or too large by the same proportion. On the other hand, the ratio of one asset to the total may falsely appear to be satisfactory because of an opposite effect of another asset on total assets.

Asset turnover

The adequacy of working capital depends on the adequacy of each of its components. The amount of net working capital and its degree of liquidity in total may appear to be satisfactory, and yet temporary financial stress can still be caused by inadequate balances of individual current assets. On the other hand, the rate of income of a business may be lessened if it carries excessive balances of individual assets. In trying to see whether the business strikes a happy medium between these two extremes, the analyst should compare the typical balance of each asset with the amount of that asset which is needed over a period of time. Such a comparison is called *asset turnover*. Its general formula is:

$$\text{Asset Turnover} = \frac{\text{Amount of Change in Asset During a Period}}{\text{Average Asset Balance During the Period}}$$

The methods of computing and using turnover rates for Cash, Accounts Receivable, and Inventories were discussed in Chapters 13, 14, and 16. The external analyst can use the same methods, except that generally he must use the actual turnover rates of the past. He does not usually have sufficiently reliable information for projecting future turnover rates.

FLOW OF WORKING CAPITAL

Earlier sections of this chapter have pointed out that liquidity and solvency are not so much conditions at a given moment as *continuing relationships* of assets to asset requirements. The discussion of the use of ratios of balances at a given date pointed out that their validity is limited because they may not be representative of balances which existed during a past period of time, or which will exist in the future.

One means of analyzing working capital which overcomes some of these objections is a detailed tracing of the *sources* from which working capital flows into the business during a period of time, and the *uses to which it is put*. This analysis of the flow of working capital shows the reasons for changes in the financial position of a business from one date to another, and it also provides valuable information about the financial policy of management.

Sources and uses of net working capital

Net working capital is the same thing as *net current assets* (current assets minus current liabilities). Analysis of the flow of net working capital is concerned with the *major sources* of net current assets which become available to a business during a period, and the major *long-term uses* to which they are put. For the purpose of this analysis, net working capital is treated as though it were a single asset, as shown in the following summary of the statement of financial position of Sound Center, Inc., on December 31, 19x3:

SOUND CENTER, INC.
Summary of Financial Position
December 31, 19x3

Net working capital (net current assets)...............	$59,900	Noncurrent liabilities..........	$ 9,500
Noncurrent assets.............	8,500	Stockholders' equity...........	58,900
	$68,400		$68,400

Net working capital has a *debit* balance, and any *increases* in it are recorded by *debits*. According to the rule of double entry, the corresponding *credit* must be to one of the *noncurrent accounts:* noncurrent assets, noncurrent liabilities, or stockholders' equity. These noncurrent accounts which are credited when net working capital increases are *sources of working capital.* Typical source transactions are:

(1) Sale of fixed assets or investment securities;
(2) Borrowing for a long term;
(3) Issuance of capital stock for net current assets;
(4) Operations of the business.

Decreases in net working capital are recorded by *credits,* and the offsetting *debits* are to *noncurrent accounts,* which represent *long-term uses* of working capital. Examples of uses of working capital are:

(1) Purchase of fixed assets or investment securities;
(2) Repayment of long-term liabilities;
(3) Retirement of capital stock;
(4) Operations of the business;
(5) Payment of dividends.

Operations of the business is listed as an example of both a possible source and a possible use of working capital. It is a *source* if the net current assets derived from revenue exceed the net current assets applied to expenses, and a *use* if the net current assets applied to expenses are the greater.

Transactions which affect only current accounts, such as the collection of accounts receivable in cash or the payment of accounts payable in cash, change the *composition* of net working capital but not its amount. Changes of this type are ignored in the analysis of sources and uses of working capital, although separate analyses of the composition of working capital, and changes therein, are often useful.

Method of determining sources and uses of net working capital[1]

One of the best methods of analyzing the major sources and uses of working capital is to *reconstruct accounting entries* to summarize the period's transactions *between current and noncurrent accounts.* Needed for this purpose are a comparative statement of financial position at the beginning and end of the period, a statement of income for the period, and a statement of retained income. Supporting schedules of fixed asset additions and retirements and of new issues and retirements of long-term liabilities and capital stock permit a more refined analysis.

---

[1] The method of analysis in this section is based on William J. Vatter, "A Direct Method for the Preparation of Fund Statements," *The Journal of Accountancy,* June, 1946, pp. 479–489.

The entries which explain the sources and uses of working capital may be recorded in T-accounts or on a transaction work sheet. T-accounts are used here, but the method of analysis in the work sheet is the same. The steps are as follows:

(1) Open a T-account for Net Working Capital and for each noncurrent asset and noncurrent equity. Also open a T-account for Change in Net Working Capital from Operations. The purpose of the last account is to explain one of the important causes of change in net working capital.

(2) On the proper side of each noncurrent account and of Net Working Capital enter the *net change* in the account from the beginning to the end of the period, as shown by the comparative statement of financial position. Draw a line across the account below the amounts of change. These are the amounts which are to be explained as sources or uses of working capital.

(a) An *increase in an asset*, a debit change, is shown on the *debit* side of the asset account, and a *decrease* is shown on the *credit* side.

(b) An *increase in an equity* is a *credit*, and a *decrease* is a *debit*.

(3) Add the changes recorded in the T-accounts to be sure that total debits equal total credits.

(4) Record a summary entry for each type of transaction which caused a change in noncurrent accounts. Identify the parts of each entry by letters or numbers. A debit to a noncurrent account may be offset by a credit (and a credit to a noncurrent account may be offset by a debit) to one of the following accounts:

(a) Another noncurrent account. Such a transaction has no effect on net working capital, but the entry should be made so that all changes in noncurrent accounts will be explained.

(b) Change in Net Working Capital from Operations. This account is debited or credited to offset a noncurrent account change which also affects *income* for the period. Its balance is later transferred to Net Working Capital. A brief explanation of the reason for the change should be entered in the account.

(c) Net Working Capital. This account is debited or credited to offset a change in a noncurrent account which also affects a *current* account, but which is not used in determining income for the period. A brief explanation of the reason for the change should be entered in the account.

(5) Compare the net changes in accounts *explained* by the summary entries in Step (4) with the *changes to be explained* which were recorded in the T-accounts in Step (2). The analysis is not complete until all changes have been explained.

(6) Prepare a formal statement from the information recorded in the Change in Net Working Capital from Operations and the Net Working Capital accounts.

Illustration of analysis of changes in net working capital

The financial statements of Sound Center, Inc., which were illustrated earlier in this chapter are used as the basis for the following explanation of the method of analyzing changes in net working capital.

Steps (1) and (2). The T-accounts which show the net changes in accounts during the year are as follows:

A, Net Working Capital

Increases		*Decreases*
Net change	900	

A, Equipment (cost)

Net change	2,500	

A, Equipment—Accumulated Depreciation

	Net change	1,000

L, Long-Term Notes Payable

	Net change	1,800

OE, Capital Stock, $50 Par

(Net change, 0)	

OE, Retained Income

	Net change	600

A, Change in Net Working Capital from Operations

Increases		*Decreases*

Step (3). Addition shows that the total of net debit changes in account balances, $3,400, is equal to the total of net credit changes.

Step (4). The summary entries are recorded here first in journal form for clearer explanation, and then are posted to the T-accounts. Actually, the journal entries are unnecessary.

(a)

A, Change in Net Working Capital from Operations..... 2,100
    OE, Retained Income...........................   2,100
    To record the tentative increase in net working capital
    equal to reported net income for the period, and to
    explain part of the change in Retained Income.

(b)

A, Equipment...................................... 2,500
    A, Net Working Capital.......................   2,500
    To record the decrease in net working capital resulting
    from the purchase of equipment.

In analyzing the flow of net working capital, it is customary to show an acquisition of a long-lived asset as though it reduced net working capital, and an increase of a long-term liability as though it increased net working capital, even though the liability was increased directly as a result of the purchase of the long-lived asset.

(c)

A, Change in Net Working Capital from Operations.....	1,000	
A, Equipment—Accumulated Depreciation.........		1,000

To adjust the tentative amount of increase in net working capital resulting from operations, recorded in entry (a). Depreciation expense of $1,000 was deducted in arriving at the reported net income of $2,100, and yet it did not require the use of net working capital. Instead, it is merely a cost expiration of a noncurrent asset.

(d)

A, Net Working Capital............................	1,800	
L, Long-Term Notes Payable....................		1,800

To record the increase in net working capital resulting from borrowing on long-term notes.

(e)

OE, Retained Income..............................	1,500	
A, Net Working Capital.......................		1,500

To record the decrease in net working capital resulting from the payment of dividends.

(f)

A, Net Working Capital............................	3,100	
A, Change in Net Working Capital from Operations.		3,100

To transfer the total amount of net working capital derived from operations to the Net Working Capital account.

The T-accounts resulting from these entries are as follows:

A, Net Working Capital

Increases			*Decreases*		
Net change		900			
Explanation of Increases			*Explanation of Decreases*		
Borrowing on long-term			Purchase of equipment	(b)	2,500
notes	(d)	1,800	Payment of dividends	(e)	1,500
Operations	(f)	3,100			4,000
		4,900			
Net increase, 900.					

A, Equipment (cost)

Net change	2,500		
(b)	2,500		

A, Equipment—Accumulated Depreciation

		Net change	1,000
		(c)	1,000

L, Long-Term Notes Payable

		Net change	1,800
		(d)	1,800

OE, Capital Stock, $50 Par
(Net change, 0)

OE, Retained Income

		Net change	600
(e)	1,500	(a)	2,100
	Net increase, 600.		

A, Change in Net Working Capital from Operations

Increases			Decreases		
Net income	(a)	2,100	Transferred to Net		
Add depreciation (which			Working Capital	(f)	3,100
does not affect net					
working capital)	(c)	1,000			
Total increase in net					
working capital from					
operations		3,100			3,100

Statement of changes in net working capital

The preparation of the following Statement of Changes in Net Working Capital from the preceding analysis is merely a formality. The necessary information can be found in the Net Working Capital and the Change in Net Working Capital from Operations accounts.

SOUND CENTER, INC.
Statement of Changes in Net Working Capital
For the Year Ended December 31, 19x3

Sources of Net Working Capital
Operations:
Net income for the period......................	$2,100	
Add depreciation expense, which does not affect net working capital but which was deducted in computing net income............................	1,000	
Total increase in net working capital from operations		$3,100
Borrowing on long-term notes payable.....................		1,800
Total increases in net working capital....................		$4,900

Uses of Net Working Capital
Purchase of equipment............................	$2,500	
Payment of dividends on capital stock..............	1,500	
Total decreases in net working capital...................		4,000
Net Increase in Net Working Capital......................		$ 900

Alternative forms and titles

Statements of the changes in net working capital often show the amount of net working capital at the *beginning* of the year, the *change* during the year, and the net working capital at the *end* of the year. They are also frequently supported by detailed statements of the beginning and ending balances of the individual current assets and current liabilities, which together comprise net working capital. These details are particularly important when there have been important shifts in the composition of current assets or current liabilities during the period.

The term *funds* is often used as a synonym of net working capital. Alternative statement titles in common use are *Statement of Sources and Uses of Funds* and *Statement of Sources and Application of Funds*.

The external analyst who does not have access to the detailed information contained in the company's ledger accounts often uses a similar method for explaining the major changes in the *cash* of the business during the year. He tries to reconstruct in summary form the net effect of transactions between cash and all other accounts, and reports the results in a *Statement of Cash Flow*.

Projecting future flow of working capital

The preceding discussion and illustration dealt with the reasons for *past* changes in the net working capital of a business. Probably most analysts are interested in this analysis as a means of projecting the working capital changes that are likely to occur in the *future*, preliminary to deciding what action they are going to take as managers, stockholders, or creditors.

The same general approach may be used in summarizing *expected future changes* in working capital. Often the information given consists of the present balances of accounts and expected future *transactions*, rather than the present and expected future account *balances*. It is easier to project the changes in net working capital by recording these expected transactions directly than by computing the differences between beginning and ending balances.

Analysis of more complex changes

The causes of the working capital changes of Sound Center, Inc., were relatively simple. The following illustrations show how more complex transactions would be reconstructed.

More than one change in a single account. The following balances are already in the T-accounts as a result of previous steps in the analysis:

A, Machinery (cost)

	Net change	2,600

A, Machinery—Accumulated Depreciation

Net change	4,000	

A, Change in Net Working Capital from Operations

	Net loss	3,000

Additional information available indicates that depreciation for the current year amounted to $6,000, and that a machine with an original cost of $25,000 and accumulated depreciation of $10,000 was sold for $7,000 cash during the year. The $8,000 loss on the sale of the machine was shown in the income statement.

The journal entries needed to analyze the changes in net working capital are:

(1)

A, Change in Net Working Capital from Operations ..	6,000	
A, Machinery—Accumulated Depreciation.......		6,000

To adjust the tentative amount of change in net working capital from operations by the amount of depreciation recorded during the period.

(2)

A, Net Working Capital..........................	7,000	
A, Machinery—Accumulated Depreciation...........	10,000	
A, Change in Net Working Capital from Operations...	8,000	
A, Machinery................................		25,000

To show as one amount the $7,000 increase in working capital which resulted from the sale of machinery, and to explain changes in three noncurrent accounts.

At this point the balances in the T-accounts would be as follows:

A, Machinery (cost)

		Net change		2,600
		(2)	25,000

A, Machinery—Accumulated Depreciation

Net change		4,000			
	(2)	10,000		(1)	6,000
Net decrease, 4,000.					

A, Change in Net Working Capital from Operations

Depreciation expense	(1)	6,000	Net loss	3,000
Loss on sale of machinery	(2)	8,000		
		14,000		
Net increase, 11,000.				

The net change in the balance of Machinery—Accumulated Depreciation has been fully accounted for.

Even though there was a net loss for the year, the net result of operations was to *increase* net working capital by $11,000. The depreciation expense entry for the year reduced net income, but it did not reduce net working capital. Instead, it reduced a *noncurrent* asset. The effect of the loss on sale of machinery was similar—a reduction of net income, but no effect on net working capital. It, too, reduced a noncurrent asset. The $7,000 of cash received for the sale of the machine is the transaction's only effect on net working capital.

There is still an unexplained change in Machinery (cost). Since there has been a $25,000 credit to the account equal to the cost of the machine sold, there must also have been a *debit* of $22,400. This was necessary to result in a net credit change of $2,600 in the account during the year. The appropriate entry is:

(3)

A, Machinery (cost)...............................	22,400	
A, Net Working Capital......................		22,400
To record the use of net working capital to purchase machinery.		

Change affecting only noncurrent accounts. The net changes of two noncurrent accounts during a year were as follows:

A, Patents

Net change	50,000		

OE, Capital Stock

		Net change	50,000

An investigation reveals that the corporation acquired a patent from an inventor and issued him capital stock in exchange. The transaction did not affect working capital at all, but the following entry should be made so that the changes of all noncurrent account balances are completely explained:

(4)

A, Patents..	50,000	
OE, Capital Stock............................		50,000
To explain the changes resulting from the issuance of capital stock in exchange for a patent.		

Start Again here

MEASURES OF LONG-RANGE SOLVENCY

Importance of long-range solvency

Prospective short-term creditors of a business are interested in its current position now and its probable current position when payments on the debt come due. If the time to maturity is short, a satisfactory current position at the date of the statement of financial position is usually sufficient indication that the company will be able to pay the loan when it is due, unless the business is incurring substantial losses. However, banks and suppliers are usually interested in maintaining a *continuing relationship* with a healthy customer. Both of these types of creditors are concerned with whether the trend of income and other financial factors of the customer are such that its financial health will last.

Even more directly concerned with the *long-range solvency* of the enterprise are its long-term creditors, such as holders of installment notes on equipment, mortgage notes, or bonds. A satisfactory current position of the borrower today may assure the lender that he will receive his interest payments promptly for a short while. This is of little comfort to him, however if the downward trend of the debtor's income and the deterioration of his current position cast doubt on his ability to pay the principal or interest several years from now.

Stockholders, too, study the factors which point to the long-range solvency of the company in deciding whether to change their stockholdings. If creditors cannot be paid, stockholders are unlikely to receive dividends. Moreover, they may suffer substantial losses in a forced liquidation or a reorganization.

Earnings coverage of debt service requirements

A business usually expects to pay the interest on loans, and often the principal as well, by using funds derived from operations. Chapter 19 pointed out briefly that the number of times the borrower has earned fixed charges in the past, and is likely to earn them in the future, is an indication of the margin of safety of the long-term creditors.

The following condensed financial summaries of the Borrower Company for the year ended December 31, 19x1, are used as the basis for later illustration.

BORROWER COMPANY
Income Statement
For the Year Ended December 31, 19x1

Revenue..	$800,000
Deduct operating expense.............................	768,750
Net income on operations...........................	$ 31,250
Deduct bond interest expense..........................	6,250
Net income before Federal income tax..................	$ 25,000
Deduct corporate Federal income tax expense.............	7,500
Net income..	$ 17,500

BORROWER COMPANY
Statement of Financial Position
December 31, 19x1

ASSETS

Current assets................................	$150,000	
Noncurrent assets............................	250,000	
Total assets....................................		$400,000

LIABILITIES

Current liabilities............................	$ 50,000	
Noncurrent liabilities:		
5% Bonds payable due in 19x9	125,000	
Total liabilities....................		$175,000

STOCKHOLDERS' EQUITY

Capital stock................................	$100,000	
Retained income............................	125,000	
Total stockholders' equity.........................		225,000
Total equities...................................		$400,000

The number of times fixed charges are earned is computed as follows:

$$\frac{\text{Net Income before Interest and Income Taxes}}{\text{Periodic Interest}} = \frac{\text{Number of Times Fixed}}{\text{Charges Earned}}$$

$$\frac{\$31,250}{\$ 6,250} = 5 \text{ times.}$$

At present, the amount of earnings available for the payment of interest is five times as large as the amount required to pay interest. Earnings available for the payment of interest could decline 80 per cent, to $\frac{1}{5}$ of their present amount, and still barely provide enough for the payment of interest.

Income tax is not deducted in computing the earnings available for the payment of interest. It is a contingent expense; there will be no income tax unless there is a net income subject to tax, after deducting interest and all other expenses.

The analyst is attempting to estimate the margin of safety with which the *future earnings* of the business will cover its *future debt service requirements*. After analyzing the past coverage as a point of departure, he should project what the coverage will be in the future, allowing for his proposed loan's effect on both earnings and interest requirements.

Availability of cash for debt service requirements

Another important type of analysis which should accompany the analysis of the number of times fixed charges are covered by earnings is the expected availability of *cash* to meet the required payments of liability principal and interest. A cash budget is the best way of making such a projection, but if one is not available, the following method gives a reasonably good approximation:

$$\frac{\text{Net Income} + \text{Depreciation and Other Charges not Requiring Working Capital}}{\text{Periodic Cash Payments of Principal and Interest on Debt}}$$
= Approximate Times Available Cash Covers Debt Service Requirements.

If major changes in current assets and current liabilities other than cash are expected, a more refined analysis is needed to project the *cash flow*.

Ratio of stockholders' equity to total equities

Another important relationship bearing on the long-range solvency of a business is the *proportion of its total equity which is furnished by stockholders.*

Most lenders hope to collect their interest and principal from a solvent business which continues in operation. However, it is a well-known fact that businesses often do fail. When a business liquidates, the creditors' claims must be paid first. After liabilities have been settled, the remaining assets, if any, are distributed to the stockholders. Stockholders are thus the final, or residual, claimants of both the income of a living business and the assets of a dying one. Any loss which occurs in disposing of the assets reduces the stockholders' equity first. The ratio of stockholders' equity to the total equities (which equal the total assets) of the business shows the relative size of the margin of safety.

For Borrower Company, the ratio is computed as follows:

$$\frac{\text{Stockholders' Equity}}{\text{Total Equities}} = \frac{\$225,000}{\$400,000} = .5625 = 56.25\%$$

This means that the total assets of the company could shrink 56.25% before there would be any loss to the creditors in liquidation. A major shrinkage might result from continued operating losses or from losses upon disposal of important assets, such as investments or buildings.

The greater the risk of decline in the assets of a business, the greater is the margin of protection which creditors need. This required margin is indirectly a protective feature for the stockholders, too, because usually no equity holder gains by a forced liquidation of a business.

If other factors remain constant, there is usually a greater risk of shrinkage in assets the longer the time period involved. Creditors stand more chance of losing on a loan due 2 years from now than one due next year, and still more chance of losing on a 10-year loan. The degree of periodic fluctuation in the income of the business also affects the safety of the loan. Electric utilities have fairly stable income because the demand for their service usually changes little in good times or bad, and substantial loans to them for long periods are considered quite safe. On the other hand, manufacturers of factory machinery often suffer wide swings in periodic income and frequent losses; consequently, long-term loans to them are relatively rare.

As in practically every other case involving analysis of the long-term solvency of a business, the analyst is trying to *predict* what the margin of safety will be in the future. In his analysis of the ratio of stockholders' equity to total equities, therefore, he should take into consideration expected *future* changes in liabilities and equities.

Summary

This chapter has emphasized the point of view of external analysts of the business, principally creditors and stockholders. These groups as well as management are concerned with the liquidity, long-range solvency, and profitability of the business, but creditors tend to lay more stress on the first two.

The amount of net working capital, the current ratio, the quick ratio, and the turnover rates of individual assets are sometimes useful indicators of the liquidity of the business, but the person who is using them needs a reliable standard of comparison. An analysis of the major sources and uses of net working capital during the period provides valuable information about the changes in the current position and their underlying causes, as well as about the policies of management. Important measures of the long-range solvency of a business are the adequacy of earnings to cover debt service requirements, and the margin of safety to creditors provided by the equity of the stockholders. In all of these analyses and interpretations, the analyst must keep in mind that the prospective *future* amounts and relationships are usually the most significant ones for his decisions.

QUESTIONS AND PROBLEMS

25-1 A banker has been requested to make a short-term loan to a business.
REQUIRED:
Why might he consider its financial results for the past more important than its budget for the future?

25-2   You are considering buying 100 shares of stock of a corporation whose stock is listed on the New York Stock Exchange.

REQUIRED:

a. What would you consider the single most important amount or comparison based on the company's financial statements? Why?
b. What would you consider the next most important amount or comparison? Why?

25-3   You are the credit manager of a manufacturing company which has been asked to extend a substantial amount of credit to a retailer for merchandise.

REQUIRED:

a. What would you consider the single most important amount or comparison based on the company's financial statements? Why?
b. What would you consider the next most important amount or comparison? Why?

25-4   As an investment officer of a financial institution you are in the process of deciding whether to purchase $100,000 of the bonds of the X Company.

REQUIRED:

a. What would you consider the single most important amount or comparison based on the company's financial statements? Why?
b. What would you consider the next most important amount or comparison? Why?

25-5   As a creditor of a business you are attempting to evaluate its liquidity.

REQUIRED:

a. Name three standards against which you could compare the present financial position of the business.
b. Explain the significance and the limitations of each of the standards which you named in (a).

25-6

REQUIRED:

State whether each of the following transactions would increase, decrease, or have no effect on (1) the amount of net working capital and (2) the current ratio.

a. Sale of merchandise on account.
b. Sale of merchandise for cash.
c. Borrowing cash on a short-term note payable.
d. Collection of accounts receivable.
e. Purchase of merchandise on account.
f. Purchase of equipment on account.
g. Purchase of equipment in exchange for long-term notes payable.
h. Declaration of dividend payable in cash.
i. Payment of dividend declared earlier.
j. Payment of accounts payable.
k. Return of merchandise to supplier for credit.
l. Issuance of capital stock for cash.
m. Acquisition of treasury stock for cash.
n. Issuance of a dividend in the form of capital stock.
o. Recording periodic depreciation.
p. Sale of used equipment for cash.

25-7

REQUIRED:

Referring to the information in Question 25-6:

a. List the letters of the items that are sources of net working capital.
b. List the letters of the items that represent uses of net working capital.

25-8

REQUIRED:

a. Itemize the sources and uses of net working capital of a partnership that would not be found in a corporation.
b. Itemize the sources and uses of net working capital of a corporation that would not be found in a partnership.

25-9

REQUIRED:

If you were given a statement of financial position for a company for December 31, 19x3, and the details of its operating and financial budgets for 19x4, explain what steps you would use in analyzing its expected flow of net working capital for 19x4.

25-10

The following are condensed financial statements taken from the annual report of Marchman, Inc., for 19x4.

MARCHMAN, INC.
Comparative Statement of Financial Position

| | Years Ended December 31 | |
ASSETS	19x4	19x3
Current assets:		
Cash.................................	$15,000	$18,000
Accounts receivable (net)...............	30,000	20,000
Inventories (FIFO cost).................	45,000	29,000
Total current assets.........................	$ 90,000	$67,000
Fixed assets:		
Equipment (cost).......................	$50,000	$40,000
Deduct accumulated depreciation.........	20,000	15,000
Total fixed assets...........................	30,000	25,000
Total assets.................................	$120,000	$92,000
LIABILITIES		
Current liabilities:		
Accounts payable........................	$11,000	$10,000
Notes payable..........................	20,000	15,000
Corporate income tax payable............	6,000	4,000
Total current liabilities......................	$ 37,000	$29,000
Long-term liabilities:		
6% Bonds payable in 19x9.....................	0	15,000
Total liabilities..............................	$ 37,000	$44,000
STOCKHOLDERS' EQUITY		
Capital stock, no par value...............	$60,000	$40,000
Retained income..........................	23,000	8,000
Total stockholders' equity....................	83,000	48,000
Total equities...............................	$120,000	$92,000

MARCHMAN, INC.
Combined Statement of Income and Retained Income
For the Year Ended December 31, 19x4

Sales...		$200,000
Deduct expenses:		
Depreciation.................................	$ 5,000	
Income tax..................................	6,000	
Interest......................................	900	
All other expenses...........................	168,100	
Total expense..		180,000
Net income........................		$ 20,000
Deduct dividends..		5,000
Addition to retained income.............................		$ 15,000
Add retained income, December 31, 19x3..................		8,000
Retained income, December 31, 19x4.....................		$ 23,000

Late in the year, the company retired the bonds at par prior to their maturity. Because of this and other significant changes in the company's financial position, management feels that a statement analyzing the major sources and uses of working capital during the year would be desirable.

REQUIRED:

a. Analyze in **T-accounts** the major causes of changes in the company's net working capital during 19x4.

b. Prepare a formal statement summarizing the net working capital changes.

25-11 The management of the Hall Manufacturing Company desires to obtain a $25,000 loan for plant expansion purposes. The bank executive would like to have some more detailed information concerning the sources and uses of the funds used in the business to aid him in reaching a decision.

REQUIRED:

From the accompanying financial statements and additional information for the year ending December 31, 19x2, you are to prepare T-account analyses and a formal statement of the flow of net working capital during 19x2.

HALL MANUFACTURING COMPANY
Income Statement
Year Ended December 31, 19x2

Net sales...		$150,000
Cost of goods sold....................................		90,000
Gross margin.......................................		$ 60,000
Operating expenses:		
Salaries...	$ 15,000	
Rent expense......................................	7,200	
Depreciation—Buildings...........................	2,000	
Depreciation—Equipment.....	1,800	
Advertising expense................................	1,500	
Loss on uncollectible accounts......................	800	
Repairs and maintenance expense....................	1,200	
Insurance expense.................................	300	
Miscellaneous expense.............................	2,200	
Total operating expenses...........................		$ 32,000
Income from operations...............................		$ 28,000

Other revenue and gains:

Interest revenue	$1,500	
Gain on sale of equipment	5,000	6,500
		$ 34,500

Other expense and losses:

Interest expense	$2,000	
Loss on sale of temporary investments	500	2,500
Net income before Federal income taxes		$ 32,000
Corporate Federal income taxes		11,000
Net income		$ 21,000

HALL MANUFACTURING COMPANY
Statement of Retained Income
Year Ended December 31, 19x2

Retained income at beginning of year	$57,000
Add net income for the year	21,000
	$78,000
Deduct dividends	10,000
Retained income at end of year	$68,000

HALL MANUFACTURING COMPANY
Statement of Financial Position
Years Ended December 31, 19x1 and 19x2

ASSETS	19x2	19x1	Increase or Decrease*
Current assets:			
Cash	$ 20,000	$ 8,000	$12,000
Temporary investments	15,000	20,000	5,000*
Notes receivable, trade	8,000	5,000	3,000
Accounts receivable, trade	42,000	32,000	10,000
Deduct estimated uncollectibles	(3,200)	(2,000)	1,200*
Accrued interest receivable	2,500	500	2,000
Inventories	57,900	56,000	1,900
Prepaid rent	—	600	600*
Prepaid insurance	600	900	300*
Total current assets	$142,800	$121,000	
Fixed assets:			
Land	$ 10,000	$ 10,000	—
Buildings (cost)	95,000	80,000	15,000
Deduct accumulated depreciation	(20,000)	(18,000)	2,000*
Equipment (cost)	50,000	40,000	10,000
Deduct accumulated depreciation	(3,800)	(5,000)	1,200
Total fixed assets	$131,200	$107,000	
Total assets	$274,000	$228,000	$46,000
EQUITIES			
Liabilities:			
Current liabilities:			
Notes payable, trade	$ 5,000	$ 6,000	$ 1,000*
Accounts payable, trade	42,000	48,000	6,000*
Corporate Federal income tax payable	11,000	12,300	1,300*
Accrued payroll taxes payable	2,000	4,000	2,000*
Accrued interest payable	1,000	700	300
Total current liabilities	$ 61,000	$ 71,000	

EQUITIES (Continued)	19x2	19x1	Increase or Decrease*
Liabilities (*continued*):			
Long-term liabilities:			
Notes payable to banks....................	$ 20,000	—	20,000
Total liabilities.........................	$ 81,000	$ 71,000	
Stockholders' equity:			
Capital stock, $50 par......................	$125,000	$100,000	25,000
Retained income............................	68,000	57,000	11,000
Total stockholders' equity................	$193,000	$157,000	
Total equities..........................	$274,000	$228,000	$ 46,000

Additional information:

Temporary investments—Securities which cost $5,000 were sold for $4,500.
Equipment—Purchased new equipment for $20,000 and sold old equipment which
cost $10,000, with accumulated depreciation of $3,000, for $12,000.

25-12 The G Company had the following unrelated transactions in 19x1:

(1) Accounts payable of $10,000 were paid in cash.
(2) The company purchased long-term investments for cash, $5,000.
(3) Sold a vacant lot that had not been used in the business for cash, $20,000.
(4) Determined that $3,000 of accounts receivable, trade were uncollectible.
(5) Declared a $4,000 cash dividend to be paid during the first week of the next accounting period.
(6) Inventory which had cost $400 was considered obsolete when the physical inventory was taken.
(7) The company borrowed $2,000 from the bank and gave a 90-day, 6 per cent promissory note.
(8) Purchased a three-year insurance policy for $1,800.
(9) The bank notified the company that a customer's check for $150 had been returned marked "insufficient funds."
(10) The owners of the company made an additional cash investment of $10,000.

REQUIRED:
Considering the above transactions separately, how would each affect the
company's

a. Current ratio?
b. Quick ratio?
c. Net working capital?

CASE 25-1. DUGAN, INC.

The accompanying account balances were taken from the financial statements
of Dugan, Inc., a retailer, for the year ended June 30, 19x2.

REQUIRED:
a. Prepare the following financial statements in properly classified form:

(1) Comparative statement of financial position.
(2) Income statement.
(3) Statement of retained income.

b. Prepare the following analyses of the company's net working capital. Round all percentages to the nearest tenth of a per cent and all ratios to the nearest thousandth.

  (1) Amount of working capital at the ends of 19x2 and 19x1.
  (2) Current ratios for the two dates.
  (3) Quick ratios for the two dates.
  (4) T-accounts analyzing the changes in net working capital during 19x2.
  (5) Formal statement of changes in net working capital.

c. Comment on any significant changes in the company's working capital. Do you consider the over-all change in working capital satisfactory? Explain.

d. Prepare the following analyses of the company's operations:

  (1) Rate of return after income tax on stockholders' equity.
  (2) Rate of return before income tax on total assets.
  (3) Turnover rate for all assets.
  (4) Percentage of net income before tax to sales.
  (5) Accounts receivable turnover rate.
  (6) Inventory turnover rate.
  (7) Number of times bond interest requirements were earned.

e. Prepare the following analyses of the company's assets and equities:

  (1) Ratio of stockholders' equity to total equities.
  (2) Per cent of each major type of asset to total assets.
  (3) Per cent of each major type of equity to total equities.

f. Comment on any significant changes in the company's long-range solvency. Do you consider the over-all change satisfactory? Explain.

	19x2	19x1
Accounts payable	$ 168,800	$ 167,500
Accounts receivable	39,000	43,400
Accrued salaries and expenses	104,300	94,500
Accumulated depreciation—buildings	105,200	90,900
Accumulated depreciation—fixtures and equipment	229,300	187,400
3% Bonds payable in 15 years	46,300	56,800
3½% Bonds payable in 20 years	179,000	192,600
4% Bonds payable in 20 years	212,000	0
Buildings (cost)	333,900	305,300
Cash	157,600	183,600
Capital stock, common—par	53,000	35,300
Capital stock, common—premium	290,000	271,600
Capital stock, preferred	56,300	62,300
Cost of goods sold	6,035,600	5,374,200
Dividends paid—common	46,700	32,600
Dividends paid—preferred	2,600	2,700
Dividends in stock to common stockholders	16,400	0
Federal and state income taxes	104,000	99,100
Federal and state income taxes payable	75,100	78,100
Fixtures and equipment (cost)	499,700	429,200
Interest expense	17,400	13,700
Inventories (lower of cost or market)	462,300	409,900
Investments—long-term	188,700	81,100
Investments—temporary	64,500	0
Land	85,200	81,900

	19x2	19x1
Notes payable due in one year..............................	0	21,900
Notes payable due after one year.........................	60,300	60,400
Operating expenses.......................................	1,101,000	983,000
Other revenue..	22,400	23,100
Prepaid expenses...	15,400	13,300
Retained income...	266,700	228,400
Sales..	7,339,600	6,548,300

CASE 25-2. TWO LARGE MAIL-ORDER COMPANIES (A)

The mail-order business in the United States has been a major factor in the advancement of retailing during the past 50 or 75 years. Two of the leaders in this field have been Sears, Roebuck and Company and Montgomery Ward & Co., Inc. Both companies have operated large retail outlets as well as mail-order houses. Their merchandise lines include clothing, shoes, dry goods, furniture, home furnishings, radios, musical instruments, jewelry, books, stationery, drugs, electrical appliances and supplies, sporting goods, paints, hardware, plumbing and heating equipment, building materials, farm equipment and supplies, and automobile tires and supplies.

A study of net sales and net income in the following schedule shows that the growth of both companies was steady and continuous during the 1940's. During the first five years of the 1950's, the sales and net income of Montgomery Ward & Co., Inc., decreased, when compared with the results of the 1940's, while those of Sears, Roebuck and Company increased.

Comparison of Operating Data[2]
(All figures are expressed in millions of dollars)

Year Ended Jan. 31	Net Sales		Earnings before Income Tax		Net Income	
	Montgomery Ward	Sears, Roebuck	Montgomery Ward	Sears, Roebuck	Montgomery Ward	Sears, Roebuck
1942	$ 632.7	$ 915.1	$ 49.0	$ 85.5	$22.4	$ 29.9
1943	635.0	867.8	51.6	87.0	20.4	24.6
1944	595.9	852.6	32.0	87.4	20.7	33.9
1945	621.0	988.8	49.1	105.6	21.3	34.2
1946	654.8	1,045.3	58.3	98.6	23.0	35.8
1947	974.3	1,612.6	80.0	171.2	42.3	100.1
1948	1,158.7	1,981.5	102.2	193.0	59.1	107.7
1949	1,212.0	2,296.0	114.6	228.7	68.3	137.2
1950	1,084.4	2,169.0	79.4	178.2	47.8	108.2
1951	1,170.5	2,556.4	141.1	303.7	74.2	143.7
1952	1,106.2	2,657.4	114.1	272.0	54.3	111.9
1953	1,084.6	2,932.3	97.3	276.1	49.6	110.2
1954	999.1	2,982.0	85.4	271.8	41.2	117.9

The statements of financial position of the two companies for the fiscal years 1955 and 1956 are presented as follows:[3]

---

[2] *Moody's Industrial Manual* 1960 (Moody's Investors Service), pp. 2152, 2566–67.
[3] *Idem.*

SEARS, ROEBUCK AND COMPANY
Balance Sheet
For the Years Ended January 31, 1955 and 1956
(In millions of dollars)

ASSETS	1956	1955
Cash	$ 190.7	$ 218.1
Marketable securities (cost)	4.5	5.1
Notes and accounts receivable (net)	569.2	483.7
Inventories (lower of cost or market)	513.4	456.6
Prepaid expenses	24.3	22.7
Total current assets	$1,302.1	$1,186.2
Investment in insurance companies	$ 4.8	$ 4.8
Latin American subsidiaries	40.6	33.3
Investment in Simpsons-Sears, Ltd.	20.4	20.4
Other investments and advances	17.8	13.2
Property, plant and equipment	414.8	400.1
Less reserve for depreciation	204.4	188.1
Net property account	$ 210.4	$ 212.0
Total	$1,596.1	$1,469.9

LIABILITIES		
Notes and accounts payable	$ 61.9	$ 55.9
Accrued taxes, including Federal income tax	219.4	200.4
Other accruals	58.0	50.6
Unfilled orders and refunds to customers	24.1	21.7
Total current liabilities	$ 363.4	$ 328.6
Long-term debt	$ 200.0	$ 200.0
Capital stock	$ 221.7	$ 227.5
Capital surplus	38.1	
Retained earnings	772.9	713.8
Total	$1,596.1	$1,469.9

MONTGOMERY WARD & CO., INC.
Balance Sheet
For the Years Ended January 31, 1955 and 1956
(In millions of dollars)

ASSETS	1956	1955
Cash	$ 20.4	$ 23.0
U. S. Government, state, and municipal securities (cost)	221.1	304.2
Receivables (net)	189.7	147.0
Inventories	278.7	216.2
Total current assets	$709.9	$690.4
Land	$ 6.8	$ 6.7
Buildings	40.1	39.9
Fixtures and equipment	25.2	25.4
Leasehold improvements	5.4	5.6
Total property account	77.5	77.6
Less depreciation and amortization reserves	46.5	46.8
Net property account	$ 31.0	$ 30.8
Total	$740.9	$721.2

LIABILITIES	1956	1955
Accounts payable....................................	$ 37.1	$ 29.4
Due customers on unfilled orders, etc................	7.3	7.3
Accrued wages and extra compensation..............	3.7	2.8
Accrued sundry operating expenses..................	2.3	2.0
Accrued miscellaneous reserves.....................	6.5	10.3
Accrued property, real estate, and sundry tax........	5.4	4.9
Accrued Federal income taxes......................	35.1	25.7
Total current liabilities...........................	$ 97.4	$ 82.4
Capital stock.....................................	$231.4	$231.4
Earned surplus....................................	412.2	407.4
Total..	$741.0	$721.2

REQUIRED:

a. From the financial information given in the comparative financial statements of the two companies, what reasons might explain the fact that Sears, Roebuck and Company increased its net income during the 1950's while the net income of Montgomery Ward & Co., Inc. decreased during the same period?

b. Compare the financial structure of the two companies. Which company do you think has the better composition of assets? Support your answer with financial ratios.

c. Compare the effectiveness with which the two companies seemed to be using their assets in 1955 and 1956.

d. Using such comparisons as you think appropriate, analyze the two companies' liquidity, long-term solvency, and profitability for both years.

e. For each analysis made in (d), state whether you think the change from fiscal year 1955 to fiscal year 1956 is an improvement or not, and why.

f. Give reasons why you think each company adopted the financial policy that it did over this series of years.

g. At the end of 1956 what recommendations for management action, if any, would you make?

h. Compare current financial reports of these two companies with those given in this case, pointing out any changes which have been made in recent years and why you think that they were made.

Chapter 26

Reappraisal of Accounting

Fra Luca Pacioli, a Franciscan monk who lived in Italy, explained the operation of double-entry bookkeeping in his *Summa de Arithmetica, Geometria, Proportioni et Proportionalita*, published in Venice in 1494. Development of the system had occurred over the preceding two centuries. The method was widely adopted and refined in the Italian cities of the day and soon spread to other western countries, where it helped to facilitate economic growth.

The developing tool of accounting was adapted largely to the internal needs of each company. It was only with the emergence of the publicly-owned corporation as an important form of business organization in the latter part of the nineteenth century that the public began to take interest in the accounting of businesses. Today the accounting of a business must serve both the internal needs of its management and the external needs of stockholders, creditors, and others who are directly concerned with its financial affairs.

Earlier chapters have attempted to present a balanced description of accounting as a useful source of financial information and an analytical tool for both management and other interested groups. The present chapter examines some of the forces which are shaping the current development of accounting, as well as some of the major unresolved problems and limitations of modern accounting.

Increasing external interest in business accounting

Ownership of large interests in American corporations by stockholders who took no direct part in management became increasingly widespread in the early decades of the twentieth century. The importance of bankers and bondholders as short- and long-term suppliers of credit to businesses also increased. More and more companies began issuing published financial statements, although their emphasis was chiefly on financial position. Assets were commonly measured in terms of their liquidating values. Many businesses did not even prepare income statements for the use of their stockholders and creditors.

The enactment of the Federal income tax law in 1913 and its revision in 1918 to recognize the accrual basis of measuring income helped to stimulate the interest of businesses in careful measurement of income. As Chapter 24 pointed out, however, the diverse objectives of income taxation and of general-purpose measurement of business income have resulted in significant differences in methods of measurement for the two purposes.

The stock market boom in the late 1920's brought about increasing interest in the measurement of business income. The market crash of 1929 led to searching examination of existing practices in selling and buying securities, as well as of financial reporting to stockholders. A special committee of the American Institute of Accountants (now the AICPA) on Cooperation with Stock Exchanges was organized to help educate the public as to the meaning and limitations of accounting reports, and to take steps to make published reports more meaningful and reliable.

The Securities Act of 1933 and the Securities Exchange Act of 1934, both outgrowths of the stock market crash and the resulting investigations, had an important influence on the requirements of accounting and on the quality of financial reporting. The latter act created the Securities and Exchange Commission, which had authority to specify the requirements for financial reports for those companies whose securities were listed on a national securities exchange, or who wished to offer securities for sale to the public.

As a representative of the interests of stockholders and of the public, the Securities and Exchange Commission has been of great assistance to the accounting profession in implementing generally accepted accounting principles in financial reporting.

The auditor's report

The Securities and Exchange Commission requires that financial statements submitted to it be accompanied by the report of the independent accountant who has examined the statements. The financial statements are prepared by the *management* of the company, and the *auditor's report* contains his opinion as to their fairness. The standard wording of this report was developed jointly by representatives of the American Institute and the New York Stock Exchange, and is used today in practically all short-form audit reports. It consists of two main parts: the *scope of the audit* and the *opinion as to the statements*, which are presented below.

(*Scope*)

We have examined the statement of financial position of *A* Company as of December 31, 19xx, and the related statements of income and retained income for the year then ended. Our examination was made in accordance with generally accepted auditing standards, and accordingly included such tests of the accounting records and such other auditing procedures as we considered necessary in the circumstances.

(*Opinion*)

In our opinion, the accompanying statements of financial position, of income, and of retained income present fairly the financial position of *A* Company at December 31, 19xx, and the results of its operations for the year then ended, in conformity with generally accepted accounting principles applied on a basis consistent with that of the preceding year.

The independent accountant must give a *qualified opinion*, stating the matters to which he takes exception, if he has not been able to satisfy himself completely as to the fairness of presentation in the statements. If the questionable matters are of such a nature, or are so material, that they would destroy the significance of an opinion on the statements as a whole, the auditor should clearly *deny an opinion*.

The purpose of the *scope* paragraph is to assure the reader of the financial statements that the auditor has observed the accepted standards of auditing, and that to the best of his judgment he has followed necessary auditing *procedures*, in making his examination.

There are three significant elements in the *opinion* paragraph, indicated by the following key words:

(1) Present fairly;
(2) In conformity with generally accepted accounting principles;
(3) Applied on a basis consistent.

If the statements *present* the financial position and operating results of the business *fairly*, in the auditor's judgment the accounting methods and measurements are suited to the nature and circumstances of the particular business entity. Businesses have some freedom of choice in selecting their own methods of accounting within rather broad limits.

Generally accepted accounting principles

The broad limits, or guides, which accountants use in determining the acceptability of accounting methods and measurements are called *generally accepted accounting principles*. There is no unanimity among accountants as to what these individual principles are. Accounting has developed to serve a useful purpose, and its underlying assumptions and concepts have evolved in response to this need. Those principles which are generally agreed upon are based upon practical logic rather than upon laws or judicial interpretations.

The broad principles of accounting which have been discussed earlier in this book are the following:

(1) Accounting is carried on for separate units of economic activity called *entities*.

(2) Accounting describes and measures the forms, sources, and changes of the economic factors and relationships of the particular entity.

(3) *Money* is an appropriate common denominator for measuring the economic results of the entity.

(4) Accounting measurements should be based upon *objectively determined evidence*, an important class of which is *realization* in market transactions.

(5) Periodic income is properly measured by matching *realized revenues* with the related *expired costs*.

(6) For purposes of accounting measurement, *continuity* of the entity for the indefinite future, rather than liquidation, is the prospect (in the absence of specific evidence to the contrary). *Cost* is therefore a proper starting point in the measurement of long-lived assets.

Major limitations of these assumptions and concepts, together with significant disagreements as to their interpretation, are discussed in later paragraphs.

Consistency

One of the purposes of the auditor's concern with the *consistency* with which generally accepted accounting principles are applied in the accounts of the entity is to assure the user that the accounting information furnished by the company at one time is comparable with that furnished at other times. This does not mean that a business cannot change to a better method of accounting, within the limits of generally accepted accounting principles. If it does change, however, it should disclose the nature of the change and its effect on the financial statements, and should provide sufficient information to permit the reader to compare the affected account balances before and after the change.

Another important purpose of *consistency* in accounting measurements is to prevent manipulation of the results. Shifting from one method to another without restriction would permit a dishonest accountant or manager to change the measurements of income and financial position to suit his own purposes.

Still another aspect of *consistency* of accounting is the comparability of information between businesses, especially between those in the same industry. The traditional position of accountants has been merely to *disclose* the method used by the particular entity, where others use equally acceptable methods which produce materially different results.

Many accountants maintain that accounting principles are far too general, and that they allow too much latitude in the selection of methods. As a result, they feel that financial statements have lost much of their meaning to management, stockholders, creditors, and others. Some of the situations in which various acceptable accounting methods may result in significantly different measurements are summarized below.

Areas of wide divergence in revenue recognition

There is wider agreement among businesses as to when revenue is realized than as to when costs expire. Still, the following major alternatives are found in business practice, and all are considered to comply with generally accepted accounting principles:

(1) Using the percentage-of-completion or the completed-contracts method of accounting for revenue under long-term construction contracts;

(2) Estimating revenue deductions for items such as sales discounts, returns, and transportation, or waiting to deduct them in the future period in which their amounts are finally determined.

Areas of wide divergence in recognition of cost expiration

Many of the disagreements among accountants and businessmen deal with the proper *allocation of costs* between accounting periods, past and future. Some important examples of alternative methods in wide use are the following:

(1) The FIFO, LIFO, average cost, specific identification, and the lower-of-cost-or-market methods of measuring the unexpired cost of inventoriable items which is allocated to future periods. By the same process, the remainder is allocated to the current period as an expired cost.

(2) The straight-line, production, declining-balance, and sum-of-the-years'-digits methods of allocating the cost of depreciable assets to the periods of their useful life.

(3) Charging research and development costs directly to expense in the period in which they are incurred, or treating them as unexpired costs to be matched against the revenue from the resulting products in future periods.

(4) Charging exploration costs and intangible development costs (costs of drilling and developing wells exclusive of the cost of tangible equipment) of oil and gas properties to expense in the period in which they are incurred, or matching them against the revenue of future periods.

(5) Allocating organization costs to the first 5 years, or treating them as assets of indefinite life.

PROBLEMS IN APPLYING ACCOUNTING PRINCIPLES

What are the limits of the accounting entity?

Earlier chapters have dealt with accounting for the business *entity*, as distinguished from the affairs of the owner or owners of the business as individuals. Assets, equities, and changes in equities resulting from income have been accounted for from the point of view of the entity.

Often the *legal form and extent* of the entity differ from the *economic realities* of the case. Chapter 7 pointed out that the owner-manager of a business which is organized as a corporation is regarded as an employee of the business, and that his salary is treated as an *expense*. On the other hand, the compensation of the owner-manager of a proprietorship or partnership is treated as a *distribution of income*. Chapter 24 explained that segments of the business activities of one individual are often incorporated separately in order to minimize income taxes. Much more important, perhaps, are the many legal reasons for separate incorporation of businesses, such as limiting the liability of the owners to the amount invested in each corporation. In addition, separate incorporation may sometimes permit more effective management of the divisions of the business.

Consolidated statements

Must the accounting concept of entity correspond to the legal concept? To protect the legal rights of the creditors of each separate corporation, yes; accounting records must respect their separate legal existence. However, it has long been recognized that there is a need for financial statements of the *business* entity, in addition to the required separate financial statements of each *legal* entity of which it is composed. The basic principles for such *consolidated financial statements* may be stated as follows:

(1) In the absence of special circumstances, consolidated statements are useful representations of financial position and results of operations when a dominant central financial interest in two or more companies exists and is accompanied by administrative control of their activities and resources.

(2) Insofar as practicable, the consolidated data should reflect the underlying assumption that they represent the operations, resources, and equities of a single entity.[1]

In applying the second principle, account balances of one company which are reciprocal to accounts on the books of the other company are *eliminated*. The debit balance in the asset, Investment in Stock of Subsidiary, on the parent company's books and the corresponding credit balances of equities on the books of the subsidiary company, Capital Stock and Retained Income (and others, if appropriate), are both eliminated from the consolidated statements. Also eliminated are accounts which show sales of one company to, and purchases from, the other; revenue of one which is an expense of the other; and receivables of one company which are payables of the other. The remaining account balances which have not been eliminated are combined in consolidated statements, showing the results of the dealings of the business entity with persons outside of the common ownership group.

Is money a common denominator?

Accounts are kept as though the significance of the monetary unit were constant from one time to another. The serious declines in the purchasing power of the dollar that have occurred in the past two decades have emphasized sharply that this assumption is often untrue. As a result of the assumption, however, costs of long-lived assets acquired in one year and recorded in terms of the then current dollars, are combined in the same accounts and added to the amounts of similar assets acquired at different times and in exchange for dollars of unequal significance.

Income, the result obtained by deducting from revenue expressed in relatively current dollars the sacrifices, or costs, which are stated in dollars of varying significance, becomes a less useful measure of the progress of business endeavor when the value of money changes substantially. Income distortions appear when goods bought in one year and sold in the following period are matched with revenues expressed in terms of a different price level; but they are much more likely to stem from long-term cost prepayments such as buildings and equipment. The nature of the distortion is illustrated by Example 1.

EXAMPLE 1: In 19x1 a company pays $5,000 for a machine which is expected to last for 5 years. In 19x3, when the price of identical machines has

---

[1] Committee on Concepts and Standards, American Accounting Association, *Consolidated Financial Statements, Supplementary Statement No. 7* (Columbus, O., The Association, 1954).

doubled and the general price level of all goods and services has risen by 50 per cent, the company rents the machine to a customer for one year for $2,200 cash. What is the income as measured by *accounting* methods in 19x3, and what is the *real* income?

SOLUTION: (a) A *conventional income statement* would summarize the 19x3 results as follows:

Revenue..............	$2,200
Deduct depreciation (⅕ of original cost)...................	1,000
Net income..	$1,200

Revenue is expressed in 19x3 dollars, depreciation in 19x1 dollars, and net income in a mixture of the two.

(b) An income statement expressed in dollars of the *same general purchasing power* would show:

Revenue...	$2,200
Deduct depreciation (⅕ of 150 per cent of original cost)......	1,500
Net income..	$ 700

The original cost of the machine in terms of 19x1 dollars is converted into the equivalent cost in 19x3 dollars by multiplying it by 150, the general price index of 19x3 (19x3 general prices are 150 per cent as high as 19x1 prices).

(c) An income statement which expresses the *current cost* of the asset which is expiring would show:

Revenue...	$2,200
Deduct depreciation (⅕ of 200 per cent of original cost)......	2,000
Net income..	$ 200

The original cost of the machine in terms of 19x1 dollars is converted into the equivalent *current cost of the machine* by multiplying it by 200, the specific price index of 19x3.

The analysis in Example 1 shows that the $1,200 net income reported by traditional accounting procedure is composed of three elements:

(1) A *management gain* of $200, based upon the excess of current revenue over the current economic significance of the use of the machine;

(2) A *price gain* of $500, resulting from the increased significance of this machine in relation to prices in general;

(3) An *illusory*, or *phantom*, *gain* of $500, resulting from the decline in the general purchasing power of the dollar.

Distortion of financial statements by changing price levels is not a new phenomenon, nor is it confined to inflation alone. Equally serious misrepresentations of the results of business activity occur during periods of price decline. Statistical analyses have revealed that price movements in opposite directions do not offset each other over time, but rather that there has historically been a long-term upward movement of prices.

In view of the instability of the monetary unit, those who prepare and those who use accounting reports have been concerned with two questions:

(1) Is the magnitude of the change in the value of the dollar sufficient to warrant giving it recognition in the accounts? and

(2) If so, how can the recognition best be accomplished?

Should accounts reflect the changing value of the dollar?

The extent of the distorting effect of changing price levels on financial statements depends partly on the rapidity of changes in general price levels, partly upon the rate of changes in specific price levels, and partly upon the rate of turnover in the accounts of a specific business. The materiality of the price-level distortion can be judged by comparing (1) the amount of the distortion in assets and equities with the total amounts of assets and equities, and (2) the amount of the distortion in income with the total amount of income.

Even in times of rather rapid changes in the purchasing power of money, conventional accounting does not materially distort the results of businesses which have relatively small amounts of long-lived assets and a rapid turnover of current assets. The problem is more significant for those businesses which have relatively large amounts of long-term assets and long-term liabilities, and it tends to increase with the length of life of those assets.

Although changing price levels have affected some businesses more acutely than others, the weight of accounting opinion is that the effect has not been great enough to justify changing the basis of accounting from historical cost. In the recent history of some other countries, the rate of price-level change has been so drastic that it was necessary to restate the amounts of long-lived assets in the accounts.

There are those who dissent strongly from the majority view that no change in the basis of accountability is now required because of price changes. Some of their suggested remedies are outlined in the next section.

How can the changing value of the dollar best be recognized?

Some of the proposals which have been advanced for modifying accounts to provide information in current dollars would involve revision of the basic accounting records. Others favor showing the effects of price-level changes in reports supplementary to the principal historical accounting statements. Some of the methods advocated are:

(1) Appraisal of properties;
(1) Rapid write-down of fixed assets;
(3) Computation of depreciation on replacement costs;
(4) Conversion of cost to a current basis by the use of:
    (a) Specific price index numbers;
    (b) General price index numbers.

Appraisal of properties. Appraisals of the current market values of business assets are sanctioned when original costs cannot be determined, when there is a significant change in the ownership of a business, and when a corporation is reorganized.

A large element of subjectivity enters into such a valuation process. The current value of a machine or of a business as a whole depends on a *subjective* estimate of the flow of net revenue from the asset throughout its future economic life, discounted to the present by means of a discount rate which is also subjective. Appraisals are often quite expensive. Moreover, unless the price level remained stable for a very long period, the revised figures would soon be out of date and the appraisal process would have to be repeated.

Rapid write-down of fixed assets. Some companies have favored accelerated depreciation and similar methods of combating the effect of inflation on their financial reports. These methods are appropriate, of course, when the asset yields greater service benefits during its earlier years. In other cases, such a remedy to the problem of inflation is only partial, to the extent that other assets and liabilities have also been affected by price movements. In addition, it is short-sighted. It may give a more realistic income figure in the period when the increased depreciation is recorded, but the error in future years in which the over-depreciated assets are still in use is compounded. These later years are not charged with the full cost of the services received from the assets, thus overstating income; and the proper unexpired cost of the assets is not shown in the statement of financial position, thus further overstating the rate of return on assets.

Depreciation on replacement cost. This method is similar to the general appraisal, the main difference being that it is advocated for specific fixed assets, rather than for the enterprise as a whole. It is supported by the argument that the amount of distributable income cannot be determined until there has been a provision for maintaining the productive capacity of the business.

In opposition to the method, it may be said that the business probably will not wish to replace the specific assets in kind, and may even choose to go into other lines of activity. Even if it does plan to replace them, nobody knows what replacement costs will be in the future, and because of technological change the replacement is almost certain to differ materially from the asset replaced. Essentially, this method would amount to applying an estimate of *future cost* against *current revenue*.

It should be made clear that the funds needed for the replacement of an asset are not provided by *any* depreciation policy, but come instead from revenue or borrowed or invested capital.

Conversion by price index numbers. The function of a price index number is to show the trend, rate, and range of increases and decreases in the prices being studied. Theoretically, there is not only a price index for every commodity, but also one for every individual, and even for every different state of his preferences.

Specific price indexes have been advocated as a means of converting the accounting data into current dollars on the ground that the average change in all prices may not reflect the impact of price level change on a particular enterprise. Numerous variations of specific index numbers have been proposed. There is a danger that in view of this diversity, the resulting measurement would not be objective. The difficulties of applying separate indexes to each asset of a business and of allowing for technological change would also be great.

General index numbers, such as the Bureau of Labor Statistics' Wholesale Commodity Index, the Consumers' Price Index, and other similar ones are already available. It is possible to construct other indexes of more general applicability. These indexes have the advantage of being compiled by an agency independent of the management, stockholders, and creditors of the business.

Complete conversion of all accounts. A complete restatement of all accounts in terms of purchasing power would reveal purchasing power gains or losses of the following kinds, none of which are shown by conventional accounting statements:

(1) Gains or losses from holding long-term assets;
(2) Gains or losses from holding monetary assets;
(3) Losses or gains from owing monetary liabilities.

In times of inflation there are losses from holding monetary assets and gains from owing monetary liabilities. In times of deflation, monetary asset holdings result in gains and monetary liabilities result in losses to the business. The existence of these factors emphasizes the desirability of maintaining working capital at just the right amount needed to conduct business. An excess would result in a needless speculative gain or loss.

Complete restatement of the accounts in current dollars would be cumbersome, and it would also cause the accountant to lose sight of historical figures which are necessary for many important purposes. In

extreme cases of inflation or deflation, however, a supplementary
analysis of the effect of price level changes is desirable.

When does realization occur?

A change in an asset or a liability is considered to be *realized* in accounting when it has become sufficiently definite and objective to justify its
recognition in the accounts. Most commonly, this recognition is based
upon an exchange transaction, but established trade practices and dependable contractual relationships are also important.

The point of sale has usually been regarded as the appropriate time for
recognizing revenue. It has been objected to because it results in recording
the entire net income or net loss in the period in which the sale occurs.
Actually, it is argued, much of the productive effort which has contributed
to this income or loss was expended in earlier periods. The sale basis of
recognizing revenue is defended on the ground that apparent gains from
production may never become real gains if the item produced is not
accepted by the market.

In some situations, the point of sale is considered to be *too early* to
recognize the realization of revenue. This is true when there are substantial risks of loss in collecting the resulting receivables, especially long-term
installment receivables, and when there are significant related costs to be
incurred in later periods. As a rule, these additional costs can be matched
with the revenue in the period of sale, with a credit to a corresponding
liability account. In extreme cases, it is perhaps justifiable to postpone
the recognition of revenue until its collection is assured. If this is done,
the related amounts of costs should also be postponed.

In recent years there has been increasing disagreement over what constitutes the *realization* of a liability, particularly such estimated liabilities
as warranties payable, pensions payable, and others which are recorded
to permit a matching of the related costs with revenue recognized in the
current period. These borderline liabilities, and also the troublesome problem of liabilities for long-term leases, received attention in Chapter 19.

A similar difficult problem of liability recognition deals with the "postponed" and "prepaid" income taxes which are caused by differences between the income reported for income tax purposes and that reported for
financial accounting purposes. Although such liability recognition has
received acceptance for some situations, there is still strong objection to
it, and there are some items to which it is not applied.

Traditionally, accountants have tended to recognize *losses* on the basis
of much less substantial evidence than that required for the recognition
of *gains*. The widespread method of writing unsold inventory items down
to *market* if *lower* than cost, but not up to market if *higher* than cost, is an
illustration.

Is cost the appropriate basis for measuring assets?

The assumption of business continuity for the indefinite future has been offered as justification of the use of acquisition cost as the initial basis for measuring assets, and for the later allocation of the expired parts of acquisition cost to the periods in which an asset's services are received.

The historical cost basis of accounting has been challenged on many grounds, including that of the changing significance of the monetary unit. Many people contend that, since *future costs* are the ones which are relevant to business decisions, the compilation of historical costs in accounting is largely a waste of time. If future costs can be determined reliably without the objective evidence of past performance, they have a point. Still, there are some important decisions, such as the distribution of shares of income and the appraisal of management performance, which make good use of historical cost information.

Chapter 17 showed how predetermined *standard costs* can be woven into the accounts for the purpose of facilitating business planning and control. The variances which are developed between the actual costs and the standards provide useful information for the latter purpose, but knowledge of actual costs is still important.

Need for accounting in making decisions

This chapter has emphasized the difficulties which the accountants of various businesses face in applying accepted accounting principles, as well as some challenges to the principles themselves. It should be stressed that the choice of accounting principles and methods does have an important effect, not just upon the way in which the financial information of a business is presented, but also upon the business actions which are based upon the accounting information.

Even if these questions as to proper principles and practices could be settled, the resulting financial information would not provide the businessman, the stockholder, or the creditor with a magic guide for making decisions. Accounting is at best an imperfect attempt to describe in financial terms the realities of an entity which has many nonfinancial aspects—the interrelationships of the people within the business with each other and with outsiders; the complex physical facilities; and the influence of political, economic, and social forces external to the business. Even if an ideal plan of accounting could be agreed upon in theory and attained in practice, many business decisions would still hinge largely upon nonfinancial factors. Nevertheless, accounting, crude as it is, is often a valuable help to those inside and outside of the entity who must make decisions relating to the entity.

Applicability of accounting to nonbusiness entities

The foregoing exposition of accounting has highlighted its role in the decisions of business managers, stockholders, creditors, and others who have significant financial interests in the affairs of a business. This emphasis has perhaps obscured the essential part that accounting plays in the financial management of nonbusiness institutions, such as governments, schools, hospitals, clubs, and other organizations whose objectives are generally to provide service, rather than to maximize the income of the owners.

Most of the features of accounting are applicable to these organizations, except for income determination in the ordinary case. Even the accounting principles of income measurement apply to those functions of governments and institutions which parallel functions of private enterprise, such as the management of governmentally-owned utilities and similar activities.

The future of accounting

The Committee on Accounting Procedure of the American Institute of Certified Public Accountants, the Committee on Concepts and Standards of the American Accounting Association, the National Association of Accountants, and other professional organizations have made noteworthy contributions to the development of accounting principles and the solution of current accounting problems in the last two or three decades. In 1959 the American Institute began a new approach to the problem of divergent accounting principles and practices by establishing an Accounting Research Division. After careful study to establish the basic postulates and principles upon which accounting rests, the Division is to make recommendations to an Accounting Principles Board, which in turn will make such recommendations as it deems appropriate to accounting practitioners.

This effort seems likely to strengthen the principles upon which modern accounting rests, and to increase the extent to which accepted accounting principles are applied in practice. In the future, however, accounting will most likely continue to evolve in response to the changing needs of business and of society in general. No doubt there will continue to be a lag between the best in theoretical principles and the preponderance of actual practice, although it is to be hoped that the lag will be shortened.

It is still very important that accurate accounts be kept of the historical financial transactions of business. To provide for a variety of later needs, the design of the accounting classification should be made carefully to permit such reclassification as is desirable.

QUESTIONS AND PROBLEMS

26-1 Some people have contended that accounting principles should be precisely defined in detail, so that the accounting profession and enterprise management can apply them to any situation which might arise, thus reducing the latitude within which the accountant must exercise his judgment.

REQUIRED:

a. Do you think that such an approach is desirable? Explain.
b. Do you think that it is feasible?   Explain.

26-2 "Accounting principles should be enacted into law, and there should be a high court which decides accounting questions or disputes."

REQUIRED:

Do you agree with the preceding recommendation? Why?

26-3

REQUIRED:

What does the term "generally accepted" mean with relation to accounting principles?

26-4 "All of the disagreement about when revenues are realized, and what specific costs should be matched against them, could be avoided if we reflected revenues in the accounts only as they were collected in cash and expenses as they were paid in cash. This method is both simple and objective."

REQUIRED:

Do you agree with this statement? Why?

26-5 "We are not justified in assuming that the business entity will continue indefinitely. Studies of business mortality rates show that a high percentage of them fail during the first year, and that many more fail in the first two or three years."

REQUIRED:

a. What effect does the assumption of continuity have upon the method of making accounting measurements?
b. Is the assumption justified in view of the high failure rate among new businesses?

26-6 In the case of a corporation, accounting assumes that the salaries paid managers who also are stockholders is an expense, to be deducted in computing income. Partners' salaries, however, are not usually deducted in determining the net income of the partnership, but are treated as distributions of income.

REQUIRED:

a. Can you justify this different treatment of partners' salaries as compared with the salaries of officers of a publicly-owned corporation? How?
b. Is the situation any different in the case of the small family-owned corporation? Explain.

26-7 Accounting describes and measures the forms, sources, and changes of economic factors and relationships in a business.

REQUIRED:

a. What are some of the important economic factors affecting the value of a business which a prospective buyer of a large interest in it should consider, but
which are not in the accounting records? Why are they not in the accounts?
b. Are any of these items which are not usually reflected in the accounts ever
properly included in the accounts of a business? Under what circumstances?

26-8 "We place too much emphasis on the market-place in accounting.
Why should we wait until a product is sold to recognize revenue, and then treat
the entire gain as though it occurred at the instant the product is sold? This denies
the value of production, and it ignores the importance of such obvious physical
changes as the growth of the timber in a forest, or the growth of cattle being
fattened for sale."

REQUIRED:

a. Do you agree with the criticism expressed in this statement? If so, what exceptions to customary accounting practices would you recommend?
b. Describe a situation in which accounting does recognize income in proportion
to production. Why is this justified under current accounting thought?

26-9 "Accountants do a pretty good job of matching the so-called *product*
costs with revenue, but their matching of many *period* costs with revenue is often
subject to question."

REQUIRED:

a. What is meant by "product" costs? Explain the accounting method used in
matching them with revenue.
b. Give an example of a period cost which you consider to be properly matched
with revenue under present accounting practices.
c. Give an example of a period cost which you consider to be improperly matched
with revenue under present practices. How would you recommend that it be
handled?

26-10

REQUIRED:

a. Is the process of assigning depreciation of long-lived assets to accounting
periods based upon amounts determined in market transactions?
b. Is the estimate made of the useful life of the depreciable asset based on objective evidence?
c. In view of your answers in (a) and (b), is depreciation accounting justified
under generally accepted accounting principles? Explain.

26-11 "We cannot base our financial accounting on predictions; it must be
based on dependable, objective facts."

REQUIRED:

a. Do you agree with this statement? Explain.
b. What exceptions are there to this policy in customary accounting practice?
How, if at all, can you justify each exception?

26-12 "When considering the problems of wide variations in accounting
methods between businesses, coupled with rapidly changing price levels, the only
financial ratio that has real meaning for the analyst is the quick ratio."

REQUIRED:

a. Do you agree with this statement? Explain.
b. If you agree, would you recommend that the financial analyst not compute any
other ratios? Why?

26-13   Early in 19x1, a business acquired for $1,000,000 some highly specialized machinery for the purpose of manufacturing a new product. The extent of market acceptance of the product was in considerable doubt, although demand was increasing steadily at the end of 19x1. If things went well, the machinery should have a useful life of 10 years, but the management of the company elected to use a conservative estimated life of 5 years in computing annual depreciation.

Sales of the new product in 19x1 were $300,000, and expenses other than depreciation amounted to $90,000. The machine was still in use in 19x7, and demand for the product continued to be strong. Sales for that year amounted to $500,000, and expenses other than depreciation were $200,000.

Average assets in use in 19x1, other than the machinery in question, were $500,000, and other average assets amounted to $800,000 in 19x7.

REQUIRED:

a. Prepare condensed income statements for the business for 19x1 and 19x7.
b. Compute the rate of return before income tax on the average assets of the business in 19x1 and 19x7.
c. How would the amounts of income and average assets for the two years have differed if the company had used an estimated useful life of 10 years for the machinery?
d. What would the rate of return have been for 19x1 and 19x7 under the 10-year estimated life?
e. What depreciation rate should have been used under the circumstances?

26-14   Some items in accounting statements are expressed in current dollars, while other items are normally expressed in dollars of a prior year or years.

REQUIRED:

a. Name the principal balance sheet items which might not be expressed in current dollars. If any part of your answer depends on the accounting procedures employed by the particular company, explain fully.
b. Name the principal items in the income statement which might not be expressed in current dollars. If any part of your answer depends on the accounting procedures employed, explain fully.
c. Name the principal items in the statement of sources and uses of working capital which might not be expressed in current dollars. If any part of your answer depends on the accounting procedures employed, explain fully.

(Adapted from AICPA Examination in Theory of Accounts, May 16, 1952.)

26-15   The general manager of the Cumberland Manufacturing Company received an income statement from his controller. The statement covered the calendar year 19x7. "Joe," he said to the controller, "this statement indicates that a net income of two million dollars was earned last year. You know the value of the company is not that much more than it was this time last year."

"You're probably right," replied the controller. "You see, there are factors in accounting which sometimes keep reported operating results from reflecting the change in the value of the company."

REQUIRED:

Prepare a detailed explanation of the accounting conventions to which the controller referred. Include justification, to the extent possible, for the generally used accounting methods.

(Adapted from AICPA Examination in Theory of Accounts, May 16, 1958.)

26-16   Company *P*, a manufacturer, organized Company *S*, a selling company, on January 1, 19x2, and immediately acquired all of the latter's capital stock for cash. During 19x2 Company *P* sold manufactured products which had cost $400,000 to Company *S* on account, charging $500,000 for them. Company *S* has paid $350,000 on the account during the year. Company *S* has no other source of supply.

The condensed trial balances of the two companies on December 31, 19x2, were as follows:

	Company *P*		Company *S*	
Cash..........................	$ 50,000		$ 20,000	
Accounts receivable..............	150,000		100,000	
Inventories......................	175,000		200,000	
Fixed assets (net)................	400,000		150,000	
Investment in Company *S*.........	250,000			
Accounts payable.................		$ 140,000		$150,000
Capital stock....................		300,000		250,000
Retained income.................		535,000		0
Sales...........................		500,000		450,000
Cost of goods sold................	400,000		300,000	
Other expenses...................	50,000		80,000	
	$1,475,000	$1,475,000	$850,000	$850,000

REQUIRED:

a. Prepare condensed financial statements for each of the separate legal entities.
b. Prepare consolidated financial statements of the business entity from the point of view of the stockholders of Company *P*.

26-17   Two of the important functions of a certain medium-sized city government are providing police protection and operating a city water works. The police department is financed from the general property taxes of the city, and the customers of the water works are charged in proportion to the metered quantity of water they use.

REQUIRED:

a. How can accounting be useful in each of these situations?
b. To what extent do you think that a modification of generally accepted accounting principles and customary practices would be needed for each?

CASE 26-1. THE CLASE COMPANY

When the 19x5 financial statements of the Clase Company, a small corporation, had been prepared by its accountants, Mr. Jason, the company's general manager, made some comparisons with the company's financial statements of 19x0. He was delighted to see that the net income before taxes had almost doubled over the five-year period, increasing from $87,000 in 19x0 to $159,000 in 19x5. Closer observation of the statements, however, showed that the company's cash balance had decreased. The comparison further disclosed that all other items on the statement of financial position had shown relatively little change with the exception of inventory, which was $68,000 higher in 19x5 than in 19x0.

Mr. Jason could not understand why the inventory had increased in dollar amount to such a large extent. It was his opinion that the quantity of inventory on hand was practically the same as it had been for the last several years. He called the company accountant into his office and asked him to bring in the inventory sheets showing the physical counts for 19x0 and 19x5. He compared the figures for the different classes of inventory, and found to his amazement that the quantities of goods in the various classes were practically the same. He then started comparing 19x0 and 19x5 costs of some of the items which the company sold, and found that some of the unit costs had more than doubled since 19x0.

Several thoughts went through his mind. The company was doing almost twice the dollar amount of business in 19x5 as it had in 19x0 with practically the same quantity of inventory. This same inventory, however, was costing the company approximately twice as much money. The company's cash account had decreased, and its other assets showed little change during the five-year period.

Mr. Jason called a conference with the accountants who had helped to prepare the financial statements. He opened the conference with these remarks: "Gentlemen, I have suddenly realized that our Income Statement shows that we are making $72,000 more profit in 19x5 than we were in 19x0. An investigation shows that the company is operating with approximately the same quantity of inventory as it was in 19x0; however the inventory for 19x5 is $68,000 higher than it was in 19x0. It seems to me that we are showing profits which we really haven't realized, since practically all of the profit is tied up in inventory which has increased drastically in cost. And the company has paid income taxes on this profit! We must continue to carry the same quantity of inventory, but it is taking more money each year to carry it. At the same time, we have to pay income taxes on this high-priced inventory.

"I have talked this over with a friend of mine and he has advised me to change the method which we are using for costing our inventory. He claims that we can use the LIFO method and reduce income taxes, because the LIFO method will result in lower net income. If this is true, I would like to see the company use LIFO in the income tax return. I don't object to the favorable showing of net income for the company's stockholders. In fact, I would like to leave the company's statements as they are. What do you gentlemen think?"

REQUIRED:

a. Draft an answer to Mr. Jason's questions, commenting on all of the points which he has raised in his discussion.
b. What factors should the Clase Company consider before adopting the LIFO method for costing inventory for income tax purposes?
c. Under what conditions would you recommend the adoption of LIFO for financial statement purposes as well?
d. On the basis of the information given, what method of inventory measurement do you recommend?

CASE 26-2. TWO LARGE MAIL ORDER COMPANIES (B)

Refer to the statements of financial position shown in Case 25-2.

REQUIRED:

a. Which items on these statements do you think were affected most by the change in the value of the dollar from 1940 to 1955–56?
b. Evaluate the effect of each item in (a) on the financial results of the companies (1) in the short run and (2) in the long run.
c. Are the net sales for the years 1942 to 1954 comparable? How could these data be adjusted to provide more useful financial information? As they are presented, show how a prospective investor in either company might be misled by using the financial data without adjustment.

CASE 26-3. NEWPORT NEWS SHIPBUILDING AND DRY DOCK COMPANY

The following item appeared in an Associated Press release:

"LATHE PURCHASED AFTER FIGURING

"Newport News, Va. (AP)—Back in 1936 the Newport News Shipbuilding and Dry Dock Company purchased a huge heavy-duty engine lathe for $6,600. In 20 years it was depreciated on the books in the amount of $6,300 and this amount set aside for replacement.

"It was sold for $3,700, making $10,000 available for replacement. The new lathe cost $36,000 and $26,000 had to be taken from profits after taxes. Taxes amounted to 54 per cent of earned profit and, therefore, $57,000 had to be earned in profits. The company figures it required $807,000 in new business to make enough to buy the new lathe."

REQUIRED:

a. In what way did the company probably "set aside the amount for replacement"?
b. Is the problem of this company an unusual one?
c. Record the entries for the sale of the old lathe and the purchase of the new one.
d. What accounting method should the company have followed during this period, if other than the one the company used? Explain.
e. Assuming that the specific prices of lathes was representative of the change in the general level of prices during this period, did the company gain or lose on the disposal of the old lathe? Explain.

CASE 26-4. UNITED STATES STEEL CORPORATION[2]

"FINANCIAL SUMMARY
As Wage Inflation Goes . . .

"For the last two decades U. S. Steel's operations have been conducted within a framework of unremitting cost inflation. This cost inflation is not unique with U. S. Steel—instead it is a matter of national concern. It has been the hope of many that the continuing cost inflation could be abated, even if complete stability could not be achieved. In this respect the year 1956 has been a disappointment. There is as yet no evidence of an abatement of cost inflation in the affairs of U. S. Steel.

"The chart in Exhibit A shows that for the best part of two decades both U. S. Steel's employment cost per employe hour and its total of all costs per employee hour have advanced at rates, compounded annually, averaging 8.1 per cent and 8.8 per cent, respectively. These advances were fully sustained in 1956.

"This current evidence supplements other reasons for believing that cost-price inflation is in danger of becoming a permanent feature of American life. Central to such conclusion is the fact that the vast power of industry-wide labor unions in compelling annual increases in employment costs far beyond increases in productivity is automatically compelling inflation. This is because, up and down the industrial production line, employment cost constitutes, directly or indirectly, the vast bulk of all costs. There is thus a natural sequence between the basic employment cost inflation and cost-covering price inflation since the latter is

---

[2] This case consists of excerpts from the 1956 Annual Report of United States Steel Corporation, which have been reprinted by permission of the Corporation.

but the reflection of the former. To the extent that product price increases are eventually reflected in cost-of-living indexes, further employment cost increases are automatically generated by reason of so-called cost-of-living clauses in wage contracts. This starts the process all over again. Inflation is rapidly becoming automatic in America. Such inflation creates serious problems for business managements. These problems center around the finding of the additional dollars that are needed to finance the ever-increasing costs of doing business.

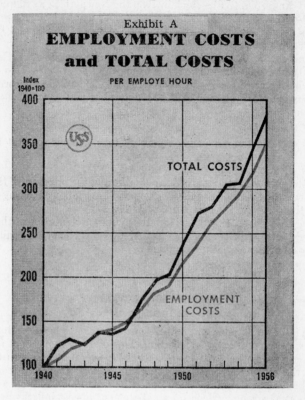

Exhibit A
EMPLOYMENT COSTS
and TOTAL COSTS

"Capital expenditures

"Nowhere is the requirement for additional dollars more evident in U. S. Steel's affairs than in the purchase of facilities. Steel making requires heavy investment in long-term facilities. Since the close of World War II U. S. Steel has engaged in a hugh modernization and expansion program. This program at the construction cost level prevailing at the end of the war would have required capital expenditures of $1.7 billion through 1956. But construction costs (see Exhibit B) have steadily risen at a rapid rate with the result that actual capital expenditures were $3.0 billion. The additional $1.3 billion, or about 75 per cent, is one measure in one area of the financing problem created by inflation. It represents additional dollars but not additional facilities.

"Inadequate depreciation

"Aggravating the problem of finding the additional dollars for expenditure for facilities is the serious inadequacy of the present Federal income tax formula for wear and exhaustion, often called depreciation. Recovery, through depreciation, of capital previously invested in facilities is essential if, through its re-expenditure, the supply and modernness of existing tools of production are to be maintained.

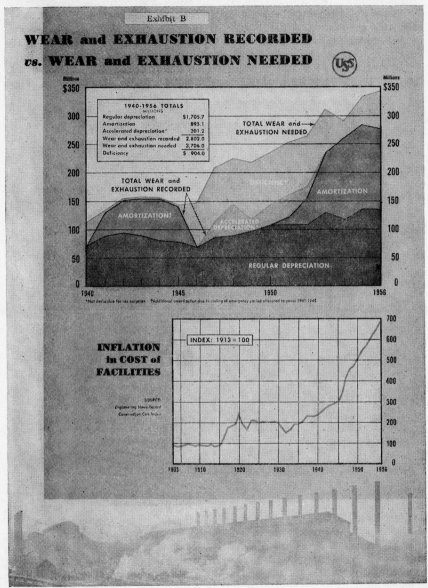

SOURCE: *1956 Annual Report of United States Steel Corporation.*

Income tax law limits the total depreciation recoverable during the life of a facility to the number of dollars originally spent for it years ago. But with the value of the dollar steadily declining the buying power originally expended cannot possibly be recovered under this unrealistic limitation. Faster recovery, such as has been permitted under certificates of necessity, tends to reduce the inadequacy which would otherwise exist; but the only real basis of recovering purchasing power would be to adjust for the change in the dollar intervening between the year of capital expenditure and the year in which depreciation is taken.

"Few people realize the extent of the deficiency in depreciation. U. S. Steel has calculated the number of dollars of wear and exhaustion that would have been needed in each year since 1939 to equal in that year's dollars the portion of the buying power originally expended which was used up in the year's production.

"In every year since 1939, as displayed in Exhibit B, the wear and exhaustion recorded, including accelerated depreciation not allowed for tax purposes, failed

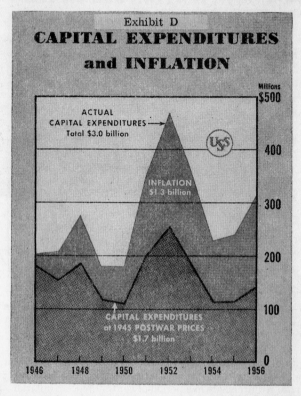

to equal that needed for recovery of buying power. The 17-year aggregate deficiency was $904 million. The Federal income tax paid, as a result of treating this deficiency and the accelerated depreciation as income for tax purposes, aggregated $608 million, or 22 per cent of the taxes paid. The $608 million for U. S. Steel and analogous amounts for all other companies, big and little, may be regarded as the hidden taxation of capital as it turns over through depreciation or, alternatively, as a hidden increase in the tax rate on true income. From the latter viewpoint it is highly inequitable, because it results in a higher rate for those industries or companies which require relatively heavier investment in longer-term facilities than the average for all industry.

"Short of legislative correction of the tax injustice or renewed granting of certificates of necessity, the depreciation deficiency is destined to become more serious. Thus U. S. Steel's wear and exhaustion recorded for 1956 was $278 million, or about $67 million short of the $345 million needed for buying power recovery. Included in recorded wear and exhaustion is $140 million of amortization which will decline and virtually disappear after 1958.

"As that happens, the depreciation deficiency will actually increase and income will seemingly increase. Since taxes will increase by over half the decline in amortization, a curious and serious situation will result: At the very time that the business appears to have greater income the cash with which to conduct it is

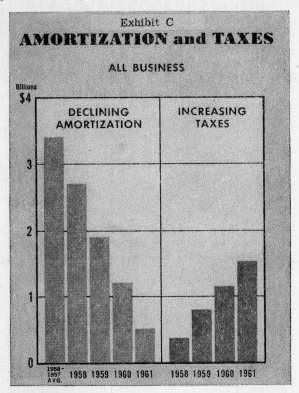

Exhibit C

AMORTIZATION and TAXES

ALL BUSINESS

diminished; and cash is what is required to cover the ever-mounting costs, to supplement the inadequate depreciation permitted, and to meet the expanding working capital requirements in a period of continuing cost inflation. The prospect is that the portion of reported income that must be regarded as "phantom" income, because it is required merely to maintain the business under conditions of continuing inflation, will increase.

"These problems are by no means unique with U. S. Steel. Thus, as shown in the diagram in Exhibit C, estimated tax deductible amortization for all business amounted to $3,400 million in 1956. If no more certificates of necessity are issued, it is estimated this amortization will decline to about $500 million by 1961. This may represent a tax windfall to the Treasury but it will also be an equivalent aggravation of the taxation of capital invested in the nation's tools of production.

"Prices

"The only continuing source of revenue that any company has with which to cover its costs and provide the income to justify its continuing existence is sales

EXCERPTS FROM U. S. STEEL'S OPERATING STORY, 1910–1956

Net tons in thousands

Year of oper.	Total ores mined	Total fluxes produced	Total coal mined	Total coke produced	Total iron produced	Ingots & castings Total production	% Capacity operated	Steel products shipped	Employment statistics No. of employes	Weekly hours	Hourly earnings	Weekly earnings
1940	34,047	15,730	29,528	16,144	18,367	22,934	82.5	15,014	254,393	36.7	.898	32.97
1941	43,318	19,176	29,076	18,563	22,321	28,963	96.8	20,417	304,248	38.1	.994	37.91
1942	52,012	20,864	32,317	19,275	23,496	30,030	98.1	20,615	335,866	38.8	1.086	42.17
1943	51,649	19,478	29,046	19,028	23,660	30,540	97.8	20,148	340,498	42.2	1.159	48.94
1944	49,842	19,208	30,709	20,503	23,445	30,815	94.7	21,052	314,888	44.2	1.257	55.53
1945	47,655	19,030	27,622	18,341	19,648	26,479	82.0	18,410	279,274	42.0	1.287	54.03
1946	37,972	20,874	24,463	15,242	15,853	21,287	72.9	15,182	266,835	35.0	1.426	49.91
1947	47,434	24,827	29,639	20,806	21,511	28,570	96.7	20,242	286,316	38.5	1.550	59.64
1948	48,926	26,870	26,795	21,237	22,228	29,292	93.8	20,655	296,785	38.2	1.680	64.21
1949	41,543	23,746	19,181	17,688	19,546	25,807	82.5	18,212	291,163	34.3	1.775	60.94
1950	46,334	26,985	22,280	20,078	23,574	31,457	98.2	22,635	288,265	37.8	1.828	69.10
1951	57,457	29,224	24,460	21,504	25,821	34,323	101.3	24,626	301,328	38.7	2.046	79.24
1952	45,660	26,571	19,241	18,023	22,022	29,436	85.0	21,133	294,263	34.7	2.265	78.53
1953	58,682	30,270	26,048	21,582	27,167	35,827	98.4	25,091	301,560	37.9	2.394	90.66
1954	37,891	25,232	22,678	18,724	20,904	28,355	73.2	20,239	268,142	35.6	2.488	88.47
1955	52,137	29,490	25,159	21,575	26,028	35,309	90.8	25,506	272,646	37.5	2.698	101.28
1956	47,439	28,586	22,991	20,615	24,633	33,402	85.2	23,911	260,646	37.1	2.926	108.47

Production data, which are grouped in broad product classifications, include all production of the materials by the operating divisions and subsidiaries and exclude all materials purchased. The average weekly hours and average weekly earnings shown are based on the average monthly number of employes receiving pay. Prior to 1929, the full time equivalent rather than the actual number of employes is shown and, for those early years, the average weekly hours, hourly and weekly earnings have been partially estimated.

EXCERPTS FROM U. S. STEEL'S FINANCIAL STORY, 1910–1956

Exhibit F

Dollars in millions

Year of oper.	Products & services sold	Employment costs	Products & services bought	Wear and exhaustion	Interest & other costs on debt	Income & other taxes	Income or loss	Preferred stock dividend	Common stock dividend	Reinvested in the business	% Income of sales
1940	1,079.1	464.3	358.3	72.6	13.6	68.1	102.2	25.2	34.8	42.2	9.5
1941	1,622.3	628.3	604.6	98.6	6.0	168.6	116.2	25.2	34.8	56.2	7.2
1942	1,863.0	782.7	673.4	128.2	6.2	201.3	71.2	25.2	34.8	11.2	3.8
1943	1,972.3	912.9	730.6	134.0	6.3	125.9	62.6	25.2	34.8	2.6	3.2
1944	2,082.2	957.2	814.4	139.0	5.0	105.8	60.8	25.2	34.8	.8	2.9
1945	1,747.3	825.5	670.1	123.4	3.5	66.8	58.0	25.2	34.8	2.0d	3.3
1946	1,496.1	704.5	560.4	68.7	4.8	69.1	88.6	25.2	34.8	28.6	5.9
1947	2,122.8	903.6	839.4	114.0	2.5	136.2	127.1	25.2	45.7	56.2	6.0
1948	2,481.5	1,035.7	1,008.9	146.0	2.4	158.9	129.6	25.2	52.2	52.2	5.2
1949	2,301.7	945.9	885.7	119.7	2.3	182.2	165.9	25.2	56.1	84.6	7.2
1950	2,956.4	1,179.4	1,118.8	143.9	2.2	296.6	215.5	25.2	92.7	97.6	7.3
1951	3,524.1	1,374.5	1,327.9	162.1	2.0	473.3	184.3	25.2	78.3	80.8	5.2
1952	3,137.4	1,322.1	1,307.6	176.9	1.9	185.3	143.6	25.2	78.3	40.1	4.6
1953	3,861.0	1,569.2	1,418.7	236.6	2.1	412.3	222.1	25.2	78.3	118.6	5.8
1954	3,250.4	1,387.0	1,134.3	261.8	5.2	266.7	195.4	25.2	85.5	84.7	6.0
1955	4,097.7	1,614.9	1,355.2	285.2	9.1	463.2	370.1	25.2	122.9	222.0	9.0
1956	4,228.9	1,681.0	1,487.5	277.6	7.7	427.0	348.1	25.2	144.9	178.0	8.2

The data are in some respects necessarily approximate, and are based on the yearly earnings reported annually to stockholders without adjustment for surplus charges and credits except that the years 1942 and 1943 reflect renegotiation settlements made in the succeeding years.

For example, taxes are as accrued before adjustments. Employment costs include pensions and social security taxes and, beginning with 1949, also include payments for insurance and other employe benefits.
ddenotes deficit.

to customers. Since the basic employment cost inflation has far outstripped productivity increases, part of the cost increase has had to be passed on to customers in higher prices. U. S. Steel's employment cost per employee hour in 1956 was three and a half times that of 1940. Steel mill finished product prices in 1956, according to the Bureau of Labor Statistics, averaged less than two and a half times what they were in 1940. As basic costs continue to be forced upward, and as the depreciation deficiency widens, management's problem of finding the dollars required to maintain the business becomes more acute.

SUMMARY OF 1956 FINANCIAL OPERATIONS   Exhibit G

Additions to working capital

Income		$348,098,916
Add—Wear and exhaustion of facilities		277,598,963
Proceeds from sales and salvage of plant and equipment		29,812,853
Proceeds from sale of common stock under Stock Option Incentive Plan		4,760,696
Total additions		$660,271,428

Deductions from working capital

Expended for plant and equipment	$311,792,037	
Set aside for property additions and replacements	225,000,000	
Reduction in total long-term debt	42,674,975	
Dividends declared on preferred and common stocks	170,103,878	
Miscellaneous deductions	2,102,834	
Total deductions		751,673,724
Reduction in working capital		$ 91,402,296

Working capital per consolidated statement of financial position

December 31, 1956	$603,739,028	
December 31, 1955	695,141,324	
Reduction		$ 91,402,296

"It is especially acute with respect to covering the depreciation deficiency because it takes two dollars, either from increased productivity or from customers in the prices they pay, to yield one dollar toward meeting the depreciation deficiency. This is because the tax authorities treat the two dollars as taxable income. To secure the additional dollars through increased productivity is most desirable, and every company competitively strives to increase productivity. To do so, however, requires heavy outlays for ever more modern and efficient equipment at the very time when equipment prices are rising and the depreciation source of funds to purchase it is undermined through taxation.

"The broader problem

"While continuing inflation presents particular problems to managements, it presents broader problems to the nation as a whole. If the American people come to accept inflation as a way of life—however reluctantly or apathetically—it is inevitable that both individuals and business will come to compete in borrowing in order to buy now and pay off later in cheapened dollars. Such tendencies are already evidenced by unprecedented increases in both consumer and business indebtedness. Expectation of inflation induces something of a flight from money into goods. This, too, is evidenced by the increasing rapidity with which the nation's supply of money is turned over, by mounting inventories and by developing overcapacity in an increasing number of industries. Expectation of inflation stimulates the urge toward speculative spending at the expense of traditional forms of thrift through which productive capital is provided, thus unbalancing the economy.

"Speculative overbuying—whether of commodities, stocks, real estate or other property—when financed through debt expanding more rapidly than income presents the historic framework out of which have come crisis and readjustment. No one wants to repeat that historic sequence, but the presence of wage inflation

---

Consolidated Statement of
FINANCIAL POSITION

Exhibit H

	Dec. 31, 1956	Dec. 31, 1955
Current assets		
Cash	$ 267,909,652	$ 249,817,576
United States Government and other marketable securities,		
at cost (approximates market)	242,239,366	317,659,464
Receivables, less estimated bad debts	314,498,132	300,576,212
Inventories *(details on page 38)*	501,283,785	475,086,019
Total	1,325,930,935	1,343,139,271
Less		
Current liabilities		
Accounts payable	389,281,706	352,944,492
Accrued taxes, less United States Government		
securities of $272,700,000 at December 31, 1956		
and $346,800,000 at December 31, 1955	254,843,551	220,861,844
Dividends payable	46,591,835	41,101,678
Long-term debt due within one year	31,474,815	33,089,933
Total	722,191,907	647,997,947
Working capital	603,739,028	695,141,324
Miscellaneous investments, less estimated losses	42,416,361	36,356,888
United States Government securities set aside		
for property additions and replacements	525,000,000	300,000,000
Plant and equipment, less depreciation *(details on page 37)*	1,877,994,847	1,873,614,626
Operating parts and supplies	45,424,240	43,208,254
Costs applicable to future periods	19,484,070	24,041,577
Total assets less current liabilities	3,114,058,546	2,972,362,669
Deduct		
Long-term debt *(details on page 38)*	245,023,677	286,083,534
Reserves for insurance, contingencies and accident and hospital		
expenses *(details on page 37)*	105,062,063	103,707,084
Excess of assets over liabilities and reserves	$2,763,972,806	$2,582,572,051
Ownership evidenced by		
Preferred stock, 7% cumulative, par value $100 (authorized		
4,000,000 shares; outstanding 3,602,811 shares)	$ 360,281,100	$ 360,281,100
Common stock (authorized 90,000,000 shares; outstanding		
53,699,617 shares at December 31, 1956, and 53,495,274		
shares at December 31, 1955)	2,403,691,706	2,222,290,951
Par value, $16% per share . . . . $ 894,993,617		
Income reinvested in business *(see page 33*		
for addition of $177,995,038 in 1956) . . . 1,508,698,089		
Total	$2,763,972,806	$2,582,572,051

---

and resulting price inflation, together with widespread expectation that they will continue, augments the danger that it might be repeated. The means by which such a prospect may be avoided merit the most careful consideration of managements, of labor leaders, of legislators—in fact, of all citizens.

"Note on Statistical Method

"The measurement of the wear and exhaustion needed was accomplished as follows: recorded wear and exhaustion (exclusive of accelerated depreciation and including only regular depreciation on amortizable facilities) for a given year was subdivided by the prior years in which the investments being depreciated were acquired. Each subdivision was then adjusted by the change in buying power of the dollar experienced from the year of acquisition to the given year, as indicated by the *Engineering News-Record* index of construction cost. Summation of the adjusted items then gave the wear and exhaustion needed to recover the proper proportion of buying power originally expended. This same process was repeated for each year, thus providing the data of wear and exhaustion needed charted in Exhibit B.

		Details of		
Exhibit I		SELECTED ITEMS		
Plant and equipment (at cost)	Balance Dec. 31, 1955	Additions	Deductions	Balance Dec. 31, 1956
Land	$ 80,568,190	$ 718,944	$ 522,240	$ 80,764,894
Plant, mineral and manufacturing . .	3,865,528,298	297,653,879	54,044,449	4,109,137,728
Transportation	598,247,827	13,419,214	33,304,514	578,362,527
Total	4,544,344,315	311,792,037*	87,871,203	4,768,265,149
Less				
Depreciation and depletion				
Plant and manufacturing properties	2,381,898,807	262,982,271	52,574,291	2,592,306,787
Transportation properties . . .	288,830,882	24,198,112	15,065,479	297,963,515
Total	2,670,729,689	287,180,383†	67,639,770	2,890,270,302
Net	$1,873,614,626	$ 24,611,654	$20,231,433‡	$1,877,994,847

*Includes expenditures of $19,386,852 for emergency facilities. Such expenditures since the beginning of 1950 total $794,741,725.
†Wear and exhaustion of $277,598,963 shown in the consolidated statement of income comprises depreciation and depletion of $287,180,383

(including amortization of emergency facilities of $140,214,592), less profit of $9,581,420 resulting from sales.
‡Includes $29,812,853 proceeds from sales and salvage of plant and equipment, less profit of $9,581,420 resulting therefrom.

"In interpreting the wear and exhaustion deficiencies that have been calculated, it should be remembered that each year's deficiency is in dollars of the buying power that prevailed in that year—not in today's dollars of diminished buying power. The $904 million aggregate deficiency for the 17-year period would be considerably greater if the deficiencies were converted into today's dollars."

REQUIRED:

a. Summarize the financial and accounting problems of U. S. Steel Corporation which are revealed by the preceding information.
b. Evaluate the Corporation's accounting policies, and its arguments in support of them. Are they in accordance with generally accepted accounting principles?
c. How would you recommend that the company's financial statements deal with these problems? Present arguments to support your recommendation.

SUGGESTED REFERENCES:

American Accounting Association, Committee on Concepts and Standards, "Price Level Changes and Financial Statements." Supplementary Statement No. 2. Columbus, O.: The Association, 1951.

American Institute of Certified Public Accountants, Committee on Accounting Procedure, *Restatement and Revision of Accounting Research Bulletins.* Accounting Research Bulletin No. 43. New York: The Institute, 1953, pp. 67–71.

Dein, Raymond C., "Price-Level Adjustment: Fetish in Accounting," *Accounting Review*, January, 1955, pp. 3–24.

Dohr, James L., "Limitations on the Usefulness of Price Level Adjustment," *Accounting Review*, April, 1955, pp. 198–205.

Jones, Ralph C., *Price Level Changes and Financial Statements. Case Studies of Four Companies*. Columbus, O.: American Accounting Association, 1955.

————, *Effects of Price Level Changes on Business Income, Capital, and Taxes*. Columbus, O.: American Accounting Association, 1956.

————, "The Effect of Inflation on Capital and Profits: Records of Nine Steel Companies." *Journal of Accountancy*, January, 1949, pp. 9–27.

Kennedy, Ralph D., and Stewart Y. McMullen, *Financial Statements: Form, Analysis, and Interpretation*. Homewood, Ill.: Richard D. Irwin, Inc., 1957, pp. 327–400.

Mason, Perry, *Price-Level Changes and Financial Statements. Basic Concepts and Methods*. Columbus, O.: American Accounting Association, 1956.

Paton, William A., "Measuring Profits under Inflation Conditions: A Serious Problem for Accountants," *Journal of Accountancy*, January, 1950, pp. 16–27.

Index